The Wiley Blackwell Companions to Religion

The Wiley Blackwell Companions to Religion series presents a collection of the most recent scholarship and knowledge about world religions. Each volume draws together newly commissioned essays by distinguished authors in the field, and is presented in a style which is accessible to undergraduate students, as well as scholars and the interested general reader. These volumes approach the subject in a creative and forward-thinking style, providing a forum in which leading scholars in the field can make their views and research available to a wider audience.

Published

The Blackwell Companion to Judaism
Edited by Jacob Neusner and Alan J. Avery-Peck

The Blackwell Companion to Sociology of Religion
Edited by Richard K. Fenn

The Blackwell Companion to the Hebrew Bible
Edited by Leo G. Perdue

The Blackwell Companion to Postmodern Theology
Edited by Graham Ward

The Blackwell Companion to Hinduism
Edited by Gavin Flood

The Blackwell Companion to Protestantism
Edited by Alister E. McGrath and Darren C. Marks

The Blackwell Companion to Modern Theology
Edited by Gareth Jones

The Blackwell Companion to Religious Ethics
Edited by William Schweiker

The Blackwell Companion to Christian Spirituality
Edited by Arthur Holder

The Blackwell Companion to the Study of Religion
Edited by Robert A. Segal

The Blackwell Companion to the Qur'ān, Second Edition
Edited by Andrew Rippin

The Blackwell Companion to Contemporary Islamic Thought
Edited by Ibrahim M. Abu-Rabi'

The Blackwell Companion to the Bible and Culture
Edited by John F. A. Sawyer

The Blackwell Companion to Catholicism
Edited by James J. Buckley, Frederick Christian Bauerschmidt, and Trent Pomplun

The Blackwell Companion to Eastern Christianity
Edited by Ken Parry

The Blackwell Companion to the Theologians
Edited by Ian S. Markham

The Blackwell Companion to the Bible in English Literature
Edited by Rebecca Lemon, Emma Mason, John Roberts, and Christopher Rowland

The Blackwell Companion to the New Testament
Edited by David E. Aune

The Blackwell Companion to Nineteenth Century Theology
Edited by David Fergusson

The Blackwell Companion to Religion in America
Edited by Philip Goff

The Blackwell Companion to Jesus
Edited by Delbert Burkett

The Blackwell Companion to Paul
Edited by Stephen Westerholm

The Blackwell Companion to Religion and Violence
Edited by Andrew R. Murphy

The Blackwell Companion to Christian Ethics, Second Edition
Edited by Stanley Hauerwas and Samuel Wells

The Wiley Blackwell Companion to Pastoral Theology
Edited by Bonnie J. Miller McLemore

The Wiley Blackwell Companion to Religion and Social Justice
Edited by Michael D. Palmer and Stanley M. Burgess

The Wiley Blackwell Companion to Chinese Religions
Edited by Randall L. Nadeau

The Wiley Blackwell Companion to African Religions
Edited by Elias Kifon Bongmba

The Wiley Blackwell Companion to Christian Mysticism
Edited by Julia A. Lamm

The Wiley Blackwell Companion to the Anglican Communion
Edited by Ian S. Markham, Barney Hawkins IV, Leslie Nuñez Steffensen and Justyn Terry

The Wiley Blackwell Companion to Interreligious Dialogue
Edited by Catherine Cornille

The Wiley Blackwell Companion to East and Inner Asian Buddhism
Edited by Mario Poceski

The Wiley Blackwell Companion to Latino/a Theology
Edited by Orlando O. Espín

The Wiley Blackwell Companion to Ancient Israel
Edited by Susan Niditch

The Wiley Blackwell Companion to Patristics
Edited by Ken Parry

The Wiley Blackwell Companion to World Christianity
Edited by Lamin Sanneh and Michael J. McClymond

The Wiley Blackwell Companion to Politics and Religion in America
Edited by Barbara A. McGraw

The Wiley Blackwell Companion to Religion and Ecology
Edited by John Hart

The Wiley Blackwell Companion to Political Theology, Second Edition
Edited by William T. Cavanaugh and Peter Scott

The Wiley Blackwell Companion to Religion and Materiality
Edited by Vasudha Narayanan

The Wiley Blackwell Companion to Wisdom Literature
Edited by Samuel L Adams and Matthew Goff

The Wiley Blackwell Concise Companion to the Hadith
Edited by Daniel W. Brown

The Wiley Blackwell Companion to Christian Martyrdom
Edited by Paul Middleton

The Wiley Blackwell Companion to Zoroastrianism
Edited by Michael Stausberg and Yuhan Vevaina

Forthcoming

The Wiley Blackwell Companion to Islamic Spirituality
Edited by Vincent J. Cornell and Bruce B. Lawrence

The Wiley Blackwell Companion to Religious Diversity
Edited by Kevin Schilbrack

The Wiley Blackwell Companion to Christianity, 2 Vols.
Edited by Nicholas A. Adams

The Wiley Blackwell Companion to the Old Testament Apocrypha & Pseudepigrapha
Edited by Randall D. Chesnutt

The Wiley Blackwell Companion to the Study of Religion, Second Edition
Edited by Robert Segal

This paperback edition first published 2020
© 2012 John Wiley & Sons Ltd

Edition history: John Wiley & Sons Ltd. (hardback, 2012)

All rights reserved. No part of this publication may be reproduced, stored in a retrieval system, or transmitted, in any form or by any means, electronic, mechanical, photocopying, recording or otherwise, except as permitted by law. Advice on how to obtain permission to reuse material from this title is available at http://www.wiley.com/go/permissions.

The right of Michael D. Palmer and Stanley M. Burgess to be identified as the authors of the editorial material in this work has been asserted in accordance with law.

Registered Offices
John Wiley & Sons, Inc., 111 River Street, Hoboken, NJ 07030, USA
John Wiley & Sons Ltd, The Atrium, Southern Gate, Chichester, West Sussex, PO19 8SQ, UK

Editorial Office
The Atrium, Southern Gate, Chichester, West Sussex, PO19 8SQ, UK

For details of our global editorial offices, customer services, and more information about Wiley products visit us at www.wiley.com.

Wiley also publishes its books in a variety of electronic formats and by print-on-demand. Some content that appears in standard print versions of this book may not be available in other formats.

Limit of Liability/Disclaimer of Warranty
While the publisher and authors have used their best efforts in preparing this work, they make no representations or warranties with respect to the accuracy or completeness of the contents of this work and specifically disclaim all warranties, including without limitation any implied warranties of merchantability or fitness for a particular purpose. No warranty may be created or extended by sales representatives, written sales materials or promotional statements for this work. The fact that an organization, website, or product is referred to in this work as a citation and/or potential source of further information does not mean that the publisher and authors endorse the information or services the organization, website, or product may provide or recommendations it may make. This work is sold with the understanding that the publisher is not engaged in rendering professional services. The advice and strategies contained herein may not be suitable for your situation. You should consult with a specialist where appropriate. Further, readers should be aware that websites listed in this work may have changed or disappeared between when this work was written and when it is read. Neither the publisher nor authors shall be liable for any loss of profit or any other commercial damages, including but not limited to special, incidental, consequential, or other damages.

Library of Congress Cataloging-in-Publication Data
The Wiley Blackwell companion to religion and social justice / edited by Michael D. Palmer and Stanley M. Burgess.
   p. cm. – (Wiley Blackwell companions to religion)
 Includes bibliographical references and index.
 ISBN 978-1-4051-9547-8 (hardcover : alk. paper)
 978-1-1195-7210-7 (paperback)
1. Social justice–Religious aspects. I. Palmer, Michael D., 1950– II. Burgess, Stanley M., 1937– III. Title: Companion to religion and social justice.
 BL65.J87W55 2012
 201'.7–dc23
                                                                                    2011046000

Cover image: © Ivelin Radkov/Alamy Stock Photo
Cover design by Wiley

Set in 10/12.5 pt Photina by SPi Global, Pondicherry, India

10 9 8 7 6 5 4 3 2 1

The Wiley Blackwell Companion to Religion and Social Justice

Edited by

Michael D. Palmer and Stanley M. Burgess

WILEY Blackwell

"A wide-ranging and engaging gathering of contributors have provided an ideal text for exploring the social justice implications of varied religious traditions. The organization – around historical and present expressions of social justice in the world religions and in the traditions of indigenous peoples, together with selected issues – is user-friendly for beginning students as well as teachers and scholars."

— **Larry Rasmussen, Union Theological Seminary**

"[The Companion's] global range, intellectual ecumenism, and attention to diverse historical contexts provides a rich resource for exploring how religious beliefs and practices engage issues of colonialism, gender justice, political struggle, healthcare, race, and the environment, among other topics ... Bringing together theoretical discussions with case studies, it opens up new pathways for exploring how global and local religions interrogate matters of historical injustice, identity, and the moral quality of public life. I recommend it enthusiastically."

— **Richard B. Miller, Indiana University**

Contents

Notes on Contributors ix
Acknowledgments xix

Introduction 1

Part I Major World Religions 13

Introduction 15

1 Buddhism: Historical Setting 17
   Mavis Fenn

2 Buddhism: Contemporary Expressions 30
   Steven Emmanuel

3 Christianity: Historical Setting 46
   Stanley M. Burgess

4 Christianity: Contemporary Expressions 61
   Curtiss Paul DeYoung

5 Confucianism: Historical Setting 77
   Joseph Chan

6 Confucianism: Contemporary Expressions 93
   Stephen C. Angle

7 Hinduism: Historical Setting 110
   O.P. Dwivedi

8 Hinduism: Contemporary Expressions 124
   Amita Singh

9	Islam: Historical Setting *Hussam S. Timani*	137
10	Islam: Contemporary Expressions *Erin E. Stiles*	153
11	Judaism: Historical Setting *Moshe Hellinger*	170
12	Judaism: Contemporary Expressions *Eliezer Segal*	190

Part II Religious Movements and Themes — 205

Introduction — 207

13	Bahá'í Faith *Christopher Buck*	210
14	The Quest for Justice in Revival, a Creole Religion in Jamaica *William Wedenoja*	224
15	The Muhammadiyah: A Muslim Modernist Organization in Contemporary Indonesia *Florian Pohl*	241
16	The Role of the Chief in Asante Society *Yaw Adu-Gyamfi*	256
17	Tibetan Monastics and Social Justice *Derek F. Maher*	268
18	Sangha and Society *Hiroko Kawanami*	280
19	*G'meelut Chasadim* (Deeds of Kindness) *W.E. Nunnally*	292
20	Hospitality *Ana María Pineda*	306
21	*Zakat:* Faith and Giving in Muslim Contexts *Azim Nanji*	319
22	Ecumenical and Interreligious Dialogue *Barbara Brown Zikmund*	330

Part III Indigenous People — 345

Introduction — 347

23	Africa: Religion and Social Justice among the Diola of Senegal, Gambia, and Guinea-Bissau *Robert M. Baum*	350
24	Australia: Religion and Social Justice in a Continent of Hunter-Gatherers *Robert Tonkinson*	361
25	Central America: A God for the Poor – Folk Catholicism and Social Justice among the Yucatec Maya *Christine A. Kray*	373
26	Europe: The Roma People of Romania *Sorin Gog and Maria Roth*	388
27	Middle East: The Kurds – Religion and Social Justice of a Stateless Nation *Charles G. MacDonald*	402
28	New Zealand: The Māori People *Rawinia Higgins*	412
29	North America: Ojibwe Culture *Gregory O. Gagnon*	425
30	Southern Asia: The Gonds of India – A Search for Identity and Justice *Sushma Yadav*	438

Part IV Social Justice Issues   451

	Introduction	453
31	Colonialism *Brigid M. Sackey*	456
32	Abundant Life or Abundant Poverty? The Challenge for African Christianity *T. John Padwick*	469
33	AIDS, Religion, and the Politics of Social Justice in Sub-Saharan Africa *Afe Adogame*	482
34	Religion, Civil Rights, and Social Justice *Paul Harvey*	496
35	Human Rights: The South African Experience *Glenda Wildschut*	507

36	The "Double-Conscious" Nature of American Evangelicalism's Struggle over Civil Rights during the Progressive Era *L.B. Gallien, Jr.*	519
37	Gender and Sexuality in the Context of Religion and Social Justice *Mary E. Hunt*	535
38	Beginning of Life *Andrew Lustig*	547
39	Death and Dying *Courtney S. Campbell*	561
40	Religion's Influence on Social Justice Practices Relating to Those with Disabilities *Ruth Vassar Burgess*	575
41	Ecology and the Environment *Laurel Kearns*	591
42	Christianity and Nonviolent Resistance *Celia Cook-Huffman*	607
43	Building Peace in the Pursuit of Social Justice *Mohammed Abu-Nimer*	620
Index		633

Acknowledgments

Books are often the collaborative effort of many people, only some of whose names appear on the cover. So it is with this *Companion*. Many people have invested time and intellectual effort to see this volume appear in print. We owe them a debt of gratitude and wish to acknowledge them here.

First and foremost, we wish to acknowledge the authors who so willingly and ably explored topics dealing with religion and social justice, and whose essays form the essential content of this *Companion*. They inspired us by the way in which they embraced their tasks, and they often surprised us with their insights.

Two colleagues at Wiley Blackwell played important roles in the development of this *Companion*. Rebecca Harkin, Religion Publisher, spoke with us at length about the original prospectus. Her interest in and commitment to the core ideas prompted us to refine the scope of the project and move toward publication. Isobel Bainton, Religion and Theology Project Editor, managed development of the book from the time the manuscripts were submitted through final production. Her organizational skills (often evident in the detailed questions she posed) made the entire process seem well ordered and manageable. We thank her.

Ryan Swan, a senior undergraduate student, provided extensive, valuable research during the early stages of the book's development. Perhaps our largest debt is to Renea Brathwaite, a PhD student at Regent University, whose knowledge of computers and software, organizational skills, ability to read critically, meticulous attention to detail, good judgment, and sense of humor all contributed importantly to this *Companion*.

Notes on Contributors

Mohammed Abu-Nimer, PhD (George Mason University), is a Professor at American University's School of International Service in International Peace and Conflict Resolution in Washington, DC. He is the Director of the Peacebuilding and Development Institute. Dr. Abu-Nimer is also the Founder and Director of the Salam: Peacebuilding and Justice Institute, and the co-founder and co-editor of the *Journal of Peacebuilding and Development*. He has written, edited, and co-authored many books, including *Peace-Building By, Between and Beyond Muslims and Evangelical Christians*; *Reconciliation, Coexistence, and Justice: Theory and Practice*; *Unity in Diversity: Interfaith Dialogue in the Middle East*; and *Peacebuilding and Nonviolence in Islam*.

Afe Adogame, PhD (Bayreuth University, Germany) is Assistant Professor in World Christianity/Religious Studies at University of Edinburgh, UK, where he teaches Indigenous Religions, African Christianity, and Religion in the new African Diaspora. His numerous publications include *Celestial Church of Christ: The Politics of Cultural Identity in a West African Prophetic-Charismatic Movement* (1999); and, co-edited, *European Traditions in the Study of Religion in Africa* (2004); and *Christianity in Africa and the African Diaspora: The Appropriation of a Scattered Heritage* (2008). His most recent books are, co-edited, *Religion Crossing Boundaries: Transnational Religious and Social Dynamics in Africa and the New African Diaspora* (2010), and (ed.) *Who is Afraid of the Holy Ghost?: Pentecostalism and Globalization in Africa and Beyond* (2011). He is General Secretary, African Association for the Study of Religion; Member, International Advisory Board of *Journal of Religion in Africa* and *African Diaspora* (Brill); and Associate Editor, *Studies in World Christianity* (Edinburgh University Press).

Yaw Adu-Gyamfi, PhD (University of Sheffield, UK) is a Senior Lecturer of Biblical Studies at Ghana Baptist University College in Kumasi, Ghana, where he regularly teaches courses in the field of Old Testament Literature, Biblical Interpretation, and Gospel and Culture. Dr. Adu-Gyamfi has delivered numerous papers on topics related to the Bible and African culture. Among his best-known works is *Leviticus 16 and Asante Odwira Festival*, which deals with the biblical faith and Asante traditional religion.

Stephen C. Angle received his BA from Yale University in East Asian Studies and his PhD in Philosophy from the University of Michigan. Since 1994 he has taught at Wesleyan University, where he is now Professor of Philosophy. Angle is the author of *Human Rights and Chinese Thought: A Cross-Cultural Inquiry* (2002), *Sagehood: The Contemporary Significance of Neo-Confucian Philosophy* (2009), and numerous scholarly articles on Chinese ethical and political thought and on topics in comparative philosophy.

Robert M. Baum, PhD (Yale University), an Associate Professor at the University of Missouri-Columbia, is currently a Residential Research Fellow at the Woodrow Wilson International Center for Scholars, in Washington, DC. He is the author of numerous articles on Diola religion, African religions, and indigenous religions. His best-known work is *Shrines of the Slave Trade: Diola Religion and Society in Precolonial SeneGambi* (1999), which received the American Academy of Religion's Award for the best first book in the history of religions. He is currently writing a history of Diola prophetic movements.

Christopher Buck, PhD (University of Toronto), JD (Cooley Law School), is a Pennsylvania attorney and independent scholar. He has taught at Michigan State University (2000–2004), Quincy University (1999–2000), Millikin University (1997–1999), and Carleton University (1994–1996). His publications include *Religious Myths and Visions of America: How Minority Faiths Redefined America's World Role* (2009); *Alain Locke: Faith and Philosophy* (2005); *Paradise and Paradigm: Key Symbols in Persian Christianity and the Bahá'í Faith* (1999); and *Symbol and Secret: Qur'an Commentary in Bahá'u'lláh's Kitáb-i Íqán* (1995/2004).

Ruth Vassar Burgess, PhD (University of Missouri, Columbia) is Professor Emerita at Missouri State University in Springfield, Missouri, where she taught courses relating to communication disorders, assisting families with individuals with disabilities, and methods of integrating positive inclusion strategies in society. Born and reared in India in a context where Hindus, Muslims, and Christians resided peacefully, Dr. Burgess brings a cross-cultural background into being. Two recent scholarly works are *Changing Brain Structure through Cross-Cultural Learning: The Life of Reuven Feuerstein* (2008) and *Shantistan* (2004). The latter is a peacebuilding curriculum that utilizes an interreligion, mediated learning, dialogic approach.

Stanley M. Burgess, is Professor Emeritus, Missouri State University. In addition to over 150 scholarly articles, he has published numerous books, including the *International Dictionary of Pentecostal and Charismatic Movements* (2002), the *Encyclopedia of Pentecostal and Charismatic Christianity* (2004), and *Christian Peoples of the Spirit: a Documentary Collection* (2011).

Courtney S. Campbell, PhD (University of Virginia), is Professor of Philosophy in the Department of Philosophy at Oregon State University, where he holds the Hundere Chair in Religion and Culture. He teaches courses primarily in the fields of biomedical ethics, death and dying, nonviolence and just war, and religious liberty. He has published nearly 150 articles on issues in medical ethics, with a particular concentration on the ethics of death with dignity, and the role of religious views in public ethical discussion. He has recently assumed a position on the board of directors of Benton Hospice, addressing ethics in hospice care and patient care.

Joseph Chan, DPhil (Oxford University), is Professor in the Department of Politics and Public Administration at the University of Hong Kong, where he regularly teaches courses in the field of political theory. His recent research focuses on Confucian political philosophy, theories of human rights, and liberalism and perfectionism. He has published articles on these topics in major journals, including *Ethics*, *Oxford Journal of Legal Studies*, *Journal of Chinese Philosophy*, *Journal of Democracy*, *Philosophy and Public Affairs*, and *Philosophy East and West*. Currently he is writing a book on Confucian political philosophy.

Celia Cook-Huffman, PhD (Syracuse University), is Professor of Peace and Conflict Studies at Juniata College, where she holds the W. Clay and Kathryn Burkholder Professorship in Conflict Resolution. Her background combines peace studies with specialized training and education in conflict transformation, nonviolence, gender, and mediation. She works as a consultant and trainer in workplace, church, and educational settings. She has received grants from Fulbright and the US Embassy Program on Bicommunal Projects, Cyprus. Her research focuses primarily on the impact of social identity on conflict and the relationship between gender issues and conflict.

Curtiss Paul DeYoung, EdD (University of St. Thomas, St. Paul, MN), is Professor of Reconciliation Studies at Bethel University in St. Paul, Minnesota. Dr. DeYoung has written, co-written, and co-edited nine books related to reconciliation and social justice issues from a faith perspective. Among these he is the author of *Living Faith: How Faith Inspires Social Justice* (2007), co-author of *United by Faith: The Multiracial Congregation as an Answer to the Problem of Race* (2003), and a co-editor for *The Peoples' Bible* (2008). His reconciliation interests have led to several visits to South Africa and Palestine/Israel.

O.P. Dwivedi, PhD (Queen's University), Fellow of the Royal Society of Canada, is Professor Emeritus, Department of Political Science, University of Guelph, Canada, where he has taught since 1967. He has published 35 books and written many articles and chapters in various professional journals and scholarly books. His research interests include environmental ethics, comparative public policy and management, and public morality. He has been consultant to the World Bank, UNESCO, WHO, UNO, UN-ESCAP, IDRC, and CIDA. He is the recipient of honorary degrees and various awards. In 2005, he was bestowed with the Order of Canada, the highest civilian honor by the Government of Canada.

Steven Emmanuel, PhD (Brown University), is Batten Professor of Philosophy at Virginia Wesleyan College in Norfolk, Virginia. Dr. Emmanuel's research interests lie mainly in the areas of intellectual history and comparative ethics. He is the author of

Kierkegaard and the Concept of Revelation (1996), *The Modern Philosophers: From Descartes to Nietzsche* (2001), and the co-editor of *Modern Philosophy: An Anthology* (2002). Dr. Emmanuel's most recent work includes a foray into filmmaking. He produced and directed an award-winning documentary entitled "Making Peace with Viet Nam" (2009), which explores the challenges of reconciliation in the aftermath of war.

Mavis L. Fenn, PhD (McMaster University), is Associate Professor of Religious Studies at University of Waterloo, Ontario, Canada, where she regularly teaches courses in the field of Buddhism and Asian religions. Dr. Fenn has published articles on Buddhist women in Canada and on Sakyadhita, the International Association of Buddhist Women. Among her best-known works is "The concept of poverty in the Pali Canon," which deals with issues of social concern in Buddhism. Dr. Fenn also serves as Acting Chair for the Department of Religious Studies. She is interested in issues of pedagogy and online technology.

Gregory O. Gagnon, PhD (University of Maryland-College Park), an emeritus faculty member of the University of North Dakota Indian Studies, is currently a research associate at Loyola University, New Orleans. He is an enrolled citizen of Bad River Reservation (Ojibwe). His *Culture and Customs of the Sioux Indians* and co-authored *Native American Studies: An Interdisciplinary Introduction* were published in Summer, 2011. Professor Gagnon teaches Chippewa History, Federal Indian Law and Policy, and Indian Issues in the Twenty-First Century. He is a consultant to four Ojibwe tribal colleges and has written articles and made presentations on various aspects of Chippewa history.

Louis B. Gallien, Jr., PhD (University of North Carolina), is Dean of the School of Education and Human Services at Oakland University, MI. Professor Gallien's research interests have centered on themes of race, gender, human sexuality, and religion in the contexts of African American culture and American evangelicalism in particular. His latest chapter, "Crossing over Jordan: Navigating the music of earthly desire and heavenly bliss in the lives of three 20th Century African American cross-over artists," appears in Alexander and Yong, *Afro-Pentecostalism and Its Changing Discourses* (2010).

Sorin Gog, PhD (Babes-Bolyai University), is Assistant Lecturer at the Faculty of Sociology and Social Work, Babes-Bolyai University, Cluj-Napoca, Romania, where he teaches Symbolic Anthropology and Social Theories. Sorin Gog has published numerous international papers on the issue of religious conversion, secularization, anthropology of religion, and anthropology of death and cemeteries. Currently he is a research fellow at Institute of Human Sciences in Vienna, Austria, where he explores the impact of the Europeanization process on religious mentalities in postsocialist countries.

Paul Harvey, PhD (University of California at Berkeley), is Professor of History and Presidential Teaching Scholar at the University of Colorado at Colorado Springs. He is the author/editor of six books, including *Freedom's Coming: Religious Cultures and the Shaping of the South from the Civil War through the Civil Rights Era* (2007), and runs the professional blog Religion in American History at http://usreligion.blogspot.com.

Moshe Hellinger, PhD (Bar-Ilan University), is Senior Lecturer of Political Science at the Department of Political Studies, Bar-Ilan University, Israel. He also teaches there at the Faculty of Law. Dr. Hellinger is the head of the Ernest and Martha Schwartz institute for Judaism, Ethics and Society at Beit Morasha, Jerusalem and a senior researcher at the Israel Democracy Institute, Jerusalem. Dr. Hellinger has published numerous articles in Hebrew and English journals on Jewish political thought in general and on Judaism and democracy and religious Zionism in particular. His book on religious Zionism will be published by Academic Press. He is currently working on a book on attitudes toward war and peace in Jewish tradition.

Rawinia Higgins, PhD (University of Otago), is a Senior Lecturer at Te Kawa a Maūi, School of Māori Studies at Victoria University of Wellington, New Zealand. Dr. Higgins is indigenous to New Zealand and comes from the Tūhoe tribal group located in Te Urewera, Eastern Bay of Plenty. Dr. Higgins is a Trustee of Te Kotahi a Tūhoe, the Treaty of Waitangi Settlement Negotiation group for Tūhoe. She has published articles and book chapters pertaining to Māori culture and society with specific emphasis on Tūhoe social justice issues, particularly the terrorism raids in Ruatoki in 1997.

Mary E. Hunt, PhD (Graduate Theological Union), is a feminist theologian who is co-founder and co-director of the Women's Alliance for Theology, Ethics and Ritual (WATER) in Silver Spring, Maryland. A Catholic active in the women-church movement, she lectures and writes on theology and ethics with particular attention to liberation issues. She is the editor of *A Guide for Women in Religion: Making Your Way from A to Z* (2004) and co-editor with Diann L. Neu of *New Feminist Christianity: Many Voices, Many Views* (2010).

Hiroko Kawanami, PhD (London University), is Lecturer in Buddhist Studies at Lancaster University, UK, where she teaches several courses on contemporary Buddhist issues in southeast Asia. Dr. Kawanami has published numerous articles in both Japanese and English on topics related to women and Buddhism, Buddhism and modernity, and the notions of power(s) in Buddhism. Her most recent works are a special issue on Burmese-Myanmar religion in *Asian Ethnology* 68: 2 (2009); and the *bhikkhuni* ordination debate: global aspirations, local concerns, *Buddhist Studies Review* 24 (2007). Dr. Kawanami has recently taught at McGill University, Canada, as Numata visiting professor in Buddhist Studies.

Laurel D. Kearns, PhD (Emory University), is Associate Professor of the Sociology of Religion and Environmental Studies at the Theological School and Graduate Division of Drew University in New Jersey, where she teaches on religion and ecology, environmental justice, religion and social movements, and the US religious landscape. Dr. Kearns has published numerous articles in journals and in volumes such as *The Blackwell Companion to Modern Theology* (2004), *The Oxford Handbook of Climate Change and Society* (2011), and *Religion, Globalization and Culture* (2007). She co-edited, with Catherine Keller, *Ecospirit: Religions and Philosophies for the Earth* (2007), and served as an assistant editor of *The Encyclopedia of Religion and Nature*. Dr. Kearns also serves on the

Sustainability Committees of Drew University and the American Academy of Religion, and on the executive committee of the Green Seminary Initiative.

Christine A. Kray, PhD (University of Pennsylvania), is Associate Professor of Anthropology at Rochester Institute of Technology in Rochester, New York, where she teaches courses in the degree programs of International Studies and Urban and Community Studies. Dr. Kray has published numerous articles on topics of religious choice and conversion in the context of economic globalization, religion and the self, international tourism, and labor migration to Cancún. She is currently working on a book project about the incorporation of Yucatec Maya refugees into the colony of British Honduras (modern-day Belize) and consequences they faced amid divergent strategies of development.

B. Andrew Lustig, PhD (University of Virginia), is the Holmes Rolston III Professor of Religion and Science at Davidson College in Davidson, North Carolina, where he teaches courses in religion and science, theological ethics, and bioethics. Dr. Lustig has co-written, edited, or co-edited 10 books on bioethics and health policy, most recently *Altering Nature: Religion, Biotechnology, and Public Policy* (2008). He is also the author of more than 175 other publications for both scholarly and general audiences. Dr. Lustig currently sits on the board of directors of the National Biomedical Research Foundation, the editorial board of *The Journal of Medicine and Philosophy*, and the advisory board of Christian Bioethics.

Charles G. MacDonald, PhD (University of Virginia), is Professor of International Relations at Florida International University in Miami, Florida, where he teaches courses in international relations, specializing in international law, the Middle East, and ethnic studies. Dr. MacDonald has published numerous articles and two books on Kurdish issues, including the jointly edited *Kurdish Identity* (2007), which deals with human rights and the political status of Kurds. Dr. MacDonald was the first president of the Kurdish Studies Association. He has spoken at scholarly international conferences on the Kurds in Brussels, Lausanne, and Washington, DC.

Derek F. Maher, PhD (University of Virginia), is Associate Professor of Religious Studies and the Director of the Religious Studies program at East Carolina University in Greenville, North Carolina. He teaches courses in Buddhism, Hinduism, and Religion and Violence. Dr. Maher has written widely on religious biography, history, and philosophy. He recently published a two-volume annotated translation of the classic Tibetan-language *One Hundred Thousand Moons: An Advanced Political History of Tibet* (2010). Dr. Maher also directs Tong-Len USA, a nonprofit organization that raises money for one of the organizations he mentions in his contribution to this volume.

Azim Nanji, PhD (McGill University), joined the Abbasi Program in Islamic Studies at Stanford University in 2008, where he also lectures on Islam in the Department of Religious Studies. He was Director of the Institute of Ismaili Studies in London from 1998 to 2008 and before that was Professor and Chair of the Department of Religious

Studies at the University of Florida. He has authored, co-authored, and edited several books including *The Nizari Ismaili Tradition* (1976), *The Muslim Almanac* (1996), *Mapping Islamic Studies* (1997), *The Historical Atlas of Islam* (with M. Ruthven, 2004), *The Dictionary of Islam* (with Razia Nanji, 2008), and *Living in Historic Cairo* (with Farhad Daftary and Elizabeth Fernea, 2010). In addition, he has contributed numerous articles on religion, Islam, and Shiism in journals and collective volumes, including *The Encyclopedia of Islam*, *Encyclopaedia Iranica*, *Oxford Encyclopaedia of the Modern Islamic World*, and *A Companion to Ethics*.

W.E. Nunnally, PhD (Hebrew Union College), specializes in Rabbinic Literature and the Dead Sea Scrolls. He holds a BA in Religion from Mississippi College, an MA in Hebrew Language from the Institute of Holy Land Studies (now called Jerusalem University College) in Israel, an MA in Old Testament from Reformed Theological Seminary, and an MPhil in Hebraic and Cognate Studies from Hebrew Union College. He has taught in Springfield, Missouri, for the past 18 years and has authored numerous books and articles. He is currently Professor of Early Judaism and Christian Origins at Evangel University.

Timothy John Padwick, PhD (University of Birmingham, UK), has for the past 15 years explored the interface between theology and its socioeconomic and political environment within the context of African Independent Churches. His research has centered on how oral/vernacular theology emerged in particular situations, how it has changed to meet emerging challenges, and how it has motivated social transformation. With Lawford Imunde, he developed the concept of "Founding Visions," which enables African Independent Churches to recover and engage with the roots of their faith and apply their findings in areas of theology, culture, HIV/AIDS, and economic development. He has also been instrumental in developing a methodology and theological approach to facilitate working with African religious movements. For many years he has served in various advisory roles to the Organization of African Instituted Churches in Nairobi, Kenya, most recently on matters of theological research and documentation.

Michael D. Palmer is a professor of philosophy at Regent University. In addition to numerous scholarly articles, book chapters, and reviews, he has published four books, including a two volume work *The Holy Spirit and Social Justice, Interdisciplinary Global Perspectives* (2019), coedited with Antipas Harris. Palmer has extensive experience teaching undergraduate and graduate courses in moral theory, social ethics, applied ethics, and philosophy of religion. He has also conducted professional workshops and seminars for educators on topics relating to religion and ethics.

Ana María Pineda, RSM, STD, is Associate Professor of Religious Studies at Santa Clara University in Santa Clara, California, where she regularly teaches courses in Latino/Hispanic theology. Dr. Pineda has published numerous articles on topics related to Hispanic ministry, popular religion, pastoral practices, and the importance of oral tradition. Dr. Pineda has served on the board of the Louisville Institute, the Academy of Catholic Hispanic Theologians of the US (ACHTUS), the Advisory Committee for the

Hispanic Theological Scholarship Initiative (HTI), and many others. She is the past president of ACHTUS, and the co-editor of *Dialogue Rejoined: Theology and Ministry in the United States Hispanic Reality* (1995).

Florian Pohl, PhD (Temple University), is Assistant Professor in Religious Studies at Emory University's Oxford College in Oxford, Georgia. His field of research is southeast Asian Islam, with a special focus on questions of contemporary religious expression and public life. Among his recent publications are "Interreligious harmony and peacebuilding in Indonesian Islamic education," in *Peace Psychology in Asia*, Christina Montiel and Noraini Noor (eds.) (2009), and *Islamic Education and the Public Sphere: Today's Pesantren in Indonesia* (2009). For the past five years, he also has been affiliated through research and teaching with the Center for Religious and Cross-cultural Studies at Gadjah Mada University in Yogyakarta, Indonesia.

Maria Roth, PhD (Babes-Bolyai University), is a Professor of Social Work at Babes-Bolyai University, Cluj, Romania. Chair of the Social Work Department, she is one of the founders of Social Work Studies in Romania. Following a nine-month residency as a Fulbright Senior Research Scholar at University of North Carolina at Chapel Hill, she returned to her home university and published books and articles in the field of child well-being, social service development for vulnerable populations, and social work methods.

Brigid Maa Sackey, PhD (Temple University), is Professor of Anthropology at the Institute of African Studies, University of Ghana, Legon. She was trained in Ghana, Germany (Philipps University, Marburg), and the United States (Temple University, Philadelphia). Her teaching, research, and publication topics include African traditional religions, Christianity and Islam in Africa, new religious movements, religion and health, women, religion and politics, and family studies. She is the author of *New Directions in Gender and Religion* (2006). She has been Deputy Director and Acting Director of the Institute of African Studies, University of Ghana, Legon, and a Research Associate and Visiting Scholar in the Women's Studies and Religion Program, Harvard Divinity School.

Eliezer Segal, PhD (Hebrew University of Jerusalem), is Professor of Religious Studies at the University of Calgary, Canada, where he regularly teaches courses in the fields of Judaism and western religions. Dr. Segal has published numerous articles and books on topics related to Jewish religious literature, law, and thought. Among his best-known works is the three-volume *Babylonian Esther Midrash: A Critical Commentary* (1994), which explores ancient rabbinic exegesis and homiletical interpretations. In addition to his academic research, he publishes works on Jewish tradition targeted at nonspecialists, maintains a popular website, and is the author of a children's book.

Amita Singh, PhD (Agra University), is Professor and Chairperson at the Centre for the Study of Law and Governance at Jawaharlal Nehru University, New Delhi. She has been the Project Director of the Governance Knowledge Centre of the Government of India and the Secretary General of the Network of Asia Pacific Schools and Institutes of Public Administration and Governance (NAPSIPAG). Her publications include several books and several research papers in peer-reviewed journals. Her most recent publications are *Governance and Poverty Reduction* (2009), co-edited with Kapoor and Bhattacharyya; *Governance and Access to Justice* (2009), co-edited with Justice Nasir Aslam Zahid, Chief Justice of Sindh High Court in Pakistan; and *Strengthening Governance in Asia Pacific* (2010), co-edited with Saber, Ahmad, and Jalal. Her scholarship focuses on issues of social and environmental justice in administrative reforms.

Erin E. Stiles, PhD (Washington University in St. Louis), is Assistant Professor of Anthropology at the University of Nevada, Reno, where she teaches courses in cultural anthropology and the anthropology of religion. Dr. Stiles has conducted ethnographic research in Zanzibar, Tanzania since 1999, and recently published a book, *An Islamic Court in Context: An Ethnographic Study of Judicial Reasoning* (2009), which looks at marital disputes in Zanzibar's Islamic courts. She has also published several shorter works on the subject. At the University of Nevada, Dr. Stiles serves on the advisory board for the Religious Studies minor.

Hussam S. Timani, PhD (University of California, Los Angeles), is Associate Professor of Religious Studies at Christopher Newport University in Newport News, Virginia, where he regularly teaches courses in the field of Islamic studies. Dr. Timani is the author of *Modern Intellectual Readings of the Kharijites* (2008), which deals with modern interpretations of the Muslim past, and has also published a number of articles and a book chapter on topics related to Islam. Dr. Timani is co-founder and serves on the advisory board of *Interfaith Forum of Hampton Roads*, which promotes Christian–Muslim dialogue. He has appeared on radio talk shows including National Public Radio's *With Good Reason* and is the recipient of the 2009 *Rumi Forum Education Award* for peace and dialogue.

Robert Tonkinson, PhD (University of British Columbia), is Emeritus Professor of Anthropology and Honorary Senior Research Fellow at the University of Western Australia. He has worked with Western Desert Aborigines since 1963 and Melanesians in Vanuatu since 1966. His publications include three monographs and numerous articles on these peoples. Among his best-known works is *The Mardu Aborigines* (1979), on traditional Western Desert Aboriginal society. His interests include religion, social change, kinship, migration, identity, and the politics of tradition. He is a long-serving member of the governing council of the Australian Institute of Aboriginal and Torres Straits Studies.

William Wedenoja, PhD (University of California, San Diego), is Professor of Anthropology at Missouri State University, where he serves as coordinator of Anthropology and as director of the MS in Applied Anthropology program. Dr. Wedenoja has been conducting research on Jamaica since 1972, publishing articles on indigenous religion, healing, possession trance, Pentecostalism, and mental illness. In recent years he has also worked on a number of community development projects in Jamaica, concerning artisanal fishing, education, tourism, environmental protection, and heritage preservation.

Glenda Wildschut is the Managing Director of the Collective Leadership Institute in South Africa. In 1995 she was appointed by President Nelson Mandela to serve as a Commissioner on the South African Truth and Reconciliation Commission, under the chairmanship of the Nobel Peace Laureate Archbishop Desmond Tutu. She served on the Reparation and Rehabilitation Committee. In 1998, she worked at the World Health Organization in Geneva, examining the role of health workers in transitional societies. She has been involved in human rights advocacy since the early 1980s, working particularly with political prisoners in South Africa and Namibia, their families, exiles, and orphaned returnee children. She pioneered the establishment of a trauma center for survivors of violence and torture – the first of its kind in South Africa. Having acquired academic and clinical qualifications in South Africa and the United States, she lectured and tutored at both the University of Cape Town and the University of the Western Cape. Glenda Wildschut serves on several boards, including the board of the Institute of the Healing of Memories, the Institute for Justice and Reconciliation, the Centre for Rural Legal Studies Home for Kids in South Africa (HOKISA), and Truth in Translation. Until recently, she was the Director of the Desmond Tutu Leadership Academy.

Sushma Yadav, PhD (University of Delhi), holds the Dr. Ambedkar Chair in Social Justice and is Professor of Public Policy and Governance at the Indian Institute of Public Administration, New Delhi, India. With more than 30 years of teaching and research experience, she has published numerous articles in books and professional journals and authored and edited 11 books, including *Social Justice: Ambedkar's Vision* (2006), *Gender Issues in India: Some Reflections* (2008), and *Culture and Politics* (1998). Recipient of the Rai Bahadur Gori Shankar Memorial Medal, the Maharshi Karve Memorial prize, and National IFJA award, she has served and is currently serving on the editorial boards and panels of referees for several peer-reviewed professional journals. She has been a visiting faculty member of the Dr. Ambedkar Study Centers of a number of universities in India. Currently, she is the Vice-Chairperson of the Research Committee and India coordinator of the International Political Science Association. At IIPA, she introduced a core course on social justice, which remains her main area of interest and expertise.

Barbara Brown Zikmund, PhD (Duke University), is retired from 30 years of teaching and administration in theological education. She has held appointments in church history and administration in five seminaries, serving as Dean of the faculty at Pacific School of Religion (1981–1990) and as President of Hartford Seminary (1990–2000). Under her leadership Hartford Seminary strengthened its long-standing programs in Christian–Muslim relations. She was a member of several ecumenical commissions, attended international interreligious conferences, and for seven years served as chair of the Interfaith Relations Commission of the National Council of Churches of Christ USA (2000–2007). She is co-editor of *Remembering Jamestown* (2010), a collection of essays exploring interreligious issues related to Christian missionary efforts in colonial Virginia.

Introduction

Michael D. Palmer and Stanley M. Burgess

Rationale for the Project

In today's cosmopolitan environment, one is struck by how much public discourse on questions of social justice is addressed (or addressable) in the arenas of politics, economics, public policy, or international affairs. Daily, news media broadcast consequential reports from any or all of these arenas: Can Egypt and Tunisia successfully transition to democratic rule? Who should pay for the economic catastrophes in Greece, Portugal, and Iceland? Should the United Nations recognize a Palestinian state? Can Tibetans ever expect to gain a measure of autonomy given the authoritarian control exerted by the People's Republic of China? When so much that is important can be framed in the language of state and economy, one wonders whether religion remains a relevant force in public discourse, especially discourse that concerns social justice.

The answer to this question is yes. Despite the fact that a growing (though still small) minority of the world's people claims no religious affiliation, religion continues to provide an important window into human motivation and aspiration on matters of consequence, including questions of social justice. While other domains of discourse (political, economic) have much to offer, religion provides both a historically important and continuingly significant perspective on social justice in at least two ways.

First, religion has social justice implications in the way it shapes what its adherents believe about their roles and prerogatives in society. Consider, for example, that historically all three of the Abrahamic religions – Judaism, Christianity, and Islam – have struggled with questions about the status of women. Are women equal to men or subordinate to them? From one generation to another, leaders in these religions, mostly men, have advanced religiously grounded views about the relative roles of men and women, and these views have affected the lives of women in profound, often negative, ways. The continuing relevance of religious discourse in matters of social justice is evident in the fact that religious dialogue over the status of women has continued into the present and is more lively and engaging than ever, with women taking the lead.

Hinduism reveals another way in which religion has social justice implications. Its caste system, which ancient sources suggest was originally established as a means to advance societal and individual well-being by arranging divisions of labor appropriate to the skills and aptitudes of the people, has for centuries perpetuated social discrimination and class oppression. Hinduism's religious ideology gave rise to a social arrangement (the caste system) that shaped how its adherents could expect to be treated by others and had deep and and negative impacts on certain of its adherents, especially the *dalits*.

Quite simply, religion has had and continues to have social justice implications. This much seems clear and worth exploring. But there is a second point that also merits attention. The way in which social justice is or is not administered has religious implications. Two examples – one ancient, one modern – illustrate this line of thought.

The ancient Hebrew Scriptures called for Jews to release slaves after six years; those who released them were expected to provide them with the necessities for living. This expectation was expressed as a commandment issued by their God: "Remember that you were a slave in the land of Egypt, and the Lord your God redeemed you; for this reason I lay this command upon you today" (Deuteronomy 15:15). What is interesting and noteworthy here is the relationship between experience and moral/theological ideology. The moral edict, the commandment, was embedded within a larger religious framework and justified by reference to a prior experience that informed the moral/religious sensibility of the people.

Among modern religious people, adherents to the Bahá'í Faith have exhibited a strong concern for social justice. Their commitments to human rights, racial unity, and women's issues are all well documented. But what is the source of this overt commitment to justice? From the beginning of the religion in the nineteenth century, Bahá'í leaders were persecuted by civil and religious authorities, mainly in Muslim countries. In the 1980s, for instance, Iran declared the Bahá'í religion to be an unlawful, criminal organization, banned it, and executed a number of its leaders. Clearly, Bahá'í moral sensibility has been shaped by historical experiences of unjust treatment.

The accounts of the ancient Jews and the modern Bahá'ís are hardly unique. Among adherents of many religions and sacred belief systems a certain theme recurs: powerful experiences of unjust (or sometimes just) treatment inform a people's moral sensibility in a way that profoundly shapes how they understand and practice their religion. Thus, to study the religion is to study more than a set of theological claims. It is also to engage a set of experiences that inform and enliven the adherents of the religion. If their experiences have social justice implications, then those implications will likely be reflected in the religion's essential ideology, norms, and narratives.

Do all religions deal with issues of social justice? The question does not admit of a simple yes or no response. Clearly, many do not use (or have not historically used) the language of social justice. At the same time, that a religion does not use (or has not historically used) the language of social justice does not mean that it has not struggled with issues that in some way qualify as social justice issues. Virtually all major religions, religious movements, faith traditions, and sacred belief systems have found ways to express what may broadly be called social justice concerns. These include beliefs and practices by which peoples and individual persons express concern for weak and vulnerable members of the community; sustain the community; treat each other fairly; resolve disputes and grievances; distribute community resources; uphold the dignity of the human person; promote peaceful interaction; enhance political or economic participation in the community; or encourage a sense of stewardship for the natural world. It is this complex set of concerns – concerns situated at the intersection of religion and social justice – that this book explores.

Overview and Arrangement of Essays

The essays in this book are arranged into four parts: (I) Major World Religions; (II) Religious Movements and Themes; (III) Indigenous People; and (IV) Social Justice Issues.

Major world religions

Essays in this part deal with the world's major religions. As discussed in the Introduction to Part I, the expression *major world religion* is not uncontroversial. Suffice it to say at this point that the term *major* refers to a religion's geographical distribution, antiquity, and cultural influence. Major religions include Buddhism, Christianity, Confucianism, Hinduism, Islam, and Judaism. This part includes twelve essays, two on each of the religions. The first essay for each religion addresses the historical development of the religion's approach to social justice; the second focuses on the religion's approaches toward and expressions of social justice in recent decades, as well as in today's world.

Religious movements and themes

Essays in this part offer examples of what social justice means and how it functions practically within a variety of religious settings. Except for the conscious effort to avoid focusing attention exclusively on one or two religions, no attempt has been made to be exhaustive or even representative, only illustrative. Each essay was chosen for a distinctive reason, which is addressed in the part Introduction. What the essays share in common is that they deal with social justice from the perspective of some religious movement or theme.

Indigenous people

Essays in this part discuss the approaches to social justice of eight indigenous peoples, each in a distinct geographical region of the world: Central America; West Africa; Australia; Southern Asia; Europe; North America; New Zealand; and the Middle East.

The expression *indigenous* is intended to identify peoples (usually relatively small in population) that have traditionally occupied specific regions of the world. As used here, the expression refers primarily to a people whose underlying organizational principle is a social relationship such as family, clan, band, tribe, or other social structure, rather than the religion or sacred belief system to which they subscribe. Thus, for example, native peoples of North American (Native Americans) are classified as indigenous people partly because they have historically occupied particular geographical regions of North America, but also because their fundamental organizational principle is the band or tribe to which their members belong, not the sacred beliefs to which they subscribe. The essays on indigenous peoples provide historical, cultural, and geographical information, but their primary purpose is to elucidate how the sacred beliefs, experiences, narratives, and social arrangements of the people in question inform their beliefs and practices about social justice.

Social justice issues

Essays in this part include a representative sampling of issues that have social justice implications and that religions address, but that are not unique to any single religion. The topics were chosen because of their importance in the contemporary conversation about social justice. The purpose of the essays is not to resolve the debates, but to deepen our understanding of the issues and to show how some (although not all) religions deal with the issues in question.

Social Justice

The Italian Roman Catholic Jesuit scholar Luigi Taparelli D'Azeglio (1793–1862) is generally credited with being the first to use the expression *social justice*. Drawing heavily on the moral teachings of the thirteenth-century theologian Thomas Aquinas, he focused mainly on problems associated with the industrial revolution of the nineteenth century.

Today, the expression *social justice* covers a broad semantic domain, both secular and religious. The word *social* suggests that social justice has to do with matters of justice at the societal level rather than the personal level. Thus, for example, social justice is not principally about individual persons acquiring the virtue justice. However, beyond this general insight clarity is difficult to achieve. The expression is in fact used in a number of ways throughout this book. Depending on the context, it can be a near-synonym for any one of several forms of justice, including distributive justice, compensatory justice, retributive justice, procedural justice, or restorative justice. In some instances it even applies to types of behavior or interaction that are known more commonly by other names, such as *potlatch*, hospitality, *zakat* (almsgiving), or *g'meelut chasadim* (deeds of kindness). In short, although it may be desirable to have a succinct definition of *social justice*, no such definition exists. Rather, we have something more akin to interlocking circles: definitions that relate to each other as members of a family (to borrow a phrase from Wittgenstein) but do not finally reduce to a univocal statement.

Social justice as distributive justice

Distributive justice (an ancient concept, explicated at least as early as Aristotle) is essentially a comparative concept, having to do with the just or fair allocation of benefits and burdens among the members of a social group. In "The concept of social justice," William Frankena (1964) expresses distributive justice as a purely formal principle: equals should be treated equally and unequals should be treated unequally in proportion to their inequality. More recently, David Miller has described distributive justice somewhat more concretely:

> Very crudely, I think, we are discussing how the good and bad things in life should be distributed among the members of a human society. When, more concretely, we attack some policy or some state of affairs as socially unjust, we are claiming that a person, or more usually a category of persons, enjoys fewer advantages than that person or group ought to enjoy (or bears more of the burdens than they ought to bear), given how other members of the society in question are faring. (Miller, 1999: 1)

Questions about distributive justice arise when available resources (e.g., food, money, education, healthcare) are insufficient to meet everybody's needs or when the available resources, even if sufficient, are allocated in a way that does not meet the needs of all members of the social group. Questions about distributive justice also arise when burdens (e.g., onerous work, inadequate shelter, care of the very young, the very old, and those with disabilities) are excessive or unfairly imposed.

Whether we use Frankena's version of the principle or Miller's, certain difficult questions inevitably emerge. For instance, the preceding discussion may suggest that it is relatively easy to determine what benefits and burdens are to be distributed. It may seem obvious, for instance, that such things as wealth, income, and opportunity must be distributed fairly. But in point of fact, cultural factors (including religion) often frame and define the benefits and burdens. These same factors may also prescribe or proscribe who or what distributes the benefits and burdens, and may even determine who qualifies for benefits or who must bear the burdens.

Distributive justice shows up as the predominant way of interpreting social justice in a number of the essays in this book. For example, in "Confucianism: Historical Setting," Joseph Chan discusses whether Confucianism contains the concepts of distributive justice and then explores whether it articulates any ethical principles governing the distribution of resources. Chan's thesis is that Mencius advanced a social ideal of "a multilayer system of care and help" and examines "its relations with other values such as justice, personal responsibility, and individual merit"(this volume: 77).

As noted earlier, some instances of behavior that go by names not commonly associated with justice might nonetheless qualify as social justice expressed as a form of distributive justice. For instance, *potlatch*, hospitality, *zakat* (almsgiving), or *g'meelut chasadim* (deeds of kindness) might be understood in this way. What is the basis for this conjecture?

The *potlatch* is a ceremony that has existed since time immemorial among the indigenous peoples of the Pacific Northwest Coast of the United States and Canada. A festive ceremony involving singing and dancing, the *potlatch* involves gift giving. As Ana María Pineda explains in her essay "Hospitality":

> While the *potlatch* ceremony may vary among the different indigenous communities of the Pacific Northwest, the primary purpose of the ritual is to redistribute wealth. The *potlatch* is thus a practical embodiment of distributive justice in which the riches of the community are shared equally by all. (This volume: 315)

In short, among this indigenous people a certain practice of gift giving – the *potlatch* ceremony – achieves the aims of social justice.

Without belaboring the point, something similar, though with interesting and important thematic variations, can be said for hospitality, the Christian practice of welcoming the stranger, which has its roots in ancient Judaism (Pineda); *zakat*, the Islamic practice of almsgiving, which is one of Islam's Five Pillars (Azim Nanji); and *g'meelut chasadim*, the ancient Jewish practice of engaging in deeds of kindness (W.E. Nunnally). In each case, people with a religious worldview or sacred belief system are called on to engage in a type of behavior that redistributes wealth and thereby aims at achieving a more just social result. Clearly, the religious or sacred worldviews that motivate and sustain such expressions of redistribution of wealth make for a very different perspective on social justice than one finds in the secular version advanced by John Rawls.

Social justice as compensatory justice

As the name suggests, compensatory justice has to do with compensating someone or some social group. To compensate is to make whole, to make fair restitution to someone or some social group that has incurred loss or suffered injury because of someone else's wrongful act. The restitution may take many forms. It could be the replacement of a lost, damaged, or destroyed item; monetary compensation; or restitution by work.

Compensatory justice is governed by social rules, some of which are explicit and codified and others of which are implicit and context dependent. For instance, typically the perpetrator of the loss or injury (not someone else) is expected to provide restitution to the victim. But what if the injury or loss occurred long ago, has persisted without remedy, and the actual perpetrators no longer survive? Is anyone then responsible to make restitution?

This and other related questions are not simply hypothetical musings. They emerge with some measure of exigency in several of the essays devoted to indigenous people. The Aborigines of Australia, the Māori of New Zealand, the Gonds of central India, the Asante of West Africa, and the Ojibwe of North America all in one way or another make claims of compensatory justice against the larger, dominant cultures in which they are imbedded. Often their grievances are related to the disposition of land that they inhabited ("owned" would be the wrong word) from time immemorial, but from which they were disinherited during periods of occupation.

Social justice as retributive justice

Retributive justice concerns the various ways in which we blame or punish people for their wrongful acts. In thinking about the fairness of blame or punishment, contemporary western theorists often look to the *conditions* under which it is just to blame or punish someone for doing wrong. They consider such factors as the person's capacity to act and relative level of knowledge. (Lack of capacity to act on one's own initiative and inability to understand the meaning of one's acts are often – though not always – regarded as mitigating or exculpating factors in ascribing responsibility.) In assessing blame or punishment, western theorists also commonly consider the relative certitude that the accused person actually committed the wrongful act. In addition, they value consistency (treating similar cases in the same way) and proportionality (fitting the punishment to the wrongdoing).

Do people in non-western societies employ a concept of retributive justice and, if so, do any distinctive features emerge? There is no simple or singular answer to this question, but Robert Baum's essay on the Diola people of West Africa presents an intriguing case study. The Diola have a highly nuanced moral code that is intimately integrated with their spiritual view of reality. For example, they arrange moral behavior along a spectrum ranging from things that are absolutely forbidden to those that are absolutely required of members of the community.

> Violations of the obligations imposed by various spirit shrines – including the penetration of sacred forests or other spirit shrine sites that one has no right to attend; violations of behavioral norms associated with gender roles (e.g., menstrual avoidances, male avoidance of maternity houses, and female avoidance of cemeteries); the taking of life outside of war; most cases of theft; witchcraft and sorcery – are all considered absolutely forbidden and are subject to spiritual sanctions by the spirit shrines or by the Supreme Being, Emitai. The spirit shrines afflict wrongdoers with specific diseases, such as leprosy, which is associated with theft, but could afflict not only the thief, but anyone in his or her family that benefited from the theft. The Supreme Being judges the moral worth of individuals when they die and determines the nature of their afterlife. (This volume: 352)

It is a distinctive feature of western moral thinking that moral evaluation – praise and blame – accrues to the individual, not to groups or collectives. The classic expression of this view is given by the British philosopher H.D. Lewis:

> If I were asked to put forward an ethical principle of particular certainty, it would be that no one can be responsible, in the proper ethical sense, for the conduct of another. Responsibility belongs essentially to the individual. (Lewis, 1971: 121)

This feature of western moral appraisal is by no means universal. Here again the beliefs and practices of the Diola people are instructive. In the words of Robert Baum:

> Underlying Diola concepts of justice is a collective sense of responsibility, reward, and benefit. In a very literal sense, in Diola society, one is one's brother's keeper. Anyone who benefits from the wrongdoing of his or her kin could be subject to sanctions. (This volume: 352)

With respect to social justice, important theoretical questions can be framed from this contrast between the so-called western approach to responsibility ascription and the collectivist approach that Baum attributes to the Diola. For instance, which view best serves social justice: a view that makes individuals the primary targets of responsibility ascription or one that holds collectives accountable? Is there in principle a way to answer this question, or is social justice so intimately integrated with the society's view of accountability (individual or collective) that the question is unanswerable? These and other related questions situated at the intersection of religion and social justice merit careful reflection.

Social justice as procedural justice

In North America, questions about procedural justice have almost exclusively to do with a debate over competing models about how to render justice in the criminal justice system. Herbert Packer (1968) made famous a distinction between two extreme positions, one called the *due process* model, the other called the *crime control* model. The crime control model places primary importance on suppressing criminal conduct through arrests, convictions, and judicial sentencing. Efficiency and economy are its hallmarks (Packer, 1968: 12–16). Its extreme alternative, the due process model, is known for its formality and strict adherence to rules. Packer describes it as unwieldy as an "obstacle course" (Packer, 1968: 16). Its principal virtues are that it presumes the accused is innocent until guilt is established and that it places a priority on formal equality of the people brought into the judicial system. Despite these laudable virtues, the due process model has engendered deep skepticism about the possibility of achieving justice, due to its inefficiency and labored formality.

Some critics charge that both models are excessively indebted to retribution theory as a philosophy of punishment. They also assert that the models assume a Hobbesian world of irreconcilable struggle (Griffiths, 1970: 371, 463). Is there a better way?

One alternative has been tried in South Africa. Following the demise of the Apartheid system of government in the 1990s and the multiracial elections of 1994, South Africa established a court-like body called the Truth and Reconciliation Commission (TRC). Based in Cape Town, the TRC was established under the auspices of the *Promotion of National Unity and Reconciliation Act*, No. 34 of 1995. The TRC's mandate was to bear witness to, record, and in some cases grant amnesty to the perpetrators of crimes relating to human rights violations, as well as reparation and rehabilitation. The TRC had a number of high-profile members, including Archbishop Desmond Tutu (chairman), Dr. Alex Boraine (Deputy Chairman), Mary Burton, Reverend Khoza Mgojo, Dumisa Ntsebeza (head of the Investigative Unit), Dr. Wendy Orr, Denzil Potgieter, Dr. Fazel Randera, and Glenda Wildschut (author of "Human Rights: The South African Experience" in this book).

How did the TRC function and was it successful? Victims of gross and detestable human rights violations were invited to testify before the TRC about their experiences; some were asked to speak in public hearings. Perpetrators of violence were also given the opportunity to testify and to request amnesty from both civil and criminal prosecution. Very commonly, perpetrators of violence faced their victims (or their victims' surviving family members) and confessed their crimes. The *procedures* of the process encouraged openness as a strategy for achieving social reconciliation – social justice.

The work of the TRC is not without its critics. Those who are committed to the retributive theory of justice remain convinced that it has not properly punished parties guilty of grave atrocities. Those who assume a Hobbesian world of inevitable struggle see it as a weak and indecisive approach to a national calamity. Nevertheless, its procedures are widely thought to have achieved important social results beyond anything that could have been achieved by more conventional approaches, such as the procedural models of due process or crime control mentioned earlier. Glenda Wildschut's essay explores the work of the Truth and Reconciliation Commission as an instrument to deal with human rights abuses, explains how the amnesty process worked, discusses the activity of the human rights violations committee and the repatriation and rehabilitation committee, and finally discusses the role of the faith communities in the ongoing work of nation building.

Restorative justice

South Africa's Truth and Reconciliation Commission appeared under the heading of *procedural justice* because it explored an alternative procedure to achieving justice outside of the usual boundaries of the state's criminal justice system. It might just as well have appeared under the heading of *restorative justice*. For the goal of the TRC's alternative procedures was to restore something that the grave injustices suffered under the Apartheid system of government had stripped away – things like trust in one's neighbors, a sense of belonging to a people and a country, and confidence in the political institutions on which the well-being of the people depends. In short, the goal of the TRC's procedures was to begin the long and arduous work of restoring the torn fabric of the society.

Restorative justice normally differs from compensatory justice in what it tries to achieve. The language of restoration is in fact sometimes used when talking about compensatory justice, but though there is no sharp or absolute line between compensatory justice and restorative justice, there is a practical distinction between the two. In practice, compensatory justice limits its attempts to restore or "make whole" to acts of exchanging products, money, or labor. If I damage your automobile, I must compensate you; that is, I must pay to have it repaired. In practice, restorative justice typically has more to do with human relationships than with property damage or loss.

Mohammed Abu-Nimer explores restorative justice in "Building Peace in the Pursuit of Social Justice." For him, *peacebuilding* is an umbrella term that encompasses the practices of conflict resolution, peace studies, and alternative dispute resolution. Each of these three distinct and irreducible areas of engagement and activism exemplifies restorative justice.

Social justice in relation to personal virtues

The discussion so far has made abundantly clear that the expression *social justice* is not univocal. But there are other complicating factors as well. For example, the expression *social justice* suggests that what it refers to is somehow different from the state of character called justice that is sometimes found in or attributed to virtuous individual human beings. In the *Republic*, for example, Plato says that the just person is someone whose soul (*psychē*) exhibits an orderly arrangement of its constituent parts: the various parts of the soul harmonize with each other under the governance of reason. According to Plato, this virtuous state of the soul is analogous to, but distinct from, justice at the societal level, which is achieved when the various constituents of society (artisans and merchants, soldiers and law enforcement auxiliaries, and political leaders) refrain from interfering with each other and instead cooperate in performing their various tasks under the rule of the philosopher-king, who in turn is governed by reason.

What appears at first glance to be a simple analogical relationship between justice as we see it in the individual citizen (a virtuous condition of the individual citizen arising from the harmonious interaction of the parts of the citizen's soul) and justice as we see it in society (the complementary and harmonious interaction of citizens under the rule of the philosopher-king) turns out to be not so simple after all. If we accept Plato's theoretical construct for the just society, the role of the philosopher-king is critical not only to good order in society, but also to the flourishing of justice (and other virtues) in the lives of individual citizens. The prospects for individual citizens flourishing in the way Plato envisions (not only having their basic physical needs met, but also flourishing in their souls) depends critically on the just rule of the philosopher-king. However, no such leader is likely to emerge on the political scene unless enough citizens of the city-state (*polis*) already embody (or at least aspire to) the kinds of personal virtues that could make for a wise and just leader like the philosopher-king. In short, while it may be useful from a theoretical point of view to distinguish justice as a virtue to which individual citizens may aspire from justice as a broader social phenomenon, the two are really quite integrally linked. Each informs and shapes the other.

Something like the interdependence of justice as the virtue of individual citizens and justice as a societal phenomenon occurs among the Asante people, who inhabit parts of present-day Ghana. Yaw Adu-Gyamfi explores these interdependencies in "The Role of the Chief in Asante Society." For example, the Asante people believe that the well-being of their society depends on establishing cordial relationships with the ancestors, on whom the living depend for help and protection. The chief fulfills an important function as intermediary: "he is the central figure at the instituted religious rituals, ensuring the maintenance of the desired harmony between the living and the ancestors" (this volume: 263). However, his authority and power derive from an elaborate process by which the community bestows its collective wisdom on the chief and invests him with the knowledge necessary to lead his people. But for the collective wisdom embodied in mid-level leaders, passed on to him through carefully planned and executed ceremonies, the chief would not and could not have their confidence that his decisions would be good for the community. While the chief is the wise leader under whose judgments his people flourish, the chief became wise only because of a complex social, political, and religious network that already had the capacity to recognize his ability, nurture his talent, and install him as the chief.

Similar interdependencies between social justice (justice at the societal level) and personal justice (justice or some other virtue of the individual) are evident in the Bahá'í Faith. As Christopher Buck says,

> The primary purpose of a Bahá'í's life is threefold: to love and worship God, to acquire virtues, and to carry forward an ever-advancing civilization.... While many of the norms or laws seem directed at shaping personal piety and refining character, their larger purpose is often to prepare followers of the religion to serve humanity more effectively. (This volume: 213)

Clearly, for Bahá'ís there is an interdependent relationship between worshiping God, acquiring personal virtues, and practicing social justice. This same kind of interdependency probably exists in other religious expressions of social justice.

The purpose here has not been to foreclose on the possible meanings of social justice, but to elaborate on some of the most prominent and obvious ones in order to stimulate interest in exploring others. For surely there are others. The essays in this book are rich in detail. The careful and perceptive reader is likely to discover comparative insights that the editors have not imagined.

References

Frankena, Willliam (1964) The concept of social justice, in *Social Justice* (ed. R.B. Brandt), Prentice Hall, Englewood Cliffs, NJ, pp. 1–29.

Griffiths, John (1970) Ideology in criminal procedure *or* a third "model" of the criminal process, *Yale Law Journal* 79(3): 359–417.

Lewis, H.D. (1971) The non-moral notion of collective responsibility, in *Individual and Collective Responsibility* (ed. P.A. French), Schenkman, Cambridge, MA.

Miller, David (1999) *Principles of Social Justice*, Harvard University Press, Cambridge, MA.

Packer, Herbert L. (1968) *The Limits of the Criminal Sanction*, Stanford University Press, Stanford, CA.

Bibliography

Barry, Brian (2005) *Why Social Justice Matters*, Polity Press, Cambridge.

Capeheart, Loretta and Milovanovic, Dragan (2007) *Social Justice: Theories, Issues and Movements*, Rutgers University Press, New Brunswick, NJ.

Clayton, Matthew and Williams, Andrew (eds) (2004) *Social Justice*, Blackwell, Oxford.

Fleischacker, Samuel (2004) *A Short History of Distributive Justice*, Harvard University Press, Cambridge, MA.

Part I
Major World Religions

Introduction

The world's population is currently about 7 billion people. The vast majority – perhaps as many as 84% – are believed to be practitioners of or adherents to a religion or a sacred belief system. About one third claim to be Christian: Roman Catholic, Orthodox, Reformed, Anglican, Pentecostal, Evangelical, and others. More than a fifth are Muslim: Shiite, Sunni, and others. Hindus make up approximately 14%. Buddhists make up almost 6%, as do adherents to other traditional Chinese religions and belief systems. Practitioners of primal-indigenous religions make up another 6%, while practitioners of all other religions, including Judaism (0.22%) and Sikhism (0.36%), make up the remaining small percentage of religious people. Up to 16% of the world's people claim to be nonreligious (www.adherents.com).

This part includes twelve essays, two on each of six religions: Buddhism, Christianity, Confucianism, Hinduism, Islam, and Judaism. The first essay for each religion addresses the historical development of the religion's approach to social justice, with attention to some or all of the following:

- *Ideology*: the authoritative beliefs, including the moral/ethical norms, that form the central conceptual framework for explaining the religion's approach to social justice.
- *Narratives*: central narratives, myths, epics, historical accounts, or other stories that tell something special about the religion's approach to social justice.
- *Practices*: the religion's celebrations, reenactments, and rituals that disclose its approach to social justice.
- *Experiences*: defining experiences that shape the distinctive social justice beliefs, stories, and practices of its adherents.
- *Social arrangements*: the religion's network of social arrangements and institutions that affect how its adherents practice social justice.

The Wiley Blackwell Companion to Religion and Social Justice, First Edition. Edited by Michael D. Palmer and Stanley M. Burgess.
© 2012 John Wiley & Sons Ltd. Published 2020 by John Wiley & Sons Ltd.

The second essay on each major religion focuses on the religion's approaches toward and expressions of social justice in today's world.

Given the prevalence and diversity of religious belief and practice throughout the world, what qualifies the six religions discussed here as *major world religions?*[1] If numbers are the (or at least *a*) determining factor, then Christianity (one third of the world's population), Islam (one fifth of the world's population), and Hinduism (16% of the world's population) are all surely major world religions. The relevance of numbers for including Buddhism (6% of the world's population) and Confucianism (exact numbers unknown) among the major world religions is less compelling. A census cannot justify including Judaism among major world religions; at 0.22% of the world's population, Judaism is tiny.

Judaism fares rather differently if viewed from the perspectives of antiquity and cultural influence, however. Despite its small population it is an ancient religion, which has had a profound impact on western culture in general and Christianity in particular. A similar case can be made for Confucianism, which today has a relatively small population but historically has had enormous cultural reach in central and southeastern Asia. For example, in many southeast Asian countries today, Confucian ideology and practices are so integral to the culture that people do not distinguish sharply between Confucianism and Buddhism.

In the end, the decision to limit the presentation of major world religions to six is somewhat arbitrary. The six presented here are surely important from the standpoint of antiquity and cultural reach. To be sure, they are not the only ancient religions. (Jain, Shintō, Daoist, and Zoroastrian religions are all ancient.) Nor are they the only ones that have shaped culture, if not globally then certainly regionally. (Shintō's historical impact on the Japanese archipelago of Hokkaidō, Honshū, Shikoku, and Kyūshū has been profound.) But each of the six religions highlighted here has a long, rich, and diverse history and each has exerted a profound impact on the larger culture.

Are there more (or fewer) than six major world religions? Is it even necessary to create a category called *major world religions?* These questions need not be answered here. The central purpose of this section is to present six religions in such a way as to invite the reader to think critically about a range of historical and contemporary issues situated at the intersection of religion and social justice.

Note

1 It is worth noting that the name *world religions* is not uncontroversial, partly because of its historical connection with European colonialism that began in the fifteenth century but reached its zenith in the nineteenth century. A religion was said to be a *world religion* if it affected social and political events around the world, presumably placing it on a par with the major European colonial powers. In time the expression fell out of favor with some and was replaced by more inclusive language such as "the world's religions."

CHAPTER 1
Buddhism
Historical Setting

Mavis Fenn

New religious movements are not created in a vacuum. They represent a response to concerns, both individual and social, that arise in particular historical circumstances. Their ability to take root, or not, depends on their ability to address these concerns in a manner that engages a significant segment of the broader population. Central to a movement's ability to attract new members is its ability to debate the issues of the day with the established order and other new groups whose ideas may differ. The seventh to sixth centuries BCE saw significant changes in the Ganges plain area of India; changes that provided great opportunity for some and great suffering for others. Debate about these changes and the possibility of certain knowledge amidst those changes as well as about why there is suffering and what our response to it should be, produced three major world religions: Hinduism, the Jain religion, and Buddhism, our concern in this essay.

The changes were multiple. The development of the iron plow allowed for the intensification of agriculture. Many people were displaced from the land and forced to move into the newly emerging cities. These cities often provided a breeding ground for disease and violence. While agriculture flourished, ownership of the land devolved into the hands of individual families. Politically, there was a shift from an oligarchic tribe/clan system to a system of kingship. Trade flourished, guilds were established, and a banking system developed. The newly emergent mercantile class had money but little status, as the established order had no place for them.

While we cannot enter the minds of the people at the time, it is not difficult to speculate about how these rapid technological, social, and political changes may have affected people psychologically. Themes of identity and the nature of change and suffering are central in the philosophical debates of the time, as are ideas regarding the proper construction of society. Dominant in India from about 1500 BCE to the present is a hierarchical social system rooted in the vision of ancient religious texts called the

The Wiley Blackwell Companion to Religion and Social Justice, First Edition. Edited by Michael D. Palmer and Stanley M. Burgess.
© 2012 John Wiley & Sons Ltd. Published 2020 by John Wiley & Sons Ltd.

Vedas. The Vedas are a collection of religious texts brought to India by the Indo-European peoples, various tribes that moved into India perhaps from about 2000 BCE onward. Some groups continued their migration to Iran, and on to Europe. The term "Indo-European" refers to the family of languages that share certain linguistic characteristics and thus to the tribes as a whole.

We cannot understand Buddhism, including its ethics and social concerns, without understanding something about the religion of the groups of Indo-Europeans whose religious vision came to dominate India.

Religious Background

The religion of one of the major Indo-European tribes that migrated into India, the Aryans, was based on a group of texts called the Vedas. These were not written texts. Sound was considered to be sacred and the chanted word was considered to be spiritually efficacious. Received by ancient sages known as *rishis*, these texts were chanted by priests and passed down to future generations through memorization.

There are four Vedas in all. The oldest is the *Rig Veda*. This contains a series of hymns to a variety of gods: gods and goddesses of nature like Ushas (Dawn); Indra, the god of war; and Varuṇa, the god of order. It also contains foundational stories such as the story of creation. While there is more than one cosmological myth, the one that has predominated is *Rig Veda* 10.90, the *Purusha Sūkta*. This hymn recounts the creation of everything and presents the worldview that came to dominate Indian religious thought to the present day.

The *Purusha Sūkta* describes creation as the product of sacrifice. The primal being, Purusha, is sacrificed and from this sacrifice the natural world, the supernatural world, the universe, and even the social order are generated. Sacrifice, then, forms the basis of the religious system. Sacrifices are made, hymns of praise to various gods are offered, and petitions for worldly blessings, long life, children, and a place in heaven are made by priests on behalf of the people, and conveyed to the gods by Agni, the god of fire. The gods, if pleased, grant the petitions. And, because sacrifice brought the cosmos into existence, repeated sacrifice maintains that order. Over time, the notion arose that if the sacrifice were performed precisely, the gods were compelled to grant their blessings; since only the priests could perform these major public sacrifices, they gained a great deal of power. As their power grew, so did the number of animals that were sacrificed.

The social order created from the primal sacrifice is hierarchical. The priestly class is dominant, the warrior or noble class comes next, then the peasant class, and finally the servant class. Because it was generated through sacrifice, the social order, like the universe itself, is considered to be eternal, unchangeable, and sacred. Due to a series of philosophical developments, not the least of which was the notion that karma (action) was not only sacrificial action but moral deed, this class system developed into the caste system and the belief that individuals were born into a specific class based on the accumulation of their moral deeds was accepted.

The environment into which Vedic religion was introduced was not a *tabula rasa*. Prior to the immigration of the Indo-Europeans, the Indus Valley was a thriving civilization with a variety of religious expressions. Archaeologists have found numerous fertility symbols, representing examples of natural, animal, and human fecundity, some dating back to about 2500 BCE. As well, they have unearthed symbols of emaciated male figures seated in meditation poses. Perhaps the most interesting find for students of Indian religions is a figure commonly known as proto-Shiva. Seated in a meditative posture, this male figure wears a helmet of bull horns, the sign of animal fertility, between which vines are growing, a sign of natural fertility. The Hindu god, Shiva, is known both as lord of the animals and for his ascetic prowess. In this figure, then, scholars have seen not only the combination of the two main themes of Indus Valley religion – fertility and asceticism – but the development of a Hindu god from the influence of the indigenous tradition on the newly introduced Vedic religion.

Transformation of Values

Our sense of identity and the comfortableness with which we accept our beliefs and practices as self-evident is rarely faced with scrutiny until we encounter those who believe and practice differently. Our encounter with *the other* frequently provokes us to contemplate who we are, what we believe, and why we do so. This need for clarification and distinction from others is not confined to individuals who may travel cross-culturally, but occurs on the larger scale as well. The differing values held by those indigenous to the Ganges Valley and those who immigrated, bringing Vedic religion with them, produced an often contentious discussion about ultimate truth, highest value, and the nature of what it meant to be human, both individually and collectively. It was that discussion that shaped and formed the foundations and outlines of Hinduism, Jainism, and Buddhism. Indeed, many Buddhist concepts were consciously conceived in contrast to Vedic thought.

Central to Buddhism is the notion of karma, which means "act." Within the Vedic context it referred to the sacrificial action of the priest. These acts were efficacious in that they produced the benefit sought. Over time and under the influence of non-Vedic religious expressions, the term took on the connotation of "moral deed." In Buddhism, our moral deeds produce consequences according to their nature, and these consequences must be experienced, if not in this lifetime then in a subsequent one. We live in a moral universe and karma is one of its laws. An act itself has several components: the intention of the action, the will to carry it out, carrying it out, and the consequences of that act. It is a complicated matter; only a Buddha can fathom its intricacies. Of primary importance is the intention of an act, a good thing given that our best intentions frequently go astray.

It is to our benefit, then, to engage in acts that will produce positive results in this life and the next. Karma is believed to condition the basic parameters of where we begin in life, the physical and mental aspects of ourselves, personality, social position, and general "luck." If one is born with a congenital condition or in poor social circumstances, this is considered to be the result of actions in a past lifetime. While one cannot change one's past, one can change one's future through consciously and consistently choosing to act positively. The result of positive acts is to be reborn better looking, in a financially secure family, and with the characteristics that make for a bright future. There are volumes of folk narratives, the *Jātaka Tales*, and numerous Sanskrit *Avadānas* that demonstrate the great benefit that may be obtained through even a small, well-intentioned act such as a poor man's gift of a bowl of gruel to an ascetic or Buddha. We will discuss this in more detail when we examine some central texts that deal with Buddhist notions of social justice.

Also transformed is the notion of sacrifice as the central religious act. As noted earlier, the scale of animal sacrifice was increasing, particularly so for the large public sacrifices held primarily by the king and other wealthy members of his circle. There were many who objected to these sacrifices on a variety of grounds: the suffering of the animals; the waste of resources; the wealth and power that accrued to the priests; and skepticism surrounding the ability of sacrifice to provide the benefits alleged. While Buddhist monks and nuns were not strictly vegetarian in India for reasons outlined below, they objected to causing harm to animals. The *Metta Sutta* notes that all beings wish to be happy and free of suffering, and there is a series of meditative exercises in which one meditates on generating and radiating loving-kindness in progressively wider circles, finally reaching "all living beings." Instead of wasting resources, Buddhist texts call for the redistribution of wealth through giving, developing the virtue of generosity. Giving is expected to occur on both a private and a public level. Instead of providing money for sacrifices, one should give to the ascetics, who were widespread at the time and who would include groups like the Buddhists and the Jains.

Acts of this type constitute the second highest form of giving, behind only the gift of self (renouncing the lay life for a monastic one) and ahead of other forms of charitable giving or activity. The newly emerging business and banking class could not only attain great respect from these alternative religious groups, but also the religious benefits that such giving would provide now and in future lives. While one could not be certain how the specific benefits would accrue in the future, in the present one was accumulating merit. The amount of merit collected depended on the giver's intention (a pure heart) and the recipient's suitability (religiously adept). As a result of implementing these guidelines, the laity became vigilant enforcers of the monastic rules. Oddly, this enforcement led to the forest monks, who spent most of their time in solitary meditation, receiving copious gifts.

The same practice also seems to have expanded the religious possibilities for poor people. Indeed, in one narrative a senior monk with great purity turns down a dinner invitation from the gods because he wishes to take his meal with some poor working people so that they can attain merit. The monastic community was considered to be a "field of merit" for the laity, and accepting a gift was viewed as an act of compassion. Monks and nuns were expected to take what they were given, with thanks, regardless of whether or not they liked the offering. A bowl of sour gruel, with or without meat, given with a pure heart by a poor man or woman, merited considerable benefit.

Within the kingship system of government, the ideal king (*cakkavattin*) not only keeps the realm safe from robbers and foreign invasion, he also pays his public administrators fairly and is required to ensure that the realm is free of poverty. These practices (not sacrifices) guarantee social and cosmic stability. The notion that the priests were inherently more moral than others and that one was born into a specific class because of one's moral actions was also challenged. All classes of society had ethical and non-ethical individuals within them. And, while Buddhism did not reject the class system per se, it rejected any notion that there was a moral component to this system of social organization. There were good and bad people within every class of society.

We get a good sense of Buddhist ideas regarding the ideal society and issues of social concern such as poverty when we examine several central texts from the Pali Canon, the only complete set of texts we possess from the early Buddhist groups and the scriptural corpus of the Theravāda branch of Buddhism geographically centered in south and southeast Asia.

Narratives

What we refer to as Buddhist *texts* were originally aural in nature; that is, they were spoken and adapted to the audience assembled to hear them. Indeed, the Buddha was said to have possessed "skill in means" for the way he tailored his message to his audience. Many texts still bear evidence of their aural origins in their repetitive nature. While scholars believe that the Pali Canon was relatively stable from the middle of the third century BCE, it was not written down until shortly before the beginning of the Common Era. Historically, the texts were not widely studied even by monks and nuns. Texts became increasingly important during the colonial period because of the emphasis Christian missionaries placed on the authority of the Bible. George Bond (1988) notes in *Buddhist Revival in Sri Lanka* that all reform movements in Sri Lanka now place emphasis on textual authority. The impact of colonialism also produced a movement of Buddhist modernism, with laity becoming more active in temple affairs and also in activities traditionally associated with the monastic community, such as meditation. Outside of Asia, Buddhism is primarily lay led, textual study is not uncommon, and meditation is the foremost religious activity.

Aggañña Sutta

It should be noted at the outset that the life of a renouncer – that is, one who renounces normal life in the world for the religious life – is always seen as the superior lifestyle choice. Indeed, in the *Aggañña Sutta*, a narrative of origins, the evolution of society is seen as part of a "fall." According to the text, originally beings were "simply beings." Made of mind, feeding on joy, self-luminous, and able to travel through the air, they were not differentiated from each other. That changed when, due to previous karma, one greedy being began to eat the forming earth and the others followed suit, causing them to see each other differently. Some perceived themselves as attractive and began to despise those whom they saw as unattractive. Thus, through a moral choice that led to craving and a dislike of others, a series of devolutions was set in motion. These devolutions included the creation of the universe as the sun and moon appeared, a consequence of beings losing luminosity, itself a consequence of ingesting matter. As we will see later, this interconnection between human moral action and the natural world is a recurring pattern.

At each stage of differentiation or evolution, moral consequences ensue and society begins to take shape. Differentiation between the sexes leads to lust, which leads to sexual intercourse. Community moral outrage at this vile and violent act leads to the establishment of family life as men and women build huts to hide their activities. Hoarding leads to poorer-quality grain that grows in clusters. This situation leads to the establishment of private property, assigning plots to individuals, which in turn leads to theft, censure, lying, and punishment. At this point, people meet and decide that things have gone far enough. They choose a leader, the finest among them, to become king and rule over them in return for a portion of their rice. This arrangement marks the beginning of society proper, stops the decline, and allows for a stable order to emerge, ironically by having the kingly rather than the priestly caste emerge first. Having detailed the formation of a class society, portraying it as a series of occupational choices, the narrative ends by praising all those who abandon class to become renouncers.

Cakkavatti Sīhanāda Sutta

Whereas the *Aggañña Sutta* presents the creation of a social contract type of kingship, the *Cakkavatti Sīhanāda Sutta* outlines the responsibilities entailed in being an ideal ruler, a *cakkavattin*, a "wheel turning" (wheel of truth and morality) monarch. It does so within the story of the fall and rise of a mythical kingdom. The fall is due to the ruler's failure to provide for the poor. The consequences of this failure ultimately provoke a holocaust. Founded by King Daḷhanemi, the kingdom flourishes for seven generations as each successor follows the "noble duty of a wheel turning monarch." The noble duty entails that the ruler embody dharma in all his affairs; provide shelter and protection for all segments of the realm, including animals and birds; ensure that no wrongdoing occurs; provide wealth for those who have none, being advised by the religieux; and not do anything that would cause the religieux to give up their practice. The eighth king, who is by all accounts a properly constituted ruler, does not follow the noble duty and the kingdom does not flourish. When this is brought to his attention by advisers and important citizens, he adjusts his behavior to follow the noble duty, with one exception: he does not provide wealth for those who have none. As a consequence, poverty becomes widespread and theft occurs. While initially the king responds to theft by providing the thieves with wealth and enjoins them to spend it on care for their families, setting up a business and making religious gifts that will benefit them now and in future lives, he later resorts to public humiliation and beheading.

From this point, a downward spiral of social disintegration, human degradation, and natural calamity is set in motion. The process is one of action–reaction, causation and result, each stage more disastrous than the previous one: because of poverty, theft; because of theft, weapons; because of weapons, murder. Moral decline is rapid and severe – including informing, adultery, lust, incest, and loss of filial and religious piety

– all due to the fact that the king failed to give wealth to those who had none. The alleviation of poverty is not a case for individual charity but one of social justice.

What is interesting here is that there is no mention of karma. Poverty does not arise from karma but from a political failure. Poverty does provoke deeds that are karmically nonproductive, negative, what we would term evil. Interestingly, the consequences of these deeds are shared by the entire populace, a general decline in attractiveness, lifespan, health, and moral behavior. Perhaps there is some notion of communal karma? In the same way as in the *Aggañña Sutta*, the quality of food and the numbers of birds, plants, and animals decline as a consequence of human immorality. This spiral culminates in an apocalyptic situation where the populace regard each other as animals, literally "acquire animal consciousness toward each other," and an orgy of bloodshed ensues. Some individuals, however, do not appear to be overcome by this delusion and they, not wanting to kill or be killed, run off and hide in the woods. When the holocaust is over, these humans emerge from their hiding places. Making the connection between evil deeds and the decline of the kingdom, they refrain from evil deeds and gradually the kingdom grows and become prosperous again, and a new righteous ruler arises, who is described in terms like those of the original King Daḷhanemi.

From the rise and fall of the kingdom we learn quite a bit. The righteous ruler appears to be the product of a righteous populace, and his job is to protect and preserve the moral community created by them. Without a stable and moral political structure, individual human moral action is at risk. While there will always be human beings who are able to maintain their humanity regardless of the chaos around them, most will become rudderless. Humankind at its worst is bestial; at its best nonviolent, rational, consensual, and morally active. Finally, human moral action is not limited, but its effects are felt within the natural order as well.

Kūṭadanta Sutta and Sigālovāda Sutta

How individuals should act in order to preserve the stability and moral tenor of society is reflected in the *Kūṭadanta* and *Sigālovāda Sutta* of the Pali Canon. The *Kūṭadanta Sutta* is a good example of the transformation of values from those of Vedic sacrifice to Buddhist notions of giving. In addition, it presents a detailed picture of how the various elements of the social order should interact with each other.

The narrative is constructed with a frame tale and a central narrative. In the frame tale, a wealthy brahmin named Kūṭadanta, who lives on land over which he has control "as if he were a king," goes to the Buddha in order to find out how to perform a very complicated sacrifice, the sacrifice in three modes with sixteen instruments. He wishes to perform this sacrifice for his benefit now and in the future; that is, he wishes to attain heaven. All the brahmanical notions of sacrifice are present. In response to his question, the Buddha tells Kūṭadanta a story about a king who approached his adviser about performing just such a sacrifice.

The central narrative then lays out all the traditional elements required for this sacrifice, but does so in terms of the qualities of the king who wishes to perform it and his adviser who directs its performance. Eight instruments of the sacrifice are described as qualities of the king: rich, pure in lineage, handsome, militarily strong, faithful, generous to the poor, one who does good deeds, and intelligent in the senses of being learned and able to think matters out. Other sacrificial instruments are the qualities of the adviser. Some qualities, virtue and wisdom, are like those of the king. Others, like knowledge of the Vedas, ritual, and grammar, are patterned on traditional priestly knowledge. Also present are representatives of the four classes of people who make up the realm. Their communal consent is stated to be an instrument of the sacrifice as well.

Given the parallel between Kūṭadanta and the Buddha and the mythical king and his adviser, it is fair to assume that the advice given in the story is meant for Kūṭadanta. The performance of the sacrifice begins with setting the stage. The king should end disorder in the kingdom, not through rigid policies of law and order, but through measures we would refer to as job-creation programs, equitable taxation, and good wages and benefits for government workers. These are elements that, taken together, we would claim today as essential ingredients for social justice. The three modes of performance refer to the state of mind in which he should conduct the sacrifices. There should be no regret for the wealth spent, no remorse that some evil people will benefit, and joy that good people will benefit. Finally, when performing the sacrifice, the king should gladden his heart in sixteen ways: he has invited the four classes of subjects, he has the eight necessary qualities for success, and his adviser possesses the four necessary qualities. Those representing the four classes of people are so impressed with this sacrifice, which does not involve any animal deaths and is conducted by volunteers, that they offer the king more money, which he refuses. They then establish, with the rest of the populace, donation centers throughout the land.

What is of note is that the narrative flow is from personal and individual to public and communal. The king asks what he should do in order to attain heaven, and he is told to act publically and in socially beneficial ways and with the consent of his subjects. Further, the actions of the populace in emulating the king produce a society that is generous, nonviolent, mutually supportive, and of benefit to the natural world (no animals are slain) as well as to its human inhabitants. In this case, the idea of society and the notion of social justice are expanded to include nonhumans.

The *Sigālovāda Sutta* deals with individual religious and moral duty. Again, it contrasts Vedic notions of worship with Buddhist ones. The narrative concerns a young man named Sigāla, a nonreligious youth who agrees to his father's deathbed wish that he worship the six directions. Sigāla does so, encountering the Buddha one morning. The Buddha informs him that his worship is inappropriate and, on request, describes what proper worship of the six directions entails. The preparation for worship section deals with individual morality. One should not destroy life, lie, steal, or engage in sexual misconduct; actions that arise from desire, anger, and ignorance. As well as removing these moral obstacles, one should not dissipate one's wealth through intoxicants, late nights out, theatrical shows, gambling, association with bad companions, and idleness. The cost of these expenditures is not simply monetary but causes ruptured relationships, illness, mental instability, and a loss of reputation. If a man engages in such behaviors, his family and property are vulnerable if he is married; if not married, he is not a good marriage prospect. Further, he becomes suspected of evil deeds, and his word is not accepted by a court of law. Finally, he does not get anything done, spends all his money, and is left with only fair-weather friends.

If he refrains from this bad behavior and corrects his moral attitude, he will acquire wealth in harmless ways and his virtue will be known to all. He manages his wealth appropriately: one quarter for himself, half for his business, and a quarter for reserve in hard times. Now, he is ready to worship the six directions.

The six directions are revealed as six sets of reciprocal relationships: parents, teachers, husbands and wives, friends and associates, servants and employees, and ascetics and brahmins. Interactions are characterized by courteousness, fairness, and care and concern for the individual, his behavior and his family and property.

The notion of social justice in Pali texts

The vision of the ideal society presented in these texts is of an individualist, mercantile society set within the context of a strong central government concerned with the preservation of order and the elimination of any obstacles to productivity. The primary obstacle to this society is poverty. The texts do not envision an equality of resources; they simply argue that everyone should have sufficient resources to care for themselves and contribute to the collective. An inability to do so produces dehumanization within the entire collective. Individuals are required to take care of themselves and to make a contribution to the whole.

As well as the interrelationship between the individual and society, there is also an interrelationship between morality and prosperity. Again, the values espoused are those of a mercantile society: hard work, thrift, and the preservation of income through refraining from wealth-dissipating activities such as gambling and drinking. All this is not surprising given that the support for Buddhist and other groups came from the newly wealthy mercantile class. That the Vedic sacrifice has been transformed into giving to religious mendicants is also not surprising given the historical context. We do note that the giving does not appear specifically to include what we would call broad social acts of charity. These are not excluded, but the emphasis is definitely on religious giving.

Mahāyāna and Vajrayāna Buddhism

Mahāyāna Buddhism, which includes traditions such as Zen and Pure Land Buddhism, was originally a monastic movement within Buddhism centered around the veneration of specific texts that appeared in India perhaps as early as the first century BCE. These new texts, while created by and for a monastic audience, do however appear to have expressed more optimism in the ability of ordinary people to make religious progress without renouncing life-in-the-world. They critique what they see as a Buddhism that has become ingrown, elitist, and insensitive to the needs of the laity. They follow the Mahāyāna, the "Great or Large Vehicle," while others follow the Hīnayāna, the "Lesser or Small Vehicle." They consider themselves to be greater in aspiration, wisdom, and compassion than the others. Mahāyāna sūtras tend to focus on two central themes: the *bodhisattva* and the notion of "emptiness." A *bodhisattva* aspires to full Buddhahood rather than what the Mahāyāna sees as the limited enlightenment of the *arhat* or perfected person extolled by the earlier schools, of which only the Theravāda remain. They do this through the development of a deeper understanding of reality, and they do so for the sake of all living beings rather than simply for personal liberation. Early Mahāyāna texts include the *Perfection of Wisdom Sūtras*, of which the *Aṣṭasāhasrikā Prajñāpāramitā Sūtra* (*Perfection of Wisdom in 8,000 Lines*) may be the earliest.

While some texts focus on celestial *bodhisattvas* who are able to help living beings through transferring their huge reservoirs of merit and through various magical strategies above and beyond the early notions of teaching and preaching, other texts such as the *Vimilakīrti Nirdeśa Sūtra* and the *Lotus Sūtra* show laypeople demonstrating deep wisdom and compassion. This expansion of the idea of what *bodhisattvas* can do to aid other beings and the greater valuation of the possibility that ordinary people can attain spiritual progress in daily life issues in the practice of laypeople taking the *bodhisattva* vow, performing spiritually efficacious deeds, and dedicating the merit from these deeds to all living beings. The *Daśabhūmika Sūtra*, which outlines the ten stages of the *bodhisattva*, states that the *bodhisattva* should learn the arts of medicine, mathematics, music, and history as a means to aiding beings. These disciplines were taught at the great monastic universities in India, which were open to monks and laymen but not nuns or laywomen.

The *Jewel Garland*, traditionally ascribed to Nāgārjuna and written to a powerful king, sets out a notion of kingship that is consonant with the one presented above in the Theravāda texts. The text urges a personal transformation that leads a ruler to contemplate what is good for his realm. As Ken Jones (2003), a prominent proponent of engaged Buddhism, puts it, Nāgārjuna's position is that the goal is a society in which there are favorable conditions for each person to move toward enlightenment or, in other words, to work out their karma. Nonviolence, including compassion for animals and abolishing the death penalty, education, and care for the poor, are advocated as good social policy.

Vajrayāna Buddhism, whose texts may be as early as the sixth century CE, was, by the tenth century, being absorbed into the university system. One of the reasons given for the growing influence of this form of Buddhism was the increasing isolation of monks from the concerns of the people. Highly sophisticated logic held sway, and education became a means of moving up in society rather than a spiritual path. Vajrayāna is a tantric form of Buddhism. Tantra refers to ritual and it is a type of Buddhism that focuses on ritual and meditation as a means to attain enlightenment. It is so closely identified with Tibet that it is often called Tibetan Buddhism. Tibetan Buddhism follows Theravāda monastic discipline, Mahāyāna philosophy, and tantric practice. As Paul Williams (1989) notes in his classic work on Mahāyāna Buddhist texts, through gestures, visualizations, and chants the practitioner transforms him- or herself into a Buddha and the surrounding world into a divine realm. The notion that *the world* is somehow dependent on our perception of it collapses the distinction between the *real* world and the *spiritual* world. Living our life in a certain way can be a "skillful means" of assisting others and our actions in this world can transform it into a Buddhist Pure

Land. These ideas find expression in a variety of ways in contemporary Buddhism, most fully in Chinese reformed Buddhist organizations such as Fo Guang Shan and Tzu Chi and in the engaged Buddhist movement.

Sociopolitical Practice

There are a few examples of rulers who have tried to establish the kind of ideal realm portrayed in the Theravāda *Cakkavatti Sīhanāda Sutta*. Aśoka was the most powerful king of his time (third century BCE) and ruled most of India. The traditional story is that he was so repelled by the violence involved in his conquest of Kalinga that he vowed to become a "righteous ruler"; that is, one who ruled by righteousness rather than force of arms. He left behind a series of edicts inscribed on rocks and pillars, which give us a feel for his policies. Some edicts promote general religious values to the populace. Aśoka forbade animal sacrifices, provided medical aid for both animals and people, and improved travel by providing way stations. He did not abolish capital punishment, but he allowed appeal and gave criminals some time to put their affairs in order. He supported religions other than Buddhism. He supervised the Buddhist monastic community. He made suggestions for reading and established officials to ensure that the practice in the monasteries was appropriate. The Theravāda tradition has Aśoka presiding over a monastic council held, in part, for the purpose of expelling heretical monks and nuns. While we cannot be certain about the dating of the *Cakkavatti Sīhanāda Sutta*, A.L. Basham (2005) believes that it was composed using Aśoka as a model for the king. Before Aśoka, Buddhism was one of many religions in India; after Aśoka, it was a major presence.

While the focus of this essay is on the historical setting of Buddhism, the example of U Nu (1907–1995), the first postcolonial Prime Minister of Burma in the mid-twentieth century, provides an example of how traditional notions of Buddhism and social concern are being translated in contemporary times. Consistent with the texts discussed above and with the example of the righteous king Aśoka, U Nu believed that the health of a nation began with the morality of its people, especially its leaders. Indeed, biographer Richard Butwell (1969) quotes U Nu as stating that democracy is really an unwritten code of personal behavior. Like Aśoka, U Nu also saw himself as a "promoter of the faith," although he supported the rights of all religious groups. He sponsored the Sixth Great Theravada Buddhist Council (1954–1956), established the *Pali University Act* (1950), and set up a Buddha Sasana (Teaching) Council to study and promote Buddhism and supervise monks. He established a cabinet post for a Ministry of Religious Affairs, and promoted the teaching of Buddhism to non-Buddhists. He encouraged the restoration of the country's pagodas, brought relics from Sri Lanka (then called Ceylon) and toured them throughout Burma, and commuted the sentences of criminals who agreed to study Buddhism. He also banned the slaughter of cattle. As was undoubtedly true in Aśoka's case, some commentators felt that U Nu's political efforts would be best served in directions other than religion. He believed that socialism and Buddhism were compatible and wished to make Burma a Buddhist state. After holding power twice, he was deposed by the army in 1962 and died in 1995 at the age of 87.

Individual practice

In individual terms, Buddhist morality has focused on the Five Precepts and giving. The Five Precepts are guidelines to moral behavior that may be understood in both a narrower and a broader sense. For example, the First Precept is to refrain from murder. More broadly, one should refrain from abusive behavior. The other precepts are to refrain from theft, sexual impropriety, lying, and intoxicants.

Buddhists make religious gifts. In early Indian Buddhism, monks and nuns made gifts of items used for religious purposes, for example a cave in which one could meditate, or religious objects. The merit of these gifts was ascribed to others, most often deceased parents. Gifts from the laity to the community of monks and nuns included food, lodging, and robes. Histories of later periods in Sri Lanka and Tibet, for example, indicate that wealthy landowners or nobles might give a portion of village labor or produce to a monastery. Valuable Buddha images are often donated in the name of a deceased parent.

Although there is some discussion regarding the canonicity of the practice, the transfer of merit generated from ritual performance to others living or dead is a longstanding practice. Prior to the rise of Mahāyāna Buddhism, merit was generally transferred to a specific individual(s). With the increasing popularity of Mahāyāna, merit was transferred to "all living beings." It is common practice for Buddhists to buy birds and fish on special occasions and free them. This practice has turned out to be problematic, however. Enterprising shopkeepers will often capture birds specifically to sell, and freeing the birds can cause them to get disoriented and fly into automobiles or become victims of predators. Recently, there has been resistance to this practice and some temples prohibit the release of fish into the temple pond.

Conclusion

Buddhist social concern is based, not surprisingly, on the interdependence of individual morality and social security. A productive, secure, and stable society is one in which individuals engage in acts that aid their spiritual progress. Through their own moral actions, they help create a secure and stable society, and their gifts to the monastic community keep religious values ever present amid the hustle and bustle of daily life. While social justice has been a less explored area than Buddhist philosophy or meditative practice, the interaction between the colonial powers and Buddhism in the late nineteenth century and the rise of Buddhist modernism have moved social concerns more to the forefront of Buddhist thought. Buddhist organizations such as Fo Guang Shan and Tzu Chi build hospitals and universities, and the primary form of Buddhism in the West is a Buddhism that combines the search for individual enlightenment through meditation with engagement in social issues from the perspective of Buddhist values.

References

Basham, A.L. (2005) Asoka and Buddhism: A re-examination, in *Buddhist Origins and the Early History of Buddhism in South and Southeast Asia, Vol. 1 of Buddhism: Critical Concepts in Religious Studies*, Paul Williams (ed.), Routledge, London, pp. 54–64.

Bond, George D. (1988) *Religious Revival in Sri Lanka: Religious Tradition, Reinterpretation and Response*, University of South Carolina Press, Columbia.

Butwell, Richard (1969) *U Nu of Burma*, Stanford University Press, Stanford.

Jones, Ken (2003) *The New Social Face of Buddhism: A Call to Action*, Wisdom, Somerville, MA.

Williams, Paul (1989) *Mahāyāna Buddhism: The Doctrinal Foundations*, The Library of Religious Beliefs and Practices, John Hinnells and Ninian Smart (eds), Routledge, London.

Bibliography

Fenn, Mavis L. (1996) Two notions of poverty in the Pāli Canon, *Journal of Buddhist Ethics*, 6: 98–125.

Fenn, Mavis L. (2006) The Kūṭadanta Sutta: Tradition in Tension in *Buddhist Studies from India to America – Essays in Honor of Charles S. Prebish*, Damien Keown (ed.), Routledge, London.

Gombrich, Richard F. (1996) *How Buddhism Began: The Conditioned Genesis of the Early Teachings*, 2nd edn, Routledge Critical Studies of Buddhism, Charles S. Prebish and Damien Keown (eds), Routledge, London.

Mitchell, Donald W. (2002) *Buddhism: Introducing the Buddhist Experience*, Oxford University Press, Oxford.

Robinson, Richard and Johnson, Willard L. (1997) *The Buddhist Religion: A Historical Introduction*, 4th edn, Wadsworth, Belmont, CA.

CHAPTER 2
Buddhism
Contemporary Expressions

Steven Emmanuel

Throughout its long history, Buddhism has demonstrated a remarkable resourcefulness, both in the way it has adapted to new cultures and in the skillful ways it has sought to promote peace and well-being in the world. Perhaps the best example of this is the contemporary movement known as socially engaged Buddhism.

As it is commonly used, the phrase "engaged Buddhism" refers to various forms of social action that have been undertaken by Buddhists to address the social, political, and economic causes of suffering in modern society. Though consciously activist in its approach, engaged Buddhism does not represent a radical departure from traditional Buddhist teachings and practice. Indeed, social activism falls well within the scope of what the Buddha called *skillful means*: sharing the *dharma* and alleviating suffering through the wise and compassionate use of methods specifically adapted to a given time, place, and situation.

Engaged Buddhism is not a unified movement, but rather a cluster of organic movements that have emerged, mainly in Asian countries, in response to problems of violence, poverty, political oppression, and environmental degradation. Leading figures include A.T. Ariyaratne (Sri Lanka), Buddhadasa Bhikkhu and Sulak Sivaraksa (Thailand), Maha Ghosananda (Cambodia), Aung San Suu Kyi (Myanmar), and the Dalai Lama (Tibet).

In the West, engaged Buddhism is perhaps most closely associated with the life and writings of Vietnamese Zen Master Thích Nhất Hạnh, who is credited with coining the English phrase. During the Vietnam War, Nhất Hạnh's work as a teacher, writer, poet, and social activist inspired thousands of Buddhists to become directly engaged in the work of peace and reconciliation. In addition to organizing and training volunteer youth for social service, he founded Tiếp Hiện (the Order of Interbeing), a new branch of Vietnamese Zen Buddhism based on the principles of engaged practice. After the war, his order continued to grow, gradually evolving into an international community of

---

The Wiley Blackwell Companion to Religion and Social Justice, First Edition. Edited by Michael D. Palmer and Stanley M. Burgess.
© 2012 John Wiley & Sons Ltd. Published 2020 by John Wiley & Sons Ltd.

lay and ordained practitioners dedicated to promoting mindful living and compassionate action in society.

Because Nhất Hạnh's writings offer one of the clearest and most fully articulated accounts of engaged Buddhist practice, they will serve as the basis of the discussion that follows.

Liberation from Suffering

The Buddha often said, "I teach only *dukkha* and the cessation of *dukkha*." Typically translated as "suffering," the term *dukkha* actually encompasses a much wider range of psychological and physical ills than the English word suggests. The Buddha often spoke of *dukkha* as the ill-being that results from craving worldly pleasures, or from attachment to things that are, by their nature, changing and impermanent. Among the primary examples mentioned in his teachings were the inevitability of aging, sickness, and death, the loss of people we love, and the disappointment we experience when our desires go unsatisfied.

The Buddha summarized his teaching on suffering in the Four Noble Truths:

1. The truth of the existence of suffering.
2. The truth of the origin of suffering.
3. The truth of the cessation of suffering.
4. The truth of the path leading to the cessation of suffering.

Liberation from suffering depends first of all on becoming fully aware that suffering is present. When we look deeply into the causes of that suffering, we find that it is rooted in craving and attachment, and that this is conditioned, in turn, by our ignorance of the true nature of things. By gaining insight into the causes of suffering, we can stop contributing to the conditions that give rise to it.

The fourth truth, known as the "Noble Eightfold Path," describes the practice that leads to the cessation of suffering. It is presented as a set of practical guidelines that promote the virtues of Right View, Right Thought, Right Speech, Right Action, Right Livelihood, Right Effort, Right Mindfulness, and Right Concentration. Briefly stated, the aim of the path is to bring our moral conduct into conformity with wisdom; that is, with a correct understanding of the nature of things. To do this requires diligence in cultivating wholesome states of mind, developing a deeper awareness of our habits and the consequences of those habits for our mental and physical well-being. According to this teaching, the insight and capacities needed to bring about the end of suffering can be realized in the practice of mindfulness. To be mindful is to be mentally alert, steady, and free from delusion. It is the form of meditation that led to Gautama Siddhartha's own enlightenment experience.

Mindfulness occupies a place of central importance in Buddhist philosophy. It is the first of the *Seven Factors of Awakening*, as well as the subject of an important early discourse known as *The Greater Discourse on the Foundations of Mindfulness*. Indeed, mindfulness is the basis of all Buddhist teaching on meditation.

As a contemplative practice, mindfulness is the activity of bringing the mind to a point of focus in nonjudgmental awareness of the present moment. In this state, it is possible to experience the way the mind constantly changes from one moment to the next, how one thought or feeling is replaced by another, and then another. To be in the present moment is to be fully aware of what is unfolding here and now, yet free from the distortions created by perception and judgment. It is a form of "letting go," of allowing things to be exactly as they are. The capacity for mindfulness is the foundation for understanding the world as it really is, and hence overcoming the ignorance, craving, and attachment that give rise to suffering. It is key to bringing about the personal transformation that leads to the complete inner peace of Nirvana.

The Monastic Ideal and Social Reform

The Buddha traveled all over northern India, sharing his teaching about *dukkha* with anyone who was willing and able to receive it. People from all walks of life joined his *Sangha*, a fourfold community that included monks (*bhikkhus*), nuns (*bhikkhunis*), and lay practitioners of both sexes (*upasakas, upasikas*). Unlike the monastic disciples, who shaved their heads, donned yellow robes, begged for their food, and assumed the vow of celibacy, lay practitioners observed a more limited set of precepts, vowing to abstain from killing, stealing, sexual misconduct, lying, and intoxication. These are known as the Five Precepts, which form the basis of Buddhist ethics. Lay practitioners could follow these precepts in their daily lives as "householders."

Taking the monastic vow meant living apart from the mainstream of society, where disciples could study and practice in a concentrated way, unobstructed by the demands of a householder's life. They renounced the materialist values of society in favor of a life of austere simplicity. This was not the extreme asceticism of the forest monks – a way the Buddha had tried and abandoned. Rather, this was a community governed by precepts designed to ensure harmony and freedom from the distractions of the outside world. The monastic way, though not easy, promised a life filled with peace and joy.

Traditionally viewed, monasticism represented the ideal form of Buddhist practice. By choosing to remain in the world, the householder maintained various attachments in the form of family, wealth, and material possessions. Of course, these attachments could only prolong and complicate the task of attaining liberation. Still, it remained possible for those who did not renounce the world in a decisive way to make progress toward enlightenment, and members of the monastic community played a vital role in this regard. Their primary responsibilities included preserving, studying, and disseminating the Buddha's teachings. They provided a living example of the ideal moral and spiritual life, encouraging lay followers in the practice of the Five Precepts.

For their part, the laity provided sustaining support for the monastic community through the donation of food, material goods, and volunteer labor. These activities provided laypeople ample opportunities to earn merit by practicing the central Buddhist virtue of generosity (*dana*).

It would be a mistake, however, to interpret the observance of the division between lay and ordained communities as a signal that the Buddha was unconcerned with the betterment of society. Despite the pronounced emphasis on attaining inner peace and personal enlightenment, the monastic ideal was never set over against concern for the well-being of society at large. The potential of Buddhism as a force for social reform was already present, if latently, in its most basic teachings.

The Buddha's spiritual journey toward enlightenment was driven not only by his personal experience of suffering, but also by his profound empathy for the suffering of the world. This empathy was only deepened by his enlightenment experience, which confirmed in a direct way that everything in the world, including suffering, exists in a condition of interdependence. In traditional Buddhist thought, suffering arises together with the causes of suffering. When these causes are no longer present, the suffering ceases. This idea is expressed in a central Buddhist teaching known as "dependent origination" or "interdependent co-arising," which the Buddha summarized this way:

> When this exists, that comes to be; with the arising of this, that arises. When this does not exist, that does not come to be; with the cessation of this, that ceases.

Despite the simplicity of its formulation, this teaching has far-reaching consequences. It follows, for example, that nothing in the world exists as a permanent, unconditioned reality – not even the self. Even those aspects of human nature that we associate with personal identity (body, feelings, perceptions, mental formations, and consciousness) exist only in interdependence with each other and with everything else. As Christopher Gowans explains, what we call the self is not ontologically distinct, not a substance-self, but rather part of an ever-changing, interdependent network of processes in the world (Gowans, 2003: 84). From the standpoint of conditioned arising, all things are said to be empty of self-existence.

Once we grasp the truth of emptiness (*sunyata*), we see that our personal suffering exists interdependently with the suffering of others. Thus, when we work to transform the conditions that give rise to suffering, either in ourselves or in society, our work contributes to the liberation of all beings. In Buddhist thought, this realization is the basis for true compassion.

Although the Buddha did not directly engage in social activism, his teachings confirmed that personal transformation in the Buddhist sense could not be separated from the transformation of society. The monks and nuns who joined the *Sangha* in search of personal enlightenment did not practice solely for their own sake. Whether teaching the *dharma*, observing the precepts, or sitting in meditation, they, too, were working to create the conditions for all beings to attain liberation.

The social dimension of Buddhist practice was greatly amplified, however, in Mahayana tradition, which held up the ideal of the *bodhisattva* (awakened being). Moved by great compassion for the suffering of the world, a *bodhisattva* is committed to being reborn until all sentient beings have attained enlightenment. This compassion flows directly from the realization that suffering, wherever it is and however it is manifested, affects all beings.

The theme of interdependence figures quite prominently in Mahayana teachings. The *Avatamsaka Sutra*, for example, is well known for its depiction of the interpenetration of all the elements of the universe. The gleaming jewels of Indra's net are but mirrors that reflect each other. Nothing happens in any part of the universe that is not felt everywhere. According to this picture, the true nature of our being lies in our identity and interdependence with everything else. In a word, the true nature of our being is "interbeing" (see Hạnh 1987a: 86f.).

Insight into the nature of interbeing is the fruit of meditation, in which we see things as they really are, free from the distorting lens of the ego-self. However, this insight reveals at the same time a moral imperative. The final chapter of the *Avatamsaka Sutra* concludes with the words of the *bodhisattva* Samantabhadra, who teaches that wisdom exists only for the sake of putting it into practice; that wisdom is only useful to the extent that it benefits all living beings. As Francis H. Cook summarizes this point:

> Not only is the reality of identity and interdependence the basis for Bhodisattva activity, but it also acts as a moral imperative, leaving the truly moral being with no option but to act in accordance with this reality. For if my own existence is unthinkable apart from the existence of this infinite other, and if my own actions touch these beings in some manner, then I must have an obligation to act in such a way that all benefit from the acts. . . . I choose for all when I choose for myself. It even reaches beyond the human so that if I throw away a paper drinking cup, I can almost hear the reverberations of a falling tree in Michigan. (Cook, 1973: 118)

From the Mahayana perspective, the translation of insight and understanding into moral praxis is regarded as a natural and inevitable development of the Buddha's core teachings. However, it was not until the twentieth century that the full flowering of the *bodhisattva* ideal would be realized in the practice of socially engaged Buddhism.

Buddhism for This World

In 1964, Nhất Hạnh published two collections of articles devoted to discussions about the role of Buddhism in Vietnamese culture and society: *Buddhism Today* (1964a) and *Engaged Buddhism* (1964b). The latter work bore the Vietnamese title Đạo Phật đi vào cuộc đời. Đạo Phật is a common way of referring to Buddhism, or the way of the Buddha. Cuộc đời means "society" or "life." Đi vào means "to enter." Thus the literal meaning is closer to "Buddhism That Enters Society." However, this and similar phrases were translated by Nhất Hạnh as "engaged Buddhism" (see Hạnh, 2008a: 31).

Written in a more scholarly style than the popular works for which Nhất Hạnh would later become known in the West, these early articles ranged over a wide variety of issues, including Buddhist education, considerations about ethics and language, the relation between religion and politics, and the existential implications of key concepts in Buddhist philosophy. His main objective, however, was to advance the idea of an "actualized" or "engaged" Buddhism.

The notion of an "engaged" Buddhism was not entirely new in Vietnam. As Nhất Hạnh noted in his first major English-language publication on the subject of the war, *Vietnam: Lotus in a Sea of Fire*: "In the 1930s, the Buddhist scholars had already discussed the engagement of Buddhism in the modern society and called it Nhân Gian

Phật Giáo, or engaged Buddhism" (Hạnh, 1967: 42). This phrase was associated with various efforts to revive Buddhism after a long period of perceived decline under French colonial rule.

The Buddhist revival movement in Vietnam had been shaped in various ways by the events of the Second World War, the rise of communism and Vietnamese nationalism, and a long military insurgency against the French (see DeVido, 2007). The most significant developments occurred at the grassroots level, in particular with the formation of a national Buddhist youth organization known as the Buddhist Youth Family (Gia Đình Phật Tử). This wing of the movement directed most of its efforts to helping Vietnam's rural poor, and was responsible for the creation of many orphanages, schools, nurseries, and hospitals throughout the provinces. This became a model for the kind of work that Nhất Hạnh and his colleagues would later undertake with the creation of the School of Youth for Social Service.

The revival movement had generated vigorous public debate concerning whether and to what extent Buddhism should be involved in the social and political affairs of the country. By the early 1960s, with the escalating involvement of the United States in Vietnam, these questions took on even greater urgency. The country was immersed in political turmoil. Buddhists were being targeted for persecution by the repressive Diệm regime, causing many to take to the streets in protest. A pivotal moment came in June of 1963, when Thích Quảng Đức called the world's attention to the suffering in Vietnam by burning himself alive at a busy intersection in Saigon. Before the war was over, more than 50 others, including monks, nuns, and laypersons, would follow Quảng Đức's example (DeVido, 2007: 251). With that event the "Buddhist Struggle Movement" was born.

Within the Struggle Movement there were those who advocated a full-on political engagement, while others opposed any form of social or political action (Hạnh, 1967: 48f.). Eventually this disagreement within the Buddhist community led to the formation of the Unified Buddhist Church of Vietnam (UBCV), which splintered off from the traditional and more conservative Vietnamese Buddhist Sangha (VBS). The UBCV advocated a more progressive agenda of social and political engagement.

Although Nhất Hạnh was a strong voice within the UBCV and an ardent supporter of efforts to renew Buddhism as a vital expression of Vietnamese cultural identity, he was not particularly interested in aligning himself with any political party, or relying on political tactics to achieve this end (see King, 1996: 349). As he saw it, all the resources for renewing and preserving Buddhism were already available within the religious tradition, which he described as "a great spiritual force in search of self-realization" (Hạnh, 1967: 47). The Buddha's teachings about suffering and interdependence already pointed to a more direct and active involvement for Buddhism in society. Nhất Hạnh's task as a writer was to clarify the theoretical framework for understanding the scope and nature of that engagement. The result was a comprehensive statement about Buddhism's response to suffering in the modern world.

The conception of engaged Buddhism advocated by Nhất Hạnh did not distinguish sharply between the social and spiritual realms. One of the major points he was concerned to make in his early writings was that the essence of Buddhism, as a living religion, can be known and understood only by the way it manifests itself as a response to the actual conditions of our social existence. In *Buddhism Today* he stressed the need to modernize Buddhism, to adapt its teachings to meet the challenges of the day. According to this view, Buddhism simply *is* the compassionate response to suffering in the world. As the conditions in a society change, so must the form of the Buddhist response:

> Each country, each time, each place, has its own form of living conditions, and living religion must change and adapt to these so that it may be a part of the social milieu of its time. The forms of Buddhism must change so that the essence of Buddhism remains unchanged . . . Being imprisoned in such forms would mean that the essence of Buddhism would be diluted and weakened, so that the discovery of new forms of Buddhism is in fact the way in which Buddhism itself may be perpetuated. (Hạnh, 1967: 94)

If Buddhism is to continue as a "living source of wisdom and peace," its principles must constantly be reinterpreted and adapted to the realities of the contemporary situation (see Hạnh, 1987b: 9).

As a spiritual and social movement, engaged Buddhism has only one goal: the cessation of suffering. To this end, we must become aware of the suffering around us:

> The natural tendency is to run away from suffering, from ill-being. We don't want to confront it so we try to escape. But the Buddha advises us not to do so. In fact he encourages us to look deeply into the nature of the suffering in order to learn. His teaching is that if you do not understand the suffering you cannot see the path of transformation, the path leading to the cessation of suffering. (Hạnh, 2008a: 32)

When we look deeply into the nature of social suffering, we begin to understand our interdependence with it. We see that the causes of suffering in society cannot be separated from the way we live, or from the institutions that we collectively create and support. This mindful awareness of our nonseparation from the suffering of others is the spiritual and moral basis for all Buddhist engagement in society.

Viewed from the perspective of interdependence, the path leading to the cessation of suffering cannot be one of withdrawal, either in the form of monastic retreat or in a practice of meditation aimed at detaching oneself from what is happening in the world. Thus, whereas tradition had dictated that the proper place for the monk (or nun) was in the monastery, Nhất Hạnh understood that "Buddhas are to be found in places of suffering." In a journal entry dated July 12, 1965, he wrote:

> Engaged Buddhism in Vietnam teaches that good works do not need to be reserved for the pagoda, but can be extended to towns and villages. . . . Buddha does not just sit in the temple anymore! Of course, the only reason he ever did was because people placed him there. But the Buddha does not want to be isolated amidst offerings of rice, bananas, and flowers. . . . Avalokiteshvara must continue to move if she is to hear and respond to the cries of those who suffer. It does not make sense for students of the Buddha to isolate themselves inside a temple, or they are not his true students. Buddhas are to be found in places of suffering. (Hạnh, 1998: 196f.)

This statement was not intended as a call to abandon the monastic life of contemplation in favor of social work. The challenge was to learn how to bring meditation into society, how to practice compassion in the presence of the suffering and devastation of war. For a *bodhisattva*, meditation is not an end in itself, but rather a preparation for "reentry into society." The task was to become aware of the suffering all around us, to recognize our nonseparation from that suffering, and to seek ways to transform the situation through compassionate action:

> When bombs begin to fall on people, you cannot stay in the meditation hall all of the time. Meditation is about the awareness of what is going on – not only in your body and in your feelings, but all around you. . . . You have to learn how to help a wounded child while still practicing mindful breathing. You should not allow yourself to get lost in action. Action should be meditation at the same time. (Hạnh, 2003a: 1)

Whereas the traditional Five Precepts of Buddhism had focused on abstaining from specific behaviors, Nhất Hạnh's idea of engaged practice placed far greater emphasis on cultivating a deeper awareness of the interdependent nature of reality:

> Therefore we have to see the real truth, the real situation. Our daily lives, the way we drink, what we eat, has to do with the world's political situation. Meditation is to see deeply into things, to see how we can change, how we can transform our situation. . . . Awakening is important. The nature of the bombs, the nature of injustice . . . and the nature of our own beings are the same. This is the real meaning of engaged Buddhism. (Hạnh, 1987a: 74)

When we look deeply into the suffering caused by war, for example, we begin to understand that we are not separate from the bombs or from the people who drop them. We are not mere observers who pass judgment on what is happening around us; we are part of it. Our being is interdependent with the bombs and the injustice. It is for this reason that Nhất Hạnh says: "The war stops and starts with you and with me" (Hạnh, 2003b: 55).

Bombs not only kill and injure living beings, they also create hatred, intolerance, and an appetite for revenge that perpetuates the cycle of violence. From a Buddhist perspective, the peace worker who goes out into the village to care for the survivors of a bombing attack must be aware that he or she cannot remain completely unaffected by it. There is always the potential for suffering to take root in the form of sadness, frustration, anger, or hatred – feelings that give rise to wrong perceptions and unskillful actions. The peace worker must therefore be mindful of these feelings, so that he or she can engage the situation with calmness, clarity, and compassion for everyone involved.

It is the practice of mindfulness that allows us to acknowledge suffering without being consumed by it, without watering the seeds of anger and hatred in ourselves, without cultivating the appetite for revenge that only perpetuates the cycle of violence and suffering. It is mindfulness that keeps us firmly grounded in the consciousness of interdependence, of the nonduality of "victim" and "victimizer," and of our nonseparation from everything that is happening (King, 2005: 30). To bring the transformative power of mindfulness into places of suffering – to *be* peace in the midst of suffering – is the practice of engaged Buddhism.

Lotus in a Sea of Fire

Apart from his writings, which provided an intellectual framework for understanding Buddhist social engagement, Nhất Hạnh brought practical leadership to the movement in a variety of ways, including the creation of a Buddhist university and an independent publishing house. The Institute for Higher Buddhist Studies (later Vạn Hạnh University) was founded in 1964 in association with the monks of Ấn Quang pagoda in Saigon; Lá Bối Press was established in Saigon during the same period.

However, Nhất Hạnh also distinguished himself as a leader of nonviolent social action. In 1964, he launched a project to establish "self-help villages" (see Hạnh, 1998: 181ff.) in some of the poorest rural areas of Vietnam. Within a year, the project had evolved into the School of Youth for Social Service (SYSS), a "rice-roots" relief corps that trained thousands of young volunteers to carry out social work in the rural villages and hamlets of Vietnam. They provided education and medicine, built schools and makeshift health clinics, taught modern farming techniques, and established cooperatives to help people find ways to become economically self-sufficient. As the war intensified, a good deal of their effort was devoted to reconstructing villages destroyed by bombing. The SYSS placed special emphasis on caring for the needs of the children of war.

All the efforts of the SYSS were aimed at promoting healing, reconciliation, and peace. While many of its members died in the course of their service, they carried out their work with a spirit of openness and tolerance, and with an unwavering commitment to the principle of nonviolence. Their work was compassion in action.

In 1966, Nhất Hạnh founded Tiếp Hiện, the Order of Interbeing, which he later described as a "spiritual resistance movement." The first members were men and women who had been working closely with him in the SYSS. The creation of the order was crucial to sustaining the continued work of the SYSS, as it provided vital spiritual support for its members during the darkest hours of the war.

The Charter of the Order of Interbeing identified four foundational principles:

1 Nonattachment from views: To be attached means to be caught in dogmas, prejudices, habits, and what we consider to be the Truth. The first aim of the practice is to be free of all attachments, especially attachments to views. This is the most important teaching of Buddhism.

2 Direct experimentation: Buddhism emphasizes the direct experience of reality, not speculative philosophy. Direct practice-realization, not intellectual research, brings about insight. Our own life is the instrument through which we experiment with truth.

3 Appropriateness: A teaching, in order to bring about understanding and compassion, must reflect the needs of the people and the realities of society. To do this, it must . . . conform with the basic tenets of Buddhism, and it must be truly helpful and relevant.

4 Skillful means (*upaya*): Skillful means consist of images and methods created by intelligent teachers to show the Buddha's way and guide people in their efforts to practice the way in their own particular circumstances. These means are called Dharma doors. (Hạnh, 1987b: 8f.)

These principles were articulated in 14 precepts (later referred to as "Mindfulness Trainings"), which served as guidelines for engaged practice. The first precept, called "The Lion's Roar," was key for framing the engaged Buddhist response to war:

Do not be idolatrous about or bound to any doctrine, theory, or ideology, even Buddhist ones. Buddhist systems of thought are guiding means; they are not absolute truth. (Hạnh, 1987b: 17)

Based on\ the insight that all suffering is rooted in the mind, in ignorance, this precept placed primary emphasis on the practice of "nonattachment to views," which meant keeping the mind free from dogmatic assumptions or ideological commitments. It recognized that peace is impossible in a situation where ideology prevents us from seeing the basic humanity of those we call our enemies, and hence from acknowledging their suffering – let alone recognizing our nonseparation from their suffering. From the Buddhist perspective, clinging to an ideology is more dangerous even than the physical weapons used in war:

In the name of ideologies and doctrines people kill and are killed. If you have a gun you can shoot one, two, three, five people; but if you have an ideology and stick to it, thinking it is the absolute truth, you can kill millions. (Hạnh, 1987a: 89)

At its heart, engaged practice is, as Nhất Hạnh suggested, a spiritual resistance movement. It is the conscious effort to transform the conditions that give rise to suffering, both in ourselves and in society, while at the same time resisting the temptation to become attached to our own limited ideas about good and evil, right and wrong. It requires that we look deeply into the interdependent nature of things in order to liberate our minds from discrimination, intolerance, anger, and fear – the roots of suffering in the world (see Hạnh, 1975).

In the context of the struggle for peace in the midst of war, the practice of nonattachment to views allows us to transcend the dualistic perspective that insists on distinguishing sharply between "victim" and "victimizer," and prevents us from seeing the interdependent nature of reality:

When we look deeply into the nature of interdependence and see that the person harming us is also a victim – of his family, his society, his environment – understanding arises naturally. With understanding there is empathy and reconciliation. Understanding always leads to love. . . . The ability to see the interdependent nature of all things leads to compassion in our hearts and keeps us from suffering, even when people betray us and cause us harm. (Hạnh, 2006: 278f.)

This move is critical to understanding the spiritual dimension of Buddhist social engagement. From the Buddhist perspective, blaming and arguing are forms of violence that perpetuate the cycle of suffering (Hạnh, 1993: 67). Our task, as peacemakers, is not to judge who is right and who is wrong, who is good and who is bad, but to try to understand the situation. It is only when we can identify with both the victim and the victimizer that we can truly act in a spirit of selfless love and compassion to bring about reconciliation (Hạnh, 1987a: 69f.). As Sallie B. King explains:

> Through identifying with both, we can overcome such a dualistic attitude toward the complexities of suffering. Through this identification with both good and bad, through meditative discovery of the impulses behind one's own "goodness" and "badness" one can finally put aside these categories and "wake up," opening one's heart to compassion. (King, 1996: 341)

This is transformation at the base. For even as the *bodhisattva* seeks to alleviate suffering in the world, this work of transforming suffering always begins in ourselves. As Nhất Hạnh succinctly expresses this point: "Peace work means, first of all, being peace" (Hạnh, 1987a: 80).

Ironically, it was the sublime ideal of selfless love and compassion that made the SYSS and the Order of Interbeing targets for violent attack. Each of the major combatants in the war interpreted the unwillingness to take sides as tacit support of the enemy. The Diệm regime actually codified this view in law, equating neutrality with pro-Communist sympathy, and hence as an act of treason (see Hạnh, 1967: 90). For all his efforts toward restoring peace in his homeland, Nhất Hạnh was forced into exile by government authorities in 1966. Nevertheless, the work he began there continued, despite the grave danger it posed to those who carried it out.

After almost 40 years in exile, Nhất Hạnh returned to Vietnam in 2005 (see Chapman, 2007). This visit was followed by two more visits, which were partly pilgrimage, partly an opportunity to see at first hand the social, political, and religious situation in Vietnam, and partly an opportunity to continue the work of healing the wounds of a war that divided families in life and in death. During a trip in 2007, Nhất Hạnh conducted a series of public memorial services for the millions who perished as a result of the war.

Although Nhất Hạnh's teachings had been officially banned by the Vietnamese government after the war, he was permitted to hold retreats, give public lectures, and publish Vietnamese translations of some of his books. He also ordained hundreds of young Vietnamese men and women eager to practice in the engaged Buddhism tradition. These monks and nuns see themselves as continuing the work of peace and reconciliation begun during the Vietnam War.

Applied Buddhism

Having lived in the West for many years, Nhất Hạnh has a deep understanding of western culture and, like the Dalai Lama, possesses a gift for communicating Buddhist ideas in a clear and accessible way. His interpretation of engaged practice has been enormously influential in shaping contemporary western ideas about Buddhism.

Buddhist practitioners in Nhất Hạnh's tradition observe the Five Mindfulness Trainings, which are a modernized version of the Five Precepts of Buddhism. These trainings represent the Buddhist vision for a global spirituality and a global ethic. Although they are intended as guidelines for the concrete realization of the Buddha's teachings on the Four Noble Truths and the Noble Eightfold Path, Nhất Hạnh stresses their universal, nonsectarian nature (Hạnh, 2008b: 10). Briefly summarized,

> The First Mindfulness Training is about protecting the lives of human beings, animals, vegetables, and minerals. To protect other beings is to protect ourselves. The second is to prevent the exploitation by humans of other living beings and of nature. It is also the practice of generosity. The third is to protect children and adults from sexual abuse, to preserve the happiness of individuals and families. Too many families have been broken by sexual misconduct. When you practice the Third Mindfulness Training, you protect yourself and you protect families and couples. You help other people feel safe. The Fourth Mindfulness Training is to practice deep listening and loving speech. The Fifth Mindfulness Training is about mindful consumption. (Hạnh, 1999: 197)

A distinctive feature of Nhất Hạnh's teaching about mindfulness is his emphasis on the importance of recognizing the forms of ill-being that are characteristic of contemporary life. These include stress, anxiety, broken families, suicide, destruction of the ecosystem, as well as the various social, political, and economic forms of suffering associated with globalization. The problems of global terrorism and global warming have been a major focus of Nhất Hạnh's work in recent years (see Hạnh, 2005, 2008b).

Mindfulness practice uses the traditional contemplative techniques of stopping (*samatha*) and looking deeply (*vipassana*) in order to cultivate both the awareness of suffering and also the insight and understanding needed to engage that suffering with compassion. The practice is first and foremost about learning how to live in the present moment:

> We run our whole life chasing after one idea of happiness or another. Stopping is to stop our running, our forgetfulness, our being caught in the past or the future. We come home to the present moment, where life is available. (Hạnh, 1999: 209f.)

In the present moment, we have a chance to become aware of how our patterns of thought, speech, and action are connected to the suffering we experience in ourselves, in our families, and in society. For example, when we look deeply into our habits of consumption – the way we consume food, energy, news, entertainment, and luxury items – we can see that it has consequences not only for our own health and happiness, but also for the health of the environment and the happiness of beings everywhere. Thus, when we practice mindful consumption, "we protect our body, our consciousness, and the body and consciousness of our family and society" (Hạnh, 1999: 97).

Many people think of meditation as something that is done only in quiet solitude, perhaps seated on a mat or a cushion, with legs folded and eyelids lowered. However,

Nhất Hạnh teaches that even the simplest of acts, such as attending to our breath, drinking a cup of tea, or eating an orange, if done with mindful concentration, can bring us freedom and happiness. By doing these things in such a way that we are truly present, we can experience a calming of body and mind that liberates us from tension and stress, and from the influence of strong emotions, such as anger and fear. According to Nhất Hạnh, "a moment of living in mindfulness is already a moment of enlightenment." As he explains:

> Suppose you are drinking some tea and you are aware that you are drinking some tea. That kind of mindfulness of drinking is a form of enlightenment. There have been many times that you've been drinking but you didn't know it, because you are absorbed in worries. . . . If you can focus your mind on the act of drinking, then happiness can come while you have some tea. . . . But if you don't know how to drink your tea in mindfulness and concentration, you are not really drinking tea. You are drinking your sorrow, your fear, your anger – and happiness is not possible. (Hạnh, 2003a: 3)

The more we practice mindfulness in our daily lives, the more we water the seeds of happiness and enlightenment in ourselves. Mindfulness deepens our insight into the interdependent nature of reality, our awareness and understanding of the causes of suffering in the world, and our capacity to transform that suffering into peace, joy, and liberation (Hạnh, 2003a: 4).

Simply stated, the practice of engaged Buddhism is the practice of mindfulness in daily life. For when we nurture peace and well-being in ourselves, we are already addressing the root causes of the conflicts that arise within families, within communities, and among nations:

> To prevent war, to prevent the next crisis, we must start right now. When a war or a crisis has begun, it is already too late. If we and our children practice *ahimsa* [nonviolence] in our daily lives, if we learn how to plant seeds of peace and reconciliation in our hearts and minds, we will begin to establish real peace and, in that way, we may be able to prevent the next war. (Hạnh, 1993: 71)

To nurture peace and well-being in ourselves is to nurture peace and well-being in the world.

In recent years, Nhất Hạnh has begun to use the phrase "applied Buddhism" as a way of talking about engaged practice in the twenty-first century. The most prominent example of this is the name of the newly established European Institute for Applied Buddhism (EIAB) in Germany. The mission of EIAB is to promote the creation of healthy, peaceful, and sustainable communities through the practice of mindfulness. In keeping with the idea that Buddhism is not just a theory but a practice that is relevant to the needs of people today, the EIAB offers specialized retreats for parents, couples, business leaders, and people in various professions, including teaching, healthcare, and law enforcement.

There is also a renewed emphasis in Nhất Hạnh's tradition on educating and organizing youth for social transformation. The "Wake Up Movement," launched in 2008, is a worldwide grassroots initiative supported by the EIAB and associated Plum Village practice centers in the United States, France, and Thailand. The aim is to empower young people to bring the practice of mindfulness into their homes, neighborhoods, and schools, where they can sow seeds of peace and reconciliation, and promote greater awareness of global issues.

According to Nhất Hạnh, "engaged" and "applied" Buddhism differ in name only: "Nowadays we are using the term 'Applied Buddhism,' which is just another way of referring to Engaged Buddhism" (Hạnh, 2008a: 36). While this may be true, the phrase "applied Buddhism" does resonate differently in a western ear. For one thing, it conveys more accurately the sense of a practical, skills-based approach to addressing the problems of life, suggesting something closer to an applied Buddhist ethics than a religious practice in the traditional sense. This is in keeping with the universal, nonsectarian character of the teachings, which are offered merely as "a guiding means" to help people learn to look deeply, in order to develop greater insight and compassion (Hạnh, 1987b: 71–77).

The inclusive nature of Nhất Hạnh's approach is no doubt part of the great appeal of his teachings in the West. For not only Buddhists, but humanists and religious believers from other faith traditions, are able to find a well of inspiration and insight in the practice of mindfulness.

Epilogue

While it is true that engaged Buddhism is not a unified movement, it has its roots in core Buddhist teachings. Interdependence, impermanence, nonself, and compassion form the conceptual nucleus at the heart of engaged Buddhist thought and practice. While these concepts may be worked out in different ways by different authors, they contribute to a shared vision of compassionate action in the service of peace and social justice – a vision that transcends any particular tradition of Buddhist thought (King, 2005: 30).

The insights of interdependence and nonself are as fundamental to Buddhadasa Bhikkhu's "Dhammic Socialism" (1986) and Sulak Sivaraksa's "Small 'b' Buddhism" (1992) as they are to the Dalai Lama's Mahayana conception of "exchanging self and others" (2005). For all three thinkers, grasping the true nature of our interbeing deepens our compassion and our sense of moral duty toward others in society; it is essential to overcoming the forces of oppression and intolerance that prevent our individual and collective awakening.

These ideas are also at the heart of A.T. Ariyaratne's conception of "Sarvodaya," which literally means "the awakening of all." Recognizing the deep interdependence between personal liberation and social transformation, Sarvodaya seeks to address the external conditions in society – the poverty and the injustice – that prevent people from understanding and overcoming the internal sources of their suffering (Ariyaratne, 1999).

In keeping with the Buddha's own description of his teaching, these writers see their task as neither more nor less than the cessation of *dukkha*. They interpret the Four

Noble Truths and the Noble Eightfold Path not as a call to retreat from the suffering of the world, but as a call to engage it with wisdom and compassion. Nirvana need not be deferred to some future supramundane existence. It is possible to touch Nirvana in the present. Working to alleviate the effects of poverty, oppression, and social injustice can make a difference here and now. This work is itself an expression of enlightenment.

Nhất Hạnh concluded his book *Vietnam: Lotus in a Sea of Fire* on an optimistic note, observing that the "spirit of openness and tolerance" characteristic of Buddhism would guarantee its ability to adapt to the situation in Vietnam and be a force for peace (1967: 94). The engaged movements that have emerged over the past 40 years offer ample evidence of the vitality of that spirit, and of the enormous potential that Buddhism holds for creating a peaceful, just, and sustainable future.

References

Ariyaratne, A.T. (1999) *Collected Works*, Sarvodaya Vishva Lekha, Sri Lanka.

Buddhadasa, A. (1986) *Dhammic Socialism*, Donald Swearer (ed.), Thai Inter-Religious Commission for Development, Bangkok.

Chapman, J. (2007) The 2005 pilgrimage and return to Vietnam of exiled Zen Master Thích Nhất Hạnh, in *Modernity and Re-Enchantment: Religion in Post-Revolutionary Vietnam*, Philip Taylor (ed.), Institute of Southeast Asian Studies, Singapore, pp. 297–341.

Cook, F.H. (1973) *Hua-yen Buddhism: The Jewel Net of Indra*, Penn State University Press, University Park, PA.

Dalai Lama (2005) *The Essential Dalai Lama: His Important Teachings*, Penguin, New York.

DeVido, E.A. (2007) Buddhism for this world: The Buddhist revival in Vietnam, 1920–1951, and its legacy, in *Modernity and Re-Enchantment: Religion in Post-Revolutionary Vietnam*, Philip Taylor (ed.), Institute of Southeast Asian Studies, Singapore, pp. 250–296.

Gowans, Christopher W. (2003) *Philosophy of the Buddha*, Routledge, London.

Hạnh, N. (1964a) *Buddhism Today* [Đạo Phật ngày nay], Lá Bối Press, Saigon.

Hạnh, N. (1964b) *Engaged Buddhism* [Đạo Phật đi vào cuộc đời], Lá Bối Press, Saigon.

Hạnh, N. (1967) *Vietnam: Lotus in a Sea of Fire*, Hill and Wang, New York.

Hạnh, N. (1975) *The Miracle of Mindfulness: A Manual on Meditation*, trans. Mobi Ho, Beacon Press, Boston.

Hạnh, N. (1987a) *Being Peace*, Parallax Press, Berkeley, CA.

Hạnh, N. (1987b) *Interbeing: Fourteen Guidelines for Engaged Buddhism*, Parallax Press, Berkeley, CA.

Hạnh, N. (1993) *Ahimsa*: The path of harmlessness, in *Love in Action: Writings on Nonviolent Social Change*, Nhất Hạnh (ed.), Parallax Press, Berkeley, CA.

Hạnh, N. (1998) *Fragrant Palm Leaves: Journals 1962–1966*, Mobi Warren (ed.), Riverhead Books, New York.

Hạnh, N. (1999) *The Heart of the Buddha's Teaching: Transforming Suffering into Peace, Joy, and Liberation*, Broadway Books, New York.

Hạnh, N. (2003a) In engaged Buddhism, peace begins with you, interviewed by John Malkin, *Shambhala Sun*, http://www.shambhalasun.com/index.php?option=content&task=view&id=1579 (accessed April 19, 2011).

Hạnh, N. (2003b) *Creating True Peace*, Free Press, New York.

Hạnh, N. (2005) *Calming the Fearful Mind: A Zen Response to Terrorism*, Parallax Press, Berkeley, CA.

Hạnh, N. (2006) *Understanding Our Mind*, Parallax Press, Berkeley, CA.

Hạnh, N. (2008a) The history of engaged Buddhism, *Human Architecture: Journal of the Sociology of Self-Knowledge* 6: 29–36.

Hạnh, N. (2008b) *The World We Have: A Buddhist Approach to Peace and Ecology*, Parallax Press, Berkeley, CA.

King, S.B. (1996) Thich Nhat Hanh and the Unified Buddhist Church of Vietnam: Nondualism in action, in *Engaged Buddhism: Buddhist Liberation Movements in Asia*, Christopher S. Queen and Sallie B. King (eds.), SUNY Press, Albany, NY.

King, S.B. (2005) *Being Benevolence: The Social Ethics of Engaged Buddhism*, University of Hawaii Press, Honolulu.

Sivaraksa, S. (1992) *Seeds of Peace: A Buddhist Vision for Renewing Society*, Parallax Press, Berkeley, CA.

CHAPTER 3
Christianity
Historical Setting

Stanley M. Burgess

Christianity has long been known for its emphasis on social justice. Because of this, it will be possible in this essay only to offer brief pericopes of social justice champions, ranging trans-temporally from ancient to modern times, and trans-spatially from eastern and western churches.

Because historical Christianity grew from Jewish roots, it is necessary to comment briefly on the Jewish "law and the prophets" in terms of the impact they had the emerging concepts of social justice. Social justice is not a goal that humans decide to strive for: it is the commandment of the just God. God commands the Israelites to create a society based on the values embodied in laws designed to ensure equality and fairness for all. The role of the prophet is to liberate those who have been crushed under the burdens of social injustice. Once liberated, they are expected to keep the covenant with God. Part of the covenant is treating others well. If you are unjust, you break the covenant. The prophets are saying to the people: God's protection is predicated on your keeping of the covenant. The prophets exhort the people to be charitable and merciful to the poor and to help those who were defenseless and needy, widows and orphans, oppressed people, strangers, and those without legal rights. They stipulate impartiality in justice, and fairness. They insist on respecting the property of others. They demand respect for every human life.

Jesus and Social Justice

Clearly, most Christians have historically looked to a Jew – Jesus of Nazareth – as the fountainhead of their concepts of social justice. He was a peacemaker, as evidenced in the Sermon on the Mount (Matthew 5:9): "Blessed are the peacemakers, for they shall be called the children of God." Again, he insists, "Love your enemies, bless them that

---

The Wiley Blackwell Companion to Religion and Social Justice, First Edition. Edited by Michael D. Palmer and Stanley M. Burgess.
© 2012 John Wiley & Sons Ltd. Published 2020 by John Wiley & Sons Ltd.

curse you, and pray for them which despitefully use you" (Matthew 5:44). Jesus even forgives his executioners as they nail him to a cross.

Jesus argues for a measure of social equality: "But when you give a feast, invite the poor, the maimed, the lame, the blind, and you will be blessed because they cannot repay you. You will be repaid at the resurrection of the just" (Luke 14:13–14). He endorses community: "Love your neighbor as yourself" (Matthew 22:39); "So in everything, do to others as you would have them do to you" (Matthew 7:12); and "If you would be perfect, go, sell what you possess and give to the poor, and you will have treasure in heaven" (Matthew 19:21). He teaches against corporate greed and the religion of wealth. In the temple courts Jesus finds men selling cattle, sheep, and doves, and other individuals sitting at tables exchanging money. So he makes a whip out of cords, and drives all from the temple area, both sheep and cattle. He then scatters the coins of the money changers and overturns their tables (John 2:14–15). "Watch out! Be on your guard against all kinds of greed; a man's life does not consist in the abundance of his possessions" (Luke 12:15). "Truly I say unto you, it will be hard for a rich man to entered the kingdom of heaven" (Matthew 19:23). "You cannot serve both God and money" (Matthew 6:24).

Jesus makes it clear that God's law can be summarized in two commandments: love God and love your neighbor (Luke 10:25–37). He explains further that "love thy neighbor" means helping people in need until they can become self-sufficient, as illustrated by the so-called Parable of the Good Samaritan. In fact, all people have a moral duty to help other people who are disadvantaged in society. Above all, he certainly practices Micah's injunction "to do justice, love mercy, and walk humbly with your God" (Micah 6:8). Jesus takes seriously Jewish law and Jewish prophets.

Throughout the past two millennia, the Christian church's love for the poor has been inspired by the Gospel expressed in the Beatitudes, by the poverty of Jesus, and by his attention to the poor. The fundamental basis for pursuing social justice goes back to the belief that every person is made in the image and likeness of God (Genesis 1:26–27), and thus has intrinsic value.

In the early church, Paul's letter to Philemon is a plea by the apostle to the owner of runaway slave Onesimus to accept him back, given his conversion to Christianity and his excellent service to Paul. This is not a revolutionary attempt to seek freedom for slaves or even manumission for Onesimus. Even Jesus does not openly promote the ending of slavery. But Paul asks Philemon to accept Onesimus back as a brother in Christ, and, if he suffered financial loss in the process, to charge Paul for that loss. Here is the suggestion that their common faith superseded social conventions of the period. The result is that Philemon frees Onesimus – a clear signal to the rest of the early church that their new community in Christ should come before old practices.

By and large, however, the first-century apostles and later Church Fathers (ca. 100–600) accept without question established social institutions. They were, after all, educated in the same schools as their pagan counterparts. For them, the promise of Christianity is in personal reform, not social reform. This only reinforces the conservative bent of their thought. From this point onward, many heretical and social revolutionary movements lead the way in demanding radical social change, including a return to the utopian regimen existing before the Fall.

Leading Social Reformers in the Early Church

The primary exception to this patristic conservatism was that numerous Church Fathers speak out on questions concerning the poor, the sickly, and the oppressed. As an example, John Chrysostom had a nonnegotiable concern for those who suffered from poverty, illness, and imprisonment. At the end of his second sermon on "Lazarus and the rich man," delivered in Antioch in the late fourth century, Chrysostom implores his audience to remember that we do not possess our own wealth, but that of the poor. However, most of the Fathers follow Augustine of Hippo in accepting the evils of inequality and slavery as punishments for sin.

The legendary St. Patrick (389–461), British missionary to Ireland, condemns the practice of slavery, at least taking other Christians as slaves. Some scholars consider him as the first Christian to do so.

Among Fathers of the Church, none is more actively involved in matters of social justice than St. Basil the Great (ca. 330–79), also known as Basil of Cappadocia. Basil enjoys the privileges of wealth, including the best education in pagan and Christian culture available in his day, studying in his native Cappadocia, Constantinople, and Athens. He becomes disillusioned with riches and vanity, and founds the monastic system in Pontus. Together with Pachomius, Basil is remembered as a father of communal monasticism in eastern Christianity. He is best known for the Basilian rule (focusing on community life, liturgical prayer, and manual labor), which remains standard for eastern ascetics even today. Basil chooses not to live in the monastery of Annisa – where he clearly is most comfortable – but rather to return to Caesarea in Cappadocia, living out his spiritual vocation as a parish priest. Against his will, Basil is made bishop in 370 CE, a position he holds until his death in 379.

In his writing "To the Rich," Basil elaborates on Christ's words to the rich young ruler in Matthew 19:16–22. He reasons that if one cannot divest oneself of wealth, one will not fulfill the law of love for one's neighbor. The more one abounds in personal riches, the more one lacks in love. Basil concludes that the one who shows no mercy cannot expect that mercy will be shown to him. Those who do not give bread will not be given eternal life.

In a second homily on the parable of the rich fool in Luke 12:16–21, entitled "I Will Tear Down My Barns," Basil insists that his readers resolve to treat the things in their possessions as belonging to others. If the rich will scatter their wealth, God will receive them and their glory will be eternal. This homily paints a picture of the suffering of poverty for his rich listeners. The poor consider taking their own children to the slave market, thinking that they might be able to avoid death from famine.

In his homily "In Time of Famine and Drought," Basil explains why God allowed famine. The reason is that the rich do not share with the poor. He suggests that the unjust contracts be torn up, so that sin might also be loosened; that debts be eliminated, so that the earth bears its usual fruits. Here Basil also addresses the poor. He encourages them to put their hope in God. He insists even that the poor give to the poorer. Finally, he concludes with a threat of hell and the final judgment for those who did not heed his warnings.

In a fourth homily, "Against Those Who Lend at Interest," Basil reminds his hearers of the numerous places in Scripture where the sin of usury is denounced. He also recognizes the terror experienced by the debtor, expecting at any moment to be seized violently by his creditor.

Basil practices what he preaches, as evidenced by the entire "New City" (later called the Basiliad) constructed on the outskirts of Caesarea in Cappadocia. Here the poor and diseased are able to receive food, shelter, and medical treatment free of charge. While Basil never refers to this place in his own writings, in the funeral oration by his friend Gregory of Nazianzus we are given a glimpse into this phase of Basil's Episcopal ministry (NPNF 2nd series 7:416):

> My subject is the most wonderful of all, the short road to salvation, the easiest ascent to heaven . . . Basil's care for the sick, and the relief of their wounds, and the imitation of Christ, by cleansing leprosy, not by a word, but in deed.

He also chose to live among the poor and afflicted in the "New City." Basil gives the impression of a bustling center of activity there: physicians and nurses, cooks and attendants, clergy and ascetics all working together to minister to the physical and spiritual needs of the sick and destitute (Epistle 94, NPNF second series 8:179–180). Clearly, this was a direct attempt to replicate the first church at Jerusalem. As Basil puts it:

> Let us zealously imitate the early Christian community, where everything was held in common – life, soul, concord, a common table, indivisible kinship – while unfeigned love constituted many bodies as one and joined many souls into a single harmonious whole. ("In Time of Famine and Drought," 8)

Historians have debated the causes for Basil's social activities, arguing that he had a wealthy background, or that his superior education led him to philanthropic ventures. In the end, however, it seems clear that his outreach to the poor and diseased, and his outspokenness on the social ills of his time, come as the result of his unfolding understanding of the Gospel, and of the necessity of understanding and applying the law of love.

Medieval Women

In the medieval West, female mystics are far more numerous than their male counterparts. It must be remembered, however, that women were strictly restricted in the ways they could act in their vocation. They could not participate in the public sacramental life of the church. They were forbidden to administer the sacraments, to hear confessions, or to grant absolution, and they were not allowed to preach. Once they had entered a convent, they were not supposed to have commerce with the secular world. Their role was to pray for the salvation of their own souls and for the souls of those in the Christian community.

That notwithstanding, religious women in the West *do* emerge as leaders in medieval society. They draw on their personal experience of the divine to provide spiritual guidance for others. Their roles as prophets, mediators, and healers constitute the one exception to women's presumed societal inferiority. They become known for their writings, as well as their efforts to reform the church, undermined as it was by schisms, intellectual aridity, and other ills. They thunder against evils in both their ecclesiastical and their secular societies, as had the prophets of old.

Their impact on medieval society is documented by numerous writers, including one observer in 1158: "In these days, God made manifest his power through the frail sex, in these handmaidens whom he filled with the prophetic spirit." (*Annales palidenses* [Monumenta Germaniae historica, scriptorium tomus 16], 90.)

One of the few autobiographies still extant from the medieval period was written by an Englishwoman, Margery Kempe (ca. 1373–after 1433). In *The Book of Margery Kempe* she deals with her answered prayers, visions, and prophetic insights, which she insists came from God. After bearing 14 children, she persuades her husband to agree to a celibate marriage that she believes was God's will for them. She travels to shrines and holy places, including the Holy Land. Margery reports an ongoing and frequent exercise of the gift of tears. She believes that her spiritual experiences give her the right to teach and advise, questionable activities for a medieval Christian wife.

At a time in which Christian wives were usually mere shadows of their husbands, bearing their children and enduring the many trials of the late Middle Ages, Margery Kempe announces her independence, both from her husband and from the expectations of her church. Like other female mystics, she represents an important avenue of power and self-affirmation for women in the Christian community. Based on their visions and intimate friendship with God, mystics such as Margery are figures of Christian authority, even though they are excluded from offices in the medieval church.

A contemporary, Catherine of Siena (1347?–1380), is able to convince the Pope to return from the "Babylonian Captivity" in France to Rome, because she believes that she has received authentic directions from God. The nuns at Helfta, founded in Saxony, Germany in 1229, are sought out by both men and women for spiritual advice, to provide information on the condition of people who had already died, and even to perform priestly duties like the forgiveness and absolution of sins. Gertrude of Helfta (1256–ca. 1302) claims to have visions in which she is told by God who has been forgiven, and that she is commanded to announce this absolution to the people involved.

Other Medieval Champions of Social Justice

Named the patron of environmentalists by Pope John Paul II, Francis of Assisi (1182–1226) is remembered for many things, including his famous "Canticle of Creation," in which he praises his brothers, the sun, the wind, and fire; his sisters, the moon and water; and his mother, the earth. He also is a friend to animals and to the poor, as well as a strong advocate for peace and nonviolence. He probably is not the author of the poem and song "Make Me an Instrument of Your Peace." Francis does not formally address the topic of social justice, because it was not a issue of his day. That notwithstanding, he lays the foundation for future Franciscan leadership through his social concerns.

Thomas Aquinas (ca. 1225–1274) is the most important systematic theologian in the Roman Catholic tradition. In his famous work, the *Summa theologica*, he incorporates the philosophy of Aristotle into Christian thought. This serves as a basis for Catholic moral theology, including Catholic social thought. Aquinas's political and social ideas are found chiefly in *Commentary on the Politics of* Aristotle, the *Rule of* Princes (he completed only a few sections), and, above all, in sections of the *Summa theologica* (especially 11.11).

Everywhere in his writings, Aquinas's basis of judgment is justice. All of society is a hierarchy of classes and ranks. In this system each man, by what Aquinas calls the principle of "distributive justice," is entitled to a share of worldly goods. Justice demands that the prices of goods and services must always be equal to their value; that is, it is unjust to sell anything at a higher price than it is worth or to buy anything at a lower price. Along with the theory of the just price is that of the just wage, a wage that would enable the worker to live decently in the station of life in which he was placed. The remuneration of the worker is to be measured not by the market value of the products, but by the extent of his needs.

Aquinas views private property as necessary for human life and as an extension of natural law. While under natural law all property is communal, he states that possession of private property is necessary because men better take care of things they possess, because possession advances order rather than chaos, and because private possession promotes a more peaceful state. He accepts an uneven distribution of private property, but also approves of the regulation of private property by the state. He argues that while the ownership of goods should be private, the use of goods must be in common – so that the poor and needy can have their share – or must be in service of the common good.

Similarly to the Bible and Aristotle, Aquinas condemns the practice of charging interest for the lending of money. In his thinking, usury, the charging of money on loans, is sinful and unnatural because money is barren and is simply invented for the purpose of exchange. At the time of the brutal Spanish conquest of the New World, Bartolomé de Las Casas (1484–1566) is an ardent defender of the Native American peoples. He affirms their inherent dignity and defends their rights in the face of genocide and slavery by their countrymen. His writing on the rights of native peoples serves as a most significant step in the history of ideas.

Pope Leo XIII names St. Vincent de Paul (1580–1660) the patron of organizations that help the poor. Vincent also works with slaves and helps to free many of them. The sick are singled out for his special nurturing. He is best remembered for organizing groups in the parishes to feed and clothe the hungry. To pay for these efforts, he organizes charitable efforts of those who were more well-to-do.

Protestant Reformers

The great Protestant reformer, Martin Luther (1483–1546), is less concerned about social justice and reform than spiritual regeneration and correct interpretation of the

Scriptures. Luther writes a book entitled *On the Freedom of the Christian* (Luther meant spiritual freedom), which is misinterpreted as a call to arms by a variety of groups with social causes. To make matters worse, Luther openly attacks fringe social reformers, such as Thomas Müntzer, for stirring up unrest among unfortunate peasants and knights. One such diatribe is his *Against the Thieving, Murderous Horde of* Peasants (May 1525). The result is a series of unfortunate events, such as the Peasants' War (1524–1526) and the execution of Müntzer.

For John Calvin (1509–1564), in contrast to Luther, social and economic matters are part and parcel of right earthly worship. Recent scholarship indicates that Calvin's concern is to improve the actual situation of the poor, although he strongly opposes any direct relation between theology and politics. At the same time, the Calvinist ethic has long been credited with spurring the spirit of industrial capitalism, as material success is linked with the possession of virtue.

On the basis of their belief that the Bible commanded the subordination of women to men, the Lutherans and Calvinists do not allow women to preach, be ordained, or participate in the governing bodies of the churches. However, in both Luther's Germany and the Reformation city of Geneva, changes in education affect the status of women. All Christians, it is said, must learn to read the Bible as the authoritative guide to faith and practice. As a result, the Reformation advances the general improvement of education for both women and men.

The Radical Reformation produces a variety of Protestants who rejected both Magisterial (teachers such as Luther, Zwingli, and Calvin) and Catholic reformers. In an age of great turmoil and violence, including that of Thomas Müntzer and the wild men of Münster, many Anabaptists choose to be nonresisting pacifists. The most important of these is Menno Simons (ca. 1496–1561), under whose able leadership Anabaptism is purged of its radical elements and gains widespread respectability. Simons teaches that true Christians receive the written Word of God, and obediently follow it through the Holy Spirit's unction. They are free from bitter partisanship, hatred, and envy. They have a lovely spirit of peace, as well as pure and upright minds.

Among early Protestant leaders, John Wesley (1703–1791) stands out as one who understands the need for social justice, and strives to achieve it. He early becomes a model of Christian activism. Motivated by a conviction that all persons are made in the divine image, and, therefore, are of equal worth, Wesley teaches social sensitivity to his Methodist followers and to others who will listen. For him, love for God results in love of neighbors. Furthermore, he does not see poverty as culpable failure or sin on the part of the poor, or as an unavoidable fate of those excluded from divine grace, as contemporary Calvinists believe. As a result, he investigates the causes of poverty, and openly denounces the guilty, while expecting diligent labor of the poor. Among all classes he promotes a sense of responsibility for eliminating social ills.

In his essay "Thoughts on the Present Scarcity of Provisions" (*Works*, 11: 53–59), Wesley argues that thousands are dying for lack of nourishment because the breweries are using up the grain supply. They suffer from high taxes arising from the public debt, and the waste of foodstuffs by those living in luxury. His concern for social justice results in the founding of dispensaries for the sick, homes for orphans and widows, schools for poor boys and girls, loan funds for small business ventures, and pension funds for "tired and worn out preachers." He has three rules: "Gain all you can; save all you can; and give all you can." He insists that Christians who love money cannot love God or their neighbors.

At the age of 81, he notes in his *Journal*,

> At this season we usually distribute coals and bread among the poor . . . But . . . they (needed) clothes, as well as food. So on this, and the four following days I walked through the town, and begged two hundred pounds, in order to clothe them that needed it most. But it was hard work as most of the streets were filled with melting snow, which often lay ankle deep, so my feet were steeped in snow water nearly from morning to evening. (*Journal*, 4: 295)

For Wesley, the most effective means of renewing society is the moral transformation of individuals. Human wickedness remains the cause of social evil. Peace and commonweal will be produced by purification from lies, injustice, lack of compassion, pride, a partisan spirit, wrath, revenge bitterness, prejudice hypocrisy, narrow-mindedness, and contentiousness. He struggles against public abuses such as smuggling, luxury, and alcoholism.

Wesley's inveterate Toryism results in his general unwillingness to call for change in the political system, fearing that he might cause or promote unrest. However, in war-torn eighteenth-century Europe, John Wesley stands virtually alone, with the exception of the Quakers, in opposing all forms of war. He is particularly aggrieved with the American colonists who had openly and violently resisted the king's government. He is suspicious of those who speak of liberty as a cover for their own limited interests. For Wesley, war is not a means of changing society for the better. He therefore appeals to the reason of the combatants.

John Wesley directly opposes slavery, as evidenced by his tract *Thoughts upon Slavery*, written in 1773. It is thought that this writing is singly responsible for the overt condemnation of slavery by American Methodism in 1790. Until this time only a small number of pamphlets written by comparatively unknown authors have been written against human slavery. *Thoughts upon Slavery* reaches 13 editions in 30 years, and even becomes part of the libraries of several greats, including George Washington.

Wesley follows up with his famous letter to William Wilberforce on February 24, 1791 – the last letter he writes before his death on Wednesday, March 2. Wilberforce, a member of Parliament, has been converted under Wesley's ministry, and is positively influenced by the founder of Methodism to take action for change. In Wesley's words, "O be not weary in well doing! Go on in the name of God and in the power of His might until even American slavery (the vilest that ever saw the sun) shall vanish away before it." Sixteen years later, in 1807, Parliament finally outlaws England's participation in the slave trade.

Because Wesley teaches that good works are the fruit of one's salvation, and not the way in which that salvation is earned, faith and works go hand in hand in Methodist theology. From the beginning, Methodists have been dedicated to the social gospel and have strived for social justice. As a result, they have been leaders in such causes as abolition, women's suffrage, labor rights, and civil rights.

William Booth (1828–1912) is one of the greatest proponents of social justice in the modern world, and an early follower of John Wesley. Booth and his wife, Catherine, are co-founders of the Salvation Army, the largest Protestant charity in the world. William Booth's father was a nail maker who was put out of business by the new machines and mass production of the industrial revolution. He tried to set up a number of building companies, but recurring trade recessions ruined him financially. In 1842 he could no longer afford his son's school fees, and 13-year-old William Booth was apprenticed to a pawnbroker.

Working for a pawnbroker brings William into constant contact with the poor and destitute, and makes him concerned to do something for them. He is caught up in the working-class movement of the day known as Chartism. He despises his trade and finds his comfort in the fervent Christianity of a group of young Methodist men who preach outdoors in the slums of Nottingham. He is converted in a Nottingham Wesleyan Chapel. When his apprenticeship concludes in 1849, he moves to London.

Booth's great love is in lay preaching, for which he has great gifts of empathy and expression. Edward Raddits, a wealthy boot and shoe manufacturer who attends the same chapel, decides to pay William's expenses so that he can devote himself unreservedly to evangelism. At a small dinner arranged by the Raddits, William meets Catherine Mumford, his future wife. They are married on June 17, 1855.

Because he lacks education, William is not able to become a Wesleyan minister. The Booths serve in pastorates in four other denominations. The last of these is the Methodist New Connection. He becomes a respected and popular preacher in his denominational home, but he increasingly feels restricted by rules that limit his evangelistic trips away from his own pulpit. He resigns as a Methodist minister. Troubled by moods of despair, he considers giving up preaching. However, two urban missionaries in East London hear him addressing the crowds at the "Blind Beggar" public house, and invite him to begin a tent mission in Whitechapel. The date of this mission, July 2, 1865, is understood by the Salvation Army as the date of its foundation. He is 36 years of age, has no steady income, with a wife and six children to support and a seventh on the way. After the tent meetings, he sets up the Christian Mission, designed to reach the poor of London's East End.

The Booths' Mission has over 60 converts during the first year, but the work is hard and dangerous, with William occasionally stoned by his enemies. Mission preaching emphasizes evangelism for the lost and holiness as an instant second work of grace for those already converted. The Booths require all permanent members to abstain totally from alcohol. The Christian Mission opens small-scale welfare programs, including soup kitchens, around London and the immediate area. By 1878 there are 57 soup kitchens.

In that year comes a change of name that brings to the organization a new image and with that a fresh appeal. Up to that time, the Mission uses a committee form of government. Yet they understand that their work is to be active spiritual warfare with Satan and his devils. Booth is their battlefield commander, and this is a "holy war" in which military imagery seems natural. Booth's private secretary, George Scott Railton, hits on the phrase "volunteer army" to describe their Mission. William crosses out the word "volunteer," replacing it with "salvation." The concept of the "Salvation Army" has been born. The military aspect is appealing to Victorian England. The Army would do battle with forces of evil worldwide. It continues to have enemies, including representatives of established denominations and many intellectuals. Brewers and tavern keepers regards the Army's temperance campaign as a mortal threat. The Salvation Army immediately has enormous appeal to the very elements that the Booths hope to reach with the gospel. By 1880 the official magazine of the Salvation Army becomes *The War Cry*. At the time of William Booth's death in 1912, the Army has spread to 58 countries worldwide.

Social concerns are never far from Booth's heart. In 1891 he publishes a controversial book about the plight of the poor in England called *In Darkest England and Way Out*. In it he outlines his program to help the poor and needy. His approach is called "The Cab Horse Charter," claiming that in England cab horses are better cared for than millions of the poorest people: "When a horse is down he is helped up, and while he lives he has food, shelter, and work."

During the preparation of this book, Catherine Booth dies of breast cancer (October 20, 1890), and *In Darkest England* is dedicated to her. From this moment onward, William Booth's innovation and effective daily leadership are diminished. He is isolated and without the wise counsel and the encouragement of Catherine, but he never loses his heartfelt compassion for the poor. In his last public address (May 9, 1912), he speaks of his dedication to eliminating social injustice:

> While women weep as they do now, I'll fight; while little children go hungry as they do now, I'll fight; while men go to prison, in and out, as they do now, I'll fight; while there is a drunkard left, while there is a poor lost girl on the streets, while there remains one dark soul without the light of God, I'll fight – I'll fight to the very end.

Modern Catholic Teaching on Social Justice

Although numerous Catholic philosophers deal with issues of social justice before the 1840s, including the great medieval thinker Thomas Aquinas, the church fails to develop a body of social thought and a program of social reform until the pontificate of Leo XIII (1878–1903). The very term "social justice" is adopted by the Jesuit Luigi Taparelli in the 1840s, largely based on the work of Aquinas. Taparelli argues that the rival economic theories –capitalism and socialism – undermine the unity of society present in Thomistic metaphysics. In addition, neither liberal capitalism nor communism is concerned with public moral philosophy.

Pope Leo XIII, Taparelli's student, in 1891 issues the encyclical *Rerum Novarum* (On the Condition of the Working Classes). Leo rejects both socialism and capitalism, defending labor unions and private property. He insists that the role of the state is to promote social justice through the protection of rights. At the same time, the church must speak out on social issues in order to teach correct social principles and to ensure class harmony. Finally, this encyclical declares that workers are not to be treated as slaves. They too are made in the image of God.

Forty years later, Pope Pius XI's encyclical *Quadragesimo Anno* (literally, "in the fortieth year") seeks a reconstruction of the social order by encouraging a living wage, and advocates that social justice is a personal virtue as well as an attribute of the social order, saying that society can be just only if individuals and institutions are just.

In 2006 Pope Benedict XVI issues an encyclical, *Deus Caritas Est* ("God Is Love"), stating that justice is the defining concern of the state and the central concern of politics, and not of the church, which has charity as its central social concern. In addition, this encyclical states clearly that the laity has the specific responsibility of pursuing social justice in civil society. The Church's role is to inform the debate, using reason and natural law, as well as providing moral and spiritual formation for those involved in politics.

Black Males in the American Abolitionist Movement

The abolitionist movement is part of the American experience since colonial times. In the 1830s it takes on a stronger and louder voice. William Lloyd Garrison usually is given too much credit for this shift. As publisher of *The Liberator* and leader of the New England Anti-Slavery Society, he wages his moral campaign against slavery. But neither the moderate voices of the antislavery movement nor the Garrisonites' either embrace or argue for total racial equality. Instead, it takes the voices of David Walker, Henry Highland Garnet, and Frederick Douglass to make the claim of total racial equality part of the national debate on slavery.

David Walker (1796–1830) is a free black, having been born to a free black mother. He early becomes involved with the nation's first African American newspaper, the *Freedom's Journal* (New York City). By 1828 he becomes Boston's leading spokesman against slavery. In 1829 he publishes his *Appeal*, which he intends to reach the enslaved men and women of the South. This pamphlet is sewed into the used clothing of sailors headed for Southern ports. The *Appeal* makes a great impression throughout the South, with the result that horrified whites offer rewards for Walker's head. In 1830 he is found dead in his home, perhaps a victim of poisoning.

A slave, Henry Highland Garnet (1815–1882), appears before the National Negro Convention in Buffalo, New York in 1843, encouraging slaves to revolt against their masters. His address is rejected, but by only one vote (William Lloyd Garrison votes against his approach). At that point he begins to favor emigration to Liberia, a country in Africa inhabited by freed blacks from the New World, which declared its independence two years earlier. He dies in Liberia two months after his arrival there.

A more famous abolitionist, Frederick Douglass (1818–1895), is born a slave on Maryland's eastern shore. After escaping a notoriously brutal "slavebreaker," he successfully escapes to Baltimore and then to New York City. In 1845 Douglass publishes his autobiography, *Narrative of the Life of Frederick Douglass, an American Slave. Written by Himself*. He breaks with the more radical Garrison, who advocated the breakup of the Union. He is active throughout the rest of his life, working for improved conditions for African Americans. In 1895 he suffers a massive and fatal stroke or heart failure.

Modern Women and Equality

Lydia Marie Child (1802–1880) is hailed by William Lloyd Garrison as "the first woman in the republic." Known for her historical novels and key antislavery works and her ardent social reform activity, Child's influence on American social policy is highly regarded. In 1824 she publishes *Hobomok: A Tale of Early Times*, a novel describing an interracial marriage between a Puritan woman and a Native American. Reviewers brand this work as "revolting ... to every feeling of delicacy." Two years later she founds *Juvenile Miscellany*, the first periodical for children in the United States. Her later writings include a two-volume collection, *The History of the Condition of Women in Various Ages and Nations* (1832–1835). In 1833, she publishes *An Appeal in Favor of that Class of Americans Called Africans*, a severe indictment of slavery that calls for immediate emancipation of slaves that leads to her being shunned socially. Later she opens her home to part of the Underground Railroad, which aids escaping slaves. In her late career, Child campaigns against the dispossession and genocide of Native Americans, and for black suffrage, equal rights for women, and religious tolerance for non-Christian faiths, as well as publicizing the plight of the white urban poor.

Elizabeth Cady Stanton (1815–1902) is an American social activist, abolitionist, temperance leader, and one of the most important leaders of the early woman's movement. In 1848 she presents her Declaration of Sentiments to the first women's rights convention, in Seneca Falls, New York. She refuses to support the passage of the Fourteenth and Fifteenth Amendments to the United States Constitution because the same rights given to African American men in these instruments are still denied to women. Instead, she concerns herself with the temperance movement, women's parental and custody rights, property rights, employment and income rights, divorce laws, the economic conditions of the family, and birth control.

The Women's Bible, written by Stanton and a committee of 26 women, is published in 1895 and 1898 to challenge traditional religious orthodox teaching that women should be subservient to men. Among its most extreme statements is that the Trinity is composed of "a heavenly Mother, Father, and Son," (in another place the Holy Spirit is described as the female principle of the Trinity) and that prayers should be addressed to an "ideal Heavenly Mother." Stanton emphasizes the fall of man, not of women. The real name of the first woman was "Life," not Eve – "the representative of the more valuable and important half of the human race" (Stanton, 2002: 27). According to Stanton, the conduct of woman was from the beginning vastly superior to that of man. Notwithstanding, men are called "sons of God," while women the "daughters of men" (Stanton, 2002: 35).

The widespread negative reaction to this book includes suffragists who are close to her, and destroy her influence in the suffrage movement. Thereafter, Susan B. Anthony takes the leadership role in the movement; at the same time, the suffragists disassociate from *The Women's Bible*.

Modern Eastern Christian and Protestant Extremes

Modern Christian movements vary on attitudes toward social justice, depending on time, place, and circumstance. To illustrate this point, I have chosen to present the writings of two twentieth-century authors, one an eastern Christian bishop from

Kerala, South India, and the other a Protestant fundamentalist, a professor at Western Kentucky University.

Metropolitan of the Orthodox Syrian Church in Kerala, South India, Geevarghese Mar Osthathios, represents the social justice of a developing country, at a time when prosperity is pitted against community and social responsibility. In his first work on the subject, *Theology of a Classless Society* (1979), Osthathios insists that it is wrong to leave the concept of a classless society to communists. Instead, it is potentially a Christian concept, quite capable of defeating the atheism of communism, if applied with courage and vision. He argues that the concept of a classless society is fully Christian, ranging from that of the Lord's Prayer, which he sees as a model of a classless society, to the Sermon on the Mount, which carries the ethical standards of a classless society. Poverty is a spiritual as well as a material condition; poverty anywhere is a threat to prosperity everywhere. The perfection of such a society may be impossible in practice, but that makes it all the more important to pray for it and to work for it.

Behind every aspect of Osthathios's social theology is the notion that the Christian Trinity is a classless society of total equality. Perfectionism is in the mystery of the Trinity, where singularity and plurality exist in the beauty of eternal *koinonia*, the sharing of love, holiness, and all that is perfectly good. If we are to express God and his love in life, we must see to it that the classless society of state, nation, and world is modeled on the life of the Holy Trinity.

In a sequel volume, *The Sin of Being Rich in a Poor World* (1983), Osthathios carries the discussion further. He shows that it is not enough to engage in mere philanthropy. Christianity has a basic ethic that is opposed to capitalism, since it postulates that all humans are God's children, made in the divine image. The very world is God's and is not to be divided up as private property. This book describes the sin of selfishness in the accumulation of wealth, in the patenting of beneficial scientific discoveries, in the luxurious lifestyle of a few in a world of poverty, and the unwillingness to share God-given resources with others.

In contrast, Ronald H. Nash's work *Social Justice and the Christian Church* (1983) presents a view of social justice that is agreeable to western capitalism and a free-market economy. It is popular among extremely conservative evangelicals who are uncomfortable with the so-called social gospel, in contrast to the "real gospel" of the born-again believers who have experienced "justification by faith." Nash has been included, not because he is an outstanding scholar, but rather because he represents views that are prominent in the West in the period before the end of the twentieth century.

Nash counters arguments that capitalism is immoral, largely based on nineteenth-century thinkers and before, with the advent of the industrial revolution and the social ills that accompanied it. He insists that the poor have always been with us, and that poverty did not begin with the advent of capitalism. It is his contention that the poor should not share equally in the profits of capitalism, because they have not shared in the risks and possible losses. Nash also counters arguments that capitalism adds to the poverty and squalor of the underdeveloped countries. Next he refutes the notion that capitalism panders to greed and selfishness.

In addition, Nash counters the so-called puritanical argument of the American economist John Kenneth Galbraith, who suggests that capitalism is immoral because it encourages individuals to waste their money on trivial, useless, immoral, or dangerous products. He finds equally useless the argument that all bad habits and bad tastes of consumers are caused by wicked producers. In short, Nash comes to the conclusion that capitalism is not inherently immoral, and that the real roots of opposition to capitalism are nonrational in nature.

Nash has especially harsh words for Jim Wallis, editor of the journal *Sojourners*. Wallis, he admits, is an Evangelical, but with strong anticapitalist leanings. Nash classifies Wallis with other "Christian Marxists" who portray the capitalist West as inherently unjust. Nash counters by declaring that state socialism has led to dehumanizing totalitarianism.

Nash then counters the notion that God is on the side of the poor and oppressed, and that God's people, if they are truly Christians, are also on the side of the needy. He does so by arguing that the one true enemy of the poor in the United States is the liberal welfare state. Any attempts to replace the oppressive institutions of Latin America with a "utopian socialist ideal" will only serve to prolong the misery of the poor.

Conclusions

In this essay we have considered a few of the many voices of Christian social awareness responding to human need during the past two millennia. As Bernard V. Brady puts it:

> tradition calls each of us to be the sort of person who acts and thinks, who responds and prays, who experiences himself or herself as an individual and as a member of multiple communities, and who lives on that vital crossroad where Christian faith meets the world. (Brady, 2008: 271)

References

Brady, Bernard V. (2008) *Essential Catholic Social Thought*, Orbis, Maryknoll, NY.

Nash, Ronald H. (2002) *Social Justice and the Christian Church*, Academic Renewal Press, Lima, OH.

Osthathios, G. Mar (1979) *Theology of a Classless Society*, Lutterworth Press, Cambridge.

Osthathios, G. Mar (1983) *The Sin of Being Rich in a Poor World*, Christian Literature Society, Madras.

Stanton, Elizabeth Cady (2002[1895]) *The Women's Bible: A Classic Feminist Perspective*, Dover Publications, Mineola, NY.

Bibliography

Abbrescia, Domenico M. (1982) *Elena Guerra, Prophecy and Renewal*, Society of Saint Paul, Makoti, Philippines.

Basil of Cappadocia (2009) *St. Basil the Great: On Social Justice*, St. Vladimir's Seminary Press, Crestwood, NY.

Booth, William (2004[1890]) *Darkest England and the Way Out*, Kessinger Publishing, Kilo, MT.

Brendlinger, Irv A. (2006) *Social Justice through the Eyes of Wesley*, Joshua Press, Ontario.

Carlen, M.C. (1990) *A Guide to the Encyclicals of the Roman Pontiffs from Leo XIII to the Present Day (1740–1978)*, Pierian Press, New York.

Clement of Alexandria (1919) The rich man's salvation, in *Clement of Alexandria*, Loeb Classical Library 92, trans. G.W. Butterworth, Harvard University Press, Cambridge, MA.

Dommen, Edward and Bratt, James D. (2007) *John Calvin Rediscovered: The Impact of His Social and Economic Thought*, Westminster John Knox Press, Louisville, KY.

Dorr, Donal (1983) *Options for the Poor: A Hundred Years of Vatican Social Teaching*, Gill and Macmillan, Dublin.

Fedwick, Paul Jonathan (ed.) (1981) *Basil of Caesarea: Christian, Humanist, Ascetic*, Pontifical Institute of Mediaeval Studies, Toronto.

Friedman, Milton (1962) *Capitalism and Freedom*, University of Chicago Press, Chicago.

Frykenberg, Robert (1981) World hunger: Food is not the answer, *Christianity Today*, December 11.

Gertrude of Helfta (1993) *The Herald of Divine Love*, trans. Margaret Winkworth, Classics of Western Spirituality, Paulist Press, New York.

Harold, Stanley (2001) *American Abolitionists*, Longmans, London.

Heitzenrater, Richard P. (ed.) (2002) *The Poor and the People Called Methodists*, Kingswood Books, Louisville, KY.

Helm, Paul (2006) *John Calvin's Ideas*, Oxford University Press, Oxford.

Hughes, Richard T. (2001) *How Christian Faith Can Sustain the Life of the Mind*, Eerdmans, Louisville, KY.

Johnston, Robert K. (1979) *Evangelicals at an Impasse*, John Knox Press, Atlanta.

Karcher, Carolyn L. (1994) *The First Woman in the Republic: A Cultural Biography of Lydia Maria Child*, Duke University Press, Durham, NC.

Lucas, J.R. (1980) *On Justice*, Clarendon Press, Oxford.

Marquardt, Manfred (1976) *John Wesley's Social Principles*, Abingdon, Nashville, TN.

Mavrodes, George (1977) On helping the hungry, *Christianity Today*, December 30.

Pontifical Council for Justice and Peace (2004) *Compendium of the Social Doctrine of the Church*, Libreria Editrice Vaticana, Vatican City.

Schaffer, David Lewis (1979) *Justice or Tyranny? A Critique of John Rawl's Theory of Justice*, Kennikat Press, Port Washington, NY.

Schuck, Michael J. (1991) *That They Be One: The Social Teaching of the Papal Encyclicals 1740–1989*, Georgetown University Press, Washington, DC.

Simons, Menno (2005[1871]) *The Complete Works of Menno Simons*, University of Michigan Press, Ann Arbor.

Williams, George Hunston (1962) *The Radical Reformation*, Westminster Press, Philadelphia.

Winston, Diane (1999) *Red Hot and Righteous: The Urban Religion of the Salvation Army*, Harvard University Press, Cambridge, MA.

Wogaman, J. Philip. (1977) *The Great Economic Debate: An Ethical Analysis*, Westminster Press, Philadelphia.

CHAPTER 4
Christianity
Contemporary Expressions

Curtiss Paul DeYoung

Wherever you find injustice in the world, there are people of faith working for social justice – and often they are Christians. Twenty-first-century Christians are working for social justice in a world with great poverty and much oppression. These contemporary expressions of Christian social justice are many and varied. This essay highlights some examples of how Christian individuals, organizations, and church communions pursue various aspects of social justice ministry.

What are contemporary expressions? For this essay, "contemporary" denotes what is current at the end of the first decade of the twenty-first century. Obviously, many of the movements and methods that are in full bloom now were initiated in the last quarter of the twentieth century. In some cases it is valuable to note people, trends, events, and movements from even earlier moments that were forerunners to present efforts. Therefore, this essay reaches back into the twentieth century to describe and give meaning to what is happening now.

"Expressions" of social justice can be observed in both words and actions. I will identify words of Scripture that are foundational for contemporary expressions of social justice and words of social justice emanating from church bodies and Christian leaders. Words of social justice include church statements, declarations, documents, educational programs, and theological writings. I will also share actions for social justice in society and in the church itself. Actions include protest movements, community development initiatives, policy advocacy, church rituals, and intentional solidarity with the poor. In the space of this essay it is impossible to include contemporary expressions from all parts of the world and within all Christian traditions. The essay is also limited in its reach by the author's knowledge, experience, and social location.

Christian expressions of social justice occur in the various strands of Christianity: Roman Catholicism, Orthodoxy, mainline Protestantism, Evangelicalism, and Pentecostalism. This essay does not discuss the various nuances and arguments on how to

---

The Wiley Blackwell Companion to Religion and Social Justice, First Edition. Edited by Michael D. Palmer and Stanley M. Burgess.
© 2012 John Wiley & Sons Ltd. Published 2020 by John Wiley & Sons Ltd.

define the tapestry of Christian faith, such as: Should Pentecostals be considered Evangelicals? Are Fundamentalists a separate category from Evangelicals? Are Anglicans a part of mainline Protestantism or are they yet another different tradition? Where do the African Independent churches or Chinese house churches fit into this paradigm? What about Quakers? Are African American denominations mainline Protestants or theologically Evangelical? The essay simply illustrates contemporary ways in which the Christian community is pursuing social justice.

Contemporary expressions of social justice address injustice in society and in the church. This can include a wide range of issues, such as poverty, AIDS, sex trafficking, racism, sexism, immigration, materialism, environment, abortion, peace, capital punishment, socioeconomic class, domestic abuse, drugs, education, female genital mutilation, genocide, healthcare, homelessness, housing, hunger, human rights, immigration, refugees, slavery, sexuality, urban challenges, land rights, water rights, jobs, living wages, incarceration – the list goes on. Each church tradition defines what issues are included on its list of social justice concerns based on the church's theology, social location, and political biases. This essay is not exhaustive in its coverage of issues. Rather, it is illustrative of how the issues are being addressed.

Of course, the church often wears two faces. There is the social justice church and there is the church aligned with an oppressing state government or a racially segregated identity. So at times the words and actions of social justice are directed at the church itself, as well as the broader society. The words and actions of social justice find their source in the words of Scripture.

The Words of Scripture

The Scriptures of most religions note the cries of oppressed people and call for social justice. Contemporary Christians seek wisdom from the Hebrew Scriptures (Old Testament) and the New Testament. In the Hebrew Scriptures, the author of Deuteronomy proclaimed:

> You shall not abuse a needy and destitute laborer, whether a fellow countryman or a stranger in one of the communities of your land . . . You shall not subvert the rights of a stranger or the fatherless; you shall not take a widow's garment in pawn. Remember that you were a slave in Egypt and that the LORD your God redeemed you from there." (Deuteronomy 24:14, 17–18)

The prophet Isaiah encouraged the people of the ancient nation of Israel to "Learn to do good. Devote yourself to justice; aid the wronged. Uphold the rights of the orphan; defend the cause of the widow" (Isaiah 1:17). The writer of Proverbs warned followers of God, "He who mocks the poor affronts his Maker" (Proverbs 17:5).

The New Testament adds force to the mandate of the First Testament. Luke quoted Jesus in his first sermon:

> The Spirit of the Lord is upon me, because he has anointed me to preach good news to the poor. He has sent me to proclaim release to the captives and recovery of sight to the blind,

to let the oppressed go free, to proclaim the year of the Lord's favor . . . Today this scripture has been fulfilled in your hearing. (Luke 4:18–19, 21)

The apostle Paul believed that the death and resurrection of Jesus produced a spiritual reality of justice and equality: "There is no longer Jew nor Greek, there is no longer slave or free, there is no longer male and female, for all of you are one in Christ Jesus" (Galatians 3:28). The author of 1 John forthrightly declared God's concern for justice, "How does God's love abide in anyone who has the world's goods and sees a brother or sister in need and yet refuses help?" (1 John 3:17).

It is not only biblical texts that inspire Christians toward social justice, it is also the narrative history contained in the Bible that informs contemporary Christians regarding how they should live lives of justice and mercy. Central to the story is the exodus event, when God liberated the Hebrew people from oppressive slavery (Exodus 1–15). This incident of God's justice was retold by each generation in various forms throughout the Hebrew Bible. "We were Pharaoh's slaves in Egypt, but the Lord brought us out of Egypt with a mighty hand" (Deuteronomy 6:21). This same narrative is central for many Christians today living in oppressive societies.

The spirit of liberation in the exodus event was made practical in the year of jubilee (Leviticus 25). It was to be a time when people were released from all debts and everyone could have a new beginning. The 25th chapter of Leviticus ended with God reminding the Hebrews that they were "my servants whom I brought out from the land of Egypt" (Leviticus 25:55). The purpose of the year of jubilee was to insert social justice as a core component into ancient Israel's system of government. The jubilee year was placed in the law of the new nation as a foundational guarantee of social justice. It seems that the ancient Israelite governments never put into practice the jubilee year legislation, however. Therefore, they reduced the exodus experience to a theological statement without any practical outcomes.

The pronouncement that God was a liberator as experienced in the exodus event and legalized in the jubilee found new voice with many of the prophets in the Bible. Isaiah is an excellent example when he wrote:

> The Spirit of the Lord God is upon me, because the LORD has anointed me; he has sent me to bring good news to the oppressed, to bind up the brokenhearted, to proclaim liberty to the captives, and release to the prisoners; to proclaim the year of the LORD's favor, and the day of vengeance of our God; to comfort all who mourn. (Isaiah 61:1–2)

When the Hebrews (or the ancient nation of Israel) rejected the ways of the God of the exodus, the prophets challenged them to return to the social justice foundation of their faith.

Jesus was raised learning the tradition of the exodus and the prophets. By quoting Isaiah 61, Jesus declared in his inaugural sermon at Nazareth that his ministry was seeking to reintroduce the social justice tradition of the Hebrew Scriptures (Luke 4:18–19, 21). The reign of God that Jesus preached and taught throughout his ministry would begin when the spirit of social justice was written on people's hearts. The exodus from Egypt defined the core understanding of religion for the Hebrews. It was during the Passover celebration of the exodus event that the death and resurrection of Jesus became the core understanding of the religious faith of the disciples (and the church to follow).

Words of Social Justice

With such a strong witness to the centrality of social justice in the Scriptures, most church communions and denominations declare a commitment to social justice. For example, the Ecumenical Patriarch Bartholomew writes,

> As Orthodox Christians, we are called to support and stand up for the innocent and defenseless victims of religious oppression, racism, and intolerance. Ultimately, we are called to work for peace in every part of the world. (Bartholomew, 2008: 135)

The Orthodox liturgy opens with prayer for peace in the world. The Orthodox Church declares its intention to work on issues of poverty, peace, racism, fundamentalism, human rights, affordable healthcare, basic education, environment, inclusiveness for people with disabilities, adequate wages for workers, refugees, abuse of women and children, sexual exploitation, and sanctity of life. Bartholomew adds,

> The transformation of the heart can and must lead to the transformation of society . . . Transformation is our only hope of breaking the vicious cycle of poverty and injustice. (Bartholomew, 2008: 151, 152)

The literature of most church communions and denominations includes statements similar to those of the Ecumenical Patriarch Bartholomew. Some speak as forthrightly as the Patriarch, and in other cases such statements are included in supportive documents. In addition to these church statements, the words of social justice are proclaimed in theological works, educational settings, and public declarations.

Theology

Debates have occurred throughout the history of the church regarding how central to church life are the concerns of social justice. Some argue that evangelism is the church's priority rather than social action – without salvation, what is the value of social justice? Others argue that social justice is the primary concern for Christians. If the church is not working for a just society, individuals will not look to the church for words of salvation. Therefore, theological inquiry regarding social justice is a significant endeavor for the church. Theologies of social justice are words that inspire acts of justice and call for social action.

Dietrich Bonhoeffer struggled to integrate his theological reflections with his social justice instincts in the early 1940s as a theologian in Nazi-controlled Germany. As he became more and more aware of the oppression and mass murder of Jewish people by the Nazi government, his theology had to become relevant to the realities of the situation. He began to see reality through the eyes of the oppressed and his theology was transformed. Most of the Christian church in Germany had aligned itself with Adolf Hitler and the Nazi government. Bonhoeffer sought to create a theology that differed significantly from an institutional church whose allegiance was turning toward the Führer. Bonhoeffer's theology was centered in a Christ for others – a Christo-centric theology of social justice. The central question for Bonhoeffer was: How could the church in the future claim any authenticity after it had sold its soul to Nazism? While in prison for his resistance to the Nazis, Bonhoeffer discerned that Christians must limit their lives of faith to two things: prayer and social justice actions. Out of this practice would emerge an authentic theology for a church committed to social justice.

In many ways, Bonhoeffer was a forerunner to what in contemporary times has emerged all across the globe as liberation theology. Liberation theology emerged in Latin America proclaiming that God had a preferential option for the poor. In 1962, Pope John XXIII at the Second Vatican Council called for "the Church to become the Church of all, and in particular the Church of the poor" (Guitierrez, 2007: 25). This pronouncement coincided with discussions occurring in Latin American Catholic churches and was given language at a conference of bishops in Medellín in 1968 (and reaffirmed at a second bishops' conference in Puebla in 1979). The pioneer theologian was Fr. Gustavo Gutierrez of Peru, who started publishing liberation theology in the early 1970s.

Liberation theology is grounded in the daily life of impoverished people. Scripture is interpreted using the lens of people's experience. It is a lived theology rather than an abstract one. It is not a theology for the oppressed, offered to them by the institutional church. Liberation theology is not a theology that calls those who are not oppressed to go and serve the poor. Rather, it is a theology that emerges from the life experiences of people who are poor and oppressed. Liberation theology is a theology of the oppressed. To fully understand liberation theology it must be lived (rather than learned or acquired in an academic setting). Perhaps a better way to understand it is to think of it as a new way of doing theology. Liberation theology is deeply rooted in the reading and application of the Bible by the poor themselves (often using the passages of Scripture noted earlier, especially the exodus narratives). This reading and application are done in a community setting and thereby avoid the limiting factor of individualism. The experience of poverty and oppression is a life text read alongside the Bible.

Liberation theology in Latin America began with a strong emphasis on socioeconomic class perspectives. It soon included issues of race and gender in its understanding of injustice and oppression. The same year that bishops were meeting in Medellín to discuss God's preferential treatment of the poor, African American priests were meeting in Detroit, Michigan, after the assassination of Martin Luther King, Jr., to declare that the Roman Catholic Church in the United States was a white racist institution. The late 1960s in the United States was a time of much turmoil and conflict related to issues of race. The Civil Rights Movement, led by many African American Protestant clergy, was facing the critique of Muslim Malcolm X and the Black Power movement. In the midst of this, African American theologians were forming a Black theology of liberation similar to the musings of Latin American theologians. James Cone became the foremost proponent. Black theology echoes many of the same biblical themes and social realities as Latin American liberation theology, but places a primary focus on blackness and white racism. It affirms the humanity, dignity, and worth of black people with a call for the liberation of blacks socially, economically, and spiritually. It calls for the liberation of white people through the dismantling of structures and attitudes of white racial superiority. Black theology also emerged in settings outside of the United States where racial hierarchies inform the systems of oppression, especially in apartheid South Africa.

Since liberation theology emerges from the grass roots as poor and oppressed people reflect on their life experiences and biblical texts, there is a diversity of ways in which liberation theology takes root. With common themes, each location has its own distinct emphases. In portions of Africa, notions of African healing have influenced the shape of liberation theology, especially given AIDS and other diseases. Asian forms of liberation theology are often molded in a multireligious context in which repressive state governments are at work. Ecological issues are also central to some forms of liberation theology in Asia. Always, though, oppression and poverty are central, as in Korean Minjung liberation theology (theology of the common people), which has become a significant social justice theology in South Korea.

Social location significantly affects the content of liberation theology. Women began to reflect theologically on their oppression. Feminist theology emerged alongside liberation theology to challenge patriarchy and sexism in the church and in society by seeking the liberation of women. Soon women who experienced oppression, not only for their gender but also due to race, culture, or socioeconomic class, began integrating liberation theology and feminist theology into hybrid forms. African American women wrote Womanist theology. Latinas in the United States developed Mujerista theology. African, Asian, and indigenous women also blended their culture and gender in their theological writings. Yet all of these forms of liberation theology retain the holistic focus on the liberation of all of humanity.

Some Native American theologians have critiqued liberation theology. The strong class consciousness of liberation theology can homogenize people into classifications such as "the poor" or "the oppressed." Central to the concerns of indigenous people are issues of land, nationhood (or peoplehood), and culture. These require a focus on uniqueness that is diminished when people are assigned to a generalized group of oppressed persons. Another critique is the use as the primary narrative of liberation of the exodus from Egypt to the "promised land." Indigenous theologians in the Americas, Palestine, and elsewhere often read their stories through the indigenous people in the Bible – the Canaanites. They are horrified that after the Hebrew people escaped oppression in Egypt, they entered Palestine and slaughtered the indigenous inhabitants. Biblical stories that inspire the liberation of some may communicate oppression to others. The book of Joshua describes in great detail the move of the Israelites into Palestine. It is a story of the conquest of the indigenous peoples of Palestine, the Canaanites and others, at God's initiative and with God's blessing. It certainly is a portrayal of God that is in conflict with the God revealed in the exodus and the God revealed by Jesus – the God of liberation and social justice.

Educational settings

Educational settings are a prime place for disseminating social justice theology and for training people as leaders in congregations, para-church organizations, and faith-based nongovernmental organizations (NGOs). The bishops' conferences in Latin American Catholicism served this purpose in the formation of liberation theology. Meetings of the Ecumenical Association of Third World Theologians (EATWOT) and the World Council of Churches have led to many initiatives on social justice. Instituted by evangelist Billy Graham, the Lausanne Movement's periodic global gatherings for Evangelicals have produced documents on social justice issues in the context of discussions on evangelism. In the United States, the Seminary Consortium on Urban Pastoral Education (SCUPE) hosts a biennial Congress on Urban Ministry and the Christian Community Development Association (CCDA) sponsors an annual conference. Both of these gatherings convene thousands of people to learn about and network for social justice.

Christian universities and seminaries also have courses, programs, and degrees in social justice. The schools of higher learning among the traditional peace churches like the Mennonites and Quakers often have peace and justice studies programs. Similar programs can also be found at Catholic universities and those linked to mainline denominations. Some programs are now called reconciliation studies and address peace and justice concerns, with the added dimension of reconciliation process and theology. Evangelical school Bethel University in St. Paul, Minnesota, offers a Bachelor of Arts program in reconciliation studies. Catholic school Trinity College in Ireland offers a Master of Arts in reconciliation studies based in Belfast, Northern Ireland. Similar degree programs are developing independently in Rwanda and Australia.

Public declarations

Another way of using words to provoke action is public declarations. These take many forms. Numerous sermons and speeches have been given calling for social action or repentance for inaction on justice issues. The orators of twentieth- and twenty-first-century Christian social justice movements are legendary. From Martin Luther King, Jr. to Oscar Romero, from Allan Boesak to Dorothy Day, from Fannie Lou Hamer to Jim Wallis, social justice orators have influenced millions of people to embrace causes for justice and peace.

Sometimes letters written by individual leaders are made public. In 1963, Martin Luther King, Jr. wrote a letter to white ministers in Birmingham, Alabama, who had criticized his actions against racial segregation titled "A Letter from a Birmingham Jail." Archbishop Oscar Romero of El Salvador wrote a letter in 1980 to US President Jimmy Carter asking him not to send military aid to the El Salvadoran government, which was oppressing the people of the country. Other times longer teaching letters have been issued from church communions. This is particularly true of the Roman Catholic Church. For example, in 1986 the US Catholic Bishops released a pastoral letter entitled

"Economic Justice for All," and in 2009 Pope Benedict XVI issued a papal encyclical, "Caritas in veritate" (charity in truth), emphasizing the importance of charity and justice.

Other forms of social justice statements include declarations that emerge out of gatherings in which issues or tactics are debated. A meeting was convened in 1973 by Evangelicals for Social Action (ESA) and other Evangelical leaders in the United States to discuss the relative importance of social justice issues, including racism, sexism, and economic injustice. After the meeting, they issued the "Chicago Declaration of Evangelical Social Concern," stating that social justice was biblical and relevant for Evangelicals. Historically, many in the Evangelical community had avoided statements and actions related to social justice because they were believed to divert energies from evangelism, which was considered the primary work of Christians. The 1973 Chicago Declaration opened the door for many organizations and initiatives to emerge among Evangelicals, including Christians for Biblical Equality (CBE) and the Christian Community Development Association (CCDA). Politically conservative Evangelicals, Fundamentalists, and Pentecostals did not follow the lead of those in Chicago. Instead, they founded organizations like the Moral Majority and the Christian Coalition and pointed their followers toward a strategy of partnership with the Republican Party to address a limited political agenda, taking action against abortion, in favor of capital punishment, and, later, against gay marriage.

The Chicago Declaration was a statement directed to an Evangelical church that was disengaged from societal issues and had in many ways missed out on involvement with the Civil Rights Movement of the 1950s and 1960s in the United States. Some of the most significant public statements have been issued in the midst of severe oppression and church-based political action. In the 1930s, Adolf Hitler and the Nazi government were systematically transforming the church in Germany into a Nazi-supporting church (with a Reich bishop). A group of dissident pastors formed what came to be known as the Confessing Church. In 1934 they issued the Barmen Declaration, which was a theological call and imperative for resisting the Nazi government's takeover of the church.

When the anti-apartheid theologians of South Africa looked for ways to speak truth to injustice, the Barmen Declaration influenced their 1985 declaration, called the Kairos Document. South African theologians of black liberation theology penned the Kairos Document to offer the church in South Africa a biblical foundation for resisting the oppressive Afrikaner government. It affirmed that God was on the side of the oppressed and called for the church to join the oppressed and seek liberation. The theology contained in the document "was in fact the classic portion of Liberation theology which had been the staple of South African radical Christianity for almost two decades by the time the Kairos Document was written" (Boesak, 2009: 350).

Another Kairos Document emerged from the pens of yet another group of Christian leaders and theologians witnessing to God's desire for social justice in the midst of oppression. In Bethlehem, the birthplace of Jesus, Christian leaders released "The Kairos Palestine Document" in 2009. Drawing on the wisdom and inspiration of the German Barmen Declaration and the South African Kairos Document, Palestinian Christian leaders issued a call for an end to the Israeli occupation of the Palestinian territories and for the church worldwide to resist this evil, which the document called a sin against God. The full title of the document was "A Moment of Truth: A Word of Faith, Hope and Love from the Heart of Palestinian Suffering." The Kairos Palestine document was a truly ecumenical effort. It was signed by the Latin Patriarch emeritus of the Roman Catholic Church for the region, the Archbishop of the Greek Orthodox Patriarchate in Jerusalem, the Lutheran Bishop of Jerusalem, Evangelical leaders, and many others.

Actions for Social Justice

The words of social justice are a form of activism. They can change the direction of movements. Words prompt action. Social justice activism has many forms. Sometimes the rituals of church life are given public meaning. At times the action takes the form of protest or the organizing of social movements. These can be local grassroots efforts, citywide events, and even national or international human rights movements. The protest action may be boycotts, sit-ins, marches, getting arrested, lobbying officials, and the like. Some actions are taken to reform the church itself. Always there is a focus on society. Other forms of social justice action can include the direct meeting of needs through humanitarian organizations, community development agencies, refugee resettlement, homeless shelters, and a host of other social service programs. Global Christian organizations like World Vision, CARITAS, and the World Council of Churches work alongside church denominations to effect social change. Sometimes Christians of privilege move into communities of need to work in solidarity with the poor to address injustice.

Rituals

The rituals of the church are expressions of Christian witness that have been used as a form of public protest or a sign of commitment to social justice. In 1968, grape pickers in the state of California were in the midst of a nearly three-year strike to improve their working conditions. The leader of the strike, César Chávez, a Roman Catholic, decided to go on a hunger strike taking only water and Eucharist wafers. For the duration of the hunger strike he lived at a gasoline station, where every evening a Franciscan priest would celebrate mass with Chávez and the growing number of protesters also staying at the site of the protest. After 25 days and the loss of 30 pounds, he ended the hunger fast. More than 6000 farm workers joined him for a mass to break the fast. Also joining Chávez was United States Senator Robert Kennedy, running for the Democratic nomination for President. That day Kennedy sat next to César Chávez – not as a politician but as a fellow Catholic resisting injustice. Together they protested injustice through the church ritual of Communion.

Archbishop Oscar Romero of El Salvador also understood the public power of the Eucharist. His friend Fr. Rutilio Grande was assassinated in 1977 due to his liberation work in El Salvador. Archbishop Romero suspended all masses in the capital city in order to celebrate just one funeral mass in the cathedral. With 150 priests concelebrating and over 100 000 people attending, the mass served as more than a memorial for his priest and friend. It was a protest against the repressive government and an act of solidarity with the poor and oppressed. Three years later, Oscar Romero would be assassinated while blessing the Eucharist in the celebration of the mass.

Prayer is another Christian ritual that finds power when wed with the struggle for social justice. In the 1980s, Christians in eastern Europe prayed and protested in order to end repressive Communist regimes. There were weekly peace prayer meetings in East Germany at the Church of St. Nicholas in Leipzig from 1982 until the fall of the Berlin Wall in 1989. Prayer was also central to anti-apartheid protests in South Africa. In his message to the South African Council of Churches (SACC) in 1984, Allan Boesak proclaimed:

> I call on all Christians and churches to set aside a day on which to pray for the downfall of this government. If the rulers will not hear the cries of the people, if they will not change, if they continue to prevent justice, let us pray them out of existence. God will hear our cry. (Boesak and Villa-Vicencio, 1986: 16)

So in 1985 the SACC issued the "Call to Prayer for the End to Unjust Rule in South Africa," calling on Christians to pray for the demise of the apartheid government. All across the nation on June 16, the ninth anniversary of the 1976 uprising in Soweto and killings of school children, people gathered in their churches and in ecumenical services to pray for an end to injustice. Shortly after this day of prayer, the Kairos Document was published tying prayer and theological reflection to the daily protest actions in the streets.

Another ritual that has been used as a symbol of repentance for injustice and as a sign of reconciliation is foot washing. The Pentecostal Fellowship of North America (PFNA) was established as an umbrella association for Pentecostal denominations in 1948; that is, for white Pentecostal denominations. The modern Pentecostal movement started as a multiracial assembly at the Azusa Street Revival in Los Angeles, California, in the first decade of the twentieth century. Yet 40 years later Pentecostals were highly segregated by race. The formation of the PFNA also seemed to ignore the fact that the largest Pentecostal denomination was the predominantly African American denomination the Church of God in Christ. In 1994 in Memphis, Tennessee, the PFNA voted to disband as an act of repentance and racial reconciliation and form a new, racially inclusive association called the Pentecostal/Charismatic Churches of North America (PCCNA). The first leader of the new group was the presiding bishop of the Church of God in Christ. In what was dubbed the "Memphis Miracle," the participants celebrated Communion together and, in a moment of spontaneity, washed each other's feet across racial lines, proclaiming their reconciliation.

An unexpected and highly shocking act of foot washing occurred in South Africa. In the late 1980s during the apartheid era, Adriaan Vlok, an Afrikaner police minister, poisoned Rev. Frank Chikane, then head of the South Africa Council of Churches. Chikane miraculously survived this attempt to kill him. Years later, in 2006, Vlok repented of his actions and sought forgiveness from Chikane by washing his feet. Many

South Africans found this action utterly ridiculous. But for Christians it held symbolic power. Adriaan Vlok also realized that there were many other people to whom he needed to repent. Primary among these was Sarafina, his family's domestic worker for 47 years. So he washed her feet, too. Rituals are powerful symbolic actions that visually speak truth and change conceptual realities. They usually have greater impact in societies where Christian rituals are common. They open the doors for even more direct action for social justice.

Acting for social justice in the church

The internal and structural realities of church communions and local congregations often reflect injustices found in society. Even with proclamations declaring themselves committed to social justice, the reality can be a different story. Many congregations claim to welcome people with disabilities, yet their buildings are not accessible. Women are told that they are full participants, but few hold leadership positions. Christians preach that all people are created in the image of God and loved by God. Yet when discussions of sexual orientation or gay marriage occur, the rhetoric becomes angry and demeaning, even hateful. The church declares that reconciliation is central to the Gospel, but most congregations are comprised of one racial, cultural, ethnic, or socioeconomic group. Because of these inconsistencies and hypocrisies, the church itself is an arena for social justice action.

Racism and ethnic division has caused some people in the church to challenge injustice within the church itself. The Confessing Church of Germany challenged the church's alliances with Nazi Germany. The Civil Rights Movement of the United States challenged the racial segregation of the church. The Uniting Reformed Church challenged the Dutch Reformed Church of South Africa in the 1980s, calling its apartheid theology a heresy. A racialized and ethnically segregated church in Rwanda collapsed in 1994 and became a leading participant in the genocide that killed over 800 000 Rwandans in a three-month period. In the African country with the highest percentage of Christians (90% identified as Christians), every denomination and church communion in Rwanda participated in genocidal actions. Individual Christian leaders protested, but the institutional church failed. Far too many massacres occurred in church buildings. Today, the church in Rwanda is going through a process of truth telling, repentance, and transformation. Efforts at reconciliation in the church can create a milieu of social justice.

One of the most turbulent areas in church life has been sexism and the role of women in leadership. The churches of the southern hemisphere are more apt to hold views that offer women only traditional roles than those in the north. Meanwhile, North American and European churches have become more progressive on gender issues. In the late 1800s, many Protestant denominations in the Holiness movement ordained women. The mainline Protestant churches did not follow until the second half of the twentieth century. Methodists ordained women in the 1950s. World Lutheranism began ordaining women in the 1950s in Europe and in the 1970s in North America, Asia, and Latin America. Pauli Murray became the first woman ordained in the

Episcopal Church in the United States in 1977. The first time she led the Holy Eucharist was in the chapel where her grandmother had been baptized as a slave, which had been built by the wealthy woman who had owned her. Liberation themes related to gender, race, and class all played themselves out in this narrative that featured women. By 1989, Barbara Harris was consecrated a bishop in the Episcopal Church. Katharine Jefferts Schori became the first female presiding bishop of the Episcopal Church in 2004. Despite these gains, women still wield little power in most church structures, while they make up a significant majority of membership in churches. Women cannot be ordained as priests in the Roman Catholic Church or the Orthodox Church. In 2004, the Orthodox Church decided that women could be ordained as deacons. Women are being ordained in Africa, Asia, and Latin America. However, there is less openness to the leadership of women, and there are several countries where churches do not ordain women. Of course, this also remains true in some North American and European conservative Evangelical, Pentecostal, and Fundamentalist churches.

One cannot write of contemporary expressions of Christian feminism without mentioning two international feminist and gender justice movements that both emerged in Minneapolis, Minnesota, in the late 1980s and early 1990s. Christians for Biblical Equality International (CBE) began with a meeting in 1987 of Evangelical theologians and leaders who were egalitarians in their view of the Bible. They met to consider how to support women leaders in Evangelicalism. The Re-Imagining Movement started with a conference in 1993 drawing 2000 individuals (mostly women) to a conference focusing on progressive Christianity and feminism. Feminist theology became a public conversation and was connected to laypeople from churches. Both movements are multidenominational with an international constituency. Although they agree on the need to address sexism and work for gender justice, theologically they are quite different. The theology of CBE is clearly Evangelical. The theology of the Re-Imagining Movement is very nontraditional, with some even calling themselves post-Christian feminists. Both use conferences to bring together sizable grassroots networks of affiliates (in the case of CBE), church members, and women. The Re-Imagining Movement had an organizational presence until 2003 through the Re-Imagining Community (and conferences have continued past 2003). CBE has become a sophisticated gender justice organization of grassroots Evangelical feminists. Interestingly, for a time both organizations had their international offices in the Minnesota Council of Churches office building.

Acting for social justice in society

For the sake of credibility in society, the church itself must practice its tenets of justice internally. Of course, social justice must also be pursued in the broader society. Christian leaders often join with larger political movements to enact societal changes. At the forefront of the US Civil Rights Movement in the 1950s and 1960s were Christian leaders such as Martin Luther King, Jr., Fannie Lou Hamer, John Lewis, Diane Nash, Septima Clark, Ella Baker, Andrew Young, Jesse Jackson, and many others. The United Democratic Front (UDF) in South Africa was launched in 1983 in Cape Town with over

10 000 people in attendance. From 1983 to 1991 the UDF brought together churches, civic associations, trade unions, student organizations, sports clubs, and other religious groups into a powerful movement against apartheid. The UDF philosophy was a mix of African nationalism, socialism, and Christianity. Christian leaders were at the forefront: Allan Boesak, Frank Chikane, Bishop Desmond Tutu, Sister Mary Bernard Ncube, and Archbishop Dennis Hurley – a mainline reformed Protestant, a Pentecostal, an Anglican, and two Roman Catholics.

Also in the 1980s, the struggle for freedom in Poland had a strong religious feel. The primary protest organization was the Solidarity trade union, led by Roman Catholic electrician Lech Walesa. A visit by Pope John Paul II in 1979 served as a catalyst for the launch of the movement. Millions of Poles attended his masses. While never criticizing the government directly, he told the people not to be afraid. This encouragement empowered the masses of people to join in protest. The next year the Solidarity trade union was formed as the first free trade union in communist Europe; 25% of the citizens of Poland were members (10 million). The gate to the Lenin Shipyard in Gdańsk, at the center of the protest, was covered with Polish flags and photos of Pope John Paul II, symbolizing the hopes of the people. The union focused on labor reform and civil rights. While fears were increasing that the Soviet Union would send tanks into Poland to end the protest, the Solidarity members were making confession to priests and taking the Eucharist in the open shipyard. Eventually, the protest movement would lead to the end of Communism in Poland and the election of Lech Walesa as president of the country in 1990.

Many protest movements emerge from the oppression and injustice faced by people at the grass roots. Others then join in support and partnership. The Christian tradition also has a legacy of people with privilege moving into communities of need to live in solidarity with the poor and work for social justice. Sometimes a voluntary vow of poverty or simplicity is taken. The Franciscans and other religious orders have a long history of such efforts. Dorothy Day started the first Catholic Worker House in 1933 in New York City, living and working among poor and homeless people, addressing their basic needs, and working for change to the systems that were causing poverty. Day also worked on peace and justice issues like the end of war and nuclear weapons. Mother Teresa began caring for poor and dying homeless people on the streets of Calcutta, India, in the 1940s. Her work soon grew into the Sisters of Charity religious order, established in 1950, with over 5000 Catholic nuns giving their lives to serve the poorest of the poor around the world in over 130 countries. In 1960, John Perkins returned to his native rural Mississippi to serve poor and segregated African Americans. His work also grew to include urban areas in a ministry that focused on racial reconciliation, relocation to places of economic challenge, and redistribution of resources. Through his example, mentoring activities, and organizational gifts, he helped launch the Christian Community Development Association (CCDA).

Sojourners began in the early 1970s as a Christian community serving and living among the poor of Washington, DC. They wanted to do more than provide social services: they hoped to change the politics of the United States. A magazine called *Sojourners* became the forum for debate, with particular emphasis in the early days on ending the Vietnam War. The name "sojourners" was understood from its biblical use to speak of God's people as present and relevant in society, but committed to the reign of God. In the early days the members shared life together through living in communal houses, combining their incomes, worshiping together, and organizing for the work of peace and justice in their neighborhood and around the world. Eventually Sojourners disbanded its intentional communities. It retained a commitment to a culture of community, but began to focus more of its efforts on political organizing.

Sojourners helped found the Call to Renewal in 1995 to unite the church in the United States to address poverty. In a unique coalition, it brought together leaders from the historical African American denominations, Roman Catholic Church, mainline Protestants, Evangelicals, and Pentecostals. The Call to Renewal effort lasted for a decade. This vast network created a major platform for Jim Wallis, the leader of Sojourners. In the midst of the contentious 2004 presidential elections in the United States, Wallis wrote a book called *God's Politics: Why the Right Gets It Wrong and the Left Doesn't Get It*. He went on a book tour following the elections that formed a movement of young people seeking new ways of viewing politics. Wallis saw politics through the lens of Martin Luther King, Jr. and the Civil Rights Movement. His focus on racism and poverty embodied black liberation theology. Wallis and Sojourners radically changed the politics of a new generation of Evangelicals, who left their parents' exclusive allegiance to the Republican party. Many of these young Evangelicals found themselves voting for Barack Obama in the 2008 election.

In the twenty-first century a group of young US Christians, many who have been influenced by Mother Teresa, Dorothy Day, John Perkins, Jim Wallis, and others, have simultaneously developed small intentional living communities among the poorest of the poor in the United States. Several of the leaders of these communities met in 2004 at an African American Baptist church in North Carolina and called their movement a "new monasticism." They agreed on a rule of life similar to early monastic Christians, but chose to live in community with the urban poor. They have sought wisdom from and relational ties to older intentional communities like Mennonite Reba Place Fellowship, Bruderhof, and the Catholic Worker.

They agreed that the 12 following marks characterized their communities:

1 Relocation to the abandoned places of Empire.
2 Sharing economic resources with fellow community members and the needy among us.
3 Hospitality to the stranger.
4 Lament for racial divisions within the church and our communities combined with the active pursuit of a just reconciliation.
5 Humble submission to Christ's body, the church.
6 Intentional formation in the way of Christ and the rule of the community along the lines of the old novitiate.
7 Nurturing common life among members of the intentional community.
8 Support for celibate singles alongside monogamous married couples and their children.
9 Geographical proximity to community members who share a common rule of life.

10 Care for the plot of God's earth given to us along with support of our local economies.
11 Peacemaking in the midst of violence and conflict resolution within communities along the lines of Matthew 18.
12 Commitment to a disciplined contemplative life (Rutba House, 2005).

Courageous Words and Actions

In 1943, the Nazis ordered Chrysostomos, the Metropolitan of Zákynthos, to provide them with a list of all the Jewish residents on his Greek island. When he brought them the list it had only one name: his own. In 1955, Rosa Parks was asked to give up her seat on a segregated bus in Montgomery, Alabama, so that a white person could sit there. She refused. In the 1980s, priests Daniel and Philip Berrigan were imprisoned because of their acts of civil disobedience against the development of nuclear weapons. In 1989, Fang Zheng was one of thousands of student protesters in Tiananmen Square in Beijing, China. His legs were crushed by a military tank during the protest and amputated after he arrived at the hospital. During the 1994 Rwandan genocide, Immaculée Ilibagiza spent 91 days hiding quietly in a small bathroom with seven other women. While in hiding she lost 40 pounds, prayed the rosary to keep rage and bitterness from overtaking her, and taught herself English using a Bible and a dictionary. On leaving she discovered that most of her family members had been murdered. Yet when encountering the killer of her mother and her brother she said, "I forgive you." Nobel Peace Prize laureate Mairead Corrigan Maguire has long been at the forefront of the Northern Ireland peace struggle. Yet in the first decade of the twenty-first century she has also participated in the Palestinian freedom movement. In 2007, Israeli security forces teargassed her and shot her with a rubber-coated bullet for protesting the construction of the security fence (called apartheid wall by Palestinians) at the West Bank village of Bil'in. In 2009, Corrigan Maguire was imprisoned by Israel for attempting to bring humanitarian aid into the Gaza Strip via ferry. Such acts of courage by Christians committed to social justice are many.

The courage to suffer for social justice is a theme drawn from the life of Jesus and the early disciples. Christian social justice activists have been brutalized. Civil rights leader Fannie Lou Hamer was arrested by white police officers in Mississippi in 1963. She was tortured by the police. When the officers recognized that Hamer was the woman who had been protesting segregation in Mississippi, they began to assault her verbally. Eventually, two African American male prisoners were ordered to beat Mrs. Hamer physically. They were joined by white policemen. By the time they had finished beating Fannie Lou Hamer, "one of her kidneys was permanently damaged, and a blood clot that formed over her left eye threatened her vision" (Marsh, 1997: 19). Hamer woke up the next morning in jail and began to sing an old spiritual, "Paul and Silas was bound in jail, let my people go." The Christian social justice activist gains a credibility that comes from a willingness to suffer for a cause. Nelson Mandela's 27 years of imprisonment in South Africa gave him a universally recognized authority as committed to social justice. Finally, words and actions for social justice by Christians have led to martyrdom for some, the ultimate sacrifice for a cause and for Christ.

References

Bartholomew, Ecumenical Patriarch (2008) *Encountering the Mystery: Understanding Orthodox Christianity Today*, Doubleday, New York.

Boesak, Allan (2009) *Running with Horses: Reflections of an Accidental Politician*, Joho Publishers, Cape Town.

Boesak, Allan A. and Villa-Vicencio, Charles (1986) *When Prayer Makes News*, Westminster Press, Philadelphia.

Guitierrez, Gustavo (2007) The task and content of liberation theology, in *The Cambridge Companion to Liberation Theology*, Christopher Rowland (ed.), 2nd edn, Cambridge University Press, Cambridge, pp. 19–38.

Marsh, Charles (1997) *God's Long Summer: Stories of Faith and Civil Rights*, Princeton University Press, Princeton.

Rutba House (2005) *School(s) for Conversion: 12 Marks of New Monasticism*, Wipf & Stock, Eugene, OR.

Wallis, Jim (2005) *God's Politics: Why the Right Gets It Wrong and the Left Doesn't Get It*, HarperSanFrancisco, New York.

Bibliography

Bednarowski, Mary Farrell (ed.) (2008) *Twentieth-Century Global Christianity, Volume 7: A Peoples' History of Christianity*, Denis R. Janz (gen. ed.), Fortress Press, Minneapolis.

Benson, Bruce Ellis, and Goodwin Heltzel, Peter (eds.) (2008) *Evangelicals and Empire: Christian Alternatives to the Political Status Quo*, Brazo Press, Grand Rapids.

Cannon, Mae Elise (2009) *Social Justice Handbook: Small Steps for a Better World*, InterVarsity Press, Downers Grove.

DeYoung, Curtiss Paul (2007) *Living Faith: How Faith Inspires Social Justice*, Fortress Press, Minneapolis.

DeYoung, Curtiss Paul (2009) *Coming Together in the 21st Century: The Bible's Message in an Age of Diversity*, Judson Press, Valley Forge, PA.

Groody, Daniel G. (2007) *Globalization, Spirituality, and Justice*, Orbis Books, Maryknoll, NY.

Hornsby-Smith, Michael P. (2006) *An Introduction to Catholic Social Thought*, Cambridge University Press, Cambridge.

Jenkins, Philip (2002) *The Next Christendom: The Coming of Global Christianity*, Oxford University Press, New York.

Marsh, Charles (2005) *The Beloved Community: How Faith Shapes Social Justice, From the Civil Rights Movement to Today*, Basic Books, New York.

Thurman, Howard (1949) *Jesus and the Disinherited*, Abingdon-Cokesbury Press, New York.

CHAPTER 5
Confucianism
Historical Setting

Joseph Chan

This essay aims to outline the early Confucian perspectives on social justice and welfare. I shall argue that early Confucian thinkers, especially Mencius, developed what I would call a perfectionist perspective that connects justice and welfare to the Confucian conception of the good life. In particular, Mencius's social ideal combines justice and care in a multileveled system in which government, family, and community all play a role. This essay will begin with a note on the origins of Confucianism and then discuss whether Confucianism contains the concepts of distributive justice and social justice, and whether there are ethical principles governing the distribution of resources. Finally, it will describe Mencius's social ideal as a multilayer system of care and help and examine its relations with other values such as justice, personal responsibility, and individual merit.

Origins of Confucianism

As a tradition of thought, Confucianism began life in China more than 2500 years ago.[1] Although its core ideas can be traced back to the teachings of Confucius (551–479 BCE), this tradition was never thought to be wholly created by Confucius himself. In fact, the original Chinese term for Confucianism, *ru-jia*, makes no reference at all to Confucius. Rather, it refers to a school of *ru*, "a type of man who is cultural, moral, and responsible for religious rites, and hence religious" (Tang, 1988: 362). Confucius himself stressed that he was not an inventor of any radically new vision of ethics or ideal society, but only a transmitter of the old tradition – the rites and social values developed in the Zhou dynasty (traditionally, mid-eleventh century to 256 BCE) and even earlier. Nevertheless, it was Confucius who most creatively interpreted the tradition that he had inherited, gave it a new meaning at a time when it had become stifling, and expounded it so

---

The Wiley Blackwell Companion to Religion and Social Justice, First Edition. Edited by Michael D. Palmer and Stanley M. Burgess.
© 2012 John Wiley & Sons Ltd. Published 2020 by John Wiley & Sons Ltd.

effectively that his views have influenced a great number of generations of *ru* to come. *The Analects*, a record of his ideas and teachings compiled primarily by his disciples and later scholars, is the most fundamental text in the Confucian tradition. However, Confucius handed down no systematic philosophy: *The Analects* left a number of basic questions undeveloped, such as those about human nature, the metaphysical grounds of ethics, and the proper organization of the state. It was Mencius (approx. 379–289 BCE) and Xunzi (approx. 340–245 BCE) who filled in the details and more systematically developed the tradition in new and different directions. The thoughts of these three thinkers, together with the early classics on which they drew, such as the *Book of History* and the *Book of Poetry*, constitute the classical tradition of Confucianism.

Confucianism has continued to evolve ever since its inception, in part as a response to the political needs of the time (as in Han Confucianism) and in part to the challenges of other schools of thought (as in Song-Ming Confucianism). Han Confucianism had made Confucian ethics and politics rigid and hierarchical, placing the father and ruler at the center of absolute power in the family and polity respectively. Song-Ming Confucianism, on the contrary, turned its inquiry inward into the human mind in order to meet the challenges of Buddhism, and constructed robust theories of the inner life of human individuals. No matter what innovations were made in these later developments, however, classical Confucianism, especially the Mencius strand, has been recognized as the canon of the tradition, something that later thinkers claimed only to appreciate, vindicate, and enrich; this was exactly the kind of moderate claim made by Confucius himself regarding his attitude toward the tradition before him. In this sense, a deep respect for tradition – thinking that it was the sages in the past who had got things right – has always been a salient mark of Confucianism.

What are the core ideas in Confucianism? And how much influence has it had? Most simply put, Confucianism holds that people should cultivate their minds and virtues through lifelong learning and participation in rituals, that they should treat their family members according to the norms of filial piety and fatherly love, and that they should show a graded concern and care for all outside of the family. Political leaders should do their best to care for the ruled and serve as moral exemplars for them. Learned intellectuals, above all others, should devote themselves in politics and education to promote the Way and help build a good society.

More will be said concerning the content of Confucian ethics later in this essay. But even this much characterization enables us to see that the Confucian vision of human life has fundamentally shaped the Chinese culture and the basic structure of society in the past 2000 years or so. Its vision, however, has extended far beyond the Chinese borders and has penetrated deeply into neighboring countries. Today, those east Asian societies that have been influenced by the Confucian culture – namely, mainland China, Hong Kong, Japan, Korea, Singapore, Taiwan, and Vietnam – have undergone modernization and been exposed to the powerful forces of global capitalism that have eroded their Confucian cultural traditions to a considerable extent. But Confucian values such as the importance of the family, respect for learning and education, and emphasis on order and harmony remain significant in these societies.

It is important to note that Confucianism has never been an established religion, although it has a strong religious dimension that stresses the harmony and unity of humanity and Heaven. The interest of Confucianism as a religious humanism lies in its concern for this world, with a clear mission to improve human life and society.[2] There was no official spokesperson for Heaven or revelation of Heaven's will in the form of a book. Confucius and other sages were not prophets, the *Analects* not the Bible. The Way had to be embodied and expounded in human action, and the teachings in the classics were never meant to be a timeless, sacred creed handed down from Heaven. This fact about Confucianism has implications for any attempt that explores its contemporary relevance. Because Confucianism has always been an evolving tradition of thought, with many self-identified participants sharing only a cluster of values, beliefs, and practical concerns rather than a set of fixed creeds, the participants are at liberty to reinterpret, revise, and further develop the tradition of thought in the way they see fit in their exploration of its contemporary relevance.

Is There a Concept of Distributive Justice in Confucianism?

Distributive justice has not attracted much attention in the contemporary literature on Confucianism. This may be due to a widely held view that there is little room for justice in Confucianism, which sees politics as the continuation of personal ethics and the state as the family writ large. In this interpretation, cultivation of virtue is more important than enforcement of justice, and benevolent leadership (*ren*) more important than the exercise of law and policy. I argue, however, that this understanding of Confucianism is heavily one-sided. Confucianism also contains fundamental *political* principles and policies, including one regarding distribution of offices and resources, and these are not reducible to family-based principles. Moreover, central to the ideal of benevolent rule is proper distribution of economic resources.

In the limited number of contemporary writings on Confucian justice, a majority argues that Confucianism cannot share the philosophical presuppositions of western conceptions of justice. A typical strategy that these writings employ is to take John Rawls's theory of justice as a point of reference, and then argue that Rawls's theory presupposes liberal conceptions of persons and community radically different from those in Confucianism. This kind of discussion, illuminating as it may be, often ends without any serious treatment of distributive justice. I believe that it is not necessary or desirable to reconstruct Confucian views through a comparison with Rawls, for doing so leads us to approach western and Confucian philosophical visions as diametrically opposed ideal types and distracts us from distributive issues that concern Confucian and western thinkers alike. Here, I hope to explore Confucian justice in a way that assumes the fewest philosophical presuppositions about human nature, personhood, and community.

Let us start with the classic formula of the idea of justice developed in Plato's *Republic*: "render to each his due." Although this broad formula leaves open what is to count as a person's due, it is not empty. It tells us several things. First, justice is a *distributive* idea. It concerns how benefits and burdens should be passed out among individuals according to some principle of rightness, and not according to some aggregative ends that make distribution a mere means (Miller, 1976: 19–20). Second, and a corollary of the first, justice is an *individual-oriented* idea. The formula "to each his due" expresses a particular way of assessing the rightness of distribution. The distribution of a benefit is to be made on the basis of the personal characteristics and circumstances of an individual involved – his or her efforts, contributions, merit, needs, well-being, or worth as a person, and so on – and not on the basis of things that have nothing to do with the individual. The same holds for the distribution of burdens. Third and last, justice expresses a *moral* idea. To give what is due to people is a moral requirement, not a matter of personal favor or grace bestowed by the distributor (Campbell, 2001: 24). In sum, the concept of justice expresses a moral concern about how individuals fare – what they ought to receive as their due – in distribution of benefits and burdens.

Is there such a concept in Confucianism? The answer, I believe, is a clear yes. The most obvious places in the classical texts where the concept of justice is at work are passages that discuss the justice of punishment and the distribution of offices.[3] Among pre-Qin masters, Xunzi (approx. 340–245 BCE) is the most explicit on the importance of justice or fairness in government affairs. For him, the activity of governing has to be "fair" [*ping*] (Xunzi, 1988–1994: 9.19a).

> Public-spiritedness and impartiality [*gong ping*] are the balance by which affairs of government are to be weighted, and the mean of due proportion [*zhung he*] is the marking line by which they are to be measured. (Xunzi, 1988–1994: 9.2)

Now Xunzi fleshes out the idea of fairness or impartiality in exactly the same way as ancient Greek philosophers do: that justice or fairness consists in rendering to each person his due according to his personal characteristics, circumstances, or conduct.

> As a general principle, every rank and official responsibility, and each reward or punishment, was given as a recompense that accorded with the nature of the conduct involved. (Xunzi, 1988–1994: 18.3)

The coming of honor or disgrace, therefore, must be a reflection of one's inner virtue [*de*] (Xunzi, 1988–1994: 1.5), offices must be matched by appropriate ability, rewards must correspond to achievement, and penalties to offenses (Xunzi, 1988–1994: 8.3). It is important to note that for Xunzi, when it comes to justice, each person should be treated as an independent individual who is separate from other individuals, including family members:

> If rank fits the worth of the individual holding it, there is esteem, where it does not, there is contempt. In antiquity, penal sanctions did not exceed what was fitting to the crime, and rank did not go beyond the moral worth of the person. *Thus although the father had been executed, his son could be employed in the government; although the elder brother had been killed, the younger could be employed. . . . Each was allotted what was his due according in every case to his true circumstances.* (Xunzi, 1988–1994: 24.3, italics mine; see also 24.4)

Nothing could show more clearly that Xunzi understands the individual-oriented feature of justice, in the sense that justice concerns the proper treatment of each individual taken separately. Mencius (approx. 379–289 BCE) and Xunzi also take justice as a moral imperative that trumps political goals such as the gaining of an empire. Mencius says that it is wrong to "kill an innocent man" or "take what one is not entitled to" in order to gain the empire, for doing so is contrary to rightness (*yi*) and benevolence (*ren*) (Mencius, 2003: 2A.2, 7A.33; see also 4B.4). Xunzi is of the same view that a gentleman (*ru*)

> would not commit a single act contrary to the requirements of justice nor execute a single blameless man, even though he might thereby obtain the empire. Such a lord acts with justice (*yi*) and faithfulness (*xin*) toward the people. (Xunzi, 1988–1994: 8.2; see also 11.1a, 4.8)

For Mencius and Xunzi, then, justice is a moral constraint on people's pursuits of goals and benefits. Justice is understood as a nonconsequentialist, nonutilitarian idea.

If my analysis is correct, then Confucianism does have the concept of (distributive) justice, and it is the same as the Platonic one: to render to each person his due. Like the Platonic concept, Confucian justice is distributive, individual oriented, and moral.

From Distributive to Social Justice

We have seen that in the Confucian texts the concept of distributive justice is at work in the discussions about distribution of honor, offices, and punishment. But how about economic matters like the distribution of land or other forms of material goods like grains? Do Confucian thinkers approach economic matters from the perspective of justice as well? Is distribution of material resources a matter of justice for Confucians?

The Confucian concept of justice reconstructed so far is close to the traditional western concept of justice, in that it links justice with a person's merit or desert. Some theorists argue that this traditional western concept – sometimes called a *meritorian* perspective of justice (Campbell, 2001: Ch.1) – is very different from the modern concept of economic or social justice. The former confines the scope of justice's concern to the civil sphere (offices, honor, and punishment), while the latter extends it to the economic sphere (material goods).[4] Samuel Fleischacker argues that major thinkers in the western tradition from Aristotle to Adam Smith held the traditional, meritorian concept of justice, and that they would reject the concept of social justice, for they did not believe that it is *the poor's due, merit, or desert* to receive allocation of material goods by society or the state (Fleischacker, 2004). Modern theorists of social justice (of the egalitarian kind), however, take the opposite view. They believe that justice morally entitles each member of a society to a level of material goods and that it is the responsibility of society – of which the government is the agent – to provide each member with material goods. On Fleischacker's view, premodern, western thinkers tend to hold some of the following views about the nature or origin of poverty, any one of which can block a transition from the traditional concept of distributive justice to the modern concept of social justice (Fleischacker, 2004: 9):

- Poverty is a punishment for sin.
- Material things do not matter, hence poor and rich can live equally good lives without any change in the material condition.
- Poverty is a blessing, enabling one to learn humility or to turn away from material obsessions.
- Poverty is a natural evil that cannot be overcome by human efforts.

If people in a society do not think that poverty is bad for an individual or that anything can be done about it, then poverty (or the distribution of material goods) will not be considered as a subject of concern for justice. Interestingly, Confucianism holds none of these views. No doubt Confucian thinkers expect people of high virtue to be able to live nobly whether in poverty or riches, and to take pride and delight in virtue rather than in material possessions (Confucius, 1992: 1.15; Mencius, 2003: 7A.21; Xunzi, 1988–1994: 2.5, 12.3). Yet none of them says that material goods do not matter to people's lives. Quite the contrary, the desire people have for material goods and wealth is natural and, if pursued within moral boundaries, legitimate. Confucius says:

> Wealth and rank are what every man desires; poverty and low station are what every man dislikes. (Confucius, 1992: 4.5)

> If wealth were a permissible pursuit, I would be willing even to act as a guard holding a whip outside the market place. If it is not, I shall follow my own inclination. (Confucius, 1992: 7.12)

Mencius affirms even more explicitly the centrality of material goods to the lives of ordinary people. In a well-known passage, he says that people who lack stable, sufficient material possessions will go astray, and that it is the responsibility of the ruler to prevent them from falling into the trap of poverty and illegal acts:

> Only a Gentleman can have a constant heart in spite of a lack of constant means of support. The people, on the other hand, will not have constant hearts if they are without constant means. Lacking constant hearts, they will go astray and fall into excesses, stopping at nothing. To punish them after they have fallen foul of the law is to set a trap for the people. How can a benevolent man in authority allow himself to set a trap for the people? (Mencius, 2003: 1A.7)

Material goods, in Mencius's view, are not only important to keep people from going astray; they are necessary conditions for them to live a good life.[5] Immediately following the passage in 1A.7 is this important one:

> Hence when determining what means of support the people should have, a clear-sighted ruler ensures that these are sufficient, on the one hand, for the care of parents, and, on the other, for the support of wife and children, so that people always have sufficient food in good years and escape starvation in bad; *only then does he drive them towards goodness.* (Mencius, 2003: 1A.7, italics mine)

For Mencius, material goods enable people to support the physical existence of themselves, their parents, and family members, which are important ethical duties. Moreover, having sufficient material means to support their family, people will

> learn, in their spare time, to be good sons and good young brothers, loyal to their prince and true to their word, so that they will, in the family, serve their fathers and elder brothers, and outside the family, serve their elders and superiors. (Mencius, 2003: 1A.5)

This is what constitutes Mencius's conception of good life, for which material goods are an important, necessary condition.

We have shown that in the view of Confucian thinkers, material goods are important to the good life, and people's desire for them is natural and legitimate. But this is not sufficient to establish that such a concern for material goods is, or can be, part of a concern of social justice. As David Miller has argued, we need some premises about the kind of society that can give rise to the circumstances of social justice.

> If we do not inhibit bounded societies, or if people's shares of goods and bads do not depend in ways we can understand on a determinate set of social institutions, or if there is no agency capable of regulating that basic structure, then we no longer live in a world in which the idea of social justice has any purchase. (Miller, 1999: 6)

If we follow Miller's understanding of the circumstances of social justice here, then we need to show that Confucian thinkers do understand society to have something like the characteristics described above.

Mencius and Xunzi do see society as a scheme for the division of labor in the production and distribution of goods that are necessary for the well-being of each and every member. Responding to the major social issues of their day, both thinkers went to great lengths to discuss issues such as poverty, differentiation of social roles and functions, inequality of income and status, and the distributive role of government. They see society as an interdependent complex that requires specialization and differentiation of occupation in the political and economic spheres. Both think that trade between "the hundred crafts" is necessary to satisfy everyone's needs (Mencius, 2003: 3A.4, 3B.4; Xunzi, 1988–1994: 4.12, 11.5b). But they also realize that if left completely on their own, free trade and the market may result in monopoly, excessive profits, and also what contemporary theorists today have called "the tragedy of the commons" in forestry and fishing, and so government interference in economic activity is necessary (Mencius, 2003: 1A.3, 2B.10; Xunzi, 1988–1994: 9.16b). More importantly, as will be shown, they believe that rulers and their governments have the capacity and the obligation to ensure fairness or equity in the management of government and economic affairs through enforcement of the right kinds of laws and policies in taxation, distribution of lands, and social welfare. So Confucian thinkers did look at society in such a way that it is *possible to conceive* that they viewed society's distributive impact on the people's well-being as a concern of social justice. However, whether these thinkers framed this concern as one of justice is a further question that requires a detailed analysis of the texts.

Justice as Sufficiency for All

Mencius is keenly aware of the seriousness of poverty and inequality of wealth in his times. He refers to the situation in which some people have "so plentiful good to be thrown to dogs and pigs," while "some drop dead from starvation by the wayside" (Mencius, 2003: 1A.3). He also says,

> nowadays, the means laid down for the people are sufficient neither for the care of parents nor for the support of wife and children. In good years life is always hard, while in bad years there is no way of escaping death. (Mencius, 2003: 1A.7)

Part of the cause is the unequal distribution of land and the inability of the government to take proper measures to redistribute land or provide the poor with material subsistence. Mencius therefore takes the equity of land distribution to be the first task of a benevolent government:

> *Benevolent government must begin with land demarcation.* When boundaries are not properly drawn (*ching*), the division of land according to the well-field system and the yield of grain for paying officials cannot be equitable (*jun, ping*). For this reason, despotic rulers and corrupt officials always neglect the boundaries. Once the boundaries are correctly fixed, there will be no difficulty in settling the distribution of land and the determination of emolument. (Mencius, 2003: 3A.3)

To use modern terminology to express Mencius's point, *economic justice is the backbone of good governance.* Now, what counts as equitable distribution of land? From the following two passages, the answer, I believe, is: an equal distribution of land *sufficient* for each person to live a good life.

> Hence when determining what means of support the people should have, a clear-sighted ruler ensures that these are *sufficient*, on the one hand, for the care of parents, and, on the other, for the support of wife and children, so that people always have sufficient food in good years and escape starvation in bad; only then does he drive them towards goodness. (Mencius, 2003: 1A.7, italics mine)

And how much land is needed for ensuring material sufficiency? Mencius tells King Xuan of Qi:

> If you wish to put this into practice, why not go back to fundamentals? If the mulberry is planted in every homestead of five *mu*[6] of land, then those who are fifty can wear silk; if chickens, pigs and dogs do not miss their breeding season, then those who are seventy can eat meat; if each lot of a hundred *mu* is not deprived of labor during the busy season, then families with several mouths to feed will not go hungry. (Mencius, 2003: 1A.7; see also 1A.3)

Mencius further elaborates on the well-field system (*ching*), which he regards as the first task of benevolent government:

> A *ching* is a piece of land measuring one *li* square, and each *ching* consists of 900 *mu*. Of these, the central plot of 100 *mu* belongs to the state, while the other eight plots of 100 *mu* each are held by eight families who share the duty of caring for the plot owned by the state. Only when they have done this duty do they dare turn to their own affairs. This is what sets the common people apart. (Mencius, 2003: 3A.3)

Mencius remarks that these calculations constitute a rough outline, and it is up to the ruler to make adjustments. But it seems clear that the well-field system contains three related principles:

1. *Sufficiency*: Each household should have an amount of land that is *sufficient* for the material well-being and ethical life of the members of the household.
2. *Equality (as a corollary of the first principle)*: The amount of land to be allocated should be more or less the *same* for every household of commoners (officials receive more land because they make a greater contribution to society).
3. *Government obligation*: It is the duty of the government to ensure that the land demarcation is "properly drawn" (*cheng*) and the division of land according to the well-field system is "equal" (*jun*).

Like Mencius, Xunzi subscribes to the principle of sufficiency and regards it as central to benevolent government (Xunzi, 1988–1994: 9.5, 10.2, 12.6). In a later book of *Xunzi*, he makes reference to something like Mencius's well-field system as a basis for sufficiency:

> A people that is not made prosperous will have no means of caring for the needs of their essential natures. . . . Hence, the way to make families prosperous is to allot five *mou* lots for the abode and one hundred *mou* for the fields, to devote one's attention to their concerns, and not to rob them of the time required for their fields. (Xunzi, 1988–1994: 27.52)

However, apart from land distribution, Xunzi also talks about income from jobs and assignments as another basis for sufficiency. He advises a ruler to

> [e]mploy the people so that they are certain to succeed in their assigned tasks; make certain that *the profits from their assigned tasks are sufficient to provide a means of living for them*. In all these to cause income to match outgo in regard to clothing, food, and the hundred other necessities of life so that with certainty the harvest surplus will be stored up at the proper season is called the "art of [achieving the plan]." (Xunzi, 1988–1994: 10.3a, italics mine)

There is an important point to note about Mencius's understanding of government obligation. Mencius thinks that if people die of starvation under a ruler, then that ruler has not only failed in his obligation but has behaved no differently than if he had killed them:

> Now when food meant for human beings is so plentiful as to be thrown to dogs and pigs, you fail to realize that it is time for collection, and when men drop dead from starvation by the wayside, you fail to realize that it is time for distribution. When people die, you

simply say, "It is none of my doing. It is the fault of the harvest." *In what way is that different from killing a man by running him through,* while saying all the time, "It is none of my doing. It is the fault of the weapon." Stop putting the blame on the harvest and the people of the whole Empire will come to you. (Mencius, 1988–1994: 1A.3, italics mine; see also 1A.4)

How to make sense of this strong condemnation of a ruler's failure to help the needy? One possible answer is that Mencius believes that it is the *people's due* to have sufficient means to live a good life, and that the government should supply this through prudent management and proper policies. So the failure of the ruler to help the needy is a serious failure in justice; that is, having no regard for people's due in economic distribution. This issue, however, raises some important questions: What is the moral foundation of distribution of resources in Mencius's thought? Is the foundation one of justice? Unfortunately, Mencius never attempts to provide an answer. But I believe that from the ideas of Mencius discussed above, we can construct a perfectionist theory of justice that justifies the distributive role of government as a duty of justice. This theory is perfectionist because its ultimate basis is a certain conception of the good life. It tries to link up Mencius's conception of the good life and the distributive role of government and social justice. The theory runs like this.

1. It is morally important that every human person can live a good life.
2. Living a good life requires sufficient material resources.
3. The natural world provides human beings with enough material resources to meet the material needs of everyone.
4. But the availability of, and access to, those resources depends on a well-ordered social structure in which the ruler (or government) plays a critical role. A well-ordered structure requires a proper set of laws and policies in land distribution, taxation, and the management of common pool resources such as forest and fish.
5. The fact that people's access to material resources is affected by the way social and legal rules are set up by the ruler and how well they are managed gives rise to a duty of justice on the part of the ruler.
6. In setting up distributive rules and institutions, the ruler has a duty of justice to provide everyone with a fair share of material resources (according to the sufficiency principle), because everyone has the capacity to lead a good life (and therefore has worth and need). In a well-ordered society, any person can claim that it is his or her due to have sufficient material resources. If the ruler fails to maintain the well-ordered structure even though natural resources are sufficient, and if as a result some people die of starvation while others have excessive wealth, then the ruler has actively committed a serious wrong of injustice (on a par with killing the starved) rather than merely a wrong in failing to help them.
7. Of course, providing everyone with a fair share of material resources is not just the ruler's responsibility alone. Everyone has a part to contribute to the government revenue through the working of the public land in the well-field system or paying other forms of tax. In other words, everyone has some responsibility in providing for everyone's due. In modern language, we can say that people have

a claim of justice to material sufficiency and an obligation to work to provide that sufficiency for all.

Many of the above statements are drawn from Mencius or at least consistent with his ideas, and so this perfectionist theory of justice can properly be called Mencian. This theory helps us see why the sufficiency principle can be a principle of social justice.

A Multilayer System of Care

Mencius's well-field system is actually a multilayer system of provision of care and help in which the family, the village or commune, and the government all play a role. We have seen that the well-field means first and foremost a fair distribution of land – government has a duty of justice to distribute to every household sufficient land to make a decent living. In this sense, it is appropriate to say that social justice is the foundation of the well-field system. One level above the foundation is the first tier of care and help, which is the family or household, the most important basic social unit in the well-field system. When people in the well-field system have enough land to plow and enough harvest to feed and clothe themselves, Mencius says, they will "learn, in their spare time, to be good sons and good younger brothers ... they will, in their family, serve their fathers and elder brothers, and outside the family, serve their elders and superiors" (Mencius, 2003: IA.5). If one needs any personal care at all, the most natural and appropriate source of help would be one's family, the prime site of care and affection. If a son is able to provide care to his parents, it would be wrong to shed his responsibility onto other people or government.

Mencius also envisages a network of *communal* relationships that serves as a second tier of help. People living in this well-field system are expected to offer mutual aid to each other:

> Neither in burying the dead, nor in changing his abode, does a man go beyond the confines of his village. If those who own land within each *ching* befriend one another both at home and abroad, help each other to keep watch, and succor each other in illness, they will live in love and harmony. (Mencius, 2003: IIIA.3)

Strictly speaking, the idea of mutual aid need not presuppose a "well-field system." The idea needs only to presuppose a small community, a village or commune, in which people reside together and interact with each other on a regular basis. Our neighbors are our second-tier caretakers, if our family members are the first-tier caretakers. The idea of mutual aid among fellow villagers coheres well with another famous saying of Mencius:

> Treat the aged of your own family in a manner befitting their venerable age and extend this treatment to the aged of other families; treat your own young in a manner befitting their tender age and extend this to the young of other families. (Mencius, 2003: IA.7)

The third tier in the multilayer system of welfare assistance is the government, which plays the role of some kind of last resort. There are two main occasions in which assistance from the government is necessary. The first is that there are people who cannot help themselves and have no family to turn to.

> Old men without wives, old women without husbands, old people without children, young children without fathers – these four types of people are the most destitute and have no one to turn to for help. Whenever King Wen put benevolent measures into effect, he always gave them first consideration. (Mencius, 2003: 1B.5)

Mencius argues that the government should give first priority to these people. But couldn't one turn to one's fellow villagers for assistance, even if there is no adult family member around to help? Why directly rely on the government? Why not first try the second tier? These questions are not considered by Mencius, and this is one issue that necessarily requires elaboration and extension of what is said in the text. One possible answer is that if a person – old or young – is unable to support herself and also permanently lacks adult family members to do so, then it would probably be too much of a burden for neighbors to support her for life. This is especially true if the neighbors are not well enough off to do so. In an agricultural economy, production is heavily affected by contingent natural factors such as weather and fertility of land. There are times when peasants do not reap sufficient harvests to maintain a good life for themselves. So this second tier may not always be able to provide long-term, stable, and sufficient assistance to the old and young fellow villagers who have no direct family support.

The second main occasion in which governmental assistance is necessary is that there are poor people who do not have enough means even to plow their land, and there are people in hunger because they do not harvest enough crops due to natural causes. If the number of these people is large, perhaps only a government can provide sufficient aid to them.[7] Mencius suggests to King Hsuan of Chi that if he is in a tour of inspection in spring, he should "inspect ploughing so that those who have not enough for sowing may be given help"; and on an autumn trip he should "inspect harvesting so that those who are in need may be given aid" (Mencius, 2003: IB.4). In another place, Mencius explicitly says that a good government should prudently collect resources (money or goods such as grains) through taxation in good times so that it would have enough to help the most needy in bad times (Mencius, 2003: IA.3). As seen above, Mencius thinks that if a government fails to assist those who die in starvation, it is morally responsible for their death. It is no excuse to blame a bad harvest caused by natural causes, because a responsible government should have prepared for the worst situation.

Mencius's principle of giving special favor to the four kinds of the needy and more generally the poor was put into practice in China. Chen Huan-Chang, author of an important but neglected book published in 1911 with the title *The Economic Principles of Confucius and His School*, wrote that in the Song dynasty (960–1279 CE), the central government established a granary in each district for the storing of rice that came from the public land as a rent. Each of the four classes of people was given rice and sometimes food and clothes. In Ming dynasty (1368–1644 CE), there were decrees to support the destitute. For example, in 1386 CE, a decree was made to the effect that:

> Among poor people, if the age was above eighty, five pecks of rice, three pecks of wine, and five catties of meat were given to each of them monthly. If the age was above ninety, one roll of silk and one catty of cotton were added to this amount annually. Those who owned some farmland were not given rice. To all the four classes – widower, widow, orphan, the solitary – six bushels of rice were given annually. (Chen, 1911: 599)

Similarly, in the Qing dynasty (1644–1911 CE), every district had an almshouse maintained by the government. Officials who failed to fulfill their welfare responsibilities would be punished.

> According to the Law Code of the Tsing [Qing] Dynasty, if the officials do not support the four classes, the very sick person and the infirm and superannuated who need public support, they shall be punished with sixty blows of the long stick. (Chen, 1911: 599)

This demonstrates, Chen claims, that the Confucian idea that government has a responsibility to help the needy and poor "has been put into actual law, and its effects differ only because of the efficiency of administration" (Chen, 1911: 599).

Inequality Arising from Merit and Contribution

Confucian justice and care permit economic inequality that arises from one's productive activity. For Mencius and Xunzi, the salary or income from one's productive activity should be based on one's merit or contribution. They do not believe in equality of outcome. Some people may legitimately get a greater reward or possess more wealth than others because of their merit or contribution. Xunzi writes that the amount and substance of one's emolument should fit one's "station":

> [T]he ancient Kings acted to control men with regulations, ritual, and moral principles, in order thereby to divide society into classes, creating therewith differences in status between the noble and base, disparities between the privileges of age and youth, and the division of the wise from the stupid, the able from the incapable. *All of this caused men to perform the duties of their station in life and each to receive his due (yi); only after this had been done was the amount and substance of the emolument paid by grain made to fit their respective stations.* (Xunzi, 1988–1994: 4.12, italics mine)

Note that Xunzi is not advocating a discriminatory, class-based hierarchy of society. Rather, he presents a hierarchy of status and emolument that is defined with reference to people's ability, not their family background. In fact, Xunzi is an advocate of class mobility based on merit. He writes,

> Although they be the descendants of kings and dukes or knights and grand officers, if they are incapable of devotedly observing the requirements of ritual and moral principles, *they should be relegated to the position of commoners*. Although they be the descendants of commoners, if they accumulate culture and study, rectify their character and conduct, and are capable of devotedly observing the requirements of ritual principles and justice, *they should*

be brought to the ranks of a prime minister, knights, or grand officers. (Xunzi, 1988–1994: 9.1, italics mine)

Mencius also endorses contribution or merit as the basis for emolument. He says that one should be paid in accordance with one's work or contribution (*gong*), not one's intention (Mencius, 2003: 3B.4). He stresses in particular that a gentleman who gives advice to the ruler deserves emolument, even though he does not engage in a productive activity like that of farmers and carpenters. This is because helping to make the prince secure and honored and to educate people to be dutiful is a kind of contribution (Mencius, 2003: 7B.32).

We have seen that once past the level of material sufficiency, Mencius and Xunzi do not object to economic inequalities that arise from personal factors such as merit and contribution, which are largely based on the possession of abilities (moral character and intelligence). Neither thinker is a "luck" egalitarian, one who believes that those who become worse off than others through no fault of their own should be compensated. Instead, both believe that desert should be based on a person's achievements and contribution.

Interestingly (and controversially), both men believe that human beings are born with the same nature, including even natural talent. "In natural talent, inborn nature, awareness, and capability, the gentleman and the petty man are one" (Xunzi, 1988–1994: 4.8). What accounts for the eventual differences in ability and moral development are two factors, one personal and the other social. The personal factor is the extent to which a person is willing to think, learn, and cultivate himself (Mencius, 2003: 6A.17; Xunzi, 1988–1994: 4.8, 4.10, 23.5b). The social factor is a person's environment and the customs of his community. "The habituation of custom modifies the direction of will, and, if continued for a long time, will alter [a person's substance]" (Xunzi, 1988–1994: 8.11, see also 4.8). Mencius also says that a person's surroundings can transform his temperament (*qi*) (Mencius, 2003: 7A.36). Although people's achievements depend in part on the environment and customs in which they grow up, neither thinker asserts that those who become worst off through such uncontrollable kinds of factors should be compensated. I suspect that even if they were shown that people are born with different levels of talent, they would still not go so far as to endorse luck egalitarianism.

Conclusion

The main principles of a Confucian perspective on social justice and welfare, if only a rudimentary one, can be summarized as follows:

1 *Justice as sufficiency for all*: Each household should have a sufficient amount of resources (land for Mencius) to live a materially secure and ethical life.
2 *Mutual aid*: Beyond the foundation of social justice, families and social networks are the first and second tier of care and help for people in need.

3 *Government's welfare assistance*: When the first two tiers cannot meet the needs of the badly off, government should provide them with direct welfare assistance.
4 *Merit and contribution*: Offices and emolument should be distributed according to people's merits and contributions. Inequality of income that arises from this source is not illegitimate.

If we put all these principles together, we can see a social ideal that nicely integrates justice, care, personal responsibility, and individual merit into a coherent system. The first principle combines justice with personal responsibility – justice requires equitable land distribution by government, but to be able to harvest it members of a household must work together and labor hard. The second principle shows that caring is an important part of the social ideal. For the Confucian conception of the good life, assistance coming from family and social ties should be preferable to governmental help, for it comes from caring and concern, and it may be more effective because the caretaker understands the needs and problems of the one who seeks assistance. More importantly, mutual aid is a valuable opportunity for the caregiver to engage in virtuous activity and for both parties to develop a valuable relationship. But when mutual aid fails or is not sufficient to help the needy, the ideal of care requires the government to step in to provide direct welfare assistance, and so the third principle comes into operation. Finally, the fourth principle makes room for economic inequality arising from the differential efforts and merits of individuals. The Confucian social ideal is a regime of justice and care, one that does not eliminate personal responsibility or individual merit.

Acknowledgment

This chapter is an integration and development of two of my published essays on the subject (Chan 2003b, 2008). I am grateful to Cambridge University Press and Rowman and Littlefield Publishers for permission to use the material in the essays. My work on this essay was supported by a grant from the Research Grants Council of the Hong Kong Special Administrative Region, China (HKU 741508H).

Notes

1 This and the next two paragraphs are adapted from Chan (2003a).
2 For a discussion on whether Confucianism is a religious tradition, see Yao (2000: 38–47).
3 Aristotle would treat the justice of punishment as an instance of corrective justice and the distribution of offices as an instance of distributive justice, although both corrective and distributive justice belong to the category of what he calls particular justice. See Aristotle's *Nicomachean Ethics*, V.
4 For a contrast of civil justice and social justice, see Passmore (1979: Ch. 2).
5 Aristotle also says that citizens of a polis should take part in common meals, which are financed through the use of communally owned land. See his *Politics* VII xi, 1330a3–13.

6 C.D. Lau notes: "As a *mu* is one nine-hundredth part of a square *li*, it works out to be somewhat less than 200 square meters" (Mencius, 2003: 9).
7 In principle, members of a community could establish a granary to support each other. But even this is not a safe guarantee, for sometimes an entire community, or communities in a region, would suffer, for a long period of time, from bad harvests and natural disasters. The idea of voluntary community granaries is explored in DeBary (1998: Ch. 5). Its history, however, was not well documented. From a historical point of view, government funded and managed community granaries were more prevalent than voluntary ones. See the discussion later in the chapter.

References

Campbell, Tom (2001) *Justice*, Macmillan, London.

Chan, Joseph (2003a) Confucian attitudes toward ethical pluralism, in *The Many and the One*, Richard Madsen and Tracy B. Strong (eds.), Princeton University Press, Princeton, pp. 129–153.

Chan, Joseph (2003b) Giving priority to the worst off: A Confucian perspective on social welfare, in *Confucianism for the Modern World*, Daniel Bell and Chaibong Hahm (eds.), Cambridge University Press, Cambridge, pp. 236–253.

Chan, Joseph (2008) Is there a Confucian perspective on social justice? in *Western Political Thought in Dialogue with Asia*, Takashi Shogimen and Cary J. Nederman (eds.), Rowman and Littlefield, Lanham, MD, pp. 261–277.

Chen, Huan-Chang (1911) *The Economic Principles of Confucius and His School*, Columbia University Press, New York.

Confucius (1992) *The Analects*, 2nd edn, trans. D.C. Lau, Chinese University Press, Hong Kong.

DeBary, William Theodore (1988) *Asian Values and Human Rights*, Harvard University Press, Cambridge, MA.

Fleischacker, Samuel (2004) *A Short History of Distributive Justice*, Harvard University Press, Cambridge, MA.

Mencius (2003) *Mencius: A Bilingual Edition*, trans. D.C. Lau, Chinese University of Hong Kong, Hong Kong.

Miller, David (1976) *Social Justice*, Clarendon Press, Oxford.

Miller, David (1999) *Principles of Social Justice*, Harvard University Press, Cambridge, MA.

Passmore, J.A. (1979) Civil justice and its rival, in *Justice*, Eugene Kamenka and Alice Erh-Soon Tay (eds.), Edward Arnold, London.

Tang, Chun-I. (1988) *Essays on Chinese Philosophy and Culture*, Students Book Co., Taipei.

Xunzi (1988–1994) *Xunzi: A Translation and Study of the Complete Works*, 3 vols, trans. John Knoblock, Stanford University Press, Stanford.

Yao, Xinzhong (2000) *An Introduction to Confucianism*, Cambridge University Press, Cambridge.

CHAPTER 6
Confucianism
Contemporary Expressions

Stephen C. Angle

Confucianism is one of the world's great moral, philosophical, and spiritual traditions. It has been a central part of the religious lives of people throughout east Asia for more than two millennia. The last century has been a particularly challenging period for Confucian thinking and practice, however. As such, it makes sense for us to begin this consideration of contemporary Confucian perspectives on social justice with some background on Confucianism itself. On that basis, we can then move on to the main topic, which we will examine in two stages: first, the range of ways in which Confucianism figured in discussions of social justice in the twentieth century; and second, specific discussion of current Confucian thinkers and their views on social justice. In the conclusion, we briefly reflect on the ways in which the contemporary views we have examined are justified. This last topic is important, because while we will see some significant areas of agreement – virtually all authors agree that Confucian social justice is intimately related to the idea of "harmony," for instance – there are also important disagreements, and assessing those disagreements requires thinking about the structure of Confucian justification.

Background to Contemporary Confucianism

The twentieth century started badly for Confucianism. In 1905, a last-ditch effort to reform a floundering empire led to the abandonment of the ubiquitous civil-service examination system based on Confucian classics, around which higher education in China had been organized for centuries. This was followed, in 1911, by the collapse of the last dynasty itself. In 1915 Chinese intellectuals inaugurated a "New Culture Movement" that sought fundamental changes to Chinese values, practices, and even the

Chinese language. In many ways this movement was a more pervasive "cultural revolution" than the later Maoist movement of that name. The values of "modern civilization" were on the rise and older traditions like Confucianism were roundly criticized. Confucianism did not die, but after the first decades of the twentieth century it would need to find new ways to be relevant in Chinese society.

After this unpromising start, the twentieth century continued to pose obstacles to any revival of Confucianism. Some political leaders tried to manipulate it as a shallow ideology of loyalty to power, while others tried to wipe it completely from the hearts of China's citizens (most notably during the 1973–1974 "Criticize Lin Biao and Confucius" campaign). There were some exceptions: philosophers and educators like Liang Shuming (1893–1988) and Mou Zongsan (1909–1995) developed Confucian ideas for the new century and sought to teach its ideals both within the People's Republic, to the limited degree that was possible, and in Taiwan, Hong Kong, and even farther afield. We will hear more about Liang and Mou below, as well as about other political and social thinkers who were significantly influenced by Confucianism even if they did not consider themselves to be "Confucian." There have, in addition, been efforts to establish Confucianism as a state-sponsored religion – notwithstanding the arguments by other intellectuals that Confucianism was valuable to modern Chinese precisely because it was not (in their view) a "religion" in the western sense. This debate was especially fierce in the early twentieth century, when the utopian Confucian thinker Kang Youwei (1858–1927) and his associates sought (and failed) to have Confucianism recognized in the constitution of the emerging republic.

The precise nature of the relationship between "Confucianism," in all its historical complexity, and the category of "religion" is not our central concern here. For our purposes, what is significant is the relation of "Confucian" values to "Confucian" texts and practices. Many influential voices within the tradition have treated neither its texts as sacred nor their authors as infallible. The tradition's founders had deep insight and sage wisdom, to be sure, but they were no more than human beings – and often were quite insistent in their texts about their own fallibility. This fallibilist attitude helps to ensure a diverse tradition with shifting emphases over the centuries, in part responding to broad changes in social and intellectual trends, not only in China but also in Korea, Japan, and elsewhere. When we look for Confucian views of social justice in the twentieth and twenty-first centuries, we will see that these interactions with other sources of value and meaning continue to be important as various thinkers struggle to define the place of Confucianism in a new and dynamic environment.

Confucianism and Social Justice in the Twentieth Century

Kang Youwei (1858–1927)

In 1902, Kang Youwei completed – but did not publish – his *Book of the Great Community (Da Tong Shu)*, which he had first begun writing in 1884 (Thompson, 1958). The utopian vision presented in this text is a good place to begin the complicated story of

Confucianism and social justice in the twentieth century, for three reasons. First, Kang's striking views are probably the most radical ideas on social justice in the entire century. Second, Kang's relationship to Confucianism is itself vexed, and will allow us to reflect more deeply on the possibilities enabled by the Confucian tradition in the modern world, and on their limits. Third, although the *Da Tong Shu* itself was not immediately influential, many of Kang's ideas and specific Confucian sources were well known and had a significant impact. At the heart of Kang's vision is a unified human world, the name of which ("Great Community" or Da Tong) and some of the content of which he gets from the early Confucian text known as the "Li Yun Pian." Kang repeatedly invokes key ideas from this ancient text, although he radicalizes them. For example, "Li Yun" contrasts the era of "Small Tranquility," in which people are concerned only for their own families and states, with the "Great Community," in which people do not confine their affection to their own parents and children. Still, "Li Yun" emphasizes the role of ritual (this is the "li" in the text's title) and clearly envisions a society in which it is precisely the fulfillment of distinct, complementary, role-based responsibilities that leads to general flourishing. Kang shares the goal but transforms the means, seeking to do away with any ritualized distinctions:

> Now to have states, families, and selves is to allow each individual to maintain a sphere of selfishness. This contradicts utterly the universal principles (gongli) and impedes progress ... Therefore, not only should states be abolished, so that there will be no more struggle between the strong and the weak; families should also be done away with, so that there will no longer be inequality of love and affection [among people]; and, finally, selfishness itself should be banished, so that goods and services would not be used for private ends ... The only [true way] is sharing the world in common by all (*tianxia wei gong*). (trans. from Hsiao, 1975: 499)

Kang argues in the various chapters of his *Book of the Great Community* for an ideal that abolishes distinctions between nations, classes, races, genders, families, and occupations, as well as the distinction between ruler and ruled. It is a radically egalitarian vision, motivated in part by Kang's great concern for the suffering in world around him. For much of his public career Kang worked toward concrete reforms that he hoped might eventually help to move both his own society and the world in the direction of his social ideal.

Readers of this volume's chapter on early Confucian conceptions of social justice (Chapter 5) will immediately note that these ideas are much more extreme than the overall view found in the classical Confucian texts. This raises a question: Even if phrases like "great community (*da tong*)" and "sharing the world in common by all (*tianxia wei gong*)" come from a text that has long been accepted as Confucian, can Kang's social justice ideal itself be called "Confucian"? One astute commentator on this matter notes that the question of whether a thinker or idea or practice counts as Confucian can be interpreted in several different ways (Hsiao, 1975: 42). Certainly, Kang's ideas are dramatic departures from the "Confucian" values and practices of his day, even if his more practical proposals were presented as gradual reforms to present institutions. However, on other grounds it seems appropriate to see Kang as Confucian. He certainly took himself to be a Confucian and was taken by some (like his important student Liang Qichao) to be developing Confucian ideas (Hsiao, 1975: 436). He argued that his ideas represented the true Confucian teachings, and offered (highly controversial) arguments aimed at removing various long-standing misunderstandings of the true Confucianism. At the same time, he was quite open about the degree to which he also drew on western sources and claimed to be articulating ideals that were objective and universal – not distinctive of or limited to China. To this day, Kang's status as a Confucian remains contested. When we come to various claims for and against the "Confucian" pedigree of social justice ideas in the contemporary world, we will have occasion to return to Kang's example.

Sun Yatsen (1866–1925) and Zhang Junmai (1887–1969)

The third reason why Kang offers us a good point of departure is that ideas he highlighted, such as "great community (*da tong*)" and "sharing the world in common by all (*tianxia wei gong*)," come to be widely discussed and widely endorsed, even by many who do not consider themselves to be Confucians at all, and even though these ideas took on different meanings in different contexts. Take, for example, Sun Yatsen, the first president of the Republic of China. Sun regarded Kang's efforts to legitimize reform through a reinterpretation of Confucianism as a scholastic and pointless exercise, but nonetheless was influenced by Kang's version of Confucianism (Bergère, 1998: 78, 392). Sun famously articulated his ideology as "Three Principles of the People"; the third principle, "People's Livelihood," bore the marks of both western socialism and Kang's more Confucian language. Sun argues that "Livelihood" is a more all-encompassing ideal than western writings on socialism – however connected it is to various socialist ideals – and concludes one of his lectures with the words: "When the people share everything in the state, then we will truly reach the goal of the People's Livelihood principle, which is Confucius's hope of a 'great community'" (Sun, 1928: 184). Another example of the ways in which Confucianism and ideas of social democracy were interlinked in the mid-twentieth century is presented by Zhang Junmai. Zhang was sincerely interested in Confucianism – he was a signatory of the 1958 New Confucian "Manifesto," which we will discuss below – but his political thinking was consciously pluralistic. At one point Zhang described his democratic socialist thought as a blend of German philosophy, English politics, and Confucianism (Fung, 2005: 327). His social and economic views were not as radical or utopian as those of Kang Youwei; he actively sought to create what he saw as a Chinese social democracy, a middle path between Anglo-American liberal capitalism and Soviet revolutionary socialism (Fung, 2005: 339). Still, his goal was "Chinese" in two senses: it was designed for Chinese circumstances, and it was based in part on Chinese (that is, Confucian) social ideals. Like his co-signatories to the Manifesto, Zhang recognized that a contemporary Confucianism would need to be different from traditional Confucianism in significant ways, but felt that the core insights of the tradition represented important human values that needed to be preserved and developed.

Liang Shuming (1893–1988)

Zhang Junmai was both a scholar and a politician, and it was primarily in the latter role that he pursued his concern for social justice. An alternative model is offered by Liang Shuming. Liang was a philosopher, an academic, and an activist. While he ultimately seems to have understood his personal convictions as more Buddhist than anything else, in his writing, teaching, and public activities he strongly identifies with Confucianism. Liang's most famous book is his 1921 *Eastern and Western Cultures and their Philosophies*, which helped to usher in a renewed attention to Confucian and Buddhist thinking. For our purposes, though, his most significant contribution lies in his efforts to theorize social justice and then to put it into practice, all of which went under the heading of "rural reconstruction." He sought to offer the "start of a new life for humanity" that would avoid the faults of the "abnormal, money-based, distorted," overly industrialized, overly urbanized civilization of the West, wherein humanity "has lost its control over matter" (quoted in Alitto, 1979: 192). He sought a balance between collectivized, technologically developed agriculture – which carried with it both economic and moral benefits – and industry. His goals were both material improvement and the moral improvement that lies at the center of Confucianism; he designed his political, social, and economic institutions to aim at these twin objectives. He saw China's (and the world's) problems as in the first instance cultural, rather than political, and felt that the institutions he advocated would have a crucial transformative effect on people's values and cultural presuppositions. One other element of his vision will be important for us to keep in mind as we go forward: on the one hand, he advocated "vigorous participation in the life of group organizations" and saw "self-rule" as vital, but on the other hand, he also embraced the Confucian commitment to moral meritocracy. His proposed solution was one-party rule, with the party both responsive to the masses and focused on cultivating the quality of its cadres (Alitto, 1979: 203). Issues of political organization go beyond our specific scope, but, as we will see below, it is impossible to keep political (in)equality completely distinct from questions of social hierarchy. At any rate, while Liang's concrete efforts in Shandong province ultimately were overshadowed by larger social and political forces, he anticipates some contemporary thinkers in his connection between the pursuit of individual Confucian virtues and broad societal reforms aimed at securing social justice for all.

Mou Zongsan (1909–1995)

We turn now to Mou Zongsan, arguably the most influential Confucian philosopher of the twentieth century. Mou left mainland China in 1949 and spent the rest of his life in Hong Kong and Taiwan; there is no question that his political and social views were shaped by his anticommunist stance. He is one of the main authors and signatories of the 1958 Manifesto to the World's People on Behalf of Chinese Culture, which argues both that the people of the world must respect and learn from Chinese cultures (and especially Confucianism), and that Confucianism itself needs to reconstruct itself by coming to embrace democracy and science. Mou has a celebrated argument (discussed in Angle, 2009: Ch. 10) showing why Confucian commitments themselves require embracing a strong form of rule of law and constitutionalism, but he has much less to say on the specific topic of social justice. In one comparatively early work he argues for an abstract connection between Confucianism and socialism. In later writings, though, while he acknowledges some defects in capitalism and therefore embraces certain protections for people's welfare, his fundamental commitment seems to be to the individual right to private property. He says: "private property is the defense line of the human individual and protects the dignity of the human being" (Mou, 1983: 183). Mou's position here is consistent with his idea that individual moral claims to authority must "restrict themselves" – that is, be limited by independent human rights – in order to avoid tyrannical impositions by self-proclaimed sages. While Mou certainly does pay some attention to the social and economic realities of his day, it is true (just as later critics will claim) that he focuses much more on the metaphysics and epistemology of moral reality than he does on issues of practical, social justice.

An east Asian development model?

Our final topic in this section is the series of claims and counter-claims made in the 1980s and 1990s concerning Confucianism's relation to capitalism and economic development. As east Asian economies flourished in the 1980s, some social scientists began to reevaluate Max Weber's well-known claims concerning Confucianism's inability to promote economic development. In Peter Berger's phrase, was there an "East Asian development model," based in part in Confucianism that could be an alternative to, or even preferable to, the development experience of the "West" (Berger, 1988)? Many voices chimed into these conversations, some supportive and some skeptical of the link between Confucianism and economic growth. A particularly important participant has been long-time Harvard professor Tu Wei-ming, who has been both cognizant of Confucianism's historical shortcomings, and yet enthusiastic about its potential to contribute to world civilization. In one of the most thorough and yet critical discussions, though, historian Arif Dirlik concluded:

> What the Confucian discussions produced was not a critique of capitalism, or of Orientalism, but their affirmations . . . Tu Wei-ming has been most prominent for articulating Confucianism as a global ideology of modernization, enhancing its hegemony. Confucianism could indeed contribute to a critique of modernity, but in defining the "core values" of Confucianism, Tu and others have refrained from any thoroughgoing critique of capitalism, portraying it instead as a remedy for the ailments of capitalism, which translates into a rendering of Confucianism as a instrument of "social engineering" to guarantee more cooperative (and docile) citizens for corporations and patriarchal families. (Dirlik, 1995: 272)

Tu would certainly not accept this characterization, and one can find some references in his work to the idea that Confucianism might help alleviate the excesses of western societies in the area of distributive justice. Still, it is fair to say that in comparison with some of the earlier Confucian-influenced thinkers whom we have canvassed in this section, Tu is relatively less engaged with the issue of social justice – like the New Confucians (such as Mou), on whose work he sees himself as building.

Contemporary Views

It has become commonplace among observers of China to talk about a revival of Confucianism in twenty-first-century China, as well as a growing interest in Confucianism abroad. Writing at the end of the century's first decade, I cannot say with any confidence in what direction these trends will develop. Perhaps in another 30 or 40 years, Confucianism will be relegated more thoroughly to the museum than it ever was in the twentieth century. There are many other possibilities, though, from Confucianism as one part of a pluralistic national (or global) moral-political discourse, to some form of Confucianism once again serving as a leading national ideology and/or religion. In this section we will canvass several different views on Confucianism and social justice, and along the way see some different visions of the place Confucianism might have in our future.

Jiang Qing's political Confucianism

In 2003, Jiang Qing (1953–) published *Political Confucianism: The Changing Direction, Particularities, and Development of Contemporary Confucianism* (Jiang, 2003). While not his first book, *Political Confucianism* was a significant departure from his earlier scholarship on the Confucian classics and represents an importantly different approach to contemporary Confucianism from the work of the "New Confucians" such as Mou Zongsan and their students. When coupled with his efforts to revive traditional Confucian educational practices by leaving his university post and founding a private academy, Jiang's writings have garnered him considerable attention as a public intellectual. Like Kang Youwei from the early twentieth century, Jiang believes that Confucianism must be institutionalized as a formally organized religion, though Jiang has a considerably more particularist or cultural nationalist view than Kang: Jiang sees Confucianism as intimately tied to Chinese history, culture, and popular practice; for him, any talk of global values or justice is problematically utopian. Still, Jiang's faith in the truth of Confucian teachings and – strikingly – in the reality of Tian (or "Heaven") as a kind of deity seem to be deeply held, and he views Confucian institutions as eventually able to have a positive impact on the rest of the world (Jiang, 2010: 14). His confidence that Confucianism must be the source of Chinese values has led him to outline a dramatically different set of political institutions from those currently in place in China (Jiang, 2010). This new political structure would have a place for the democratic expression of people's views, but the upper two houses of its tricameral legislature would be designed to give voice to learned Confucians with special insight into moral reality, on the one hand, and to experienced representatives of Chinese cultural and social institutions, on the other. This is one indication that Jiang views a contemporary Confucian social order as significantly nonegalitarian.

Before looking further at the antiegalitarian aspects of Jiang's position, it makes sense to focus first on what he says about the core issues of economic justice. This is a much less developed side of Jiang's thinking than the political, but his views are clear enough and, in light of what we have seen from Confucianism in the twentieth century, quite interesting. He sets aside Kang Youwei's idea of a "great community" as an ideal in which Confucianism "believes" but with little immediate practical relevance (Jiang, 2010: 256). Following one of the trends discussed above, Jiang insists that Confucianism instills practical virtues that lead to economic development, just as Weber claims that Protestantism does. In a few brief sentences, furthermore, Jiang asserts that Confucianism is consistent with modern market economics because it has always supported freedom of economic exchange and opposed all forms of monopolization (Jiang, 2003: 364). At the same time, however, he is conscious of the problems engendered by markets and is worried about the alienation that a dominance of economic values can engender. He is concerned both about the alienation of people from themselves – because as mere economic instruments, they cannot attend to or realize their full human natures – and about the alienation of people from nature, which becomes a mere means to the realization of economic value and no longer a sacred existence in which we share mutual affection and reverence (Jiang, 2003: 365–366). Without offering many details, Jiang argues that Confucian values like harmony, concern for others (*youhuan yishi*), and opposition to economic inequity (*bujun*) can enable us to avoid market failures and alienation, if these values are primary and the pursuit of profit – which is perfectly legitimate, in moderation – is secondary. Essentially, his argument is that markets, contractual relations, and profit are fine, so long as the institutions of moral education are functioning properly throughout the society (Jiang, 2003: 314–320).

The basic meaning of "harmony" is complementary differences, and it is important to note that Jiang definitely does not advocate egalitarianism. In his view, many status and identity distinctions have deep bases in the nature of the cosmos. Without the complementary differences between male and female, for example, life would be impossible. Following certain classical Confucian sources, he takes this to be a metaphysical and value-laden point, rather than merely an issue of biology (Jiang, 2003: 215). Marriages not founded on the idea of "difference" between men and women lose their sacred significance and, he suggests, as a result are collapsing in the modern world (Jiang, 2003: 227). This is one specific instance of a broader theme, namely the importance of rituals (*li*) and the status/rank distinctions they underwrite (Jiang, 2003: 291–294). Jiang's vision of society, like his outline of Confucian politics, is markedly hierarchical. He does not explicitly address the degree to which economic inequality can be allowed to track these other forms of inequality; his talk of harmony is certainly meant to suggest that economic differences should not be stark enough to have an impact on people's flourishing, but the concrete implications of such references to "harmony" are unclear. Jiang's emphasis on "ritual" is an important side of his overall project to revive what he calls "political" Confucianism: he argues that the institutional aspects of the Confucian tradition were too quickly abandoned by even the advocates of Confucianism in the twentieth century. He also argues that Confucian rituals are unlike class or other status distinctions that one sees in the West: because rituals are suffused with personal human feeling (rather than being based, for example, in an impersonal, external legal code), they lead to status differences that are less oppositional and harsh (Jiang, 2003: 322). According to Jiang, ritual- and harmony-based status distinctions can actually contribute to social justice.

Kang Xiaoguang's humane government

The next two thinkers whom we will consider are both influenced by Jiang Qing, though in the realm of social justice they go in somewhat different directions. We will first consider Kang Xiaoguang. Born in 1963 and initially trained in physics, Kang is a social scientist and public intellectual who has become persuaded that China must replace its communist ideology with a soft authoritarianism based on Confucianism. His writings are passionate and incisive, sparkling with insight and argumentation that draw on many sources. Kang's main Confucian sources include the classical canon (especially Mencius), some Han dynasty developments, Kang Youwei, and Jiang Qing. Kang does not have a pedigree as a scholar of Confucianism, and it can sometimes seem that he has seized on Confucianism as a means to his ends, rather than visualizing his ends from the perspective of Confucianism in the first place. This fact hardly makes him irrelevant to our topic, though: as we saw in the section above on the twentieth century, Confucianism can figure in people's thinking about social justice in a variety of complex ways.

Kang occupies an intriguing position in the contemporary Chinese political scene. On the one hand, he is deeply unhappy with failings of the current regime in the area of social justice and is concerned that China's present political system lacks legitimacy. Kang writes of an alliance of political, intellectual, and economic elites that is leading to increased corruption, inequality, a rise in the power of organized crime, and other social maladies; he sums it up by saying that these elites are robbing the masses (Kang, 2005: xiv). He (quite rightly) sees that such a system cannot possibly be legitimate in any type of Marxist framework. On the other hand, Kang does not see liberal democracy as the cure for these ills. He accepts and seeks to justify authoritarian, one-party rule. His goal, therefore, is to show how a version of authoritarianism can both deal effectively with the social justice problems he has identified, and simultaneously be legitimate in its own terms. His basic idea is to show that a certain type of authoritarian, "cooperativist," welfare state can be justified through a commitment to Confucianism.

Following Mencius, Kang calls his recommended solution to China's ills "humane government (*renzheng*)." He asks: Can humane government both preserve China's current strengths (relatively efficient economic growth, political stability, and national unity) while remedying its shortcomings (social injustice and lack of legitimacy)? His answer is affirmative. For instance, he says that Confucianism can happily accept many roles for economic markets, and offers the well-known "theory of Confucian capitalism" – discussed earlier in the context of Tu Wei-ming's support for this idea – as evidence for such a compatibility. Humane government will tackle social justice problems from two directions: at the level of values, it prioritizes humane concern for others; and at the level of institutions, it builds in a variety of structures that limit inhumanity and injustice (Kang, 2005: xliii). One side of this is a unification of moral, religious, and political values, which, Kang says, enabled traditional Chinese society to be so stable for so long. Other aspects are distinctly modern but supported, according to Kang, by Confucian values. It is not hard to see why the institutions of a welfare state, for example, are consistent with the classical Confucian commitment to the well-being of the masses. Kang also emphasizes the idea of corporatism, according to which different "classes" in society will have a significant degree of internal democracy and "self-rule (*zizhi*)," even though the broader political system will be strictly hierarchical, ruled by a moral-intellectual Confucian elite (Kang, 2005: 99). The result of all this is supposed to be a "blended" and "balanced" polity that promotes growth while protecting the interests of all classes in society. It is Confucian because its basic values (e.g., "humaneness") and thus legitimacy derive from a Confucian framework.

Fan Ruiping's reconstructionist Confucianism

Fan Ruiping's *Reconstructionist Confucianism: Rethinking Morality after the West* (Fan, 2010) shares with Jiang Qing and to some degree with Kang Xiaoguang an enthusiasm for Confucian ritual and other fairly specific forms of life. Like Jiang, Fan sets his version of Confucianism up against the "New Confucianism" of Mou Zongsan and others. Fan identifies his "reconstructionist Confucianism" with the "project of reclaiming and articulating moral resources from the Confucian tradition so as to meet contemporary moral and public policy challenges" (Fan, 2010: xi). According to Fan, philosophers like Mou advocate greater changes than Fan himself; in fact, they strive to "recast the Confucian heritage in light of modern Western values." As a result, Fan alleges that the "Confucian heritage is in great measure colonized by modern Western notions" as the New Confucians engage in "naïve presentism" in order to "read social democratic concepts into Confucianism" (Fan, 2010: 106 n2, 108 n8). This is a strong critique, though not – in my view – a justified one. I have argued elsewhere (Angle, 2009) that Mou does not simply read contemporary western concerns into Confucianism, but rather presents an argument that Confucianism for its own deep reasons must develop the resources of law and rights in a way that the tradition had previously never fully realized. Just like Fan, in fact, Mou argues for a change to the tradition. He claims to give us good Confucian reasons for the change.

Let us look, then, at key elements of Fan's view of social justice. At the center of Fan's understanding of Confucianism is the family. Family interests are more important than individual interests; shared family decision making is the model for exercising judgment; and roles within the family are the models for all human relationships. Indeed, Fan says that the main Confucian social ideal is to treat all people as relatives (Fan, 2010: 29). Within the family, some relationships and responsibilities are stronger than others, and these inequalities undergird the broader antiegalitarianism for which Fan argues. He sees the individual development of love and virtues as critical, but these are constituted via roles and relationships with close family members. Many of these same themes have been developed by other scholars in recent years. What is striking and controversial are the subtle normative conclusions that Fan seems to draw from them. For instance, he argues in various places that the "natural" and "normal" type of family is heterosexual. The Confucian notion of the family, he says, "supports a web of sex- and age-specific orders of authority and obligation" (Fan, 2010: 100, see also 32). It is worth noting, though, that nothing about gender distinctions or roles actually follows from the general picture of families as meaning- and identity-constituting institutions. Only if we add that the specific external forms in which families were traditionally arranged in China continue to have normative priority can we conclude that a reconstructed Confucianism should be heteronormative and patriarchal. In his extensive treatment of ritual (*li*), Fan does in fact argue for considerable stability of ritual forms, as well as emphasizing that "Confucian rituals provide the specific content to Confucian ethics. Without attending to the Confucian rituals, Confucian ethics would be too abstract to stand clearly" (Fan, 2010: 171). It is thus possible to read him as arguing that the traditional gender roles must remain constant. Fan's detailed discussion of when and how ritual forms can change is valuable and deserves more attention than I can give it here. I worry, though, that he has tied the values of reconstructionist Confucianism so closely to the practices of traditional Chinese society that he risks contemporary irrelevance. Furthermore, he is in danger of endorsing forms of discrimination that are increasingly rejected around the world and that have no deep justification in Confucian values (as Sin Yee Chan and others have shown; see Chan, 2000).

It is impossible to read very many pages of Fan's book without noting his strong endorsement of private property and capitalism. Part of the context, quite explicitly, is his critique of socialist China, but what makes his position unusual is that he tries to ground arguments against even modest welfare state policies in an alleged Confucian support for free-market capitalism. In pursuit of this ambitious goal, Fan makes some points that are well taken; certainly, the often-heard claim that Confucianism is flatly opposed to commercial activity and profit is mistaken. But in trying to read support for a modern, private-property economy back into the Confucian classics, he stretches the texts beyond recognition. For example, consider Mencius's famous statement that common people without *hengchan* – typically translated as constant livelihood – will not have *hengxin*, or constant heartminds. (In contrast, virtuous people will have constant heartminds even in straitened circumstances, a sentiment that is confirmed elsewhere in the text.) Fan proposes to read *hengchan* instead as "private property," which then allows him to conclude that Mencius believes that a publically owned economic system will lead to "more immoral or even tragic outcomes" (Fan, 2010: 65–66), since those without private property will stop at nothing. The problems with this reading, however, are numerous. Most basically, *heng* simply does not mean "private." Secondly, Fan acknowledges that even in Mencius's idealized "well-field" system, the land that commoners cultivated for themselves could not be bought or sold: it belonged to the ruler. Finally, reading *hengchan* as "private property" renders the reasoning of the rest of the passage and the meaning of *hengxin* otiose. I think that we must conclude that Fan has overreached himself. Free-market capitalism – and modern socialism or welfare state capitalism, for that matter – are simply too different from the socioeconomic arrangements considered in the ancient Confucian texts. It is quite plausible to say that some form of capitalism is *consistent* with the Confucian tradition, though many of the views we have already examined here argue that there is considerably more concern for a welfare state-like "safety net" than Fan is willing to acknowledge. In any event, Fan's stronger claim that Confucianism *requires* free-market capitalism is simply unconvincing.

Sor-hoon Tan's synthesis of Dewey and Confucius

The contemporary views we have examined so far all share a significant antiegalitarianism, but not all contemporary Confucian thinkers downplay the value of equality. A nice example of this comes in the work of Singaporean philosopher Sor-hoon Tan. In *Confucian Democracy: A Deweyan Reconstruction* (Tan, 2004) and in more recent essays, Tan has endeavored

> to offer East Asians who are increasingly open to diverse global cultural influences a way out of the false dilemma of having to choose between their Confucian heritage and a democratic way of life. Confucian democracy modernizes Confucianism with democratic values and modifies democracy with Confucian concerns. (Tan, 2009: 1)

Tan's approach depends on finding a version of democratic thinking that is both attractive and comparatively resonant with Confucian concerns, and also ensuring that the resulting dialogue between democracy and Confucianism is genuinely open and creative, rather than simply reading the values of one onto the other. She suggests that John Dewey's understanding of democracy, which is an ethical and social ideal constituted by values of community, equality, and liberty, serves much better as a partner with Confucianism than other, more institution-driven definitions of democracy. It is the constitutive role of equality in this picture that makes her work so interesting from the perspective of social justice.

Two things need to be clarified before going further. First, someone who does not find the ideal of democracy at least somewhat attractive will not be drawn into Tan's approach. To be sure, much of what she says about Confucianism could stand independently as an interpretation of the Confucian texts, but a key premise of her argument is that Confucianism is not sealed off from other value systems, nor does commitment to Confucianism seal one off from viewing and valuing things from other vantage points. Even in classical China, people were not confined to a single view, as the cross-pollinization among putatively "Daoist," "Confucian," "Mohist," and "Legalist" texts makes clear. To the extent that one sees the idea that "we Chinese are and must be only Confucians" in the background of the writings of Fan Ruiping or Jiang Qing, Tan challenges it on both factual and methodological grounds. Secondly, to say that equality is a constitutive value of democracy is not to say that democracy demands the kind of extreme egalitarianism that eliminates all inequalities. Tan writes, "The debate about equality as a value is over which inequalities are justifiable and which are to be ignored, avoided, or eliminated" (Tan, 2009: 13). Why is significant equality important to democracy? Tan says:

> without equality, members of a community could not participate meaningfully in governing themselves, and whatever negative liberty is permitted would be available in reality only to the rich and powerful. (Tan, 2009: 19)

Furthermore, since Deweyan democracy is committed to the moral growth of individuals and the flourishing of community, it is relevant that too much inequality would stifle such possibilities.

With these points in mind, we can now turn to Tan's specific arguments concerning equality. One important thread of her argument is summarizing the concerns with significantly unequal distribution that one can find in the classical Confucian corpus. Following Joseph Chan's analysis (on which see Chapter 5 this volume), she begins by noting the roles played by a principle of sufficiency (the masses must have sufficient means to provide for themselves and their families) and a principle of priority to the worst off (Tan, 2009: 16). She goes beyond Chan, though, to argue that at least according to one key *Analects* passage (6:4), need rather than merit is prioritized in the distribution of resources. Tan also finds evidence in other early Confucian sources that inequalities of virtue and merit are not supposed to be translated directly into equivalent inequalities of distribution. She adds:

> A person with the Confucian virtue of ren would certainly share what she has earned with her abilities and merits with those who are worse off than herself, even when they do not fall below "sufficiency" level, and spend it on various projects aimed at improving people's lives (and not just in material terms). This will lead to a more egalitarian social outcome than a straightforward meritocracy, or even one tempered only by the sufficiency principle and priority for the badly off. (Tan, 2009: 18)

In short, the classical sources offer various reasons to resist wide disparities between the haves and the have-nots.

The other side of Tan's argument is to critique rigid notions of meritocracy — both in theory and in Chinese practice – and to suggest an alternative understanding of the Confucian social ideal. She highlights some of the well-known problems with meritocracy. For example, it is difficult to see how examinations can be fair, given the often unjustified differences in resources and education that underlie candidates' preparations; similarly, rewarding those who are more capable will tend toward increasing inequality and the unfairness of the system, with respect to opportunities to improve for those individuals coming from families that have been less successful in the past. Tan emphasizes that these are not just marginal problems with the practice of meritocracy, but fundamental challenges to the very idea of meritocracy, since great material inequality would mean that even talented have-nots will fail to compete successfully with mediocre elites, thus leading meritocracy to defeat itself (Tan, 2009: 14). What can be done about this? Tan's answer is that the Confucian social ideal should not be understood as demanding a rigid social hierarchy. Rather,

> The social roles in ideal Confucian societies are unequal only to the extent required by functional differentiation. Inequalities are domain-specific and there can be no single roster presenting a totalistic ranking from superior to inferior . . . An individual's abilities and accomplishments vis-à-vis others also change as she goes through different stages of her life, during which she learns, catches up with and even overtakes others in her expertise, and in turn will one day be overtaken by others. The complex crisscrossing and overlaying of diverse and changing inequalities prevent a society from becoming stratified. (Tan, 2009: 16)

This notion of distinct and dynamic inequalities bears some comparison to Michael Walzer's idea of "complex equality," according to which inequalities in one realm are not unjust so long as they do not translate into inequalities in other realms (Walzer, 1983). Tan's claim, remember, is not that Confucians did or should endorse complete egalitarianism. Their valuing of equality can be seen in their rejection of some kinds or degrees of inequality. To the extent that Confucians value equality, they can readily embrace a Deweyan kind of social democracy, with its constitutive value of equality. We can also view this from the other direction: to the extent that one is committed to the development of democracy (which depends on a degree of equality), one has an incentive to develop Confucianism along the lines that Tan has emphasized.

Daniel Bell and "left Confucianism"

My final case in this section is what the Canadian political theorist Daniel Bell has started calling "left Confucianism." Bell says, "Left Confucianism attempts to combine the socialist with the Confucian tradition in a way that allows Confucianism to enrich and change socialism" (Bell, 2010: 93). We saw in the previous section considerable interest, earlier in the twentieth century, for the idea that Confucianism and socialism might be mutually supportive. In recent decades in the People's Republic of China, both academics and public intellectuals have discussed the possibility of reconciling socialism and Confucianism, though the reflections have tended to either be very abstract or somewhat superficial. It makes sense, then, to take Bell's suggestions seriously.

Before looking at their substance, though, it will first be helpful to clarify the nature of "left Confucianism." Bell himself seems a bit conflicted. In some places, he explicitly refers to it as an "interpretation" of Confucianism – an interpretation that was advocated both by historical Confucians (such as the seventeenth-century scholar Huang Zongxi; see Bell, 2008, xv) and by contemporary figures (here he references Jiang Qing). In other places, he says things like this:

> To the extent that Confucianism will be appropriate for the modern world, it needs to be reconciled with left-egalitarian values . . . The future lies in some sort of "left Confucianism" that combines Confucian and socialist values. (Bell, 2008: 178)

In this context, "Confucian leftism" might be at least as appropriate as "left Confucianism." Indeed, the key tenets that Bell puts forward are left-egalitarian ideas that have been inflected by Confucianism, rather than the other way around.

Bell lists six characteristics (not meant to be exhaustive) of left Confucianism, all of them "traditional socialist values" (Bell, 2010: 93). The ones most relevant to our concerns are "concern for the disadvantaged," "concern for basic material well-being," "solidarity with strangers," and "global justice." We have already seen that the first two of these have regularly been taken to be central to the Confucian conception of justice. Bell adds some significant observations. For example, he says that according to Confucians, "being disadvantaged is not just about lacking money. Equally serious is the absence of family members and friends" (Bell, 2010: 94). More importantly,

> Confucians are realists in the sense that they take for granted that power relationships and social hierarchies will exist in all large-scale societies. They worry less than Western liberals do about these relationships and hierarchies, particularly when they are based on age and achievement. If a choice must be made between social and economic equality, then Confucians would choose economic equality and make social inequality work to support it. (Bell, 2010: 95)

As was the case with Tan, when Bell speaks of economic equality, he is not referring to complete equality, but to the idea that inequalities must be moderate and justified. Similar to Jiang Qing, he holds that the Confucian idea of shared ritual is key to enabling social inequality to support (relative) economic equality:

> By participating in common rituals, those with more status develop feelings of care for the others and thus become more willing to do things in their economic interest. (Bell, 2010; see also Bell, 2008: Ch. 5).

"Solidarity with strangers" and "global justice" are central socialist values; many leftist movements have in fact insisted on very strong versions of these ideas. One contribution that Confucianism can make would be to moderate what might otherwise be an overly radical objective. For instance, Confucians do not aim at a universal solidarity in which everyone is treated equally, but rather a "graded love" in which strangers are treated well, but not with the degree of love shared among family members. Confucian attention on the family informs global justice, too: Bell says that left Confucians would insist that the interests of ancestors and descendants be considered, rather than narrowly focusing on the interests of the current generation. This could potentially have benefits for complex issues like climate change and historical preservation (Bell, 2010: 96–97). Of course, there are real questions about how either of these ideas is to be implemented; one of the persistent complaints about Confucianism in the twentieth century is that it does a poor job of adequately motivating solidarity with and concern for strangers. Some have charged that Confucianism is directly responsible for contemporary China's ongoing struggle with corruption, though exponents of Confucianism reply that only a superficial or perverted form of Confucianism could be employed to justify corruption (e.g., Guo, 2007; Liu, 2007). In any event, and no matter whether we think of Bell's topic as left Confucianism or Confucian leftism, it seems clear that the project of bringing Confucianism and socialism into dialogue has the potential to bear significant fruit.

Conclusion

The figures we have just canvassed do not exhaust Confucian-inspired thinking about social justice in the contemporary world. Another important thinker is Joseph Chan, author of Chapter 5 in this volume, who has begun to limn his own contemporary Confucian views of social justice in recent essays (Chan, 2003, 2008). Still, the theories we have examined here provide the general outlines of contemporary Confucian thinking about social justice. The central trope is harmony: differences among individuals are accepted (and even embraced), so long as these differences contribute to both individual and social flourishing, and as long as the differences are not too great. Confucian social justice thus can coexist with different sorts of hierarchies, so long as the hierarchies are open, flexible, and dynamic.

Why is it important that any social inequalities have this limited character? Tan puts a stress on the constitutive role of equality in democracy, but even though this is correct, it is not a *Confucian* reason, and thus one might wonder whether Confucians really are obligated to limit inequality in the way just described. An alternative argument would stress the fundamental Confucian commitment to each individual's moral transformation. Each person can, in principle, become a sage; all of us should strive to better ourselves. Excessive inequalities – whether social, political, or economic – would stand in the way of individual moral improvement. This is not to say that the downtrodden can never reach great moral heights, but it is certainly the case that systematic oppression limits opportunities for moral growth (arguably, for the oppressors as well as for the oppressed) (Tessman, 2005). Confucianism must therefore oppose oppression.

Historically, Confucianism has tended to stress individual moral education and be less attuned to systematic problems. We see this also in several of the authors just discussed: Jiang Qing, for example, seems to think of moral education as the main contribution of Confucianism to avoiding alienation and market failures. Confucians need to step back from the particular and notice – and then attend to – challenges to the realization of their ideals that are rooted in broad social, economic, and political institutions. This critical attitude must encompass the "ritual" realm. Most Confucians correctly see the recognition of ritual's importance as one of the great insight of the tradition, but ritual is also vulnerable to rigidity and oppression. Only by embracing an activist, social-critical role can Confucians today adequately justify their stance on social justice – both to themselves as Confucians and to whatever other dialogue partners they engage with in our dynamic, pluralistic social world.

References

Alitto, Guy S. (1979) *The Last Confucian: Liang Shu-ming and the Chinese Dilemma of Modernity*, University of California Press, Berkeley.

Angle, Stephen C. (2009) *Sagehood: The Contemporary Significance of Neo-Confucian Philosophy*, Oxford University Press, New York.

Bell, Daniel A. (2008) *China's New Confucianism: Politics and Everyday Life in a Changing Society*, Princeton University Press, Princeton.

Bell, Daniel A. (2010) Reconciling socialism and Confucianism? Reviving tradition in China, *Dissent*, Winter: 91–102.

Berger, Peter (1988) An east Asian development model? in *In Search of an East Asian Development Model*, Peter Berger and Hsin-huang Michael Hsiao (eds.), Transaction Books, New Brunswick, NJ, pp. 3–11.

Bergère, Marie-Claire (1998) *Sun Yat-sen*, Janet Lloyd (trans.), Stanford University Press, Stanford.

Chan, Joseph (2003) Giving priority to the worst off: A Confucian perspective on social welfare, in *Confucianism for the Modern World*, Daniel Bell and Chaibong Hahm (eds.), Cambridge University Press, Cambridge, pp. 236–253.

Chan, Joseph (2008) Is there a Confucian perspective on social justice? in *Western Political Thought in Dialogue with Asia*, Takashi Shogimen and Cary J. Nederman (eds.), Rowman and Littlefield, Lanham, MD, pp. 261–277.

Chan, Sin Yee (2000) Gender relationship roles in the *Analects* and the *Mencius*, *Asian Philosophy* 10(2): 115–132.

Dirlik, Arif (1995) Confucius in the borderlands: Global capitalism and the reinvention of Confucianism, *Boundary* 2(22): 229–273.

Fan, Ruiping (2010) *Reconstructionist Confucianism: Rethinking Morality after the West*, Springer, Dordrecht.

Fung, Edmund S.K. (2005) State building, capitalist development, and social justice: Social democracy in China's modern transformation, 1921–1949, *Modern China* 31(3): 318–352.

Guo, Qiyong (2007) Is Confucian ethics a "consanguinism"? *Dao: A Journal of Comparative Philosophy* 6(1): 21–37.

Hsiao, Kung-chuan (1975) *A Modern China and a New World*, University of Washington Press, Seattle.

Jiang, Qing (2003) *Zhengzhi Ruxue: Dangdai Ruxue de zhuanxiang, tezhi, yu fazhan* [Political Confucianism: The Changing Direction, Particularities, and Development of Contemporary Confucianism], Harvard-Yenching Academic Series, Sanlian Shudian, Beijing.

Jiang, Qing (2010) Zhengzhi Ruxue Xubian – Wangdao zhengzhi yu Rujia xianzheng: Weilai zhongguo zhengzhi fazhan de Ruxue sikao [A Sequel to Political Confucianism – Kingly Politics and Confucian Constitutionalism: Confucian Reflections on the Future Development of Chinese Politics], unpublished.

Kang, Xiaoguang (2005) *Renzheng: Zhongguo zhengzhi fazhan de disantiao daolu* [Humane Government: A Third Road for the Development of Chinese Politics], Global Publishing Co., Singapore.

Liu, Qingping (2007) Confucianism and corruption: An analysis of Shun's Two Actions described by Mencius, *Dao: A Journal of Comparative Philosophy* 6(1): 1–19.

Mou, Zongsan (1983) *Zhongguo Zhexue Shijiujiang* [Nineteen Lectures on Chinese Philosophy], Xuesheng Shuju, Taibei.

Sun, Yat-sen (1928) *San Min Chu I: The Three Principles of the People*, Frank W. Price (trans.), Commercial Press, Shanghai.

Tan, Soor-hoon (2004) *Confucian Democracy: A Deweyan Reconstruction*, SUNY Press, Albany, NY.

Tan, Soor-hoon (2009) Why Confucian Democracy?, unpublished.

Tessman, Lisa (2005) *Burdened Virtues: Virtue Ethics for Liberatory Struggles*, Oxford University Press, Oxford.

Thompson, Laurence G. (1958) *Ta T'ung-shu: The One-World Philosophy of K'ang Yu-wei*, George Allen and Unwin, London.

Walzer, Michael (1983) *Spheres of Justice: A Defense of Pluralism and Equality*, Basic Books, New York.

CHAPTER 7
Hinduism
Historical Setting

O.P. Dwivedi

This essay discusses the Hindu approach to social justice, giving special attention to Hinduism's caste system. The story of the caste system is controversial, complex, and at times contradictory. Ancient sources suggest that it was originally established as a means to advance societal and individual well-being by arranging divisions of labor appropriate to the skills and aptitudes of the people. The caste system has historically played a role in sustaining Hindu culture and intellectual tradition, especially when the society suffered the onslaught of foreign elements. So arguably, the caste system has, in part, served a positive cultural role.

However, it is inarguable that for centuries the caste system has also needlessly perpetuated social discrimination and class oppression. In this respect its impact on Hindu culture has clearly been far from favorable. In response, individuals, organizations, and movements have sought at various times to reform the caste system. This essay will explore both the beneficial and disruptive aspects of the Hindu caste system, as well as the people, organizations, and movements that have attempted to reform it.

Defining Caste: *Varna* and *Jati*

The word "caste" originated from the Latin *casta* for a rank, group, breed, race, or kind. When the Portuguese came to India in the fifteenth century, they applied the term *casta* indiscriminately to various social and vocational groups that existed in western India. The term stuck, as the British rulers used it to denote entire social structures within Hindu culture.

More recently, David and Julia Jary (2000) have defined caste as a form of social stratification involving a system of hierarchical and closed endogamous layers, to which eligibility is ascribed, and within which social contact and mobility are restricted. H.H. Risley (1915: 67) defines caste as

> a collection of families or groups of families bearing a common name, claiming common descent from a mythical ancestor, human or divine, following the same hereditary calling, and regarded as forming a homogeneous community.

Generalizing, then, a caste is an endogamous and hereditary subdivision of a society that creates and maintains a hierarchical social stratum.

We must think more contextually to really understand caste as it appears in Hindu culture. Instead of "caste," the two specific terms used in the Hindu social and religious lexicon are *Varna* and *Jati*.

Ancient Indian society was founded on the classification of the entire society into four occupational *Varnas* (castes), and the division of the life of each individual into four *Ashramas* (stages).[1] *Varna* appears as a concept during the Vedic period[2] (2500–1000 BCE) and is mentioned in Hindu scriptures such as the *Dharmashastras* (legal codes compiled about 600–300 BCE). For example, in *Purush-sukta* of *Rig Veda*, the hymn says that all the four *Varnas* sprang respectively from the mouth, arms, thighs, and feet of the Supreme Being, and as such the division of society into four classes is to be considered as natural and God ordained (Devi, 1999: 37). *Varna* ("division") denotes the classification of Hindu society, based on occupation, into four groups.[3] It also implies a system of social stratification and specifies that different groups of people have different social rankings. During the Vedic and Upanishadic period, *Varna* was not based entirely on heredity, which was thought to be dependent on the consequences of one's *Karma*. The *Chandogya Upanishad* (Book V, Ch. X: 7), the *locus classicus* regarding the Hindu caste system, states:

> Those who have led a life of good conduct, will be born as a *Brahman*, a *Kshatriya*, or a *Vaishya*, but those who have led a life of evil deeds, will be born as others (including *Chandala*, an outcaste) or be born in an animal-life.

The system of *Varna* was intended to allow Hindus to excel in their professions according to their natural capabilities and tendencies. People were divided into the following groups:

1 *Brahmans* (Brahmins, in the anglicized version): educators, trainers, priests, theologians, philosophers.
2 *Kshatriyas*: rulers, defenders from enemy attacks, military, administrators.
3 *Vaishyas*: producers of wealth and prosperity, businessmen, traders, professionals.
4 *Shudras*: artisans, service providers, and laborers.

This meticulous division of people according to their occupation enabled every occupational element of society to contribute and thus to demonstrate their indispensability and interdependence with one another. Each group depended on the others for its well-being and for the sustenance of the society. The *Bhagavad Gita* (4: 13 and 18: 41) explains that the four *Varnas* were created in keeping with the distribution of *Guna* (attributes) and *Karma* (actions/deeds), and that each person – simply by performing his or her caste-related profession and thus serving the society – could thereby achieve *moksha* (soteriological liberation; ultimate release from earthly bondage; 18: 44–45). The *Varnas* incorporated the fourfold functional and hierarchical divisions of the social fabric of Hindu society (*Gita*, 4: 5), including the various subcastes of the four main *Varnas*.[4] No caste exists in isolation, because it is relevant only in the context of the complementary caste components of society as a whole.

How did the system of the *Ashramas* and *Varnas* work in practice? The *Kshatriyas*, advised and supported by the priests (*Brahmans*), exercised ruling authority. The *Vaishyas* and *Shudras* were exempt from any military service, although they provided material and resources to the *Kshatriyas* who protected the society. Since the *Brahmans* were the instructors of governance and military training, they were often appointed as commanders of the army.[5] While the upper two castes worked together to govern the land, the *Vaishyas* (merchants and traders) provided the needed financial and material support. Thus, these three castes dominated the power structure of the Hindu society for centuries.

At the village level, priests charged fees for officiating at religious functions, rituals, and worship. *Kshatriyas*, being the rulers and landlords, maintained order, while the *Vaishyas* controlled business and the trades, and the *Shudras* provided support services to all as barbers, blacksmiths, water drawers, potters, skinners, and midwives. Laborers received money or a portion of the harvested crop. Thus everyone, from *Brahmans* to *Shudras*, was offered interdependent support within the village or village clusters.

Later, *Jati* (a social category, based on four *Varnas*, composed of subcastes in which each *Jati* maintains restrictions for taking food together with other *Jati* people and entering into inter-*Jati* marriage), came into use to identify traditional occupational subgroups within the *Varnas* (Kinsley, 1993). The term *Jati* appears to have been fully used during the British period, particularly from 1769 when the Governor of Bengal issued instructions to his British revenue-collection officers not to interrupt the indulgence and privileges of each caste (Devi, 1999: 122); however, it was after 1871 that the first country-wide census undertaken revealed the caste-based demographic data. Once a person was born in one *Jati*, a change to another *Jati* was not possible. For example, a person born as a *Brahman* remained a *Brahman* throughout his life and was expected to carry out the priestly profession as prescribed in religious books; the same was true for all other *Jatis*. *Varna* was further divided into two categories: *Savarna* and *Avarna*. *Savarna* consisted of four major castes (including *Shudras*), while *Avarna* included conquered people, servants, and *Yavans* (non-Aryan invaders from the west, including Greeks, Persians, and others). Thus, in the beginning, *Shudras* were counted as *Savarna*, although later this classification was limited to the upper three castes. Others, called *Ati-shudras* (lower than Shudras), were deemed less civilized than *Shudras* and were grouped as untouchables, living at the periphery of the village or in a secluded hamlet.

These divisions, over time, were gradually institutionalized, resulting in people being confined inextricably to specific professions at birth – effectively destroying the previous flexibility by which individuals were free to choose their own line of work. With this shift, Hindu society's degradation, fragmentation, and disintegration began.

Early Egalitarianism in the Caste System

During the Vedic period, Hindus were taught that the main purpose of life on earth was to live not just for themselves but also for others. This orientation was called *Vasudhaivkutumbakam* (treating all living beings on earth as a part of their extended family or household). Each person was encouraged to contribute to society by choosing a vocation consistent with the specific inclinations and abilities that one possessed.[6] The choice of a vocation determined one's duties and material rewards, which were to be used to take care of one's family needs. The key legal text, *The Book of Manu* (Book 7, verse 35), dictates that the position of the king was created by God to protect the *Varnas* and *Ashramas*. No room was left for overlapping responsibilities, meaning that caste/*Jati* divisions became closed groups, with each caste managing its own affairs (Venkatesananda, 1992: 195). People were known for their expertise. A single family might have members in all four *Varnas*. Society permitted individuals to choose their work and occupation freely, without any attendant social restriction, stigma, or taboo.

Various safeguards were put in place to avoid rigid social stratification in ancient India. For example, the *Yagyavalkya Smriti* (*Acharadhyaya*,Ch. IV: 91–95), stipulated that intermarriages could take place between individuals from the four *Varnas*. Moreover, this *Smriti* states that when it comes to giving a place of honor to someone in an assembly, the following sequence ought to be respected: a scholar, a ruler, an elderly person, a relative, and a wealthy person. However, if a *Shudra* has one of these attributes, he is entitled to receive the same honor as his counterpart in a higher caste (*Acharadhyaya*, Ch. IV: 116).

Moreover, *Shudras* were not confined to a life of servitude. The same *Smriti* (verse 120) says that if a *Shudra* is unable to take care of his family due to the nonavailability of caste-related work, he can learn and perform one of the professions meant for *Vaishyas*.

Even more striking, the *Mahabharata* (Shanti Parva, Ch. 189: verses 4, 8) says that "Brahmanhood" is not to be recognized based only on birth in a *Brahman* family. If attributes such as truthfulness, generosity, humility, and freedom from hatred and wickedness are found in an individual, then he also ought to be treated as a *Brahman*. A virtuous *Shudra* should receive the same respect as a *Brahman*.

Later Changes in the Caste System

As Hindu society became larger, and the production and distribution of goods and services became more complex, vocation guilds appeared to enhance efficiency and to protect rights. This shift, in essence, brought about the advent of hereditary castes, which were further entrenched as a result of the tendency jealously to keep secret the oral traditions of caste-related trade skills. The appearance of strong caste guilds led to the emergence of various internal elites, and eventually of upper castes, which used their power to consolidate governance for following generations.

Over time, this caste elitism began to destroy the cohesive fabric of Hindu society (Pandey, 1972: 74). The *Shudras* (referred to as Scheduled Caste in the Indian constitution) were discriminated against, exploited, and humiliated, and as a result they became financially and socially handicapped.

In addition to the four major castes, another group, comprising the tribes of various forest and hill peoples, collectively nicknamed *Achhoot* (untouchables), came into being. In the past, they were relegated to the lowest social status, faced the worst socioeconomic conditions, and were treated with apathy by those who belonged to any of the other castes. Mahatma Gandhi called them *Harijans* (children of God) and spoke vigorously against the victimization of these downtrodden people (Sharma, 1999: 47).

The problems outlined above clearly raise social justice issues that beg to be addressed. This, too, is a question that must be considered contextually. We thus turn to the question: How is social justice understood within the Hindu cultural milieu?

Defining Key Hindu Concepts Related to Social Justice

According to David Miller (1999), social justice cannot be defined as a set of principles that apply universally in all situations and contexts, nor can it be measured along a single metric such as human welfare or individual liberty. Thus, one should be cautious about applying non-Hindu standards of social justice to a Hindu cultural setting. While the equivalent to the western term "social justice" did not exist in historical India, the current term *Sarvodaya* (Sanskrit for "awakening of all") refers to the goal of effecting changes in the social-political and economic structure to create social responsibility and equity.

Moving further back in the history of the culture, however, the following five justice-related terms from Hindu religious scripture set the stage for understanding the Hindu framework for thinking about social justice: *Dharma, Niti, Nyaya, Karma,* and *Punarjanma*.

Dharma is one of the most important and untranslatable terms in the Hindu, Buddhist, and Jain religious vocabulary. Coming from the Sanskrit root word *Dhar* (sustain), *Dharma* has been interpreted variously as a religious code of behavior, a divine system of morality and righteousness, and conformation to one's cosmically allotted duty and nature (Radhakrishnan, 1968). It is a comprehensive term, incorporating benevolence to humanity, moral restraint (*yama*), and observance of duty or obligation (*niyama*). *Yama* requires the active avoidance of violence (*ahimsa*), dishonesty, falsehood, jealousy, avarice, and other vices. *Niyama* includes purification of the body and soul, contentment, study of sacred books, religious worship and activity, and performance of family and social responsibilities. *Dharma* also denotes the sustaining of the principles of social harmony through the preservation, progress, and welfare of humanity.

As explained in the *Mahabharata*: "*Dharma* exists for the welfare (*Abhyudaya*) of all living beings; hence, that which sustains the welfare of all living beings is unquestionably *Dharma*" (*Mahabharata*, Shanti Parva, Ch. 109: verse 10).

Dharma can thus be considered as an ethos that holds the social and moral fabric together by building individual and group character, and giving rise to harmony and understanding in our relationships with one another.

More specifically in terms of social justice, *Dharma* ought to be interpreted in terms of *Niti* and *Nyaya*. *Niti* indicates "justice" in Sanskrit in terms of organizational propriety and correct behavior. *Nyaya* refers more to a comprehensive concept of "realized justice." Thus, *Niti* requires one to perform one's duty unconditionally, while *Nyaya* considers the consequences of one's actions before and after decision making.

We see the tension between *Niti* and *Nyaya* in the debate between duty-based and rule-bound reasoning and humanistic, consequence-sensitive reasoning that is played out in the dialogue between the warrior Arjuna and the avatar Krishna in the *Bhagavad Gita*. Here the tension is resolved Brahmanically in the direction of maintaining rigidity of the caste system: *Niti* and Krishna's insistence that one must do one's duty to one's caste holds sway. This predilection of deontology (duty-based ethics) over consequentialism is typical of Hindu thought; the Hindu scriptures lean more on *Niti* than on *Nyaya* in defining social justice.

Any understanding of *Dharma*, *Niti*, and *Nyaya* remains incomplete, however, apart from linkage with the concepts of *Karma* and *Punarjanma* (rebirth). The term *Karma* comes from the root *kri*, which means "to do," and thus has a general connotation of "action." In its broadest sense, it applies also to the effects of actions. Each act, willfully performed, leaves a consequence in its wake. These consequences, also called *Karma-Phala* (fruits or effects of action), always remain with us, even though their impact may not be felt immediately. Moreover, every action creates its own chain of reactions and events, some of which are immediately evident, while others manifest only later – perhaps in a subsequent incarnation. *Dharmic* (righteous) actions generate beneficial results, while *Adharmic* (unethical) actions create harmful effects. One of the implications of the truth of *Karma* is that one should be prepared to face and overcome the karmic obstacles that arise as a result of one's actions in both the present life and future lives.

The pairing of the doctrines of rebirth (*Punarjanma*) and *Karma* provides the Hindu theological explanation of the origin and nature of human sufferings such as disease, untimely death, poverty, and caste inequality. Hindu theologians use these doctrines to justify the birth of persons in lower castes. According to this view, members of a lower caste committed some negative karmic act in a previous life, resulting in their present low status in society. Slowly, the concept had the effect of justifying the miserable conditions of many persons in Hindu society. For example, *Manusmriti* (Book 12:verse 9) says that the consequence of a sinful action is a low-caste birth in the next life. In this way, the concepts of *Karma* and *Punarjanma* became ideological mechanisms justifying social disparity (Upadhyay, 1978: 173). Using the *Karma*–rebirth doctrines, Hindu theodicy seems to legitimize the continuing existence of the class structure of the social oppressor and socially oppressed.[7]

It must be noted, however, that Hindu religious experience, doctrine, and practice also reflect a counter-interpretation to the aforementioned Hindu theodicy. The rituals and dramas of *Ram Lila* (a drama depicting Lord Ram's life) and *Raas Lila* (a drama relating to Lord Krishna's life in Vrindavan and Mathura) disclose a different Hindu approach to social justice. The ubiquitous *Ramayana*, one of the two greatest epics of the Hindu religious literature, was written by Valmiki (a *Shudra*) in Sanskrit, and thus was not initially accessible to the common people. When Tulsidas rendered it into a local dialect, it was enacted in villages as a drama that went on for weeks.

Shri Ramcharitmanas contains a story about Shabari, an untouchable woman who was a devotee of Lord Rama (the seventh God-incarnation). When Shabari discovered that her Lord was passing by, she invited him – along with his wife Sita and his brother Lakshman – into her hut, and fed him by her own hand. Shabari said, "I am the lowest of the low in the community, and even then you graced my place." In reply Lord Rama said, "I recognize no caste or kinship other than that of devotion. For me, caste, kinship, lineage, piety, reputation, fame, wealth, strength, family, achievements, and education are meaningless if a person lacks devotion to the Lord" (*Shri Ramcharitmanas*, book 3, Doha 35, verses 1–4). Whenever this drama was performed, persons belonging to the lower castes felt edified, and drew on it to find courage to ask for due compensation from upper-caste employers.

Raas Lila, which was initially performed in Mathura and Vrindavan, speaks of the various acts of Lord Krishna (the eighth God-incarnation). This drama has Lord Krishna (who was born in the *Yadava* clan, not one of the upper three castes) being worshiped by people of all castes. In another story from the *Mahabharata*, Lord Krishna declines a dinner invitation from the royal house of Kauravas, while he accepts an invitation to eat with Vidur (a son who was born to a low-caste woman).

These examples illustrate the catholicity of the Hindu religion and show that despite the rigidity of its social mores, the religion accorded proper recognition to individual merits and virtues, irrespective of a person's birth caste.

Hindu Law: The *Smrities*

In ancient India, Hindus were governed by a set of laws, which came through *smrities* (recollected wisdom) such as *Manusmriti* and *Dharmashastras* and laid down criminal and civil procedures based on the notions of *Nyaya* and *Niti*. The concept of law in that period was different from that of modernity. Besides various laws governing criminal, civil, and family-related cases, which were heard by the king, each caste or community had its own codes of conduct, although provisions were in place for an appeal to the royal court in certain cases. The king personally administered justice, but he was advised by the court-appointed priest, called *Raj-purohit* (royal priest), or by a group of learned *Brahmans*. Due regard was also paid to caste and family customs. In cases where a person who was to be punished lived far away from the capital, the king would appoint an officer to administer a reprieve or punitive justice.

Problematically, from a modern perspective, the *Dharmashastras* prescribed different punishments for different castes for the same offense. Harsher punishment was reserved for *Shudras*. For example, in Kautilya's *Arthshastra* (Book IV, Ch. 13: 236), written around 321 BCE, if a *Shudra* committed adultery with a *Brahman* woman he was to be burnt, while a *Kshatriya* was to be fined heavily and the *Vaishya* was to be deprived of his property. On the other hand, if a man committed adultery with a lower-caste woman, he was to be banished from the kingdom or demoted to the caste of the woman.

A shift in this level of inequity occurred with the advent of the *Panchayat* system, the provision of justice by an assembly of five notable elders from the same community who settle disputes according to a caste-approved code of conduct. Most caste-related cases were settled by the caste *Panchayat*. *Panchayats* provided oversight and ensured the betterment of a caste, punished social transgressors, and prevented interference from other castes. The most severe punishment was excommunication from the community. When inter-subcaste disputes arose within a caste, a joint *Panchayat* was called to find a mutually agreeable solution. If there was a dispute between a lower and a higher caste, the case was sent to the court of a king for final settlement. However, with the arrival of the British, such dispute settlements were abandoned.

Social Justice and Early Reform Movements

With the passage of time and changes in society, it was natural that there were several attempts to reform the Hindu caste system. The first major attempt was by Lord Krishna, who during the *Mahabharata* made the following pronouncement: "The fourfold *Varnas* have been created based on the differences in individuals' abilities and functions" (*Gita*: 4: 13). However, Krishna explains later that despite being born in any *Varna*, a person devoted to his prescribed *Karma* can achieve salvation (18: 45).

Still, caste rigidity persisted. Around the sixth century BCE, anti-Vedic religious movements such as Buddhism and Jainism began to challenge the Brahmanical ascendancy. Heretics, who believed "neither in the Vedic gods nor in the Vedic *dharma* as regulated by the system of castes and orders of life," started appearing (Hazra, 1962: 248). For these reformers, little importance was given to prevailing Brahmanical rules and the value of scriptures. These reforms were buoyed by an influx of casteless foreigners such as Greeks, Shakas, Pahlavas, and Kushans, with their non-Brahmanical customs and manners.

Buddhism and Jainism arose in part due to the excessive control of the society by upper castes, with their severe rituals and customs. Moreover, the ritualistic and magical power of *Brahmans* was shaken by the presence of invaders, who seemed unaffected by their power. The spiritual masters of these new religions – Mahavir Jain and Gautama Buddha – rejected the validity of caste. They set the goal of religion as spiritual liberation, and caste was merely an obstacle to this goal. Buddha propagated the doctrine of the equality of all – including gender equality. Beginning with the reign of Emperor Ashoka (274–232 BCE), Buddhism spread across India and weakened the power of caste.

However, by the seventh century CE Buddhism was in decline, and a Hindu monk, Shankaracharya from South India, reestablished the Vedic hegemony and Hindu religious practices (including the caste structure) all over India. Thereafter, various reform efforts were made by saints of the *Bhakti* (devotion) movement, including Ramanuja, Madhava, Ramananda, Kabir, Ravidas, Nanak, Tukaram, Sri Chaitanya, Namdev, and

Dadu. They raised their powerful voices against injustice and condemned caste distortions in unequivocal terms (Chopra, 1962: 637). These spiritual leaders opposed the monopoly of *Brahmans* in religious matters, and encouraged the people to abandon caste exclusiveness, to elevate the status of women, to downgrade the oppressive rites and rituals, and to limit the excesses of polytheism. Nevertheless, *Brahmans* jealous of their status and other castes of their crafts (such as *Kshatriyas* for their martial arts), prevailed in stifling attempts at reformation. Neither Buddhism, Jainism, nor the efforts of various reformers during the middle ages could shake the strength and solidarity of the caste groupings.

Social Justice and Modern Reform Movements

With the advent of British rule, and particularly after the promulgation of uniform codes of legal procedures (such as the Civil Procedure Code of 1859, the Indian Penal Code of 1860, and the Code of Criminal Procedure of 1861), educated Hindus launched various reforms, including the Arya Samaj and Brahmo Samaj movements of the nineteenth century, which advocated a complete overhaul of the socio-religious framework of Hindu society. Gandhi's momentous influence in the twentieth century continued this trajectory.

Arya Samaj was founded in 1875 by Swami Dayananda, who came from a Gujarati orthodox Hindu *Brahman* family. He espoused a "protestant" Hinduism that emphasized monotheism and the *Vedas*, and opposed the caste system and Brahmanical orthodoxy (Talbot, 2000: 35). His major contentions were that the hereditary caste system among Hindus was evil and that it had no justification according to Vedic scriptures. In his view, the *Varna*, as taught in the *Vedas*, was the fourfold division of society based on the physical and mental capabilities of individuals. He also regarded women as equal to men and held that the practice of categorizing people as untouchable was not only un-Vedic but also sinful.

Arya Samaj opened up its temples to all castes and religions, invested the so-called untouchables with the sacred thread (thus declaring them to be equal with other caste members), and rejected the religious need for a Brahmanic priest, thus removing any intermediary between the individual and God. The Samaj also argued for widow remarriage, and advocated a policy of education for all, but especially for women. The Arya Samaj movement infused Hindus with new faith and dynamism as they began to take renewed pride in their religion. However, the movement's influence remained concentrated in north and northwest India.

The Brahmo Samaj was created in 1828 through the efforts of celebrated social reformer Raja Ram Mohan Roy. The Brahmo Samaj opposed *sati* (the immolation of Hindu widows on their husbands' funeral pyres), the practice of polygamy among some wealthy Hindus, idol worship, and the degradation of widows. Roy argued that these customs did not originate, and were not sanctioned, in the Vedic scriptures. Despite hostility from orthodox Hindus, Roy and his associates succeeded in 1829 in getting Lord William Bentinck, the Governor-General of India, to pass a regulation that criminalized *sati*. Brahmo Samaj was also eventually instrumental in granting widows the right to remarry, and curbing polygamy, which was abolished through the Hindu Code Bill in 1954.

When Mahatma Gandhi was invited to study the status of untouchables in Madras Province in 1925, he found the situation most abhorrent, and declared the treatment of untouchables to be a great blot on Hinduism. He called untouchables *Harijans* (children of God) and declared that there would be no independence in India so long as the curse of untouchability continued to stain Hinduism (Wolpert, 2000: 310).

At that time, Dr. B.R. Ambedkar, the leader of the untouchables in India, joined the Gandhian movement and declared with Gandhi

> that henceforth, amongst Hindus, no one shall be regarded as an untouchable by reason of his birth, and those who have been so regarded hitherto, will have the same rights as other Hindus in regard to the use of public wells, public schools, public roads and other public institutions. (Wolpert, 2000: 320)

Other political leaders supported this change. Thus, when India received its independence from the British, constitutional guarantees of equality and certain special privileges were established for all of the depressed classes (identified in the constitution as Scheduled Castes), as well as for other oppressed classes.

The reform movements discussed here had some initial success in changing Hindu society, but it was only when India gained its independence that the framers of the constitution seized the opportunity to include specific legal provisions to remove untouchability and make discrimination punishable by a jail term. With acceptance of social justice and civil liberty as fundamental principles of state policy, the Indian constitution assisted the *Shudras* and other oppressed classes to claim equal status politically and socially. Of course, their numerical strength also helped them in the democratic process, as Indian political parties catered to this group for votes.

The Social Status of Castes Today

Social inequality is not unique to Hindus, but the key difference is the form in which it has become rigidly institutionalized in the vastness and complexity of Hindu culture. If the caste system is not seen from a racial perspective, but rather is viewed as being occupational in nature (as various western Indologists have argued; see Morton Klass, 1980, and Heinrich von Stietencron, 1991), then the "discrimination based on functional differences are more easily eliminated than if based on racial differences" (Sharma, 1999: 72).

Race and caste discrimination was declared illegal after India gained independence from the British in 1947. For the past six decades *dalits* (*Shudras*) and other oppressed classes have received special privileges to better their social, economic, and political status in the country. Still, in the villages caste discrimination continues to exist. The centuries-old custom of castes takes time to eradicate. Independent India has tried to overcome this injustice. This is evident not only in institutional and legal systems, but also in the prevailing social interaction among all castes of Hindus – although, admittedly, more so among the Indian diaspora than in the nation itself.

Until a few decades ago, the caste system restricted people of different castes from eating together, socializing, and marrying. Restrictions on intermingling (e.g., giving and accepting food or drink) and on marriages were imposed not only between major castes but even among subcastes. For example, until the late 1960s, Kanyakubja and Saryuparin *Brahmans* would not allow their children to marry or even share meals. The reason set forth for such restrictions was to maintain the purity of each subcaste. Castes members were also not allowed to choose, or to change their occupation.

When the British came and introduced legal reform, many *Brahmans*, tempted to work for new masters rather than for Muslim rulers, discarded their caste restrictions and entered British Raj employment. This practice marked the beginning of a slow decline of caste dominance in Hindu society. But it was not until the independence of India in 1947 that the most significant reforms took place, and casteism declined rapidly, especially in cities and urban centers. Soon, practices such as not allowing themselves to be touched by members of lower castes and not eating in close proximity to members of other castes while traveling became a thing of the past.

By the 1980s, political realities further weakened the hold of the caste system as lower castes attempted to liberate themselves from the domination of the upper castes. Being in the numerical majority in most geographical areas of India, the disempowered castes used the power of the electorate to better their social and economic position. They secured their share in government employment, and were appointed to senior policy positions through job quotas. They also gained admission to educational and professional institutions. This trend indicates that in a few years' time, the hold of the caste system in India will be on the way out, and in its place an economic class system akin to the western world will emerge – one in accord with the ethos of globalization and human rights.

Conclusion

Hindus in ancient India made a supreme effort to understand the fundamental meaning and purpose of life through contemplation and meditation, and realized that life was a kind of pilgrimage in search of the infinite and eternal supreme. They divided individuals in a society according to aptitudes and attributes, so that each unit could attend to its own duty for the well-being of the whole social organism, and they divided the life span into four stages, so that the individual could harmoniously pursue the goal of spiritual realization. The very fact that Hindu society, with spiritual freedom as its goal, endured for thousands of years, notwithstanding the incursions of cultures and religions different from its own, is a testimony to the essential validity of its principles (Chakladar, 1962: 579).

It should be noted that much of the wondrous diversity of Indian life is due in part to the caste system, despite a thousand years of invasion and centuries of foreign rule (Bhaskarananda, 1994: 27). Among Hindus, the *Brahmans*, as the "custodians of culture," have used their influence to keep the *Varna* functioning properly. For that they enlisted the support of the *Kshatriyas* and *Vaishyas*, as well as the legislative power of the state to suppress revolt and to subdue non-Vedic corruptions of *Varna* system. These measures created a composite faith, brought social stability, and thus preserved the *Dharma* as practiced in earlier times, and protected the culture from complete annihilation, unlike what happened in Egypt, Persia, Indonesia, and other places, whose ancient civilizations were completely destroyed. However, these acts of preservation also resulted in a degenerative system of oppression toward, and control over, the lower castes.

Admittedly, whether due to a weakness inherent in its ideal or owing to centuries of external aggressive cultural onslaught, Hindu culture eventually created a protective layer via the caste system. This reaction resulted in the creation of sometimes oppressive conservatism, sanctions, caste conventions, and prohibitions. Only with the emergence of democratic governance and the establishment of an appropriate institutional design following India's independence in 1947 were many of the defective and harmful conventions and caste restrictions legally abolished. However, the sheer politics of voter strength had already given the lower castes the ability to undo the injustices of the past.

Ultimately, the success of democracy in India will not depend merely on having the most appropriate institutional structures. It will depend also on behavioral patterns and "the working of political and social interactions" (Sen, 2009: 354). The pursuit of justice demands that society not only ask how things have happened, or are happening, but how they can be improved. This is precisely the challenge facing Hindu society and its religion in the twenty-first century.

Notes

1 The concept of the four *Ashramas* ("stages") had as its focus the *Dharmic* stages of development of the individual human life span: (1) *Brahmacharya*: student life (up to age 25) devoted to general studies and trained to enter the respective profession of the student's family; (2) *Grahastha*: householder stage (between the ages of 25 and 50), during which one earns a living, provides for the family, excels professionally, and brings wealth and prosperity to family and nation; (3) *Vanprastha*: the stage (50–75 years of age), when the individual (or both the wife and husband together) begins to retire from active professional life and devote time to the welfare of society in general; and (4) *Sanyasa*: (age 75 onward), a time for contemplation, meditation, renunciation of worldly pleasures and desires, attaining equanimity of mind, and serving others. The stage of *Sanyasa* was primarily for *Brahmans*. *Kshatriyas* and *Vaishyas* stopped at the stage of *Vanprastha*. For *Shudras*, there was no such requirement to enter into the *Vanprastha* or *Sanyasa* stage.
2 Historical dates for various Hindu scriptures and other religious books are from Panduranga Vaman Kane (1973) and A.S. Altekar (1958).
3 *Varna* may also be translated as "color." In this sense, it was used during the Vedic period to differentiate Aryans and *Dasas* (servants).
4 Each upper caste was divided into *Gotras*. Each *Gotra* is named after a Vedic sage to whom a member of a Gotra is said to be able to trace his family lineage through the male line. A higher *Gotra* male may marry a woman from a lower Gotra and still retain his original status, but a higher *Gotra* woman loses her previous status when marrying a lower *Gotra* man.
5 For example, Drona was the Brahmin martial arts teacher of both of the warring *Pandavas* and *Kauravas* clans in the *Mahabharata* epic. A more contemporary example are the

Brahmin "Peshawas" of the seventeenth and eighteenth centuries, who commanded the ruling Marathas army in western India for many years.

6   The taxonomy of caste came to predicate even the specific temperamental, moral, ethical, and spiritual qualities of adherents of the various castes. For example, a *Brahman* was to possess the attributes of serenity, purity, austerity, and uprightness appropriate for a self-disciplined teacher and a spiritual guide. *Kshatriyas* were to evince heroism, firmness, resourcefulness, and administrative skills. *Vaisyas* were to have the skills and inclinations appropriate to agriculture, commerce, and trade; while *Shudras* were likewise to have the natural proclivity and aptitude to provide manual labor and support services (*Manusmriti*, Book 1: 88–91).

7   The Hindu sacred texts called the *Puranas* are 36 in number. They contain historical and geographical records as well as rituals related to devotion (*Bhakti*), such as fasts and other caste-specific norms. Most of the *Puranas* defend the caste system. However, the last *Purana*, *Bhavishya Mahapurana* (Bramha-parva, Ch. 40–45), is critical of the prevailing caste system in medieval India. It devotes five chapters to examining whether birth in a higher caste is due to one's *Karma*. For example, this *Purana* (Bramha-parva, Ch. 44, verse 31) says, "If a *Shudra* is well-mannered and has outstanding characters, he is better than a *Brahman*, while a wicked and morally-wrong *Brahman* is to be considered worse than a *Shudra*." Further, it instructs that by birth, all human beings belong to only one species – humanity (verse 33). If any division or favoritism among people occurs, it must be based on the *Karma* and competence of a person, not on birth. The *Bhavishya Mahapurana* took a "heretical" step in criticizing the caste system of India, although the system remained entrenched for centuries.

References

Altekar, A.S. (1958) Vedic society, in *The Cultural Heritage of India*, Vol. 1, Suniti Kumar Chatterji, *et al* (eds.), Ramkrishna Mission, Institute of Culture, Calcutta, pp. 221–233.

Bhagavad Gita (1971) Gita Press, Gorakhpur, India.

Bhaskarananda, Swami (1994) *The Essentials of Hinduism*, Viveka Press, Seattle.

Chakladar, H.C. (1962) Some aspects of social life in ancient India, in *The Cultural Heritage of India*, Vol. 2, C. P. Ramaswamy Aiyer (ed.), Ramkrishna Mission, Institute of Culture, Calcutta, pp. 557–581.

Chopra, P.N. (1962) Some experiments in social reform in medieval India, in *The Cultural Heritage of India*, Vol. 2, C.P. Ramaswamy Aiyer (ed.), Ramkrishna Mission, Institute of Culture, Calcutta, pp. 627–639.

Devi, Shakuntala (1999) *Caste System in India*, Pointer Publishers, Jaipur, India.

Hazra, Rajendra Chandra (1962) The Puranas, in *The Cultural History of India*, Vol. 2, C.P. Ramaswamy Aiyer (ed.), Ramkrishna Mission, Institute of Culture, Calcutta, pp. 240–270.

Jary, David and Jary, Julia (2000) *Sociology*, 3rd edn, HarperCollins, Glasgow.

Kane, Panduranga Vaman (1973) *Dharmashastra Ka Itihas*, Vols I, IV and V, Uttar Pradesh Hindi Sansthan, Lucknow, India.

Kinsley, David R. (1993) *Hinduism: A Cultural Perspective*, Prentice Hall, Englewood Cliffs, NJ.

Klass, Morton (1980) *Caste: The Emergence of the South Asian Social System*, Institute for the Study of Human Issues, Philadelphia.

Mahabharata (1988) Manmatha Nath Dutt (trans.), Parimal Publications, Delhi.

Miller, David (1999) *Theories of Social Justice*, Harvard University Press, Cambridge, MA.

Pandey, D. (1972) *The Arya Samaj and Indian Nationalism*, S. Chand, New Delhi.

Radhakrishnan, S. (1968) *Religion and Culture*, Orient Paperbacks, New Delhi.

Risley, H.H. (1915) *The People of India*, W. Thacker and Co., London.

Sen, Amartya (2009) *The Idea of Justice*, Belknap Press of Harvard University Press, Cambridge, MA.

Sharma, U. (1999) *Caste*, Open University Press, Philadelphia.

Stietencron, Heinrich von (1989) Hinduism: On the proper use of a deceptive term, in *Hinduism Reconsidered*, Gunther D. Sontheimer and Hermann Kulke (eds.), Manohar Publications, New Delhi, pp. 11–27.

Talbot, Ian (2000) *India and Pakistan*, Arnold, London.

Upadhyay, Govind Prasad (1978) *Brahmanas in Ancient India*, Munshiram Monoharlal Publishers, New Delhi.

Venkatesananda, S. (1992) *The Eternal Religion*, Anand Kutir Yoga Centre, Cape Town.

Wolpert, Stanley (2000) *A New History of India*, Oxford University Press, New York.

Bibliography

Bhavishya Maha-Puranam (1995) Pandit Baburam Upadhyay (trans.), Hindi Sahitya Sammelan, Allahabad, India.

Chhandogya Upanishad (1971) *The Thirteen Principal Upanishads*, Robert Ernst Hume (trans.), Oxford University Press, London, pp. 177–274.

Cox, Oliver C. (1970) *Caste, Class and Race: A Study in Social Dynamics*, Monthly Review Press, New York.

Kautilya's Arthshastra (1967). R. Shamasastry (trans.), Mysore Printing and Publishing House, Mysore, India.

Manusmriti (1979) Hargovinda Shastri (ed.), Chowkhamba Sanskrit Office, Varanasi, India.

Pandey, Raj Bali (1949) *Hindu Samskaras: A Study of Hindu Sacraments*, Vikrama Publications, Banaras, India.

Post, Kenneth H. (1995) Spiritual foundations of a caste, in *Hindu Spirituality: Vedas through Vedanta*, Vol. 1, Krishna Sivaraman (ed.), Motilal Banarasidass, Delhi, pp. 89–105.

Prabhavananda, Swami (1956) *Religion in Practice*, George Allen and Unwin, London.

Sharma, Arvind (2003) *Hinduism and Human Rights*, Oxford University Press, New Delhi.

Sooryamoorthy, Radhamany (2006) Caste system, in *Encyclopedia of the Developing World*, Vol. 1, Routledge, New York, pp. 252–256.

Tulsidas (1982) *Shri Ramcharitmanas*, Gita Press, Gorakhpur, India.

Yagyavalkya Smriti (1996) Ganga Sagar Rai (ed.), Chawkhambha Sanskrit Pratishthan, Delhi.

CHAPTER 8
Hinduism
Contemporary Expressions

Amita Singh

After more than a dozen reform movements and more than 60 years of living with a Republican Constitution, Hinduism is still confronted with the social evils of casteism, untouchability, and bride burning. The spirit and content of the Constitution shine out in its Preamble as India being a "Sovereign, Socialist, Secular, and Democratic Republic." The four fundamental principles defining the spirit of the Indian Constitution are "Justice, Liberty, Equality, and Fraternity to assure dignity to all individuals." While these principles exist presumably by virtue of a Hindu majority in this country that cherishes spiritual and intellectual freedom of resistance and denunciation as natural symptoms of human existence, yet the strengthening of these ideals through the travails of Indian democracy in the last 60 years speak volumes of the high sense of justice among average Hindus.

However, there exists a deep gulf between the Hindu philosophy interpreted from a variety of ancient Hindu scriptures and the on-the-ground realities of Hindu practices and social rituals. The idea of justice moves around the dispersed Hindu society, one segment of which has largely discarded the outdated and unconstitutional social practices under the influence of many reform movements that took place during the nineteenth and twentieth centuries. The other segment has resisted the pressures of change and has lived through numerous dogmatic interpretations of ancient scriptures. Thus these two parts are like two streams within a Hindu society, one extremely modern and global in outlook and the other very medieval and reactionary. While the former protects and chaperones diversity, internal debates, and substantive equality in society, the latter has grown in power to divide the society on grounds of caste, religion, and gender by referring to random quotes from ancient Hindu literature. The coexistence of two segments manifests itself in a nation full of irresolvable diversities of caste, linguistic groups, and religious sects (e.g., Vaishnavas who worship Vishnu, Shaivaites who worship Shiva, and thousands of other groups who worship one or the other form of gods and goddesses). The constant but nonacrimonious tug-of-war between the modern and the medieval system of beliefs is the essence of Hinduism, but is too complex to be easily or fully understood by an outsider, especially those from the occidental part of the globe. Hinduism carries with it the norms and practices of a more than 5000-year-old evolutionary social history, leaving enormous breathing space for every individual and every faith to grow and advance. This study attempts to understand the idea of justice as it unfolds within the changing dynamics of Hinduism in the contemporary world.

Caste and Untouchability

Caste continues to exert an interesting influence on Hindu society. Studies on caste discrimination have exposed the two most influential social justice trendsetters in India, one being the Supreme Court (Venkatesan, 2000) and the other being an icon of higher education in India, the Jawaharlal Nehru University (Santhosh and Abraham, 2010: 27). Despite the rejection of untouchability by the Constitution and several social reform movements in the history of modern India, which are discussed in the latter part of this essay, many Hindus continue to practice it.

Caste discrimination has been endemic to Hindu society, and even in present times the *Shudras*, who are untouchables for being the lowest in the caste hierarchy, have been given many titles during the period of social reform. Gandhi called them *Harijans* (the children of God); present-day researchers call them *dalits* or the "depressed classes," as the focus of research has been more on the circumstances and situations that have led to their oppression. When the British decided to bring "self-rule" to India through the *Government of India Act* of 1935, they used the term "Scheduled Castes" for the first time in order to reserve seats for them in the provincial legislatures. The *Government of India (Scheduled Castes) Order* of 1936 constituted the first list of all depressed classes in the British-administered provinces. The Constitution of independent India reproduced this British understanding of the depressed classes in articles 341 and 342 and on that basis prepared its first list of castes and tribes via two Orders passed in 1950, The Constitution (Scheduled Castes) Order and The Constitution (Scheduled Tribes) Order. Since then, Scheduled Castes and Scheduled Tribes (SC/ST) has become the title for a population mix of all "depressed classes," which is around 25% (24.4% in the 2001 census).

With the execution of the Constitution in 1951, all Scheduled Castes and Scheduled Tribes appeared more polarized, but they suffer from exclusion in all community and social activities. They are not allowed to stay in the main village, to drink water from the same well or even the riverside, or to be seen during certain auspicious occasions held in upper-caste houses. The impact of caste on mainstream society culminated in the worst form of human practice, untouchability, which continues even today in independent India despite Article 17 of the Constitution, which makes untouchability a punishable offence. Yet every year there are more than 62 000 human rights violations, the majority of whom are on *dalits* (suppressed, depressed, or lower castes). The National Commission for Scheduled Castes and Scheduled Tribes reveals horrifying data of more than 115 million *dalit* children in slavery and at least two *dalit* women and children raped every hour. Article 17 is the only fundamental right enshrined in the Constitution that constitutes a punishable offence. This right was further strengthened by the *Untouchability (Offences) Act*, enacted in 1955 and later amended by the *Protection of Civil Rights Act* in 1976.

Navsarjan, a nongovernmental organization (NGO) in *dalit* research, found that cases involving untouchability practices often led to acquittal of the offender for want of sufficiently strong support legislation. The necessary supporting legislation came in 1989 when *The Scheduled Castes and the Scheduled Tribes (Prevention of Atrocities) Act* was passed and the need for setting up special courts and special government prosecutors was upheld. Since then a flood of legislation has struck the courts and, as Navsarjan has recorded, more than 5000 cases were filed in the State of Gujarat alone.

During the British period, the *dalits* were rechristened Scheduled Castes, Scheduled Tribes, and Other Backward Classes. They continue to be trapped in poverty and social exclusion. Article 338 was inserted into the Constitution to provide for a Commissioner for SC and ST, which after the Constitution's Sixty-fifth Amendment was able to set up a National Commission for the Scheduled Caste and Scheduled Tribes. In 2002, this Commission was split into two separate National Commissions, one for the Scheduled Castes and the other for the Scheduled Tribes. Hindu society has by and large accepted these legal and institutional changes in principle, even though there are serious differences in the strategies being adopted by political leaders to implement them.

Many scholars in present times have started investigating the paradoxes of Hindu beliefs. For example, Gopal Guru (2009: 51) has tried to analyze the paradox within the doctrine of Panchmahabhuta or the five elements of life (sometimes referred to as the five principles: earth, sky, fire, water, and air), as propounded in the Sankhya School. He argues that if these five principles are the cause of the very organic existence of everybody and apparently are endowed with the internal purity of every human being, then they would also bring about an ontological unity of all human bodies, which should make them worthy of respect without discrimination. Similarly, Sarukkai (2009: 39–48), in his interesting analysis of untouchability using psychological tools, has exposed the paradox of the act of touching and being touched, which makes the evil practice irrelevant. Such studies by contemporary political and legal experts have been the basis and the driving force of the movement for the rights of those socially trapped in the lowest and the most underprivileged hierarchy of caste.

A consolidated movement against the idea of justice in the caste system and knowledge was trapped under the control of the Brahmins, the highest caste in the social hierarchy accepted as the repositories of information in Sanskrit, the language of the elites, in which all Hindu scriptures were written. All leaders of these movements (from Buddhism and Jainism in ancient India to the Bhakti Movement in medieval India) preached liberation from Brahmanism and Sanskrit scriptures, so that ordinary human beings are brought into the mainstream of decision making about their future. These movements rejected caste and violence in any form wherein human relationships suffered and disturbed the movement of the soul toward its final destination. Tulasidas's translation of the ancient Sanskrit text *Ramayana*, written by Valmiki in the language of the masses known as Ramacharitmanas, launched a movement that opened the doors of the "god" to ordinary human beings, who had earlier been prohibited from reading it. This had a tremendous impact on the understanding as well as the practice of substantive justice in Hindu society. This was a period when many Shudra religious leaders like the Nabhadas and Raidas, along with agnostic and secular believers like Kabirdas, exposed the irrelevance of brahamanical rituals (social practices designed by the highest caste, which was revered as the repository of knowledge), such as the cruel ritual of animal sacrifice and preventing *Shudras* from entering temples or having meals with the upper castes.

Kabirdas, the lead reformer of medieval India, was presumed to be of Muslim origin because an Arabic name was inscribed on his hand when he was discovered by Ramananda in the waters of the river Ganges. He was brought up in his *ashram* (school) against the wishes of all the Brahmins and *Kshatryias* (the warrior class of kings), who were fellow students. In his famous work *Bijak* ("The Seedling," Kabir, 2002) he mentions two constituents: *Jeevatman* (the human soul) and *Paramatman* (the ultimate soul or the Lord). True salvation comes in their union. As he writes in the *Songs of Kabir* (Kabir, 2008), "The simple union with the Divine Reality was independent of the rituals." He eradicated many embedded paradoxes of Hinduism and proclaimed:

> God was neither in "Kaba" [Muslim pilgrimage in the Arab region] nor in "Kailash" [Hindu pilgrimage over the Himalayas]. Those who sought Him need not go far; for He awaited discovery everywhere, more accessible to the washerwoman and the carpenter than to the self-righteous holy man. (Kabir, 2008: Poems I, II, XLI)

Kabir was most forceful in clearly denouncing scriptures, rituals, and priests as dead things intervening between the soul and its love. This movement diluted caste divisions to reinstate the human soul with its vision of fairness in treating a sinner and granting proportionate penalties. Kabir has one of the widest followings of Hindus in India. Some religious sects have even tried his reinvention for the sake of the democratic and secular health of India in a new form called Shirdee Saibaba.

Two leading reform movements, namely Brahma Samaj, founded by Raja Ram Mohan Roy and later Devendra Nath Tagore in 1828, and Dayananda Saraswati's Arya Samaj, founded in 1875 at Rajkot in Saurashtra, were the torchbearers of modern Indian society. Roy wanted to introduce the Hindu religion to western science and institutions, with the hope of eradicating some of the most barbaric social practices and evil customs through analytical reasoning. In the face of the utter devastation of Hindu society through the caste hierarchy, superstitions, religious rites, and gross idolatry, in his book *Gifts of Monotheists* (1809) Roy rejected the worship of idols or the image of gods, polygamy, and the abusiveness of the caste system. Arya Samaj wanted to win back Hindus who had converted to Christianity and Islam. It questioned the alienation and exclusion of *Shudras* from the mainstream and thereby suggested education and livelihood for them. The main plank of religious reform was the *Shuddhi* (purification) process, or "the voluntary reconversion of Hindus from other religions" on the pretext that the orthodoxy of Hinduism had forced them to join those other religions. Brahmo Samaj and Arya Samaj lie at the base of secular India, because of which the country has been able from time to time to marginalize the forces of religious fundamentalism.

The politics of contemporary India have brought to the surface many less acknowledged movements, which have brought about the complete transformation of Hindu society. The rise of *dalit* leaders like Kansi Ram and Mayawati in the Brahmin belt of India, known for sending the most prime ministers to Delhi, cannot be ignored in the prospective advance of Hinduism. Many marginalized thinkers, such as Mahatma Phule (1824–1890), have been reintroduced. For Phule, education was a weapon of progress. He opened schools for the education of non-brahmins, untouchables, and women. His emphasis on the education of the *Shudras* is well explained in his own words:

> for want of education intellect deteriorated; for want of intellect morality decayed; for want of progress wealth vanished; for want of wealth Shudra perished and all these sorrows sprang from illiteracy. (Kshirsagar, 1994)

It was due to Phule's influence that the Woods Despatch of 1854, also known as the Magna Carta of education for the *dalits* in India, declared "open access to all castes" as the first official policy of the British Parliament in India. Influenced by this current of change, the Maharaja of Baroda opened schools for the *dalit* Hindus, and the Maharaja of Kolhapur made the first attempt to reserve 50% of the seats for *dalits* in the state administration in 1902. A remarkable feat of his leadership were the Hujur Orders of 1919, which ensured that no otherwise qualified *dalits* could be denied admission to schools, and if any official or a teacher had a problem abiding with this, he was asked to submit his resignation within six weeks from receipt of the order (Thorat and Kumar, 2008: 19). Since then efforts have been pursued more systematically, from the Southborough Committee to the constitutional reforms of the 1930s and later the Constitution of independent India. Bhimrao Ambedkar and Rao Bahadur Sriniwasan submitted a memorandum in 1931 demanding special representation to provincial and federal legislatures.

As India approached independence, one man who understood that charitable and mission-led local movements alone cannot bring sustainable change in the Hindu caste hierarchy was the towering personality of Ambedkar. He understood that the basic legal document of the country's governance, the Constitution, should be made strong enough to declare caste-based divisions illegal and subject to the strictest of penalties. He also knew that the upper castes have centuries-old vested interests that can never be overcome without affirmative action such as reserved positions for the *dalits* in governmental agencies and educational institutions. He dominated the Constituent Assembly debates and the making of the Constitution for a post-British India. He was instrumental in developing a theory of the caste system in 1916, which in 1948 was advanced into a theory of untouchability, thus inspiring a new discourse on the origin of *Shudras* that could strongly campaign for the eradication of caste in the Constitution.

With the achievement of independence, many legislative changes were brought about in the direction of the spirit of the Constitution. Untouchability had already become a policy concern in the Morley Minto reforms of 1909. Ambedkar's efforts demonstrate how these interventions shook Hindu society at its fundamental structure of caste. It was not easy for many social reformers to accept this change. Even Gandhi, who debated the issue of separate electorates for the untouchables in 1932 with Ambedkar, did not in the end sign the document that finally emerged from the debate. A smaller respite arrived in a resolution that followed the debate: it granted equal rights to *dalits* in the use of public wells, schools, roads, and other public institutions (Galanter, 1969).

Indian Constitution and Caste Discrimination

The Constitution of India has made efforts in redefining Hindu law and practices in view of its relevance in a modernizing and forward-looking Hindu society. Besides economic and religious equality, the Constitution guarantees social equality. Social equality is assured through Article 15, which prohibits discrimination on grounds of religion, race, caste, sex, and place of birth. This law represented a revolutionary inclusion in the Constitution, since most Hindus were still not prepared to share their kitchens or professional places with the untouchables. Gandhi had worked hard to bring down this irrational divide within Hindu society by calling all human beings *Harijan* (children of God) and launching a strong movement within India against colonial rule. In post-independence India these caste-based divisions also brought difficult legal questions to the judiciary. One such battle started in 1951, when a brahmin girl, Champakam Dorairajan, was denied admission to a medical college in Madras (*Champakam Dorairajan vs State of Madras*, AIR 1951, SC 226), even though she had achieved the requisite qualifying marks. She filed a writ petition to the Madras High Court against her discrimination based on caste. The court upheld her claim and struck down Communal Government Order No. 2208, 1937, which allocated seats in educational institutions on the basis of caste. However, the government, in support of social justice, ruled in favor of substantive equality by bringing the first amendment to the Constitution in 1951. Clause (4) was added to Article 15: "Nothing in this article or in article 29(2) shall prevent the state from making any provisions for the advancement of any socially and economically backward classes of citizens or for Scheduled Castes and Scheduled Tribes." This addition to the Constitution can be viewed as a turning point in the ancient Codes of Hinduism, which structured justice around the four castes as the very foundation of Hindu society. Chapter IV of the Constitution, the Directive Principles of State Policy, Article 42, grants "special protection" to socially deprived people.

Article 17 takes another revolutionary step to declare the practice of untouchability as an offence punishable under law, which is well supported by the *Protection of Civil Rights Act* of 1955. Even though the conviction rate of those practicing untouchability has been very low, the constitutional changes have proven to be a deterrent to inhumane practices against vulnerable people. The constitutional sections dealing with caste and untouchability resulted in battles between the legislature and the judiciary in the early republic due to the Supreme Court's reactionary stand on the denial of reservation based on caste. In *Balaji vs State of Mysore* (AIR 1963, SC 649), the court again tried to prevent the government from proceeding toward a caste-based affirmative action plan. However, the court also prevented the issue from being politicized in Parliament by putting a cap of 50% on reservations for students from Scheduled Casts and Scheduled Tribes. Ruling that "backwardness" is not just confined to the categories listed, it diverted attention away from castes to backwardness so that the affirmative action initiatives of the government also have to benefit the other castes. It was only in 2005 that another Clause (5) was added to Article 15 after the 93rd amendment, enabling the state to make special provisions for Backward Classes.

The state under *The Protection of Civil Rights Act* of 1955 has taken several penal measures against institutions and individuals found violating the abovementioned sections of the Constitution. By the 1990s the courts began to show signs of progressive litigation and since then they have upheld convictions for preventing injustices against the Scheduled Castes and Scheduled Tribes. One such case is the *State of Karnataka v. Appa Balu Ingle* (1993), in which the court upheld the conviction of Appa Bala for an atrocity under Sections 4 and 7 of the 1955 Act, preventing a lower-caste person from filling water from a bore well. Currently reservation for the deprived castes is not only confined to educational institutions but extends to the Parliament, State Assemblies, and all local bodies of the country (Article 330/332). An institutional protection against atrocities has been created under Article 338/338A and Article 339; a National Commission for the Scheduled Castes and Scheduled Tribes has also been created to prevent atrocities against *dalits* or the "oppressed."

Caste Injustices in Public Institutions

Despite a detailed legal framework to eradicate caste discrimination and atrocities against SC/ST classes, most leading institutions continue to practice these in a subtle and covert manner. Thus caste-based discrimination continues to afflict the country's leading government institutions. The Supreme Court has shown shocking disregard of constitutional requirements in the appointment of judges. In 1998 the President of India, K.R. Narayanan, made an extraordinary comment on one file relating to appointments of judges to the Supreme Court:

> While recommending the appointment of Supreme Court Judges, it would be consonant with constitutional principles and the nation's social objectives if persons belonging to weaker sections of society like S.C.s and S.T.s, who comprise 25 per cent of the population, and women are given due consideration.

He further wrote:

> Eligible persons from these categories are available and their under-representation or non-representation would not be justifiable. Keeping vacancies unfilled is also not desirable given the need for representation of different sections of society and the volume of work which the Supreme Court is required to handle. (*Frontline*, February 12, 1999)

In 60 years of independence and constitutional remedies for discrimination, Justice Ratnavel Pandian, in the famous Advocates on Record Case (1993), lamented the prejudice occurring against women, Other Backward Classes, Scheduled Castes, and

Scheduled Tribes in the appointment of judges to the Supreme Court. A study of the recruitment process under Article 16(4), which enabled the state to make provision for the reservation of judges from the Backward Classes in the Supreme Court, indicates discrimination in the appointment of judges. Even the former Chief Justice K.G. Balakrishnan, who belongs to the Scheduled Castes category, had been initially rejected for elevation to the Supreme Court; he was finally elevated in 2002.

Similar to the highest judiciary of the country, the apex institution of higher education, Jawaharlal Nehru University, also presents an ugly face of caste prejudice. One student, Saurabh Kamal, was constantly harassed by a group of upper-caste students in the university. His brother, Amritashva Kamal, intervened to protect him from verbal and physical abuse, but both the brothers were openly beaten and dragged out of the hostel where they were staying. While the university took disciplinary action against the upper-caste student, Mahendra Kumar Chauhan, by rusticating (or removing from the university) him and his friends for four semesters, Amritashva Kamal was debarred from admission to the university in the future. The Delhi High Court in its judgment wrote:

> Sadly the stark reality of caste prejudice has been highlighted in this case. There is no more justice when the victim and the oppressor are treated alike. As where the lion and the lamb are afforded the same treatment, [that] the Vice Chancellor of the University has chosen to support such a stand and apparently "applied his mind" is alarming to say the least.

The judgment advised the university to admit Amritashva Kamal and pay him damages within two weeks. The university challenged the judgment in the higher court and has shown no intention of admitting him, despite his very high score in the written entrance examination. The Equal Opportunity Office of the university shares the problem of an increasing number of caste-discriminated students and the failure of the university administration to take a progressive approach to the problem. The constant emphasis of the courts on recognizing the right to free compulsory education as the most important of all the fundamental rights (Art. 21 A) and as indispensable for the exercise of other fundamental rights added a mission to the policy. In this context, it is also worth noting that recently the role of the Supreme Court has favored the affirmative policy of reservations and capacity building (*Amritashva Kamal v JNU & Anr*, W.P [C] 4980/2007; *Avinash Singh Bagri and Ors v Registrar IIT Delhi* (2009), 8 SCC 220), in sharp contrast to its postindependence inclination to favor excellence and merit (*State of Madras v Smt. Champakam Dorairanjan*, AIR 1951, SC 226).

The courts have shown a scintillating inclination for relevance in interpreting law while deciding cases on caste prejudices in professional institutions, and this trend has become a major factor in transforming contemporary thinking in Hinduism, as the philosophy adapts itself to global changes within the society.

Gender Justice in Hinduism

The constitutional position of women appears to be quite strong under Article 15(3), due to which the state has been proactively passing acts like the *Dowry Prevention Act* and the *Domestic Violence Act* of 2005. Equal pay to women for equal work was upheld by the Supreme Court in the case of *Randhir Singh v Union of India* 1982 SC 0234 (Writ Petition 4676/1978), which directed the state to enforce such laws through constitutional remedies granted under Article 32. Since 1992 women have been provided with 33% reservations in rural and urban local government bodies.

A study of marriage rituals and practices in a Hindu community highlights the community's attitude toward dowry, divorce, and widows. A large section of the Hindu community continues to sustain the Brahmin (highest caste in the Hindu hierarchy) superiority, patriarchy, and exclusion of single women (unmarried, divorced, or widows). Hinduism has varied perceptions about womanhood and the status of women. One of the Hindu writings, *Brahatsamhita*, by Varamhira, says that women are naturally superior to men because all men are born from women, women are more faithful to their spouses, and they follow *Dharma* (code of good conduct) more than men (Chapter 72). Within the same Hindu philosophy there is a record collection of literature in which women are talked about in the same terms as animals, idiots, and untouchables (*Dharmashastras*). It is interesting that the desire to have a son in the family has even led the *Vedas*, specifically the *Brahadanayaka Upanishad*, to suggest special ceremonies for the birth of a son. However, one cannot altogether blame the *Vedas* for advocating a patriarchal family system, in as much as the same text (6.4.17) describes a number of rituals for the birth of a brilliant daughter.

Religion has accorded a decisive place to women in a Hindu society. No religious ceremonies or family rites can be completed without the woman of the house. India sustains this pride in having the first woman author, the first woman doctor, the first woman lawyer and attorney, and even the first woman who divorced her husband to study medicine. Gandhi's call to women during the freedom movement and Netaji Subhash Chandra Bose's admittance of women soldiers to the Ajad Hind Fauz provide ample proof that it is not the Hindu religion but the obsolete Codes that have perpetuated patriarchy and blind faith in traditional Hindu life.

Marriage ceremonies bring out gender discrimination in its worst forms. Modern Hindu girls have started opposing the idea of dowry and *Kanyadaan* (*Kanya* is daughter and *dana* is giving away); a Hindu home traditionally treats a girl as somebody else's treasure, to be some day given away through this ceremony (Panikkar, 1961: 57). In the words of Yaska's Nirukta, "They give away to others the female children. There exist dana (give away), vikraya (sale) and atisarga (abandonment) of the female but not of the male." A Hindu home would celebrate the birth of a son, while that of a daughter is generally treated as a nonevent. Most religious ceremonies and wedding blessings start with "Be the mother of the males" (*putravati bhava*). This practice is encouraged by the fact that, even though Hindu society is changing, the rituals of birth (*annaprasan* or initiation for solid food intake, and *namkaran sanskara* or name-giving ceremony), death (lighting the funeral pyre and related 13-day ceremonies involving rituals from the *Garuda Purana*, a sacred book to Hindus), and property purchase (*bhumi pujan* or land worship; *griha pujan* or house worship) have to be conducted by a male member of the house. If a woman is single, she unequivocally becomes an outcaste, as she can neither participate in rituals nor host rituals at her home. Hence a spinster, a widow, or a divorced woman immediately becomes an outcaste in a traditional Hindu society. Even in contemporary times, these practices are followed avidly in some regions like

West Bengal, where they discard such single women to places of religious worship such as Vrindavan and Mayapuri. Many organizations, such as the Women's Guild of Ms. Mohini Giri and the National Commission of Women, a statutory body of the government of India, have taken drastic steps to rehabilitate women who have been thrown out of their homes. Social reforms and constitutional changes have raised the age of marriage and given women the right to own their matrimonial share of property, or even their husband's property in case of abandonment. Measures such as allowing women to divorce their husbands or widows to remarry have been abhorred by the ancient Hindu Codes, since they disturb the concept of the indissoluble marriage and at the same time negate the concept of the permanence of family ties, or what in the language of religious texts is referred to as "*gotra* conversion" or absorption of a woman into the husband's family by abandoning her own family ties completely. *Gotra* is a Hindu description of the lineage of a family or a clan. As part of the sacrosanct marriage, "A widow who does not remain a member of her late husband's family repudiates the conception of Hindu marriage" (Panikkar, 1961: 59–60).

Many later authors of the medieval and postmedieval era, including many social reformers, continued to promote this understanding in the treatment of women. Tulsidas, the celebrated author of the Hindu scripture *Ramcharitmanas*, which even today is the single most important influence over the Hindu psyche, sums up the status of woman in a couplet: "*Dhol, Ganwar, shudra, pashu nari, yeh sab taran ke adhikari*" (an idiot, illiterate, untouchable, animal, and the woman are worthy to be reprimanded). The reemergence of the Khap Panchayats (caste-based community councils of villagers) in some parts of India in the last decade has passed penal directives against women who tried to break through tradition. In the last two years many villages in northwestern India, which are relatively more prosperous than the rest of the country, have protested against the independence given to Hindu women in the *Hindu Marriage Act* of 1955 and many of its associated Acts, such as the *Hindu Succession Act* of 1956, the *Hindu Minority and Guardianship Act* of 1956, and the *Hindu Adoptions and Maintenance Act* of 1956. The legacy of Manu continues to haunt the lives of Hindu women, especially the underprivileged ones who are forced to live in tradition-bound rural India.

Raja Ram Mohun Roy may be remembered as the widows' messiah, since he raised the bogey of legislative reforms to eradicate *sati* and promote widow remarriage, the latter the most revolutionary aspect of his action plan. After her husband's death, a Hindu widow was unwanted in her family home. Most Hindu customs were designed in a manner that made the appearance of widows during the occasion inauspicious and a bad omen for the family. Hence if the widow did not leave the home willingly, she would be forcibly taken away to any of the religious pilgrimages, such as Vrindawan or Varanasi, and made to stay there for the rest of her life. Considering the early age of marriage at that time in history, most women were widowed at a very early age and hence suffered enormous sexual and physical abuse once they were discarded from their families. This is one of the reasons why to this day prostitution has been at its highest in Hindu religious places.

Some regions of the country practiced *sati* (burning the widow with her husband's dead corpse). The rebellion against *sati* started during the late eighteenth century. *Sati* continues to be practiced in Rajasthan despite severe opposition by the people and a ban under law. In 1987, Roop Kanwar, an 18-year-old married *rajput* woman in the Sikar district of Rajasthan, succumbed to *sati*. This barbaric incident of burning to death an unwilling young widow not only shocked the people of India, but also infuriated women's groups across the world. More exasperating was the aftermath, when the local administration was found to be supporting the family of the husband, which was coercing immolation on the girl. Hindus of that region went in large numbers to worship at the pyre where the widow was forced into self-immolation, hence glorifying the frightful and unconstitutional incident. Since then many women of every age group have been committing *sati* in and around that area.

Treatment of widows is another residual scar of the ancient legacy of Hindu society, despite Ishwar Chandra Vidya Sagar, a social reformer who brought about the *Widow Re-marriage Act XV* of 1856. Many old men, some even on their deathbed, married prepubertal girls, who were soon left behind as widows in their maternal homes. There was also a festival called Akshaya teej that was celebrated during the rainy season across the country as a child marriage day. Sometimes girl babies under one year of age were married to a young boy or infant male; child mortality being high, these girls were mostly widowed before consummation. Being widows, they were subsequently subjected to torture, violence, and untold miseries through starvation and social exclusion. Most of them ran away from home, only to give themselves up to prostitution. Bengal was the worst region for the treatment of women and thus also had the highest number of prostitutes. Shockingly, in the conservative Calcutta of 1853, there were more than 12 000 prostitutes (Sarkar, 1977).

Independent India has achieved a substantial amount of legal equality for women, with the new breed of statesmen and legal scholars like Jawaharlal Nehru, Madan Mohan Malaviya, and Bhim Rao Ambedkar emphasizing the role of women as equals in the Indian Constitution (Articles 14–17). Ambedkar's fortnightly magazines *Mooknayak* ("leader of the dumb") and *Bahishkrit Bharat* ("excluded India") were women centric in many ways, in that they rejected child marriage, widow remarriage, and *sati*. A legislative revolution in support of women was suggested in Ambedkar's article "The rise and fall of Hindu women." Roy also directed women to live a clean and healthy life with washed clothes. In his address to a congregation of more than 3000 *dalit* women at Mahad in 1927, he made a passionate effort to empower them against caste- and gender-inflicted violence.

Much of the effort made by social and gender justice activists during the period of colonial India is reflected in many articles of the Constitution. Article 51A(e) imposes a duty on every citizen in India to renounce practices that undermine the dignity of women. Even Section 14 of the *Hindu Succession Act* of 1956 has been modified to bring about the economic empowerment of Hindu women. The *Dowry Prohibition Act* of 1961 was later amended in 1986 to add Article 304-B in the Indian Penal Code, which brought criminal liabilities to the perpetrators of crimes against women. Articles 15(3) and 39(a) stipulate that the state shall not discriminate on grounds of sex. This prohibition has recently been extended to a path-breaking transformation of Indian society by amending Article 377 of the Indian Penal Code to extend civil rights to transgender people. Moreover, the courts have finally ruled that homosexuality is not a crime. A large number of women's organizations spread across the country try to invoke Article

2(f) of CEDAW (the UN Convention on the Elimination of All Forms of Discrimination against Women), under which states are obliged to take all appropriate measures, including legislation, to abolish or modify gender-based discrimination in their existing laws, regulations, customs, and practices.

Conclusion

Despite strong affirmative action to bring the Scheduled Castes and Scheduled Tribes into the mainstream of Indian social life, the official machinery of the justice system in India, including the police and the courts (especially the lower courts), continues to treat the *dalits* and women as classes that should be kept in subordination. The administration continues to view them as subclasses, which has also been a dominant reason for the failure of many inclusive policies brought about under Clause 4 of Article 15, which enabled the state to grant compensatory discrimination for those at the lower end of the caste hierarchy. Many of the legal changes, such as the abolition of untouchability under Article 17 or the setting up of institutions for the protection against caste discrimination under Articles 338 and 339 or for the protection against gender discrimination under the *National Commission for Women Act* 1990 have increased access to justice for those discriminated against. These legal actions alone do not strengthen the accessibility of justice to them, since the implementation of these provisions is dependent on the public support of the electorate.

There has been a strong critique of the ancient Hindu Codes by radical thinkers from the time of Roy to Ambedkar, but the most sustaining features of Hindu philosophy have been aptly summarized by Shashiprabha Kumar (1999, 2008). These features include nonviolence or *Ahimsa*, the cosmic unity of all living beings, universal brotherhood, and peace (*sarvadharmasambhavah*). The freedom of faith, its methodology and strategy available to an average Hindu has inadvertently broadened and diversified the idea of justice through a self-corrective process and escaping dogmatism, or what Amartya Sen (2009: 403) referred to as the "trap of parochialism." Still, Hinduism has a long way to go before it is able to extinguish caste (and its associated injustices) from the social order. Jawaharlal Nehru (1889–1964), the first Prime Minister of independent India, lamented, "Many of us still live in the ancient past regardless of what is happening around us." He pleaded that many of the Hindu myths and dogmas be "discarded in favour of the realities of today" (1928: 370).

Acknowledgment

The author acknowledges the valuable inputs received from Prof. Shashiprabha Kumar in the final drafting of this paper. Professor Kumar is a renowned scholar of the "Vedas" and a Professor of Indian Philosophy at the Centre for Sanskrit Studies, JNU. The author is immensely benefitted by the deep analytical insight of Professor O. P. Dwivedi who encouraged discussions on most of the semantic complexities preventing an understanding of ancient Hindu writings.

References

Galanter, Marc (1969) Untouchability and the law, *Economic and Political Weekly* January: 131–170.

Guru, Gopal (2009) Archeology of untouchability, *Economic and Political Weekly* 12 September: 49–56.

Kabir (2002) *Bijak*, Linda Hess and Shukdev Singh (trans.), Oxford University Press, Oxford.

Kabir (2008[1915]) *Songs of Kabir*, Easy Reading Series, Rabindra Nath Tagore (trans.), Forgotten Books, Charleston, SC.

Kshirsagar, R.K. (1994) *Political Thought of Babasaheb Ambedkar*, Intellectual Publishing, New Delhi.

Kumar, Shashiprabha (1999) *Facets of Indian Philosophical Thought*, Vidyanidhi, Delhi.

Kumar, Shashiprabha (2008) Vedic vision of inclusiveness and interconnectedness, *Voice of Sankara* 33(1): 97–120.

Nehru, Jawaharlal (1928) Swaraj and socialism, *The Hindu*, August 11.

Panikkar, K.M. (1961) *Hindu Society at Cross Roads*, Asia Publishing House, New York.

Santhosh, S. and Abraham, Joshil K. (2010) Caste injustice in Jawaharlal Nehru University, *Economic and Political Weekly*, June 26.

Sarkar, Nikhil [Sripantho] (1977) *Bat tala*, Ananda, Calcutta.

Sarukkai, Sundar (2009) Phenomenology of untouchability, *Economic and Political Weekly*, September 12: 39–48.

Sen, Amartya (2009) *The Idea of Justice*, Allen Lane, London.

Thorat, S. and Kumar, Narendra (eds.) (2008) *B. R. Ambedkar: Perspectives on Social Exclusion and Inclusive Policies*, Oxford University Press, Delhi.

Venkatesan, V. (2000) Judiciary and social justice, *Frontline* 17(21): 14–27.

Bibliography

Ambedkar, B.R. (1990) *Annihilation of Caste*, Arnold Publishers, Delhi.

Bühler, G. (trans.) (1886) *The Laws of Manu* [Manusmṛti], Vol. 25 of *Sacred Books of the East*, Max Müller (ed.), Oxford University Press, Oxford.

Carson, Rachael (1962) *Silent Springs*, Hamish Hamilton, London.

Manu (1920) *Manu Smriti: The Laws of Manu with Bhasya of Medhatithi*, Ganga Nath Jha (trans.), University of Calcutta, Calcutta.

CHAPTER 9
Islam
Historical Setting

Hussam S. Timani

> You who believe, uphold justice and bear witnesses to God, even if it is against yourselves, your parents, or your close relatives.
>
> The Qur'an 4:135

> No, he does not believe in Allah, nor in the Day of Judgment, he who eats his full at night while his neighbor is raked with hunger.
>
> The Prophet Muhammad

Social justice is one of Islam's basic tenets that is closely associated with the belief of the Unity of God (*Tawhid*). Monotheism "makes for a just and coherent moral universe, since God . . . never does any wrong (*Zulm*) to anybody; rather, God in the Qur'an is an ethical construct associated with the concepts of truth and justice" (Barlas, 2002: 96). The Qur'an commends Muslims to lead a pious life, and Islamic piety can be achieved not solely by personal or individual piety but by striving hard (performing jihad[1]) collectively and personally to eliminate injustices. It is reported that the Prophet Muhammad once said: "Whoever takes a piece of the land of others unjustly, he will sink down the seven earths on the Day of Resurrection" (Bukhari, 1997: 3.43.634). Thus, Islamic theological and religious teachings are centered on the concept of justice, and all the duties that the Qur'an prescribes eventually lead to establishing justice in one's own community. Unlike some expressions of Christianity in which people's relationship with God is vertical – that is, the belief in Jesus for personal salvation in the hereafter – in Islam this relationship is horizontal – that is, be just to yourself and do justice to others so that society can be saved here and now. This essay will provide an overview of the economic and social conditions in Arabia at the eve of the rise of Islam and will discuss how the Qur'an responded to these conditions and hence provided guidance for eradicating the ills and injustices of that society.

The Wiley Blackwell Companion to Religion and Social Justice, First Edition. Edited by Michael D. Palmer and Stanley M. Burgess.
© 2012 John Wiley & Sons Ltd. Published 2020 by John Wiley & Sons Ltd.

Social Injustice in the Pre-Islamic Era

At the eve of the birth of Islam during the seventh century, Arabia was a tribal, chaotic, and lawless land. The inequalities between members of society were reflected in the separation between the elite, who owned most of the wealth, on the one hand, and the rest of the people, who were largely poor and deprived of wealth, on the other. The poor were neglected and discriminated against and women were treated as the property of men. Slavery existed on a large scale and female infanticide was a common practice. Moreover, because there was no common law to be enforced by a central authority, chiefs of local tribes served as the sources and enforcers of law. Life had little value, and killing another human being was not a crime. When members of a tribe killed a person from another tribe, justice was exacted in the form of revenge by killing anybody in the murderer's tribe.

Most of the injustices were committed against the most vulnerable in the society. For instance, families sometimes denied their female children basic rights and justice by burying the girls alive before they reached the age of six. Families that practiced this cruel tradition believed that "females were flawed" (Ahmed, 1992: 41) and would bring shame and dishonor to both the tribe and the family when they became adults. For example, when two tribes fought each other, the winning tribe would resort to anything to humiliate the defeated tribe. One way to inflict humiliation was to dishonor the tribe by raping young virgin women. Thus, some of the victims' families believed that by getting rid of the girls, they could eliminate potential problems before they occurred. Also, families that were unable to support more than one or two children commonly preferred to raise boys rather than girls, because boys were regarded as more valuable: they could fight for the tribe, herd the cattle, carry the family's name and legacy, and provide for their families when they grew up. Moreover, because Mecca was the commercial center of Arabia, slavery was highly valued, and slaves were badly treated and denied basic human rights. Thus, it was the inequalities, the injustices, and the dire social and economic conditions of the time – rather than the religious and theological conditions – that the Qur'an targeted in the formative years of Islam.

The beginning of Islam was the call for social justice in society. Karen Armstrong has argued that Islam "was first received by the Arabs of Mecca in an atmosphere of cut-throat capitalism and high finance" (Armstrong, 1992: 68). "The new prosperity of Mecca," she added, "drew people's attention to the disparity between the rich and the poor and made them deeply concerned with problems of social justice" (Armstrong, 1992: 68). In fact, the Qur'an neither defined the economic system of pre-Islamic Arabia nor proposed a new economy. Rather, the Qur'an spoke against social and economic injustices, and the message, if read in totality, calls for the eradication of these injustices. For instance, the Qur'an allows the ownership of property and the accumulation of wealth on the condition that the believer must share his wealth with the rest of society, especially the poor. God always reminds the wealthy that their wealth belongs to God. Because they have no authority over it, the wealthy are expected to share their wealth with those who are in need as well as let the poor have for themselves what is "just and reasonable" (Qur'an, 4:6). These qur'anic teachings were outright condemnations of the unjust social and economic system of pre-Islamic Arabia. One may also argue that, since the message of the Qur'an does not overtly prohibit accumulating wealth, it tolerated an unrestrained economic system. I contend that while it generally tolerated a free economic system, it also strongly discouraged such a system. In this respect the message of the Qur'an on unfettered markets paralleled its approach to many practices, such as slavery, which it tolerated but simultaneously discouraged, anticipating that they would gradually be eliminated. Therefore, the Qur'an allowed a grace period to end these practices because, as many scholars argue, its aim was "to reform the old Arab code of honor with which the Quraysh [the most prominent tribe in Mecca] were familiar" (Armstrong, 1992: 92). Thus, the Qur'an had to compromise and allow time for change.

Although the Qur'an did not abolish the old economic system of Mecca, its main message required believers to "strive to create a just society, where the vulnerable are treated decently" (Armstrong, 1992: 92). As Armstrong puts it, Muslims are

> intolerant of injustice, whether this is committed by one of their own rulers . . . or by powerful Western countries. The early message of the Qur'an is simple: it is wrong to stockpile wealth to build a personal fortune, but good to give alms and distribute the wealth of society. (Armstrong, 1992: 92)

The Qur'an ordered people to reform their society, taught them to adopt new ways of thinking, and gave them incentives to undergo social changes.

The notion of the Last Judgment assumed a central role in the message of the Qur'an and compelled the wealthy to take responsibility, because they will be judged based on their deeds before God. The Qur'an warned the Quraysh that on the Last Day their wealth will not help them, for everyone will come naked to face God's judgment. "Neither their possessions nor their children will be any use to the disbelievers against God" (Qur'an, 3:10; also 3:116). People will be asked why they did not take care of the poor, the orphans, and those who are in need. They will be asked why they accumulated wealth and did not share it with the poor. Early qur'anic verses proclaim that feeding the poor is an act of piety as well as an identifying trait of those who will be saved on Judgment Day (Qur'an, 90:13–20). The fire of Hell is in store for those who do not believe in God and for those who "never encouraged feeding the hungry" (Qur'an, 69:34). Righteous are those who "give food to the poor, the orphan, and the captive" (Qur'an, 76:8). Therefore, the Qur'an threatened those who did not believe in God and the Last Day and who refused to commit to the egalitarian message of the new religion. As mentioned earlier, women, orphans, and female children suffered with the poor from the injustices that plagued pre-Islamic Arabia. The existence of slavery by itself speaks to the injustices of that society. The message of Islam addressed these ills and provided solutions to them.

Promulgating the worship of God and the essentials of justice are two of the Qur'an's main purposes. It provides rules to govern human life and moral standards, and is also a source of healing and a cure for social illnesses. The Qur'an refers to itself as the "straightest way. It gives the faithful who do right the good news that they will have a great reward . . ." (Qur'an, 17:9). The Prophet Muhammad declares: "The Qur'an is a definite decree distinguishing between the truth and falsehood . . . Whoever judges by it judges justly and whoever calls to it calls to truth" (quoted in Unal, 2008: xvii). Also, the Prophet declared in a *hadith* that "there are seven categories of people whom God will shelter under His shadows on the Day when there will be no shadow except His. [One is] the just leader [*imam 'adil*]" (quoted in Kamali, 2002: 108). God spoke through His Messenger in a divine *hadith* (*hadith qudsi*)[2] saying: "O my servants! I have forbidden injustice for Myself and forbade it also for you. So avoid being unjust to one another" (quoted in Kamali, 2002: 108). The Qur'an also declares that "God commands justice, doing good, and generosity" (Qur'an, 16:90), requires believers to "adhere to justice" (Qur'an, 5:8), and assures man that God has sent messengers "with clear signs, the Book and the Balance, so that people could uphold justice" (Qur'an, 57:25). Thus, one may argue that the message of the Qur'an is first and foremost a social guide aimed at leading humanity to happiness.

The Qur'an prescribes that Muslims make their *zakat* (almsgiving) to fulfill one of the mandated five pillars of Islam.[3] In order to make their *zakat* acceptable to God, believers must give to the needy out of their belongings an amount that ensures that they themselves will not have need to receive alms. This rule prevents those who give from making an excessive gift, thereby inflicting injustice on themselves. Believers also must not remind those to whom they have given something of the kindness they have done to them. Reminding them would cause humiliation on the part of those who receive and would boost the giver's pride. In Islam, any person who commits an act that would humiliate a fellow human being is regarded as having committed an act of injustice. For this reason, believers must not announce or make their *zakat* public (Qur'an, 2:271, 4:38). Doing so is considered an act of pride, which goes against the message of justice and humility in the Qur'an.

To establish and maintain justice in society, believers must pursue a life balanced between pairs of extremes: boasting in pride and suffering in humbleness; greedy and spendthrift; and excess in worship and having little or no faith at all. God "has set the balance so that you may not exceed in the balance: weigh with justice and do not fall short in the balance" (Qur'an, 55:7–9). Thus, a balanced society is a requirement for social justice.

Wasat, meaning middle course or moderation, is a qur'anic term that defines the concept of justice. It appears in the Qur'an in the context of bearing witness: "We have made you [believers] into a just (*wasat*) community, so that you may bear witness [to the truth] before others and so that the Messenger may bear witness [to it] before you" (Qur'an, 2:143). Most qur'anic commentators interpret this verse to mean that God requires Muslims to be a moderate community; that is, "in the middle," avoiding excess. *Wasat* is related to just faith, which means a balanced faith: neither praying too much (lest their faith have no practical impact) nor too little (lest their action lack piety); neither giving too much (lest they impoverish themselves) nor too little (lest they fail to address the needs of the poor). "They are those who are neither wasteful nor niggardly when they spend, but keep to a just balance (*wasat*)" (Qur'an, 25:67). In sum, the term *wasat* means '*Adl*: a middle course in one's behavior in religious, social, and economic realms of life.

Since, according to the Qur'an, it is God who both provides for believers and commands believers to share their wealth with others, Muslims believe that God will not allow believers to become poor because they share with others. In early Islam, this assurance from God and the belief that God will provide contributed to widespread participation among the believers to help the needy, the poor, and the orphans. As a result, social justice was extended to almost everyone in society.

For Muslims, believers must share with others because what they share is not their own property but God's property (Qur'an, 57:7). "Those who give, out of their own possessions, by night and by day, in private and in public, will have their reward with their Lord: no fear for them, nor will they grieve" (Qur'an, 2:274). The Qur'an mandates that believers must spend not only out of their goods, but also out of whatever they have. For instance, those who do not have the means to make a financial contribution may fulfill the *zakat* pillar by "a kind word and forgiveness [which] is better than a charitable deed followed by hurtful [words]" (Qur'an, 2:263), by contributing their time in community service, by giving a piece of advice, or by teaching, among other things. The Qur'an insists that believers perform *zakat* as a form of religious duty. According to W. Montgomery Watt, *Zakat* is a personal morality that transcends personal piety to show a concern for social welfare (Watt, 1961: 42–43). In the words of Muhammad Husayn Haykal:

> The believers are brethren; no man's *iman* [belief] is complete until he wishes for his neighbor that which he wishes for himself. The believers love one another by virtue of God's light and grace. The duties of zakat and charity are intimately related to this fraternal feeling. (Haykal, 1976: 536)

Islam's main concern is justice for all, and the religion is more connected to many aspects of social life. Therefore, *zakat* is a religious duty that is more connected to social justice and to the sustenance of others than to being only an act of personal piety.

Islam's concerns for the salvation of the society as a whole can be seen in Muslims' behavior after establishing the first Islamic community in Medina. Many scholars often ask: Why, after going to Medina, did "Muslims not live quiet, secluded, upright lives, worshipping God as they pleased?" Why did they attack Meccan caravans on the road between Syria in the north and Mecca? Why was Muhammad not satisfied until he had to return to Mecca and destroy the old polytheistic and economic system (Watt, 1961: 43)? In fact, Muhammad's concern was not to convert everyone to Islam, but to abolish the system that perpetuated injustices. He returned to Mecca to save the poor, the slaves, orphans, women, the oppressed, and the deprived, more than to convert individuals to a new religion. This motive can be seen in his behavior when he entered Mecca. The Meccans, who eight years earlier had persecuted Muhammad's followers, threatened his life, and chased him out of the city, were not only left unmolested but were also given amnesty and not forced to join the new religion. The Meccans were surprised to see the Muslims not bothering them in a society where the unspoken but long-practiced rule was that the victorious tribe would wreak havoc on the defeated one. Not demanding of, or forcing, them to accept the message of Islam testifies to the fact that the message of the Qur'an was less concerned with personal piety and more interested in replacing the old and unjust system with a just and fair one. Also, in the last sermon he delivered before his death, Muhammad gave instructions to the Muslims requiring them to preserve the ideals of justice. He began by praising God and, turning to people, he said:

> Remember that you will indeed meet your Lord, and that He will indeed reckon your deeds. Thus do I warn you. Whoever of you is keeping a trust of someone else shall return that trust to its rightful owner. All interest obligation shall henceforth be waived. Your capital, however, is yours to keep. You will neither inflict nor suffer inequity. God has judged that there shall be no interest. . . . Every right arising out of homicide in pre-Islamic days is henceforth waived . . . O Men, to you a right belongs with respect to your women and to your women a right with respect to you . . . Do treat your women well and be kind to them . . . Nothing shall be legitimate to a Muslim which belongs to a fellow Muslim unless it was given freely and willingly. Do not, therefore, do injustice to your own selves. O God, have I conveyed Your message? (quoted in Haykal, 1976: 486)

Thus, Muhammad's last words and final message to the community emphasized the importance of implementing social justice in the new society. This, one may argue, is a clear indication that social justice not only was at the heart of the message of Islam but also transcended personal piety, at least during the time of the Prophet.

The individualistic tendency that plagued society was one of the social injustices that the message of Islam aimed to eradicate. Although the tribal society of pre-Islamic Arabia valued solidarity (*'asabiyya*) and, in the hard desert conditions, members of a tribe worked together to overcome hardships, this notion of solidarity, according to Watt, lost its essence and was replaced with individualism. The trend to individualism was peculiar to the tribes of Mecca and "was mainly due to the growth of commerce" (Watt, 1961: 49). To maintain and ensure the growth and survival of their businesses, merchants elevated their interest rates, which negatively affected all their customers, including their own friends and relatives. The Prophet himself was not immune. "Muhammad suffered from this . . . because his uncle Abu-Lahab had friends among the great merchants who induced him to turn against his nephew" (Watt, 1961: 49). But the rise of individualism in the tribal society of Arabia had its most profound effect on the most vulnerable members of the community: widows and orphans.

> The successful merchant thought only of increasing his own power and influence . . . and was no longer prepared to carry out the chief's traditional duty of looking after the poor members of the clan. (Watt, 1961: 49)

As individualism replaced the tribal system of solidarity, Watt argues, the tribal chief was no longer able to perform his duty in providing for the weak in his tribe. In the old tribal system of solidarity, the chief collected the booty taken on raids and distributed it among the weak. However, when the "merchant gained his fortune not from raids but by his own shrewdness, the old traditional moral code [could] no longer oblige him to help the poor" (Watt, 1961: 49–50). Thus, the Qur'an spoke against both tribal solidarity and the trend of individualism and sought to replace them with a communal solidarity as a way to bring justice to everyone in the community.

Social Justice in the Qur'an

The message of the Qur'an sewed the seeds for social justice, equality, and human rights in Islam. The term justice appears numerous times in the Qur'an in different Arabic forms: *'adl, qist, mizan*. "Say, 'My Lord commands righteousness (*qist*).' Among those We created are a group of people who guide with truth and act justly according to it" (Qur'an, 7:29, 181; also 10:4, 47; 11:85; 16:76; 39:75; 40:20, 42; 49:9; 51:6, 12; 60:8; 65:2). The concept of justice, therefore, occupies a central role in the Qur'an and is as important to Islam as the concept of love (*agape*) in the New Testament is to Christianity. The social injustices of the time demanded a drastic social reform. Qur'an 107:1–3 severely denounces the abuses of the weak: "[Prophet], have you considered the person who denies the Judgment? It is he who pushes aside the orphan and does not urge others to feed the needy." Qur'an 104:1–3 warns those who abuse their wealth: "Woe to every fault-finding backbiter who amasses riches, counting them over, thinking they will make him live forever."

Although the Qur'an values wealth as "God's bounty" (Qur'an, 62:10) and holds economic prosperity as among God's highest blessings (Qur'an, 106:1–4), it reminds believers that wealth is only an illusory pleasure and only a brief enjoyment (Qur'an, 3:185, 197). Those who abuse their wealth and neglect the poor are hypocrites: "So woe to those who pray but are heedless of their prayer; those who are all show and forbid common kindness" (Qur'an, 107:4–7). People are also required to be just in the distribution of wealth and to be honest when making business transactions: "Give full measure: do not sell others short. Weigh with correct scales: do not deprive people of what is theirs. Do not spread corruption on earth" (Qur'an, 26:181–183).

The Meccans contended that the wealth they had amassed was rightfully theirs and they could dispose of it any way they wished. Against these claims, the Qur'an insisted that the poor and the destitute should rightfully share in their wealth (Qur'an, 51:19). Its concern for public welfare led to the revelation of two important measures: the banning of usury (charging excessive interest and hence increasing one's wealth illegitimately at the expense of other people) and the imposition of the *zakat* tax (the distributive justice of wealth). The Qur'an says:

> Whatever you lend out in usury to gain value through other people's wealth will not increase in God's eyes, but whatever you give in charity, in your desire for God's approval, will earn multiple rewards. (Qur'an, 30:39)

It makes clear that those who do not share their wealth are greedy and will suffer the consequences of their greed. Those who "give out of what We have provided for them" (Qur'an, 2:3) will be rewarded on the Last Day. To spend (Arabic: *Yunfiq*) on others is always used in the Qur'an to mean spending freely on, or giving as a gift to, others.

Islamic teachings mandate that for justice to prevail, Muslims must not fall to corruption, their own desires, favoritism, nepotism, and the like. The Prophet said:

> Muslims constitute one brotherhood, hence nothing shall be legitimate to a Muslim that belongs to a fellow Muslim unless it was given freely and willingly because despising others or exploiting others may be tantamount to injustice to yourselves. (quoted in Hasan, 2007: 52–53)

Qur'an 4:135 says:

> You who believe, uphold justice and bear witness to God, even if it is against yourselves, your parents, or your close relatives. Whether the person is rich or poor, God can best take care of both. Refrain from following your own desire, so that you can act justly – if you distort or neglect justice, God is fully aware of what you do.

In this verse, the Qur'an warns believers not to allow the rich man to prejudice them in his favor or against him and not to favor out of compassion the poor man at the expense of the truth. The Qur'an also instructed Muhammad not to yield to some of the rich and powerful, who believed that it was beneath their dignity to listen to the Prophet's teaching in the company of the poor and the lowly, who gathered around him. In response to their wishes that Muhammad would send these poor and lowly away, the following verse was revealed:

> Do not drive away those who call upon their Lord morning and evening, seeking nothing but His Face. You are in no way accountable for them, nor they for you; if you drove the believers away, you would become one of the evildoers. (Qur'an, 6:52)

Justice for slaves

Islam established equality and justice for all regardless of ethnic, racial, and religious backgrounds, and some qur'anic injunctions extended social justice to slaves. The racial discrimination that prevailed in pre-Islamic Arabia caused[4] the revelation of Qur'an 49:13:

> People, We created you all from a single man and a single woman, and made you into races and tribes so that you should recognize one another. In God's eyes, the most honored of you are the ones most mindful of Him.

One of the causes for this verse to be revealed was when Muhammad asked Bilal, a black slave, to call the Muslims to prayer. A certain Muslim objected, saying: Is there not someone else other than this black slave to call the Muslims to prayer? Hence, the verse above was revealed. In the Farewell Pilgrimage, Muhammad reminded Muslims:

> Believers are brothers. Your God is one, and your father is one. We are all children of Adam and Adam was dust. The most righteous in God's eyes is the one with the most piety and

consciousness of God. There is no difference between an Arab and a non-Arab except in piety. (quoted in Hasan, 1991: 152)

Also, the Qur'an says: "Behold, God bids you to deliver all that you have been entrusted with unto those who are entitled thereto, and whenever you judge between people, to judge with Justice" (Qur'an, 4:135; 5:8; 60:8; 5:42; 4:105, 135; 42:15; 6:115; 16:90; 4:58). Qur'an 5:8 states:

> O you who have attained to faith! Be ever steadfast in your devotion to God, bearing witness to the truth in all equity; and never let hatred of anyone lead you into the sin of deviating from justice. Be just: this is closest to being God-conscious.

Moreover, there are a number of verses directing and requiring Muslims to free their slaves by establishing certain rules and tactics to achieve that goal. Qur'an 58:3 mandates that those who divorce their wives by *Zihar* [by saying to their wives "you are as unlawful to me as my mother"], then wish to go back on the words they uttered, should free a slave before they touch each other. Qur'an 2:177 makes it clear that the freeing of a slave is the highest piety:

> Goodness does not consist in turning your face towards East or West. The truly good are those who believe in God and the Last Day, in the angels, the Scripture, and the prophets; who give away some of their wealth, however much they cherish it, to their relatives, to orphans, the needy, travellers and beggars, and to liberate those in bondage.

(The phrase "to liberate those in bondage" also occurs in Qur'an, 4:92; 5:89; 9:60.)

The concept of the freeing of human beings from bondage may also apply to the freeing of a human being from the bondage of debt or of great poverty. Thus, by making the concept of the freeing of people from bondage an essential act of piety, the Qur'an redeemed people from debt, extreme poverty, and slavery. In addition, the Prophet stated that, in the sight of God, the freeing of a human being from slavery is among the most praiseworthy acts that a Muslim can perform.

Justice for women

Women were "among those oppressed whom God comes to vindicate and liberate" (Barlas, 2002: 20). The message of the Qur'an teaches that both wife and husband have equal rights and should exercise these rights to serve each other and maintain justice and peace: "In accordance with justice, the rights of the wives [with regard to their husbands] are equal to the [husbands'] rights . . ." (Qur'an, 2:228). Qur'an 24:6 protects women who are falsely accused of adultery: "As for those who accuse their own wives of adultery, but have no other witnesses, let each one four times call God to witness that he is telling the truth." The Qur'an also established measures to ensure justice to both men and women on divorce. Qur'an 2:229, 231, 233 says:

> Divorce can happen twice, and [each time] wives either kept on in an acceptable manner or released in a good way. It is not lawful for you to take back anything that you have given to your wives. When you divorce women and they are about to reach the end of their waiting-term, then either retain them in a fair manner or let them go in a fair manner. But do not retain them against their will in order to hurt them. And the divorced mothers may nurse their children for two whole years, if they wish to complete the period of nursing; and it is incumbent upon him who has begotten the child to provide in a fair manner for their sustenance and clothing. No human being shall be burdened with more than he is well able to bear.

According to Islamic law (*Shari'a*), the wife also has a right to initiate divorce. The dissolution of a marriage at the wife's instance is called *khul'*. In this case, the courts acknowledge the right of a wife to obtain dissolution of her marriage by returning to the husband the dower (*mahr*) she received from him at the time of marriage. Although the wife is allowed to initiate the dissolution of her marriage, *khul'* can never be enforced unless the husband consents to it (Coulson, 1994: 137–138). This law, which is based on qur'anic injunctions and *hadiths* (Muhammad's sayings), helps women opt out of bad marriages. Likewise, it does justice to the husband by requiring the wife to return to him her dower, since he was not the one who initiated the divorce. Also, based on qur'anic injunctions and *hadiths*, a woman is recognized as a full and equal partner with the man. She has full rights to seek education and knowledge, to express herself freely (Qur'an, 58:1–4; 60:10–12), to enter into contracts, to engage in trade and business, and to earn and possess wealth and property. If she is wronged or harmed, she is entitled to the same compensation as a man in the same situation (Qur'an, 2:178; 4:92–93). Furthermore, Muhammad recognized that no social reform is possible without the inclusion of women in the social reconstruction of society and without the cooperation of all men and women in mutually helping one another. He also realized that no society is "viable where women do not enjoy rights as well as duties" (Haykal, 1976: 321).

Furthermore, the Qur'an established the basic principles of the Islamic law of inheritance for daughters and other females.

> For the male heirs is a share out of what parents and near kindred leave behind, and for the female heirs is a share of what parents and near kindred leave behind, whether the inheritance be little or much – a share ordained by God. (Qur'an, 4:7)

In pre-Islamic Arabia, women were forbidden from inheriting. Thus, by mentioning the female heirs separately, the Qur'an stresses that women must have a right to inheritance as well. Although the laws prescribe the share of a daughter at half the share of the son, this apparent inequality of inheritance meant a real equality, since the financial obligations of men far exceeded those of women. For instance, on marriage, the man was expected to provide his bride with a marriage gift or dowry, which becomes hers exclusively and remains her property if she is divorced, provided that her husband initiated the divorce. The woman, however, is not required to present any gifts to her husband on marriage.

The Qur'an extended justice to girls by abolishing female infanticide, one of the cruelest and most unjust practices of pre-Islamic Arabia. For example, Qur'an 6:151 warns parents not to kill their female children for fear of poverty; Qur'an 16:58–59 and 81:8–9 also speak to that effect:

> When one of them is given news of the birth of a baby girl, his face darkens and he is filled with gloom. In his shame he hides himself away from his people because of the bad news he has been given. Should he keep her and suffer contempt or bury her in the dust? How ill they judge! When the baby girl buried alive is asked for what sin she was killed.

Thus, the above verses protected girls and extended to them the right to life.

Justice for orphans

The Qur'an brought certain rights and justice to orphans[5] and elevated their status in society. Islam demanded that believers must "stand firm for *qist* (justice) to orphans" (Qur'an, 4:127) and must not come near the orphan's property, except to improve it or increase it. Until orphans reach maturity, "give full measure and weight, according to justice" (Qur'an, 6:152). The word *A'dilu* (be just) is used here. Qur'an 4:2 mandates that the property of the orphans must remain theirs, and no one has the right to consume their property by mixing it up with their own. The Qur'an threatens those who consume the property of the orphans wrongfully with the fire of Hell (Qur'an, 4:10). Qur'an 4:3 warns:

> If you fear that you will not deal fairly with the orphan girls, you may marry whichever women seem good to you, two, three, or four. If you fear that you cannot be equitable [to them], then marry only one, or your slave (female war captive): that is more likely to prevent you from doing injustice.

This verse was revealed after the battle of Uhud (625 CE), when the Muslim community was left with many orphans and widows and some female captives of war. These teachings instruct Muslims to marry as many as four of these orphans, widows, and war captives, because by marrying them, they will be compelled to protect their interests and their property. Thus, these verses protected the orphans, widows, and war captives from being exploited and ensured that their "treatment was to be governed by principles of the greatest humanity and equity" (Ali, 2001: 184).

Justice in matters of public property

The mishandling of public property is another form of social injustice committed against society, and the Qur'an speaks against such corruption. Qur'an 2:188 says: "Do not consume your property wrongfully, nor use it to bribe judges, intending sinfully and knowingly to consume parts of other people's property." The words "people's property" may mean public property, and the use of public property for vain use is considered greed. This form of greed may lead to committing injustice against the public. When contracting a debt for a fixed term, the Qur'an mandates that the parties involved record it in writing (Qur'an, 2:282) so that no one will suffer injustice. Likewise, it warns against committing injustices toward individuals in matters of inheritance. Qur'an 2:180 says:

> It is ordained for you, when death approaches any of you and he is leaving behind much wealth, to make bequests in favor of his parents and close relatives in accordance with what is fair: this is binding on all who are conscious of God.

The Arabic for "much wealth" is *khayr*, meaning "abundance" and not simply "property." Thus, the injunction is that those who leave *khayr* behind should make it clear in their will how the inheritance should be distributed among the deserving members of their family. Dying without leaving a will creates confusion among the next of kin of the deceased person, increasing the likelihood of an unfair and unjust distribution of wealth. Leaving a will is pleasing to God because it leads to a just conclusion. If injustice is committed due to an unfair distribution of wealth, the deceased person who owned the wealth will be held accountable in front of God for not distributing the wealth fairly among the inheritors (Timani, 2008: 64).

Retributive justice

The establishment of retributive social justice is also central to the message of the Qur'an. Qur'an 2:178 says:

> O you who have attained to faith! Just retribution is ordained for you in cases of killing: the free for the free, and the slave for the slave, and the woman for the woman. And if something [of his guilt] is remitted to a guilty person by his brother, this [remission] shall be adhered to with fairness, and restitution to his fellow man shall be made in a goodly manner.

The term *qisas*, Arabic for "just retribution," means also *musawah*; that is, making one thing equal to another. In this instance, *qisas* should not be understood as "retaliation" – a common practice in pre-Islamic Arabia – but as making the punishment equal (or appropriate) to the crime. Thus, *qisas* is frequently employed in the Qur'an and can have but one meaning: if a free man has committed the crime, the free man must be punished; if a slave has committed the crime, the slave must be punished. In other words, whatever the status of the guilty person, he or she alone is to be punished in a manner appropriate to the crime, for God loves those who judge in fairness (Qur'an, 5:45). The term *qisas* also appears in Qur'an 17:33:

> Do not take life, which God has made sacred, except for just cause. If anyone is slain unjustly, We have given his heir authority to demand (*qisas* [retribution] or to forgive): but let him not exceed bounds in the matter of taking life: for he is helped (by the law).

Qur'an 6:151 also forbids taking a life "otherwise than in the pursuit of justice." This phrase refers to the execution of a legal punishment or to killing in self-defense. In the above verses, the heir of the slain person is given the right to demand *qisas*, but he must not exceed the limits of the law. Muslim commentators see this verse as extending justice to both the heir of the slain person and the person against whom *qisas* is sought, as both are helped by the law. In matters of judging among people when crimes are committed, the Qur'an lays down injunctions for fair and just judgment: "When you judge between man and man, that you judge with justice" (Qur'an, 4:58). Qur'an 6:152 and 16:90 say:

> Behold, God enjoins justice, and the doing of good, and generosity towards [one's] fellow-men; and He forbids all that is shameful and all that runs counter to reason, as well as envy; [and] He exhorts you [repeatedly] so that you might bear [all this] in mind.

Laws of equality

The Qur'an also provides laws of equality (Qur'an, 2:178) if two groups of believers fall to fighting, and demands that there should be peace between them. However, if one group commits an act of aggression or goes on acting wrongfully toward the other, the Qur'an mandates that the oppressors should be fought until they submit to God's command and then a just and even-handed reconciliation between the two of them should be reached (Qur'an, 49:9 and 60:8). Also, the Qur'an protects the innocent until proven guilty (Qur'an, 24:12–13), makes a false charge against an honorable woman a crime, and debars those who bring false accusations for life from giving evidence (Qur'an, 24:11). Furthermore, according to qur'anic injunctions, there is no crime if the act was committed under compulsion (Qur'an, 16:106). The punishment should be commensurate with the offence and not more severe (Qur'an, 2:194), and no one can be held responsible for the offence of an other (Qur'an, 42:15).

Social Justice in Early and Medieval Islam

The preceding qur'anic injunctions and the conception of social justice in Islam influenced early and medieval rulers and jurists as well as scholars, to the extent that it dominated the legal and scholarly domains. The concept of social justice was reflected in letters, legal documentation and correspondence between rulers and judges, and it was a topic for discussion and debate among Islamic scholars and jurists as well. The following excerpt, taken from a letter written by Umar b. al-Khattab (d. 644 CE), the second caliph (successor to Muhammad), illustrates how rulers tried to implement justice in society and how scholars defined the term. In it he sets forth the duties and functions of a judge.

> [T]he administration of Justice is a duty. The Court must observe equality between the parties so that the weaker party may expect justice and the stronger may not expect

concession. The burden of proof is on the plaintiff and the defendant may be put to oath, but let this not defeat the ends of justice and law. If you have decided a case, then after due care and thinking you may revise your decision. If you are doubtful in a point which is mentioned in the Qur'an and *Hadith* then think over it again and again and then apply "*Qiyas*" (a process of deduction). When a party wants to tender evidence, then fix a time limit, and, if he proves his case, then decide accordingly. All Muslims are fit to be witnesses except those who have received the prescribed punishment (flogging) for *Hadd* (fornication, adultery) and those who have tendered false evidence. (quoted in Mannan, 2005: 46)

Furthermore, medieval Muslim scholars saw social justice as the only way to maintain the unity of God and that of the Muslim community. They saw in social justice a set of principles and practices that would preserve the individual in society and promote and strengthen God's rule on earth. Abu Hamid Muhammad al-Ghazzali (d. 1111 CE), an influential scholar, believed that a harmonious, well-ordered cosmos created by God requires a good and just government. A good government is a divine gift and may not endure without a just monarch or ruler who is accountable to God "to bring development and prosperity to the world through justice and equitable rule" (quoted in Mehmet, 1997). Al-Ghazzali's ideal state consists of a social being whose satisfaction demanded moderation (avoidance of extremes) and respect for and tolerance of others. In this ideal state, accumulation of excess wealth, conspicuous consumption, and unfair trade practices are to be avoided (Mehmet, 1997). For al-Ghazzali, justice is the highest quality of the ruler, and justice requires

> a careful and constant balancing of qualities "that have to be linked in pairs if they are rightly to be used: intelligence must be coupled with knowledge, wealth with gratitude, charity with kindness, effort with [good government], when [good government] comes, all the qualities must go with it." (quoted in Mehmet, 1997)

This ideal state is based on laws and is ruled by a wise monarch, "whose heart is an abode of justice" (quoted in Mehmet, 1997).

The Qur'an is often not specific about how social justice should be implemented, nor does it lay down a detailed path as to how it may be established. Ibn Qayyim al-Jawziyyah (d. 1350), a jurist and Qur'an commentator, declared:

> Justice is the supreme goal and objective of Islam. God has sent scriptures and messengers in order to establish justice among people. Any path that leads to justice is an integral part of the religion and can never be against it.

Although the Qur'an demands justice, there is no specific "route that leads to it," Ibn Qayyim contends, "or the means by which it can be obtained, nor has [God] declared invalid any particular means or methods that can lead to justice." Ibn Qayyim adds:

> The Lawgiver has not confined the ways and means of attaining justice, or any of its signs and indications . . . He declared justice as His overriding objective and also explained some of the means of attaining it, but then commanded that it should be the basis, generally, of all adjudication and government.

Like Ibn Qayyim, Yusuf al-Qaradawi (b. 1926), a world-renowned Egyptian scholar, states that the Qur'an and the *Sunnah* (Muhammad's tradition) "do not lay down any specific manner for how [social justice] should be implemented" (quoted in Kamali, 2002: 109, 110).

Conclusion

This essay has discussed the development of the Islamic ideals of social justice and has attempted to demonstrate that the fundamental message of the Qur'an was a direct response to the injustices (*zulm*) of the time. When Islam emerged in Arabia in the seventh century, its main concern was to eradicate the social injustices of the pre-Islamic era, bring full rights to the oppressed, and establish equality among individuals. The Muslim's duty to pay *zakat* and practice generosity was expected to transcend personal piety by showing a concern for social welfare. Islam worked to redeem the poor, orphans, women, and the oppressed here and now. In its formative years, Islam emphasized the implementation of justice in society rather than the conversion of people to the new religion. The Qur'an required believers to take care of their fellow human beings as a prerequisite for an eternal life in heaven. This teaching demonstrates that Islam was less concerned with instituting monotheism than with redeeming the oppressed; freeing the people from slavery, debt, and poverty; and giving rights and dignity to the weak. Thus, Islam emerged as a social reform movement that commanded people to serve each other, by which they could fulfill their religious duty of worshiping God.

Although the Qur'an came on too strong on the issue of social justice and equality, Muslim societies have failed to achieve this qur'anic goal. For example, in Medieval Islam – and in much of the Muslim world today – when the community was vulnerable to domestic and foreign threats, what became required of the ruler was strength rather than justice. On achieving power, the ruler legitimated his rule by demonstrating his ability to defend the integrity of the Muslim community. Even al-Ghazzali defended the ruler's legitimacy with regard to power despite injustices in society. As al-Ghazzali put it: "a hundred years of injustice are better than a day of chaos" (quoted in Barazangi *et al.*, 1996: 25). Finally, the declarations of prominent figures in Muslim countries today, that Muslims are still trying to bring justice and equality to their societies, are a testimony to the present realities in the Muslim world.

Notes

1 The Arabic term "jihad" literally means effort, striving, or struggle. To worship God, pray five times a day, take actions against injustice, feed the poor, etc. requires efforts (inner or greater jihad). Lesser or outer jihad is the armed struggle to defend the Muslim community.
2 Prophetic *hadiths* (*hadith nabawi*) are Muhammad's own sayings, while divine *hadiths* (*hadith qudsi*) pertain to the sayings of the Prophet through the medium of divine inspiration. *Qudsi* means holy or sacred.
3 Islam requires believers to fulfill their religious duties by practicing the five pillars: (1) *Shahadah* (testimony): To testify that there is no god but God and that Muhammad is the

messenger of God; (2) *Salat* (prayer): to pray five times a day; (3) *Sawm* (fasting): to fast during the month of Ramadan from sunrise to sunset; (4) *Zakat* (almsgiving): to pay alms or poor tax; and (5) *Hajj* (pilgrimage): to go on a pilgrimage to Mecca at least once in a lifetime, if affordable.
4 Various qur'anic verses were revealed to Muhammad in particular events and circumstances in history. These verses are known as the caused revelations or *Asbab al-nuzul*. The Arabic word *asbab* is the plural of *sabab*, meaning "reason," "cause," or "occasion," and *nuzul* means to descend, send down, or reveal. Thus, *asbab al-nuzul* is the knowledge about the reasons of the revelations; that is, knowledge about particular events that are related to the revelation of particular qur'anic verses.
5 The orphans referred to here are girls, widows, and female war captives.

References

Ahmed, Leila (1992) *Women and Gender in Islam*, Yale University Press, New Haven, CT.

Ali, Abdullah Yusuf (2001) *The Meaning of the Holy Qur'an*, Amana Publications, Beltsville, MD.

Armstrong, Karen (1992) *Muhammad: A Biography of the Prophet*, HarperCollins, New York.

Barazangi, Mimat Hafez, Zaman, M. Raquibuz, and Afzal, Omar (1996) *Islamic Identity and the Struggle for Justice*, University of Florida Press, Gainsville.

Barlas, Asma (2002) *"Believing Women" in Islam: Unreading Patriarchal Interpretations of the Qur'an*, University of Texas Press, Austin.

Bukhari, Muhammad Ibn Isma'il (1997) *Sahih al-Bukhari*, Muhammad Muhsin Khan (trans.), Darussalam, Riyadh.

Coulson, N.J. (1994) *A History of Islamic Law*, Edinburgh University Press, Edinburgh.

Hasan, Hasan Ibrahim (1991) *Tarikh al-Islam* [History of Islam], Dar al-Jeel, Beirut.

Hasan, Samiul (2007) *Philanthropy and Social Justice in Islam*, A.S. Noordeen, Kuala Lumpur.

Haykal, Muhammad Husayn (1976) *The Life of Muhammad*, 8th edn, Isam'il Ragi A. al-Faruqi (trans.), North American Trust Publications, Oakbrook, IL.

Kamali, Mohammad Hashim (2002) *Freedom, Equality, and Justice in Islam*, Islamic Texts Society, Cambridge.

Mannan, A. (2005) *Social Justice under Islam*, Reference Press, New Delhi.

Mehmet, Ozay (1997) Al-Ghazzali on social justice, *International Journal of Social Economics* 24(11): 1203–1218.

Timani, Hussam (2008) *Ultimate Journey: Death and Dying in the World's Major Religions*, Steven J. Rosen (ed.), Praeger, Westport, CT.

Unal, Ali (2008) *The Qur'an*, Tughra Books, Clifton, NJ.

Watt, W. Montgomery (1961) *Muhammad: Prophet and Statesman*, Oxford University Press, Oxford.

Bibliography

Abdelkader, Deina (2000) *Social Justice in Islam*, International Institute of Islamic Thought, Herndon, VA.

Ahmad, Shaikh Mahmud (1975) *Social Justice in Islam*, Institute of Islamic Culture, Lahore.

Asad, Muhammad (2008) *The Message of the Qur'an*, Book Foundation, Watsonville, CA.

Haleem, Abdel M.A.S. (2005) *The Qur'an*, Oxford University Press, Oxford.

Khadduri, Majid (1984) *The Islamic Conception of Justice*, Johns Hopkins University Press, Baltimore, MD.

Qutb, Sayyid (1953) *Al-'Adalah al-ijtima'iyah fi'l-Islam* [Social Justice in Islam], Maktabat Misr, Cairo.

Shujaat, Mohammad (2004) *Social Justice in Islam*, Anmol Publications, New Delhi.

CHAPTER 10

Islam

Contemporary Expressions

Erin E. Stiles

This essay examines expressions of social justice in modern Muslim contexts. Since the nineteenth century, Muslim intellectuals and activists from many parts of the world have emphasized justice, social justice, and the maintenance of social welfare as core values of the Islamic tradition. Nineteenth- and twentieth-century thinkers and reformers urged the renewal of Muslim societies and stressed the need not only for resistance to European imperialism in Muslim lands, but also the necessity for internal reform to address the plight of the disadvantaged in Muslim communities. A common thread that united many of these reformist thinkers was the need to reconsider the sacred sources of Islam, specifically the *Qur'an* and the *hadith* reports of what the Prophet Muhammad said and did, in light of their relationship to the historical context in which they were revealed and vis-à-vis changes in the modern era.

We can follow this thread through to discussions of gender justice, which has been a major component of the modern expression of social justice in Muslim contexts. In recent years, scholars and activists have considered the status of women and gender relationships in the sacred sources and within the broader Islamic tradition in light of modern values regarding social justice. A related issue is the significant efforts at legal reform in the Muslim world that have taken place over the past several decades. Much of this has focused on reforming shari'a, Islamic law, to reflect modern standards and address the inequities inherent in classical formulations of Islamic law; many of these reforms have focused on remedying gender inequities in the shari'a.

An issue that has received increasing attention in recent years is the question of the relationship between Islam, social justice, and the environment. At a time when those who suffer most from the effects of environmental degradation are living in poor countries that have had the least to do with human impact on climate change, environmental advocates are increasingly talking about environmental concerns as questions of social justice within an Islamic framework.

The Wiley Blackwell Companion to Religion and Social Justice, First Edition. Edited by Michael D. Palmer and Stanley M. Burgess.
© 2012 John Wiley & Sons Ltd. Published 2020 by John Wiley & Sons Ltd.

Nineteenth- and Twentieth-Century Reformers and Social Justice

In many parts of the Muslim world, significant reform and revival movements began in the nineteenth century and continued into the twentieth. Issues of social justice were a component of many of these movements. Many reformers were worried not only about the rapid expansion of Western imperialism, but also about the declining power of Muslim countries in the face of rising European economic and political power and about the status and well-being of Muslims in their home communities. Drawing many of these activists and reformers together was their belief in the commitment of Islam to justice and social welfare. Many argued that it is the duty of all Muslims to be active in this world, not simply focused on the next, and thus to care for and respond to the needs of the most unfortunate members of society. In a recent article on justice in modern Islamic thought, Gudrun Kramer has argued that in modern scholarship and commentary, justice is viewed as one of the top values – if not the primary value – of Islam (Kramer, 2007).

Among nineteenth- and twentieth-century reformers, we see a common concern with what were regarded as the misplaced priorities of the '*ulama*' – those scholars who were educated in a traditional Islamic manner and were thus the holders of centuries of religious knowledge. Reformers often argued that the '*ulama*' were too steeped in tradition and in medieval modes of thought to concern themselves with the cares and problems of the modern world. To many reformers, the traditionalism of the '*ulama*' indicated a stark disregard for the emphasis on social welfare required by Islam. To remedy this perceived neglect, many reformers argued for the necessity of reconsidering the sacred sources in light of contemporary times, rather than relying on scholarly thought from the Middle Ages.

Jamal al-Din al-Afghani (1839–1897) was a prominent and influential nineteenth-century activist and reformer who was a sharp critic of western imperialism and an advocate of Muslim unity worldwide. A somewhat mysterious figure, al-Afghani claimed to be from Afghanistan, though scholars think it is likely he was born into a Shi'i family in Iran (Keddie, 1983). It is possible that al-Afghani concealed his birthplace to make his teachings more appealing to Sunni Muslims; if so, his decision was certainly in keeping with his criticism of sectarianism in Islam and his political call for all Muslims to join together to bring about a needed renewal of Muslim societies and resist western imperialism. Al-Afghani is often credited with initiating the move toward pan-Islamism and anti-imperialism in Muslim lands.

In many ways, al-Afghani was a social and political activist more than he was a religious reformer (Keddie, 1983). We can see possible roots of later reformers' efforts at social justice in his contention that the work of a devout Muslim was in this world, not simply in focusing on the next:

> Islam is concerned not only with the life to come. Islam is more: it is concerned with its believers' interests in the world here below and with allowing them to realize success in this life as well as peace in the next life. It seeks "good fortune in two worlds." In its teachings it decrees equality among different peoples and nations. (al-Afghani, 2007: 19)

In keeping with this idea, al-Afghani was critical of the '*ulama*' as holding back the development of Muslim peoples by not engaging with the pressing issues of the day.

Furthermore, he saw no conflict between Islam and scientific advances. Indeed, he argued that the 'ulama' were responsible for hobbling Muslim society by rejecting scientific development as simply a "European" matter (Keddie, 1983: 107).

One of al-Afghani's contemporaries, the Indian thinker and writer Sir Sayyid Ahmed Khan (1817–1898), was also a proponent of reform, although he and al-Afghani differed considerably. A reformer who was perhaps best known for promoting western-style education and cooperation with the British, Ahmed Khan's views were controversial, and al-Afghani stridently criticized them as derived from British attempts to control the Indian population and mindset (Hourani, 1983: 126). Al-Afghani's critiques are laid out in his "Refutation of the Materialists" in which he censures Ahmed Khan's "materialist" views on the grounds that they placed nature above all – even the divine – and evaluates his approach to reform as too western oriented (Keddie, 1983). Furthermore, al-Afghani argues that religion is good for people "because it supports the social fabric" (Hourani, 1983: 73) and that a belief in God, or a Creator, keeps social order (Hourani, 1983: 81): "without doubt religion is the basic link of the social order, and without religion the foundations of civilization could never be firm" (Hourani, 1983: 131).

Al-Afghani's influence was widespread, and one of his followers was the modernist thinker Muhammad 'Abduh (1849–1905). In his native Egypt, 'Abduh was a prominent figure who was exiled for political reasons for several years, but later returned and eventually became the Grand Mufti of Egypt. As a follower of al-Afghani, whom he had met when he spent some time in Egypt, 'Abduh also wanted to address the decline of Muslim societies and, like his mentor, argued that while it was important to respond to foreign challenges, it was also imperative to address problems facing Muslim societies from within. 'Abduh viewed the Prophet Muhammad's mission as the founding of an ideal society based on the maintenance of the rights and duties of those living within it (Hourani, 1983: 148). Like al-Afghani, he saw no problems with the coexistence of human reason and divine revelation, and argued that Islam had always been compatible with scientific knowledge. Islam could thus be the moral foundation even for a modern society (Hourani, 1983: 140).

'Abduh was critical of the traditional way in which 'ulama' were trained and instead advocated a return to *ijtihād* – the principle of independent legal reasoning. He argued that the possibility of change is inherent in the Islamic tradition, that reason and revelation were compatible, and that it was necessary to rethink the sacred sources through *ijtihād* in light of contemporary needs and modern issues. A compelling example of this approach is 'Abduh's argument against polygamy: he contended that while polygamy may have been suitable during the time of the Prophet and the early Muslim community, it was not appropriate in contemporary Egypt, and was far more likely to cause problems in modern society than to solve any social ills. In addition, he argued that according to the *Qur'an* monogamy was clearly preferable to polygamy. He based this interpretation on verses 4:3 and 4:129, which state that polygamy is permissible only if a man is able to treat all wives equally, but that no man would be able to do so (Esposito, 2001: 48).

Another Egyptian advocate of reform who was highly influenced by Muhammad 'Abduh was Qasim Amin (1865–1908), who was interested in improving educational opportunities for young people, including women. In 1899, he published a book on the emancipation of Egyptian women, and argued that the decline of Muslim societies could be traced to a decline in social virtue, which in turn resulted from a lack of education. Improvement could begin within the family, and Amin argued for at least a primary education for women so that they would not be utterly dependent on men (Hourani, 1983: 164). Like 'Abduh, he was skeptical of polygamy and articulated the potential harm of the practice in the modern context. Despite his advocacy of women's education, he has been criticized for simply replacing an Islamic model of patriarchy with a western model of patriarchy (see Ahmed, 1992: 161).

Social Justice and Hasan al-Banna, Sayyid Qutb, and the Muslim Brotherhood

Hasan al-Banna (1906–1949), the Egyptian founder of the highly influential movement called the Muslim Brotherhood (founded in 1928), was a prominent advocate of social justice and argued for the importance of addressing the needs of the poor and the oppressed in society through institutional measures. Al-Banna was critical of the increasingly dependent relationship between the West and nonwestern countries, and he viewed western values and ideals as detrimental to Muslim societies. As a result, he called for revitalizing Muslim society through Islamic means. Like many other reformers, he advocated a return to the sacred sources of the Islamic tradition, and he viewed Islam as a comprehensive way of life that addressed social issues and thus had the potential to alleviate societal ills.

An important part of al-Banna's thought was that Islamic society should be just and that concrete measures must be undertaken in order to achieve social justice. To this aim, al-Banna advocated *zakat* as a means of redistributing wealth and as a model of Islamic social justice. *Zakat* is one of the "five pillars" of Islamic religious practice and can be described as a type of almsgiving that is incumbent on all adult Muslims; the primary recipients of *zakat* are the poor, and *zakat* is regulated by the state in some countries today. Al-Banna was highly concerned with the moral dimensions of economic activity, and argued that economics without reference to social justice and morality violated the teachings of God (Mitchell, 1969: 250). The Brotherhood adopted this sentiment, and its members advocated the unique nature of Islamic economics, in that it kept in mind the necessity of establishing and maintaining social justice (Mitchell, 1969: 251). The capitalist economy of Egypt was criticized as bringing harm to the masses and exploiting the poor. To the Brotherhood, "the corollary, or end, of moralistic economic behavior is social justice – the important foundation of the Islamic state" (Mitchell, 1969: 251). The Brotherhood also criticized the *'ulama'* for not responding to the needs of the modern age and the encroachment of foreign powers and had thus "permitted Egypt to fall into religious, cultural, political, economic, social, legal and moral decadence and impotence" (Mitchell, 1969: 212).

One of the best-known members of the Brotherhood was Sayyid Qutb (1906–1966). In his book *Social Justice in Islam* (Qutb, 1953[1948]), which became a primary intellectual reference point for the Brotherhood, Qutb places great emphasis on the Islamic imperative for concern with worldly matters, including the welfare of humanity, and argues for an Islamic means to cure the ills of Egyptian society. Early in the work, Qutb differentiates Islam from Christianity, which he refers to as a religion left in "pious isolation" from its early history, and concerned only with matters of conscience, not of the world (Qutb, 1953[1948]: 23). In Islam, on the other hand, he argues that there is no separation between life and society, and that therefore Islam "prescribes the basic principles of social justice" (Qutb, 1953[1948]: 33). Qutb's views on social justice are as follows:

> Above all other things, it is a comprehensive human justice and not merely an economic justice; that is to say, it embraces all sides of life and all aspects of activity. It is concerned alike with perception and conduct, with the heart and the conscience. The values with which this justice deals are not only economic values, nor are they merely material values in general; rather they are a mixture of moral and spiritual values together. Christianity looks at man only from the standpoint of his spiritual desires and seeks to crush down the human instincts in order to encourage those desires. On the other hand, Communism looks at man only from the standpoint of his material needs; it looks not only at human nature, but also at the world and at life from a purely material point of view. But Islam looks at man as forming a unity whose spiritual desires cannot be separated from his bodily appetites and whose moral needs cannot be divorced from his material needs. It looks at the world and at life with this all-embracing view which permits of no separation or division . . . Thus, in the Islamic view, life consists of mercy, love, help, and a mutual responsibility among Muslims in particular, and among all human beings in general . . . (Qutb, 1953[1948]: 45)

In order to build the social order, then, a people must reconnect with Islam. Qutb places great emphasis on mutual responsibility as the core of social justice and argues that the foundations of justice are the following:

1. Freedom of conscience.
2. Equality of all men.
3. Mutual responsibility of society.

Although Qutb links the necessity of paying *zakat* to the idea of mutual responsibility, it is important to note that he does not demand outright equality of wealth as essential in striving for social justice. Kramer has recently pointed out that there is also a prominent emphasis on equity or fairness rather than complete equality among contemporary thinkers on justice in Islam (Kramer, 2007). In other words, although there is a religious imperative to ensure a certain level of well-being for all members of society, it is not necessary to redistribute resources so that all have equal wealth.

The Muslim Brotherhood can be considered as both a social and a political movement, with the overarching aim to reform society along Islamic principles. The movement has at times taken radical, even violent, measures to do so and was often at odds with the Egyptian state and at times banned; both al-Banna and Qutb were executed by the state. Since the inception of the movement, however, there have also been undertakings relevant to a quest for social justice. The protection of and advocacy for laborers was one such aim. The Brotherhood assisted in forming labor unions, participated in strikes, and also advocated for labor by publicizing cases of exploitation of workers by foreign companies. In this sense, Richard Mitchell argues that the Brotherhood was fulfilling one of al-Banna's early requests: that the workers be protected from the rapaciousness of foreign companies (Mitchell, 1969: 279). In the 1940s, laborers were invited to join meetings of the Brotherhood to protest the government's lack of involvement in protecting workers and to share ideas about how to mobilize for effective change.

Education was another major focus of social reform for the Brotherhood. It was concerned with both the poor quality and the increasing fragmentation of education in Egypt, and aimed to reform the existing educational system and to establish new schools. Although the Brotherhood had a social welfare division and aided the poor in rural and urban areas, it was education that was viewed as the promise for building a better society in the future (Mitchell, 1969: 292). Unsurprisingly, a main goal was reforming schools along an Islamic basis and incorporating Islamic studies into the government schools. Another important goal was unifying the curriculum in order to prevent the division and dissolution of society, which was viewed as a potential problem stemming from the curricular differences between the religious and secular schools. Although the Brotherhood established its own schools, these remained largely informal (Mitchell, 1969: 287).

Islam, Social Justice, and the State

Many thinkers in the contemporary period have taken up the question of whether, according to Islam, the modern state can or should preserve social justice. Many have argued that it is indeed a duty of the modern state to ensure social justice to the best extent possible. Sayyid Qutb, for example, argued that the state should have enough power to ensure the social welfare of the citizenry – Muslim rulers should have powers enabling the ruler to provide for the "general welfare" (Mitchell, 1969: 239). Another member of the Brotherhood, Muhammad al-Ghazali, also argued that the state had certain powers to provide for the welfare of society, and could even restrict certain religiously grounded rights when they were deemed contrary to the general welfare of society (Mitchell, 1969: 240).

In writing on political theory and Islam, the influential South Asian scholar and politician Abu-l-'Ala Mawdudi (1903–1979) argued that the purpose of the Islamic state is to guarantee social justice and that the appropriate system for establishing social justice is laid out in the *Qur'an*:

> The object of the state is not merely to prevent people from exploiting each other, to safeguard their liberty and to protect its subjects from foreign invasion. It also aims at evolving and developing that well-balanced system of social justice which has been set forth by God in His Holy Book. (Mawdudi, 2007: 266)

Like many others, Mawdudi took up the practice of *zakat* as a means of achieving social justice and contended that although humans have the God-given right to acquire private property, doing so is not a paramount value, and is mitigated by the requirements of paying *zakat*.

More recently, the Saudi Arabian economist M. Umer Chapra (b. 1933) has argued that it is the duty of the Islamic state to provide a reasonable standard of living for those residing in the state (Chapra, 2007: 243). However, similar to the position of Sayyid Qutb, Chapra does not mean that differences in earning or wealth are not permissible. Instead, he takes up the challenge of answering where the state should get these resources, and he argues that *zakat*, taxes, and natural resources can all be considered viable means of providing for the needs of the citizenry. Chapra argues that there is an essential focus on the importance of social welfare in Islam and notes that because the well-being of the community is paramount in the tradition, individual freedoms must be curtailed if those freedoms infringe on the maintenance of social welfare.

Gender Justice in Muslim Contexts

One of the most significant areas in which the issue of social justice has come to the fore in Islamic contexts in recent years concerns gender justice. Muslim thinkers and activists from Malaysia to the United States have been reconsidering the status of women vis-à-vis the Islamic tradition and have argued for and striven to advance women's rights within an Islamic framework. Scholars have argued that the Islamic sources stress a model of gender equity, and activists have used this as a foundation to struggle for law and public policy to ensure women's rights. What is perhaps most notable about these efforts is that they have sought to promote and preserve gender justice through the framework of Islam: as with the other reformers we have discussed, they view justice – including gender justice – as an essential Islamic value. For example, in the recent volume *Progressive Muslims on Justice, Gender, and Pluralism*, editor Omid Safi writes that from the viewpoint of progressive Muslims,

> Muslim women own their God-given rights by the simple virtue of being human . . . Gender justice is crucial, indispensible and essential . . . Gender equity is a measuring stick of the broader concerns for social justice and pluralism. (Safi, 2003: 11)

One notable early movement was the Egyptian Feminist Union (EFU), formed by Huda Shaarawi (1879–1947) in the early 1920s. Shaarawi was an educated, upper-class woman who is perhaps best known for symbolically removing her veil in an Alexandria train station in 1923. She had just returned from a women's conference in Rome, and she encouraged women to cast off their headscarves in a quest for liberation. The EFU was organized to advocate for educational, political, and legal rights for women in the new Egyptian state. Similar movements advocating for women's rights were formed in Turkey, Iran, and Kuwait, among other countries (for a brief overview, see Badran, 1995). In Pakistan, for example, a women's group formed to protest the Hudood Ordinance of 1979, a very strict law that called for harsh punishments for certain criminal offenses; the law is perhaps most notorious for failing to differentiate rape and adultery.

In recent years, Muslim feminist scholars have stressed that gender equity is inherent in the sacred sources of the Islamic tradition. The Moroccan sociologist Fatima Mernissi is well known for her feminist approach to Islam and her study of *hadith* reports concerning women and gender relations. In *The Veil and the Male Elite: A Feminist Interpretation of Women's Rights in Islam* (Mernissi, 1991), she contends that some of the most misogynistic *hadith* reports were fabricated. She methodically investigates, for example, the oft-quoted *hadith* used to deny women's activism in politics or the public realm: "Those who entrust their affairs to a woman will never find prosperity." Based on her research, Mernissi asserts that even though this *hadith* is considered legitimate today, legal scholars in the past did not agree on its validity, and many did not consider it sufficient to deny women the chance to participate in political affairs (Mernissi, 1991: 61). Another prominent scholar in this area is the American Amina Wadud, who is perhaps best known for her book *Qur'an and Woman: Rereading the Sacred Text from a Woman's Perspective* (Wadud, 1999). In her reading of the *Qur'an*, she concludes that there is no inherently greater value placed on either women or men, and that the relationship between men and women is portrayed as one that is equitable and based on mutual dependence – not one of men's control over women. Other contemporary scholars have argued for the need to rethink feminism in Muslim contexts. Sa'diyya Shaikh, for example, argues for the need to "transform feminism" in order to reject colonial-era feminist views of Muslim women as a victimized and helpless other and to embrace a multiplicity of feminisms and feminist activisms. Shaikh writes that, "In the last analysis, Islamic feminism is . . . one of the most engaged contemporary responses to the core Qur'anic injunction for social justice of our time" (Shaikh, 2003: 159).

In addition to such scholarly work, there are numerous organizations currently working to promote gender justice in Muslim communities worldwide. One notable example is the Malaysian Sisters in Islam (SIS), which formed in 1988 in an effort to empower Malaysian Muslim women and to develop women's rights in an Islamic framework through legal means and public policy. SIS views women's position in Islam as one of equality and seeks to uphold this ideal in the face of inequitable social and cultural practices. According to the organization's website:

> Our efforts to promote the rights of Muslim women are based on the principles of equality, justice and freedom enjoined by the *Qur'an* as made evident during our study of the holy text. We uphold the revolutionary spirit of Islam, a religion which uplifted the status of women when it was revealed 1400 years ago. We believe that Islam does not endorse the oppression of women and denial of their basic rights of equality and human dignity. We are deeply saddened that religion has been used to justify cultural practices and values that regard women as inferior and subordinate to men and we believe that this has been made possible because men have had exclusive control over the interpretation of the text of the *Qur'an*. (http://www.sistersinislam.org.my)

The research arm of the organization states its objectives as discerning – in the face of discrimination against women on the grounds of and often in the name of religion – whether religious sources truly dictate the inferior status of women. Textual research done by SIS did not find this to be the case, and this conclusion proved foundational for advocacy projects.

One such project concerns polygamy. SIS contends that Islamic family law should reflect the realities of modern life and in 2004 began a project to research the effects of polygamy on Malaysian families. In a series of press releases from the 1990s and early 2000s, SIS argued that there are "popular misconceptions" about polygamy in Islamic contexts and that the "clear intention of the *Qur'an* is to restrict polygamy" (Sisters in Islam, 2007: 198). Similar to the arguments of Muhammad 'Abduh and other modernist thinkers, SIS emphasized that the *Qur'an* clearly shows a preference for monogamy and concluded that polygamy is not a right, but a responsibility to be undertaken only under a very specific set of circumstances and with specific conditions attached, which were outlined in the socio-historical context of the early Muslim community – a time of warfare when orphans needed to be cared for (Sisters in Islam, 2007: 198). In 2003, SIS issued a release in support of a new requirement in one Malaysian state that all parties to a proposed polygamous marriage – the wife, the husband, the potential new bride, and her guardian – appear before court to assess the ability of the man in question to be just and equitable to both wives. SIS also urged the implementation of several procedural measures, one of which was ensuring that the following four conditions be met before a polygamous union was permitted: "just and necessary, financial means, equal treatment and no harm caused to the existing wife" (Sisters in Islam, 2007: 201).

Women Living Under Muslim Laws (WLUML) is an international network that was developed in the 1980s to protect and promote women's rights and equality, and to provide contacts and resources to women throughout the world who live under "laws and customs said to derive from Islam" (http://www.wluml.org/). WLUML states as one of its goals the attempt to link women with regional organizations around the world that strive to work for women's rights. A similar organization, Women in Islam, founded in 1992 in response to the acts of violence committed against Muslim women in Bosnia, also advocates for women's rights and social justice. Among the many goals of the organization are encouraging scholarly activity among Muslim women, combating stereotypes of Islam and Muslim women, mediating conflict through education and awareness building, and promoting social justice worldwide through increased cross-cultural understanding (http://www.womeninislam.org/about.html).

Karamah, Muslim Women Lawyers for Human Rights, is a human rights organization based in the United States that aims to pursue gender justice and women's empowerment through educating Muslim women throughout the world in Islamic law and leadership skills. In addition to advocating for women's rights from both the perspective of Islamic and American law, Karamah runs an annual program to train women in law and leadership, with the aim that they can enact positive change in their home communities. According to the organization's website,

> Karamah seeks to transform the archaic conception of women's status within some Muslim communities to reflect better the egalitarian Qur'anic worldview of gender equity and humanity. Such a conceptual transformation, along with tangible reforms and

constructive discourse, will improve the treatment of women and ensure that they take an active part in governing their lives. (http://www.karamah.org/home.htm)

Islamic Law and Social Justice in the Modern World

Over the past century, many thinkers have considered the relevance of sacred sources to issues of social justice in the modern context, and many have called for a reinterpretation of these sources in light of modern ideals. Asaf A.A. Fyzee (1899–1981), an Indian expert in law and jurisprudence, has specifically argued that shari'a must conform to modern notions of social justice (Fyzee, 2007: 156). To this end, there is a need for reinterpretation of the *Qur'an* in light of the historical setting of its revelation and of modern realities. Law is something that can be changed, and Fyzee outlines procedures for examining the law in light of change in the modern world. Islamic personal law, for example, should be examined vis-à-vis modern legal thought, and interpreters of the law should consider the way in which "the rules be sustained, amended or repealed so as to conform to modern concepts of social justice and to promote the social well-being of the Muslim community as an integral part of the society in general" (Fyzee, 2007: 156). Efforts at reinterpreting the law are perhaps most significant in the realm of family law. Some of the notable areas of reform have been women's rights in marriage and divorce, women's financial rights in marriage, and limiting or restricting polygamous marriages.

In the modern period, reformers have emphasized using principles of Islamic jurisprudence like *ijtihād*, independent legal reasoning, to reform Islamic law in light of modern ideals. Reformers advocating *ijtihād* were critical of *taqlid*, adherence to the legal reasoning and writings of scholars from centuries past, and we have seen that this formed some of the basis for reformers' criticism of the '*ulama*'. Many thinkers have also noted the importance of the legal idea of *maslahah* (or *istislah*) – the public interest – in interpreting the law (Kramer, 2007: 22). The principle is that in matters regarding social welfare, the Qur'anic ideal is justice, and thus the public welfare or the public interest must be considered above all else. Both *ijtihād* and *maslahah* are often described as methodologically appropriate in Islam to reform the law in order to reflect modern times and contemporary notions of social justice, and were advocated by thinkers like Muhammad 'Abduh

> so that in the event that a particular social need was not covered by specific shari'a texts, a jurist using his reason might interpret the law in light of the public interest. The result was a method by which Islamic law might continuously and comprehensively be adapted to changing social needs. (Esposito, 2001: 145)

Today, many Muslims live in states that provide for Islamic law and Islamic courts in some capacity. In most places, Islamic law courts have jurisdiction only over family or personal status matters like marriage, divorce, and inheritance. In recent decades, many states have taken measures to address inequities in the law – particularly regarding gender – to reflect modern values. In many states, these reforms took place with the codification of law, which was often quite different from the way in which Islamic law had historically been interpreted (Mayer, 1995: 468). Many reforms aimed at equalizing men's and women's rights in marriage and divorce, and these reforms were sometimes accomplished by requiring marriages and divorces to be conducted through the state instead of within the Muslim community, or at least registered with state offices. Esposito notes that these reforms indicated a change to regarding marriage not simply as a matter between individuals, but as something that should be regulated by the state, and furthermore addressed "the question of social justice for women before the law by expanding and protecting their rights to actively participate in the processes of marriage and divorce" (Esposito, 2001: 93).

Some notable reforms took place relatively early in the twentieth century. In 1915, the Ottoman Empire passed two laws granting women greater rights in divorce. In 1917, the *Ottoman Law of Family Rights* was passed, which included elements from each of the four Sunni schools of law, granted even greater divorce rights to women, and served as a model for other reform efforts in the Middle East (Esposito, 2001: 51). In the 1920s in Egypt, similar laws were enacted that gave women additional divorce rights, on the basis that judges could adopt laws from more liberal schools of Islamic law than the school that was traditionally adhered to in Egypt. The laws also restricted a man's right unilaterally to divorce his wife (Esposito, 2001: 56). Later, under President Anwar Sadat in 1979, personal status law was reformed by presidential decree in an effort to give women and men more equitable rights in divorce, child custody, and maintenance (Fawzy, 2004). This law, called Jihan's Law after the president's wife, gave women the right to maintenance from husbands even if a woman worked outside of the home without his consent, and the right to divorce husbands who took another wife. It also gave women much greater custody rights over their children. The law was controversial, however, particularly because it guaranteed women the right to seek divorce when husbands married additional wives. Interestingly, it was not only men who opposed the new law, but also women, many of whom argued that it contravened shari'a (Fawzy, 2004: 36). In 1985, the Supreme Court rejected these new laws on the grounds that the president had issued them at a time when the People's Assembly was not in session (Fawzy, 2004: 38). A modified version of the 1979 law was passed in the same year that reflected the concerns of those who had opposed the original law. For example, a woman who requested a divorce on the grounds that her husband had married another wife now had to establish that she had been injured by this development; the original law did not impose this burden.

In 2000, another highly controversial law concerning divorce was introduced in response to increasing pressure from feminists and the fact that many Egyptians deemed the existing laws unacceptable in the modern era. Among other measures, the law permitted a womzn to seek a type of divorce known as *khul'* from a judge if she would relinquish her financial rights vis-à-vis her husband. *Khul'* is a widespread type of Islamic divorce, though it is understood and applied somewhat differently in different contexts; under the circumstances described in Egypt, it is known as judicial *khul'*. The new law also deemed *talaq*, male unilateral divorce by repudiation, invalid unless such a divorce was witnessed and registered with the proper authorities. This law raised opposition from various sources, primarily on the grounds that it contravened shari'a. Essam Fawzy argues that this law is a significant step forward in terms of women's rights. However, he notes that there remain some drawbacks: for example, the fact that it takes a woman a great length of time, possibly up to several years, to obtain a divorce that she has requested. Importantly, Fawzy also notes the impact of consciousness raising:

> legal reform alone does not suffice to guarantee women's rights, but rather, awareness of the law has to be raised. Many women, especially those from the poorest economic classes, are not aware of what rights the law does protect and have no possibility of putting its positive aspects to use. (Fawzy, 2004: 88)

Legal reform was underway in many other countries, and several reforms aimed at making divorce more equitable were also enacted. With the advent of formalized legal codes, the right of men to divorce their wives through unilateral repudiation has been restricted to a great degree in some places. Several countries, including Morocco, Yemen, and Malaysia, require all divorces to take place in the courts; and while Jordan and Libya permit repudiation, the divorce must be registered for it to take effect. In Indonesia, the 1974 Marriage Law provided for constraints on Islamic marriage and divorce law, although the law that eventually passed was weaker than that proposed due to opposition from religious conservatives (Mayer, 1995: 470). Several countries have aimed to restrict polygamy in an effort to enhance social justice. Tunisia has perhaps taken the boldest measures, in that it abolished polygamy entirely and gave men and women equal rights in divorce in the 1950s. In banning polygamy, the government argued that although the practice may have been considered acceptable at one point in Islamic history, it is not acceptable in the modern period; the argument drew a parallel to slavery (Esposito, 2001: 101). In 1981, the law was amended to provide divorced women with support comparable to what they would have received during their marriages.

Although fewer reforms have been undertaken in the realm of inheritance law, Somalia was notable for reforming inheritance law to give men and women equal standing; women were entitled to the same share that men received, rather than one half, as stipulated in classical Islamic law (Esposito, 2001: 110). The 1992 Compilation of Islamic Law in Indonesia (*Kompilasi Hukum Islam di Indonesia*) also reformed inheritance law by including provisions contrary to classical Islamic law and standard jurisprudence (Bowen, 2003: 17, 134–138).

Abdullahi Ahmed an-Na'im, a professor of law at Emory University, has called for a reformation of Islamic law in light of changes in the modern world. He argues that Muslim peoples have the right to self-determination and governance by Islamic law, so long as the latter does not infringe on the rights of others (an-Na'im, 1990). According to an-Na'im, Muslims should have the prerogative of living in societies that recognize Islamic public law as well as private law. As we have seen, the majority of states that recognize Islamic law do so only in the realm of private, family matters. An-Na'im takes up the question of Islamic public law and the issue of human rights, which he refers to as "those rights recognized by and promoted through international laws and institutions" (an-Na'im, 1990: 161). He contends that through reform, Islamic public law can be made compatible with modern conceptions of human rights. Specifically, this sort of reform would require a way to reinterpret the sacred sources to eliminate bias against women and non-Muslims. The methodology he embraces involves disregarding certain sacred texts that are deemed relevant only to a particular phase in Muslim history in favor of other texts. An-Na'im is strongly influenced by the reform movement of Sudanese Ustadh Mahmoud Mohamed Taha, who argued that certain portions of sacred texts are not, and should not be considered, applicable in the modern world. Taha was an advocate of what he termed "the evolution of Islamic legislation" (An-Na'im, 1990: 34), a principle of interpretation of the sacred sources of Islam in which certain verses or texts from the *Qur'an* and *sunna* (the example of the Prophet Muhammad) that are deemed no longer relevant to the modern period are disregarded in favor of the "eternal message" of the *Qur'an* regarding issues such as justice (an-Na'im, 1990: 180).

An outgrowth of this work and a recent example of a movement concerned primarily with the subject of human rights and Islam is the "Rights at Home" project. A joint effort organized by an-Na'im and Laila al-Zwaini through the former Institute for the Study of Islam in the Modern World at Leiden University, this project aimed to consider human rights in various Muslim contexts and to raise awareness about human rights and shari'a through workshops in countries throughout the Middle East, Africa, and Asia. The workshops focused on educating people about their basic rights according to Islam and the norms and laws of their home societies, and building networks of Muslims who are committed to social change.

Islam, Social Justice, and Philanthropy

There are, of course, many organizations working on issues relevant to social justice beyond gender issues and legal reform. The Aga Khan Development Network (AKDN) is a good example of a contemporary, philanthropic organization that attempts to remedy the plight of the poor the world over by supporting projects to improve health, education, and economic development. Although the foundation is committed to an Islamic idea of ethics, Muslims are not the only recipients of aid. Under the leadership of the Aga Khan, the spiritual leader (imam) of the Nizari Ismaili branch of Shi'i Islam, the AKDN is an umbrella organization for many agencies and programs that are concerned with all kinds of social issues, and collectively attempts to improve the living conditions of the poor around the world. According to the mission described on the AKDN website:

> In Islam's ethical tradition, religious leaders not only interpret the faith but also have a responsibility to help improve the quality of life in their community and in the societies amongst which they live. (http://www.akdn.org/)

Islam and the Environment

In recent years, Muslim thinkers have also turned their attention toward the relationships among Islam, social justice, and environmental degradation. One of the first to consider the question of the relationship between religion and the environment from an Islamic perspective was the philosopher Seyyid Hossein Nasr, who published a book entitled *Man and Nature: The Spiritual Crisis of Modern Man* in 1966. Nasr criticized western forms of modernity that lacked respect for the earth as leading to environmental crisis. He argued for a reconsideration of the relationship between humanity and the natural world from the perspective of several religious traditions, including Islam.

More recently, others have taken up the question of the relationship between modernity and environmental degradation, and have notably called this degradation a form of injustice. These thinkers have argued that the injustice stems from the fact that many of the people who are most directly affected by the environmental crisis live in impoverished parts of the world and have had far less to do with causing the crisis than their counterparts in wealthier countries (Foltz, 2003). For some thinkers, the behavior leading to the environmental crisis is distinctly un-Islamic. Yasin Dutton, for example, argues that global forms of capitalism that are based on interest are responsible for the decimation of the environment and are also distinctly un-Islamic due to the religious prohibition on usury (Dutton, 2003: 331).

Drawing on the notion of justice as a core Islamic value and Qur'anic injunctions proclaiming humanity's stewardship of the earth, contributors to the recent volume *Islam and Ecology: A Bestowed Trust* (Foltz et al., 2003), based on the proceedings of a 1998 conference at Harvard University, agree that achieving justice in society will mitigate environmental problems. Editor Richard Foltz writes:

> It is no accident, therefore, that for the most part our writers are more immediately concerned with issues of social justice and the human relationship with the Divine than they are with the state of the environment per se. Environmental problems exist, to be sure, but in the perspective of many Muslim thinkers, environmental degradation is merely a symptom of the broader (and, to a Muslim concerned not just with this world but also the next, more alarming) calamity that human societies are not living in accordance with God's will. A just society, one in which humans relate to each other and to God as they should, will be one in which environmental problems simply will not exist. (Foltz, 2003: xxxix)

Similarly, Adnan Z. Amin notes:

> the traditional concern of Islam for social justice and care for the poor, orphaned, and the widowed has a broader relevance that embraces concern for the natural environment as well. Protection of land and proper treatment of biodiversity are now being advocated by Islamic scholars and teachers. (Amin, 2003: xxiii)

In recent decades, some Muslim countries have instituted policies in an effort to curb environmental degradation, and this action has sometimes been taken within a specifically Islamic framework. Foltz claims that Iran may offer "the strongest evidence of an applied Islamic environmental ethic in the world today" (Foltz, 2003: 259). The Iranian Department of the Environment argues that there is an Islamic basis for the measures taken to protect the environment, and Foltz notes that the constitution resulting from the 1979 revolution included this commitment to environmental protection by forbidding any activities, "economic or otherwise," that jeopardize the environment (Foltz, 2003: 261). In response to environmental problems, such as the severe pollution in urban areas like Tehran, the Department of the Environment instituted a policy aimed at curbing population growth significantly, which includes requirements for couples to take family planning classes before marrying (Foltz, 2003: 261). Foltz notes the proliferation of environmental NGOs in Iran that have led to increasing awareness of environmental issues among Iran's population, some of which specifically note the link between environment and social justice issues and others of which, while not explicitly Islamic, aim to promote the idea of Islamic stewardship of the earth as laid out in the *Qur'an* and *hadith* literature.

Conclusion

For over a century, Muslim thinkers have emphasized social justice and the safeguarding of social welfare as foundational values of the Islamic tradition. A key thread that has united scholars and activists in their efforts to strive for a more just society has been the argument that the sacred sources of the Islamic tradition must be reconsidered in light of modern attitudes and values. These efforts are clearly illustrated in work on gender justice and in reforms of Islamic family law. Also, in addition to significant efforts at institutional reform and public policy, we have seen that campaigners for social justice have not underestimated the power of raising awareness to encourage Muslims around the world to learn about their rights within the Islamic tradition and the primacy of social justice within Islam, and to use this knowledge to effect change in their home communities.

References

Ahmed, Leila (1992) *Women and Gender in Islam*, Yale University Press, New Haven, CT.

Aga Khan Development Network (n.d.) http://www.akdn.org/ (accessed April 20, 2011).

Al-Afghani, Jamal al-Din (2007) Islamic solidarity, in *Islam in Transition: Muslim Perspectives*, John J. Donohue and John L. Esposito (eds.), Oxford University Press, Oxford, pp. 16–19.

Amin, Adnan Z. (2003) Preface, in *Islam and Ecology: A Bestowed Trust*, Richard C. Foltz, Frederick M. Denny, and Azizan Baharuddin (eds.), Harvard University Press, Center for the Study of World Religions, Cambridge, MA, pp. xxxiii–xxxvii.

An-Na'im, Abdullahi Ahmed (1990) *Toward an Islamic Reformation: Civil Liberties, Human Rights, and International Law*, Syracuse University Press, Syracuse, NY.

Badran, Margot (1995) Feminism, in *The Oxford Encyclopedia of the Modern Islamic World*, Vol. 2, John L. Esposito (ed.), pp. 19–23.

Bowen, John R. (2003) *Islam, Law and Equality in Indonesia*, Cambridge University Press, Cambridge.

Chapra, M. Umer (2007) The Islamic welfare state, in *Islam in Transition: Muslim Perspectives*, John J. Donohue and John L. Esposito (eds.), Oxford University Press, Oxford, pp. 242–248.

Dutton, Yasin (2003) The environmental crisis of our time: A Muslim response, in *Islam and Ecology: A Bestowed Trust*, Richard C. Foltz,

Frederick M. Denny, and Azizan Baharuddin (eds.), Harvard University Press, Center for the Study of World Religions, Cambridge, MA, pp. 323–340.

Esposito, John L. with DeLong-Bas, Natana J. (2001) *Women in Muslim Family Law*, Syracuse University Press, Syracuse, NY.

Fawzy, Essam (2004) Muslim personal status law in Egypt: The current situation and possibilities of reform through internal initiatives, in *Women's Rights and Islamic Family Law: Perspectives on Reform*, Lynn Welchma (ed.), Zed Books, London, pp. 15–95.

Foltz, Richard C. (2003) Islamic environmentalism: A matter of interpretation, in *Islam and Ecology: A Bestowed Trust*, Richard C. Foltz, Frederick M. Denny, and Azizan Baharuddin (eds.), Harvard University Press, Center for the Study of World Religions, Cambridge, MA, pp. 249–280.

Foltz, Richard C., Denny, Frederick M., and Baharuddin, Azizan (eds.) (2003) *Islam and Ecology: A Bestowed Trust*, Harvard University Press, Center for the Study of World Religions, Cambridge, MA.

Fyzee, Asaf A.A. (2007) The reinterpretation of Islam, in *Islam in Transition: Muslim Perspectives*, John J. Donohue and John L. Esposito (eds.), Oxford University Press, Oxford, pp. 151–156.

Hourani, Albert (1983) *Arabic Thought in the Liberal Age 1798–1939*, Cambridge University Press, Cambridge.

Karamah (n.d.) http://www.karamah.org/ (accessed April 20, 2011).

Keddie, Nikki (1983) *An Islamic Response to Imperialism: Political and Religious Writings of Sayyid Jamal ad-Din "al-Afghani,"* University of California Press, Berkeley.

Kramer, Gudrun (2007) Justice in modern Islamic thought, in *Shari'a: Islamic Law in the Contemporary Context*, Abbas Amanat and Frank Griffel (eds.), Stanford University Press, Palo Alto, CA, pp. 20–37.

Mawdudi, Abu-l-'Ala (2007) Political theory of Islam, in *Islam in Transition: Muslim Perspectives*, John J. Donohue and John L. Esposito (eds.), Oxford University Press, Oxford, pp. 262–270.

Mayer, Ann Elizabeth (1995) Modern legal reform, in *The Oxford Encyclopedia of the Modern Islamic World*, Vol. 3, John L. Esposito (ed.), Oxford University Press, New York, pp. 464–472.

Mernissi, Fatima (1991) *The Veil and the Male Elite: A Feminist Interpretation of Women's Rights in Islam*, Addison-Wesley, Reading, MA.

Mitchell, Richard P. (1969) *The Society of the Muslim Brothers*, Oxford University Press, Oxford.

Nasr, Seyyid Hossein (2007[1966]) *Man and Nature: The Spiritual Crisis of Modern Man*, Kazi Publications, Chicago.

Qutb, Sayyid (1953[1948]) *Social Justice in Islam*, trans. John B. Hardie, revd Hamid Algar, Islamic Publications International, New York.

Safi, Omid (ed.) (2003) *Progressive Muslims on Justice, Gender, and Pluralism*, OneWorld Press, Oxford.

Shaikh, Sa'diyya (2003) Transforming feminism: Islam, women and gender justice, in *Progressive Muslims on Justice, Gender, and Pluralism*, Omid Safi (ed.), OneWorld Press, Oxford, pp. 147–162.

Sisters in Islam (n.d.) http://www.sistersinislam.org.my (accessed April 20, 2011).

Sisters in Islam (2007) Chronology of a struggle for equal rights, in Islam *in Transition: Muslim Perspectives*, John J. Donohue and John L. Esposito (eds), Oxford University Press, Oxford, pp. 197–202.

Wadud, Amina (1999) *Qur'an and Woman: Rereading the Sacred Text from a Woman's. Perspective*, Oxford University Press, New York.

Women in Islam (n.d.) http://www.womeninislam.org/about.html (accessed April 20, 2011).

Women Living Under Muslim Laws (n.d.) http://www.wluml.org/ (accessed April 20, 2011).

Bibliography

Donohue, John J. and Esposito, John L. (eds.) (2007) *Islam in Transition: Muslim Perspectives*, Oxford University Press, Oxford.

Safi, Omid (ed.) (2003) Introduction: The times they are a-changin' – a Muslim quest for justice, gender equality and pluralism, in *Progressive Muslims on Justice*, Gender, and Pluralism, Omid Safi (ed.), One World Press, Oxford, pp. 1–29.

CHAPTER 11
Judaism
Historical Setting

Moshe Hellinger

Jewish religious tradition manifests itself in several different domains: sacred texts (Hebrew Bible, Talmud, the prayer book); discussions and interpretations of these texts through the ages; ceremonies and festivals that are celebrated in the Jewish yearly cycle; the observance of the rules governing daily life for individuals and communities mandated by the halakhah (Jewish law); communal institutions that have existed throughout Jewish history; andstories, myths, symbols, and heroes that exemplify religious faith and obedience to God. In all of these spheres, the concept of social justice is endemic – inseparable from the Jewish creed.

One of the major features of Judaism is its public character. Whereas the value of the individual is acknowledged and celebrated, Judaism places great emphasis on the strong bond between the individual and the community; that is, on the crucial role of the community in the life of the individual. Traditionally and by the very terms of Jewish discourse, being part of the Jewish collective means belonging to the Jewish people as well as to the Jewish religion.

This unique compound core of Judaism, whereby the collective Jewish identity is both religious and national, has significant consequences. Consider the following examples of Jewish "collectivism":

1 According to Jewish tradition, a person is considered a Jew if born to a Jewish mother (an ascriptive biological trait, by virtue of which the individual automatically joins the Jewish people as a quasi-familial collective entity) or if he becomes a Jew through a religious conversion ceremony and vows to observe the *mitzvot*, the religious commandments (a spiritual personal trait). The proselyte is considered a Jew for all intents and purposes and may view the Hebrew Patriarchs as his/her own forebears as s/he joins not only the Jewish religion but also the Jewish collective.

The Wiley Blackwell Companion to Religion and Social Justice, First Edition. Edited by Michael D. Palmer and Stanley M. Burgess.
© 2012 John Wiley & Sons Ltd. Published 2020 by John Wiley & Sons Ltd.

2   According to Jewish tradition, a Jew is bound by 613 *mitzvot*, of which 248 are positive and 365 are negative. Many of these commandments are imposed on the community as a whole, such as the duty to appoint magistrates. Moreover, many of the obligations originating in the Oral Law ensure that the individual will be part of the community, for example the duty to recite the congregational prayer three times a day.

This collective aspect of Judaism bears directly on the issue of social justice. Throughout Jewish history, not only was the individual personally required to help the weak, there also were clear-cut public obligations to do so. The community was required to provide educational, health, and welfare services, raising the necessary funds partly through institutionalized public taxation.

Furthermore, the intimate bond between Judaism and morality as it emerges from the Pentateuch, and even more so from the prophetic books, accords great weight to social justice. Jewish religious tradition views morality – divinely ordained morality – as a guide for the individual and society alike; and in this context, justice functions both as a religious virtue and as a personal and collective religious duty (Cohen, 1972).

Theology and Justice in Judaism

The biblical basis for an egalitarian notion of justice is found in the first chapter of Genesis, where the creation of the world reaches its peak in the creation of man in the image of God:

> And God said, Let us make mankind in our image, after our likeness, and let them have dominion over the fish of the sea, and over the birds of the sky, and over the cattle, and over the whole earth, and over every creeping thing that creeps on earth. So God created mankind in His image, in the image of God He created him; male and female He created them. (Genesis 1:26–27)

In the world of Judaism, the theological postulate concerning the relationship between God and His creation, and especially between God and man, is the starting point in all moral, social, and political issues. Therefore, this postulate is also central to the concept of justice, and particularly to social justice (Goodman, 1988: Ch. 1). The biblical verses describing the creation of man convey the connection between the unique individual aspect of every person and the universal aspect, which emerges from the fact that Adam and Eve, the prototypes of humankind, were created in the image of God. The same verses have also led to a dialectic of human dignity and humility before God (Soloveitchik, 1982: 211–212; Hartman, 1985: Chs. 2, 3). This idea is vividly captured in Psalms:

> How majestic is thy name in all the earth ... When I behold thy heavens, the work of thy fingers, the moon and the stars which Thou hast ordained; what is man that Thou art mindful of him, mortal man that Thou hast taken note of him? Yet Thou hast made him

little less than divine, and adorned him with glory and majesty. Thou hast made him master over thy handiwork, laying the world at his feet. (Psalms 8:2–7)

Human dignity derives from the creativity and majesty of God, but can also be interpreted as signifying basic equality. Humility, at the other pole, plays an important role in all streams of Judaism that adhere to the rabbinic saying "Be very, very humble" (Mishnah, Avot [Sayings of the Fathers], 4:4). In the teaching of R. Israel Bal-Shem-Tov, founder of the Hassidic movement (in the second half of the eighteenth century) and his disciples, humility becomes the dissolution of the self in the Divine (Schatz-Oppenheimer, 1968: Ch. 2).

Humility before God entails a certain measure of respectful humility in approaching the universe and confronting ecological issues, but its major moral implication concerns interpersonal relations. In fact, the moral regulation of the traditional Jewish society is governed by the dictates of God and implemented through cleaving to God and emulating His ways (*Imitatio Dei*): "You shall be holy, for I, the Lord your God, am holy" (Leviticus 19:2). As the sages assert: "Be thou like Him; just as He is gracious and compassionate, so be thou gracious and compassionate" (BT [Babylonian Talmud], Shabbat 133b). Another homiletic interpretation of the sages, based on the biblical verse "You shall walk after the Lord your God . . . and hold fast to Him" (Deuteronomy 13:5), elucidates this notion of cleaving to God and emulating Him. The Talmud asks:

> Is it then possible for a human being to walk after the *Shekhinah* (the Divine Presence) . . . But [one can] walk after the attributes of the Holy One, blessed be He. As He clothes the naked, so do thou also clothe the naked . . . (BT, Sotah 14a)

Writing in the same vein, Maimonides suggested:

> In this way did the prophets attribute to God such terms as long-suffering, abundant in beneficence, just and right, perfect, mighty, and powerful, as well as others, for example, to proclaim that they are good and straight paths, and that man is obligated to follow them, and to be like unto Him, in proportion to His power. (Mishneh Torah, Laws Concerning Ethics, 1:6)

Thus, to a large extent, the notion of emulating God finds its expression in the close connection among the concepts of *tsedek* (justice), *tsedakah* (charity), and righteousness. As suggested by R. Moshe Avigdor Amiel, the Chief Rabbi of Tel Aviv in the 1940s, "Even the concepts of moral and legal justice originate in one single source: 'As He . . . so do thou' – as He executes justice, so do we have to execute justice" (Amiel, 1975: 5). Similarly, Israeli Supreme Court Justice Haim Cohen established a connection between the Jewish notions of *Imitatio Dei* and justice (Cohen, 1991: 19).

Abraham, the Father of the Jewish nation and of monotheistic faith, followed this path: "For I have singled him out, that he may instruct his children and his posterity to keep the way of the Lord by doing *tsedakah* and *mishpat* [by practicing charity and justice]" (Genesis 18:19). Significantly, in this first mention of *tsedakah* in the Bible, the word appears in connection with justice (Weinfeld, 1995: Ch. 6), and this co-occurrence has repercussions for the notion of social justice (see later in this chapter). It is no coincidence that the connection between charity and justice also emerges in the portrayal of the exemplary ruler of the Kingdom of Judea from the perspective of biblical historiosophy: "David reigned over all Israel, and David executed judgment and justice (*tsedakah*) among all his people" (II Samuel 8:15).

The Jewish Notion of Social Justice

One of the major issues in every discussion of Jewish religious tradition is the profound and irresolvable tension between two conflicting orientations that are at the core of Judaism: universalistic individualism and Jewish–particularistic collectivism. This tension has had a strong impact on Jewish approaches to social justice.

The Jewish universalistic viewpoint emphasizes the common ground of all humanity as the essential first stratum on which any collective identity of the Jewish people must be built. By contrast, the particularistic position places Jews at the center of Creation. For strong particularists, Jews possess immanent spiritual uniqueness, indeed intrinsic superiority over all others. Jewish tradition incorporates some elements of both these perspectives as crucial components of Jewish identity, but the relative weight accorded to each of these principles varies in the different formulations of Jewish philosophy.

The *locus classicus* for the universalistic position is the creation of human beings "in God's image" (Genesis 1:26), which is elaborated on and reinforced in many rabbinic sources, for example in the Mishnah, Avot 3:18. On the other hand, we find that the nation of Israel is a "Kingdom of priests and a holy nation" (Exodus 19:6), "a nation that dwells alone" (Numbers 23:9). Even more explicitly: "For you are a holy people . . . and God has chosen you to be his treasured people from all the nations that are on the face of the earth" (Deuteronomy 14:2). Israel should be a cohesive national community in which individuals bear responsibility one for another (BT, Shavuot 39b).

This ambivalence is even present in the renowned phrase "love thy neighbor as thyself" (Leviticus 19:8), which has been interpreted in both contexts: Does "neighbor" mean Jews specifically or is it a universal call for brotherhood? (Simon, 1975). There are also two versions of a well-known *mishnah*: "He who saves one soul/one soul of Israel it is as if he saved the whole world" (Mishnah, Sanhedrin 4:5).[1]

Critical for universalistic propensities in the classical Jewish sources is the narrative of Noah (a non-Jew), who makes a universal covenant with God (Genesis 9). According to the Talmud, this Noahide covenant obliges all humankind to observe seven basic laws:

1 Prohibition of idolatry.
2 Prohibition of murder.
3 Prohibition of theft.
4 Prohibition of sexual promiscuity (adultery, homosexuality, bestiality, incest).
5 Prohibition of blasphemy.
6 Prohibition of eating the flesh taken from an animal when it was alive.

7 The commandment to promulgate just laws that will be enforced by an honest judiciary whose duty it will be to enforce the first six laws (BT, Sanhedrin 56a).

These laws are not limited to the very curt enumeration of the seven commandments themselves; rather, each one forms the heading for a cluster of related and implied rules that constitute the binding statutes for all humankind, in all places and at all times. Living by their lights earns non-Jews the appellation of "righteous gentiles," who are entitled to heavenly rewards (Lichtenstein, 1981; Novak, 1983).

Maimonides (1138–1204) was the most influential of those supporting the universalistic position. He attributed the "chosenness" of Israel to the acceptance of the Torah at Mount Sinai rather than to some immanent holiness limited exclusively to Jews (Blidstein, 1997). The most universalistic views during the Middle Ages were expressed by Rabbi Menachem Ha'Meiri (1249–1315), who, not surprisingly, was deeply influenced by Maimonides (Halbertal, 2000). On the other hand, there is no dearth of sources in support a particularistic point of view. The conceptual worlds (to choose only a few) of Rabbi Judah Halevi (1075–1141), the Maharal (Rabbi Judah Loew ben Bezalel of Prague 1520–1609), and most especially the various Kabbalistic schools distinguished between Jews and gentiles in very substantial ways (Novak, 1995).

This bifurcated vision reaches into the modern era as well. Key figures in the world of Jewish thought in the last 250 years, including Moses Mendelssohn, Rabbi Shimshon Raphael Hirsh, and Hermann Cohen, championed a universalistic vision. On the other hand, much of contemporary Orthodoxy and certainly Ultra-Orthodoxy tends to a particularistic outlook. Hasidism, in particular, has proclivities toward particularism.

A notion of social justice that represents the individual–universal aspect of Judaism would strongly oppose any approach bent on restricting social justice only to Jews, with no sensitivity to universal injustice and distress. This notion relies on the prayer "*Aleinu le-Shabe'ah*" ("It is incumbent upon us to praise the Lord"), recited by Jews three times a day. The prayer spells out the need "*letakein olam*" (to perfect the world and restore it to its pristine condition; to make the world a better place) "by the Almighty sovereignty." Indeed, several contemporary Jewish denominations, in particular the non-Orthodox and the Modern Orthodox, embrace this approach, insisting that it is incumbent on every Jew to make his or her own contribution toward *tikkun olam* (Diament, 1997), and doing so first and foremost by fighting for the cause of universal social justice (*Tikkun Magazine*, Core Vision).

On behalf of this Jewish religious call, many rabbis joined the civil rights movement under the leadership of Martin Luther King, Jr. Others invoked it in opposing apartheid in South Africa. For those responding to this call, the major moral lesson taught by the Holocaust is the duty to protest against oppression, racial discrimination, and genocide. It is no coincidence that in the last hundred years, the percentage of Jews involved in world movements for social justice has been substantially higher than their proportion in the world population.

In the Israeli context, such Jewish religious interpretations would question the value of populating and settling all the territories of Greater Israel by setting it against the high moral toll incurred by infringing on the rights of the Palestinian residents, who are entitled to a state of their own. In this respect, the position of R. Moshe Avigdor

Amiel is noteworthy. Commenting on the inequality of the Arab citizens of the newly founded Jewish state, he said:

> Not only does the Torah have compassion for the individual members of the Jewish people. It also spreads its wings over the individuals from the other nations who come to find shelter with us, even though such compassion may entail some hardships for the Jewish population.... the Torah also requires us to practice love, to love the stranger with all our heart and soul – "thou shalt love him as thyself" (Leviticus 19:34) ... Now if a small country completely surrounded by enemies legislates equal laws for the stranger and the citizen, it greatly undermines its very own edifice. Nevertheless, the Torah sanctioned this great undermining of the whole existence of the state in favor of the liberty of individual strangers, who chose to settle down in this small state, of all places. (Amiel, 1975: 36–37)

Apparently, there is great similarity between the Jewish interpretation of social justice and the individualistic liberal conception, which strives for all-encompassing civil equality (Rawls, 1971; Barry, 1989; Dworkin, 2000), Nonetheless, the Jewish notion of justice differs from the latter in several respects:

1. Unlike contemporary liberalism, it is based on the notion that all men are created in the image of God. One must bear in mind, however, that John Locke's theory of natural rights, which laid the foundations of liberalism, establishes a connection between the value of the individual and the biblical theological perception of the creation of man in God's image (Locke, 1988: Ch. 5; Dunn, 1993: Ch. 2).
2. It is based on the notion of duty toward God rather than on human or social rights. In fact, commitment to God lies at the heart of Judaism, and it is from this commitment that the duty to one's fellow men derives (Cover, 1987). In performing this duty, the other's rights are acknowledged, but the emphasis is not on the recipient's rights but rather on the obligations of the giver. These obligations fall under the category of "commandments between man and man," but a considerable portion of the "commandments between man and God" also concerns the proper conduct toward one's fellow men. Notwithstanding the above, some scholars believe that Jewish tradition has indeed formulated a conception of human rights (Cohen, 1988; Novak, 2004: Ch. 1).
3. Unlike liberal thought from Kant to Rawls, which concerns the role of humans as abstract rational agents, Judaism is concerned with one's fellow men as deserving affection ("Beloved is man, who was created in the Divine image," Mishnah, Avot 3:18) and even love ("Love thy neighbor as thyself," Leviticus 19:18). A Jewish notion of justice based on individual–universal assumptions strives to view the other as a unique individual, with whom it is desirable to have a lively dialogue.

In contrast to the above, a Jewish notion of social justice that adopts the collective–particularistic perspective would place an emphasis on the Jewish communal sphere. Jewish communality reaches its peak in the biblical notion of the covenant. The particular covenants between God and Abraham, Isaac, and Jacob are transformed into the collective–particularistic Sinaitic covenant between God and the people of Israel, through which the Israelites became a nation and accepted the yoke of the Torah. As suggested in Elazar's studies (1995–1998), the Jewish notion of the covenant has significantly contributed to western notions of the social contract and to the American federalist approach.

Yet, there is a difference between the perception of the covenant as a contract between individuals – as suggested in Anglo-American thought – and its perception as the grounding for personal relationships within the community of Jewish brotherhood. Whereas both perceptions have a theological basis, in Jewish political tradition the relationship between God and man finds its expression not merely in the personal domain but also, and primarily, at the level of the community. Jewish tradition likened the relationship between the Jewish collective and God to the relationship of lovers, in which the bride is *Knesset Yisrael*, the spiritual community of Israel. This metaphor of everlasting betrothal, which represents the ongoing dialogue between the Jewish community and God, is epitomized in the traditional and kabbalistic interpretations of the Song of Songs. Moreover, it is this kind of love that is supposed to be the model for interpersonal relations within the covenantal community. It is therefore not surprising that thinkers who accentuate the collectivist component in Jewish identity view the organic Jewish collective as the origin of the laws concerning charity. Thus, for instance, the Maharal, one of the outstanding Jewish thinkers of the Jewish particularistic school of thought, wrote the following:

> Since he [your Jewish fellow man] is your brother, how can you not have compassion for him? Man has compassion for him who is his brother. And if he ignores him, pretending that he is not his brother, he separates himself from Israel, who are one nation. And because Israel are one nation, they have one God . . . Therefore the word *tsedakah* contains two pairs of brothers [successive letters]: *tsadi* and *kof*, as well as *daled* and *heh*. (Maharal, 1972: 172)

Thinkers with a strictly particularistic orientation are opposed to adopting egalitarian attitudes toward Israeli Arabs (Harlap 1957; Aviner, 1987), an outlook that is widespread in the Orthodox rabbinical world (Liebman, 1993).

The Concept of Tsedakah in Judaism

General remarks

The distribution of goods has become one of the most salient ideological issues in the modern era. In fact, the division into Right and Left has to do with the respective differences between those who support the capitalist free market and those who embrace more egalitarian social positions. The basis for the leftist–socialist positions as they developed in Europe during the nineteenth century is the perception of man as a social creature. True sociability, so it is claimed, emerges when a community maintains relations of equality and solidarity among its members. Within the socialist Left there are various nuances between the more radical wing, which subscribes to revolutionary or anarchist approaches aspiring to obliterate private property altogether, and the more moderate social-democratic wing, which is in favor of gradual reforms that would reduce the gaps between the rich and the poor and introduce a larger measure of solidarity and equality into society. The proponents of capitalistic positions, on the other hand, usually emphasize the priority of the individual in relation to society and the importance of realizing one's potential, including the freedom to own property. However, as suggested by the debate in American society between the liberal Left (liberalism in the strict sense of the current American term) and the liberal Right (libertarianism), adopting an individualistic point of departure does not necessarily rule out strong disagreements about concepts of justice (Susser, 1995: Chs. 3–5).

Perhaps the most outstanding representatives of this controversy between liberalism and libertarianism in the political thought of the second half of the twentieth century are John Rawls and Robert Nozick. Rawls has formulated a notion of justice that supports the existence of an extensive welfare state, in which, on the basis of individualistic starting positions, freedom of ownership can be drastically reduced through legislation and liberal public policy. Nozick, on the other hand, believes that violating the freedom of ownership through taxation of the well-to-do in favor of the weak amounts to moral injustice (Rawls, 1971; Nozick, 1974).

An attempt to elicit an unequivocal stand on these issues from Jewish religious tradition is highly problematic. As in other major matters, the canonical Jewish texts, along with their interpretations throughout the generations, lend themselves to various positions. Nevertheless, the dominant tendency, discernible in the sacred texts as well as in the way of life and communal institutions, was to approve of private property, or at least not to object to it. At the same time, the tradition promoted social awareness and made efforts to assist the weak through personal commitment to giving charity and through mandated measures designed to reinforce social justice.

Briefly put, although Jewish religious tradition does not cultivate socialist tendencies, neither does it support extreme liberal capitalist ideas.

Restrictions on private property derive from the two elements discussed earlier: viewing the individual as an integral part of a Jewish collective that derives its strength from mutual solidarity; and the close connection in Judaism between theology and the notion of justice – that is, both the creation of man in God's image and the standing before God as the center of human existence have moral consequences that have an impact on the Jewish notion of social justice.

Let us now turn to a more detailed account of the notion of social justice as it emerges from the principal voices in Jewish tradition.

The Hebrew Bible and the Talmud do not disapprove of accumulating possessions as long as it is done honestly and moderately. Talmudic literature makes numerous references to ownership, by which is meant the possession of objects and slaves alike. In fact, the halakhah has lengthy discussions regarding various kinds of possessions, how to protect private property, and how to penalize those who violate it. In Sefer Kinyan (Book of Acquisition), the twelfth book of Mishneh Torah, Maimonides codified the laws concerning the ownership of property. Ownership is also the subject matter of Hoshen Mishpat, one of the four volumes of Shulhan Arukh (the Set Table), which was written by Rabbi Joseph Karo in the sixteenth century and has been widely acclaimed as a major *halakhic* source ever since.

In Judaism wealth is viewed as a gift from God, which must be used for the purpose of fulfilling the *mitzvoth* and performing acts of charity. Thus the Talmudic sages denounced those who pursued wealth and possessions for their own sake, warning them, "the more possessions, the more concern" (Mishnah, Avot 2:7). At the same time, Judaism sees no problem in gaining wealth and material success. Abraham, Isaac, and Jacob, the three Hebrew Patriarchs, were very rich men (Genesis 24:1, 26; 30:43) and according to the Talmud, the Divine Presence is more likely to rest on a wealthy man than on a poor one, provided that he also excels in other things (BT, Shabbat 92a). Owning property is thus taken for granted, possibly because it is associated with the importance attached to human individuality. According to the Mishnah:

> Man was created singly ... to show the greatness of the Holy One, blessed be He. For if a man strikes many coins from one mold, they all resemble one another. But the King of Kings, the Holy One, blessed be He, made each man in the image of Adam, and yet not one of them resembles his fellow. Therefore every single person must say, "For my sake was the world created." (Sanhedrin 4:5)

This uniqueness, which is infused with a distinct sense of individuality ("For my sake was the world created"), encompasses a variety of human capabilities in all areas of life. Economic enterprises fall under this same category. Moreover, most of the traditional Jewish thinkers insist that human beings have free choice, a notion that Maimonides made crystal clear in the introduction to his commentary on the Mishnah, Avot:

> But the truth of the matter, beyond any doubt, is that all of man's actions are in his own hands. If he wants to do something, he can; and if he does not want to, he does not have to.... Now people often mistakenly believe that a person is compelled to do certain things that are actually open to choice, for example, marrying a particular woman or acquiring a certain amount of money by stealing, but that is incorrect. (Maimonides, 2008: 124, 126, 138)

The importance attached to taking initiative, which also extends to accumulating possessions, is combined in Jewish tradition with the glorification of work. In Judaism, the duty to work is a religious value. Work is not perceived as the degrading burden of lesser creatures, as it was in the classical world. Quite the contrary, it is a worthy virtue leading to happiness: "Happy is everyone who fears the Lord; who walks in his ways. For thou shalt eat the labor of thy hands; happy shalt thou be, and it shall be well with thee" (Psalms 128:1–2). And in the Talmudic exegesis:

> R. Hiya bar Ami said in the name of Ulla: He who enjoys his own labor is greater than the one who fears Heaven. For of him who fears Heaven it is written, "Happy is the man who fears the Lord," whereas of him who enjoys his own labor it is written, "Happy shalt thou be, and it shall be well with thee." "Happy shalt thou be" in this world "and it shall be well

with thee" in the world to come. But of him who fears heaven "and it shall be well with thee" is not written. (BT, Berakhot 8a)

Maimonides concludes his systematic discussion of charity in his Laws Concerning Gifts to the Poor by stating a duty to take from the public coffers when life is at risk, but forbidding it when driven by the wish to avoid hard work (Maimonides, 1979, Laws Concerning Gifts to the Poor, 10:19).

Judaism never presented poverty as an ideal. As early as during the Rabbinic period, the Rabbis and the Church Fathers held radically different views concerning poverty. Hieronymus acknowledged this difference when he wrote: "Search in all the Jewish synagogues and you will not find one rabbi teaching the community to loathe wealth or praising poverty" (Urbach, 1951: 18).

According to various decisors (legal adjudicators), the Jewish notion of justice prohibits providing for the poor in cases when they can earn their livelihood by finding work (Ariel, 2004: 33–34; Levy, 2009). Based on various Talmudic sources, Maimonides rules that this prohibition also applies to religious functionaries (Maimonides, 1979: Laws Concerning Gifts to the Poor, 10:18; Laws concerning Torah Study, 3:10). Eventually, Maimonides' stringent ruling to refrain from paying salaries to rabbis and religious judges was rejected, and quite rightly so, in acknowledgment of their services to the community. In present-day reality, Ultra-Orthodox Jews educate men to devote many years to religious studies, even after their marriage, and to rely on the support of their community or (especially in Israel) on the welfare state's taxpayers' money. This practice is often presented as a natural extension of a long-standing tradition when, in fact, it is an "invention of tradition" of the kind characterizing the modern and postmodern world.

On the other hand, we find that Jewish religious tradition attaches great importance to *tsedakah*, a concept that combines two different aspects: charity and justice. Thus, the *mitzvah* of *tsedakah* imposes on the individual the duty to have compassion for the weak in society. In this vein, the Torah repeatedly insists on helping the poor man, the fatherless, the widow, and the stranger among us. However, practicing *tsedakah* also means pursuing justice, an obligation that is binding on the individual as well as on the society as a whole, along with its institutions. Jewish tradition in no way shares the libertarian capitalistic claim that helping the weak is mainly a matter of voluntary compassion on the part of individuals, with either diminished involvement of the state, through coercive measures (according to most capitalists), or no involvement at all (according to extreme libertarians such as Nozick). Nor is social justice perceived in Judaism as something impersonal, regulated by bureaucrats, as is the case in leftist, social-democratic views. Judaism accords great weight to the individual face of the recipient of charity and makes sure that he or she is treated with warmth and dignity by the community.

The Jewish approach to charity is antithetical to capitalistic libertarianism in two other ways: its restriction of individualism, given the centrality of the theocentric element in Judaism; and its acceptance and support of human social tendencies in general and within the Jewish people in particular. Let us consider these two dimensions separately.

Theological basis of social commandments

Canonical Jewish sources point to the unquestionable theological basis of various social commandments, and the starting point is again the creation of humanity in God's image. The human dignity of a member of a decent society cannot be realized in an environment where rapacious capitalism is rampant. The emphasis on human respect and dignity is a central element in the association of human beings; it is required to establish a relationship with God and with others. This point recurs in several commandments (Deuteronomy 21:22–23; BT, Berakhot 19b, Megillah 3b, and so on). Its crucial role in the laws of charity is evident, for instance, in the law requiring the community to give to the poor man according to his perceived needs in clothing, house furnishings, and marriage expenses, all according to his dignity (Maimonides, 1979: Laws Concerning Gifts to the Poor, 7:3, 6). Only from this perspective can we understand the significance of mandated charity, in diametrical opposition to libertarian worldviews. The Jewish view asserts that establishing social mechanisms to collect money for charitable purposes is a necessary condition for the existence of a Jewish community (Maimonides, 1979: 9:1). This is obviously not charity in its commonly accepted meaning, but rather charity in the sense of justice. Both these denotations are included in the Hebrew term *tsedakah*, but the word itself, as noted earlier, derives from *tsedek*, justice.

The second element that creates a close bond between theology and social justice is that, according to the biblical outlook, the entire world is God's property (Falk, 2001: Ch. 5). People do have a right to private property, but this right is limited because both they and their works belong to God: "The silver is mine and the gold is mine, says the Lord of hosts" (Haggai 2:8). The reason for the *halakhic* requirement that every Jew bless God before enjoying the material pleasures of food and drink is that the world belongs to God, and only after the blessing is this enjoyment not considered a form of theft (BT, Berakhot 35).

This attitude underlies various social commandments in the Torah, many of which concern the agrarian realm. God requires landowners to refrain from reaping the corners of their fields so that the poor can glean (Leviticus 19:9–10). The principle whereby people do not have ownership of the land emerges mainly in the requirement that the land lie fallow in the seventh year, and even further in the law requiring that the land be returned to its original human owners in the jubilee year. The Torah explains these edicts as follows: "The land shall not be sold forever: For the land is mine; for you are strangers and sojourners with me" (Leviticus 25:23).

This deep sense that human beings do not truly own their property is counterintuitive to the feelings of landowners in an agrarian society. More than any other factor, private ownership of land strengthens the experience of entrenched stability. In order to subvert this feeling, the Torah commands that the first fruits of the field be offered to God, thus preventing landowners from developing a sense of arrogant superiority over the poor. A community abiding by the injunctions of Rabbinic interpretation, then, can take from the rich even when they themselves do not freely wish to give, without thereby incurring moral injustice.

No wonder, then, that the Torah so blatantly infringes on the right to private property. Apart from the agrarian commandments noted above – the sabbatical and the jubilee and abstention from reaping the corners of the field and collecting the gleanings – several other social commandments are also intended to reduce economic gaps: the ban against land transfers between tribes, the extension of the sabbatical year to financial debts, the obligation of tithing for the benefit of the poor, restricting the ability to collect debts from the poor (a lender cannot enter the house of a poor borrower and collect a bond on a debt), and so forth.

The differences between an agrarian society and one in the twenty-first-century era of globalization are obvious. The religious declaration, however, is unequivocal. It takes a stand against a rapacious capitalist society placing at the center a "self" who acts on the belief that personal achievement and personal rights can be restrained only to a limited extent and only through the artificial legal means of a political society. As noted above, Judaism, unlike Catholicism, objects to making poverty an ideal. Yet, and contrary to the erroneous perception suggested by sociologists such as Karl Marx and Werner Sombart, Judaism does not call the capitalist a hero.

The Jewish view opposed to libertarianism is summed up in the Rabbinic saying: "He who says, 'What is mine is mine and what is yours is yours' – this is the common type, though some say that this is the type of Sodom" (Mishnah, Avot 5:10). The formulation "what is mine is mine and what is yours is yours" is in fact the essence of libertarian capitalism. For the Mishnah, however, an outlook that turns society into a collection of entities bereft of any social attachments is equivalent to Sodom, which the Bible takes to be a symbol of social callousness:

> Behold this was the iniquity of thy sister Sodom: she and her daughters had pride, surfeit of bread, and abundance of idleness, and yet she did not strengthen the hand of the poor and needy. (Ezekiel 16:49)

Compulsion in social justice

A central point in the notion of Jewish social justice is that voluntary personal assistance should go hand in hand with communal, institutional, and state assistance, which is to be funded by mandated charitable contributions. To a large extent, this imperative is tied in with the social aspect of Jewish identity. Whereas Judaism does not espouse socialist positions that oppose private ownership, neither does it condone extreme individualistic approaches that are compatible with predatory capitalism. According to Rabbi Shimshon Raphael Hirsch, the leader of the Neo-Orthodox community in Germany in the second half of the nineteenth century and one of the most important Bible commentators in the last generations, this approach is already implicit in the most prominent biblical source on the duty to assist the poor:

> If there be among you a poor man, one of your brethren within any of your gates in your land which the Lord your God gives you, you shall not harden your heart, nor shut your hand from your poor brother: but you shall open your hand wide to him, and shall surely

lend him sufficient for his need, in that which he lacks. Beware that there be not an unworthy thought in your heart, saying, the seventh year, the year of release, is at hand, and your eye be evil against your poor brother, and you give him nothing; and he cry to the Lord against you; for it shall be reckoned to you as sin. You shall surely give him, and your heart shall not be grieved when you give to him. Because for this thing the Lord your God shall bless you in all your works, and in all that to which you put your hand. For the poor shall never cease out of the land; therefore I command you, saying, you shall open your hand wide to your brother, to your poor, and to your needy, in your land. (Deuteronomy 15:7–12)

Hirsch's commentary on this text reflects a deep understanding of the need for three levels of action – the individual and the family, civil society, and the state – on the issue of charity:

> The duty to satisfy the requirements of the poor in every direction has on the one hand brought about the necessity to make the care of the poor a matter to be taken in hand by every Jewish community for the purpose of which it is authorized to levy a forced tax on the means of its members, but, on the other hand makes this duty by no means accomplished by this, but opens up an untiring noblest benevolent sphere of private charitable deeds and voluntary relief societies. The task which the duty of Jewish tsedakah imposes is so serious and so great that only the combination of these three factors, the community, the societies, and private individuals working together can come near to accomplishing it. (Hirsch, 1971: Commentary on Deuteronomy 15:7, 272)

In fact, Hirsch interprets the sources in reference to how charity was actually practiced in the medieval and early modern Jewish communities of the Diaspora. These well-established communities enjoyed substantial autonomy and operated much like the modern welfare state. Let us consider more deeply the three levels of action practiced in these communities.

The three levels of action

The first level The laws of charity in the biblical passage begin from feelings of personal compassion and move to official normative formulations. The personal attitude toward the poor draws largely on the quasi-familial feeling of community membership. These personal and familial feelings, however, are the basis on which the framework for state and public obligations must be built in order to preclude the perception that charity is a strictly voluntary, moral issue. The complexity of the Jewish notion of charity bears heavily on the modern democratic welfare state, because the latter erodes identity and communal ties while intensifying abstract, universal, civil, and social rights.

The strong personal dimension in the obligation of charity conveys the quasi-familial feeling of solidarity underlying the religious obligation. Although this stance may involve a considerable price in terms of increasing clannishness, that is not necessarily the case. Halakhah relates to circles built from the more intimate to the general. According to Maimonides,

> A poor man who is one's relative has priority over all others. The poor of one's own household have priority over the other poor of his city, and the poor of his city have priority over the poor of another city, as it is said (Deuteronomy 15:11): "Unto thy poor and needy brother, in thy land." (Maimonides, 1979: Laws Concerning Gifts to the Poor, 7:13)

Nehamah Leibowitz, a well-known Bible commentator in the second half of the twentieth century, explained this approach as follows:

> The Torah does not wish love of humanity or patriotism to be built up at the expense of our obligations to those nearer to us. These broader ties of country and universal brotherhood will not be implanted by the uprooting of natural links of affection but, on the contrary, the way to love of others, to love of humanity chosen by the Torah is by constant widening of the human circle, of parental love for their children eventually including the children of others, gradually embracing not only near kin but also those near in physical proximity, those among whom we happen to live. We are therefore commanded to live in mutual brotherhood with them. Our love will thus eventually embrace our people and then mankind. (Leibowitz, 1976: 210–211)

Note that Martin Buber and Emmanuel Levinas, among the most influential twentieth-century Jewish thinkers in non-Jewish circles in the realm of ethics, bolstered the personal dimension that is so strong in Jewish tradition. According to Buber, true dialogue between man and God and other men based on the I–thou relationship is a leitmotif of Jewish tradition (Buber, 1970).

The emphasis on the personal dimension in society's attitude toward the weak is also evident in the *halakhic* requirement to take into account the subjective needs of the person who requires assistance. The distress of a person who is not accustomed to a life of luxury is different from that of someone who has been ruined, and is therefore entitled to support for certain amenities as well (Maimonides, 1979: Laws Concerning Gifts to the Poor, 7:3). This law acknowledges that someone who has been reduced to poverty from high status will face a moral as well as a financial crisis. Indeed, the sense of being at a dead end has often led people used to economic independence to genuine tragedy.

Personal charity has another significant side, represented by the requirement that the caring attitude toward the poor include concern for the individual's emotional state:

> He who gives alms to a poor man with a hostile countenance and with his face averted to the ground loses his merit and forfeits it, even if he gives as much as a thousand golden coins. He should rather give with a friendly countenance and joyfully. He should commiserate with the recipient in his distress . . . He should also speak to him prayerful and with comforting words. (Maimonides, 1979: Laws Concerning Gifts to the Poor, 10:4)

The second level In the traditional Jewish community, the second circle is evident in the existence of various types of grassroots organizations such as synagogues, burial societies, and study groups. Groups focusing on specific charitable purposes – providing dowries for poor brides, heating homes, teaching poor children, and so forth – are worth noting in the present context (Bergman, 1944; Katz, 1993: Ch. 16). According to Rabbi Jonathan Sacks, the Jewish communal tradition is vital to the development of balances that can restrain radical liberal individualism from tearing down the foundations of the civic society. Expanding this system of balances in a modern democratic liberal culture requires an equilibrium between the discourses of rights and civic commitments (Sacks, 1997: Chs. 13, 20).

Joint action within voluntary frameworks working for the benefit of the other, who is perceived as a unique being, is invaluable for bridging gaps of identity, culture, and ways of life. The similarity between the *halakhic* and the Aristotelian outlooks is prominent in this context. Aristotle holds that virtue is acquired through practice. To acquire the virtue of charity, then, a man must practice many acts of charity, and the more such acts he performs, the stronger his virtue (Aristotle, 1953: Book II).

The third level Compassion and solidarity make up only one side of the Jewish idea of *tsedakah*, since it is balanced by the obligation, and even the mandate (or commandment), to engage in this pursuit. We now find ourselves in the objective-legal domain of the concept of *tsedakah* (Tamari, 1987, 1995; Novak, 2004: Ch. 7). As I noted above, the concept appears in the Bible for the first time in a legal context and is identified with the path adopted by Abraham: "For I know him, that he will command his children and his household after him, and they shall keep the way of the Lord, to do tsedakah and judgment" (Genesis 18:19).

Jewish commentators and decisors in the last 1000 years have built this broad perspective on the foundations laid down in the Talmud (Hellinger 1999, 2009; Safrai, 1995: Chs. 2, 6). The power of the public in the world of the Jewish community when it comes to enforcement of *tsedakah* was based primarily on two foundations: the authority of the citizens of the city to mandate individual behavior for the sake of the city; and the authority of the Jewish court to enforce community public administration.

The Talmudic discussion regarding payments incumbent on a town's residents that can be collected even by force culminates in halakhic and aggadic exchanges about the laws of *tsedakah* and the greatness of its virtue (BT, Bava Bathra 17a). Maimonides clarifies the measure of coercion involved: "He who refuses to give alms, or gives less than is proper for him, must be compelled by the court to comply" (Maimonides, 1979: Laws Concerning Gifts to the Poor, 7:10). The leading halakhist in the last 500 years, Rabbi Joseph Karo, in his treatise Beth Yosef, cited a responsum by the most prominent halakhic figure in fourteenth-century Spain, R. Shlomo ben Aderet (known as Rashba). Rashba says that under ordinary circumstances, charity should be collected according to the level of one's income (Beth Yosef, Yoreh Deah, Hilkhot Tsedakah, #250, s. v. nish'al).

The aims of tsedakah

According to the halakhic conception, the ideal manifestation of charity is to help the poor become independent. The Bible ties the obligation of lending money to the poor to the prohibition of taking interest on the loan, since interest would preclude attainment of the aim – freeing the poor from their plight: "If you lend money to any of my people . . . you shall not be to him as a creditor, neither shall you lay upon him interest" (Exodus 22:24). Indeed, Maimonides numbers the obligation of lending to the poor in the list of 613 commandments (Maimonides, The Book of Commandments, Positive Commandment 197). He turns this commandment into the linchpin of his charity laws and from it develops a general approach about the need to create work that will enable the poor to extricate themselves from the vicious circle of destitution (Maimonides, 1979: Laws Concerning Gifts to the Poor, 10:7).

The obligation to help people support themselves is intended not only for those who have lost their livelihood but also – and mainly – for those who are not yet really poor and can, if assisted, avoid economic penury. As usual, the Torah reminds us of the equality between the Jewish and non-Jewish inhabitants of the land, including the matter of the prohibition against taking interest:

> And if your brother grow poor and his means fail with you, then you shall relieve him, though he be a stranger or a sojourner; that he may live with you. Take you no usury of him, or increase: but fear your God; that your brother may live with you. (Leviticus 25:35–36)

In his exegesis of this commandment, Rashi cites a parable illustrating the importance of providing assistance before the final collapse:

> Do not let him fall because it will be hard to lift him up, but support him from the moment his hand slips. What is this to be likened to? To the burden on an ass. As long as it is still on the ass, one man alone can hold it and keep it there. Once it has fallen down, five men will not lift it. (Rashi on Leviticus 25:36)

In the current economic reality, preventing economic collapse may well require setting a minimum wage that will genuinely enable a dignified life. At the same time, those who are unwilling to make an effort and prefer to live at the expense of others or the state must be denied support.

A society characterized by true solidarity will show greater readiness to bear the burden of caring for the poverty stricken and will assist many to extricate themselves from poverty and develop a sense of self-respect. A society that does not invest in its members pays a heavy price in the collapse of social frameworks and in the turning of its weaker strata to crime. The greater the economic gaps, the greater the delinquency, and the same is true of assistance to underdeveloped countries. Therefore, giving food to prevent hunger, however required, is not the most significant form of aid. The main thrust should be to encourage the West, which has so blatantly exploited these societies, to enhance occupational opportunities in underdeveloped countries, while monitoring the implementation of industrialization initiatives on an ongoing basis.

In a modern country, the best and most effective way to prevent a life of poverty and decline into crime is to foster high educational standards. Jewish tradition has always stressed the significance of study and education. Among the various obligations incumbent on a father, the Talmud mentions the teaching of a craft, and R. Judah states that anyone who does not teach his son a craft is as if he had taught him to be a bandit (BT, Kiddushin 29a).

In practice, when fathers failed to provide education for their sons, the community took responsibility for their educational needs. Down through the ages, one of the central manifestations of the Jewish conception of social justice was the practice of investing in education. Such investment was funded by private acts of charity as well as by raising contributions through institutionalized imperatives. There are scarcely any parallels to the situation in which, more than 2000 years ago, a religious outlook dictated compulsory education for all schoolchildren, including those of poor families, within the framework of religious institutions, principally the synagogues. The reason for this was obvious: the obligation of studying Torah was incumbent on everyone, so the entire community was mobilized to ensure that no male child was excluded. The well-known saying of the sages, "Take heed of the poor, for Torah comes from them" (BT, Nedarim 81a), sets the stage for investing in the education of poor children. This approach can serve as the basis for supporting extensive public education, which is the most important aspect of social justice if the goal is to extricate the poor from the cycle of poverty rather than simply offer them short-term and limited assistance.

Naturally, there was a considerable gap between the theoretical vision and the reality in practice. The Jewish communities saw the emergence of a class of rich men, who oftentimes abused the poor, but the basic Jewish ethos has remained the same: establishing acts of charity and deeds of kindness, both as a philanthropic activity and as a well-regulated mechanism for channeling funds to help the needy. This ethos has persisted in various Jewish communities to this day. These communities feed the hungry in charity kitchens and offer free housing to the homeless. Charities also provide basic healthcare (*bikkur holim*); care of the elderly (*moshav zekeinim*); and assistance to children in distress (*megadlei yetomim*) (Bergman, 1944: Ch. 8).

It is no coincidence that central figures in Zionist thought, including Theodor Herzl, Berl Katzenelson, and Ze'ev Jabotinsky, despite the ideological differences among them, stressed the importance of establishing a highly developed social system in the Jewish state. One of the most crucial actions taken by David Ben-Gurion, the key figure in the founding of the state of Israel and its first prime minister, was the creation of an extensive system for helping the needy, thereby making Israel one of the most outstanding welfare states in the West.

Since 1985 Israel, like other western countries, has been moving in the direction of liberal capitalism, an ongoing process that reached its peak at the beginning of the twenty-first century. This movement has resulted in huge economic gaps within Israeli society, among the highest in the western world, a state of affairs that is incompatible with the vision of social justice as manifested in the texts and the history of Jewish religious tradition.

Conclusion

When closing his discussion of charity in the Mishneh Torah, Maimonides noted:

> It is our duty to be more careful in the performance of the commandment of almsgiving than in that of any other positive commandment . . . The throne of Israel cannot be estab-

lished, nor true faith made to stand up, except through charity, as it is said (Isaiah 54: 14), "in righteousness shalt thou be established." (Maimonides, 1979: Laws Concerning Gifts to the Poor, 10:1)

Commenting on this Maimonidean law, Urbach argued that in Jewish communities, "organized and free charity reduced inequality between its members and removed enviousness. Acts of charity intensified mutual responsibility and internal unity, as well as the ties between the various communities" (Urbach, 1951: 27). Even if we adopt a more critical view of the Jewish community in exile, it will still emerge as a unique setting of social existence in difficult and sometimes terrible circumstances, which was unquestionably helped by normative social commitments as well as by personal and communal solidarity.

Note

1 According to a well-known scholar of rabbinical thought, the original text referred to every soul and not only to the souls of Jews (Urbach, 1988). The literal reading of the Mishnah also supports the version that speaks of the significance of saving a human soul as such, since it takes its supporting textual verse from the Creation story. On the image of the human creature and its universal aspects in the rabbinic world, see Urbach (1979: Ch. 10).

References

Amiel, Rabbi Moshe Avigdor (1975) Our social justice and our legal and moral justice, in *Between a Man and his Friend: Human Relations in Judaism*, Rabbi Moshe Avigdor Amiel, Rabbi Zalman Baruch Rabbinikov, and Rabbi Eliahu Yung (eds.), Mossad Harav Kook, Jerusalem [Hebrew].

Ariel, Yaacov (2004) The world is built by Hessed': An ideal Israeli society, *Zohar* 19: 23–34 [Hebrew].

Aristotle (1953) *The Nicomachean Ethics*, J.A.K. Thomson (trans.), Penguin, Harmondsworth.

Aviner, Elisha (1987) The status of the Ishmaelites in the state of Israel according to the Halacha, *Tchumin* 8: 337–362 [Hebrew].

Barry, B. (2005) *Why Social Justice Matters*, Polity Press, Cambridge.

Bergman, Rabbi Yehuda (1944) *Tsedakah in Israel: Its History and Institutions*, Tarshish, Jerusalem [Hebrew].

Blidstein, Gerald (1997) Tikkun olam [Repairing the world], in *Tikkun Olam: Social Responsibility in Jewish Thought and Law*, Orthodox Forum Series, Chaim I. Waxman and Nathan J. Diament (eds.), Jason Aronson, Northvale, NJ, pp. 17–59.

Buber, Martin (1970) *I and Thou*, Walter Kaufmann (trans.), T&T Clark, Edinburgh.

Cohen, Haim (1988) *Human Rights in the Bible and the Talmud*, Defense Ministry, Tel Aviv [Hebrew].

Cohen, Haim (1991) *The Law*, Bialik, Jerusalem [Hebrew].

Cohen, Herman (1972) *Religion of Reason out of the Sources of Judaism*, Simon Kaplan (trans. and ed.), Ungar, New York.

Cover, Robert M. (1987) Obligation: A Jewish jurisprudence of the social order, *Journal of Law and Religion* 5: 65–74.

Diament, Nathan Jay (ed.) (1997) *Tikkun Olam: Social Responsibility in Jewish Thought and Law*, Orthodox Forum Series, Jason Aronson, Northvale, NJ.

Dunn, J. (1993) *Western Political Theory in the Face of the Future*, Cambridge University Press, Cambridge.

Dworkin, R.M. (2000) *Sovereign Virtue: The Theory and Practice of Equality*, Harvard University Press, Cambridge, MA.

Elazar, D.J. (1995–1998) *The Covenant Tradition in Politics*, Vols. I–IV, Transaction Publishers, New Brunswick, NJ.

Falk, Ze'ev W. (2001) *Hebrew Law in Biblical Times: An Introduction*, 2nd edn, Brigham Young University Press, Provo, UT.

Goodman, L.E. (1988) *Judaism, Human Rights, and Human Values*, Oxford University Press, New York.

Halbertal, Moshe (2000) Ones possessed of religion: Religious tolerance in the teachings of the Me'iri, *Edah* 1(1): 1–24.

Harlap, Yaacov Haim (1957) Selling houses and lands in the land of Israel to non-Jews, *Hamaayan* 37: 57–74 [Hebrew].

Hartman, David (1985) *A Living Covenant: The Innovative Spirit in Traditional Judaism*, Free Press, New York.

Hellinger, Michel (1999) Charity in Talmudic and Rabbinic literature: A legal, literary, and historical analysis, PhD dissertation, Bar-Ilan University [Hebrew].

Hellinger, Michel (2009) On poverty and the policy for its restriction in Rabbinical writings, *Shmaatin* 175: 138–154 [Hebrew].

Hirsch, Samson Raphael (1971) *The Pentateuch*, Isaac Levy (trans.), Judaica Press, New York.

Katz, Jacob (1993) *Tradition and Crisis: Jewish Society at the End of the Middle Ages*, Bernard Dov Cooperman (trans.), New York University Press, New York.

Leibowitz, Nehamah (1976) *Studies in Shemot: The Book of Exodus*, Aryeh Newman (trans.), WZO, Jerusalem.

Levy, Shlomo (2009) Giving charity to a poor man that can work and support himself, *Techumin* 30: 57–62 [Hebrew].

Lichtenstein, Aaron (1981) *The Seven Laws of Noah*, Rabbi Jacob Joseph School Press, New York.

Liebman, Charles S. (1993) Attitudes toward democracy among Israeli religious leaders, in *Democracy, Peace, and Israel-Palestinians Conflict*, Edy Kaufman, Shakri B. Abed, and Robert L. Rothstein (eds.), Lynne Rienner, Boulder, CO, pp. 137–144.

Locke, John (1988) *Two Treatises of Government*, Peter Laslett (ed.), Cambridge University Press, Cambridge.

Maharal, Rabbi Judah Loew ben Bezalel of Prague (1972) *Netivot Olam*, Jerusalem [Hebrew].

Maimonides, Moses (1963) *The Guide of the Perplexed*, Shlomo Pines (trans. and ed.), University of Chicago Press, Chicago.

Maimonides, Moses (1979) *The Code of Maimonides: The Book of Agriculture*, Isaac Klein (trans.), Yale University Press, New Haven, CT.

Maimonides, Moses (2008) On Human Nature, in *The Eight Chapters of Rambam*, Yaakov Feldman (trans. and ed.), Targum Press, Southfield, MI.

Mendelsohn, Moses (1983) *Jerusalem or On Religious Power and Judaism*, Allan Arkush (trans.), University Press of New England, Hanover.

Novak, David (1983) *The Image of the Non-Jew in Judaism: An Historical and Constructive Study of the Noahide Laws*, E. Mellon Press, New York.

Novak, David (1995) *The Election of Israel: The Idea of the Chosen People*, Cambridge University Press, Cambridge.

Novak, David (2004) *Covenantal Rights: A Study in Jewish Political Theory*, Princeton University Press, Princeton.

Nozick, Robert (1974) *Anarchy, State, and Utopia*, Basic Books, New York.

Rawls, J. (1971) *A Theory of Justice*, Belknap Press of Harvard University Press, Cambridge, MA.

Sacks, Jonathan (1997) *The Politics of Hope*, Jonathan Cape, London.

Safrai, Ze'ev (1995) *The Jewish Community in the Talmudic Period*, Zalman Shazar Center for Jewish History, Jerusalem [Hebrew].

Schatz-Oppenheimer, Rivka (1968) *Hsidism as Mysticism*, Magnes, Jerusalem [Hebrew].

Simon, Ernst (1975) The neighbor (*Re'a*): Whom shall we love? in *Modern Jewish Ethics* Marvin Fox (ed.), Ohio State University Press, Ohio, pp. 29–56.

Soloveitchik, Joseph Dov (1982) *Words of Thought and Assessment*, Elinar, Jerusalem [Hebrew].

Susser, Bernard (1995) *Political Ideology in the Modern World*, Allyn and Bacon, Boston, MA.

Tamari, Meir (1987) *With All Your Possessions: Jewish Ethics and Economic Life*, Free Press, New York.

Tamari, Meir (1995) *The Challenge of Wealth*, Aronson, Northvale, NJ.

Tikkun Magazine (n.d.) Tikkun's core vision, http://www.tikkun.org/nextgen/tikkuns-core-vision (accessed April 10, 2011).

Urbach, Ephraim E. (1951) Political and social tendencies in Talmudic concepts of charity, *Zion* 16: 1–27 [Hebrew].

Urbach, Ephraim E. (1979) *The Sages: Their Concepts and Beliefs*, Israel Abrahams (trans.), Harvard University Press, Cambridge, MA.

Urbach, Ephraim E. (1988) "Whoever saves a single life": The chronology of a textual version, the changes of censorship, and the affairs of publishers, in *From the World of the Sages*, Magnes Press, Jerusalem, pp. 561–579 [Hebrew].

Weinfeld, Moshe (1995) *Social Justice in Ancient Israel and in the Ancient Near East*, Magnes Press, Jerusalem.

CHAPTER 12
Judaism
Contemporary Expressions

Eliezer Segal

Although the ideal of justice remains a central concern for the Jewish religion in all generations, the attitudes of Jewish thinkers or activists in the post-Enlightenment age are more likely to be shaped by the prevailing values of the surrounding society than by their engagement with a distinctively Jewish tradition. I have therefore chosen to focus this presentation on two seminal twentieth-century thinkers whose ideas and sensibilities were deeply rooted in the teachings of Jewish religious works: Rabbis Abraham Isaac Kook and Abraham Joshua Heschel.

The spiritual and intellectual trajectories of Rabbis Abraham Isaac Kook (1865–1935) and Abraham Joshua Heschel (1907–1972) reveal many remarkable similarities. Both were the products of the intensely traditional Jewish religious milieus of eastern Europe. Each received a conventional rabbinic ordination certifying his erudition in the Talmud and Jewish religious law. Kook was an outstanding student of the celebrated Volozhin Yeshiva (talmudic seminary) in Lithuania (Yaron, 1974: 13; Dresner and Kaplan, 1998: 47–48).

In the family background of each was a strong influence of Hasidism, that powerful charismatic movement of popular mystical piety that had been founded by Rabbi Israel Ba'al Shem Tov in eighteenth-century Ukraine. Rabbi Kook's maternal grandfather had been an adherent of the Kapust branch of the movement, whereas Heschel was heir to the distinguished hasidic dynasties of Apta (Opatow) founded by his eighteenth- and nineteenth-century namesake, as well as that of Berditchev (Dresner and Kaplan, 1998: 4–9). As an ideology that was based in large measure on the teachings of the Kabbalah, Hasidism tended to focus on the theurgic or symbolic aspects of Jewish observance rather than on social ethics (Segal, 2005: 41–42), notwithstanding the widespread tendency of later popularizers to portray the Ba'al Shem Tov and his successors as champions of the poor against the wealthy establishment (Rosman, 1996:

The Wiley Blackwell Companion to Religion and Social Justice, First Edition. Edited by Michael D. Palmer and Stanley M. Burgess.
© 2012 John Wiley & Sons Ltd. Published 2020 by John Wiley & Sons Ltd.

116–119, 176–179). To take one instructive example, both Kook and Heschel equate the Good with harmonious unity, whereas Evil is identified with division, contentiousness, and disunity – a perspective that would seem to derive from kabbalistic usage (Kook, 1924: 9: 6 (34–35); Scholem, 1961: 235–239; Heschel, 1972: 120; Bokser, 1978: 71).

Both men spent formative stages of their lives in central or western European centers where they acquired a genuine interest in developments in European intellectual currents (see Goldman, 1991; Rosenak, 2007a: 119 n. 48, 135–143). In Rabbi Kook's case, it would appear that he was most strongly influenced by the historicist ideologies of Hegel (cf. Yaron, 1974: 105 n. 40; Rosenak, 2007a: 130), Marx (Yaron, 1974: 37–38 n. 3), and Darwin (Yaron, 1974: 224–225; Bokser, 1978: 304 ff.). Heschel's philosophical antecedents are to be sought principally among the exponents of religious existentialism and phenomenological approaches to religious experience (cf. Dresner and Kaplan, 1998: 115–136).

Discovering the Bible

Both Kook and Heschel were students of the Hebrew Bible. While this might sound superfluously self-evident when one is speaking of Jewish religious scholars, it was not obvious at all in their cultural environment. The predominant religious curriculum that had evolved among Ashkenazic Jews since the Middle Ages had been so ardent about placing the Talmud at the center of its religious culture that, typically, the Bible was rarely studied on its own merits (Talmage, 1987; Kanarfogel, 1993). The scriptural texts that were taught in the schools were the ones that were incorporated into the liturgy – mainly the Torah (the Five Books of Moses), which was the source of the 613 commandments on which rabbinic Judaism is founded and which are read in the synagogue over the course of each year. Notwithstanding ongoing attempts by leading religious authorities to raise the profile of biblical and Hebrew studies in the Jewish schools, the only exposure that many eastern European Jewish students had to the Bible was through the rote learning and translating of the weekly lections from the Torah, along with the authoritative eleventh-century commentary by Rashi (Rabbi Solomon ben Isaac of Troyes) that consisted largely of interpretations selected from the Talmud and ancient midrashic works. The remaining parts of the Hebrew Bible received little or no attention (Stampfer, 1988). The section classified as the "prophets" (which includes historical books as well as the books that recorded the teachings of the prophets of ancient Israel) was known to most Jews by virtue of the individual passages that are appended to the Torah reading on sabbaths and festivals (*haftarah*); consequently, they were likely to be approached as mere supplementary commentaries to the themes in the Torah lections (Dresner and Kaplan, 1998: 23, 27).

With the advent of modernism and the influences of the European and Jewish Enlightenment ideologies since the latter part of the eighteenth century, there was a revival of interest in the study of the Hebrew Bible in its entirety, whether as a way of undermining the stifling hegemony of the traditionalist rabbinic leadership, or in recognition of the fact that Christian reverence for the Hebrew Scriptures was a crucial factor in creating a climate of acceptance for Jews in European society (Shavit and Eran, 2007). At any rate, this revived interest in biblical studies had limited success in penetrating the traditionalist ranks of the Polish and Russian Jewish communities – especially after it had been stigmatized as quasi-heretical, and therefore subversive, by conservative factions. Therefore, there is something quite remarkable in the fact that Rabbis Kook and Heschel derived meaningful inspiration from their study of the whole Bible, and particularly from the teachings of the great prophets of ancient Israel.

The Aggadah

Closely related to this phenomenon is the fact that both religious teachers attached much importance to the "aggadah" component of the rabbinic corpus. The classic texts of ancient rabbinic literature were divided up into two main topical groupings: halakhah, which analyzed the technical intricacies of religious law; and aggadah, which embraced everything else, but whose main focus was the homiletical expositions of Scripture as they had been embodied in sermons delivered to synagogue audiences on sabbaths and festivals (Segal, 2009: 48–54). Aggadah is the genre to which one most readily turns in search of moral values, spirituality, theological doctrines, and most of the other features that western culture normally classifies as "religious." While there is evidence that already in antiquity halakhah had a somewhat higher status in the rabbinic program of study, in modern times aggadah was virtually eliminated from the curricula of the *yeshivot* (talmudic seminaries), especially those that followed the "Lithuanian" model that stressed profound and incisive analysis of talmudic law. Like the marginalization of biblical studies, the dismissal of aggadah can be ascribed to a number of factors, such as the prestige that attached to students who mastered the intellectual complexities of the Babylonian Talmud and its commentaries, or a wish to avoid some of the thorny theological questions that might be provoked by intensive pondering of aggadic texts. Heschel took an extreme position in opposition to this trend, insisting that it is the aggadah that ultimately defines the religious significance of the halakhah, whether in its totality or with respect to the interpretation and application of specific precepts (Heschel, 2005; Brill, 2006: 5–7; Kaplan, 2007: 207–209).

Rabbi Kook understood prophecy and aggadah as being very similar in their essences. He wrote:

> prophecy and the holy spirit emanate from the innermost parts of the human being, and from within it it flows out to everything that has anything to do with the world. Similarly with regard to Aggadah, it flows out of a person's spiritual core and then it also arranges its matters with respect to the external aspect of the world.[1]

Thus, both Kook and Heschel were opposing the dominant attitudes of their cultures when they actively proposed that the aggadah be reclaimed and assigned a central position in the Jewish religious corpus, especially as a repository of ethical values (Bokser, 1978: 13–14; Rosenak, 2007b: 137–138).

Prophetic Justice

Zvi Yaron identifies prophecy as one of the principal factors that had an impact on Kook's distinctive blending of mysticism with vital concerns for society and nature. Prophecy injected into Judaism a moral passion and a deep concern for the plights of humanity and society, including a consciousness of how urgent it is to correct social inequities and strengthen justice on the practical plane (Yaron, 1974: 110–111). In explaining the context for Kook's attitude toward prophecy, Avinoam Rosenak observed that in the medieval Jewish philosophical tradition, the concept of prophecy had taken on an additional meaning alongside its social-historical dimension: rationalist thinkers perceived it as the culmination of a process of moral, metaphysical, and intellectual discipline that was required to bring the individual to a state of receptivity to communications from God. This doctrine differs radically from the simple sense of the biblical narratives, where the prophets are often simple, uneducated figures who are compelled to take up their calling out of an overpowering divine imperative. In his teachings Kook integrated both models of prophecy, stressing as well its special connections to the Holy Land and to the messianic era (Rosenak, 2007b: 136–137). Evidently he had experienced moments of spiritual elevation of his own that he regarded as prophetic revelations (Rosenak, 2007a: 117–119, 127–128).

Heschel chose to write his doctoral dissertation for the University of Berlin on the subject of the prophets of the Bible (Dresner and Kaplan, 1998: 163–171, 198–202). The dissertation was completed in 1933 and published as a book two years later under the tightening grip of the Nazi terror (Dresner and Kaplan, 1998: 173–181). His fascination with the prophetic ethic coincided with his growing conviction that the philosophical path was unable to provide a credible metaphysical underpinning to the basic questions of human life and values. These, he came to believe, could be more effectively achieved through the study and emulation of those divine spokespersons of ancient Israel, the *nevi'im* [=prophets]. Notwithstanding the need to conform to the prevailing academic norms of source-critical biblical research, Heschel did utilize his dissertation as a platform for making an outspoken argument (at least, as a historical claim about the prophets' thinking) for the idea of a "God of Pathos" who has a very real concern for the affairs of his creatures as they reveal themselves in the successes and failings of history (Sherman, 1970: 31–37; Brown, 1985: 125; Merkle, 1985; Dresner and Kaplan, 1998: 129–132, 163–164). He had the dissertation translated into English in an extensive revision in 1962 (Kaplan, 2007: 210–213). In the Introduction to that edition he recalled that "the most important outcome of the inquiry has been for me the discovery of the *intellectual relevance of the prophets*" (emphasis in original). He contrasted their passion with the fruitless aridity that typified the philosophical climate he had encountered himself as a student of philosophy; and he described his growing realization that "some of the terms, motivations and concerns which dominate our thinking may prove destructive of the roots of human responsibility and treasonable to the ultimate ground of human solidarity" (Heschel, 1962: 1: xiv–xv; Brown, 1985: 133; Dresner and Kaplan, 1998: 14–15).

Though he was ostensibly describing a bygone historical phenomenon from the ancient Near East, it is clear that Heschel was presenting the message of the ancient prophets as one whose relevance has not diminished in the modern world. Central to that message was the conviction that "the primary way of serving God is through love, justice, and righteousness" (Heschel, 1962: 1: 195, 197, 198). God's principal concern is with the "material needs of widows and orphans" (Heschel, 1962: 1: 197):

> righteousness is not just a value; it is God's part of human life, *God's stake in human history*. Perhaps it is because the suffering of man is a blot upon God's conscience; because it is in relations between man and man that God is at stake. (Heschel, 1962: 1: 198)

Theology and Justice

Arguably, Rabbi Kook's most concerted discussion of ethical questions is to be found in his treatise *The Lights of Repentance* (1924) (cf. Bitty, 1998). Though the direct authorship cannot be completely ascribed to him (it was assembled by his son Zvi Yehudah Kook from his father's notes), it was printed with the elder Kook's approval during his lifetime and appears to be consistent with his known views. In this work, composed in the rabbi's characteristic mixture of flowery rabbinic Hebrew and modern neologisms, he examines the traditional religious concept of repentance, in the sense of turning away from sin and coming back to God's correct path as defined by the Torah. Kook expands this concept into an all-inclusive trajectory that begins from the spiritual malaise of the individual, and then leads the confused soul to the finding of spiritual direction and the improvement of one's true religious character, which will culminate in national and universal redemption (Kook, 1924: 4:10 (12); Bokser, 1978: 52–53).

In Kook's awkwardly poetic style, it is not always possible to know with certainty whether he is speaking about justice and righteousness as ethical principles governing interhuman social relationships or as theological concepts in their kabbalistic sense of divine attributes. According to the kabbalistic symbolism, Justice (*Din*, *Gevurah*) is the divine power that manifests itself in punishment and in choking off the descent of celestial blessings into the human world (Scholem, 1961: 213). As such, justice is associated with a metaphysical divisiveness that prevents the actualization of the complete unity that defines ultimate redemption (Kook, 1924: 12:10 (53); Bokser, 1978: 87–88). Kook's mystical universe is so pervaded by the divine light that at times he portrays evil as illusory, a sort of veil that is necessary to channel the undifferentiated light (Kook, 1924: 16:12 (93); Bokser, 1978: 124–125).

To a much more decisive and unmistakable degree, Heschel placed the quests for social justice and compassion at the center of his theology. While this is not the appropriate place to recapitulate all the subtleties of his philosophy, there are a number of theological points that must serve as essential background to a proper appreciation of Heschel's ethical thought. My main source for this description is his 1951 treatise *Man Is Not Alone: A Philosophy of Religion* (Kaplan, 2007: 118–120). In that work, Heschel began from the experiential and undeniable assumption of a "radical amazement" that places human beings in an existential relationship with the "ineffable" God. It is this stance that allows us to perceive our surroundings as constituting "the universe" in the literal sense of an all-embracing, coherent entity. This fundamental perception, Heschel argues, cannot be the result of any scientific analysis. "The idea of the universe is a metaphysical insight" (Heschel, 1972: 104). Though all existing things share in a "kinship of being," man, as a being with a conscious soul, possesses a crucial distinctiveness that transcends the generic commonalities of being or of nature (Heschel, 1972: 105). The recognition of human brotherhood, with all the implications it has in the realms of ethics, compassion, and mutual responsibility (Heschel, 1972: 121), makes sense only as a corollary of the unifying monotheistic principle.

> It is only in the mirror of a divine unity, in which we may behold the unity of all; of necessity and freedom, of law and love. It alone gives us an insight into the unity that transcends all conflicts, the brotherhood of hope and grief, or joy and fear, of tower and grave, of good and evil. (Heschel, 1972: 108, 226)

It is typical of Heschel that, alongside his theological formulation of this premise, he also cites a source from the prophet Malachi (2:10) "Have we not all one father? Has not one God made us? Then why do we break faith with one another, every man with his fellow, by dishonoring our time-honored troth?" (Heschel, 1972: 120). He invokes the prophets as his precedent for the idea that God is not a distant or abstract supernatural being, but rather is identical with "justice, mercy; not only a power to which we are accountable, but also a pattern for our lives" (Heschel, 1972: 133). Often the prophets established their social agendas of justice and righteousness in opposition to what many still see as the main concerns of "organized religion," such as cult, worship, solemnity, or devotion.

In a similar vein, Heschel argues that "we could not own the power for goodness if it were lacking in God. If there is morality in us, it must eminently be in God. If we possess the vision of justice, it must eminently be in God" (Heschel, 1972: 132). Furthermore, while people may need some discipline in order to enable them to live up to their ideals ("the idea of justice and the will to justice are not twin-born"; Heschel, 1972: 51), Heschel's world was clearly not built on the classic dualistic antagonism between our altruistic moral conscience and our selfish physical instincts. Rather, he believed that it is possible to educate people so that the desire for justice becomes a natural part of our thinking that is stronger than the will to do or to tolerate evil.

Religious and Secular Ethics

Modern philosophy has acknowledged since at least as far back as David Hume that scientific discourse can not legitimately progress from descriptive statements about what is to prescriptive statements about what ought to be. For many, the "is–ought problem," "fact–value distinction," or "naturalistic fallacy" (as formulated by G.E. Moore) precludes the possibility of a purely secular ethic.

Kook and Heschel shared very similar views about the relationships between religious and secular ethical sensibilities. Kook's views were very much colored by his personal encounters with the idealism of the young Zionist pioneers in Palestine, who were strongly motivated by secular, antireligious ideologies, especially Marxist socialism, and who saw their activities as a rejection of the antiquated religious values with which they had grown up in Europe (Bitty, 2005; Rosenak, 2007a: 134–135). Indeed, the Orthodox religious establishment of the day declared an ideological war against Zionists as outright heretics whose values stood in irreconcilable opposition to the Torah. Rabbi Kook, however, recognized that the Zionists' passion for justice was fundamentally a religious one, even if they themselves did not acknowledge that fact.

> We would not be upset if some sort of social justice could be established without the slightest inkling of a religious reference; because we are aware that the very desire for justice in whatever form it may take is essentially the most illuminating divine influence. (Iggerot RAIa"H, 1: 143, cited by Yaron, 1974: 39)

In other writings he deeply regretted people's failure to appreciate that ethical sensitivity is, at its root, a spiritual capacity that is implanted in the human soul, an inescapable striving for absolute goodness. In the ultimate scheme of things, secular ethics alone are not capable of bringing people to complete perfection, which remains a religious objective.[2]

Universal Justice

Kook believed that a striving for justice is integral to the human psyche. "The moral instinct demands from man righteousness and goodness," though we must struggle to actualize the ideal of absolute justice in the world (Kook, 1924: 5:6 (15); Bokser, 1978: 54–55). If we succeed in that endeavor, then the divine light will embrace all mankind and all reality "in everything that is capable of containing the quality of morality" (Kook, 1924: 13:2 (57); Bokser, 1978: 92). It is in this grand context that Rabbi Kook includes glimpses of a world in which universal justice may be realized. The process begins with "the individual and communal soul, the global and the universal souls, like a fearsome lioness crying out in its torments for a total repair, for an ideal reality" (Kook, 1924: 4:1 (8); Bokser, 1978: 49). He speaks of a "general repentance" that entails the elevation and repair of the whole world; as well as "all those cultural improvements by means of which the world is removed from its desolation, social and economic life-structures" (Kook, 1924: 4:3 (9), see also 15:12 (86); Bokser, 1978: 49, see also 118). Ultimately, it is the combined repentance of individuals that will translate into the general vanquishing of evil and ignorance (Kook, 1924: 15:11 (91–92); Bokser, 1978: 118). In the redeemed world, evil will be eradicated by means of the voluntary repentance of the wicked (Kook, 1924: 16:12 (94); Bokser, 1978: 124).

It should be noted as well that Rabbi Kook is rare, if not unique, among traditional Jewish thinkers in his insistence on establishing "justice for animals" in a way that leads to vegetarianism, an ideal whose roots he discerns in the biblical dietary laws (Bokser, 1978: 317). And yet, though he has come to be widely perceived as Judaism's most illustrious vegetarian, Rosenak has demonstrated that this image is a false one that was imposed on him and the works published under his name by prominent disciples who did indeed practice vegetarianism. Rabbi Kook evidently envisaged universal vegetarianism as an aspect of the future redeemed world, but he believed that it should not be implemented in the present (Rosenak, 2007b: 358–364).

In Kook's eschatological doctrine, true to the traditional Jewish visions of redemption, the people of Israel are to play an essential role in ushering in the utopian age. Following rabbinic and kabbalistic usage, the Jewish national spirit is personified as "the congregation of Israel." "The soul of the congregation of Israel is absolute justice, in whose realization is contained all practical moral goodness" (Kook, 1924: 4:7 (10), 13:1 (56); Bokser, 1978: 50, 91). The national dimension of the repentance process will include healthy civic values: "political order and love for the improvement of the community in good manners and tolerance" (Kook, 1924: 4:9 (12), 14:30 (74); Bokser, 1978: 52, 107). Israel will stand at the vanguard of what will become a universal repentance and redemption (Kook, 1924: 5:9 (16), 17:1 (94); Bokser, 1978: 55, 126).

For all his stress on the primacy and spiritual superiority of Israel in the redemption process, the dominant tone of Kook's eschatological vision appears to be universalistic – though there are some significant exceptions. (See Bokser's discussion [1978: 12–13], texts on pp. 136–137, 210, and so on.)

Heschel's model of the just society is essentially a universalistic one in all important respects (Dresner, 2002: 16–17). Although he very frequently quotes sources from the Bible, from the hasidic masters, or from other Jewish traditions, *Man Is Not Alone* is true to its subtitle "a Philosophy of *Religion*" and not a philosophy of *Judaism*. Its principal message is addressed to humanity in its entirety – and there is a powerful sense of urgency that the message must be shared by all peoples. In fact, Heschel evinces pointed hostility to the historical tendency of institutional religions to emphasize the differences between them: "Parochial saintliness may be an evasion of duty, an accommodation to selfishness" (Heschel, 1972: 237).

Law and Justice

In his discussions about the biblical ideal of justice, Heschel noted that Hebrew used two different lexical roots to convey the relevant concepts, producing the nouns *mishpat* and *tsedek*, conventionally rendered as "justice" and "righteousness" respectively. Though the two terms are often employed interchangeably, there is a sense to which justice refers to a "mode of action," especially by acting in accordance with the law, whereas righteousness denotes a type of personality that cultivates concern for others (Heschel, 1962: 1:200–201). While much of the wrath of the biblical prophets was directed against the abuse of the legal system by those in power, neither they nor Heschel wished to diminish the importance of a judicial system that administers the law fairly. After all, civil and criminal law were essential components of the divinely revealed Torah; and accordingly, what secular laws regard as crimes are now classified as sins (Heschel, 1962: 1:217). Nevertheless, Heschel insisted that "righteousness goes beyond justice" (Heschel, 1962: 1:201). Justice by itself is not a sufficient vehicle for imprinting God's will on society and history. Because of their righteous personalities, the prophets were often reactive – protesting against the injustices and oppressions that they witnessed around them. Apart from some significant exceptions (like Moses, Deborah, and Samuel), prophets did not occupy positions of judicial authority, but stood on the margins, remonstrating and condemning the abuses of the ruling establishment. Citing Deuteronomy 16:20, Heschel declares: "The demand is not only to respect justice in the sense of abstaining from doing injustice, but also to strive for it, to pursue it" (Heschel, 1962: 1:207). In a society that succeeded in implementing true justice and righteousness, there would likely be no need for prophets.

Thus, in the opening address that he delivered at the National Conference on Religion and Race in 1963, at the height of the American civil rights struggle, Heschel admonished his audience:

> Most of us are content to delegate the problem to the courts, as if justice were a matter for professionals or specialists. But to do justice is what God demands of every man: it is the supreme commandment, and one that cannot be fulfilled vicariously. Righteousness must dwell not only in the places where justice is judicially administered. There are many ways of evading the law and escaping the arm of justice. (Kaplan, 2007: 215–218)

In a similar setting at another conference on race, he declared:

> There are no administrative solutions to spiritual problems. The United States Senate, the courts, and the laws will only enable us to embark upon the task; it will remain a challenge to our wisdom, to our power of love to complete the task. (Heschel, 1966: 91, cf. 106; Kaplan, 2007: 219–220)

Clearly, the exploitation of the judicial system as an instrument of racial oppression was very much part of the American social landscape at that time; however, Heschel's statement was not merely a response to contemporary conditions. It reflected a coherent philosophical position at which he had arrived on its own merits. As is well known, Heschel achieved international prominence during the 1960s for his activism on social and political issues, chief among them being the struggles against racial segregation and discrimination and the opposition to the Vietnam war. At the famous Alabama civil rights protest march from Selma to Montgomery in 1965, Heschel stood in the front row along with Dr. Martin Luther King, Jr., subjecting himself to considerable risks to his safety (Kaplan, 2007: 220–224). From 1965, he was in the forefront of the religious opposition to America's war in Vietnam. He was a founding member of the National Emergency Committee Concerned about Vietnam, and participated actively in numerous rallies against the war (Kaplan, 2007: 300–310). His activist engagement was also directed toward causes like the rights of the Jews of the Soviet Union, the security of the state of Israel, and the treatment of the elderly (Dresner, 2002: 21–22; Kaplan, 2007: 202, 225–229, 313–318). Acquaintances testified that this public profile did not come naturally to his scholarly, retiring personality, but that he was compelled to act by his religious commitment to justice and compassion (Sherman, 1970: 11–14; Dresner and Kaplan, 1998: 22; Kaplan, 2007: 198). In this respect as well, Heschel's conflict paralleled that of Rabbi Kook, who expressed intense frustration at the need to occupy himself with public affairs when his personal desire was for a life of solitary scholarship (Rosenak, 2007a: 133–134, 141–143).

Unlike Heschel, Rabbi Kook's vision of social justice did not draw its primary inspiration from the image of the indignant prophet fulminating at the city gates and at the hubs of political power. It sometimes had more in common with the spirit of a platonic state that is founded on a substratum of equitable laws. Evidently, he did not feel that true justice can be achieved in a piecemeal manner by correcting individual wrongs. Nothing short of a universal reorganization of society's structures and laws can accomplish this goal in a satisfactory way. For Kook, of course, the source of those perfectly wise laws was the Torah, as expounded according to the classic rabbinic interpretations, encompassing both the 613 commandments that were revealed through Moses at Mount Sinai and the oceans of exegetical and supplementary material contained in the "oral Torah" preserved in the Talmud and codes of religious law. The fulfillment of the repentance process demands adherence to the minutiae of observance in accordance with the written and unwritten Torahs (Kook, 1924: 13:2 (57), see also 16:11 (91); Bokser, 1978: 92, see also 123). Yaron (1974: 110–111) observes how for Kook the greatness of the halakhah is to be found in the way in which it translates the divine spirit into a day-to-day regimen of practical discipline, thereby deepening Judaism's involvement in human civilization.

More specifically, Kook subscribes to the attitude of traditional rabbinic culture when he equates authentic repentance with the intense scholarly study of civil and criminal law. It is this endeavor that will "remove all the obstructions to the heart in life and establish divine justice on a dependable foundation" when it is supplemented by other domains of the Torah, especially those that deal more broadly with moral and philosophical matters (Kook, 1924: 13:4 (58); Bokser, 1978: 93). (Rabbi Kook does nonetheless acknowledge that interpersonal problems are best dealt with practically rather than theoretically [Kook, 1924: 14:15 (68); Bokser, 1978: 103].) Menachem Klein has argued that Kook's preference for scholarship over prophecy as a way of life was a consequence of the fact that, from a historical perspective, prophecy had failed in its quest to achieve a permanent transformation of the world, whereas the halakhic scholarship of the rabbis has succeeded to a great extent in shaping and guiding Jewish life for many centuries (Klein, 1986; cited by Rosenak, 2007b: 138).

There is nevertheless another, very different direction to be discerned in Kook's writing that has been characterized as "antinomian." In these passages he contrasts the cold, impersonal character of talmudic scholarship with the animated spirit of aggadah and prophecy, presenting the former as a relic of the stunted development of exilic Judaism (Rosenak, 2007a: 120–123, 129).

It is questionable whether these contrasting attitudes can be fully reconciled, and they may well reflect shifts in Rabbi Kook's thinking or reactions to differing circumstances or target audiences. Rosenak has argued that the halakhic system that Kook envisages as the basis for his ideal just society will be one that has undergone a revolutionary transformation as the legal system is rejuvenated in the spirit of prophecy and aggadah (Rosenak, 2007b: 139). At any rate, *Lights of Repentance* is directed primarily at individual Jews who are seeking to correct moral flaws and strengthen their religious personalities. As such, it often appears that the references to social justice and other forms of interpersonal ethics are being presented not as social goals that ought to be pursued for their own sakes, but rather as aspects of the individual's moral perfection (e.g., Kook, 1924: 14:29 (73–74); Bokser, 1978: 107).

In Yaron's synthesis of Kook's philosophy, which contains a chapter devoted to his social teachings, one finds very little explicit information about the topic. For example, Kook wrote extensively about the biblical sabbatical and jubilee years, in which the rights of private ownership are overridden and purchased property reverts to its original owner, who sold it out of economic need. The Torah grounds this law in God's declaration "for the land is mine, no land shall be sold permanently" (Leviticus 25:23). And yet Kook is very restrained about deriving a political or social theory from this precedent, preferring to characterize the sabbatical years as times of spiritual renewal. Only one source quoted in Yaron's book deals directly with the issue and asserts:

> without determining which social system is endorsed by the Torah, it is possible to state with certainty that the consistent observance of all the laws of the Torah in the social and economic domain without compromise, would not tolerate the existence of a system based on private ownership.

This quotation, however, is cited from a listener's private notes and does not appear in any of Rabbi Kook's published works (Yaron, 1974: 162–164). Kook does, however, insert a remark about "the legal inequity in the ownership of property" into his allegorical interpretation of the Torah's prohibition of mixed wool and linen (Deuteronomy 22:11; Bokser, 1978: 320).

Kook and Heschel: Explaining Their Differences

To be sure, religious and philosophical positions cannot automatically be reduced to their historical contexts, particularly when we are dealing with original, creative thinkers of the calibers of Kook and Heschel. Nevertheless, I think that an awareness of the historical settings in which they wrote does contribute to a clearer understanding of some of the issues that distinguish their approaches to social justice.

Rabbi Kook flourished at the beginning of the twentieth century, during a time when western thought was still heady in its faith in progress as an inevitable force that made each generation superior to the previous one (Nisbet, 1980) and that would imminently be arriving at its glorious culmination (Gellman, 1991: 53, 159, 161, 214, etc.; Rosenak, 2007a: 137–138). The perception that history is preset in a divinely guided direction that leads toward the "end times" was fundamental to ancient prophetic teaching, and in the nineteenth century it had been given secular revisions, as a metaphysical working out of the Spirit in Hegel, as the class struggle giving way to the classless society in Marx, or as the evolutionary path to higher biological adaptability in Darwin. Even the modernist exponents of the Jewish Enlightenment appealed to utopian assumptions as a way of justifying the introduction of far-reaching changes in religious practice and theology, by arguing that their times were radically different from anything that the Jewish past had hitherto encountered (Meyer, 1988: 59). Rabbi Kook integrated these views with kabbalistic eschatological themes and with Zionist ideology to produce an outlook that was, in its historical setting, typically optimistic. The secular doctrines that stood at the forefront of the Zionist movement in Palestine were imbued with socialistic ideals of equality and concern for the downtrodden proletariat and peasantry, so these were not issues that had to be placed at the top of Kook's ethical agenda (Bitty, 2005). Jews were on the threshold of restoring their sovereignty and, Kook presumed, this would be accompanied by the restoration of their divinely authored judicial system. In Europe and even in the land of Israel, the Jewish societies with which Kook was familiar were subject to foreign control, existing on the peripheries of states that differed from – and were likely hostile to – the values of Judaism. However, the nations of the world were acquiring a level of enlightenment that would allow them to appreciate the greatness of Israel's Torah and to emulate its sublime values. When the Torah will be removed from the ritualistic compartmentalization that characterizes the exile, and restored to its fitting place as the comprehensive legal system of a utopian society, then injustices will disappear and humanity will be freed to pursue its proper spiritual vocation.

Rabbi Kook died in 1935, before the full extent of Nazi and Stalinist atrocities were discernible, or perhaps even imaginable, and before the Jews of Israel declared independent statehood and were launched into a prolonged military conflict with the Arab world.

Heschel, on the other hand, was an eyewitness to the rise of Nazism in Germany and the rest of Europe. He was himself deported from Frankfurt to Warsaw in 1938 and narrowly succeeded in escaping to England months before the Nazi invasion (Dresner and Kaplan, 1998: 266–290). Most of his immediate family were murdered by the Nazis (Dresner and Kaplan, 1998: 306). Unlike the dominant perception among traditionalist Jews, which viewed the Holocaust as but the latest and most intense manifestation in a millennial pattern of Christian antisemitism, Heschel saw it as a disturbing and perhaps inevitable consequence of modern humanity's distance from the basic values and moral sensitivity of true religion. In 1944, while the war and genocide were still in progress, he wrote:

> Let Fascism not serve as an alibi for our conscience. We have failed to fight for right, for justice, for goodness; as a result we must fight against wrong, against injustice, against evil. We have failed to offer sacrifices on the altar of peace; now we must offer sacrifices on the altar of war. (Sherman, 1970: 45–46; Dresner, 1985: 21; Fierman, 1990: 17; Kaplan, 2007: 46, 120; cf. Faierstein, 1999)

The mindset that confronted Heschel in postwar America was in many ways a negative image of what Kook had encountered in Palestine during the early twentieth century. Heschel found American society to be mired in complacency, materialism, nationalistic insularity, and insensitivity to spiritual messages. Thus, when confronted by the moral outrages of racial segregation and the Vietnam war (Kaplan, 2007: 214–234, 298–313), both of which were being perpetrated in a democratic state that was governed by the rule of law, it is not surprising that Heschel found himself unready to equate the prophetic ideals of righteous justice with the mere enforcement of a legal regime, equitable though it might be. Unlike the situation in the Old World, the Jewish minority in America in the latter half of the twentieth century was able to identify with and participate fully in the social and political life of its country.

Although it is true that theological and ideological thinkers typically have limited influence among the Jewish public, the teachings of Rabbis Kook and Heschel continue to have a broad readership. Rabbi Kook's writings have acquired quasi-canonical status in the religious Zionist stream of Israeli culture, including the state religious school system. In those circles, the principal focus is often placed on his eschatological and nationalistic views, and yet the fact remains that his full corpus is studied quite widely, including his ideals of ethics and justice. There is no comparable institutional backing behind the philosophy of Abraham Heschel, and yet the eloquent charm of his writing and the passion of his message have attracted a large audience in the English-speaking world. Whether by mapping out the equitable structures of a messianic society or by honing our sensitivity to the injustices of our contemporary world, each thinker in his own way has played a crucial role in transmitting and interpreting the heritage of traditional Jewish religious values to coming generations.

Notes

1 Kook (2007a: 137), citing a version of Kook's text that was not subjected to emendation by his editor and son-in-law Rabbi David Cohen (cf. Schwartz, 2002: 198–234; Rosenak, 2007a).
2 See sources assembled by Yaron (1974: 39–40, 43). In n. 8 he compares Kook's position to that of Heschel.

References

Bitty, Yehudah (1998) Qavvei Yesod Le-Hitpattehut Haguto Shel Ra'Ia"H Quq, MA thesis, Hebrew University of Jerusalem, http://www.daat.ac.il/daat/mahshevt/biti/shaar-2.htm (accessed April 19, 2011).

Bitty, Yehudah (2005) Yaḥasav shel Ha-Ra'Ia"H Quq 'im Anshei Ha-'Aliyyah Ha-Sheniyyah: Hebetim Historiyyim Ve-Ra'ayoniyyim, *Mayyim Middalyav* 16: 295–314.

Bokser, Ben Zion (ed.) (1978) *Abraham Isaac Kook: The Lights of Penitence, The Moral Principles, Lights of Holiness, Essays, Letters, and Poems*, Classics of Western Spirituality, Paulist Press, New York.

Brill, Alan (2006) Aggadic man: The poetry and rabbinic thought of Abraham Joshua Heschel, *Meorot: A Forum of Modern Orthodox Discourse* 6(1): 1–21.

Brown, Robert McAfee (1985) "Some are guilty, all are responsible": Heschel's social ethics, in *Abraham Joshua Heschel: Exploring His Life and Thought*, John C. Merkle (ed.), Macmillan, New York, pp. 123–141.

Dresner, Samuel H. (1985) Heschel the man, in *Abraham Joshua Heschel: Exploring His Life and Thought*, John C. Merkle (ed.), Macmillan, New York, pp. 3–17.

Dresner, Samuel H. (2002) *Heschel, Hasidism, and Halakha*, Fordham University Press, New York.

Dresner, Samuel H. and Kaplan, Edward (1998) *Abraham Joshua Heschel: Prophetic Witness*, Yale University Press, New Haven, CT.

Faierstein, Morris M. (1999) Abraham Joshua Heschel and the Holocaust, *Modern Judaism* 19(3): 255–275.

Fierman, Morton C. (1990) *Leap of Action: Ideas in the Theology of Abraham Joshua Heschel*, University Press of America, Lanham, MD.

Gellman, Ezra (1991) *Essays on the Thought and Philosophy of Rabbi Kook*, Fairleigh Dickenson University Press, Rutherford, NJ.

Goldman, Eliezer (1991) Rabbi Kook's ties to European thought, in *Meḥkarim ve-'Iyunim: Hagut Yehudit be-'Avar uva-Hoveh*, Magnes Press, Jerusalem, pp. 115–121.

Heschel, Abraham Joshua (1962) *The Prophets*, Harper and Row, New York.

Heschel, Abraham Joshua (1966) *The Insecurity of Freedom: Essays on Human Existence*, Farrar, Straus and Giroux, New York.

Heschel, Abraham Joshua (1972) *Man Is Not Alone: A Philosophy of Religion*, Octagon Books, New York.

Heschel, Abraham Joshua (2005) *Heavenly Torah: As Refracted Through the Generations*, Gordon Tucker and Leonard Levin (trans.), Continuum, New York.

Kanarfogel, Ephraim (1993) On the role of bible study in medieval Ashkenaz, in *The Frank Talmage Memorial Volume*, Barry Walfish (ed.), Haifa University Press, Haifa, pp. 1: 151–166.

Kaplan, Edward (2007) *Spiritual Radical: Abraham Joshua Heschel in America, 1940–1972*, Yale University Press, New Haven, CT.

Klein, Menachem (1986) The principles of Rabbi A. Y. Kook's ideological concept of the Jewish law, in *In His Method, Studies in Rabbi A. Y. Kook's Doctrine*, H. Hamiel (ed.), World Zionist Organization, Jerusalem, pp. 153–166.

Kook, Abraham Isaac (1924) *Orot Ha-Teshuvah*, Jerusalem.

Merkle, John C. (1985) Heschel's theology of divine pathos, in *Abraham Joshua Heschel: Exploring His Life and Thought*, John C. Merkle (ed.), Macmillan, New York, pp. 66–83.

Meyer, Michael A. (1988) *Response to Modernity: A History of the Reform Movement in Judaism*, Oxford University Press, Oxford.

Nisbet, Robert A. (1980) *History of the Idea of Progress*, 2nd edn, Basic Books, New York.

Rosenak, Avinoam (2007a) Hidden diaries and new discoveries: The life and thought of Rabbi A. I. Kook, *Shofar: An Interdisciplinary Journal of Jewish Studies* 25(3): 111–147.

Rosenak, Avinoam (2007b) *Prophetic Halakhah: Rabbi A. I. H. Kook's Philosophy of Halakhah*, Magnes Press, Jerusalem.

Rosman, Murray Jay (1996) *Founder of Hasidism: A Quest for the Historical Ba'al Shem Tov*, University of California Press, Berkeley.

Scholem, Gershom G. (1961) *Major Trends in Jewish Mysticism*, Schocken, New York.

Schwartz, Dov (2002) *Faith at the Crossroads: A Theological Profile of Religious Zionism*, Brill Reference Library of Ancient Judaism, Vol. 7, Brill, Leiden.

Segal, Eliezer (2005) Rabbi Eleazar's Perutah, *Journal of Religion* 85(1): 25–42.

Segal, Eliezer (2009) *Introducing Judaism*, Routledge, New York.

Shavit, Jacob and Eran, Mordechai (2007) *The Hebrew Bible Reborn: From Holy Scripture to the Book of Books – A History of Biblical Culture and the Battles over the Bible in Modern Judaism*, Walter de Gruyter, Berlin.

Sherman, Franklin (1970) *The Promise of Heschel*, Lippincott, Philadelphia.

Stampfer, Shaul (1988) Heder study, knowledge of Torah, and the maintenance of social stratification in traditional east European society, *Studies in Jewish Education* 3: 271–289.

Talmage, Frank (1987) Keep your sons from Scripture: The Bible in medieval Jewish scholarship and spirituality, in *Understanding Scripture: Explorations of Jewish and Christian Traditions of Interpretation*, Clemens Thoma and Michael Wyschogrod (eds.), Stimulus, New York, pp. 81–101.

Yaron, Zvi (1974) *The Philosophy of Rabbi Kook [Mishnato Shel Ha-Rav Kuk]*, Jewish Agency, Jerusalem.

PART II
Religious Movements and Themes

Introduction

Part II explores social justice as it is worked out in a variety of religious movements and themes. Representing a broad religious and cultural diversity, the essays illustrate not only significant variation in approaches to social justice, but also some notable points of commonality.

Christopher Buck's "Bahá'í Faith" describes a relatively recently founded religion (nineteenth century) that places high value on social justice, an emphasis due in part, no doubt, to the fact that leaders and people have experienced severe persecution almost continuously. Even today, Bahá'ís suffer persecution in countries like Iran. Yet as important as social justice is for Bahá'ís, it is not the chief good. According to Buck, "In the Bahá'í hierarchy of values social justice directs thought and action to a higher principle and to a grand vision of a future world commonwealth" (this volume: 211). Social justice (the preferred term is *social action*) is a means to a larger end: a grand vision of a future world commonwealth.

In "The Quest for Justice in Revival, a Creole Religion in Jamaica," William Wedenoja explores the way in which social justice is sought and achieved through a particular form of revivalism distinctive to Jamaica. This essay is important because it illustrates the important role that an indigenous religion plays in sustaining culture and achieving social justice goals internal to the culture of an indigenous population. However, also it illustrates a more general feature of the Caribbean region: the prominent role of indigenous religions in all aspects of public life.

When westerners think of Islam, they often think of places like Saudi Arabia, Iraq, or Iran. Indonesia may not come readily to mind. But Indonesia is the home of more Muslims than any country in the world, and, as Florian Pohl tells us, the Muhammadiyah, which is located in Indonesia, is one of the largest Muslim mass organizations worldwide. Up to 30 million Indonesians identify with this social welfare organization's modernist agenda, which involves, among other things, providing edu-

---

The Wiley Blackwell Companion to Religion and Social Justice, First Edition. Edited by Michael D. Palmer and Stanley M. Burgess.
© 2012 John Wiley & Sons Ltd. Published 2020 by John Wiley & Sons Ltd.

cational and healthcare services. In the Muhammadiyah, religion and social justice intersect.

The Asante people occupy a part of present-day Ghana in West Africa. In "The Role of the Chief in Asante Society," Yaw Adu-Gyamfi explores the important role that the chief has played and continues to play in Asante life. More than simply a political leader or a warrior, the chief is a source of moral wisdom and spiritual discernment for the community, which he receives by communicating with the ancestors. But the chief is himself also the product of a process that calls on the accumulated wisdom of the community and the tradition it bears. Before the chief assumes his leadership role – before he is installed on his stool (his tribal throne) – he must be instructed by elders who know the tradition.

Derek Maher's essay, "Tibetan Monastics and Social Justice," and Hiroko Kawanami's "Sangha and Society" come to us with themes from the Buddhist tradition. The story that Maher tells falls into three parts. The first part begins in the seventh century, when Buddhism was first introduced into Tibet from India. This part of the story explains how Buddhism, over time, assimilated itself to the particular climate, geography, and culture of Tibet, and how the Buddhist monks and nuns made themselves integral to Tibetan life. The second part of the story begins with the Chinese occupation of Tibet in 1950. During this part of the story, the monks and nuns played an increasingly prominent role in political protest against the occupation. The Dalai Lama was also forced into exile. The third part of the story Maher calls "the globalization of Tibetan Buddhism," a name that refers to a series of internationally acclaimed public events that have taken place since the Dalai Lama gained global celebrity status on being awarded the Nobel Peace Prize in 1989.

In "Sangha and Society," Hiroko Kawanami tells a related but different narrative, in which Buddhists in various Asian countries in modern history have endured violent political conflicts and have experienced considerable brutality and suffering. According to Kawanami,

> In various stages of national development, Buddhist faith in Asian countries has seen diverse expressions in the public arena. It has given its adherents a specific worldview, cosmology, an ethical code of conduct, and a moral resource to assert a national identity, especially during the time of colonial rule and struggle for independence, and even a rationale to impose hegemony on others to the extent of justifying the use of violence. (This volume: 280)

Within this social setting, the monastic community called the Sangha has traditionally played a complicated role. Unquestionably, it has given Buddhists a moral foundation for social stability, legitimation, and security. But also, Kawanami says, "in its role as public vehicle to articulate people's voices and sentiments, it has in some contexts promoted a particular religious agenda detrimental to other faiths and ethnic groups"(this volume: 280).

The essays by W.E. Nunnally, "*G'meelut Chasadim* (Deeds of Kindness)"; Ana María Pineda, "Hospitality"; and Azim Nanji, "*Zakat*: Faith and Giving in Muslim Contexts" all deal with social justice in ways that go beyond anything that can be captured in a moral rule or a religious commandment. In each case, the person to whom the directive is given ("Be kind," "Welcome the stranger," "Give generously") is expected to do more than behave correctly. A certain attitude or disposition is called for as well: kindness, a welcoming spirit, a generous heart. These are dimensions of the moral life that bring questions of social justice into close conversation with virtue ethics, character ethics, feminist ethics, and the ethics of care, all of which have received much attention from philosophers, theologians, and moral theorists over the past 30 years.

The last essay in Part II, Barbara Brown Zikmund's "Ecumenical and Interreligious Dialogue," deals with the difficult problem of interreligious tension. Zikmund believes that tension arises when "missionary religions" (e.g., Buddhism, Christianity, Islam) attempt to proselytize people from other religions. In her essay, she reviews the history of attempts at ecumenical and interreligious dialogue aimed at easing the tension. She concludes with a brief review of Karen Armstrong's 2009 challenge to religious people in the *Charter of Compassion*, a document that affirms the centrality of compassion to all religious, ethical, and spiritual traditions, and that calls on each of us to treat others as we wish to be treated. For Zikmund, the central themes of the *Charter* summarize what is best and right about interreligious dialogue and interreligious commitments.

CHAPTER 13
Bahá'í Faith

Christopher Buck

The Bahá'í religion had established ethical and social principles for the ennobling of individuals and the ordering of societies well before "social justice" emerged as a dominant value in modern democracies. Indeed, the Bahá'í Faith claims to be a religion "endowed with a system of law, precept, and institutions capable of bringing into existence a global commonwealth ordered by principles of social justice" (Bahá'í World Centre, 1993: 107). In the Bahá'í hierarchy of moral values, social justice ranks as a central and guiding principle. The distinctively pragmatic Bahá'í approach is to promote social justice through coordinated initiatives of "social action."

Bahá'ís generally prefer to speak of "social action" rather than "social justice" because they view the former as proactive and the latter as reactive. Social action, as they speak of it, anticipates social issues and addresses them prospectively; social justice aims at remediating injustices that have already occurred. Seen in this light, engaging in social action could be expected to reduce the need to redress social injustices. If "social justice" is conceived broadly (i.e., not simply as remedial or corrective), then "social action" is the name that Bahá'ís use to articulate a proactive model for achieving social justice. This proactive orientation to social justice involves acting on the basis of a vision and core values to reorder society by means of a multifaceted, systematic, and progressive plan of social engagement: multifaceted in that it involves undertaking different kinds of initiatives and projects simultaneously around the world; systematic in that it involves coordinating complementary initiatives and programs; and progressive in that it extends successful local and regional initiatives to communities around the globe.

The centrality of justice in Bahá'í thought is evident in the declarations of the religion's early leaders. Its founder, Bahá'u'lláh (1817–1892), elevated justice by linking it in several ways to God and by citing its practical utility: "The best beloved of all things in My sight is Justice … turn not away therefrom if thou desirest Me, and neglect it

---

The Wiley Blackwell Companion to Religion and Social Justice, First Edition. Edited by Michael D. Palmer and Stanley M. Burgess.
© 2012 John Wiley & Sons Ltd. Published 2020 by John Wiley & Sons Ltd.

not that I may confide in thee." "By its aid thou shalt see with thine own eyes and not through the eyes of others, and shalt know of thine own knowledge and not through the knowledge of thy neighbor." "Ponder this in thy heart; how it behooveth thee to be. Verily justice is My gift to thee and the sign of My loving-kindness. Set it then before thine eyes" (Bahá'u'lláh, 1978: 37). 'Abdu'l-Bahá (1844–1921), Bahá'u'lláh's son and appointed successor, who led the religion from 1892–1921, also accorded justice a special status: "Justice . . . is a universal quality"; and "justice must be sacred, and the rights of all the people must be considered" ('Abdu'l-Bahá, 1969: 159).

But social justice is not an end in itself. In the Bahá'í hierarchy of values, social justice directs thought and action to a higher principle and to a grand vision of a future world commonwealth. "The purpose of justice," Bahá'u'lláh declared, "is the appearance of unity among men" (Bahá'u'lláh, 1978: 67). In other words, social justice is a means to a higher end, unity, which Bahá'ís view as an organizing principle for their entire system of community norms and practices, which will, in turn, transform society on a global scale. They describe this unity not as rigid uniformity or slavish conformity but as "unity in diversity" – a social culture in which diversity can flourish.

Historical Setting and Formative Experiences

Bahá'í concern for social justice appears repeatedly in the religion's sacred writings as well as in many of its institutional documents and policy statements, including those of the Bahá'í International Community, a religious nongovernmental organization (NGO) with consultative status at the United Nations. But the impetus for the religion's concern for social justice lies in the experiences of its founding leaders and the more recent experiences of its adherents in countries whose regimes are hostile to the religion.

Officially designated today as the "Bahá'í Faith," the Bahá'í religion was founded in 1844 CE by the Báb ("the Gate," a spiritual title taken by Sayyid 'Alí-Muḥammad Shírází, 1819–1850) and further elaborated by Bahá'u'lláh ("Glory of God," a spiritual title adopted by Mírzá Ḥusayn-'Alí Núrí, 1817–1892), a Persian nobleman born to a high-ranking vizier and grandee. The Báb, by advancing independent prophetic claims and by revealing a code of laws, the Persian *Bayán* (thereby asserting the independence of his own religion and undermining an obsolete Shí'í orthodoxy and corrupt clerical order), paved the way for, and openly foretold, the advent of an even greater religious figure, whom most Bábís accepted as Bahá'u'lláh. The Bábí religion thus evolved into the Bahá'í religion, which is why both the Báb and Bahá'u'lláh are considered to be the co-founders of the Bahá'í Faith.[1] A number of the laws revealed by the Báb were, in fact, modified by Bahá'u'lláh and incorporated into the *Most Holy Book* (*Kitáb-i-Aqdas*).

Born in 1817 to a high-ranking minister of the Shah in Tehran, Bahá'u'lláh was incarcerated in a subterranean dungeon in 1852 because he was a leader of the proscribed Bábí religion, where he experienced his first visionary/revelatory moments of prophetic inspiration. He was exiled to Baghdad in 1853, to Istanbul (Constantinople) and Edirne (Adrianople) in 1863, and finally to 'Akká (Palestine, now Israel) in 1868.

These successive experiences of exile, infused with a clear sense of destiny and messianic purpose, seem to have galvanized his vision of international order and world peace that would later prove to be distinguishing features of his ministry and lifework. For example, one of the signal events of Bahá'u'lláh's ministry was the public proclamation, directed to the world's political and religious leaders, of his mission to unify the world, a proclamation that stands as one of the first international peace missions of modern times.

Bahá'u'lláh's experiences lent further impetus to his international call for nonviolent ways of resolving conflicts among peoples, nations, and religions. Beginning in September, 1867, he addressed individual and collective letters ("epistles") to world leaders, including Queen Victoria of England, Kaiser Wilhelm I of Prussia (now Germany), Czar Alexander Nicholas II of Russia, Emperor Napoleon III of France, Emperor Franz Joseph of Austria, Sulṭán 'Abdu'l-'Azíz of the Ottoman Empire, Náṣiri'd-Dín Sháh of Persia (now Iran), and the Presidents of the Americas collectively. In these letters, Bahá'u'lláh summoned leaders and their nations to disarmament, reconciliation, justice, and the "Most Great Peace." To the leaders of the Zoroastrian, Jewish, Christian, and Muslim faiths, he revealed epistolary "Tablets," calling these leaders to religious reconciliation and inviting their recognition of Bahá'u'lláh as the promised messiah of all religions.

On his death in 1892, Bahá'u'lláh was succeeded by his eldest son, 'Abdu'l-Bahá (1844–1921). Like Bahá'u'lláh, 'Abdu'l-Bahá's approach to social justice was informed by his father's prophetic vision, reinforced by his experience as a prisoner and exile for most of his life as he accompanied his father throughout his successive exiles, and enlightened by an innate wisdom that Bahá'u'lláh accentuated in appointing 'Abdu'l-Bahá as his successor, interpreter, and exemplar. 'Abdu'l-Bahá was liberated by the Young Turks Revolution in 1908. From 1911 to 1913 he traveled to Europe, North Africa, and North America, promulgating his father's principles of social justice and world unity.

If imprisonment, exile, and revelatory experiences intensified the consciousness of early Bahá'í leaders, persecution has kept social justice at the forefront of thinking among contemporary adherents to the religion. This is true nowhere more vividly than in Iran, where some 300,000 Bahá'ís constitute the country's largest non-Muslim minority religion. Persecution of Bahá'ís in Iran has taken place ever since the religion's inception there in the mid-nineteenth century. Repression of the Bahá'í community continues to be official government policy. As a result, Bahá'ís have been targets of discrimination and violence. Since Iran's 1979 Islamic Revolution, more than 10,000 Bahá'ís have been dismissed from government and university posts. Bahá'ís in Iran are systematically denied jobs, pensions, and the right to inherit property, and the government of Iran has prosecuted a systematic campaign to deny Bahá'ís rights in what one independent scholar has described as "suspended genocide" (Momen, 2005).

Following the 1979 Islamic revolution, the Iranian regime tried to eradicate the Bahá'í Faith as a viable religious organization by executing its leaders. In 1981, the state, dominated by the clergy, executed all nine members of the National Spiritual Assembly of the Bahá'ís of Iran. In 1984, and again in 1986, Iranian authorities executed the majority of the members of the new National Spiritual Assembly of the

Bahá'ís of Iran, which had been elected to replace the martyred members of that same council.

In 1983, Iran declared the Bahá'í religion to be an unlawful, criminal organization and banned it. In strict conformity with the Bahá'í religious commitment to obey civil authorities, the National Spiritual Assembly of the Bahá'ís of Iran complied with the Iranian ban on organized Bahá'í activity by suspending its administrative network. Following suspension of its formal system of democratically elected local and national councils, the Bahá'í community in Iran managed its affairs by an informal seven-member national committee, known as the "Yaran" ("Friends"). In February 2009, Iran announced the trial of the seven Yaran, charged with "espionage on behalf of Israel," "insult to the sacredness of Islam," and "propaganda against the regime"; they were sentenced in 2010 to 20-year prison terms.

The persecution of Bahá'ís in Iran has served to reinforce, for the members of the worldwide Bahá'í community, the need for precisely the kinds of principles of social justice and unity that have been central tenets of their religion since its inception. It has also bolstered their commitment to live by the principles they espouse. Thus, for example, when the members of the National Spiritual Assembly of the Bahá'ís of Iran were executed in 1981, 1984, and 1986, the Bahá'í community responded not with violence but with elections: they elected members to replace their martyred colleagues.

Bahá'ís at the Grassroots Level

The Bahá'í Faith enjoins followers of the religion to observe a number of social norms (laws) drawn from the *Most Holy Book*. For instance, Bahá'í social norms require commitment to family and fidelity in marriage, and place a high value on productive work, which, when performed in the spirit of service, is regarded as worship of God. Bahá'ís are also expected to abstain from alcohol and narcotics and, in general, to lead healthy lives. The primary purpose of a Bahá'í's life is threefold: to love and worship God, to acquire virtues, and to carry forward an ever-advancing civilization.

While many of the norms or laws seem directed at shaping personal piety and refining character, their larger purpose is often to prepare followers of the religion to serve humanity more effectively. Thus, for example, "backbiting" (speaking maliciously of another person who is not present) is forbidden, not simply as a matter of personal integrity, but because it is socially corrosive and undermines the larger goal of social unity.

The proscription of negative personal behaviors such as backbiting illustrates a simple but important point in Bahá'í social and moral thought: Bahá'ís aspire to provide an integrated system of values and socio-moral principles aimed at achieving unity among all people. Most behaviors that are specifically forbidden, allowed, or required by religious law fall under some larger principles (often related to social justice), and these overarching principles aim at achieving the ultimate principle, which is "unity in diversity" within the framework of a world commonwealth, leading, in time, to a golden age of world civilization.

The gradual introduction of four "core activities" – devotional meetings, study circles, children's classes, and junior youth groups – has had an important transformative influence on recent Bahá'í community life. Devotional meetings, regular gatherings of individuals for prayer and worship, are considered an essential practice for the spiritual health and well-being of a community. Study circles consist of small groups of people, who regularly meet to study the Bahá'í sacred writings in a sequence of courses developed by the Ruhi Institute, guided by a trained facilitator, and supplemented by artistic, service, and social activities aimed at developing skills and capacities to help build spiritually and morally grounded neighborhoods and communities. Neighborhood children's classes provide a moral framework that assists children to achieve excellence in material, intellectual, and spiritual aspects of life. Junior youth groups, populated by young people between the ages of 12 and 14, are guided by an "animator" (an older youth who acts as a peer facilitator). The purpose of the group meetings is to develop young people's powers of expression, sharpen their capacity to understand the moral implications of their thoughts and actions, and engage them in service to their communities. All of these activities inculcate Bahá'í principles of social justice and encourage their creative application at the grassroots level.

When the Bahá'í community was relatively small, its contribution to social well-being was naturally limited. In 1983, however, the Universal House of Justice announced that the growth of the Faith had given rise to the need and opportunity for a greater involvement in the life of society. Since that time, Bahá'ís began to engage more systematically in social and economic development projects of varying degrees of complexity. Now, Bahá'í efforts to contribute to social transformation have widened to include participation in the public discourse on issues of concern to humanity, such as advancing ideal international relations, instituting infrastructures needed to sustain world peace, systematically eliminating prejudices of all kinds, empowering youth spiritually and morally, and promoting social justice through social action. These Bahá'í endeavors have steadily increased over the past 25 years and will grow in scope and influence in the future.

While there is a mystical dimension in Bahá'í spiritual life, there are no esoteric teachings reserved for a spiritual elite. Each Bahá'í is expected to embark on a quest toward spiritual perfection in an effort to draw ever nearer to the "Great Being." This is achieved, in part, by acquiring virtues, which in turn produce noble character leading to good deeds. Good deeds must be properly motivated, which is to say, they must spring from pure intentions. Proverbially, one's heart must be "in the right place" while doing "the right thing." The link between pure motives and noble deeds is the well-formed (virtuous) character. For Bahá'ís, the great example of virtuous character is 'Abdu'l-Bahá, one of whose titles is "the perfect Exemplar."

Institutions, Affiliations, and Initiatives

The themes of justice and unity are evident in many of the Bahá'í Faith's institutions as well as in its national and international affiliations and initiatives.

In the *Most Holy Book* (*Kitab-i-Aqdas*, which is the core Bahá'í code of laws), Bahá'u'lláh called for the establishment of a local House of Justice in every community. To distinguish these "Houses of Justice" from institutions with an agenda for political power, 'Abdu'l-Bahá gave them the temporary title of "Spiritual Assemblies." Each nine-member local and national Spiritual Assembly is charged with overseeing the growth and welfare of the Bahá'í community within its jurisdiction. Each national spiritual assembly, as mandated by its constitution and bylaws, is tasked with fostering unity among the various elements of society within its power to do so and to advance the work of social and economic development.

As declared in its Constitution, the mission of the Universal House of Justice, the supreme governing institution of the Bahá'í Faith, is "to do its utmost for the realization of greater cordiality and comity amongst the nations and for the attainment of universal peace"; "to safeguard the personal rights, freedom and initiative of individuals"; "to give attention to the preservation of human honour, to the development of countries and the stability of states"; "to provide for the arbitration and settlement of disputes arising between peoples"; and "to foster that which is conducive to the enlightenment and illumination of the souls of men and the advancement and betterment of the world" (Universal House of Justice, 1973: 5). These duties elaborate on and reinforce the more general themes of justice and unity to which the religion is committed.

The Bahá'í International Community, formed in 1948 as a nongovernmental organization (NGO) at the United Nations, represents an association of democratically elected national and regional spiritual assemblies. Serving as the voice of the worldwide Bahá'í community in international affairs, the Bahá'í International Community focuses on four core areas, each related to social justice:

1   Promotion of a universal standard for human rights.
2   Advancement of women.
3   Promotion of just and equitable global prosperity.
4   Development of moral capabilities.

It also defends the rights of Bahá'ís in countries where they are persecuted, such as in Iran and Egypt.

In 1970, the Bahá'í International Community was granted consultative status (now called "special" consultative status) with the United Nations Economic and Social Council. It was granted a similar status with the United Nations Children's Fund in 1976 and with the United Nations Development Fund for Women in 1989, the same year it established working relations with the World Health Organization. The Bahá'í International Community views its work with these and other organizations and offices (e.g., the United Nations Environment Program; the Office of the High Commissioner for Human Rights; the United Nations Educational, Scientific and Cultural Organization; and the United Nations Development Program) as primary channels for promoting Bahá'í social justice values at the international level.

On the 60th anniversary of the founding of the United Nations (October 2005), the Bahá'í International Community issued *The Search for Values in an Age of Transition*, a document that articulates its recommendations on democracy, human rights, collective security, and development. In it, the Bahá'í International Community endorses democracy not simply as an expression of majority rule, but as a form of political governance in which the rights of the governed are respected, leaders function transparently, principles of fairness and equality of opportunity are observed, and decisions are predicated on assessment of community needs. In the view of the Bahá'í International Community, a democracy that satisfies these criteria qualifies as good governance and is essentially an expression of social justice. Moreover, these criteria are not limited by any legal or jurisdictional boundaries, but are universal in scope and applicability.

Engaging the Global Community

One way in which Bahá'ís engage in proactive social justice (social action) is by supporting, participating in, or partnering with United Nations initiatives. For instance, Bahá'í representatives provide leadership in a number of United Nations-related bodies, including the Values Caucus, the Commission on the Status of Women, the Commission on Sustainable Development, the Committee of Religious NGOs, the NGO/Department of Public Information Executive Committee, and the Millennium NGO Network for UN reform.

Bahá'ís also partner with regional or national organizations to effect change at the international level. Established in 2002 in The Hague, Netherlands, the International Criminal Court (ICC) is mandated to try individuals accused of war crimes, crimes against humanity, and genocide. In an effort to achieve the full support of the United States for the ICC, the world's first permanent court, the National Spiritual Assembly of the Bahá'ís of the United States decided to become a founding member of the Washington Working Group for the International Criminal Court (WICC) and the American Coalition for the International Criminal Court (AMICC). The Faith and Ethics Network of the ICC was created to promote awareness of the Court and to support justice and reconciliation efforts in countries where the ICC conducts investigations and prosecutes cases. A Bahá'í representative currently serves as co-chair of this international interfaith coalition.

Bahá'ís also initiate activities of their own in order to demonstrate how local and international social action projects complement each other. The following sections highlight several such social justice (or social action) projects.

Advancement of women

For Bahá'ís, establishing the equality of men and women is one of the most basic ways to reorder societies. Bahá'í writings draw an analogy between the ideal working relationship between men and women and the way the wings of a bird function together. The bird's flight is possible only if it can effectively coordinate its wings, and that can happen only if both wings are equally strong and fit. Similarly, Bahá'ís believe, human relationships will be maximally effective only if men and women, as the respective "wings of a bird," are equally empowered to perform their roles. Consistent with the "wings" imagery and the supporting ideology found in Bahá'í sacred writings, the Bahá'í International Community has identified the advancement of women toward equality with men as one of its four core values. Thus, in *The Search for Values in an Age of Transition*, the Bahá'í International Community asserts that a healthy democracy must be founded on the principle of the equality of men and women (and, by extension, the equality of all peoples). Commending the international community's commitment to democracy, the Bahá'í International Community stresses that ideal democracy is good governance – an essentially moral exercise – which can only come about with the full participation of women and minorities.

The Bahá'í effort to realize its vision for gender equality illustrates the way in which the religion pursues complementary local, national, and international plans of action. At the local level, the National Spiritual Assembly of the Bahá'ís of the United States developed a manual, *Guidelines for Spiritual Assemblies on Domestic Violence*, to provide informed, consistent, and explicit guidance on domestic violence to local Bahá'í councils (known as Local Spiritual Assemblies). The same National Spiritual Assembly also encouraged Bahá'ís to urge their American congressional representatives to support ratification of the United Nations' Convention on the Elimination of All Forms of Discrimination against Women.

Wealth equity

"Tell the rich of the midnight sighing of the poor, lest heedlessness lead them into the path of destruction, and deprive them of the Tree of Wealth," Bahá'u'lláh counseled (Bahá'u'lláh, 1985: 39). The words of the founder vividly convey the historical Bahá'í concern for the poor and the needy. In Bahá'í thought, economic values must be measured by human values, which is to say, justice requires that economic policies and practices must serve society's most disadvantaged citizens. Thus, Bahá'ís are committed to the elimination of extremes of wealth and poverty by such practices as profit sharing among workers, redistribution of wealth through system of graduated income taxation, voluntary sharing of one's wealth for the betterment of society, and equitable distribution of the world's resources.

As with the strategy they have adopted toward gender equality, Bahá'ís approach issues of poverty on multiple fronts. For instance, at the local level, Bahá'í communities have launched more than 1700 development projects worldwide, including more than 600 schools (with over 400 village tutorial schools) and seven radio stations broadcasting educational, health, and agricultural programs, all aimed at mitigating the effects of poverty. Internationally, the Bahá'í Office of Social and Economic Development, an agency of the Bahá'í World Centre in Haifa, Israel, monitors the progress of Bahá'í-inspired development programs worldwide. The Office provides advice and support for these projects, and facilitates collaborative undertakings with like-minded organizations as well. Bahá'ís also actively cooperate with several international relief organizations, economic development organizations, and the World Health Organization.

Environmental issues

In "Seizing the Opportunity: Redefining the Challenge of Climate Change" (2008), the Bahá'í International Community states that "a need for new approaches centered on the principles of justice and equity is apparent." Bahá'ís regard environmental concerns as social justice issues to the extent that they influence one's capacity to promote healthy physical conditions for human beings while developing sustainable economies.

As with other social issues, the Bahá'í International Community has addressed environmental issues in several ways. For instance, as one response to global warming, which is seen as having a cumulative impact through industrial and other carbon-based emissions and thus threatens the planet's future as a whole, Bahá'ís established the International Environment Forum in 1997. The Forum, a nongovernmental, professional organization with more than 200 members in 56 countries on five continents, promotes the application of spiritual and ethical principles to the global challenges of the environment and sustainable development. Accredited by the United Nations as a scientific and technological organization to the World Summit on Sustainable Development (Johannesburg, 2002), the Forum networks with a wide array of organizations with similar missions and sponsors annual conferences. Also, in 2009, the Bahá'í International Community endorsed the "Interfaith Declaration on Climate Change."

Interfaith relations

The Bahá'í concern to nurture interfaith relations flows directly from its commitment to the overarching principle of unity. Bahá'ís place a high premium on interfaith relations that conduce to widening the circles of unity in human society. One of their most prominent initiatives was launched by the National Spiritual Assembly of the Bahá'ís of the United States, which in 1949 instituted an annual "World Religion Day." Then, as now, the third Sunday of January each year was designated for this celebration. The first World Religion Day was held on January 15, 1950, and was observed by Bahá'í communities across the United States. For Bahá'ís, World Religion Day serves as an occasion to highlight what they regard as the essential harmony of the world's religions, and to raise awareness of the contributions of Bahá'í principles in promoting religious reconciliation and confraternity. Celebrated with interfaith dialogue, conferences, and other events that advance mutual understanding (or what scholars call "spiritual literacy"), Bahá'ís see World Religion Day as an occasion to foster transconfessional affinity among religions and, most importantly, to promote the idea and ideal of world unity. World Religion Day, which Bahá'ís consider a natural expression and extension of their emphasis on the unity of religions, races, and nations, is now observed internationally.

Some other prominent Bahá'í interfaith initiatives have been launched by the Universal House of Justice, an institution that directs the spiritual and administrative affairs of the global Bahá'í community, and by the Bahá'í International Community as a nongovernmental organization. In 2000, in a session of the Millennium World Peace Summit of Religious and Spiritual Leaders at the United Nations (the first assembly of prominent religious leaders ever held in the United Nations), Albert Lincoln, Secretary-General of the Bahá'í International Community, called on the world's religious leaders to identify those "core values that are common to all religious and spiritual traditions" (Bahá'í International Community, 2000). Two years later, the Universal House of Justice issued a public letter, "To the World's Religious Leaders" (2002), in which it charged that the interfaith movement has lacked "both intellectual coherence and spiritual commitment," to the extent that the "greater part of organized religion stands paralyzed at the threshold of the future, gripped in those very dogmas and claims of privileged access to truth that have been responsible for creating some of the most bitter conflicts dividing the earth's inhabitants." Describing the Bahá'í community as "a vigorous promoter of interfaith activities from the time of their inception," the letter claims that interfaith activities in general will be of limited value, unless and until "interfaith discourse" honestly addresses, without further evasion, "that God is one and that, beyond all diversity of cultural expression and human interpretation, religion is likewise one." The letter also calls on religious leaders to acknowledge that "religion and science are the two indispensable knowledge systems through which the potentialities of consciousness develop."

The Bahá'í International Community has also participated in a number of interfaith organizations, including the North American Interfaith Network, the Council for a Parliament of the World's Religions, the Tripartite Forum on Interfaith Cooperation for Peace, and the Committee of Religious Non-Governmental Organizations at the United Nations.

Human rights

International law is informed by a set of universal moral norms, which include certain entitlements (rights) that individuals are believed to possess and that are commonly regarded as transnational; that is, beyond the legal jurisdiction of any single state. In 1948 the United Nations adopted a Universal Declaration of Human Rights and thus became the first international body in history to issue a collective proclamation expressing a consensus on core values as they relate to the rights of all people. While the Declaration is not a legally binding treaty, some of its provisions have come to be embodied in international law in such instruments as the International Covenant on Civil and Political Rights (ICCPR) and the International Covenant on Economic, Social and Cultural Rights (ICESCR), adopted by the General Assembly in December 1966. Together with the United Nations' Universal Declaration of Human Rights, the Covenants are referred to as the "International Bill of Human Rights."

Informed by their own experiences (Bahá'ís have historically been the victims of abuse and persecution, primarily in the Middle East) and by their sacred writings (Bahá'ís believe that human rights are ultimately God-given), Bahá'ís sought to influence the crafting of the United Nations' Declaration of Human Rights. To this end, the National Spiritual Assembly of the Bahá'ís of the United States and Canada presented

A Bahá'í Declaration of Human Rights and Obligations to the first session of the United Nations Commission on Human Rights in February, 1947 at Lake Success, New York. This statement broadly addressed human rights in seven categories: the individual; the family; race; work and wealth; education; worship; and social order. In 1995, the Bahá'í International Community presented another statement on human rights and social justice, *The Realization of Economic, Social, and Cultural Rights*, for the 47th session of the Sub-Commission on Prevention of Discrimination and Protection of Minorities Geneva. While the influence of these documents is unclear, there is no doubt that they express a longstanding and fervently held conviction among Bahá'ís that the protection of human rights remains a moral priority of the highest order.

Since 1985, American Bahá'ís have taken prominent leadership roles in pressing the United States to ratify international human rights treaties, including the International Covenant on Civil and Political Rights, the United Nations Convention to Eliminate Racial Discrimination, the United Nations Convention against Torture, and the United Nations Convention against Genocide. Current ratification efforts focus on the Convention on the Elimination of All Forms of Discrimination against Women as well as the Convention of the Rights of the Child. Bahá'ís currently serve on the steering committees of the Campaign for US Ratification of the Convention on the Rights of the Child and the Working Group on the Ratification of the Convention on the Elimination of All Forms of Discrimination against Women.

Race unity

Bahá'í efforts to eliminate racial prejudice stand at the center of their efforts to eradicate prejudice of all types. In 1921, the National Spiritual Assembly of the United States and Canada inaugurated a series of "race amity" conferences throughout the United States. Alain Locke (1885–1954) – the first African American Rhodes Scholar (1907), leader of the Harlem Renaissance (1919–1934), and prominent American Bahá'í (1918–1954) – helped organize the first such conference in the nation's capital.

Bahá'í "race amity" initiatives were as radical as they were historic. These events took place during the period of legal segregation in the United States known as the Jim Crow era, described by some as America's apartheid system. While many politically liberal Americans of the time advocated abolishing Jim Crow laws and endorsed racial tolerance, Bahá'ís went much further and urged interracial harmony, even intermarriage. Locke saw not only the need for authentic reconciliation between the races but also its promise: "If they will but see it, because of their complementary qualities, the two racial groups (Black & White) have great spiritual need, one of the other" (Locke, 1933: 50).

Bahá'í efforts to eradicate racial segregation and promote harmonious race relations continued throughout the second half of the twentieth century. In 1957, in order to foster ideal race relations, the National Spiritual Assembly inaugurated Race Unity Day on the second Sunday in June. (This event is now recognized by the United Nations.) In 1991, the United States National Spiritual Assembly issued *The Vision of Race Unity*, a statement addressed to all Americans. Since racism is a global issue, the National Spiritual Assembly also urged the United States to ratify the International Convention on the Elimination of All Forms of Racial Discrimination (CERD), which it finally did in 1994. In 1997, the National Spiritual Assembly broadcast a video, *The Power of Race Unity*, to audiences across America via several networks, including the Black Entertainment Network. Similar efforts, all animated by the impulse to eradicate racism and promote racial harmony, have been undertaken by Bahá'í communities in other countries around the globe. Specifics vary from place to place, but they share a common strategy: the way to eliminate racism is to foster a genuine appreciation of diversity by nurturing a new global consciousness, which the Bahá'í religion seeks to encourage individually, institutionally, and internationally. Appreciation of racial diversity promotes racial justice, which is a species of social justice.

Conclusion

On May 28, 1942, in NBC's nationally broadcast radio show "Town Meeting of the Air" on the question "Is there a spiritual basis for world unity?", Bahá'í philosopher Alain Locke observed that such venerable ideals as world unity, world order, and the brotherhood of man have long "wandered disembodied in the world – witness the dismembered League of Nations." Criticizing "superciliously self-appointed superior races" and "self-righteous creeds and religions expounding monopolies on ways of life and salvation," Locke stressed that social justice must be approached pragmatically if world peace, which is predicated on social justice, is ever to be realized:

> The fact is, the idealistic exponents of world unity and human brotherhood have throughout the ages and even today expected their figs to grow from thistles. We cannot expect to get international bread from sociological stone, whether it be the granite of national self-sufficiency, the flint of racial antagonisms, or the adamant of religious partisanship. . . . The question pivots, therefore, not on the desirability of world unity, but upon the more realistic issue of its practicability. (quoted in Buck, 2005: 179)

Locke's statement, while not directly referencing the Bahá'í Faith, captures the essence of the distinctively pragmatic Bahá'í approach, which is to promote social justice through coordinated initiatives of "social action" at local, regional, and international levels, while reorienting human consciousness through a global outlook.

Bahá'í social justice practices and strategies are animated by religious conviction, global orientation, and moral fitness globally translated into local initiatives – orchestrated under the auspices of a democratically elected administration, and informed by social principles nuanced by moral and pragmatic considerations. Where possible, Bahá'ís prefer to engage in proactive "social action" rather than remedial forms of social justice. Either way, social justice is not an end in itself, but a means to achieve a grand vision: that peoples of diverse backgrounds, races, and religions can live in unity, even as they respect each other's differences. Questions of international peace, human security, and equitable access to goods, services, and knowledge are all interrelated. Social justice, therefore, is a means to an end. World unity, in the Bahá'í conception of it, is the appropriate and desirable end or goal of social justice.

Note

1 With an estimated 5.5 million adherents, the Bahá'í religion is relatively small in numbers, yet is the second most widely diffused religion in terms of the number of countries in which Bahá'í communities have been established. Significant Bahá'í communities exist in 235 countries and territories, of which 182 are organized as national (or regional) affiliates, with more than 12 500 organized local communities. The religion's global scope is mirrored in the diversity of its adherents, with above 2100 distinct ethnic and tribal groups represented. The Bahá'í World Centre is located on Mt. Carmel in Haifa, Israel. The Universal House of Justice, democratically elected every five years, oversees the global Bahá'í community from the Holy Land. The essence of the Bahá'í teachings may be summed up in these words of Bahá'u'lláh: "The well-being of mankind, its peace and security, are unattainable unless and until its unity is firmly established" (Bahá'u'lláh, 1978: 167).

References

'Abdu'l-Bahá (1969) *Paris Talks: Addresses Given by 'Abdu'l-Bahá in Paris in 1911–1912*, 11th edn, Bahá'í Publishing Trust, London.

Bahá'í International Community (2000) *Complete Statement Submitted by Albert Lincoln to the Millennium Summit*, Bahá'í World Centre, Haifa, http://info.bahai.org/article-1-1-2-2.html (accessed April 10, 2011).

Bahá'í International Community (2005) *The Search for Values in an Age of Transition: A Statement of the Bahá'í International Community on the Occasion of the 60th Anniversary of the United Nations*, http://www.bic-un.bahai.org/05-1002.htm (accessed April 10, 2011).

Bahá'í World Centre (1993) The *Kitab-i-Aqdas*: Its place in Bahá'í literature, *The Bahá'í World 1992–93*, Bahá'í World Centre, Haifa.

Bahá'u'lláh (1978) *Tablets of Bahá'u'lláh Revealed after the Kitab-i-Aqdas*, Bahá'í Publishing Trust, Wilmette, IL.

Bahá'u'lláh (1985) *The Hidden Words of Bahá'u'lláh*, Bahá'í Publishing Trust, Wilmette, IL.

Buck, Christopher (2005) *Alain Locke: Faith and Philosophy*, Kalimat Press, Los Angeles.

Locke, Alain (1933) *The Negro in America*, American Library Association, Chicago.

Momen, Moojan (2005) The Bábi and Bahá'í community of Iran: A case of "suspended genocide"? *Journal of Genocide Research* 7(2, June): 221–241.

Universal House of Justice (1973) *The Constitution of the Universal House of Justice*, Bahá'í World Centre, Haifa.

Universal House of Justice (2002) *To the World's Religious Leaders*, Bahá'í World Centre, Haifa.

Bibliography

'Abdu'l-Bahá (1978) *Selections from the Writings of 'Abdu'l-Bahá*, Research Department of the Universal House of Justice (ed.), Marzieh Gail *et al.* (trans.), Bahá'í World Centre, Haifa.

Bahá'í International Community (1992) Sustainable Development and the Human Spirit: Based on the Statement "The Most Vital Challenge," presented to the Plenary of the United Nations Conference on Environment and Development, Earth Summit, Rio de Janeiro, Brazil, June 4, http://info.bahai.org/article-1-9-2-14.html (accessed April 10, 2011).

Bahá'í International Community (1995) The Prosperity of Humankind, http://info.bahai.

org/article-1-7-4-1.html (accessed April 10, 2011).

Bahá'í International Community (2005) Bahá'í International Community Response to the Secretary General's Report, In Larger Freedom: Towards Development, Security and Human Rights for All, http://bic.org/statements-and-reports/statements/bahai-bic-response-secretary-report-large-freedom (accessed September 27, 2011).

Bahá'í International Community (2006) A New Framework for Global Prosperity: Bahá'í International Community's Submission to the 2006 Commission on Social Development on the Review of the First United Nations Decade for the Eradication of Poverty, http://www.bic-un.bahai.org/pdf/06-0101.pdf (accessed April 10, 2011).

Bahá'í International Community (2008) Seizing the Opportunity: Redefining the Challenge of Climate Change: Initial Considerations of the Bahá'í International Community, http://bic.org:8081/bic_clean/bic/statements-and-reports/bic-statements/seizing-opportunity-redefining-challenge-climate (accessed October 4, 2011).

Hanson, Holly (1996) The process of creating social justice, in *Toward the Most Great Justice: Elements of Justice in the New World Order*, Charles O. Lerche (ed.), Bahá'í Publishing Trust, London.

Huddleston, John (1991) *The Search for a Just Society*, George Ronald, Oxford.

Lerche, Charles O. (ed.) (1996) *Toward the Most Great Justice: Elements of Justice in the New World Order*, Bahá'í Publishing Trust, London.

Lerche, Charles O. (ed.) (2004) *Healing the Body Politic: Bahá'í Perspectives on Peace and Conflict Resolution*, George Ronald, Oxford.

National Spiritual Assembly of the Bahá'ís of the United States (2004) *In Service to the Common Good: The American Bahá'í Community's Commitment to Social Change*, http://www.bahai.us/in-service-to-the-common-good (accessed April 10, 2011).

Schaefer, Udo (2007) *Bahá'í Ethics in Light of Scripture, Vol. 1: Doctrinal Fundamentals*, George Ronald, Oxford.

Shoghi Effendi (1971) *The Advent of Divine Justice*, 3rd edn, Bahá'í Publishing Trust, Wilmette, IL.

Walbridge, John (n.d.) Aqdas. Kitáb-i- (*al-Kitáb al-Aqdas*, The Most Holy Book), http://bahai-library.com/walbridge_encyclopedia_kitab_aqdas (accessed September 27, 2011).

CHAPTER 14

The Quest for Justice in Revival, a Creole Religion in Jamaica

William Wedenoja

Revival is an indigenous religious tradition in the island of Jamaica. It is also one of many "Creole" or African diaspora religions found throughout the Americas, including Vodou in Haiti, Santeria in Cuba, Shango in Trinidad, Conjure and Hoodoo in the United States, and Candomble in Brazil. Revival most closely resembles the Shouters or Spiritual Baptists of Trinidad, Barbados, and the Windward Islands. Like them, Revival is principally an African-derived religion, although it is Christian as well. All are products of European colonialism, the African slave trade, the sugar plantation, and Christian missionization, as well as conditions of oppression, deprivation, marginalization, and cultural dissonance; that is, they are responses to often extreme conditions of social injustice.

Jamaica is a mountainous island, roughly the size of the state of Connecticut, located in the Caribbean Sea, about 90 miles south of Cuba. It was initially and rather densely inhabited by an Amerindian people known as the Taino, who called it Xaymaca or Yamaye. Christopher Columbus discovered the island on his second voyage to the New World in 1494, saying that it was "the fairest island that eyes have beheld." The first Spanish settlement was established in 1509. In 1655 the British invaded Jamaica, and Spain formally ceded it to Great Britain in 1670. By then the Taino were virtually extinct, due to European contact. Sugar plantations were introduced in the late seventeenth century, and Jamaica became the largest producer of sugar in the world in the early 1700s. Approximately 750 000 slaves were eventually brought from Africa to meet the labor needs of the plantations. The slave trade was abolished in 1808, and the slaves were emancipated in 1838. Consequently, about 98% of the Jamaican population – which numbers about 2.8 million today – is of African descent. The country received its independence from Great Britain in 1962, after more than 300 years of slavery and 450 years of colonial rule.

The Wiley Blackwell Companion to Religion and Social Justice, First Edition. Edited by Michael D. Palmer and Stanley M. Burgess.
© 2012 John Wiley & Sons Ltd. Published 2020 by John Wiley & Sons Ltd.

Jamaica is a relatively poor postcolonial nation with many social problems. There is a large gap between rich and poor. The economy has stagnated over the past decade. The country has become increasingly dependent on tourism as agriculture, mining, and manufacturing have faltered. Over half of the population now lives in three urban areas, where ghetto communities are controlled by gangs, which have a powerful influence on politicians. Crime and violence are major concerns. The criminal justice system is failing, as police are widely believed to be corrupt and abusive, and witnesses are afraid to testify in courts. The educational system is inadequate, as are shelter and nutrition. Nonetheless, Jamaica has produced a vibrant culture, known throughout the world for its creativity, particularly in music and dance.

The Religious Landscape

Jamaica is an extremely Christian, mostly Protestant, society. The first church in Jamaica was the Anglican Church of England, which was originally supported by the colonial government and served the interests of white planters. The first missionaries, Moravians, arrived in 1754, followed by Methodists, Baptists, and Presbyterians in the early 1800s, the Quakers and the Salvation Army in the late 1800s, and American churches such as the Church of God and other Pentecostal and Evangelical groups as well as the Seventh Day Adventists in the early twentieth century. All of these churches have taken on a distinctively Jamaican character that sets them apart from their parents, most notably in an enthusiastic form of worship centering on song and dance.

Jamaica has also produced several indigenous religions, derived from African cultures but influenced to varying degrees by Christianity. They are Myalism and the Native Baptists, now defunct, their successor Revival, an Afrocentric offshoot of Revival called Rastafari, and Kumina, a predominantly African and non-Christian religion. Over the years, scholars have distinguished two forms of Revival, Revival Zion and Pukkumina or Pocomania. The former is supposedly more Christian and the latter more African. On the other hand, scholars have been hard-pressed to find a group that claims to be Pukkumina. The word "Pocomania" is often used derisively with reference to Revival, which has historically been marginalized and sometimes sensationalized by colonial whites and the mixed-race middle class. Revival is frequently associated with a healing practice called Balm. It is also important to note the presence of Obeah, the practice of African-derived magic, and "Science," a form of magic inspired by the De Laurence Company of Chicago that is typically mixed with Obeah. All of these religious traditions constitute a single system in the Jamaican context. They represent the range of choices open to the individual, and people often participate in more than one of them. In addition, these traditions compete with each other, react to each other, and borrow from each other. It would be a mistake to try to understand any one of them apart from this context.

The orthodox churches (including Anglican, Baptist, Congregationalist, Methodist, Moravian, Presbyterian, and Catholic) lost ground throughout the twentieth century, declining from 82% in the 1943 census to 25% in the most recent census, in 1991. Pentecostals grew dramatically, from 4% to 29% during the same period. The

Adventists also grew significantly, from 2% to 9%. There has been a surprising increase in the percentage of people claiming no religion, from 4% to 24%. While no reliable figures exist on the number or percentage of people affiliated with indigenous churches, the percentage claiming "other" or "not stated" in the latest census was 10%. One reason for this lack of data is that information on membership in indigenous churches is not solicited. Another is that followers of indigenous churches often claim to be Anglican or Baptist, and indeed often are; they carry a dual allegiance, because of the social stigma attached to Revival in particular.

At any rate, in my experience there is likely to be a Revival church in every community. Nowadays it may well be in disguise, however. Many Revival churches have affiliated with American denominations, most notably the African Methodist Episcopal Zion church. Others have joined newer Jamaican denominations with a Pentecostal or evangelical façade. In any case, the influence of Revival on peasant and lower-class life has been considerable, far more than the number of churches and adherents would suggest; indeed, for a hundred years it was the heartbeat of the Jamaican peasantry.

Studying Revival

The study of Revival began with Martha Warren Beckwith, a pioneering American folklorist who received her MA and PhD in anthropology under Franz Boas, the celebrated founder of American anthropology, and served for many years as Research Professor in the Folklore Foundation at Vassar College. Beckwith made four visits to Jamaica between 1919 and 1924, "collecting" in eight of Jamaica's fourteen parishes and publishing ten books and articles from this research, including an article specifically on Revival (1923) and a book, *Black Roadways* (1929), which devotes six chapters to Jamaican peasant religion. The famous anthropologist Melville Herskovits, known particularly for his studies of African "survivals" in African American cultures, identified *Black Roadways* as "the first ethnographic study of the life of any New World Negro people which, to my knowledge, has been attempted" (Herskovits, 1930: 333), concluding that it "shows clearly the great amount of African culture that has held over in Jamaica in spite of the oppressions of slavery" (Herskovits, 1930: 338).

George Eaton Simpson, formerly professor of sociology and anthropology at Oberlin College, devoted his career largely to the study of African and African-derived religions. He came to Jamaica to study Revival in 1953, having previously studied Vodou in Haiti, and later went on to study the Shango religion and the Spiritual Baptists of Trinidad and the Yoruba religion in Nigeria. Unlike Beckwith, who focused on the rural peasantry, Simpson studied the lumpenproletariat of West Kingston. Although he was in Jamaica for only seven months, he collected an amazing amount of information, presented in his detailed monograph *Jamaican Revivalist Cults* in 1956. In addition, he issued *Jamaican Cult Music*, a recording of Revival music, on the Folkways label (1954), and was perhaps the first scholar to write on the Rastafari movement. Simpson's analysis of Revival reflects the theoretical frameworks of his day in its focus on the functions and dysfunctions of the religion as well as African "survivals." He was a strong advocate of the Africanist views of Herskovits.

Edward Seaga began his study at about the same time as Simpson, if not before. The son of Lebanese parents, Seaga was raised in Jamaica, but went to Harvard for a Bachelor's degree in Social Relations. Following graduation in 1952, he returned to Jamaica and embarked on a study of indigenous religion and healing practices, particularly Revival, before entering politics in 1959. His 1969 article "Revival Cults in Jamaica" is well known and very influential, as it was published in the popular magazine *Jamaica Journal* and reached a wide audience. It also appeared during Seaga's rise to political prominence. His other contribution to the study of Revival is a Folkways record, *Folk Music of Jamaica* (1956), which includes recordings of Revival services and notes on the religion. Seaga became Minister of Culture and ultimately Prime Minister of Jamaica, as well as serving as leader of the Jamaica Labour Party for decades. He steadfastly promoted Revival throughout his political career, which may have given him some credibility as one who, although not black, understood and was close to the average Jamaican.

Donald Hogg came to Jamaica and did fieldwork on Revival in the summers of 1955 and 1956, as a graduate student at Yale University. He spent a total of only seven months in Jamaica, focusing on Revival, first in the urban area of Spanish Town, then in a rural village in the parish of St. Mary. He produced an excellent dissertation (1964), the chief contribution, in my view, being a 131-page section on the history of religion in Jamaica.

The well-known Jamaican scholar Barry Chevannes produced a Master's thesis in sociology on Jamaican "lower-class" religion in 1971, with a focus on Revival. He subsequently wrote a PhD dissertation in anthropology and then a book on the Rastafari movement, as well as several articles on Revival (1971b, 1978, 1995), emphasizing more recently the continuities between Revival and Rastafari and the contributions of the former to the latter. Chevannes collaborated with the anthropologist Jean Besson in an article on Revival in 1996 and a book on Jamaican religion in 1998.

My introduction to Revival took place in 1972 in a Jamaican market, where I encountered a woman in a uniform preaching and singing, accompanied by drummers. Returning to the center of the island in 1975, I was befriended by a Revival leader and prominent healer, and spent the next 15 months engaged in an intensive ethnographic study of her congregation, which formed the basis for my PhD dissertation (Wedenoja, 1978). Over the past 34 years, I have made 20 additional trips to Jamaica, always visiting this church, more as a friend than as a researcher, having gone on to other research projects. Nevertheless, I have had the privilege of not only an intimate view, as "Brother Bill," but a very longitudinal one as well.

Emanuela Guana did fieldwork on Revival in 1992 and wrote a Master's thesis on it for Louisiana State University (1993), publishing an excellent if general article on the religion in 1994. Joseph Murphy (1994) produced a fine overview of Revival, based largely on previous studies. Dianne Stewart (2005) offered a more theological reflection on the African-derived religions of Jamaica, including Revival, which she sees as liberation movements. And the African Caribbean Institute of Jamaica, a government research center, released a fine multimedia CD-ROM on indigenous Jamaican religions, featuring Revival (2007). We are fortunate to have a number of extensive studies over such a long period. One thing we can learn from them is that Revival varies regionally, over time, and even from one congregation to another in the same time and place. In spite of this research, Revival is hardly known outside of Jamaica.

It is also important to note some artistic contributions to our understanding of Revival. Mallica Reynolds (1911–1989) is certainly one of the most prominent Revival leaders in Jamaican history. "Kapo," as he was affectionately known, had a congregation in Trench Town, the focus of Seaga's research and that of Simpson, and he was also a notable intuitive artist; his paintings and sculptures figure prominently in the National Gallery. Bernard Stanley Hoyes is a contemporary artist, raised in Jamaica in a Revival household but now working in Los Angeles, who has produced a magnificent series of paintings of Revival services. The late Rex Nettleford, formerly Vice-Chancellor of the University of the West Indies, choreographed Revival performances for the National Dance Theatre (Nettleford, 1969). And Sylvia Wynter, professor emeritus of Spanish at Stanford University, produced a novel, *The Hills of Hebron* (1962), about the intimate life of a Revival group.

Origins of Revival[1]

An extensive system of sugar plantations, based on slavery, began to form in Jamaica in the late 1600s and reached its height at the end of the eighteenth century. The colonial population included white estate owners, merchants, managers and overseers, a much greater number of black slaves, for the most part working on the plantations, and a small group of mulattos of mixed parentage and intermediate social status. The slaves transported from Africa included religious specialists such as priests, diviners, healers, spirit mediums, sorcerers, and witches. The Church of England was the official church, but it served the interest of the planters and ignored the slaves, who maintained their African beliefs and practices and developed a new, Creole culture, mixing traditions from numerous tribal backgrounds and adapting them to the needs of slave life. The linguist Mervyn Alleyne (1996) has argued that the dominant African influence was Akan speakers, mainly Twi and Asante, also known at the time as Coromantees.

The first indigenous religious tradition to be recorded was Obeah, which included beliefs and practices about spirits, particularly "duppies" or the dead. "Obeahmen" were powerful, feared, and respected spiritual figures in slave communities. They fashioned fetishes or "guards" to hang in fields and protect crops from thieves. They concocted potions and charms to influence events and harm or bewitch other people. They diagnosed and treated illnesses, using herbal and magical remedies. They recovered lost souls, predicted the future, and avenged insults. Whites came to see Obeah as a threat, as Obeahmen were skilled in poisons and they also led numerous slave revolts. It was believed, for example, that Obeahmen rubbed the bodies of rebels with a powder to make them invulnerable in Tacky's Rebellion in 1760.

Obeahmen performed a ritual called the "Myal Dance," administering a drink to a subject that appeared to kill him, and then resurrecting him with a tonic while assistants danced around the subject, in a circle, stamping the ground loudly with their feet. This so-called Myalism apparently united slaves from different estates and ethnic groups and figured in numerous revolts. However, the Myalists were also skilled at herbal remedies and often employed in plantation infirmaries in the latter years of the eighteenth century. In addition, they offered protection from duppies and Obeah.

George Lisle, a freed slave and Baptist minister from Georgia, came to Jamaica in 1783 with a group of Loyalists fleeing the American Revolution. In 1784 he established the Jamaica Baptist Free Church, commonly known as the Black Baptists, in Kingston. Lisle used a leader-class system, organizing converts into "classes" and appointing lay leaders to guide them. His church grew rapidly; however, some of his leaders deviated from his teachings and broke away to form so-called Native Baptist groups, emphasizing visions, dreams, dance, and possession, presumably based on Myalism.

The first Christian missionaries, the Moravians, arrived in 1754, followed by the Methodists in 1789. George Lisle appealed to the British Baptist Society for assistance with his work, and a missionary was sent from England in 1814. The Baptists adopted his leader-class system and quickly grew to be the most popular mission. Missionaries from the Church of Scotland came in 1819, encouraged by white planters who saw the Methodists and Baptists as dangerous. For the most part, missionaries embraced the growing movement in England for the abolition of the slave trade (which occurred in 1808) and improved conditions of servitude, frequently interceding on behalf of slaves.

A rumor spread among slaves in 1831 that the King had issued a "free paper," which was being withheld by their masters. A Baptist deacon by the name of Samuel Sharpe used the leader-class system to organize a strike to demand freedom and fair wages following the Christmas holiday. The strike quickly turned to revolt, the most serious in Jamaican history. After the militia put down the revolt, 312 slaves were tried and executed, Sharpe among them. The so-called "Baptist War" was blamed on missionaries who were then attacked by whites, who tarred and feathered some and set fire to chapels. Baptist missionaries met in Kingston in 1832 to formally declare their opposition to slavery, and sent representatives to England to press their case for emancipation, which was passed by Parliament in 1833.

Actual emancipation did not take place until August 1, 1838, after a transitional period of so-called Apprenticeship. One of the most significant consequences of emancipation was the creation of a free black peasantry. Jamaica is a mountainous country and the plantations were located largely on the coastal lowlands and the central valleys. Unlike some of the smaller islands, there was plenty of uninhabited land in the interior, and perhaps a third of the freedmen literally "took to the hills" to become small farmers. Freedmen were prepared for this, as they had grown vegetables on "provision grounds" during slavery, and they had established an internal marketing system across the island where they could sell their surplus. Missionaries, especially the Baptists and the Methodists, worked hard on behalf of the freedmen; in particular, they purchased land for their congregations and created about 60 "free villages," intended to be church-centered communities of yeoman farmers.

The great expectations that must have been aroused by emancipation were completely dashed in the postemancipation period. The sugar industry virtually collapsed. Plantations fell into disrepair, were sold for a fraction of their previous value, were auctioned off in bankruptcy, or were abandoned. Estate owners did not have money to hire the freedmen, and turned to indentured servants from India and China, further reducing the labor demand. In addition, more than 8000 Africans were brought to

Jamaica as indentured servants, particularly to the southeastern parish of St. Thomas, where their ancestor religion, known as Kumina, persists to this day.

The end of slavery did permit freedmen to practice religion more openly. The widespread distress of the time was expressed in the form of rampant accusations of Obeah and a resurgence of Myalism with Christian elements. "Angel men," claiming to be on a mission from God to cleanse the land of Obeah before Christ's return, sought guidance in dreams and visions. The angel men recovered lost "shadows" (souls) and revealed Obeahmen, who were beaten and forced to confess and repent. During the "Great Myal Procession" of 1841–1842 exorcisms were held on at least 20 estates, and there were recurrences in 1845, 1848, 1849, and 1852.

The Baptist missionaries, inspired by a religious awakening in the United States, attempted to counter Myalism by holding special fasting and prayer meetings, triggering the "Great Revival" in 1860. The churches were filled with people seeking redemption from sin – for a time. But the revival took an increasingly ecstatic form in 1861, following the Myalist tradition. People gathered to sing and dance and angels possessed the dancers, giving them spiritual powers such as prophecy, divination, and healing. And they sought out Obeah and Obeahmen. The missionaries rejected what they perceived to be pagan "fanaticism," but lost many of their followers to a new indigenous religion called Revival, a unique combination of Myalism, the Native Baptists, and missionary Christianity.

In October of 1865, an apparently spontaneous uprising involving indigenous religion took place in the town of Morant Bay, where Paul Bogle, a Native Baptist deacon, disrupted a trial and later resisted arrest. Soon after, he and his supporters fought a battle with the militia, burning down the courthouse and killing 15 whites, including the Custos and some magistrates. The Governor declared martial law and the rebellion was brutally suppressed. Bogle and 354 others were executed.

Revival focused particularly on healing in the late nineteenth and early twentieth centuries, albeit with a militant edge. Stewart, "the Haddo Doctor," claimed that Christ had given him the gift of healing and operated a popular "balmyard" or healing center in the 1880s. The Revival "Captain" "Warrior" Higgins baptized converts in the Hope River near Kingston and offered herbal tonics at his "Millenium Hospital" in the 1890s. He also denounced other churches, ministers, and white authorities. Myalism returned in 1896 in the form of "Convinced Doctors" who sought out Obeah, removed spells, and cured the sick with consecrated water. In the same year, on the opposite end of the island, people flocked to Revival "Shepherds" offering "Jesus Medicine" from healing springs. Full gospel Holiness churches entered the scene from North America at the turn of the century, forbidding the use of medicine, tobacco, pork, jewelry, alcohol, coffee, and tea; promising salvation through the baptism of the Holy Spirit; and using prayer, olive oil, and the laying on of hands to heal the sick. The Revival leader Solomon Hewitt staged a mock crucifixion in 1914 and "rose from the dead" at Easter. "Doctor" David Bell dispensed healing mud at his "Faith Healing Church of God" and referred to whites as "liars, thieves, hypocrites."[2]

The Revival movement came to a climax with the prophet and healer Alexander Bedward. Working in Panama in 1885, the "Son of God" appeared and told him to return to Jamaica, where he became an elder in the church of a Revival leader known as Shakespeare. In 1891, Bedward received a calling to use the waters of the Hope River to heal the sick. Thousands came to hear him preach and be cured. In 1894, he built a chapel in August Town, outside Kingston, for his Jamaica Native Baptist Free Church. Pilgrims carried jugs of his healing water around the island. In 1895, Bedward accused the government of oppressing black people and called on the people to "remember the Morant War." He was charged with sedition and arrested, but acquitted on grounds of insanity. Following the great earthquake and fire in Kingston in 1907, Bedwardites warned of Judgment Day. In 1920, Bedward announced that he was Jesus and threatened to bring the world to an end because the government refused to allow his ministers to perform marriages. He said that he would ascend to heaven on December 31 and destroy the white race. Thousands quit their jobs and came to August Town to join the new kingdom of Bedwardism, but the appointed day passed without event. The following year Bedward led a march on Kingston to protest a government order for eviction. He was arrested on the way, tried, and sentenced to an insane asylum.

The militant emphasis in Revival was channeled into an offshoot in the 1930s, the well-known Rastafari movement, which embraced Emperor Haile Selassie of Ethiopia as the black messiah. Revival came to emphasize spirit possession and healing. Increasingly, it faced competition from Adventists and Pentecostals. In a quest for respectability, Revivalists often held membership in Baptist or Anglican churches too. In the 1960s, entire congregations often affiliated with African American denominations such as the National Baptists and the AME Zion. By the 1970s, Revival churches were incorporating Pentecostal forms of worship, and even adopting Pentecostal names. During the 1980s, small white American fundamentalist and evangelical denominations actively recruited Revival congregations as missions. Currently, Revival has re-entered popular culture and is enjoying great popularity, largely due to its influence on popular music, which seems to be having an effect on worship as well. Amplified reggae music is replacing traditional drums and tambourines, while Revival beats are entering the popular music dancehall. I recently attended a service at a very popular Revival church, which I would characterize as "reggae Revival" due to the music, where the young minister wore dreadlocks like a Rasta. Revival is also becoming popular with the intelligentsia, who now see it as an authentic African "survival" or "roots" religion.

Portrait of a Revival Congregation

The Revival tradition is made up of a large array of cultural beliefs, practices, and symbols. Each leader draws on this array, creating a unique combination for his or her own congregation and often adding something new to the mix. Therefore, the observer will find something unique about every Revival group, and much that is familiar from other groups as well. Leaders are constantly adding new beliefs, practices, and symbols to the Revival tradition. There is, of course, a process of selection. Some innovations spread rapidly, while other elements, even long-standing ones, fade away. It is, therefore, a constantly evolving tradition that is impossible to describe in its entirety. There is obviously variation over time, evident in published reports from different periods. But there also seems to be significant regional variation. Jamaica is a small but remarkably diverse place, perhaps because it is so mountainous. For example, in the east end of the island Kumina seems to have influenced Revival significantly, whereas in Central Jamaica the key influence is Pentecostalism. In keeping with the above remarks, I will offer a portrait of one Revival group, which I have come to know intimately over three decades, rather than attempt a generalized description.

I am going to call this church Gilead, as churches often have names in Jamaica. Gilead is located in a medium-sized farming village in the mountains in the center of the island. It sits prominently on a hilltop in a valley and can be seen easily from most parts of the village, so everyone can observe its comings and goings. The leader lives in a large two-story house just below the church, along with several church "workers" and some tenants. There is a cement wall around the house. We pass a small shop near the entrance that is operated by the church. A large cloth "banner" is stretched over the gate to the driveway, welcoming visitors. Entering the yard, there is a "seal" to our right. This is a sacred place, attracting spirits. We see a wooden pole standing about 5 feet tall, surrounded by a circle of cement. There is a wooden platform of two crossed boards on top of the pole, supporting a vase of croton leaves, a glass of water with a plant called leaf-of-life in it, some oranges, and a green flag. To our left is a flower garden, possibly containing some medicinal and spiritual herbs.

Like most guests, we have a formal audience with the leader in the parlor of her house. She will quickly begin to recite her "story," something I would call an "oral diploma," stating how she was called to be a religious leader and a healer through spiritual experiences. She has recited this countless times to clients and guests over the decades. We notice some banners and religious inscriptions and pictures on the walls, as well as a painted conch shell under the coffee table. In the next room is an "office" where she meets privately with patients. There is a glass of water with leaf-of-life on the table there, along with a painted wood sword and a Bible.

The Reverend "Mother" Jones (a pseudonym) says that she was sickly as a child, suffering from malaria and typhoid fever. As an adolescent she would sometimes faint and have visions. Spiritual people told her she had a gift, but she ignored it until she was struck with paralysis and received a vision to start a healing ministry, guided by "the Spirit." In the Revival tradition, God sends "orders" to his people and they must obey, possibly suffering death otherwise. Mother Jones started her ministry in 1950, building a small "booth" and preaching and healing, relying on "the Lord" for guidance. She has been remarkably successful. The vision she was given was detailed, and she has executed it carefully. The church building has evolved gradually for decades and is now quite substantial.

There are about 60 active members in the congregation. Most of the leaders are men, but three-fourths of the members are actually women. In the beginning, they were poor to working class, but increasingly, middle-class people have been coming to the church. In addition, members often experience social mobility and generally stay with the church. The members constitute a close, tight-knit community, held together by devotion to Mother Jones, who has almost total control, when she chooses to use it. Some of the members are relatives. Some were children she "grew" at her house for others. Some are former patients. Mother Jones and her membership are adamant "Christians," meaning that they don't smoke or drink or curse, and they don't go to "rum shops," choosing to live the good, clean life that is necessary to receive "the Spirit."

There are many positions of leadership in the church, but it is necessary to "have the Spirit" to hold one. Most of the prominent positions, such as pastors, deacons, and elders, are held by men. However, Revival offers more positions to women than other churches. In Gilead there are deaconesses, missionaries, evangelists, leadresses, a secretary, and, formerly, an "armor bearer," the "right hand" to the leader. The head of a Revival church is typically called a "captain" or a "daddy" if male and a "mother" if female. In addition, there may be a warrior, a cutter, a searcher, a hunter, a waterman, and so on.

Women are required to cover their heads in a Revival church, and they almost always "wrap head" in a turban, that of an ordinary member being white and that of officers often colored and occasionally fitted to a peak. Men who are leaders will sometimes "wrap head" too. Dress in church and out should be modest. Young men wear white shirts and ties and older men often a black suit. Women always wear long dresses, the members' being white and the leaders' generally colored, often fitted with a prominent waistband, sash or apron, and lace edging. A pencil is sometimes pushed halfway into the turban. Scissors may be tucked into the waistband "to cut destruction." Mother Jones wears a whistle around her neck to control the "bands" or congregation.

The church or "mission house" sits on top of a hill, and it too is surrounded by a concrete wall. We enter through a gate under another banner. To our right is another seal, a concrete circle with a tall flagpole to attract "pilgrims" and "spirits." Patients coming to healing service will be asked to walk counterclockwise around this seal, reciting the 23rd Psalm, to remove any "destruction" they may carry before entering the church. There are always church "workers" in dresses and turbans to greet visitors when a service is being conducted.

Inside is another seal, the "inner seal," a wooden post on wooden legs standing toward the front of the church, in front of the pulpit, with an elaborate chalk circle around it, about 8 feet in diameter. There is typically a vase of leaves on top of the post, and at the base often an enamel basin of water. The altar to the right of the pulpit contains a gold cross, flowers, a glass of water, leaf-of-life, an open Bible, a hymnal, a candle in a silver holder, fruits, a clock, and a kerosene lantern, laid out on a white tablecloth. To the left are pews for the choir and behind the pulpit are chairs for Mother Jones, the pastors, and other leaders. Biblical inscriptions adorn the walls and a vase of consecrated water called "the medicine" sits on a small table. Other ritual paraphernalia include oils and perfumes to attract spirits, a ruler and a wooden sword "to cut and clear destruction," a small flag on a pole "to flog the banner" and chase demons away, a 6-foot tall wooden cross to carry in baptismal processions, painted stones that carry power, and a shepherd's crook.

Gilead holds "divine worship" every Sunday morning and an "evangelistic" service that evening. Once a month, there is a communion service on Sunday morning and a "fasting service" on a Thursday. A "healing service" is conducted every Monday, generally for the benefit of clients or patients, not members, although "workers" in the church conduct the service. Occasionally, Gilead will march through the community and conduct a street meeting. There are evening "rallies" to raise money several times a year. A river baptism is held, early on a Sunday morning, before divine worship, approximately once a year. Gilead holds an annual "convention," lasting a week. Other churches from the area and from Kingston are invited, and two services are conducted every day, with different guests and guest preachers. Generally, Jamaicans from New York and possibly Canada or England return home for the event. The most distinctive service in the Revival tradition is, however, the "table." Gilead typically holds four tables a year, for different reasons: one to honor the leader, one for patients, one for members, and one on New Year's Day. A table will begin around noon and "break" before midnight. A rectangular table will be placed in the center of the church, covered with a tablecloth, and spread with a tiered wedding cake, vases of leaves and flowers, fruits, breads baked in special shapes, particularly that of a dove, bottled soft drinks, and occasionally "spirits" such as ginger wine. Tables are the longest and most dramatic celebrations in Revivalism.

Every service, regardless of purpose, will generally include announcements, prayers, readings from the Bible, and the singing of slow, monotonous hymns from the *Redemption Songbook* as well as many "lively choruses." Indeed, the main thrust of a service is to enliven the congregation, principally through simple rhythmic songs, which people sing loudly and stand and dance to. Choruses are accompanied by instruments if possible. Traditionally, these included two handmade goatskin drums, a bass and a snare called a "rattler," as well as tambourines, shakers, triangles, scrapers, and handclapping. Now it is more common to find electric guitars, a keyboard, and a trap set. Members are also called on to stand and give "testimonies," which are always formulaic recitations rather than personal confessions. There is usually a sermon, interrupted frequently by song and dance. The sermon should be spontaneous or inspired rather than prepared, and is judged according to the sentiments expressed and its emotive force.

The Revival view of the world is that there is a host of spirits to attend to. Some of them are essentially moral and benevolent, including Old Testament prophets and New Testament apostles, as well as biblical angels and archangels who work with God and Jesus. Some Revivalists also recognize a dove spirit, an Indian spirit, a fish spirit, and an African spirit. Revivalists rely heavily on spirits for guidance. They serve as messengers, bringing warnings and lessons in dreams and visions as well as in possession experiences. Revivalists also recognize the figure of Satan, fallen angels, and demons, which are their nemeses, as well as spirits of the dead, called "duppies," which can be put to bad use by Obeahmen.

Spirit possession is central to Revival, as it is to most African and African-derived religions. In many services several participants will generally be "in the Spirit," in different ways, as "the Spirit," the Holy Ghost, or an "angel" touches them or moves them.[3] Spirit possession is necessary for a successful service. The most dramatic and distinctive form of possession is a ritual called "shouting." During a service, while people are singing and dancing to a chorus, one person will be taken by the Spirit and start to stamp a foot and exhale loudly. Others will join in, forming a circle, and start to dance in a counterclockwise direction. Lifting their arms above their heads, they will then thrust forward and stamp the right foot on the ground, exhaling loudly. The stamping is known as "trumping," and involves trampling bad spirits under foot. The exhalation or overbreathing is called "groaning" or "sounding," and the trumping and groaning together are called "laboring in the spirit." This ritual can go on for 30–90 minutes as the "bands" travels on a synchronized journey in the spirit world, "drilled" by a leader. As the shouting begins, singing turns to humming and then subsides entirely, being replaced by the overbreathing. The music stops too. Toward the end, the humming and then the singing and music pick up again as the spiritual journey comes to a close.

Revivalists fight a constant battle against demonic forces. During a service the Cutter may "flog" a flag back and forth around the church to chase out demons, make slashing motions with her hands, or even joust with demons using a wooden sword. Sometimes glass bottles of soda are thrown at spirits, bursting of course, and the congregation then "turns the roll," rotating in a counterclockwise direction to avoid the "destruction" released. Their main nemesis is the Obeahman, someone who can conjure duppies from the grave and "set hand" on others for gain, and the people who employ him. Much illness and misfortune is blamed on Obeah. When individuals feel they have a "spiritual" problem, they often seek the help of Revivalists, particularly leaders who practice a form of folk healing called "Balm."

Gilead is a well-known "balmyard," a place for spiritual healing. This is announced by the flagpole in front of it. Every Monday morning 20–30 patients come for a healing service. Behind the church is another seal ground. Beyond it is a room where patients are bathed and another where Mother Jones meets with clients to give them a "reading." She often stares into a glass of water with leaf-of-life in it, and a diagnosis and treatment come to her mind. She also frequently performs automatic writing, scribbling esoteric characters on a piece of paper taken from an exercise book, which is then cut up and folded and given to the patient to be placed near their affliction, as a prayer. She may prescribe "bush teas" or "roots" (herbal tonics), which are traditional, but she is just as likely to prescribe patent medicines from the pharmacy or rub oils and perfumes on a client. Mother Jones's special gift, however, is simply to draw the suffering of the patient into her own body.

Revivalists distinguish between "temporal" and "spiritual" illnesses, and specialize in the latter. Spiritual illnesses are caused by spirits, which may be controlled by people with malevolent intent. They may also be punishments caused by offending the ancestors, or failure to live a godly life. In most cases, spiritual illnesses involve interpersonal relations: people you have slighted, people who begrudge you, envy you, and so on. A healer will explore patients' social dynamics and counsel them on how to live properly and deal with their relationships. The successful healer is therefore a talented counselor. I visited a healer who offered spiritual assistance in gaining a visa to travel to the United States, a notoriously difficult process. In recent years there have also been stories in newspapers about gangsters seeking magical assistance in court cases from healers and Obeahmen.[4]

Social and Practical Justice

My understanding of social justice is that it entails the idea of a just world (however we might define "just"), commonly understood as a world in which every person can enjoy dignity, respect, freedom from coercion, equal opportunity, access to resources, and fulfillment of their basic needs. It is obvious from the history of Jamaica that it was a grossly unjust society under slavery as well as colonialism. While this laid the foundation for a free and independent society that is still inherently unjust, it also engendered a passionate concern for social justice, expressed in the words and deeds of Jamaicans such as the activist Marcus Garvey, the singer Bob Marley, and former Prime Minister Michael Manley.

A panel on the topic of religion and social justice in the Caribbean was organized by anthropologist Stephen D. Glazier for the annual meeting of the Society for the Scientific Study of Religion in 1983, and published in the journal *Phylon* (volume 46, issue 4, 1985). The panel focused on the so-called folk religions of the Caribbean. Glazier, who has studied the Spiritual Baptists of Trinidad, provided an introduction, anthropologist Erika Bourguignon discussed Haitian Vodou, sociologist George Eaton Simpson spoke on the Rastafari of Jamaica, and anthropologist Merrill Singer, who has studied Cuban Santeria, was the discussant.

The panelists agreed that we cannot make statements about the position of these religions on social justice because they are "incredibly fragmented" and "lack denominational chains of command" (Glazier, 1985: 285), are "characterized by a striking amount of local and regional variation" and "have no well-defined doctrine" (Bourguignon, 1985: 292). Bourguignon also noted the instrumental orientation of West African religions, saying that they are concerned largely with specific events and problems, like illness, rather than "theological speculations." At any rate, it is clear that Caribbean religions, including Revival, are a direct response to injustice, particularly in the form of slavery, colonialism, capitalism, and now perhaps globalization, and that they have had to struggle against domination, oppression, exploitation, deprivation, racism, and poverty.

In his introductory remarks, Glazier observed that Caribbean folk religions began as what sociologist Vittorio Lanternari famously called "religions of the oppressed," but "they have not remained as such" because they "have joined the establishments" (Glazier, 1985: 283), thereby forfeiting the moral authority necessary "to advocate effectively for social justice" (Glazier, 1985: 285). Simpson, for example, remarked that Rastafari was initially a subversive force, focusing on issues of race and class, but it later turned to the question of identity, embracing Africa and Africanness, becoming a way of life that is concerned with the personal dignity and self-worth long denied to black people in colonial societies. Much the same can be said of Revival. But does this imply that neither is any longer concerned with social justice?

Bourguignon suggested that we need to look for justice in the interactions between spirits and humans. For example, the acquisition of wealth by means of sorcery may lead to spiritual sanctions, such as illness and misfortune, because this is seen as an unfair or illegitimate use of spiritual power. Singer added that "Magic . . . is an available, acquirable power that literally allows the victim or his proxy to take justice into his own hands when necessary" (Singer, 1985: 297). He went on to make what I think is a useful distinction between *social* justice and *practical* justice. We tend to think of social justice as a collective action aimed at redressing social injustice, such as a demonstration, a boycott, or a revolt. Practical justice, on the other hand, seeks fairness in "the affairs of everyday life" (Singer, 1985: 297), including jealousy, squabbles, insults, and common misfortunes.

Jamaicans are descendants of those who were taken forcibly from their lives and villages in west and central Africa, sold into miserable slavery, grossly abused for the comfort and profit of others, and treated as inferior. Emancipation freed them to a world of persistent poverty, powerlessness, and neglect under colonial governance. Jamaicans gained political freedom and equality with independence in 1962, albeit in a highly stratified society that has struggled if not floundered economically. Obeahmen and Myalists fought against slavery, Revivalists against colonialism and poverty, and Rastafari against racism and capitalism. Yet the poor majority still contend with poverty; illiteracy; lack of opportunity; inadequate housing, education, nutrition, healthcare, and other necessities; and unequal access to wealth, status, and power. They live a reality that may seem to have little justice, other than that which can be sought personally, with a prayer, a hex, or increasingly with a gun.

The sociologist Orlando Patterson, discussing colonial Jamaica, remarked that "one hesitates to call it a society since all that it amounted to was an ill-organized system of exploitation" (Patterson, 1969: 70). Slaves lived under the almost absolute rule of their masters, with few rights that were enforced. Nor did they begin to receive much support from Christian churches until the early 1800s. But slaves developed their own informal forms of practical justice and social control, including ostracism and derision, and sometimes kept their own courts, managing conflicts among themselves. Slaves often responded to oppression by refusing to work, running away, engaging in violence, or committing suicide.

Obeah was a major force for practical justice in slave communities. Illness, death, and misfortune were commonly imputed to malicious acts of Obeah. But Obeahmen also had spiritual power "for the cure of disorders, the obtaining of revenge for injuries or insults, the conciliating of favor, the discovery and punishment of the thief or the adulterer, and the prediction of future events" (Edwards, 1985[1794]: 20). Bryan Edwards, writing in 1794, related that "when a negro is robbed of a fowl or a hog, he applies directly to the Obeah man or woman; it is then made known among his fellow blacks that *Obi is set* for the thief" (Edwards, 1985[1794]: 21). In these examples, it appears that Obeah was an amoral system that nonetheless could be used in the interest of practical justice. Later, Myalism seems to have provided a moral framework for Obeah. In addition, as we have seen, Obeah played an important role in the pursuit of social justice, particularly in the form of revolt, as perhaps every slave revolt in Jamaican history – and there were many – was instigated or led by an Obeahman, usually an African, fighting for freedom from enslavement.

The indigenous religions of Myalism, the Native Baptists, Revival, Bedwardism, and the Rastafari served the poor majority, largely after emancipation, and challenged the status quo, including the colonial government and the plantocracy. Like Obeah, they also gave rise to revolts and rebellions, notably the Baptist War and the Morant Bay Rebellion. The Great Revival can be seen as a symbolic rebellion against Christian missionaries. Indigenous religion was clearly the main instrument for social justice until the rise of trade unions and political parties in the 1930s. It was also the main instrument for practical justice, as it still is.

Revival was at the center of an indigenous black counterculture from its inception in 1861 until the 1950s at least. Today, however, it is largely a thaumaturgical religion, more concerned with personal health and well-being than with social justice. Much the same can be said for the orthodox, evangelical, and pentecostal churches in Jamaica, which focus on sin, morality, and personal redemption. Other, more secular institutions, including trade unions, political parties, and nongovernmental organizations, took on the fight for social justice in the twentieth century, as Jamaica became an independent, democratic nation.

Currently, the Revival church is concerned mainly with the needs of its members, not society at large. It provides followers with ritual techniques for spiritual power, but this power should only be used for good; that is, in a just manner. Members must "walk good" and live a "clean" life if they want to "receive the Spirit" and gain its benefits. Spirits help people solve problems and they provide power to do so, but they do so generally according to moral principles. Failure to receive the Spirit, and illness and misfortune in general, are interpreted as punishments for immorality. Illegitimate use of a gift of the Spirit may lead to a "warning" from a spirit or loss of the gift.

The leader of a Revival congregation is responsible for the moral and spiritual guidance of his or her followers, and has the power and authority to punish members. This responsibility includes settling disputes and counseling individuals according to moral principles. Mother Jones has always been the moral arbiter for her people and a moral exemplar for the community at large, being widely respected and warmly regarded. That is, she is seen as someone who serves the interest of moral rather than legal justice, someone who upholds the values rather than the laws of society.

The spiritual power of Revival is open to the public through the practice of Balm or healing (although that is technically a violation of the Obeah laws). The healer and her workers will do their best to combat the "destruction" of every patient through rituals, baths, and "medicines." The healer also offers moral guidance on living in the world. Herbs and spirits are not enough; to be healed one must live a good life too, in harmony with family and neighbors.

Colonial society condemned any and every expression of Africanity as uncivilized and superstitious. Obeah and Myalism were demonized, probably because they threatened white domination. Revivalism and Bedwardism were patronized and ridiculed by newspapers, harassed by government authorities, and deprived of rights extended to western churches, such as a license to marry. Nevertheless, as the Jamaican sociologist Stuart Hall (1992) noted, Caribbean religion is "a site of cultural resistance," a space within which Caribbean peoples, dominated by European colonizers, could define their own lives and create their own culture rather than accept that imposed on them. The research of scholars is slowly giving Revival and other Creole religions the legitimacy and respect they deserve. Our study demonstrates that Revival should be taken seriously as an integral and authentic part of Jamaica's history and cultural heritage, which is itself a form of social justice long denied.

Notes

1 This section is an abridged version of my article "The origins of Revival, a Creole religion in Jamaica" (Wedenoja, 1988).
2 The information in this paragraph comes largely from Elkins (1977).

3 See my article "Ritual trance and catharsis: A psychobiological and evolutionary perspective" (Wedenoja, 1990) for a detailed examination of "ceremonial spirituality."
4 My article "Mothering and the practice of 'Balm' in Jamaica" (Wedenoja, 1989) offers a more in-depth discussion of healing, with emphasis on the psychodynamics of gender.

References

African Caribbean Institute of Jamaica/Jamaica Memory Bank (2007) *Afro-Jamaica Religions: Kumina, Revival & Rastafari*, CD-ROM, African Caribbean Institute of Jamaica/Jamaica Memory Bank, Kingston, Jamaica.

Alleyne, Mervyn (1996[1988]) *Africa: Roots of Jamaican Culture*, Research Associates School Times, Chicago

Beckwith, Martha Warren (1923) Some religious cults in Jamaica, *American Journal of Psychology* 34: 32–45.

Beckwith, Martha Warren (1969[1929]) *Black Roadways: A Study of Jamaican Folk Life*, Negro Universities Press, New York.

Besson, Jean (1998) Religion as resistance in Jamaican peasant life: The Baptist church, Revival worldview and Rastafari movement, in *Rastafari and Other African-Caribbean Worldviews*, Barry Chevannes (ed.), Rutgers University Press, New Brunswick, NJ, pp. 43–76.

Besson, Jean and Chevannes, Barry (1996) The continuity-creativity debate: The case of Revival, *New West Indian Guide/Nieuwe West-Indische Gids* 70(3/4): 209–228.

Bourguignon, Erika (1985) Religion and justice in Haitian Vodoun, *Phylon* 46(4): 292–295.

Chevannes, Barry (1971a) Jamaican Lower Class Religion: Struggles against Oppression, MSc (Sociology) thesis, University of the West Indies, Mona.

Chevannes, Barry (1971b) Revival and black struggle, *Savacou* 5: 27–37.

Chevannes, Barry (1978) Revivalism: A disappearing religion, *Caribbean Quarterly* 24(3/4): 1–17.

Chevannes, Barry (1995) *Rastafari and Other African-Caribbean Worldviews*, Rutgers University Press, New Brunswick, NJ.

Edwards, Bryan (1985[1794]) African religions in colonial Jamaica, in *Afro-American Religious History*, Milton C. Sernett (ed.), Duke University Press, Durham, NC, pp. 19–23.

Elkins, W.F. (1977) *Street Preachers, Faith Healers and Herb Doctors in Jamaica 1890–1925*, Revisionist Press, New York.

Glazier, Stephen D. (1985) Religion and social justice: Caribbean perspectives, *Phylon* 46(4): 283–285.

Guana, Emanuela (1993) Doing Spirit Work in Jamaica: A Performative Approach to Revival Zion and Kumina. MA thesis (Department of Geography and Anthropology), Louisiana State University.

Guana, Emanuela (1994) Revival Zion: An Afro-Christian religion in Jamaica, *Anthropos* 89: 517–528.

Hall, Stuart (narrator) (1992) Iron in the Soul, Episode 1 in the film series *Portraits of the Caribbean*, a Barraclough Carey production for BBC Television in association with Turner Broadcasting System.

Herskovits, Melville J. (1930) Review of *Black Roadways: A Study of Jamaican Folk-Life* by Martha Warren Beckwith, *Journal of American Folklore* 43(169): 332–338.

Hogg, Donald (1964) Jamaican Religions: A Study in Variations, PhD dissertation (Department of Anthropology), Yale University.

Murphy, Joseph M. (1994) Revival Zion in Jamaica, in *Working the Spirit: Ceremonies of the African Diaspora*, Beacon Press, Boston, MA, pp. 114–144.

Nettleford, Rex (1969) Pocomania in dance-theatre, *Jamaica Journal* 3(2): 21–24.

Patterson, Orlando (1969) *The Sociology of Slavery*, Sangster's Book Stores, Kingston, Jamaica.

Seaga, Edward (1956) *Folk Music of Jamaica*, Ethnic Folkways Library Album No. FE 4453, Folkways Records & Service Corporation, New York.

Seaga, Edward (1969) Revival cults in Jamaica: Notes towards a sociology of religion, *Jamaica Journal* 3(2): 3–13.

Simpson, George Eaton (1954) *Jamaican Cult Music*, Ethnic Folkways Library FE 4461, Folkways Records and Service Corporation, New York.

Simpson, George Eaton (1956) Jamaican revivalist cults, *Social and Economic Studies* 5(4): 321–441.

Singer, Merrill (1985) The concept of justice in the religions of the Caribbean, *Phylon* 46(4): 296–299.

Stewart, Dianne M. (2005) *Three Eyes for the Journey: African Dimensions of the Jamaican Religious Experience*, Oxford University Press, New York.

Wedenoja, William (1978) Religion and Adaptation in Rural Jamaica, PhD dissertation (Department of Anthropology), University of California San Diego.

Wedenoja, William (1988) The origins of Revival: A Creole religion in Jamaica, in *Culture and Christianity: The Dialectics of Transformation*, George Saunders (ed.), Greenwood, New York, pp. 91–116.

Wedenoja, William (1989) Mothering and the practice of "Balm" in Jamaica, in *Women as Healers: Cross-Cultural Perspectives*, Carol Shepherd McClain (ed.), Rutgers University Press, New Brunswick, NJ, pp. 76–97.

Wedenoja, William (1990) Ritual trance and catharsis: A psychobiological and evolutionary perspective, in *Personality and the Cultural Construction of Society*, David K. Jordan and Marc J. Swartz (eds.), University of Alabama Press, Tuscaloosa, pp. 275–307.

Wynter, Sylvia (1962) *The Hills of Hebron*, Simon and Schuster, New York.

Bibliography

Simpson, George Eaton (1957) The nine night ceremony in Jamaica, *Journal of American Folklore* 70: 329–335.

Simpson, George Eaton (1960) The acculturative process in Jamaican Revivalism, in *Selected Papers of the Fifth International Congress of Anthropological and Ethnological Sciences: Men and Cultures*, Anthony F. C. Wallace (ed.), University of Pennsylvania Press, Philadelphia, pp. 332–341.

Simpson, George Eaton (1970) *Religious Cults of the Caribbean: Trinidad, Jamaica, and Haiti*, Institute of Caribbean Studies, University of Puerto Rico, Rio Piedras.

Simpson, George Eaton (1985) Religion and justice: Some reflections on the Rastafari movement, *Phylon* 46(4): 286–291.

CHAPTER 15

The Muhammadiyah
A Muslim Modernist Organization in Contemporary Indonesia

Florian Pohl

With about 25 to 30 million Indonesians identifying with its modernist agenda, the Muhammadiyah is one of the largest Muslim mass organizations worldwide. It is primarily a social welfare organization dedicated to serving the community in education and healthcare. When the Special Region of Yogyakarta on the Indonesian island of Java was struck by the May 2006 earthquake that left close to 6000 people dead, many more injured, and hundreds of thousands homeless, the Muhammadiyah was among the leading nonstate actors to coordinate relief efforts in response to the tragedy. It relied on its nationwide network of hospitals, clinics, schools, and volunteers to support the relief efforts. Muhammadiyah hospitals and clinics addressed the medical needs of the injured, far beyond their regular capacities, setting up triages in the courtyards and dispatching medical service teams into the most seriously affected areas to the south of the city. Muhammadiyah University of Yogyakarta as well as many Muhammadiyah schools in the area were transformed into local headquarters for the coordination of relief operations. Emergency supplies of water and food, including fortified biscuits and baby formula, arrived at these institutions, were stored, and then loaded onto trucks for distribution. Hundreds of Muhammadiyah volunteers and trained medical staff poured in from various parts of the country, arriving on busses to assist the rescue efforts in many of the hardest-hit areas, such as Bantul to the south of Yogyakarta.

The relief efforts in which the Muhammadiyah was involved in the 2006 Yogyakarta earthquake are not an isolated incident of humanitarian work, but go to the heart of the Muhammadiyah's mission as a religious, educational, and social movement. The role the Muhammadiyah played in the relief efforts and the strategies it employed resembled those undertaken in response to the devastating tsunami that had destroyed large stretches of Indonesia's Aceh province just 17 months earlier. Similar to what one could witness in Yogyakarta, the Muhammadiyah had been at the forefront of the

---

The Wiley Blackwell Companion to Religion and Social Justice, First Edition. Edited by Michael D. Palmer and Stanley M. Burgess.
© 2012 John Wiley & Sons Ltd. Published 2020 by John Wiley & Sons Ltd.

national response to this devastating natural disaster. These activities are coordinated by the Muhammadiyah's social welfare department, which has been an integral part of the movement's organizational structure since its beginnings. It was set up in an effort to coordinate relief efforts in response to the volcanic eruption of Mount Kelud in East Java, and some of its initial relief activities aimed at alleviating the harsh social conditions of the poor and especially orphans in the city of Yogyakarta where the organization was founded (Noer, 1973: 78–79).

It is important, then, to understand that these relief efforts are not peripheral to the self-understanding of the Muhammadiyah, but are intimately connected to its mission as a social welfare organization. Since its founding in 1912, the Muhammadiyah has functioned primarily as an independent civic organization that combines a modernist theological program for Islamic reform with an outspoken agenda for social welfare. It has established itself as a shaping influence in Indonesian civil society through modernizing Muslim education, as well as through providing medical services such as hospitals, clinics, orphanages, and maternity houses and through promoting civic values of inclusiveness, moderation, and tolerance.

Dutch Colonialism and Middle Eastern Modernist Thought

The Muhammadiyah originated in the early twentieth century as part of the larger Muslim modernist reform movement that embraced a variety of social, educational, and political organizations. These voluntary organizations emerged largely in response to Dutch colonial rule and the unequal treatment of Indonesian Muslims at the hands of the Dutch in areas such as politics, education, and commerce.

Rich in natural resources, particularly spices, Indonesia was gradually colonized by the Dutch, who had first established trade missions to Indonesia in the seventeenth century. One of the obstacles to their colonial rule the Dutch sought to overcome was the perceived loyalty of the Indonesian population to Islam. The Dutch tried to counter indigenous resistance associated with Islam through a policy aimed at cultural association. This intended to strengthen the cultural connection of the colonies with the Netherlands, through which the loyalty of colonial subjects was to be ensured. Western education and missionary efforts at Christianization were two of the preferred means through which the success of the colonial project was to be ensured. "Western education," as Benda explains, was considered "the surest means of reducing and ultimately defeating the influence of Islam in Indonesia. In competition with the attraction of Western education and cultural association, Islam could not be but the loser" (Benda, 1958: 27). Colonial policy favored the work of Christian missions in Indonesia through support for the establishment of schools and hospitals as means to convert Muslims to Christianity (Hasbullah, 1995: 72–73). Educational laws that gave members of the indigenous elite preferred access to Dutch education and employment, as well as strong economic competition from the Dutch and non-Muslim groups such as the Chinese, further disadvantaged the majority of Indonesian Muslims. By the beginning of the nineteenth century, many Indonesians had become acutely aware that traditional medicine and schools in the Muslim community were ill equipped to compete with the overwhelming force of Dutch colonialism and the advances of the Christian missions. Reform and change were needed at all levels of society in order to respond to the challenges.

At the turn of the nineteenth century, a Muslim modernist movement developed in Indonesia that sought to instigate reform. The introduction of reformist ideas in Indonesia was inspired at least partially by modernist thought from the Middle East, where thinkers such as Muhammad Abduh had argued for the need to overcome the perceived backwardness of the Muslim community by purging itself of outdated customs and by aligning its practices and beliefs with modern life. The movement found institutional expression in different civic organizations that embodied reformist ideas and sought to empower the Indonesian Muslim community. A great diversity of strategies and emphases could be observed among these groups, some of which focused on social and educational issues and often consciously embraced the strategies of the Dutch Christian missionary movement, with its establishment of schools and hospitals. By contrast, Sarekat Islam, an organization that developed from an Islamic trading association, sought to promote the economic development of the Muslim community and propagated overtly political goals for national independence (see Kahin, 1952).

The diversity within the modernist movement, however, did not indicate an absence of significant overlap and agreement on fundamental questions. Early twentieth-century Muslim modernist organizations such as the Muhammadiyah, Persatuan Islam, and Sarekat Islam all advocated religious purification and Islamic orthodoxy. Although Dutch colonial policies provided a common external frame of reference for the modernist movement, its activities were geared primarily to the inside, targeting traditionalist practices and beliefs. Reformist Muslims saw ignorance and superstition among the Islamic traditionalists as responsible for the backwardness of the Muslim community and sought to eradicate them. The modernist movement embodied a rational and scientific expression of Islamic thought that stood in strong contrast to the practices and beliefs of traditionalist Muslims, who represented a time-honored way of being Muslim in Indonesia. The latter exhibited syncretistic tendencies, an openness to local customs, and a predilection for mystical expressions, as could be seen in the veneration of the graves of saints and offerings to the spirits of ancestors, as in the case of the *slametan* ritual (see, e.g., Geertz, 1960: Ch. 6). The Muhammadiyah emerged as one of the period's leading reformist organizations that opposed such practices as irrational and superstitious and sought to modernize Indonesian Islam through purification of doctrine and practice.

Religious Reform and Social Activism

The Muhammadiyah was founded in Yogyakarta in 1912. Its origin is connected to the life and thought of its founder, Ahmad Dahlan (1868–1923). Dahlan came from a family of respected Muslim scholars and officials in Yogyakarta and received a religious education in the traditional disciplines of Islamic learning. Like many figures in the early reformist movement, Dahlan spent parts of his educational life in the Middle East. After his participation in the *hajj* pilgrimage in 1890 and a year of study in the Hejaz, he returned to Mecca in 1903, where he stayed for nearly two years. In addition to the study of Qur'anic exegesis and Islamic law, his time in Mecca also brought him into contact with the thought of Muslim modernist thinkers such as Jamal al-Din al-Afghani (1838–1897) and Muhammad Abduh (1849–1905), whose reformist thought hence influenced his own. The emphasis on the sole authority of the Qur'an and the traditions of the Prophet Muhammad or the Sunna, the rejection of the uncritical acceptance and imitation of past interpretations, and the quest to purify doctrine and practice in the Muslim community of improper innovations were all part of the reformist agenda evident in Dahlan's thought and action when he returned to Indonesia.

The reformist character of Dahlan's work was visible in his attempt to eliminate practices within the Indonesian Muslim community that he perceived as out of step with the two sacred sources of the Qur'an and the Sunna. Concentrating initially on outward practices such as the proper direction of prayer as well as the improvement of hygiene standards, he sought to counter local traditions and customs that lacked proper Islamic justification and that he held responsible for weakening the fabric of Islam and keeping Muslims from prosperity and progress. Central among these were mystical practices, especially the veneration of saints and pilgrimages to their gravesites, which were popular among a wide spectrum of Javanese peoples. Dahlan described these practices as *Tahayul* (myths), *Bid'ah* (innovations), and *Chorafat* (superstitions), and used the acronym for tuberculosis (TBC) to refer to them while advocating that they, like the fatal disease, be wiped out. Despite the obvious polemics, it would be wrong to assume that Dahlan pursued an overly confrontational modernization campaign. Although he was firm in his opposition to what he perceived as un-Islamic customs, gentle patience and trust that his ideas, when given the proper space and time, would convince others of the erroneous nature of their ways were part of his strategy to implement his modernist vision. A robust level of tolerance for a diversity of opinions and practices within the community has remained a characteristic of the Muhammadiyah that Dahlan founded.

Education and the madrasah

From its inception, the expressed target of the Muhammadiyah's activities was the purification of the Islamic faith from syncretistic elements in order to overcome the perceived backwardness and poverty of the Muslim community. It thus linked social activism for modernization and progress with an explicitly theological agenda for religious reform. The Muhammadiyah's social mission has been carried out primarily through the development of modern schools, hospitals and clinics, orphanages, and related charitable activities.

The modernization of Muslim education was one of Dahlan's critical concerns that mirrored Muhammad Abduh's educational reform in Egypt. Not only was it important as a response to Dutch colonial and Christian missionary schooling, with its emphasis on marketable skills, but it also fulfilled a central role in nurturing a new cadre of modern Muslims conversant with the Muhammadiyah's teachings and values. The establishment of educational institutions was thus an integral element in the program to spread modernist Islam. Similar to other modernist organizations, the Muhammadiyah maintained its own network of HIS (*Hollandsch-Inlandsche School*) and other educational institutions modeled on Dutch schools that developed a strong focus on the sciences and technology (Noer, 1973: 306). More importantly, it championed a new reformed religious school, the *madrasah*. The *madrasah* operated as a religious day-school with a graded class system based on the European model, in which secular subjects were taught alongside traditional religious ones.

With its emphasis on modern subjects and organization, the *madrasah* differed sharply from another institution of religious learning in Indonesia, the Islamic boarding school or *pesantren*, which had been the principal educational institution for traditionalist Muslims prior to the modernist movement. Unlike the *madrasah*, the *pesantren* was an Islamic boarding school in which students focused on Qur'an recitation and the study of classical books in various fields of Islamic sciences. Learning took place under the guidance of the charismatic *pesantren* leader or *kiai*, whose authority rested on his erudition in Islam and on the belief that he possessed special spiritual and mystical powers that made him a source of blessing (Dhofier, 1999: 25). The absence of a fixed curriculum, a graded class system, formalized exams, or state-recognized certification in the *pesantren* allowed students to choose the educational activities they found most appropriate, as well as their level of involvement in them.

In contrast to the traditional and informal learning environment of the *pesantren*, the *madrasah* embraced modern educational and organizational methods and approaches and freely emulated European models in its educational system, as long as these were beneficial for the Muhammadiyah's modernization program and not in direct contradiction to central Islamic tenets. Although religious subjects formed the larger part of the curriculum, learning consciously embraced the sciences, and instruction in European languages was added in most schools. Whereas *pesantren* students sat on the floor around the *kiai*, listened to his explanations, and were focused on memorization, the *madrasah* had classrooms with blackboards, desks and chairs, formal textbooks and exams, and a full teaching staff. It emphasized understanding, and provided students with definite grade levels that resulted in formal degrees. With its modern organization and promise of individual socioeconomic success while maintaining a strong sense of religious identity throughout the curriculum, the Muhammadiyah soon challenged the monopoly of the *pesantren* as the standard for Islamic education in the Indonesian Muslim community.

The Muhammadiyah's educational network continued to expand in the independence period (post-1949). It remains one of the largest providers of private schooling in Indonesia today. Already during the colonial period, the state recognized the potential of the *madrasah* to help satisfy the growing demand for modern education through its successful combination of religious and formal subjects. And in so far as the education within Muhammadiyah schools could be shown to comply with general guidelines set forth by the colonial administration, Muhammadiyah schools were eligible to receive government subsidies similar to those obtained by Christian missionary schools. Initially, the ratio of subjects differed among the institutions, but it generally aimed at about 60% general and 40% religious instruction (Boland, 1982: 113). This trend of toleration coupled with limited state support continued after Indonesia achieved independence, although no attempts were made to bring the state and the private sector together during the first two decades under President Sukarno. From the 1970s onward, however, the state increased its efforts to incorporate Islamic schools into the national education system, and many *madrasah* institutions began to employ a curriculum sanctioned by the Department of Religious Affairs, thus qualifying their graduates to continue their education in the public sector at postsecondary level (Azra *et al.*, 2007: 186).

Through the continued upgrading of the curriculum, the Muhammadiyah schools today have been fully incorporated into the national education system, although in some cases supplementary classes in Islamic disciplines may be offered in addition to the government curriculum. A similar trend can be seen in postsecondary education. The largest private provider of higher education in Indonesia, the Muhammadiyah maintains not only thousands of *madrasahs* but also an extensive network of colleges and universities throughout the country, through which Ahmad Dahlan's reformist agenda of educational modernization has been carried forward.

Women in the Muhammadiyah and Aisyiyah

Another area in which the educational work of the Muhammadiyah differed from the traditionalists was in the Muhammadiyah's focus on the training and education of women. Similar to the Middle Eastern reformists such as Abduh, Ahmad Dahlan had made the education of women a priority. Women received training in the Islamic rules that govern worship in order to overcome the indigenous syncretistic ways and to align women's ritual life with more universally Islamic norms of piety. This meant abiding by the requirements for ritual purity that excluded women from attending services in the mosque during their menstrual cycles. Attention was also paid to proper dress in order to meet Islamic modesty requirements. Educational programs for women, however, went beyond instruction in orthodox ritual and doctrinal matters to include literacy education. The emphasis on literacy reflected the modernists' concern for a direct reading of the Islamic sacred sources, unmediated by tradition or charismatic authority. Individual responsibility for the study of religious texts and for learning fundamental religious teachings was thus extended to all members of the Muslim community, which allowed women to become active participants in religious life and independent readers of religious texts. Despite the strong link between literacy and the modernist concern for correct ritual practice, the educational measures afforded women possibilities of social and economic participation within and outside the Muhammadiyah.

Within the Muhammadiyah, women played a central role in the expansion of the organization's educational network and its health services. This was achieved initially through the establishment of a women's organization, Aisyiyah, which continues to be among the largest Muslim women's organizations worldwide today. Initiated by Ahmad Dahlan himself, Aisyiyah began as an independent organization of Muslim women, but was incorporated into the Muhammadiyah during Dahlan's lifetime (Alfian, 1969: 245). Next to the establishment of women's mosques and the facilitation of women's study groups, the primary areas of its work have been in religious education and health. Aisyiyah's educational focus is placed on teaching small children, and it maintains its own network of preschools and kindergartens. Another significant area of involvement is the training of women for professions traditionally assigned to females, including teachers and medical professionals. A teacher training college has been associated with Aisyiyah since the early beginnings, as well as educational facilities that train women to become midwives, nurses, and physicians. Employment opportunities are provided by the network of clinics and maternity houses that Aisyiyah maintains to assist women on questions of family planning, childcare, and nutrition. Although Aisyiyah is not in charge of any of the hospitals or educational institutions beyond the preschool level, its members furnish a large proportion of the staff in these institutions. Despite the strong emphasis on the training of educators and healthcare professionals, Aisyiyah's social and educational work has also strengthened women's participation in public life. It has allowed women to pursue careers in politics, medicine, and trade, and many Aisyiyah members have obtained influential positions in their communities as well as in the wider Indonesian society.

When evaluating these accomplishments, it is important to remember that the ideological frame within which Aisyiyah operates differs markedly from the contemporary western discourse on gender equality and emancipation. Aisyiyah was initiated not by women but by the Muhammadiyah's male founder, with the stated objective to support the modernist purification campaign, not emancipation. And despite the Aisyiyah's autonomous status, it is part of the larger Muhammadiyah structure that, through policies shaped by its national boards and congresses, sets the acceptable limits for Aisyiyah's articulation of gender roles and expectations. Although many of the requirements and regulations concerning women can be seen to reinforce norms of gender segregation and thus to limit women's full participation, White has pointed out that the stress on more universally acceptable norms of piety allowed Muslim women to assert their right to participate in these areas of religious and social life (White, 2004: 87–94). A similar point is made by van Doorn-Harder (2006), who describes the active participation of Aisyiyah women in the process of reinterpreting Islamic teachings on women's roles and rights. Mostly through informal channels such as private study circles led by women preachers and Qur'an readings, known as *pengajian*, women were able to discuss alternative readings and encourage each other to draw on these when discussing critical issues such as polygyny or divorce with their husbands at home (van Doorn-Harder, 2006: 6). In other instances, such as in the debate over the permissibility of birth control, women's influence on the development of legal thought has been more explicit. Before the Muhammadiyah's male scholars declared birth control permissible in 1971, Aisyiyah scholars and preachers had exerted a shaping influence on grassroots opinion through their informal study circles and public sermons on the issue (van Doorn-Harder, 2006: 12–13).

One of the most visible examples of Aisyiyah's public influence that shows both the organization's success and its limitations is its harmonious family model (*keluarga sakinah*), an ambitious family planning program that took effect in 1985 (van Doorn-Harder, 2006: 114–124). The program protected women's rights to basic birth control, secured protection from polygyny, and spelled out the husband's duties and responsibilities. In its emphasis on women's basic rights it was far reaching for its time, but stopped short of true emancipation and equality. Articulated within the Muhammadiyah frame, the program represented and was confined by the gender roles propagated by the organization's male leadership, which continued to privilege women's domestic responsibilities as mothers and wives. Based on the assumption of essential differences between the sexes, the program emphasized the complementary nature of the relationship between the spouses, in which the woman's domestic role under the guidance of her husband remained primary. The idea of static gender roles and the lack of full equality have inspired the resistance of a younger generation of women in Muhammadiyah, who incorporate more openly than the older generation new gender theories and paradigms. These younger activists are often affiliated with Nasyiatul Aisyiyah, which began as part of Aisyiyah's activities in religious formation, education, and vocational training for young women in the 1930s. Nasyiatul Aisyiyah remained a branch of Aisyiyah until the mid-1960s, when it established itself as an autonomous organization within the larger Muhammadiyah structure. It has since sought to construct a new Islamic identity for young Muslim women in Indonesia, at times in conscious distinction from the positions found among the older generation of Aisyiyah members (see, e.g., Syamsiyatun, 2007). Despite tensions and limitations for Aisyiyah and Nasyiatul Aisyiyah that result from their connection with the Muhammadiyah, it is significant to note that the Muhammadiyah's organizational structure has opened up and guaranteed women a place in which they can operate publicly and influence the direction of Islamic teachings on women in Indonesia.

The Muhammadiyah as a Modern Civic Organization

The integration of groups such as Aisyiyah into the larger institutional structure not only demonstrates the Muhammadiyah's success and growth from a local Javanese organization to one of the largest Muslim modernist organizations worldwide, but also reveals its modern pedigree as an independent voluntary organization. By the 1930s, within a decade after Dahlan's death, the Muhammadiyah had grown to incorporate new organizations for married and unmarried women (Aisyiyah and Nasyiatul Aisyiyah) and their equivalent for young men (Pemuda Muhammadiyah), a scout movement (Hizbul Wathan), and later a student organization (Mahasiswa Muhammadiyah Indonesia), through which it carried out many of its religious, educational, and health activities (Alfian, 1969: 263). Organizational growth was paralleled by geographical expansion that saw the establishment of Muhammadiyah branches outside of Java in West Sumatra, Aceh, and Makassar. Today's efficient administrative structure reflects the Muhammadiyah's growth. Departments for education, healthcare, Islamic law, preaching, economic development, property administration, and publishing are responsible for overseeing social and religious activities at provincial and local levels. Their work is directed by the Muhammadiyah's Central Board (Pimpinan Pusat Muhammadiyah), which sets up official guidelines and supervises the work of all branches. The hierarchical and centralized structure is a model of modern efficiency and transparency.

Echoing modernist ideals, membership is voluntary and largely unpaid. Different from the traditionalist Nahdlatul Ulama, in which the charismatic authority of the *kiai* passes from teacher to student and often from father to son or son-in-law, individual status within the Muhammadiyah is, by and large, based on merit, not on ascription or family ties. The advantages that modern organizational structures, methods, and techniques have afforded the Muhammadiyah can also be detected in its emphasis on healthcare. The improvement of health services available to the general public had been a major concern of Dahlan's modernization agenda. As early as 1918, the Muhammadiyah established a medical clinic in Yogyakarta, and has since developed an impressive network of clinics and hospitals throughout the archipelago. Alwi Shihab (1995) observed that the Muhammadiyah's strategies to advance Indonesian society in areas such as education and healthcare resembled those found in Dutch Christian missionary movements of the nineteenth century. Whether in conscious emulation of Christian missionary strategies or as a means to counter the Christian influence, the Muhammadiyah's efforts marked a significant departure from traditional Islamic ways to take care of the poor through individual charity. The establishment of clinics and orphanages to address social and medical needs went beyond the traditional *zakat* (almsgiving) system and put modern organizational techniques in the service of Islamic goals.

Promoting civil society

Different from other reformist movements such as Persatuan Islam, the Muhammadiyah has generally kept itself separate from politics, pursuing its goal of building a Muslim society through social and educational programs. Its primarily nonpolitical, missionary agenda allowed for greater toleration by the Dutch and enabled the Muhammadiyah to receive some government support for its schools. After Indonesia gained political independence in 1949, the Muhammadiyah continued to refrain from direct involvement in the political sphere, although it became a driving force behind the establishment of the Masyumi (Majlis Syura Muslimin), the largest Islamic political party in postindependence Indonesia, and many of its members occupied positions of leadership within the party structure (Ward, 1978). In part as a result of the changed political climate under President Suharto's New Order regime (1965–1998), which heavily restricted the institutions of political Islam, the Muhammadiyah reasserted its nonpolitical mission as a sociocultural movement during its national congress in 1971 (Fuad, 2002: 150). The decision placed the Muhammadiyah in the sphere of civil society, where it has continued to improve the well-being of Indonesian society through the provision of educational programs and healthcare facilities. In organization and ideological orientation, as Mitsuo Nakamura has pointed out, the Muhammadiyah displays many characteristics of a nongovernmental organization or NGO (Nakamura, 2005: 223). Through its nonpolitical and nonprofit orientation along with the breadth of its social activism, the Muhammadiyah strengthens the nongovernment public sphere and adds to the infrastructure of democracy.

Although the Muhammadiyah offers its members invaluable opportunities for civic participation, it should be acknowledged that its civil society-building potential is not uncontested. The Muhammadiyah's unwillingness to condemn or dissociate itself from the Darul Islam revolts in the early decades of the republic (Boland, 1982: 54–75), its hesitation to speak out against the communist killings during the political upheavals and violence of 1965–1966 (Cribb, 1990), and its often ambiguous position in the Ahmadiyya controversy (Beck, 2005) have cast a shadow over the Muhammadiyah's civility-enhancing roles within Indonesia's pluralist society. In addition, there has been a deep gap and mutual suspicion between traditionalists and modernists in Indonesia along the lines of Muslims affiliated with either the traditionalist Nahdlatul Ulama or the modernist Muhammadiyah. More recently, however, and coinciding with the transformation to democratic rule, there have been instances in which the two organizations have joined hands. A remarkable example was their united support for the Peoples Voter Education Network (Jaringan Pendidikan Pemilu untuk Rakyat [JPPR]), through which both organizations cooperated in comprehensive voter education campaigns and the monitoring of presidential elections (Bush, 2005).

Efforts at creating trust across ideological and communal boundaries and at promoting a public discourse marked by civility and respect for the rights of others are particularly significant in light of the recent emergence of interethnic tensions and sectarian violence within Indonesia's multiethnic and multireligious society. Through the continual upgrading of its educational programs and curriculum materials, the Muhammadiyah has shown itself responsive to questions of religious and cultural diversity. Many of the Muhammadiyah's institutions of higher learning have earned a reputation for advancing progressive Islamic understandings of pluralism, democracy, and human rights. In 2003, the Muhammadiyah implemented a mandatory civic education program on all its university campuses that was modeled after the successful courses developed in the state Islamic university system. The program emphasizes the Muhammadiyah's self-understanding as a social welfare organization and takes a clear stance in opposition to demands for an Islamic state. The course materials incorporate issues such as gender equality, democracy, and human rights, and also pay attention to teacher training and instructional methods that foster participatory learning and critical thinking (Jackson and Bahrissalim, 2007: 47–51). The program's success has led the Muhammadiyah to transfer the civic education courses into its nationwide network of secondary schools. Beyond programmatic developments on the national level, sensitivity to diversity and differences is replicated in local initiatives at Muhammadiyah institutions. A particularly visible example is the work of the Center for Cultural Studies and Social Change at the Muhammadiyah University of Surakarta, which has developed a program entitled "Muslim Tolerance and Appreciation for Multiculturalism," geared toward the development of a multicultural theological paradigm for religious education in Muhammadiyah schools and mosques (Baidhawy, 2007: 22).

Achievements and challenges

The Muhammadiyah's systematic efforts at community development, its internally democratic and participatory structures, and its commitment to Islamic values of equality and justice contribute to the organization's civil society building and democracy-enhancing qualities in contemporary Indonesia. First, the Muhammadiyah's achievements in community development through its social programs in healthcare and education have provided millions of Indonesians with crucial services that the state has been unable to supply. The Muhammadiyah schools, as well as its nationwide network of colleges and universities, give students access to education. The adoption of state-certified curricula in most Muhammadiyah schools has also facilitated the transfer of students between different educational institutions in the national system. It has become increasingly common to find graduates from Muhammadiyah secondary schools who have been able to make the transfer into graduate and postgraduate programs at secular and state universities. Furthermore, the clinics, maternity houses, nursing homes, and hospitals that operate under the Muhammadiyah's name tend to the needs of a wide spectrum of Indonesian society, both urban and rural, who otherwise would lack access to health services.

Second, next to the promotion of people's welfare, the Muhammadiyah offers its members invaluable opportunities for civic participation and the practice of democracy. Adding to the democratic infrastructure of Indonesian society, the Muhammadiyah promotes transparent lines of authority, elections and meritocracy, and the accountability of its leadership from the local to the national levels. The development of its activities and programs relies not on autocratic directives from the national leadership, but on a bottom-up approach that draws on resources available in local communities. As Fuad points out, although the often divergent local initiatives are held together and shaped by the organization's national leadership, the Muhammadiyah's organizational structures privilege grassroots initiatives for the implementation, financing, and management of local projects (Fuad, 2002: 146–147).

Finally, institutional virtues such as transparency and accountability point to the civic values that the Muhammadiyah adds to the public discourse. Having initially focused its energies on the modernization of Islamic doctrine and the purification of Islamic practices, the Muhammadiyah has placed a growing emphasis on questions of public morality (Abdullah, 2001: 51). Apart from the checks and balances vis-à-vis unregulated state power and the crippling effects of corruption that continue to plague Indonesia's political process, the Muhammadiyah has demonstrated commitment to inclusive goals such as religious tolerance, socioeconomic justice, gender justice, and political emancipation. In addition to examples of the programmatic developments in the area of education described above, the decision on local culture by the Muhammadiyah's national congress in 2000 signaled an unprecedented level of accommodation that promotes an open and inclusive political climate in which a robust civil society can grow.

Despite the Muhammadiyah's strong potential for civil society building, the organization confronts a number of challenges as it seeks to respond to the enormity and rapidity of social change in Indonesia's new era of democratization. Its responses have been encumbered by conservative tendencies that result from the formalization of the Muhammadiyah's structures, rules, and teachings since its inception almost a century ago. In her work on women in the Muhammadiyah and Nahdlatul Ulama, van Doorn-Harder points in particular to a past loss of vitality concerning questions of gender in the Muhammadiyah (van Doorn-Harder, 2006: 78). This perception is echoed by other observers such as Syamsiyatun, who has remarked on the unwillingness of the Muhammadiyah and Aisyiyah to take seriously the new theories on feminism and gender that had become part of the academic discourse in Indonesia in the 1980s (Syamsiyatun, 2007: 81). Reluctance on the part of the Muhammadiyah to address new questions that have arisen for Indonesian women professionally and domestically was in part influenced by governmental policies under Suharto's New Order. In an effort to depoliticize the women's movements, the Indonesian government actively promoted a gender ideology that confined women to their roles as mothers and housewives.

Reluctance in the Muhammadiyah directly to deal with gender issues began to change in the 1990s, as part of wider renewal efforts initiated by the organization's leadership. Under the direction of Amin Abdullah, then chair of the Majlis Tarjih responsible for producing religious opinions or *fatwas*, the Muhammadiyah opened up its religious discourse to new social, economic, and intellectual developments, better to address the sweeping social changes that were taking place. Intentional efforts were made to include gender perspectives in the review of the organization's leadership structure and overall religious vision. Since then, women have made some gains within the Muhammadiyah. Recognizing the significance of women's interpretations of the sacred sources, the Majlis Tarjih was opened up to women in 1995. In 2002, a similar decision was made to give women the opportunity to run for office in the Muhammadiyah's Central Board (Pimpinan Pusat Muhammadiyah), the organization's highest religious council. However, the number of women elevated by these decisions into positions of leadership in the Muhammadiyah has remained small. Despite vibrant debate, the 45th Muhammadiyah Congress in 2005, held only every five years, did not elect any women members to the Central Board. While these developments indicate a persistent division in views on gender questions between the official discourses promoted on the Muhammadiyah's leadership level and the more conservative mainstream (Dewi, 2008: 175), they also serve as a reminder that the struggle for women's equality, although carried out within the organizational structures of the Muhammadiyah, is part of a larger discourse shaped by multiple forces, including the strictures of religious and cultural patriarchy and the policies of the state.

Additional challenges arise from the paucity of economic resources that confronts the Muhammadiyah. The East Asian financial crisis of 1997–1998 left the Indonesian economy devastated and the currency destabilized. The recovery process has been slowed by rising unemployment and high fuel prices. Since the Muhammadiyah relies on donations and member contributions, the economic situation affects the organization's ability to conduct its healthcare and educational activities. In some of these areas, cooperation with the state offers the Muhammadiyah a way to address funding shortages. If and when a Muhammadiyah school adopts a state-certified curriculum, it is, for instance, entitled to receive state subsidies for its teaching staff. Although organizational independence from the state does not have to be constructed in opposition to the state, such cooperative strategies have raised questions of state interference and oversight and have led to renewed debates within the Muhammadiyah over its proper relationship to the state and the political realm (Fuad, 2002: 148–155).

Questions about the Muhammadiyah's involvement in the political process have become more pressing with the fall of the New Order in 1998. The new democratic environment has given the Muhammadiyah greater freedom to get involved directly in the political process. Under the leadership of Amien Rais, then the organization's chairman, the Partai Amanat Nasional (National Mandate Party [PAN]) was formed and gained a large following among Muhammadiyah members. Past elections have allowed Muhammadiyah members to win seats in the House of Representatives as candidates for PAN and other political parties. These developments have reinvigorated debates within the Muhammadiyah over potential dilemmas that party politics can cause for the organization's social and cultural roles in promoting the values of civil society (Abdullah, 2001: 50–51). Despite the ongoing debate over the questions raised by the involvement of its members in politics, the official position of the Muhammadiyah has been to assert its nonpolitical nature as an Islamic social welfare organization. This position finds expression in the fact that the Muhammadiyah leadership required Amien Rais to relinquish his chairmanship when he assumed the leadership of PAN. Moreover, although its constituency is almost entirely made up of Muhammadiyah members, PAN maintains no formal connections with the Muhammadiyah, but remains a secular party open to all Indonesians.

Conclusion

Over the past years the Muhammadiyah has consistently affirmed its commitment to democratic reform and participation within the political process, spoken out against the formation of an Islamic state, and instead promoted the establishment of a Muslim civil society dedicated to inclusiveness, moderation, and tolerance. This position stands in continuity with a long tradition of political neutrality, financial independence, and grassroots orientation. The organization's rich intellectual culture, over time, has shown the ability to bring forth creative and independent thinkers, such as Amin Abdullah, Amien Rais, and Ahmad Syafii Maarif. All of them have played important roles in opposing the oppressive politics of the Suharto regime, while rejecting the idea of an Islamic state and steering the Muhammadiyah toward support for pro-democracy reform. Despite varying levels of cooperation with the state, the Muhammadiyah has remained one of the leading nonstate actors in pursuit of the common good, offering its members rich opportunities for civic participation. A social welfare organization, it exerts its influence well beyond its membership in the wider Indonesian society, which it serves in education and healthcare.

One will have to be careful not to make any unbending predictions about the future of democracy in Indonesia. More than three decades of authoritarian government have endangered the country's rich culture of tolerance, and its political economy remains vulnerable in light of endemic corruption, the weakness of the law, widespread poverty, and numerous regional conflicts. Despite decades of authoritarian rule, Indonesian Islam exhibits a strong civil-pluralist tradition that Robert Hefner (2000) has described as "civil Islam." Its forces boast a network of individuals and organizations that strengthen the process of democratization and develop concepts of inclusive citizenship. The Muhammadiyah should be included in this tradition. The observation that the Muhammadiyah is a Muslim voluntary organization consistently engaged in social welfare activities instead of the promotion of Islam on the political level adds to the growing body of scholarship that calls into question the notion of an incommensurability of Islam with democratic politics, civil society, and action for the common good.

References

Abdullah, A.M. (2001) Muhammadiyah's experience in promoting civil society on the eve of the 21st century, in *Islam and Civil Society in Southeast Asia*, M. Nakamura, S. Siddique, and O.F. Bajunid (eds.), Institute for Southeast Asian Studies, Singapore, pp. 43–54.

Alfian (1969) Islamic Modernism in Indonesian Politics. The Muhammadiyah Movement during the Dutch Colonial Period (1912–1942), PhD dissertation, University of Wisconsin, Madison.

Azra, Azyumardi, Afrianty, Dina, and Hefner, Robert W. (2007) Pesantren and madrasa: Muslim schools and national ideals in Indonesia, in *Schooling Islam: The Culture and Politics of Modern Muslim Education*, R.W. Hefner and M.Q. Zaman (eds.), Princeton University Press, Princeton, pp. 172–197.

Baidhawy, Z. (2007) Building harmony and peace through multiculturalist theology-based religious education: An alternative for contemporary Indonesia, *British Journal of Religious Education* 22(1): 15–30.

Beck, H. (2005) The rupture between the Muhammadiyah and the Ahmadiyya, *Bijdragen tot de Taal, Land-en Volkenkunde* 161(2–3): 210–246.

Benda, H.J. (1958) *The Crescent and the Rising Sun: Indonesian Islam under the Japanese Occupation of Java, 1942–1945*, W. Van Hoeve, The Hague.

Boland, B.J. (1982) *The Struggle of Islam in Modern Indonesia*, Nijhoff, The Hague.

Bush, R. (2005) Islam and civil society in Indonesia, paper presented at the CSID Sixth Annual Conference on Democracy and Development: Challenges for the Islamic World, Washington, DC, April 22–23, https://www.csidonline.org/documents/pdf/6th_Annual_Conference-RobinBush.pdf (accessed April 19, 2011).

Cribb, R. (ed.) (1990) *The Indonesian Killings, 1965–1966: Studies from Java and Bali*, Monash Papers No. 21, Monash University, Centre of Southeast Asian Studies, Clayton, Victoria, Australia.

Dewi, K.H. (2008) Perspective versus practice: Women's leadership in Muhammadiyah, *Sojourn* 23(2): 161–185.

Dhofier, Z. (1999) *The Pesantren Tradition: The Role of the Kyai in the Maintenance of Traditional Islam in Java*, Program for Southeast Asian Studies, Tempe, Arizona.

van Doorn-Harder, P. (2006) *Women Shaping Islam: Reading the Qur'an in Indonesia*, University of Illinois Press, Urbana.

Fuad, M. (2002) Civil society in Indonesia: The potential and limits of Muhammadiyah, *Sojourn* 17(2): 133–163.

Geertz, C. (1960) *The Religion of Java*, Collier-Macmillan, Chicago.

Hasbullah (1995) *Sejarah Pendidikan Islam di Indonesia: Lintasan Sejarah Pertumbuhan dan Perkembangan*, Raja Grafindo Persada, Jakarta.

Hefner, R.W. (2000) *Civil Islam. Muslims and Democratization in Indonesia*, Princeton University Press, Princeton.

Kahin, G.M. (1952) *Nationalism and Revolution in Indonesia*, Cornell University Press, Ithaca, NY.

Nakamura, M. (2005) Muhammadiyah faces the challenge of democracy, in *Muhammadiyah Menjemput Perubahan: Tafsir Baru Gerakan Sosial-Ekonomi-Politik*, Mukhaer Pakkanna and Nur Achmad (eds.), Penerbit Buku Kompas, Jakarta, pp. 215–229.

Noer, D. (1973) *The Modernist Movement in Indonesia, 1900–1942*, Oxford University Press, London.

Jackson, Elisabeth and Bahrissalim (2007) Crafting a new democracy: Civic education in Indonesian Islamic universities, *Asia Pacific Journal of Education* 27(1): 41–54.

Shihab, A. (1995) The Muhammadiyah Movement and Its Controversy with Christian Mission in Indonesia, PhD dissertation, Temple University, Philadelphia.

Syamsiyatun, S. (2007) A daughter in the Indonesian Muhammadiyah: Nasyiatul Aisyiyah negotiates a new status and image, *Journal of Islamic Studies* 18(1): 69–94.

Ward, K.E. (1978) *The Foundation of the Partai Muslimin Indonesia*, Modern Indonesia Project, Southeast Asia Program, Cornell University Press, Ithaca, NY.

White, S.J. (2004) Reformist Islam, Gender, and Marriage in Late Colonial Dutch East Indies, 1900–1942, PhD dissertation, Australian National University.

CHAPTER 16
The Role of the Chief in Asante Society

Yaw Adu-Gyamfi

Asante people are a subset of the Akan, who migrated to present-day Ghana. We can trace the rise of the early Akan centralized states to the thirteenth century, which may be related to the opening of trade routes established to move gold throughout the region. It was not until the end of the seventeenth century, however, that the grand Asante kingdom emerged in the central forest region of Ghana, when several small states united under the chief of Kumase in a move to achieve political freedom from the Denkyira. The name "Asante" is derived from ɛsa (war) and nti (for the sake of). Thus, for the sake of war, various chiefdoms came together to fight their archenemy, the Denkyira king. After their victory, the people strengthened the loose alliance and became a unified state. Their primary aim of coming together to fight gave them their name, ɛsanti.

Asante chieftaincy has been transformed through various stages from the precolonial era through the colonial period (1874–1957 CE) to the present. In the precolonial period, chiefs had considerable influence and exercised great sovereignty within their areas of jurisdiction; their authority in both spiritual and secular matters was almost unlimited. During the colonial period, they became practically subagents of the colonial government in the areas of local government and judicial settlements. Various laws and statutes ratified by the colonial authority prescribed the chief's political role. In the early phase of the postcolonial era (1957 onward), the role that chiefs played in local government under the colonial era was modified in the interest of modern democracy. During the period between 1960 and 1966, chiefs were subjected to the control of the central government through the enactment of such legislation as the *Chieftaincy Act of 1961* (Act 81).

In this essay, I focus attention principally on the traditional role of the chief, by which I mean the genuinely traditional political, religious, and socioeconomic role, uncon-

---

The Wiley Blackwell Companion to Religion and Social Justice, First Edition. Edited by Michael D. Palmer and Stanley M. Burgess.
© 2012 John Wiley & Sons Ltd. Published 2020 by John Wiley & Sons Ltd.

taminated by colonial or postindependence modifications or distortions. However, we cannot discuss the role of the chief without paying attention to the Asante social structure within which chieftaincy operates.

Asante Social Structure

The perception of an individual person in Asante society is paramount for understanding the chief and his role. After all, individuals together form a society and chieftaincy is an institution that takes place in a specific sociocultural context. In addition, the way in which a community views the structure and operation of the world has connections with its religious beliefs and practices. A worldview is a means by which a society tries to structure the world and human existence within it. Religion is an objective awareness of, and a response to, the transcendent in whom individuals and societies believe and on whom they absolutely depend. Chieftaincy functions within this awareness in Asante society. We shall therefore examine the Asante cultural orientation with specific attention to its sociopolitical structure and religious worldview.

The concept of a person

Sociopolitical structure is based on the confederation of people and people groups. Therefore, it is imperative to begin with the Asante conception of the individual person. The Asante believe that a person is composed of four elements: the *mogya* (blood) that links a child with its mother; the *ntorɔ* (male totemic spirit) that connects a child with the father; the *sunsum* (spirit) that describes a person's personality; and the *ɔkra* (soul) that connects a person with *Nyame* (the Supreme Being). The *mogya* and the *ntorɔ* underlie an individual's connection with society. The *ntorɔ* forms a unique spiritual bond between father and child and links the individual with his or her father's family and to a deity of the father, which requires observance of certain taboos and the performance of certain rituals on certain days. People of the same *ntorɔ* have some common personality traits and share common greetings and responses. However the *ntorɔ* does not define descent; it is neither an exogamous nor a corporate group, nor do jural or political rights or duties derive from paternal descent.

On the other hand, the *mogya* determines a person's succession to offices or property, jural rights and obligations. The Asante social structure is, therefore, matrilineal. Descent is traced through the mother, for the traditional conception is that physical continuity between one generation and another is maintained by the *mogya*, which is transmitted through her. An individual is legally identified with his or her maternal relatives: a person's grandmother and her brothers and sisters, a person's mother and her brothers and sisters, and the person's own brothers and sisters (Busia, 1951: 1). The matrilineal descent has its most important religious significance in the Asante's reverence for the *nsamanfoɔ* (ancestors). Ancestor veneration emphasizes the unity of matrilineal ancestry.

Any discussion about chieftaincy in Asante needs to begin from the center of the Asante sociopolitical system, the *fiefo* (house-folk), because the position and power of subchief, chief, paramount-chief, and finally the Asantehene (king of Asante) are modeled after the family unit. The *fiefo* expanded into the *abusua* (lineage) and the *abusua* into the *ɔman* (state). These social units form the levels of sociopolitical organization among the Asante people in ascending order.

Social levels

The basic unit of the Asante social structure is the *efiefo* (household). A person is born into this social group, which consists of a woman (A), her children (both males and females), and the children of her daughters (not the children of her sons). In the household, the senior male, often the uncle or brother of woman A, is the head, *efie-wura* (house-master). He performs the roles of master, judge, and priest of the household. As master, he is the administrator of all the family property and custodian of the family tradition. As judge, he is the arbitrator in the family quarrels; and as priest, he mediates between the ancestors and gods and the family.

This social unit is a democratic one. In one sense, it is communal; thus, the family owns property. However, individuals have the right to enjoy family property. Most importantly, even though the *fie-wura* is the arbitrator, his interference in family disputes is influenced by the opinions of the inhabitants of his household, who are consulted, so that his decisions seldom represent his own arbitrary commands. His judgments in cases of dispute are possibly initially only backed up by religious sanctions. It is believed that his judgments derive not from his own store of wisdom but from his ancestors (Rattray, 1929: 5).

Many such extended families together form a lineage. An extended family consists of the family of woman A and the children of her sisters (not her brothers), say woman B and woman C. This unit consists of all the members of the social group lineally descended from one common ancestress – a group of people united by *mogya korɔ* (common blood). Thus, the lineage is a group of men and women who trace their descent in the matrilineal line to a common ancestress. Some lineages, especially those of chiefs, trace their ancestry as far back as 10 or 12 generations and have several branches (Busia, 1951: 2). In a village, individual lineages are geographically grouped to form what is commonly known as *abrɔno* (wards). The lineage is composed of freeborn and descendants of *nnonkɔfoɔ* (slaves), *nnwowa* (pawns), and *nnomum* (war captives). Members of every lineage form a cult group in relation to their own ancestors.

As in the family unit, the most senior man in the lineage becomes the head, *abusua panin*. The *abusua panin* is the political head. He maintains amicable relations within the group, settles lineage disputes, and represents the ancestors, who are the custodians of the lineage laws and customs. He has a stool as a symbol of his office, which acts as a connection between the dead and the living. He is also the priest of the lineage, who mediates between the ancestors and the living. By virtue of his position as head and priest, he is highly respected. Disrespect toward him is treated as an offense against the ancestors; restoration of harmony can be achieved only by slaughtering a sheep and pouring a libation. He is the custodian of lineage land.

The lineage organization is defined and sanctioned primarily through the religious belief and ritual system that centers on ancestral cult. Although the descent groupings are formed through female lines, ritual observance focuses on the spirits of deceased male members incarnated in carved wooden stools. During a man's assumption of full social maturity, he purchases a stool, which is considered an exclusive possession and an extension of his personality. On his death, this object is placed in a special room that serves as a common repository for the lineage as a whole. Every six weeks, special *adae* ceremonies are held, during which sacrifices are offered to the ancestors.

From household head to chieftaincy

In the course of time, various lineage groups in a locality came together under the head of one particular lineage to form a chiefdom. Often, this lineage is the one that first settled at the locality. The head of the lineage becomes the *Odikro* (herdsman) or *Ɔhene* (chief) of the community, and the lineage becomes the royal family through which successive chiefs are elected. The other lineage heads form the council of the chief. The chief becomes the political, religious, and social leader of the village or town. His stool becomes superior to the stools of the lineages. The chiefdom as a whole is a cult group in relation to the chief's ancestors. The central motive is the solidarity and continuity of chiefdom life.

For many generations in Asante society, this process of amalgamation went on in independent localities, and in this manner numerous chiefdoms grew up under different, independent chiefs who often were rivals. Further amalgamation occurred that brought various chiefdoms in a larger locality together, either by war or cooperation, to form a Territorial Division under the chief of one particular chiefdom. This territorial head became the *Ɔmanhene* (paramount chief) and the other chiefs formed the council of the territory. Finally, various Territorial Divisions later came together through conquest and cooperation under the *Kumasehene*, who was also the head of the Kumase Territorial Division. The *Ɔmanhene* of this territorial division became the *Asantehene* (the Asante king) and the various paramount chiefs formed the *Asanteman* (Asante state) council. As in the case of the chiefdom, the Asante state as a whole is a cult group in relation to the *Asantehene's* ancestors.

Thus, an Asante community is organized on the basis of a social contract by which people come together to form a state or nation with the belief that through their united efforts, they can realize their common aspirations for peace and security, which are essential for their physical and spiritual welfare and progress, both as individuals and as a community. It is for these objectives that the people agree communally to submit to a chief or king to rule their lives and to organize and control activities within their society.

As the state became more centralized, Asante chiefs, paramount chiefs, and kings sought to promote the perception that power emanated from a central source by placing themselves at the nexus of relations between the natural, social, and supernatural worlds, making chieftaincy indispensable to the functioning of the social order. As a result, for instance, the office of a chief's *nsumankwahene* ("chief of medicines") coordinates the workings of all the priests. The chief then becomes ɔkomfo panyin (chief priest) of the society. It is believed that in times of interregnum, even spirit possession ceases until a new chief is installed and all *akomfoɔ* (pl. of ɔkomfoɔ, priest) in the state swear allegiance to the new chief (Akyeampon and Obeng, 1995: 503, 507–508). In his capacity as priest, the chief functions as the ultimate public mediator of Asante religion.

Asante Society and the Ancestors

Any discussion of Asante chieftaincy is incomplete without mention of the ancestors, which complete the prolific life that the cosmology of the Asante represents. The ancestors occupy a very important place in Asante society. The Asante believe in the continued existence and influence of the departed fathers of the family, lineage, clan, and nation. The ancestors are believed to be present, watching over the household, lineage, clan, and nation. They are directly concerned in all the affairs of the family and property, giving abundant harvests and fertility. They are the guardians of the tribal traditions and history (Parrinder, 1961: 115).

The Asante believe that the ancestors, who founded society, facilitate and maintain the welfare of the living. They are expected to be lively and active in the affairs of the living, providing them with children, good harvests, and good health. They are involved in birth, marriage, sickness, relationships, reunion, family needs, and other personal, family, household, lineage, and state concerns. In addition, their activity is directed toward "restoring order and discipline in compliance with the norms of right and duty, enmity or piety, whenever transgressions threaten or occur" (Fortes and Dieterlin, 1965: 136). Thus, they provide the sanctions for the moral life of the group by laying down customs and taboos to govern the behavior of the group and to maintain its stability. It is believed that the ancestors offer advice through dreams, visions, or ghostly visitations.

Belief in ancestors regulates the political system. The ancestral cult creates a link between religion and politics. The Asante symbol of political authority, the blackened stool, serves as the shrine of the ancestral spirits. The stool is the symbolic link between the ancestors and the living. The occupant of the stool, the chief or king, is the living representative of the ancestors (Danquah, 1952: 135). As founders of society, the land belongs to the ancestors, because they owned it and worked it, either by conquest or by settlement. Therefore, prior to the colonial era land could never be sold outright in Asante tradition.

The land tenure system is centered on the belief in ancestors (Fortes, 1950: 254, 256; Busia, 1951: 47). Family, lineage, clan heads, and the chief/king all act as custodians of the land, and no one has the right to sell the land. In addition, since the land links the ancestors with their living descendants, to leave one's ancestral land implies leaving one's roots of heritage, because "where we bury our dead is our home" (Steyne, 1989: 85).

The Asante Chief

His selection

In Asante society, when a chief dies a successor is chosen within 40 days. This practice prepares the new chief to perform 40th-day rituals for the deceased chief. The new chief is elected from the royal family. The king makers ask the *Ɔhemaa* (the queen mother), who is the recognized authority on the genealogy of the stool family, to nominate a candidate. As the custodian of the "royal register," she decides whether a candidate is eligible or not. Her nominee is subject to the approval of the council. If the queen mother's first nominee is not accepted, she proposes another. If her second is also not accepted, she still retains the right to nominate a third, but this one is her last. If her third nominee also proves unacceptable, the electors are authorized to nominate a candidate, and assuming that this candidate is eligible, the queen mother is obligated to endorse the electors' choice.

His enstoolment (coronation)

After he is selected, the chief-elect is taken to "an unknown place" (*banmu* = inside the hut, the burial house of the previous chiefs/kings) for 40 days prior to his installation and enstoolment. This confinement is a period of "education" for the chief-elect (Obeng, 1988: 43–44). He learns the complex tapestry of Asante custom and regal life, such as walking mannerisms, controlling his speech and thoughts, learning when to smile and when to look serious or gloomy, and managing the affairs of the palace. In addition to serving an educational purpose, the 40-day period is also a time when the spirits of the dead chiefs are invoked to communicate with and bless the chief-elect.

At the end of the 40-day period, the chief-elect is led into the stool house, where blackened stools are kept and where the spirits of the ancestors are believed to be present in great measure. In the stool house, he is lowered and raised three times on the blackened stool of the most renowned of his ancestors. He is then enstooled. By means of an ancient ritual, the new chief receives a new name, the name of one of the royal ancestors. In the stool house, in front of the royal stools, the new chief is blindfolded and asked to select one of the stools. He takes the name of the owner of the stool he selects.

The person of the chief

The ceremony of enstoolment closely associates the chief with the ancestors. It also sets him apart and distinguishes him from other members of the nobility (Mulago, 1969: 145). By means of the ceremony, his person and position are made sacred (Busia, 1951: 36–39). The sacredness of the chief is emphasized by the belief that it is God who appoints a chief. The Asante believe that, although human beings enstool the chief, God appoints him, a belief that is captured in an ancient maxim: *Onyame na osi hene* ("It is God who appoints a king"). In view of this belief, on the day of installation, the community expresses its gratefulness and thanksgiving to God for the new chief by offering God a sheep (*nyame-dwan*: God's sheep), which is killed in the open yard in front of the stool house in thanksgiving to God.

In addition, the chief's sacred position is emphasized by various taboos. He must not strike, or be struck, lest the ancestors bring misfortune on the community. He must never walk barefooted, lest when his sole touches the ground some misfortune befall the community. He should walk with care not to stumble. When he stumbles, sacrifice has to be offered to avert an expected calamity. His buttocks should not touch the ground, which again brings misfortune (Busia, 1951: 26–27).

As God's appointee, the chief is believed to be the savior of his community. In Asante, the chief symbolizes a big tree and an umbrella, because he offers shade and protection (McCaskie, 1989: 424). When a chief/king dies, the representational protection afforded by both the shade tree and the umbrella is threateningly stripped from the culture. Hence, on his death, the people say, "*dupon keseɛ atutu*" (a mighty tree has fallen) and "*Nana atu ne kyineyɛ*" (Nana [the chief] has removed his umbrella). The chief is also closely identified with the fertility of crops and people, which guarantees the continuity of Asante society. Some titles of the chief depict his association with providence and protection (Danquah, 1952: 10): he is *Otumfuɔ*, the powerful, perhaps the all-powerful or the almighty; *Daase-sensa* and *Daaseberɛ*, universal provider and benefactor, who makes provision for the welfare of all his people tirelessly (*berɛ*) and infinitely (*ensa*); *Katakyi*, the great warrior and hero, though he may never himself have gone to war or won any battle; *Ɔbaatan*, mother (of children); *Ahuabobrim*, "vision of awe and reverence"; *Serɛmusei*, "king of the desert," (the lion); *Ɔsei*, the destroyer; and also *Agyeman*, defender of the nation.

As the result of his status, a chief is expected to exhibit the spirit of patience, clemency, and equanimity. He ought not to eat and drink in public, should avoid casual arguments with ordinary people, and should, above all, avoid sexual intrigues.

The Roles of the Chief

The new status of the chief defines his roles in the society. In occupying the stool, the Asante chief combines religious, political, and socioeconomic leadership. Thus, the office of chiefship is clearly composite.

Religious role

As one who sits on the stool of the ancestors, the chief is also priest-chief. He alone has power and authority to gather all the lineages and to sacrifice to the ancestors and God on their behalf. He is the "high priest" of the ancestral cult and performs religious rituals on appointed days and times.

The chief is the central figure at organized religious ceremonies such as the *Adae* and the *Odwira*. *Adae* is a religious ceremony performed every six weeks. On such a day, the chief enters the stool house with some of his attendants, including the chief stool carrier (*nkonuasowuafohene*). In the stool house, in front of the blackened stools, water is poured on the floor, inviting the spirits to wash their hands. The chief then offers *ɛtɔ* (mashed yam or plantain) to the ancestral spirits. The chief speaks to the ancestors as follows:

> Today is *Adae*
> Come and receive this food; and visit us with prosperity
> Permit the bearers of children to bear children
> Grant health to your servants
> Grant health to the Queen-mother
> Grant health to the nation
> Let no evil come upon the town
> To him who wishes evil, let evil fall upon himself. (Sarpong, 1971: 64–65)

When these words have been spoken, a sheep (*odwan*) is brought to the stool house. The chief addresses the ancestral spirits in the same words as those he used when offering the *ɛtɔ*, only substituting *odwan* for *ɛtɔ*. He then draws a knife and slaughters the sheep. Some of the blood is used to smear each of the stools in silence. He then deposits pieces of the fat from the entrails and the lungs on the center props of the blackened stools and the head and parts of the intestines are placed before the stools. The remaining part of the sheep is roasted, which the chief places on each stool. A libation is then poured.

The *Odwira* is an annual festival of purification of the community. It is celebrated at the end of the Asante calendar year to purge the community of all evils committed against the spirit beings before it enters into the coming year. The chief performs a series of rituals in the stool house, royal mausoleum, at sacred rivers, and other places. Various articles of religion and the entire palace are purified with the blood of sheep. *Odwira* cannot be celebrated without the chief.

Moreover, in times of crisis such as famine and epidemic, it is the responsibility of the chief to initiate a search for the religious cause and the possible solution. He provides ritual materials and leads in performing rituals to avert the calamity.

As the chief priest, the chief controls all traditional priests and priestess through his *nsumankwaahene* (head of the priests and priestess), and all shrines belong to him. The importance of the religious position of the chief comes into play when he dies. When the chief dies, spirit possession ceases in his jurisdiction. Thus, the spirits of the gods do not "come upon" the *akomfoɔ* (priests/priestess) until a new chief is installed and the *akomfoɔ* have sworn their allegiance to the new chief. This underscores the fusion of religious and political power in the chief.

In sum, the Asante belief that the well-being of the society depends on establishing cordial relationships with the ancestors, on whom the living depend for help and protection, shows that the chief fulfills an important function as intermediary. He is the central figure at the instituted religious rituals, ensuring the maintenance of the desired harmony between the living and the ancestors.

Political role

With the chief's religious role comes his political function, which is related to his religious role. The chief is more than a secular ruler; his credentials are mystical and are derived from antiquity (Fortes and Evans-Pritchard, 1987: 16). The "mythical credentials" of the chief explain the political role of ancestors in Asante society. The chief's authority in the Asante's political system is the authority of the ancestors. The Asante description of the chief as "the one who sits on the stools of the ancestors" (Busia, 1951: 36) means that the chief rules on behalf of the ancestors, who continue to lead the society.

Asante traditional society sacralizes authority and political office. Therefore, an Asante chief is not just a person who can impose his will on his people. He is also the center of their political relations, the symbol of their unity and distinctiveness, and the embodiment of their most fundamental values.

As political head, the chief is the commander of the army and is thus responsible for delivering his people from their enemies in battle. In Asante society, the chief leads his people to war. In precolonial days, the military role of the chief was important because of the frequent incidents of interethnic wars or the normal process of acquiring territory for statehood. Nevertheless, in this role, the welfare of the people was dominant. Any chief who ignored the welfare of his people forfeited their trust and was liable to deposition. The maxim Ɔdehyeɛ anko a akoa dwane ("If the royal does not fight, the ordinary person refuses to fight") shows that the Asante people expected their chiefs to lead them boldly and to embody the values that defined them as a people.

Socioeconomic role

As head of the community, the chief is responsible for maintaining social order by dealing with antisocial acts within the community. To achieve this, he is a legislator and arbitrator. He settles disputes between his subchiefs on matters of inheritance, succession, and land. Individuals and families also seek the chief's arbitration when necessary. In his role as arbitrator, the chief maintains a court, where he acts as the chief justice and members of his council sit as jurors.

One aspect of the chief's social role is the distribution of land. Economically, *mogya* (blood) entitles an individual Asante to the right of inheritance and claim on property, including the control of land. Land is ordinarily the property of the lineage, and tradition ascribes a sacred significance to land.

First, the Asante believe that the Earth (*Asaase*) has spiritual power, and *Asaase Yaa* is the female name that personifies the spirit of the Earth. In Asante society, a female born on Thursday is called *Yaa*. Thus, *Asaase Yaa* is a female deity, although she is sometimes regarded as a hermaphrodite (Rattray, 1923: 135). She is spoken of and treated with respect in Asante society because from Earth the people acquire their livelihood. The prominent place of *Asaase Yaa* in Asante religious thought is seen in drum texts (Nketia, 1968: 43–44), offerings, and taboos accorded to her, which depict the people's "sense of dependence" (Busia, 1951: 40). Libation and prayer are offered to her before a grave is dug; before excavation for the foundation of a house, a builder pours a libation and invokes the blessing of *Asaase Yaa*. Moreover, the people's dependence on Earth was expressed in the ancient Asante custom of a farmer offering the Earth a sacrifice of yam and fowl at the beginning of cultivation.

Work is forbidden on *Asaase Yaa's* sacred day, Thursday. In some Asante traditional communities, Thursday is still observed as a day of rest for the earth. No one is to till the earth in reverence of *Asaase Yaa*. The land has to be propitiated if a woman delivers a child in the bush. Any spilling of blood is a defilement of *Asaase Yaa*.

Second, the Asante believe that land belongs to the ancestors or local deities and so is held in trust for them. The belief in ancestral ownership makes the living temporary possessors of land, which is destined to pass to generations yet unborn. Land is an ancestral trust, committed to the living for the benefit of the whole community, in particular the unborn generations. As a result, the chief is the custodian of the land, and it is his responsibility to make sure that land is worked by the members of the kinship group and inherited only by that unit. A well known Asante saying sums it all up: "The farm is mine, but the soil belongs to the stool." Although sectors of such land may be leased to others for seasonal agricultural production, the land remains within the family and usually is not sold entirely.

The religious significance of land places the chief in a position to make sure that justice is upheld in land issues. As the religious head and the representative of the ancestors, the chief is obliged to settle land disputes so that families do not lose their ancestral lands to others. Failure to do so attracts the wrath of the spirit beings, especially the ancestors, on the chief, the community, and the guilty party.

In addition to its religious importance, the land plays a major economic role in Asante society, which makes equity in land distribution very important. Land distribution is important because it forms the primary basis of "capital" in the economic life of Asante society and so holds a prominent place in the Asante system. One cannot live without access to land; without it, one is left to die of hunger. Descendants are to live to perpetuate the lineage, and the thing to live on is the land. Asante society cannot be guaranteed continuous existence without insurance; perpetual availability of land is a guarantee of that insurance. In the old days, and in modern rural communities today, the chief's responsibility was and is to apportion land to strangers who want to settle in the community. Even during colonial rule, land allocations – mostly in the form of usufructs, confiscation, taxation, and rights – were matters controlled by the chiefs and their councils; and most disputes about these issues were resolved by Native Courts presided over by the same chiefs and councillors (Rathbone, 2000: 13).

Another social function of the chief is to uphold human rights. Traditional Asante society guarantees human rights. Rights such as ownership of property and the right to life are protected within the community. Traditionally, these rights are vested in the community through its head, the chief. Actions that violate the sanctity of the community are seriously censured. The right of the community to continue in existence is so important that such acts as the pollution of the community's source of water and violation of other environmental taboos are severely punished. The chief, with the priests and priestesses, enforces prescriptions and laws regarding these taboos.

In addition, in precolonial days, the chief was expected to attend to the rights of slaves. Slavery in Asante was described as "a state of servitude guarded by rights" (Kingsley, 1901: 398). Although the slave's life was his master's, a master could not kill his slave, whatever his offense, without the full consent of the central authority, the chief. To kill a slave without the consent of the chief's judiciary in Asante society was regarded as an act of murder, and the offense was liable to be punished as such. In addition, the master could not mutilate his slave without permission from the chief. The rights of a slave, among other things, included the right to marry, own property, own a slave, swear an "oath," be a competent witness, and ultimately even become heir to his master (Rattray, 1929: 38).

The owner of a slave was ultimately responsible for all the acts of his slave, and, in consequence, he became responsible for the debts and torts of his slave's wife. A slave could bring and win successful actions against a chief. When mistreated, a slave could run away and seek sanctuary by throwing himself on the mercy of a god or the ancestors at the *barim* (mausoleum). He could swear an oath that some other master must take him. Moreover, a recaptured slave was not necessarily punished but was made to "drink the gods" before the chief that he would not run away again (Rattray, 1929: 41–42). Importantly, it was strictly forbidden, with severe sanctions, for outsiders to point to the origins of a slave, because a man of slave origin could be made counselor, councillor, or spokesperson if he combined enterprise with honesty and good conduct.

Thus, in Asante society, the chief was both protector and advocate of slaves. He saw to it that slaves were not mistreated and deprived of their rights. He served as a check on slaveholders so that they could not abuse their authority over their slaves. Finally, the chief sought the assimilation of slaves, making them full members of society.

Conclusion

In this essay, I have shown that chieftaincy is an important institution in Asante society; community life in total centers on the chief. Before the advent of colonial rule, the chief's role encompassed many functions, which revolved around the basic themes of guiding, protecting, defending, and providing for the needs of the society he served. He was the intermediary between the departed ancestors, the living, and the yet unborn. These holistic functions involved religious, military, legislative, executive, judicial, social, and cultural features. In contemporary Asante society, the chief continues to perform many of these roles.

To be sure, today the Asante chief does not – indeed, cannot – function as he did in precolonial times. He is neither the military leader nor the legislator that his precolonial forebears were. Moreover, his judicial functions and executive powers are much diminished. However, these facts do not warrant concluding that the chief has no meaningful role in the modern era. On the contrary, he has a vital role to play both in his local domain and at the national level. This role is recognized in Ghana's central government system: the chieftaincy was given legal status in the 1992 Constitution. In addition to his providing religious direction to the people, the Constitution assigns chiefs both statutory and nonstatutory roles. His statutory functions include the collection, refinement, codification, and unification of customary laws; adjudication in chieftaincy disputes; compilation of lines of succession to offices in the various traditional areas; and appointment of representatives to various government statutory bodies. The nonstatutory functions include settling disputes through arbitration; mobilizing people for development purposes; and superintending annual festivals.

Apart from these constitutional roles, chiefs have the moral obligation to contribute to the welfare of their people. Because chiefs are regarded as symbols of unity, they are constitutionally barred from active involvement in partisan politics. But they do play an important role nonetheless. These days, for instance, a chief is expected to lead his people in organizing self-help activities and projects, and to take the initiative in establishing institutions and programs to improve the welfare of his people in areas such as health, education, trade, and economic or social development. In sum, chiefs continue to play a pivotal role in religion, politics, and development – a role that enhances democracy, sustains good governance, and promotes justice and social cohesion.

References

Akyeampong, E. and P. Obeng (1995) Spirituality, gender, and power in Asante history, *International Journal of African Historical Studies*, 28(3): 481–508.

Busia, K.A. (1951) *The Position of the Chief in the Modern Political System of Ashanti*, Oxford University Press, London.

Danquah, J.B. (1952) Obligation in Akan society, *West African Affairs* 8: 3–15.

Fortes, M. (1950) Kinship and marriage among the Ashanti, in *African Systems of Kinship and Marriage*, A.R. Radcliffe-Brown and Daryll Forde (eds.), Oxford University Press, London, pp. 252–284.

Fortes, M. and Dieterlin, G. (eds.) (1965) *African Systems of Thought*, Oxford University Press, Oxford.

Fortes, M. and Evans-Pritchard, E.E. (1987) *African Political Systems*, London: KPI.

Kingsley, M.H. (1901) *West African Studies*, Macmillan, London.

McCaskie, T.C. (1989) Death and the Asantehene: A historical meditation, *Journal of African History* 30(3): 417–444.

Mulago, V. (1969) Vital participation, in *Biblical Revelation and African Beliefs*, K.A. Dickson and W. Ellingworth (eds.), Lutterworth, London, pp. 137–158.

Nketia, J.H.K. (1968) *Our Drums and Drummers*, State Publishing Corporation, Accra.

Obeng, E.E. (1988) *Ancient Ashanti Chieftaincy*, Ghana Publishing Corporation, Accra.

Parrinder, E.G. (1961) *West African Religion*, Epworth, London.

Rathbone, R. (2000) *Nkrumah and the Chiefs*, Reimmer, Accra.

Rattray, R.S. (1923) *Ashanti*, Clarendon, Oxford.

Rattray, R.S. (1929) *Ashanti Law and Constitution*, Clarendon, Oxford.

Sarpong, P.K. (1971) *The Sacred Stools of the Akan*, Ghana Publishing Corporation, Accra.

Steyne, P.M. (1989) *Gods of Power: A Study of the Beliefs and Practices of Animists*, Touch Publications, Houston.

CHAPTER 17
Tibetan Monastics and Social Justice

Derek F. Maher

Buddhism, which has for centuries been little more than a historical relic in India, the country of its birth, has always survived as a cultural export by adapting to local contexts. As the practices, ideology, mythology, and philosophical language of Buddhism spread throughout Asia, it found a broad array of diverse social settings in which it took root, responding to local values, adjusting to contemporary needs, resonating with indigenous iconography and legends, and conversing creatively with ideologies already in place. By being adaptable in these ways, Buddhism served the new populations who embraced it and, along the way, it came to be expressed in ever-changing patterns. As Buddhism took shape in Tibet, it did so within the confines of forms that already existed, including the limitations and inspirations embedded within the prevailing martial outlook of its leadership; the unlettered nature of Tibetan society; the sparse population, high altitude, severe climate, limited agriculture, and forbidding topography of the Tibetan Plateau; the predominant economy that was reliant on animal husbandry and trade; and dozens of other significant factors that distinguish Tibet from many of its neighbors. Even more significantly, the reception that Buddhism received in Tibet and the particular character it assumed were profoundly influenced by Tibetan beliefs and practices concerning the sacred nature of the landscape, its permeation by sundry spiritual forces, the efficacy of rituals and utterances in influencing those forces, and the status of human beings in relation to those dimensions of experience, all factors that constitute the central elements of the pre-Buddhist Bön religion.

These adaptive strategies are critical to the success of a transplanted religion since, if the new religious outlook does not address some previous problem in a society or if it does not help a society improve itself in some way, it is unlikely to be accepted in a new home. For the Tibetans, Buddhism offered two substantial advantages. First of all, the warlike Tibetans had encountered many neighbors through their raiding and conquests, and they found that many of the people in the larger region maintained cultures that were more sophisticated and refined, that were richer in resources and artifacts, and that afforded their members a better life. Since the very cultures they admired also embraced Buddhism, the religion seemed to them to promise a means of advancing their culture. Similarly, but likely on a far less conscious level, Buddhism also was able to help Tibet transform from an aggressive warrior nation with a low level of social organization to an agent of social betterment in the region, and the monks and nuns of Tibet were always the most motivated actors in this transformation. This latter process, however, unfolded only very slowly.

Introduction of Buddhism to Tibet

Legendary accounts depict the seventh-century Tibetan King Songtsen Gampo (*srong btsan sgam po*, 605/617–650) as initiating the real cultural transmission of Buddhism into Tibet. His marital alliances with Buddhist princesses from both China and Nepal inaugurated the process of transmitting Buddhist ideas, artifacts, scriptures, and people to Tibet, an effort that occupied much of the next 500 years. It was under that same king, according to later accounts, that a minister named Tönmi Sambhoṭa (*thon mi sam bho ṭa*, seventh century) traveled to northern India in the company of many other young men in order to undertake a systematic study of both Buddhism and the Sanskrit language. Tönmi Sambhoṭa is credited with inventing a Tibetan script based on the Indian Gupta script, writing a grammar after Indian models, and beginning the extensive project of translating canonical scriptures into Tibetan by translating several sutras and tantras. He is marked out as a special hero in Tibetan memory because of the significant part he played in this cultural transfusion.

While these earliest Buddhist activities helped to establish the foundation for the full-fledged Buddhism that would come to dominate Tibetan culture subsequently, the new religion initially remained the preserve of the royal elite. Buddhism was embraced as part of a package of cultural imports – including medical knowledge, geomancy, astrology, calendrical systems, and writing, in addition to religious ideas – that was appropriated by Tibetans in their quest to emulate the cultivated and refined peoples who were among their neighbors. Rather than offering a coherent religious outlook, however, the first hints of Buddhism that reached Tibet served mainly to provide the court with a cultural confidence and social sophistication that they admired in nearby lands, particularly China and India.

The ripening of Buddhism as a serviceable religion that would be embraced by the public would be a gradual process, punctuated by occasional bursts of startling changes, that would help Tibetans to gain insights into Buddhisms from abroad and to formulate their own versions of it. Over time, Buddhism would permeate more levels of society, the formal institutions would develop, the canonical literature would be translated and digested, a homegrown scholasticism would emerge, and Tibet would become one of the places in Asia that is perhaps the most thoroughly influenced by the teachings of the Buddha. Most significantly, Buddhism can be said to have become ensconced in Tibet only when the institution of monasticism had finally been established there in the eighth century, when three famous visitors to Tibet precipitated the rapid development of Buddhism in the country in dramatic ways.

Śāntarakṣita (725–788) was a brilliant scholar-monk who had been invited to Tibet by King Trisong Detsen (*khri srong lde btsan*, 742–796) in order to promote the development of Buddhism. Perceiving significant opposition from both the anti-Buddhist ministers and, more ominously, the indigenous Bön deities, Śāntarakṣita found himself unable to gain significant traction in his missionary activity. He urged the king instead to invite the yogically powerful Padmasaṃbhava (eighth century) to come to Tibet so that he could subdue the deities then in opposition. Vivid Tibetan narratives recount the spiritual struggles undergone by Padmasaṃbhava before he was able to bind the Bön deities as protectors of Buddhism. This having been achieved, we are told, Tibet was pacified and the ground was safe for the emergence of monastic Buddhism (Zangpo, 2002). The first monastery in Tibet was consecrated at Samyé in 776, and either just before or just after that, a group of seven Tibetan monks was ordained by Śāntarakṣita. Kamalaśīla (d. 763), the famed Indian disciple of Śāntarakṣita, visited Tibet thereafter, and according to equally elaborate narratives, he defeated a Chinese monk named Hoshang Mahāyanā in 794, thereby establishing that Tibetans would henceforth follow Indian Buddhism and not the forms they had been receiving from China. King Trisong Detsen and his successors built networks of monasteries across Tibet, and gradually ordained monks began to occupy them.[1] Eventually, those lineages branched out in spidery webs to the point at which perhaps as many as a seventh of the male population of the plateau had donned robes.[2]

Tensions between the imported religion, Buddhism, and its indigenous predecessor, Bön, continued even as the newcomer thrived under royal patronage. By the middle of the ninth century, traditional histories indicate that outright conflict erupted when Lang Darma (*glang dar ma*, 803–842) assumed the throne after deposing his brother, the great patron of Buddhism, King Relpachen (*ral pa can*, 806–838) in 836. These histories depict King Lang Darma as the figurehead of a Bön revival movement seeking to blunt and reverse the proliferation of Buddhism. A pogrom reportedly ensued, due to which Buddhist statues, scriptures, buildings, and institutions were destroyed, and institutional Buddhism fell into decline as informal local patterns of relations between teachers and students went underground. Ultimately, in 842, a tantric yogi named Pelgyi Dorjé (*dpal gyi rdo rje*, ninth century) avenged the harm done to Buddhism by assassinating Lang Darma. Not all elements of these accounts can be verified, but the story appears to be the sort of narrative that might be constructed by Buddhists as a way of retrospectively explaining why the ascent of Buddhism was not continuous, but rather suffered the occasional interruption.[3] These sorts of narratives are composed by the victors; that is, by Buddhists who were anxious to legitimize and validate retrospectively the Tibetan embrace of a foreign religion. As part of their effort to reinforce the benefits of Buddhism, the pre-Buddhist period was depicted as a brutish, violent, and ignorant era in which unbridled spiritual forces directed early Tibetans in uncivilized behavior. A potent parallel is to be found in Muslim discussions of the pre-Islam *jahiliyah*. period, or the period of ignorance of God's will, which early authors relished in depicting in horrible detail.

Classical Monastic Buddhism[4]

Despite the setback in the ascent of Buddhism in the ninth century, it continued to inspire various groups in society, and some monastic lineages remained unbroken. As the most acute forms of suppression diminished, monastic ordination lineages were revitalized. Slowly, figures such as Tsang Rapsel, Yo Gewajung, and Mar Śākyamuni served to extend a renewed form of monastic Buddhism throughout Tibet, and the grand-scale monasteries familiar to students of Tibetan history began to emerge. However, during the four-century period following the 842 death of Lang Darma, neither political nor religious authority was unified. In that period of decentralized rule, regional centers of religious authority appeared and geographically focused monastic lineages came to be established in distinct locations across Tibet. The transmission of Buddhism into Tibet was advancing through the extensive translation projects, the exchange of Buddhist visitors between India and Tibet, and the organization of the Tibetan canon.

The most notable figure during this period was the Indian luminary from Bengal named Atiśa (982–1054), whose numerous translations served to advance the establishment of formal monastic Buddhism. Perhaps more importantly, he helped to reform a splintered form of Buddhism that he saw as lacking a firm ethical foundation, and he advanced a genre of literature in Tibet, called "Stages of the Path," through which he hoped to systematize Buddhism. His *Lamp for the Path* grounds all of Buddhist practice on the altruistic service of other beings.[5] This consciousness echoed another fundamental Indian text of even greater popularity in Tibet, *Guide to the Bodhisattva's Way of Life* by Śāntideva (eighth century) (Śāntideva, 1997). Together, these works helped to define the outward-looking service orientation that came to characterize Tibetan Buddhism.

In the thirteenth to fifteenth centuries, large-scale monastic cities began to flourish, particularly under the Geluk School of the Dalai Lamas. These monasteries, many with populations numbering in the thousands, helped to establish Buddhism at the center of every dimension of life in Tibet. The daily schedule, the annual calendar, and the cycle of life all revolved around Buddhist rituals and were imbued with Buddhist values. In this way, the quest for social justice was animated by the altruistic disposition of Atiśa and Śāntideva. Monks and nuns, on an individual basis, came to be preoccupied with serving social ends, and recording such service became a standard element of monastic hagiographies. For example, the treasure revealer and mystic Tangtong Gyelpo (*thang stong rgyal po*, 1385–1464) built a series of iron bridges in Tibet as a means of serving the public. The third Panchen Lama Lozang Pelden Yeshé (1737–1780) voluntarily invited smallpox into himself during a widespread outbreak on a visit to China, from which he died in 1780. It became a tradition, commencing in 1562, that each of the thousands of monks attending the annual Great Prayer Festival in Lhasa would carry stones to reinforce the Jowo Dam nearby. Biographies of great monastic figures are rife with accounts of vast donations dedicated to feeding the poor. Service to society became a standard element of monastic life.

Monasticism under the Red Army

Just as Buddhism assumed distinctive forms when it encountered the unique environment of Tibet, similarly Tibetan Buddhism has undergone dramatic changes since the Chinese occupation of Tibet began in 1950, as new forces prevailed on it. Within the country, tremendous pressures were exerted in the initial decade of the 1950s, during which the Tibetans attempted to accommodate the new political reality of a massive and ever-increasing military occupation. At the level of the public experience, customary patterns of travel were affected by Chinese policy, monasteries had to operate under the watchful eye of Chinese soldiers, the traditional daily and yearly rituals were curtailed, and shifts in the economy compelled changes in customary patterns of patronage. At the most elevated levels of Tibetan society, the Chinese presence utterly transformed religious life. Along with the nobility, the monastic elite had been one of the most powerful constituencies in the country prior to the Chinese invasion. The curtailment of monastic authority undermined one of the most distinctive features of the Tibetan state, that is, that it had relied on a fusion of religious and political functions. Moreover, the Chinese dominance over Tibet throughout the 1950s called into question the status of the Dalai Lama, around whom so much of Tibetan identity and national mythology revolved. Since Tibetans regard the Dalai Lama as an incarnation of the *bodhisattva* Avalokiteśvara, the threatening posture of the military compound being built in Lhasa caused Tibetans to feel that their inspired leader, and therefore the nation itself, was imperiled. When the Dalai Lama was invited to the military compound in March 1959 and his customary guard was specifically not included in the summons, his rush into exile became necessary.

Meanwhile, back in Tibet, due to both Maoist agrarian reforms in the 1950s and especially the 1960s and the Cultural Revolution from 1966 to 1976, Tibetan Buddhism and particularly monasticism were systematically dismantled. Thousands of monasteries, nunneries, temples, hermitages, and other Buddhist institutions were destroyed, often razed completely. Through struggle sessions conducted by the Red Guard, disciples were forced to denounce their teachers and in some cases murder them, while monks and nuns were compelled to break their vows by having sexual intercourse in public. Vast bonfires consumed entire libraries of sacred literature, and religious paintings and statues were sold on the international art market. Senior monks, nuns, religious artists, and others capable of perpetuating the established customs of the Tibetan people were confined to prisons and work camps, where many died under the burden of their labor. The free expression of religion was strictly forbidden.[6] In a real-life echo of the narratives about Buddhism being suppressed under King Lang Darma, Tibetan Buddhism went deep underground.

Following the death of Mao Zedong and the arrest of the Gang of Four in 1976, the communist government's policy under Deng Xiaoping toward Tibet was liberalized beginning in 1978, and slowly it became possible for Tibetans to start to rebuild what had been destroyed by the Chinese.[7] Monasteries that had lain in ruins for as many as 30 years began to be rebuilt with volunteer labor and with donations from the Tibetan people. Texts were printed, monks enrolled in monasteries, and public displays of Buddhist practice became more common. Still, official participation in Buddhist institutions was carefully curtailed by the Chinese authorities, and a number of important traditional sites were managed as little more than tourist destinations. Yet, the thaw permitted a constricted revival of Buddhism in isolated contexts.

For example, Drepung Monastery, founded in 1416, had been the largest monastery in the world in the early twentieth century, containing as many as 10 000 monks at its height in 1950. It had long enjoyed a prominent status in Tibetan society, even serving as the home to the Dalai Lama at certain points in history. Even in the twentieth century, it remained a locus of political influence and power, due to which it was a target of the earliest Chinese military units arriving in Lhasa, and much of it was destroyed in 1951. The financial infrastructure that supported the monastery was disassembled by the Chinese in 1959, with customary forms of income disallowed by the Chinese, such as rent on lands owned by the monastery, interest on loans, and the like. The physical structure was further demolished in the Cultural Revolution. By the end of that chaotic period, only 300 monks remained. With the reforms of the Deng period, however, buildings were reconstructed and monastic life was resumed beginning in 1981; by the 1990s, a new financial structure was in place that enabled some scholar monks to resume the full-time study and debate regimen that had formerly occupied so many. In 1993, nevertheless, there were only 437 monks enrolled at Drepung Monastery, and the official cap was set at 600. Since the 1980s, monks and nuns living in Tibet have played leading roles in the political protests against the Chinese occupation. Their leadership in the protests in 1989 and the early 1990s has been expertly documented (Schwartz, 1994), although the full story of monks' and nuns' involvement in the 2008 demonstrations leading up to the Beijing Olympics has yet to be told.[8]

In a different environment in eastern Tibet, another form of Buddhist revivalism came into being when the most severe restrictions on religious life were relaxed. In the Golok region of Kham, a charismatic religious teacher named Khenpo Jikphun (*mkhan po 'jigs phun*, 1933–2004) developed a rural-based revival movement that employed long-lived religious narratives as a vehicle of promoting Tibetan self-identity under communist rule. As a form of religious revival and political resistance, he deployed the Tibetan tradition of treasure discovery (*gter ston*) in which an acknowledged master is regarded as being able to extract texts, statues, or other meaningful objects from the landscape. Even though they are considered to have been concealed in the long distant epic past, these treasures are found to have contemporary significance, in the present case even appearing to offer advice on how to live under an irreligious communist regime. Mythic history is thus retrieved and made relevant to contemporary life. In this case, Khenpo Jikphun's narratives harken back to the era of King Gesar of Ling, the subject of Tibet's ancient and continually renewed epic. The revealed treasures also provide ritual practices that have immediate currency among the lama's burgeoning followers. Through revealing these voices from the past and retrieving Tibet's mythic past, Khenpo Jikphun provided his followers with a self-understanding that enabled them to reinvigorate a religious life that had been disrupted since the Chinese invasion and the subsequent oppression, that is, in David Germano's evocative phrase, he remembered the dismembered body of Tibet (Germano, 1998).

For many monastics and other Tibetans living under Chinese authority, the perpetuation of Buddhism itself constitutes a quest for social justice. In light of the history of Chinese efforts to undermine and displace Buddhism, to sever the cultural threads that connect current Tibetans to the meaning they used to find in their expression of Buddhism, and to curtail the rights of Tibetans, many people in Tibet feel that they are defiantly standing up to their oppressors merely by studying the literature, religion, history, or arts of their ancestors. It is often through religious communities themselves that Tibetans are able to help one another, instead of being able to rely on the Chinese government for services. Thus, Tibetans provide a sort of social service infrastructure for one another, which is regarded as an expression of Buddhist values of compassion and loving-kindness. This was evident, for example, in the earthquake that struck eastern Tibet on April 14, 2010, when Tibetan monks and nuns took the lead in rescuing survivors and providing services for them afterward (Lipes, 2010).

The Exile Experience

In the wake of the Dalai Lama's escape to India in 1959, 80 000–100 000 Tibetans followed him, many of them monastics fleeing the destruction of monasteries, nunneries, and temples that ensued. Tibetans living in exile in India and other locales in the Himalayan region have had to adapt to new circumstances, being influenced by novel experiences and ideas, and having to reconfigure themselves to respond to a broad range of changes. In India and elsewhere in the Himalayan region, monks and nuns have helped to shape and define the exile experience. In the initial chaos, people struggled with ill-health, lack of food, and a complete absence of infrastructure. The Indian government and some prominent Tibetans who had already been living in India for a period of years, the Dalai Lama's elder brother Thubten Norbu and the great historian Tsepon Shakabpa among them, worked to elaborate the basic necessities of a life as refugees.

Only over time did these short-term efforts shift in light of the awareness that their exile would be prolonged. An old fort on the border with Bhutan – where the British had previously imprisoned Mahatma Gandhi, Jawaharlal Nehru, and other activists for Indian independence – was provided as a gathering place for Tibetan monks and nuns to assemble, amid hot and humid jungle conditions, malarial swamps, and poisonous snakes. On this inauspicious foundation, the bare outlines of Tibetan monasticism were preserved until more permanent quarters could be established (Wangmo, 2005). Eventually, large tracts of land in south India were provided by the Indian government, and now thousands of monks occupy newly founded monasteries, nunneries, and schools in Bylakuppe, Dalhousie, Dharamsala, Mundgod, Sarnath, and elsewhere.

In the exile communities located in India and other places, Tibetan monks and nuns have sought to reestablish many of the monasteries and nunneries that were meaningful to them or their parents' generation back in Tibet. Hence, many of the most important institutions have been reborn in India and the neighboring regions. The aforementioned Drepung Monastery has been reestablished in Mundgod, Karnataka, in south India, and now houses 5000 monks, many of whom are engaged in the same rigorous scholastic curriculum that characterized the mega-monasteries back in Tibet.

Just as those large monasteries used to be financed by patronage from Chinese emperors or Mongolian khans, their new iterations are now supported in part by streams of patronage from the West. Many of the specialized monasteries have also been reestablished in exile, including, for example, the Nechung Monastery near the Dalai Lama's home in Dharamsala, which is home to an oracle that has advised Dalai Lamas for centuries. Mountain hermitages and retreats are scattered throughout the Himalayan region, as they used to be in Tibet. And nunneries of ancient pedigree have new homes on the west side of the Himalayas.

Some of these fresh versions of old religious centers are being refashioned in attenuated form due to the new financial constraints of living in a foreign land without the social infrastructure that existed in old Tibet. Yet other cases seem to have been reinvigorated by the exile experience. An example of the latter is found in the Tibetan Nuns Project, which is sponsored by the Dalai Lama, the Tibetan Women's Association, and an array of western supporters, including Elizabeth Napper, a well-known American scholar of Tibetan Buddhism. The organization supports 700 nuns at more than half a dozen nunneries from all of the main orders of Tibetan Buddhism, including the Dolma Ling Nunnery located near Dharamsala, India. In Tibet, nuns did not have the opportunity to receive a traditional Buddhist education, as was routine for the more scholastically inclined monks, but the nuns of Dromo Ling study with top-notch teachers and debate the standard array of topics in a rigorous and challenging 17-year curriculum.[9]

Other Tibetan Buddhist monks and nuns living in exile have defined new ways of expressing the Buddhist values they learned in more traditional monastic settings by engaging in what amounts to social work. Partly inspired by the social activism of Gandhi and the Indian independence movement, by western nongovernmental organizations, and by Christian aid organizations, these people are part of the movement known as Socially Engaged Buddhism. The Dalai Lama himself participates in an organization called the International Network of Engaged Buddhists (INEB), which he co-founded with Thich Nhat Hanh of Vietnam and Buddhadasa Bhikkhu of Thailand. The organization conducts an international conference biannually, which is described on its Facebook page:

> Simple monks and abbots, nuns, academics, teachers, students and social justice activists gather for meditation, mutual inspiration and presentation of their activities. The themes and aims of the networking are broad, including: social justice and promotion of peace, human and animal rights, environment, food sovereignty and global challenges of sustainability, alternative economics, inclusive education, right to livelihood, addictions and drug treatment, development and health assistance, palliative care, AIDS care and prevention, elimination of discrimination based on gender, sexual orientation, race and ethnic status, ordination of women, Sangha support and reform, as well as interfaith dialogue. (INEB, 2011)

Tibetan Buddhists living in exile have established numerous organizations that seek to address similar issues in their own communities. The Sakya Hospital in Dehradun, India, serves both the monks from the Sakya monastery and the Indian and Tibetans who live in the area. A monk living in Bylakuppe in south India has established a school for disabled children. Perhaps the most well-articulated example of Socially Engaged Buddhism is to be found in Tong-Len Charitable Trust, founded by a young Tibetan monk named Jamyang. Named after a meditative practice used to generate compassion by sending out helpfulness (*tong*) and taking on the suffering of others (*len*), the organization serves the poorest people living in the Dharamsala area of Himachel Pradesh: low-caste, tribal people who have been internally displaced from other regions of India. In existence since 2001, Tong-Len provides medical services to 3000 people in 6 slums throughout the region, as well as educational and limited vocational services to a single slum with 700 residents. Tong-Len's motto, "Compassion in Action," conveys the sense that the Buddhist value of cultivating a compassionate disposition toward all sentient beings must be manifested in personal activities that enhance the lives of others. The organization has attracted the attention of the Dalai Lama, and he now sponsors one of its projects, a daily meal for the smallest children in the main slum community. Jamyang and the 20 staff members use the opportunity presented by having so many of the slum children gathered together by providing classes before and after that noon meal is served. In addition, 40 children from the community now live full time in a youth hostel and attend a high-quality English-medium school. Without engaging in any type of proselytization, staff members work to alleviate poverty, relieve suffering, and provide the skills and resources to become self-sufficient.[10]

Every day, five Tibetans slip out of Tibet to visit or stay long term in exile communities in India or elsewhere. Frequently, parents sneak out of Tibet in order to deposit their children at the network of schools in India called Tibetan Children's Village, so that the children can be educated in an environment of religious and cultural freedom. Others undertake the risky and forbidden journey so that they can learn Tibetan traditions, whether artistic, medical, religious, or otherwise, as a way of resisting Chinese assimilation and cultural destruction. These efforts to preserve culture and perpetuate tradition are experienced by Tibetans as a righteous imperative. Tibetans still in Tibet and those in the exile communities interact with one another across a permeable threshold, collaborating in their joint objective of actualizing justice in an untenable situation.

Globalized Tibetan Buddhism

The arrival of Tibet in the international consciousness was demonstrated by the celebration of the International Year of Tibet in 1991, the Free Tibet concerts headlined by the Beastie Boys and Rage Against the Machine between 1996 and 2001, campus organizations like Students for a Free Tibet, and worldwide groups like the international Tibet Network. Tibetan Buddhism has indeed become a globalized phenomenon, particularly since the Dalai Lama gained international celebrity status on being awarded the Nobel Peace Prize in 1989. He has his own website (www.dalailama.com), maintains a Twitter account (@DalaiLama), and travels the globe at a steady pace to make the world aware of Tibet's plight, to dispense religious teachings, and to engage others in a transnational interreligious, and often supra-religious, conversation.[11] The Dalai

Lama deploys the prestige of his international standing to promote social justice, peace, and environmentalism around the world. He takes every opportunity in public pronouncements and personal audiences to advance causes of social justice, including, for example, his Nobel Peace Prize address, the negotiating positions he advances with the Chinese, his proposal to designate Tibet as the world's largest environmental refuge, and his numerous philanthropic efforts.

Tibetan monasticism has also become internationalized, with both traditional and brand new monasteries operating important Buddhist centers around the world, including the Institute of Buddhist Studies in Ithaca, New York, operated by Namgyal Monastery, the Dalai Lama's ritual monastery; the Center for Tibetan Buddhist Studies, Practice, and Culture located in Atlanta, Georgia and affiliated with Emory University; and the Sakya Buddhist Centre of London. These organizations seek to advance both the academic study of and spiritual engagement with Tibetan Buddhism within the international community.

There are also worldwide networks of centers that transcend anything that existed in Tibet, but that serve as quasi-monastic institutions in the globalized forms of Tibetan Buddhism, including, for example, the Foundation for the Preservation of Mahayana Tradition, the New Kadampa Tradition-International Kadampa Buddhist Union, or Chögyam Trungpa's organization, called Vajradhatu. Although each of these organizations arranges its teachings in nontraditional ways, they all train western adherents and supporters in topics traditionally studied by Tibetan monks, despite the fact that the adherents may not have taken vows as monks. These organizations also operate numerous service organizations in India and elsewhere, many of them educational or medical in their mission.

Although it is no longer necessary to continue refuting the old supposition that Tibet was isolated from the rest of the world, it is true that Tibet was not an active participant in many of the vital changes sweeping the globe in the modern period. Still, all of that has changed now that traditional Tibetan institutions in exile are being shaped in part by international visitors and patrons, fundraising journeys through Europe, East Asia, and North America, advanced communication technologies, and globalization. Nuns in India have cellphones, Facebook pages, and email accounts. Monks attend international conferences, study science, and participate in cognitive psychology experiments at American and European universities. Traditional sacred music and dance have been adapted as spectacles for paying customers abroad. Participants in Buddhist groups in the West host visits by prominent lamas and then travel to their home monasteries in South Asia. Tibetan monasticism in exile is very much in flux.

Buddhism has remained a vital and lively tradition by continually responding to the ever-changing forces that prevail on it. A specific set of forms developed in Tibet in light of existing circumstances and, throughout the centuries, Tibetans have perpetually renewed their traditions so that they could continue to draw meaning from their lives. Like all Buddhist traditions, they have sought to manifest compassion and loving-kindness for others as a core dimension of enacting the Buddhist life. The particular vehicles of expressing these values for Tibetans have long been conditioned by the special circumstances that have framed their lives; now Buddhist monks and nuns, both inside of Tibet and beyond, find themselves engaged in social work, political activism, environmental advocacy, and cultural preservation, among other activities.

Notes

1 These events, which form the foundation of Tibet's self-understanding, are recounted in numerous ancient legendary texts and in more recent scholarly works, for example Gyaltsen (1996) and Kapstein (2006), respectively.
2 Estimates vary on the percentage of Tibetans who were either monks or nuns prior to the Chinese invasion that eventuated in the disruption of Tibetan monasticism. Johnston (2000) indicates that 10–15% of the male population were monks and 2–5% of the female population were nuns prior to 1959. However, it can safely be said that a higher percentage of the Tibetan population was in robes than in any other time or place in the world.
3 Some scholars have argued that narratives about Lang Darma are fictional or at least exaggerated. See, for example, Yamaguchi (1996).
4 In this section, I am following Tsepon Shakabpa (2010), primarily Chapters 2 and 3.
5 A fine contemporary commentary on this text is to be found in Rinchen and Sonam, (1997).
6 Still a classic of the period, John Avedon's *In Exile from the Land of Snows* (1984) recounts many of these details through eye-witness accounts.
7 Tsering Shakya (1999) clearly described both the impact of the Cultural Revolution in Tibet and the evolution of official policy in the 1980s and 1990s.
8 This paragraph and the previous one are based on Melvyn C. Goldstein's "The revival of monastic life in Drepung Monastery" (Goldstein, 1998).
9 Information about the Tibetan Nuns Project was derived from its website as well as field visits. See www.tnp.org.
10 My understanding of Tong-Len Charitable Trust comes from extensive field studies over the past five years. I am writing a book tentatively entitled "Compassion in Action: Socially Engaged Buddhism among Tibetan Exiles in India."
11 As one of dozens of potential examples, see the volume Dalai Lama *et al.* (1991), recounting a conversation between the Dalai Lama and scholars of Buddhism on the one hand and psychologists, psychiatrists, and other neurobiologists on the other, in which efforts were made to understand similarities and differences in the ways the mind is understood.

References

Avedon, John F. (1984) *In Exile from the Land of Snows*, Alfred A. Knopf, New York.

Dalai Lama, Benson, Herbert, Thurman, Robert A.F. *et al.* (1991) *Mind Science: An East-West Dialogue*, Wisdom Publications, Boston.

Germano, David (1998) Remembering the dismembered body of Tibet: Contemporary Tibetan visionary movements in the People's Republic of China, in *Buddhism in Contemporary Tibet: Religious Revival and Cultural Identity*, Melvyn C. Goldstein and Matthew Kapstein (eds.), University of California Press, Berkeley, pp. 53–94.

Goldstein, Melvyn C. (1998) The revival of monastic life in Drepung Monastery, in *Buddhism in Contemporary Tibet: Religious Revival and Cultural Identity*, Melvyn C. Goldstein and Matthew Kapstein (eds.), University of California Press, Berkeley, pp. 15–52.

Gyaltsen, Sakyapa Sonam (1996) *The Clear Mirror: A Traditional Account of Tibet's Golden Age*, McComas Taylor and Lama Choedak Yuthok (trans.), Snow Lion Publications, Ithaca, NY.

International Network of Engaged Buddhists (2011) http://www.facebook.com/sulak.sivaraksa#!/INEB.BuddhistNetwork?v=info (accessed January 9, 2011).

Johnston, William M. (2000) *The Encyclopedia of Monasticism*, Routledge, London.

Kapstein, Matthew T. (2006) *The Tibetans*, Blackwell, Oxford.

Lipes, Joshua (2010) Monks aid rescue bid: Tibetan monks join earthquake efforts in northwestern China, *Radio Free Asia Web*, April 4, http://www.rfa.org/english/news/china/rescue-04152010161807.html (accessed January 28, 2011).

Rinchen, Geshe Sonam, and Sonam, Ruth (1997) *Atisha's Lamp for the Path to Enlightenment*, Snow Lion Publications, Ithaca, NY.

Śāntideva (1997) *A Guide to the Bodhisattva's Way of Life*, Vesna A. Wallace and B. Alan Wallace (trans.), Snow Lion Publications, Ithaca, NY.

Schwartz, Ronald D. (1994) *Circle of Protest: Political Ritual in the Tibetan Uprising*, C. Hurst & Co, London.

Shakabpa, Tsepon Wangchuk Deden (2010) *One Hundred Thousand Moons: An Advanced Political History of Tibet*, Derek F. Maher (trans. and ed.), Brill, Leiden.

Shakya, Tsering (1999) *The Dragon in the Land of Snows: A History of Modern Tibet since 1947*, Columbia University Press, New York.

Tibetan Nuns Project (2011) www.tnp.org (accessed January 9, 2011).

Wangmo, Jamyang (2005) *The Lawudo Lama: Stories of Reincarnation from the Mount Everest Region*, Wisdom Publications, Somerville, MA.

Yamaguchi, Zuiho (1996) The fiction of King Dar-ma's persecution of Buddhism, in *Du Dunhuang au Japon: Etudes chinoises et bouddhiques offertes a Michel Soymie*, Jean-Pierre Drege (ed.), Librairie Droz, Geneva, pp. 231–258.

Zangpo, Ngawang (2002) *Guru Rinpoche: His Life and Times*, Snow Lion Publications, Ithaca, NY.

Bibliography

Davidson, Ronald M. (2005) *Tibetan Renaissance: Tantric Buddhism in the Rebirth of Tibetan Culture*, Columbia University Press, New York.

Dreyfus, Georges B.J. (2003) *The Sound of Two Hands Clapping: The Education of a Buddhist Monk*, University of California Press, Berkeley.

Kapstein, Matthew T. (2000) *The Tibetan Assimilation of Buddhism: Conversion, Contestation, and Memory*, Oxford University Press, New York.

Kvaerne, Per (1984) Tibet: The rise and fall of a monastic tradition, in *The World of Buddhism: Buddhist Monks and Nuns in Society and Culture*, Heinz Bechert and Richard Gombrich (eds.), Thames and Hudson, London, pp. 231–270.

Maher, Derek F. (2008) The rhetoric of war in Tibet: Toward a Buddhist just war theory, *Journal of Political Theology* 9(2): 179–191.

Samuel, Geoffrey (1993) *Civilized Shamans: Buddhism in Tibetan Societies*, Smithsonian Institution Press, Washington, DC.

CHAPTER 18
Sangha and Society

Hiroko Kawanami

The very idea of a religious tradition called "Buddhism," which unites the diversity of beliefs and concepts, local practices, and communities throughout much of Asia and the West, is a relatively recent development. The contemporary image of pan-Buddhism emphasizing universal principles of peace, nonviolence, and compassion has emerged in the last half-century in the process of the globalization of Buddhism. Today, a new modernist Buddhism is advocated by Buddhist teachers such as the 14th Dalai Lama of Tibet, Thich Nhat Hanh, a Vietnamese monk, and the late Maha Gosananda of Cambodia, who have all been its popular promoters, appealing to the international community with universal principles. However, contrary to its tranquil outward image, Buddhist countries – including Cambodia, Burma/Myanmar, Sri Lanka, Japan, China, and Tibet – have suffered violent political conflicts in modern Asian history, and Buddhists have experienced their own share of brutality and suffering. In various stages of national development, Buddhist faith in Asian countries has seen diverse expressions in the public arena. It has given its adherents a specific worldview, an ethical code of conduct, and a moral resource to assert a national identity, especially during the colonial rule and struggle for independence, and even a rationale to impose hegemony on others to the extent of justifying the use of violence. The monastic community, called the Sangha, has traditionally given Buddhists a moral foundation, legitimation, and security, but in its role as a public vehicle to articulate people's sentiments, it has in some contexts promoted a particular religious agenda detrimental to other faiths and ethnic groups.

It may be the aspiration of all Buddhists to achieve a harmonious and rounded life, dedicated to nonviolence as a means to liberate themselves from suffering. At the same time, Buddhists regard human beings as prone to ignorance, self-centeredness, greed, anger, and hatred – propensities that make it easy for people to make poor decisions, which in turn cause suffering (directly or indirectly). To counteract these negative

---

The Wiley Blackwell Companion to Religion and Social Justice, First Edition. Edited by Michael D. Palmer and Stanley M. Burgess.
© 2012 John Wiley & Sons Ltd. Published 2020 by John Wiley & Sons Ltd.

human propensities, Buddhists encourage people to develop mindfulness, compassion, and wisdom. The moral endeavor to overcome the causes of suffering is what is believed to sustain the notion of justice in society. Numerous ethical guidelines shape the moral decisions that Buddhists make, but chief among them is the precept of "non-harm." This precept calls attention to the sacredness of life and encourages a virtuous outlook that inclines one not to inflict harm on others. However, as we shall see, in Buddhist engagement with issues that concern the collective interests of society, there have been many expressions of radical activism that contravene this fundamental principle.

One Chinese author wrote, "Justice is like colored balls in a magician's hand, changing color and shape all the time, beneath the light of politics" (Qiu Xiaolong, 2000: 352–353). Buddhist monks in particular have been at the forefront of protest movements. On June 11, 1963, Thich Quang Duc, a Vietnamese monk, burnt himself to death in the lotus position at a downtown intersection in Saigon, and his example was soon followed by several Buddhist monks in their attempt to call attention to the political oppression and suffering endured by the Vietnamese people. Many more went on hunger strikes and staked their lives to protest against the injustice and violence inflicted on them. Monks, due to their unique position at the intersection of this-worldly and other-worldly concerns, have been prominent in public protests as well as in conflict resolution, promoting dialogue between warring groups and factions. Nonetheless, in the context of war, nationalism, and political conflict, they have also found themselves thrust into situations that forced them to adopt a political stance, in either opposing the regime or siding with it. This essay examines how the notion of justice is apprehended by the Sangha and society by introducing examples from recent events in Sri Lanka and Myanmar, and raises the fundamental question as to whether justice is ultimately compatible with the Buddhist principle of non-harm.

What Is the Sangha?

The Sangha, which originally meant "assembly," was established soon after the Buddha attained enlightenment over two and a half millennia ago. Initially, it was a loose grouping of wondering ascetics who lived in forests and practiced meditation and austerities. These "homeless" mendicants gradually took up residence in large monasteries built by lay supporters. Fraternities of monks developed out of monastery schools, and transactions with society became very much part of their religious lives. In the middle ages the Sangha changed its nature to become a monastic institution with defined objectives, a set of monastic rules, and a concrete status structure (Ishii, 1986: 5–6). Buddhist kings, who saw the benefit of having a solid moral foundation for the state, acted as "supreme defenders of faith," and the Sangha developed under royal patronage. However, monks suffered from the loss of their traditional patrons as kings were deposed under the colonial administration in the nineteenth century, which resulted in a spiritual vacuum, sectarianism, and fragmentation of the Sangha. Moreover, the changing social and political climate in the twentieth century placed new demands on the Sangha to be more socially engaged; thus monks could no longer concentrate on religious matters that concerned only their "salvation."

Buddhism in the Theravādin tradition adhered to in countries in south and southeast Asia is referred to as Sāsana, normally translated as "Dispensation" or "message," implying the Buddha's doctrinal legacy preserved in the Pāli canon and embodied in the Sangha. Southern Buddhists take pride in the Sangha, which has survived over the centuries with minimal change to its institutional structure and they regard their tradition as uncorrupted and closest to its earliest forms. In the face of predictions that the Buddha's Sāsana would eventually decline, this concept has given them in particular a sense of collective destiny and a self-perception of being the "true" custodians of Buddhism. The Sangha in particular has played an important role in reinforcing this sense of religious pride by promoting itself as a unifying cultural symbol and asserting moral leadership in times of national crises.

Eastern Buddhists as well as western Buddhists, however, regard the traditional Sangha as elitist, male centered, and even anachronistic in its mode of living, especially because it excludes female members from positions of authority. One of the largest Buddhist organizations in the West, Friends of Western Buddhist Order, established in the 1960s in the United Kingdom, has promoted an inclusive view of the Sangha so that members do not have to renounce their secular status to become part of the community. The Sangha in a nontraditional context has had to change in order to make the community more accessible to new Buddhist adherents, who do not always appreciate the traditional implications of monasticism. Nonetheless, hundreds and thousands of monks adhering to a lifestyle of sexual abstinence, nonpossession, and nonpleasure continue to be supported by lay congregations in a large area of southeast Asia, south Asia, and regions of the Himalayas, and the Sangha continues to provide a focal point for their Buddhist activities.

Monastic Rules, Precepts, and Morality

Buddhist monks are revered and admired by Buddhist laypeople not only because they are learned and authoritative, but because they strictly adhere to the moral conduct regulated by the Vinaya. The Vinaya is a set of monastic rules and regulations: 227 rules in the Theravādin Vinaya in southeast Asia; 250 in the Dharmaguptaka Vinaya followed in China, Japan, Korea, and Taiwan; and 253 in the Mūlasarvāstivāda tradition adhered to in Tibetan Buddhism. Some of these rules were laid down originally by the Buddha to achieve a harmonious community so that his disciples could concentrate on the task of disseminating his "message." They were systematically compiled later to govern minute details of daily conduct in transactions among themselves and with the wider society. The celibate lifestyle in particular was instituted as a way to impose control on members and to focus their energy on the collective ideals of the Sangha. The Sangha, a democratic institution run on the seniority principle, is required to regularly hold a disciplinary ritual to recite the Pātimokka rules and its members confess to each other if any of the rules were transgressed. The gravest offences (called Pārājika), which include the violation of celibacy rules, murder of parents, falsely claiming to possess supra-mundane powers, and inciting schism in the Sangha, merit expulsion from the community.

While monks are encouraged to study and meditate, lay Buddhists are expected to observe the Five Precepts (refraining from killing or harming life, stealing, sexual misconduct, lying, and taking intoxicants) and to endorse ethical ways of living that maintain a harmonious relationship in society. In this way, although monks and lay Buddhists adhere to a different set of ethical rules, there is an interdependent relationship that sustains the foundation of Buddhist worship. Lay devotees also take additional vows such as celibacy, fasting in the afternoon, and abstaining from drinking alcohol, dancing, and singing on special religious days. Modesty, restraint, simplicity, and mindful deportment are also integrated as essential components of normative ethical behavior.

The common view in Buddhism is that morality is instrumental in achieving higher wisdom and that if one follows its ethical code, developing compassion and nonattachment, among many virtuous traits, one can embark on the right path toward final liberation. As one learns to cultivate virtues and progresses on the prescribed moral ladder, ethical choices are expected to become increasingly less difficult. Every intentional act is believed to have its karmic consequences. Thus Buddhists reason that one's present state in the cosmic and social hierarchy is the result of one's past deeds. For example, a monk in his superior state of detachment is regarded as having achieved this state as a result of his past meritorious deeds. Similarly, a beggar has earned precisely the state in which he finds himself. Therefore, those presently endowed with fortune, health, beauty, or position of power are seen to be reaping the result of past actions and accrued merit. Likewise, the poor and the needy have achieved what they deserve. These results may appear to be unfair to those unfamiliar with the Buddhist logic, but Buddhists accept their lot and devote themselves either to offsetting the store of demerit or enhancing the karmic store by following the ethical guidelines. To them, karma is not a static concept that confines one to a given state, but seen as a dynamic process in which one has to work continuously toward improving one's moral position. And although the karmic process may take much longer than one life, justice carried out as the consequence of one's action, either positive or negative, is believed eventually to catch up.

Sangha and Society

In Buddhist countries, especially in the southern tradition, the monastic community has provided education and social mobility for bright and ambitious boys from rural areas. It is still customary for boys from Buddhist families to spend a few weeks as novices in monasteries, and adults also become ordained temporarily to spend their time in quiet contemplation. Sometimes a male enters the monastery before marriage or conscription as a transitional stage in life. In recent decades, it has become acceptable for girls in Myanmar to become temporary nuns, but it was never normative for a woman to become a nun in Buddhist societies. The most meritorious act for her is to send her son into the Sangha. In monasteries, children are taught the fundamentals of

Buddhist morality: both the merits of acceptable behavior in society and karmic retribution that follows from unacceptable and immoral deeds. From a young age, they learn to respect the monks and senior members in society; to lay prostrate in front of them; and to speak with honorific vocabularies. They are also taught to overcome selfish impulses and desires, which would result in antisocial consequences and human suffering. In this way, children are taught to value Buddhist ethics and to internalize the habits associated with becoming a responsible adult.

Members of the monastic community, especially monks, are seen by the laity as a supreme "field for merit." *Visuddhimagga*, a Buddhist commentary written by Buddhaghosa, a Ceylonese monk in the fifth century, states that the Sangha is "worthy of offerings, of oblations, of gifts, and of reverential salutation, the world's peerless field of merit" (1923: 252). Obviously, not all monks are worthy, but the Sangha is generally seen as a symbol of other-worldly virtues whose members are expected to be righteous and law-abiding. For a lay householder, the ultimate goal of nirvana (a state or condition free from all suffering and misery) is regarded as virtually unattainable in a single lifetime. Thus the support that he or she gives to the monastic community is believed to be the best way to enhance the chances of a better rebirth. Ishii explains, "offerings and alms given to the Sangha are believed to be the most effective means of gaining happiness, or more correctly, of enhancing one's position in the cosmic hierarchy" (1986: 17). Supported by lay devotees and society, monks can focus their efforts on religious work such as meditation, learning the scriptures, as well as conducting ritual and giving moral advice to the laity whenever required. In this way, the interlocking of these two distinct worlds – Sangha and society – functions as a prerequisite for achieving the respective goals of both parties, maintaining a complementary system for religious worship.

Buddhism and the State

Buddhism involves a deeply ingrained sense of natural order grounded in the cosmic order of the universe, and concepts such as state, social order, and hierarchy are all imbued with profound symbolic meanings. Buddhist monarchs in the history of south and southeast Asia have upheld the ideal of *dharmaraja*, a "righteous king," and looked to the model of King Asoka in the third century BCE. Asoka was known to have renounced military force and aggression on converting to Buddhism and became a respected ethical king. Following his model, the Buddhist king was expected to be righteous and just, to adhere to the principles of nonaggression and generosity, and ensuring the moral purity of the Sangha. In return, monks provided him with an important legitimating principle that gave moral stability to the country.

Buddhist countries in Asia do not share the social and intellectual trajectory of European Enlightenment in the West, deriving from the Christian belief in the fundamental equality and rights of man granted by God. Buddhist soteriology originated in a rigidly stratified society in ancient India, and although emerging out of the Buddha's critique of the hereditary model of Brahmanism, there has been little questioning of the royal and ecclesiastical power of the king. Even after Buddhist monarchs were forced into exile or effectively removed by the colonial powers in the nineteenth century, Buddhist kingship retained its mythical status, revered as the symbolic linchpin in society and almost sacrosanct in the popular belief. In Thailand, which is one of the few remaining countries with a continuous line of Buddhist kings, the monarch, although now constitutional in position, continues to reside at the apex of society, revered as almost godlike by the public. The present king, Bhumibol, commonly known as King Rama the 9th, is the longest-serving monarch in Thailand. He has presided over almost 30 prime ministers (many of them army generals) during his reign since 1946 and also used his royal influence to resolve political conflicts and mitigated many coup attempts. The king in his role is expected to establish a coterminous relationship between the state and Sangha, and to safeguard peace and prosperity for the people.

It is deeply problematic, however, if the political ruler violates his moral duties, bringing disorder and forfeiting his position of righteousness. In the eyes of Buddhists, even royal power has to be exercised justly, since everyone is entitled to fair treatment before the *dharma*. If the king does not fulfill his designated honorable role, the role expected of a monarch, his subjects are, at least in principle according to Buddhist scriptures, entitled to remove him. The notion that everyone is endowed with a different moral position in the cosmic and social hierarchy has stipulated the notion of social duty and responsibility, providing guidelines for acceptable behavior in sustaining social order.

Sangha in Sri Lanka

In Sri Lanka (formerly Ceylon), the long history of colonial domination and challenges of Christian missionaries hostile to Buddhism led to a revivalist movement uniting the Sinhala Buddhists and resulting in a new Buddhist awareness in the early twentieth century. (Sinhalese, who are Buddhists and speak the Sinhala language, are the majority ethnic group of Sri Lanka.) Buddhism's modernist orientation emphasized the rational and philosophical features of Buddhist teachings and played down so-called superstitious practices condemned by missionaries, in an attempt to present Buddhism as a united religious tradition that could stand up to modern demands. Such modernist ideals were further refined by Anagāriaka Dharmapala – half monk, half lay Buddhist activist – who wore a mendicant robe and lived a celibate lifestyle of nonpossession. Influenced by the social ideals of the Theosophical Society, he imbued monks with a sense of social responsibility by promoting this-worldly objectives and practical goals. Despite the general view that monks should not be involved in politics on the grounds that doing so would undermine their other-worldly status, Buddhist monks in Sri Lanka emerged as a forceful and articulate group during the nationalist struggle in the 1940s. In their unique position, they could appeal to the Sinhala sentiments for self-determination and foster a sense of collective mission by drawing from their ancient religious and cultural tradition. The respected scholar Walpola Rahula was one of the monk leaders who combined leftist politics and Buddhist scholarship, advocating the view that it was within the remit of the Sangha to oppose measures detrimental to the "common good." He endorsed the right of monks to identify with public affairs that were conducive to the general welfare of the people and publicly justified their political activism in the decolonization process (Tambiah, 1992: 25–26). However, Rahula did not realize then that the same argument of religious patriotism could be applied in the postindependence period to assert Sinhala majority rule and eliminate ethnic minorities who did not share their Buddhist cultural heritage in Sri Lanka.

The modern construction of Sinhala Buddhist identity had its source in the political appropriation of *Mahāvamsa* (the Great Chronicle), which was a historical text with mythological components that carried canonical authority for Sinhala Buddhists. This text narrates stories of heroic ancient kings such as King Dutthagamani, who defended the island of *Dharma* from the threat of *damilas* (foreign influences); in other words, the Tamils. Bartholomeusz (2002: 34), who has examined the effect of religious narratives in shaping people's moral views, states that *Mahāvamsa*, which uplifted the perception of the island to an almost divine status, effectively gave rise to "Buddhist fundamentalism" in Sri Lanka. The perpetuation of the notion of "chosen people" in its mythological history has made Sinhala Buddhists believe that they were entrusted with a mission to conserve and protect the Sāsana, giving rise to a strongly chauvinistic trend in Buddhism. The aspirations to protect and promote Buddhism and the nationalist sentiments were fused from early on in Sri Lankan politics, giving supremacy to the rights of Sinhala Buddhists that seems to have subsequently polarized the population.

Out of a population of 20 million Sri Lankans, Sinhalese-speaking Buddhists make up almost 75%; 18% are Tamil minority, mostly Hindus; and the rest are Muslims, Christians, and animists. Since independence in 1948, successive governments have enacted policies in the course of nation building that aimed at preferential treatment of the Sinhala Buddhist majority. The religious rhetoric of *dharma yuddhaya* (dharma war or righteous war) came to be used frequently after Prime Minister Bandaranaike was assassinated by an angry Buddhist monk on September 26, 1959. Bandaranaike had earlier campaigned on a "Sinhala-only" policy, but shifted his position to comply with some of the Tamil demands. Tambiah says that achieving Sinhalese national unity was a recurring theme in the political discourse since the time of the Buddhist revival movement in the early twentieth century (1992: 105). Some monks, who were against any form of devolution to grant regional autonomy to the Tamils, justified the use of violence by fanning religions sentiment for unification. They called on the Sinhala population to take action against the Tamil separatists and encouraged them to "meet one violence with another" in their fight to protect Buddhism and the Island (Bartholomeusz, 2002: 68). It seems that the Sangha took its role as "defender of the faith" rather seriously. The monks' inflammatory rhetoric incited fear of the "other" among the Buddhist majority, and their appeal for self-preservation exacerbated a religious fervor that prevailed in the political discourse during the height of armed conflict with the Tamils in the 1980s and 1990s.

Although Sinhalese Buddhists had enjoyed political dominance since independence, the Tamils were not newcomers to the island, having lived and shared its history since as early as the second century BCE. As a result of a state policy that promoted majority rights, however, Buddhism was given a prominent position and Sinhala became the official language alongside English. In contrast, Tamils were excluded from power and marginalized socially; their language was removed from state education; and Tamil youths who were denied access to higher education joined militant organizations such as the Liberation Tigers of Tamil Eelam (LTTE), established in 1976. When the temple in Kandy that enshrined the holy Buddha's tooth relic was bombed in 1983, the conflict developed into a full-scale civil war. The incident enraged the monks, who became even more vocal in their religio-political rhetoric in supporting the use of violence against the Tamil aggressors (Bartholomeusz, 2002: 8). The notion of "just religious war," derived from the urge to fulfill a religious duty to protect the island and Sinhala sovereignty, became openly endorsed by senior monks, and in this respect Buddhism became appropriated by politically defined ends. A vicious cycle of violence ensued for almost 30 years, which came to an abrupt end in May 2009 when the Sri Lankan Army offensive shelled the strip of narrow coastline where the remnants of Tiger resistance were trapped and killed off the last Tamil opposition. The war, which resulted in hundreds of casualties and the displacement of almost one million Tamils, was completely unjustifiable from the Tamil point of view.

Sangha in Myanmar

Monks in Myanmar have been at the forefront of protest movements and have rallied resistance at many critical junctures in modern history. Following the conquest by the British, they resisted the deposal of the last Buddhist king in 1885 and the separation of religion and state that followed. Since then, monks participated prominently in political protests in the 1920s and 1930s, during the struggle for independence in the 1940s, and in the nationwide uprising during 1988–1990. Successive governments have gone to great lengths both to harness the Sangha and to sideline monks from the country's social and political affairs, depriving them of voting rights in the Constitution of 1974 and in the draft Constitution of 2008. However, as recent demonstrations have made clear, monks have continued to be at the forefront of protest movements and involved themselves actively in the country's political process.

Today, in a population of 50 million, more than 85% of Myanmar's people are Buddhists, including some of the ethnic minority groups: Shans, Mons, Karens, and Arakanese. Myanmar Buddhism belongs to the older school of Theravādin, meaning the "way of the elders," and adheres to a tradition that upholds monasticism as its moral and religious foundation. There is a large contingent of Buddhist monks, estimated at almost half a million, and 40 000 nuns. An interdependent relationship exists between the monastic members and lay Buddhists: monks and nuns are dependent on their lay donors for material support and they in turn conduct rituals and provide moral guidance to their lay congregation.

In a vacuum of social and legal infrastructure, censored speech, and curtailed freedom, the monastic community has functioned as a voice that informs public life in Myanmar society. For advice and leadership, people look up to monks and nuns, who are viewed as nonpartisan and just, with a combined spirit of independence and compassion. In their capacity as public venues, monasteries have also brought people together from all walks of life and provided safe havens for open political discussions. Therefore, although monks and nuns are not invested with civil and political rights, they have been very much part of civil society. Whenever there is conflict in the locality, monks are summoned to mediate or resolve it, since the authorities are often absent or incompetent to deal with problems on the street. The participation of a large number of monks in times of political crises and natural disasters is seen as not only reassuring but almost indispensable for preventing cities from descending into anarchy in the absence of appropriate social infrastructure.

The military regime, on the other hand, has devoted considerable resources since the early 1990s to rebuilding its relationship with the monastic community and to legitimating its political foundation. Attention was directed at historically important monuments and sacred pagodas to promote the cultural and religious heritage of the country (see Schober 2005). In addition, the government took on an active role to reward both monks and nuns for their contribution to the Sāsana by granting them honorary titles in elaborate state-sponsored ceremonies. The regime, as Houtman has pointed out, has been especially concerned about the charismatic monks, whose popularity was seen to threaten and "erode the regime's control over the country" (Houtman, 1999: 121). In order to dissipate their influence and popularity, the military rulers adopted a hands-on policy intended to appease as well as control the Sangha. The plan was to acknowledge the religious work of the monks, with an overall intention of diffusing the potential tension that could destabilize the country.

Events in 2007

In September 2007, many thousands of Buddhist monks began marching in Yangon, Myanmar's former capital and largest city. Monks, who live by receiving alms from the general public and who witnessed the country's economic hardship by the decreasing food intake in their begging bowls, started to protest in sympathy with the people against the sudden increases in costs of public transport, staples, and oil, which were causing distress and impoverishment. The protests were triggered by an alleged beating of a monk by local council officials in the northern town of Pakokku. Angered by the aggression of the officials toward their fellow monk, the monks held some of them hostage and demanded a public apology. When no apology was forthcoming from the authorities, the monks launched protests, which soon spread to other cities. Pakokku, a small provincial town, is an important center for monastic learning with many large monastery schools. Through its network of monastic students and alumni, word spread within days to monks in Yangon, Mandalay, and other parts of the country, including the states of Shan, Mon, and Arakan, which further alarmed the authorities. Senior monks remained resolutely silent despite repeated requests from the authorities to intervene. Their silence sent a clear signal to junior monks and students, who are fiercely loyal to their teachers, that they condoned their active political engagement.

As monks led the demonstrations, ordinary people lined the streets forming a long chain of arms to protect them from violence inflicted by soldiers. Monks walked with overturned begging bowls to show their defiance and refused to accept food or donations from soldiers or anyone related to the military. This tactic, called *patta nikkujjana kamma* in the Pali language, meaning "excommunication," deprived the aggressors of any chance to accumulate merit and spread a powerful message in a Buddhist culture where merit making is considered essential for achieving a better rebirth. In fact, this was seen as the ultimate moral rebuke, implying that the monks no longer wished to be recipients in the "field of merit." As a result, the military regime and families of government officials could no longer sow the seeds for future prosperity. The monks' action threatened effectively to remove the condition that sustained the religious foundation of political power. More than 100 000 people took to the streets in the hope of bringing down a repressive regime. As demonstrations gained momentum, video images of defiant citizens started to seep out to the international media through internet and satellite connections, which unsettled the generals to the core. Soon after, the army moved in, targeting primarily the monks, whom they considered to be the instigators, by beating and arresting them. One monk said: "Raiding the monasteries is like raping Buddhism. This is an unspeakable offense against the religion (Sāsana)" (Human Rights Watch, 2009: 39). The brutality and violence, and especially the lack of sensitivity toward their religious symbols, appalled the Myanmar population.

The protests were quelled quickly under heavy army presence and showed the limitations of the Sangha as an effective opposition movement. Nevertheless, the disciplined and nonviolent manner in which the monks conducted themselves raised their public profile as the moral conscience of the people, both in Myanmar and in the international community. And although unintentionally from its point of view, the Sangha has come to represent an alternative power base for the people and a potential challenge to the military regime.

Conclusion

The monks in Myanmar were probably spurred into political activism by a deep sense of crisis that engulfed them, that unless they as custodians of the Buddhist religion took the initiative, the unstable political and harsh economic situation under the present regime would precipitate a further decline of the Sāsana and lead to more suffering for their people. However, their religious aspirations and ideals being ultimately world renouncing, monks could not have served the political objectives of the public and instigate a regime change. Nevertheless, recent incidents show how a religious faith embedded in the moral fabric of society can challenge an oppressive regime and even threaten to destabilize it. Ironically, this was made possible because both Sangha and the state, although in opposition, shared fundamental religious values, understood the consequence of their actions, and upheld a vision of a unified Buddhist state. Interestingly, the chants recited by monks throughout the demonstration were directed at the well-being of the whole nation, sending out *mettā* (loving-kindness) to safeguard against aggression and solicit protection for their fellow participants in a turbulent situation surrounded by armed soldiers. Myanmar monks steadfastly adhered to the principle of non-harm, both in upholding the dignity of the Sangha and in standing as a symbol of Buddhist resistance.

The Sri Lankan case reveals another face of Buddhism. The combined ideology of nationalism, religious patriotism, and ethnicity has promoted a particular type of militant Buddhism, with monks employing political rhetoric to promote violence at the expense of the non-Sihala and non-Buddhist population. Unfortunately, in contemporary Sri Lanka this tactic reduced justice to a narrow concept applicable only to the Buddhist segment of the population. This case raises two questions. First, can the concept of *Dharma* war ever be reconciled with Buddhist principles, since the first precept that prohibits killing or harming of life under any circumstances remains the core principle of social justice for Buddhists? Second, can the concept of justice be widely applied to non-Buddhists, people whose well-being in this case was not given due consideration? It is conceivable that Sinhala Buddhist monks were spurred into an aggressive stance by an impending sense of crisis and an instinct for self-preservation. However, their behavior suggests a more sinister motive and shows clearly that Buddhist monks do not always act on lofty moral principles that elevate them above worldly politics. In Sri Lanka, at least, monks endorsed a morally dubious militant campaign on the cynical pretext of protecting the interests of their "own people," and Buddhism in this case has served only to legitimate a partisan political cause.

One may say that monks are only human. Without the traditional system of checks and balances offered by Buddhist kingship or political authorities looking after the interests of monks, the Sangha is always in danger of compromising its position as a symbol of Buddhist moral values. For an ideal relationship of interdependency and mutual benefit between Sangha and society to be achieved, much depends on the Buddhist monks both expressing publically and living out their best moral ideals following the monastic guidelines. However, as more demands are placed on the Sangha to be both above politics and also active in social affairs that concern the interests of its lay constituents, monks increasingly labor under the pressure to find a right balance in their engagement with society. Many see a positive contribution of Buddhism when the internal quest for spiritual perfection and the external pursuit for social justice are interlinked. When the monks are virtuous and wise, they provide society with a moral foundation for social cohesion and stability. But if they misappropriate their position of authority to benefit only Buddhists, they introduce instability into society. After all, in Buddhism one is made to realize the working of karma, according to which everyone reaps the consequence of their actions, and the doctrine of dependent origination (*paticca samupāda*), according to which all beings are interdependent. If one accepts the premise of such interdependence, then in the long term the common good, liberty, and social justice may become realized not only as one's own interest but as everyone's right.

References

Bartholomeusz, Tessa J. (2002) *In Defense of Dharma: Just-War Ideology in Buddhist Sri Lanka*, Routledge Curzon, London.

Buddhaghosa (1923) *The Path of Purity (Visuddhimagga)*, Pe Maung Tin (trans.), Pali Text Society, London.

Houtman, Gustaaf (1999) *Mental Culture in Burmese Crisis Politics: Aung San Suu Kyi and the National League for Democracy*, Institute for the Study of Languages and Cultures of Asia and Africa, Tokyo.

Human Rights Watch (2009) The resistance of the monks: Buddhism and activism in Burma, *Human Rights Watch Report*, 22 September, http://www.hrw.org/en/reports/2009/09/22/resistance-monks (accessed April 19, 2011).

Ishii, Yoneo (1986) *Sangha, State, and Society: Thai Buddhism in History*, Peter Hawkes (trans.), University of Hawaii Press, Honolulu.

Qiu Xiaolong (2000) *Death of a Red Heroine*, Soho Press, New York.

Tambiah, Stanley J. (1992) *Buddhism Betrayed? Religion, Politics, and Violence in Sri Lanka*, University of Chicago Press, Chicago.

Bibliography

Deegalle, Mahinda (ed.) (2006) *Buddhism, Conflict and Violence in Modern Sri Lanka*, Routledge, London.

Gombrich, Richard F. and Gananath, Obeyesekere (1988) *Buddhism Transformed: Religious Change in Sri Lanka*, Princeton University Press, Princeton.

Keown, Damien (ed.) (2000) *Contemporary Buddhist Ethics*, Curzon, Richmond.

King, Sallie B. (2005) *Being Benevolence: The Social Ethics of Engaged Buddhism*, University of Hawaii Press, Honolulu.

Schober, Juliane (2005) Buddhist visions of moral authority and civil society: The search for the post-colonial state in Burma, in *Burma at the Turn of the Twenty-First Century*, Monique Skidmore (ed.), University of Hawaii Press, Honolulu, pp. 113–132.

CHAPTER 19

G'meelut Chasadim (Deeds of Kindness)

W. E. Nunnally

The Hebrew phrase *g'meelut chasadim* is an idiomatic phrase that may be translated loosely as "kind deeds" and even more loosely as "good works." It evidently originated in Palestine within Pharisaic/rabbinic circles. Although it does not appear in the Hebrew Bible and many later Jewish works, it is well attested in Rabbinic literature (written material generated in the schools of the rabbis in antiquity). The phrase is used to refer to the good deeds of truly righteous Jews who performed them with the proper attitude and motivation. Foremost among these behaviors were actions taken on behalf of those in need (Babylonian Talmud Sanhedrin 104a: "For thus is the way of the doers of *g'meelut chasadim*: to run after the poor"). Among the most ancient statements preserved in Rabbinic Literature is the statement of Simeon the Righteous (fourth to third century BCE), "By three things the world is upheld: by the Torah, by the temple service, and by *g'meelut chasadim*" (Mishnah Avot 1:2). That this teaching was attributed to an authority as early and as revered as Simeon is a testimony to the importance the early Jewish community placed on these acts of kindness. Some five centuries later, Rabbi Judah (head of the Sanhedrin and compiler of the Mishnah, the first collection of Rabbinic literature to attain written form) declared that anyone who neglected to perform *g'meelut chasadim* was actually neglecting the cardinal doctrine of Judaism (Ecclesiastes Rabba 7.1.4). Other rabbinic authorities opined that those who do not practice *g'meelut chasadim* are not even fit to be members of the Jewish community (Babylonian Talmud Yevamot 79a). Rabbinic leaders would go on to declare that "the Torah begins with *g'meelut chasadim* and ends with *g'meelut chasadim*" (Babylonian Talmud Sotah 14a).

Actions that Constitute *G'meelut Chasadim*

Quite the opposite of a vague attitude or philosophy of life, the phrase *g'meelut chasadim* came to include certain specific, almost stereotypical actions toward those in need.

Among these actions were clothing the naked, feeding the hungry, burying the dead (cf. Tobit 1:16–20, 2:2–8, 14, 4:7b–11, 16–17, 12:8b, 9b, 13; Josephus Antiquities of the Jews 1:14–21, etc.), dowering the bride of a poor family, visiting the sick, showing hospitality to travelers, and giving alms to the poor (see later in this essay). The Talmuds distinguish between mere almsgiving and *g'meelut chasadim*, explaining that almsgiving only involves the giving of money, whereas *g'meelut chasadim* involves the giving of money and of oneself (Babylonian Talmud Sukkah 49b; Jerusalem Talmud Peah 1:1). Because *g'meelut chasadim* was much more comprehensive in scope than almsgiving, the early rabbis concluded that it was the greater of the two (Babylonian Talmud Sukkah 49b).

Almsgiving

Of all the categories of *g'meelut chasadim* listed above, by far the most prominent among them is the Jewish practice of *tsadakah* or "almsgiving." The principles on which this institution was based can be found in the Law of Moses. Legislation contained in the Torah had already made mandatory the support of the poor and the vulnerable of Israelite society at a time when farming was the predominant trade. Thus, the form such support took is expressed in passages like Leviticus 19:9–10:

> Now when you reap the harvest of your land, you shall not reap the very corners of your field, neither shall you gather the gleanings of your harvest. Nor shall you glean your vineyard, nor shall you gather the fallen fruit of your vineyard; you shall leave them for the needy and for the stranger. I am the LORD your God. (cf. also Leviticus 23:22)

Deuteronomy 24:19–22 adds:

> When you reap a harvest in your field and have forgotten a sheaf in the field, you shall not go back to get it; it shall be for the alien, for the orphan, and for the widow, in order that the LORD your God may bless you in all the work of your hands. When you beat your olive tree, you shall not go over its boughs again; it shall be for the alien, for the orphan, and for the widow. When you gather the grapes of your vineyard, you shall not go over it again; it shall be for the alien, for the orphan, and for the widow. And you shall remember that you were a slave in the land of Egypt; therefore I am commanding you to do this thing.

The former passage suggests that the motivation for this act of benevolence is rooted in the nature of Israel's God, who is compassionate toward those in need and expects his covenant community to exhibit that same character trait. The latter passage suggests a different but complementary motivation: empathy with the plight of the oppressed because of shared human experience.

However, neither the term "almsgiving" nor the particular practice it represented was popularized by specific commandments in the Hebrew Bible (the Christian "Old Testament"). Rather, it became a prominent feature of Judaism in the Intertestamental Period, largely due to the process of urbanization. During the periods of Greek and

Roman domination of the Jewish people, the demographic trend was toward greater and greater urbanization, which resulted in smaller and smaller percentages of the population owning farmland and producing crops. At the same time, an "artisan" class was developing and increased trade activity was producing more "businessmen." How were Torah-observant members of the Jewish community to obey these commandments when they owned no farmland and had no agricultural produce? Even more important, on what basis could this growing moneyed class help the increasing number of urban poor?

The religious leadership interpreted and applied the principles taught in the Torah passages above to this new situation, and the practice of "almsgiving" was born. The antiquity of the association between the earlier agricultural laws and the resulting practice of almsgiving can be seen in the writings of Philo of Alexandria (circa 20 BCE–circa 50 CE), who noted that almsgiving is a commandment found in the Torah (De Virtutibus 82–85)! The first-century Jewish historian Josephus Flavius (37 to circa 105 CE) also argued that the Torah is superior to the "constitutions" of all other nations, owing to its emphasis on justice, righteousness, and egalitarian nature (Antiquities of the Jews 1: 14–21). As an example, he paraphrases and expands the words of the Torah to say,

> The duty of sharing with others was inculcated by our legislator [Moses] . . . We must furnish fire, water, food to all who ask for them, point out the way, not leave a corpse unburied . . . show consideration even to declared enemies . . . He has given us such a thorough lesson in gentleness and humanity that he does not even overlook animals. (Against Apion 2: 211, 213)

On the other hand, he mentions that "gleaning rights" were still being exercised in his day. He notes with approval the inclusion of all travelers, Jewish or gentile, who were allowed to exercise "gleaning rights" while on their journeys (Antiquities of the Jews 4:234; cf. also 4:235–238; Deuteronomy 23:24–25; Matthew 12:1).

Eventually, however, almsgiving eclipsed the more cumbersome, agriculturally oriented commandments as a means of fulfilling the requirements of the Torah and at the same time providing support for the less fortunate members of Jewish society. In fact, entire tractates of the Mishnah (circa 200 CE, the earliest rabbinic material in written form) are dedicated to detailed discussions of this form of philanthropy.

In contrast, the term *eleamosunae* appears in late, pagan Greek literature and is best translated as "sympathy." It is derived from *eleos*, which is used exclusively to refer to an emotion rather than a moral responsibility to another person. In Jewish literature written in Greek, however, these words are used to reflect the content of Hebrew words like *chesed* ("[deeds of] covenant loyalty"), *rachamim* ("[deeds or expressions of] mercy"), and *tsadakah* (literally, "righteousness," but within the context of benevolent giving, "almsgiving"), all of which refer not to emotions, but to specific actions of help as expressions of covenant loyalty, mercy, love, and compassion toward the less fortunate (cf. Mishnah Avot 1:2, etc.). In Jewish literature written in Greek, the context is almost always religiously motivated charitable giving. It should not be overlooked that these words are also often used to describe the various attributes of God. The intended implication, therefore, is that those who practice properly motivated almsgiving are exhibiting the most prominent characteristics of the deity, a point that is made in many rabbinic texts.

Motivations for the Performance of *G'meelut Chasadim*

Despite the importance Early Judaism placed on these actions, nowhere are they governed by specific scriptures in the Torah. Early rabbinic authorities concluded that the absence of specific biblical legislation on the amount of *g'meelut chasadim* expected was intentional on God's part and intended to amplify rather than restrict their performance (Mishnah Peah 1:1). Further, the origin of *g'meelut chasadim* was intended to be the free will of the person doing such actions rather than obligation arising from requirements. They were to be motivated by love, compassion, and mercy (Babylonian Talmud Sukkah 49b; Bava Batra 10a), and are never to be performed with the intent to receive something back in return (Mishnah Avot 1:3; Tanchuma VaYechi 3). Nor are they to be performed publicly with the intent to impress others with one's piety (Mishnah Shekelim 5:6; Ecclesiastes Rabba 12.14.1; cf. Matthew 6:1–4).

Nevertheless, great rewards were indeed promised to those whose lives produced such actions. Their sins would be forgiven (Avot d'Rabbi Natan A 4); they would be saved from *Gehenna* (a common rabbinic term for "Hell"); they would be freed from the sinful inclination (Babylonian Talmud Avodah Zarah 5b); they would be reconciled with God; and they would be called "sons of God" (Babylonian Talmud Bava Batra 10a; cf. Matthew 5:9, 39–45). Ultimately, they would be ushered into heaven (Midrash Tehilim to Psalm 118:20) and would behold the face of God (Midrash Tehillim to Psalm 17:15; cf. Matthew 5:7–8).

Major Figures and Groups in Jewish History Who Promoted *G'meelut Chasadim*

Hillel the Elder

Perhaps the most important figure in rabbinic times to encourage *g'meelut chasadim* was the great teacher Hillel the Elder. Hillel was born in Babylonia (Tosefta Negaim 1:16; Sifra Tazria 9:16; Babylonian Talmud Pesachim 66a; Sukkah 20a), but came to Israel to pursue Torah study under the greatest teachers of the time: Shemiah and Avtalion (Mishnah Avot 1:12). As a new immigrant to Israel, he was so poor that once he almost froze to death outside the house of study (Babylonian Talmud Yoma 35b). These humble beginnings evidently had a profound impact on Hillel and can be seen in the things he chose to emphasize in his personal life and teaching. Although he was eventually promoted to the presidency of the Sanhedrin (*nasi*) and thus became the head of the Pharisaic movement (Tosefta Pischa 4:13; Jerusalem Talmud Pesachim 6:1; Babylonian Talmud Avodah Zarah 9a; Pesachim 66a), he never lost sight of the days in which he struggled as a poor immigrant. Even after his rise to prominence, Hillel voluntarily chose poverty and earned his living as a common day laborer (Avot d'Rabbi Natan A 6; Babylonian Talmud Sotah 21a; Yoma 35b; cf. Mark 6:3; Matthew 8:20; Acts 18:3; 2 Corinthians 6:10). Rabbinic Literature places the dates of his rule at 30 BCE–10 CE (Babylonian Talmud Shabbat 15a), which makes him a contemporary of Herod the Great and Jesus. Hillel and the "school" he founded eventually played the lead role in forming what would become "normative Judaism" (Babylonian Talmud Eruvin 13b; Sukkah 28a).

Hillel considered love of God and fellow man to be the foundational teaching of the Torah and the fundamental principle of Judaism (Babylonian Talmud Shabbat 31a; cf. Matthew 22:37–40; Galatians 5:14). He taught that the requirement to demonstrate love was rooted in the fact that man is created in the image of God (Leviticus Rabba 34:3; cf. the Hillelite views expressed later in Sifra Kedoshim 4:3; Genesis Rabba 24:7; etc.). He is therefore credited with popularizing an earlier teaching (Tobit 4:15) known today as the "Golden Rule" ("That which is hateful to you do not do to your fellow man. This is the summation of the Torah, and the rest is just a commentary on it. Therefore, go and learn it," Babylonian Talmud Shabbat 31a; cf. Sifra Kedoshim 4:12). Targum Jonathan says that he based this teaching on Leviticus 19:18, "You shall love your neighbor as yourself – I am the LORD." This same foundation of loving fellow human beings based on loving God underlies early Christianity, which points to the same Torah passages for support (Matthew 7:12; 22:36–40; cf. Romans 13:8; Galatians 5:14; 1 John 4:20–21).

Closely related to this is Hillel's teaching that all of life is sacred, and that no distinction should be made between "sacred" activities and "secular" activities. Rather, Hillel taught, "All your deeds should be done for the sake of Heaven," including in the "all" such mundane activities as bathing and relieving oneself (Avot d' Rabbi Natan B 30; Leviticus Rabba 34:3). Therefore, true believers should see every aspect of their lives as opportunities for worship. This teaching alone had tremendous influence on the leaders and literature of early Christianity (Matthew 10:42, 25:34–45; 1 Corinthians 10:31; Ephesians 6:6–8; Colossians 3:17, 22; 1 John 3:17; James 1:27, etc.).

Another foundational principle of Hillel was the pursuit of peace. He taught "Love and pursue peace" and "Increase peace" (Mishnah Avot 1:12, 2: 8; cf. Matthew 5:9; Romans 12:18; Ephesians 2:17). Hillel overcame his adversaries by gentleness and humility (Babylonian Talmud Eruvin 13b) and even lowered himself to the position of a slave in order to serve his fellow man (Tosefta Peah 4:10; Babylonian Talmud Ketubot 67b; cf. John 13:4–17; Philippians 2:5–7). This approach to conflict may have been learned from his teachers, Shemiah and Avtalion, who advised making peace with Herod the Great when he was besieging Jerusalem (Josephus, Antiquities of the Jews 15: 1–3). Under this influence, his students taught, "Thus if someone curses [you, then you] should answer with the blessing, 'Peace be upon you'" (Kallah Rabbati 3; cf. Matthew 5:44; Luke 6:28; Romans 12:14). His premier student Yochanan ben Zakkai taught,

> He who establishes peace between man and his fellow man, between husband and wife, between city and city, between nation and nation, between family and family, between government and government should be protected so that no harm should come upon him. (Mekhilta d'Rabbi Ishmael BaChodesh 11)

Because of his consistent pursuit of humility and peace, numerous scholars on this period have seen Hillel as the antitype to the egocentric, despotic, violent, oppressive, worldly ruler, Herod the Great.

In practical application, these foundational principles required that Hillel emphasize leniency in judgment (Mishnah Avot 2:5). He taught a view of divine judgment that within the Academy came to be called "measure for measure" (Mishnah Avot 2:7; Babylonian Talmud Sukkah 53a; cf. Matthew 7:2). In his understanding, if a man exhibited prejudice or was unnecessarily harsh in passing judgment, God would dispense the same measure of judgment back to him. Instead, he taught, "Judge not your fellow man until you have come into his place" and "Judge your fellow man toward the side of the scale of merit [i.e., when in doubt, give the benefit of the doubt to the accused]" (Mishnah Avot 2:5; Derekh Eretz Zuta 3; cf. Matthew 7:1; Romans 14:10). Our modern "presumption of innocence" legal principle is an outgrowth of this approach to jurisprudence.

Further, Hillel set an example of seeking out the poor, sinners, and gentiles, making the way to God as accessible to them as to the righteous (Mishnah Avot 1:12, 2:5; Avot d'Rabbi Natan A 3, B 4, 126; Babylonian Talmud Ketubot 16b; Shabbat 31a; Soferim 16:9). He said, "Be among the disciples of Aaron . . . loving [all] mankind and bringing them near to the Torah" (Mishnah Avot 1:12). He is thus seen as generally more lenient than his more stringent peer Shammai. One way in which the tradition describes the vastly different approaches of these two contemporaries is as follows:

> Raise up many disciples [earlier sages had taught in Mishnah Avot 1:1]. The School of Shammai held that a man should only teach someone who is intelligent and cultured, from a good religious family, and wealthy. The School of Hillel said "Teach all men, because many sinners in Israel were attracted to the study of the Torah and became good people and some even came to be counted among the righteous and the chasidim." (Avot d'Rabbi Natan A 3; cf. Avot d'Rabbi Natan B 4)

Even more to the point, Hillel challenged his fellow scholars to align and interact with the rest of the community, "Do not keep yourself aloof from the community" (Mishnah Avot 2:5; cf. also Tosefta Berachot 2:21). Instead, he encouraged involvement in groups that would band together to do good deeds (Babylonian Talmud Hagigah 9b). In Hillel's private life, he also demonstrated the same concern for the underprivileged. One tradition relates,

> Our rabbis have taught on tannaitic [early rabbinic] authority . . . They say of Hillel the Elder that for a certain poor man of well-to-do parents he bought a horse to ride on and a slave to run before him. Once he couldn't find a slave to run before him, so he ran before him for three miles. (Tosefta Peah 4:10; Babylonian Talmud Ketubot 67b; cf. Matthew 5:41)

Concern for the poor so pervaded the atmosphere of his home that his wife once gave an entire meal that had been prepared specially for his house guest to a poor man who begged food at their door (Derekh Eretz Rabba 6). Hillel taught, "He who multiplies *tsadakah* [religiously motivated benevolent giving to the needy] increases peace" (Mishnah Avot 2:7; cf. Isaiah 32:17). Always a paradigm of balance, however, Hillel also emphasized personal responsibility (Mishnah Avot 1:14).

Gamaliel I

Rabban ["our master"] Gamaliel *HaZaken* ["the elder"] was a grandson of Hillel the Elder who eventually became the head of the School of Hillel. He flourished in the first half of the first century. As leader of the party of the Pharisees, he was the president (*nasi*) of the Sanhedrin (Babylonian Talmud Shabbat 15a). He was the first of only seven authorities in all of rabbinic history to be distinguished by the title *Rabban* ("our teacher/master"). He may thus be understood as the greatest living authority and most revered figure in Judaism during the period 20–50 CE.

As the head of the School of Hillel, Gamaliel was the leader of the most lenient and most popular version of Judaism. In his rulings on matters of Jewish law, he consistently applied his principled leniency to matters of everyday life to ease the burden on women and on the poor. His rulings were commonly based on the guiding principles of "promotion of the common good" and "promoting the ways of peace" (Mishnah Gittin 4:2–3; Rosh HaShanah 2:5; Yevamot 16:7; Orlah 2:12; Babylonian Talmud Ketubot 10b, 28b, etc.). This same benevolent, lenient personality moved a Sanhedrin bent on passing a sentence of death on the apostles to reduce the penalty to mere flogging (Acts 5:34–40).

Like his grandfather Hillel, Gamaliel was responsible for many *takkanot* ("repairs," "corrections," or "adjustments" intended to ease the burden of Torah observance), many of them bearing the formula "for the benefit of humanity." This was especially the case in matters that affected women (Mishnah Gitttin 4:2–3). Although the language of *g'meelut chasadim* is not heard in connection with Gamaliel as often as it is with Hillel, his overall approach to life and his guiding principles strongly suggest that he carried on his grandfather's emphasis on such acts' importance. Further, his student Saul/Paul (cf. Acts 22:3) was clearly an ardent proponent of *g'meelut chasadim* as a means of reflecting the image of God in service to humankind (see under the heading "Early Jewish Christianity").

Yochanan ben Zakkai

Yochanan ben Zakkai (John, the son of Zakkai [pure, innocent, righteous; cf. "Zaccheus" in Luke 19:2–10]) was a rabbinic authority who died circa 80 CE. He was a student of both Hillel and Shammai (Mishnah Avot 2:8; according to rabbinic tradition, Hillel prophesied that Yochanan would be his successor, cf. Jerusalem Talmud Nedarim 5:6; Avot d'Rabbi Natan B 28). Whether this tradition is true or not, it is clear that he became the most influential rabbi of the generation that experienced the crushing defeat of the Jews in the First Revolt (66–73 CE) and the destruction of the temple in Jerusalem (70 CE). Consequently, he is one of only seven rabbinic authorities to be given the honorific title *Rabban* ("our master," versus Rabbi, "*my* master").

As the leader of the Sanhedrin after the temple was destroyed (Babylonian Talmud Gittin 56b), it fell to ben Zakkai to provide leadership and forge a way forward for the Jewish people, who no longer had the benefit of the temple, the priesthood, and the sacrificial system. One issue that came up almost immediately was how sin was to be forgiven and reconciliation with God was to be restored in light of the fact that the sacrificial system was no longer operational. The following story describes the way he resolved the dilemma:

> Once when Rabbi Yochanan ben Zakkai was leaving Jerusalem, Rabbi Joshua was walking behind him and saw the temple in ruins. Rabbi Joshua said, "Woe be unto us that this place has been destroyed, the place where atonement was made for the sins of Israel." [But Rabbi Yochanan ben Zakkai said,] "No my son. Don't you know that we have another means of making atonement that is like it? And what is that? It is kind deeds of covenant loyalty, as it is said, 'For I desire covenant loyalty [*chesed*, a term related to the *chasadim* of *g'meelut chasadim*] and not sacrifice' [Hosea 6:6]." (Avot d'Rabbi Natan A 4)

Amazingly for this time period, Yochanan ben Zakkai appears to have elevated good deeds to a status previously reserved in mainstream Judaism only for the temple sacrifices: now good deeds had the power to bring atonement! In addition, he had the creativity to connect this radical departure back into the ancient tradition with an appropriate proof text. To be sure, before ben Zakkai's time, smaller groups among the Jewish people had already made the paradigm shift from animal sacrifices to the sacrifices of obedience, money, goods, and self (Tobit 4:11, 12:9; 1QS Community Rule 9:4–5; 4Q174 Florilegium/Midrash on the Last Days 3:6b–7a; Acts 10:4, etc.). However, it was left to the genius of ben Zakkai to lead the nation as a whole into this new approach to forgiveness and to bring the performance of *g'meelut chasadim* to the pinnacle of prominence in mainstream Judaism.

In dealing with other matters of established tradition, ben Zakkai showed himself no less innovative. For example, he discontinued the centuries-old practice of requiring wives suspected of adultery to drink the "waters of bitterness" (Mishnah Sotah 9:9, cf. Numbers 5:11–31). The Talmud's explanation for this act suggests that ben Zakkai understood the wives as being no more guilty than the husbands (Babylonian Talmud Sotah 47b; cf. John 8:7). Similarly, he revoked the exemption of the aristocratic priests from paying the half-shekel temple tax (a rabbinic enactment based on Exodus 30:13–16; cf. Matthew 17:24–27), which was required of the common people (Mishnah Shekalim 1:4). Other examples of his concern for equity include his ruling on restitution:

> God shows consideration for the dignity of human beings. [For stealing] an ox, since it walks with its [own] legs, the thief must repay fivefold. [For stealing] a sheep, since he has to carry it on his shoulder, he [only] has to repay fourfold! (Tosefta Bava Kama 7:10; Mekhilta d'Rabbi Ishmael Nezikin 12)

Like his predecessors, in his interpretations and applications of Scripture ben Zakkai demonstrated his emphasis on the doing of good deeds to those in need. Concerning

Proverbs 14:34, "Righteousness exalts a nation, but sin is a disgrace to a people," he provided the contextual paraphrase, "Benevolence [kind deeds of covenant loyalty] on the part of a nation has the atoning power of a sin-offering" (Babylonian Talmud Bava Batra 10b). Interpreting Ecclesiastes 9:8, he stated, "White garments and costly oils are not meant here, for the gentiles have plenty of these. Rather, it speaks only about [fulfillment of] precepts [of the Torah], good deeds, and [Torah] study" (Ecclesiastes Rabba 9.8.1; cf. Avot d'Rabbi Natan A 4, cited in full earlier in this essay). Not content to leave the concept of good deeds in the realm of theory, he once chided impious Jews of his own generation for being unwilling to repair the roads and streets to make the journeys of pilgrims easier as they came to Jerusalem to observe the feasts (Mekhilta d'Rabbi Ishmael BaChodesh 1).

Gamaliel II

Gamaliel II (died prior to 116 CE), also called Gamaliel of Jamnia/Jabneh/Yavneh, succeeded Yochanan ben Zakkai as the head of the Sanhedrin and leader of the Jewish people about 80 CE. He was the grandson of Gamaliel (see earlier in the essay), and great-grandson or great-great-grandson of Hillel (also discussed earlier). As such, he was viewed as royalty, descended from King David, and rightful ruler of the people (Babylonian Talmud Ketubot 62b; Jerusalem Talmud Taanit 4:2; Genesis Rabba 98:8). He too eventually earned the title Rabban ("our master," versus Rabbi, "my master"), a title borne only by himself, his father, his grandfather, Yochanan ben Zakkai, and three others.

In his public life as *nasi* ("president") and head of the Sanhedrin, he evidently viewed positions of leadership not as opportunities to dominate but to serve, "Do not think that dominion is being offered to you. Rather, slavery is being offered to you, perpetual slavery to the needs of your people" (Babylonian Talmud Horayot 10a). Therefore, it is not surprising that Gamaliel II took lengthy trips to many cities around the land of Israel to inquire as to the economic welfare of the Jewish population (e.g., Tosefta Terumot 2:13, etc.). Rabbinic Literature is replete with instances in which he interceded with the Roman government when decrees were issued that would make the lives of the Jewish people more difficult than they already were after the crushing defeat of the First Revolt (Sifre Devarim 43; Jerusalem Talmud Sanhedrin 7:13; Babylonian Talmud Makkot 24a–b; Sotah 49b; Bava Kama 83b; Deuteronomy Rabba 2.24, etc.).

Although not all of Gamaliel's rulings were in favor of the poor and disenfranchised (e.g., Mishnah Peah 6:6), the vast majority of them were. For example, he rescinded a previous rule (Mishnah Sheviit 1:1, cf. 3:8) forbidding plowing in the year prior to the Sabbatical Year (Exodus 23:10–11; Leviticus 25:1–22) and allowed cultivation of the fields in the sixth year (Jerusalem Talmud Sheviit 1:1, 7; cf. Tosefta Sheviit 1:1). He relaxed restrictions on the consumption of stored foodstuffs during the seventh year (Tosefta Sheviit 6:27; Jerusalem Talmud Sheviit 9:3). He encouraged extending rather than limiting the number of times per day that poor people could come into the fields and glean (Mishnah Peah 4:5; cf. Jerusalem Talmud Peah 4:3). He exempted sharecroppers from certain tithes (Mishnah Hallah 4:7; Jerusalem Talmud Hallah 4:4; Maaserot

5:5). In contrast to traditional practice, Gamaliel accepted the testimony of a woman without further proof that she lost her "tokens of virginity" due to an accident and not due to fornication (Mishnah Ketubot 1:6–7). He forbade any Jew from profiting from the theft of a gentile's goods, a practice that was previously allowed (Sifre Devarim 344; Jerusalem Talmud Bava Kama 4:3; Babylonian Talmud Bava Kama 38a). He also rescinded the previous ruling that exempted a Jew from liability if his ox gored the ox of a gentile, recognizing this as unjustly discriminatory (Jerusalem Talmud Bava Kama 4:3). He once reset precedent by giving a gift of bread to a gentile (Tosefta Pischa 2:15; Jerusalem Talmud Avodah Zarah 1:9), which previous rabbinic instruction never allowed (Jerusalem Talmud Avodah Zarah 1:9). Many other rules were changed under his leadership in the direction of making the lives of common people easier (Tosefta Avodah Zarah 3:5; Sotah 15:8; Babylonian Talmud Sotah 49b, etc.).

At one point in his career, Gamaliel II sought to remove the wall of legislation that previous generations had erected to prevent interaction between Jews and Samaritans, going so far as to permit testimony to be received from a Samaritan (Mishnah Gittin 1:5; Tosefta Gittin 1:4). He bemoaned the increase of corrupt judges, perjured witnesses, informers, evil doers, and "seekers of revenge" in the period after the First Revolt (Esther Rabba Proem 9; Babylonian Talmud Makkot 24a).

Events within the personal life of Gamaliel II attest to the same level of concern for the bereaved, the poor, and the marginalized. When a neighbor lost her only son, he wept alongside her until his eyelashes fell out (Babylonian Talmud Sanhedrin 104b; Lamentations Rabba 1.2.24). Other stories depict his deep compassion toward suffering (Babylonian Talmud Shabbat 104b; Lamentations Rabba 1.2.24; Lamentations Zuta 1:2). He was very careful to give the tithe intended for the support of the poor (Mishnah Maaser Sheni 5:9; cf. Jerusalem Talmud Maaser Sheni 4:6; Maaserot 3:4). Gamaliel II loaned money or seed to his impoverished tenants, always receiving back the least possible amount in payment (Mishnah Bava Metsia 5:8; Jerusalem Talmud Bava Metsia 5:6). He extolled the virtues of those who worked with their hands (Tosefta Kiddushin 1:11) at a time when rabbinic authorities were shunning the "working poor." He insisted on being buried in simple attire to reverse the custom of elaborate burial garments that had become burdensome to poor people (the "great takkanah," Tosefta Niddah 9:17; Babylonian Talmud Ketubot 8b). Breaking with the rabbinic conventions of his day, he was even willing to pronounce a blessing on seeing a beautiful gentile woman (Jerusalem Talmud Avodah Zarah 1:9)!

With respect to the affairs of his own home, Gamaliel demonstrated the same principles that governed his public life. He regularly provided food for his day laborers (Tosefta Demai 3:15; Jerusalem Talmud Demai 3:1). He owned slaves, as was common at that time, but he made every effort to honor them (Mishnah Sukkah 2:1) and treated them like members of his own family (Mishnah Berachot 2:7). He set aside an earlier prohibition and required that his slaves be referred to as "Mister So-and-so" and "Madam So-and-so" (Jerusalem Talmud Niddah 1:4; cf. Babylonian Talmud Berachot 16b, which reads "Father So-and-so" and "Mother So-and-so") and was always looking for reasons to liberate them according to the rules of the Torah (Jerusalem Talmud Shebuot 5:6; Babylonian Talmud Bava Kama 74b). He often practiced hospitality, feeding many people (Tosefta Yom Tov 2:13, 14). To model humility, this leader of the nation would take on himself the responsibility of a slave and serve guests, and in so doing is compared favorably in the literature with Abraham and even God Himself (Sifre Devarim 38; Babylonian Talmud Kiddushin 32b).

In all these ways, Gamaliel II consistently demonstrated one of the guiding principles of his life, "As long as you yourself are compassionate, God will show you mercy" (Mishnah Bava Kama 9:30; Tosefta Bava Kama 9:30; Jerusalem Talmud Bava Kama 8:7).

The Essenes

The Essenes were a pre-Christian Jewish sect that, although relatively small in number, were nevertheless held in high esteem by the Jewish population in Palestine. The first-century author Philo of Alexandria tells us:

> They were taught . . . love of God, [love] of virtue, and [love] of man. . . . their love of man [was demonstrated] in their kindliness, their equality, [and] their fellowship passing all words. For no one had his private house, but shared his dwelling with all; and, living as they did in colonies, they threw open their doors to any of their sect who came their way. They had a storehouse, common expenditure, common raiments, common food eaten in common meals. This was made possible by their practice of putting whatever they each earned day by day into a common fund, out of which also the sick were supported when they could not work. (Philo of Alexandria Quod Omnis Probus Liber Sit 83–87)

From Philo's description alone, it would appear that Essenic philanthropy was restricted to members of their sect. The first-century Jewish historian Josephus, however, sheds light in addition to that supplied by Philo, which demonstrates the true extent of the sect's good will. He states, "there is, in every city where they live, one appointed particularly to take care of strangers, and to provide garments and other necessaries for them" (Josephus, History of the Jewish War 2:125). Later in the same passage, he adds that all members of the group are free "to assist those that want it, and to show mercy; for they are permitted of their own accord to afford succor to such as deserve it, when they stand in need of it, and to bestow food on those that are in distress" (Josephus, History of the Jewish War 2:134). The larger context of this passage reveals that the assistance these Essenes were providing was being offered to outsiders, not to members of their own group. Elsewhere, Josephus reinforces the same view of the outward focus of the sect's acts of benevolence: "before he is allowed to touch their common food, he is obliged to take tremendous oaths; that, in the first place, he will exercise piety towards God; and then, that he will do righteousness towards men" (Josephus, History of the Jewish War 2:139).

Therefore, these sectarians were also putting into everyday practice the same philanthropic principles practiced by the members of mainstream Judaism, and the impetus for both groups was the same: the teachings of the Hebrew Bible. Although neither they nor Josephus use the Pharisaic/Rabbinic phrase *g'meelut chasadim* (the Dead Sea Scrolls do employ the root *gamal*, but in an entirely different context) to refer to these good works done toward others, the content and motivations of their actions were the same.

John the Baptist

While John the Baptizer is usually thought of in light of his connection with Jesus and the birth of Christianity, he is actually an intertestamental Jew, who was known and revered by the Jewish community of his contemporaries. The Gospels testify to his popularity among the Jewish population of Palestine (Matthew 3:5, 21:26; Mark 1:5, 11:32; Luke 3:7, 20:6; John 3:23, 25–26), as does the independent Jewish witness Josephus, "others too joined the crowds around [John the Baptist]" and "the verdict of the Jews was that the destruction of Herod's army was a vindication of John" (Antiquities of the Jews 18:118–119).

As an intertestamental Jew, John's teaching mirrors that of other intertestamental Jewish leaders and sects. For example, when the crowds that had come to him for ritual purification and spiritual guidance asked how they were to live as a result of their renewed relationship to God, the Baptizer responded, "Let the man who has two tunics share with him who has none; and let him who has food do likewise" (Luke 3:10–11). Although this passage has no parallel in the other Gospels, it is evidently authentic, since Josephus also attests to the same egalitarian emphasis in John's ethical teaching. He summarizes, "He was a good man and had exhorted the Jews to lead righteous lives, to practice righteousness towards their fellows and piety towards God" (Antiquities of the Jews 18:117). The term "righteousness" in this context is code for "almsgiving," the Greek *dikaiosunase* being a literal translation for the idiomatic Hebrew *tsadakah*. The same idiom appears twice in places like Matthew 6:1–2 and 2 Corinthians 9:7–10, whose contexts refer to benevolent giving to those in need (cf. also Psalm 112:9, etc.).

The Relationship of *G'meelut Chasadim* and Right Standing with God

For the sake of context and perspective, it is appropriate to consider the role played by *g'meelut chasadim* ("good works" or "good deeds") in the process of achieving right standing with God. For more than a century, most of Christian (and especially Protestant) scholarship has understood early Judaism to have been a religion that viewed salvation as the result of human works. Sanders, however, surveyed the entire corpus of early Jewish literature and found that with one possible exception (4 Ezra), Judaism has taught that good works did not accomplish righteousness, but were rather the expected byproduct thereof (Sanders, 1987: 292, 296–298, 382–383, 395–396, 427, 550). In other words, Sanders concluded that in early Judaism as in early Christianity, salvation (right standing with God) was exclusively the result of God's gracious work toward humankind, and that salvation produced good works rather than the other way around.

Early Jewish Christianity

It should come as no surprise, therefore, that early Jewish Christianity adopted the Jewish emphasis on *g'meelut chasadim* wholesale as the only appropriate response to

God's gracious actions toward humankind. It is reflected at every developmental level in the canon of the New Testament. Jesus not only encouraged almsgiving, feeding the hungry, visiting the sick and imprisoned, and care for others in need (Matthew 5:16, 6:3–4, 14:16, 22:39–40, 25:34–40, etc.); he also role-modeled such behavior (Matthew 14:19–21, 15:32–38; Acts 10:38, etc.). Paul and those under his influence promoted the same ethos, presumably influenced by the teachings of Jesus and that of Rabbinic/Pharisaic Judaism (Romans 12:13; 2 Corinthians 8:14, 9:7–8; Galatians 6:9–10; Ephesians 2:10, 4:28; Philippians 2:4; Colossians 1:10; 2 Thessalonians 2:17; 1 Timothy 2:10, 5:10, 6:18; 2 Timothy 2:21, 3:17, Titus 2:7, 14, 3:1, 8, 14, etc.). The remainder of the New Testament likewise reflects the same emphasis (Hebrews 10:24, 13:1–3; James 1:27, 2:14–17; 1 Peter 2:12, 3:13; 3 John 11; Revelation 2:19, etc.).

G'meelut Chasadim in Later and Current Jewish Thought and Practice

As is the case in most other areas of Judaism, current thought and practice have been powerfully shaped by the Hebrew Bible and the traditional teachings of the great sages of Judaism after the biblical period. The same emphases seen in the Hebrew Bible and rabbinic circles were coopted in the later Talmudic, Gaonic, Medieval, Renaissance, and Enlightenment periods, and continue unabated in most segments of modern Judaism today. For example, in the movement known as Kabbalah (Jewish mysticism), it was expected that pious Jews perform charitable acts in order to combat the evil present in the world and to "repair the world" (*tikun-olam*) from its current ills. This motivation can still be seen in the "Alenu" prayer that appears in the Jewish Prayer Book.

Another motivation for *g'meelut chasadim* is noted by Moses ben Maimonides (1135–1204 CE). At one point he writes,

> The perfection in which man can truly glory is attained by him when he has acquired (so far as this is possible for man) the knowledge of God, the knowledge of His providence, and of the manner in which it influences His creatures in their production and continued existence. Having acquired this knowledge, [man] will then be determined always to seek lovingkindness, justice, and righteousness and thus to imitate the ways of God. (Guide of the Perplexed 3:54)

Similarly, the later Kabbalistic author Moses Cordovero (1522–1570 CE) wrote at the beginning of his Tomer Devorah, "It is proper for man to imitate his Creator, resembling Him in both likeness and image [and] the chief Supernal image and likeness is in deeds." In other words, as in other religious expressions such as Christianity, the good deeds of Jews continued to be motivated by the desire to imitate the attitudes and acts of the God they served.

Yet another motive for the performance of good deeds is simply the desire to obey the commands of God as set forth in Scripture. This view is evidenced among all Jewish groups and throughout the various historical periods, and remains a prominent feature of Judaism today. Throughout its literature, the sages of Judaism have consistently taught that there is no special favor or merit that is earned by the performance of good deeds; rather, the Jew who is involved in *tikun-olam* and *g'meelut chasadim* is merely doing his or her duty.

It must be admitted that statements to the contrary can also be found within Jewish literature. From biblical to modern times, the view occasionally heard is that the performance of *g'meelut chasadim* has the capacity to bring divine blessing and even the forgiveness of sins. Such expressions can also be traced back to the Tannaitic Period and figures like Rabban Yochanan ben Zakkai (see earlier in this essay) and are still seen in the Prayer Book, one example being the prayers of the High Holiday liturgy. It must be observed, however, that the desire to gain divine favor is not the only (or even the most prominent) motivation for the doing of good deeds. Again, to draw from the distinction made by Sanders in reference to early Judaism, the primary emphasis within Judaism is that good deeds are done because of one's relationship to God, not in order to establish one.

That performance of *g'meelut chasadim* remains a central tenet of Judaism today is easily observable in recent studies of philanthropic trends. A study conducted in 2003 that was subsequently reported in the *Jewish Journal* revealed that Jews comprised 24.5% of donors who contribute more than $10 million per year to charity. In 2006, *Business Week*'s "50 Most Generous Philanthropists" revealed that 30% of the top 50 givers in the United States are Jewish, despite the fact that Jews comprise only 2% of the general population. Further, both studies indicated that the majority of this philanthropic giving did not go to causes that were specifically Jewish in nature.

Reference

Sanders, E.P. (1987) *Paul and Palestinian Judaism: A Comparison of Patterns of Religion*, Fortress Press, Philadelphia.

Bibliography

Bultmann, Rudolf (1983) Eleos/eleeow, in *Theological Dictionary of the New Testament, Vol. 2*, Gerhard Kittel (ed.), Eerdmans, Grand Rapids, MI, pp. 447–487.

Buxbaum, Yitzhak (1994) *The Life and Teachings of Hillel*, Jason Aronson, Northvale, NJ.

Nunnally, W.E. (2000) Gamaliel, in *Eerdmans Dictionary of the Bible*, David Noel Freedman (ed.), Eerdmans, Grand Rapids, MI, pp. 481–482.

Nunnally, W.E. (2000) Hillel, in *Eerdmans Dictionary of the Bible*, David Noel Freedman (ed.), Eerdmans, Grand Rapids, MI, pp. 591–592.

Siegel, Seymour (2007) *Imitation of God*, in *Encyclopaedia Judaica, Vol. 9*, Keter, Jerusalem, pp. 732–738.

CHAPTER 20
Hospitality

Ana María Pineda

Driving the Pacific Coast Highway to San Diego, one is struck by the beauty of the landscape, the sea breeze flavoring the air, the expansiveness of the ocean bordering the highway. Posted highway signs create a visual litany of the many towns and cities that make up southern California. Along the way, more signs indicate rest stops, fast food eateries, places for overnight lodging, and gas stations. There are signs to alert drivers to the crossing of agricultural machinery, domesticated animals, and even wildlife such as deer and elk. These signs put us on our guard so as to avoid any danger to ourselves. On a long drive, the periodic appearance of signs tends to create a rhythm that almost lulls us into taking them all for granted.

As I draw closer to the southern border of our state and, in fact, of our county, a new sign appears that breaks into the complacency of my drive. It is not a sign warning about road conditions or crossing hazards, but a yellow, diamond-shaped sign depicting in dark silhouette human beings on the run: a family in flight. Like the Holy Family of the Gospels seeking safety in Egypt, the modern family in flight not only crosses California highways, but traverses every nation of the globe. It is a family in search of a place to live, to work, to love, to grow, and to flourish safely – a family in search of hospitality.

This desperate human journey is not new. It is written across time and place. It is an agony experienced throughout human history. The documents of all major religions and faith traditions have addressed the plight of those seeking hospitality or refuge.

Hebrew Scriptures and Just Treatment of the Stranger

The moral imperative to welcome the stranger is ancient. The concern for the most vulnerable persons in society is an integral part of the Hebrew tradition. That this

---

The Wiley Blackwell Companion to Religion and Social Justice, First Edition. Edited by Michael D. Palmer and Stanley M. Burgess.
© 2012 John Wiley & Sons Ltd. Published 2020 by John Wiley & Sons Ltd.

concern was at the heart of Hebrew identity is evidenced in the preponderance of writings dating back to the sixth century BCE. In recent times, however, scientists have discovered a fragment of what is considered the earliest-known Hebrew text.[1] The inscription dates back to the tenth century BCE during the reign of King David. On a reconstructed 6 inch by 6½ inch trapezoidal piece of pottery, the message with some missing letters reads:

> [Y]ou shall not do [it], but worship the [Lord]
> Judge the sla[ve] and the wid[ow]
> Judge the orph[an] [and] the stranger,
> [Plead for the infant/ [plead for the po[or and] the widow.
> Rehabilitate [the poor] at the hands of the King
> Protect the po[or and] the slave/[supp]ort the stranger.

In this selection, the word "judge" indicates a decision in favor of a petitioner. The word "plead" means to intercede for a supplicant. The discovery of this ancient Hebrew text lends weight to the view that the ancient Hebrew tradition was biased toward the most fragile members of society: the stranger, the widow, and the orphan. The text is four centuries older than what was previously known. Scientists working on this discovery believe that it is a statement regulating society, indicating how slaves, widows, and orphans should be treated. The Hebrew society of that era had to "protect," "rehabilitate," and "support" the poor, the fragile, and the dispossessed. The ancient Hebrew community was morally obligated to provide practical assistance to the infant, the poor, the widow, and the stranger. Anyone perceiving the needs of the most vulnerable in society had to implore, even beg, for just treatment for the vulnerable members of the extended family. And, in a most telling manner, those who were political leaders, like the king, must rehabilitate and restore the fragile members of society to respected and fruitful lives.

The Hebrew Scriptures tell the story of the descendants of Abraham and Sarah, who answered God's call to journey far from home in search of a promised land. After years of exile and slavery in Egypt, their descendants were a refugee people, wandering in a wilderness. Later still, they were again forced into captivity and sent off to a distant land. The experience of exile was deeply and irrevocably etched in the memory of the people and led to a profound awareness of justice and compassion for refugees and nomadic people on the move. Consequently, the Hebrew Scriptures are filled with directives regarding the just and merciful treatment of strangers.

> You shall count seven weeks; begin to count the seven weeks from the time the sickle is first put to the standing grain. Then you shall keep the festival of weeks to the Lord your God, contributing a freewill-offering in proportion to the blessing that you have received from the Lord your God. Rejoice before the Lord your God – you and your sons and your daughters, your male and female slaves, the Levites resident in your towns, as well as the strangers, the orphans, and the widows who are among you – at the place that the Lord your God will choose as a dwelling for his name. Remember that you were a slave in Egypt, and diligently observe these statutes. (Deuteronomy 16:9–12)

It is this memory of the experience and plight of the stranger that requires a generous outpouring of hospitality, especially to those who are most vulnerable and exposed to danger.

Hospitality here is identified not simply as charity but more profoundly as justice. As a matter of Jewish law the most vulnerable among them – the sojourners, the widows, and the orphans – were not only to be protected from physical harm but also provided with provisions. Communal structures included immediate provisions for them. In addition, every third year, a Jubilee year, a tenth of the produce raised was to be given as a tithe toward the support of the resident aliens, the widows, and the orphans of the community: in order "that the Levites, because they have no allotment or inheritance with you, as well as the resident aliens, the orphans, and the widows in your towns, may come and eat their fill so that the Lord your God may bless you in all the work that you undertake" (Deuteronomy 14:28–29).

The Christian Tradition and Catholic Social Teaching

Developing from the Judaic tradition, the ancient Christian tradition continues to uphold the dignity of all human beings and the need to act justly, especially toward those who are most vulnerable. Believers are constantly reminded of their responsibility to act justly toward the stranger.

> For the Lord your God is God of gods and Lord of lords, the great God, mighty and awesome, who is not partial and takes no bribe, who executes justice for the orphan and the widow, and who loves the strangers, providing them with food and clothing. You shall also love the stranger, for you were strangers in the land of Egypt. (Deuteronomy 10:17–19)

At the heart of the Christian tradition is the understanding that we are all made in the image and likeness of God. This truth demands a posture of respect for each human being regardless of state in life, life circumstances, or any other factor that contributes to the diversity of the human family. A hospitality that is fully expressed and lived out is restorative; it re-establishes right and just relationships among all human beings.

A hospitality that is truly just upholds the dignity of all humans because each is made in the image of God. A proper and just hospitality ensures that all human beings enjoy basic political, social, and economic security.

> Christian love of neighbor and justice cannot be separated. For love implies an absolute demand for justice, namely a recognition of the dignity and rights of one's neighbor. Justice attains its inner fullness only in love. Because every man [person] is truly a visible image of the invisible God and a brother [sister] of Christ, the Christian finds in every man [person] God himself and God's absolute demand for justice and love. (Synod of Bishops, *Justice in the World*, 1971)

Genuine hospitality must promote both the common good (the good understood collectively) and the good of each person (the good understood distributively). Since

Christians believe that the universal family has no boundaries, they have an obligation to promote the rights and dignity of each and every human being. Furthermore, this moral posture obliges them to give particular care to those members of the universal family that are the most vulnerable and fragile. In the words of the New Testament:

> I was hungry and you gave me food; I was thirsty and you gave me drink; I was a stranger and you made me welcome; naked and you clothed me; sick and you visited me; in prison and you came to see me . . . I tell you solemnly, in so far as you did this to one of the least of these brothers of mine, you did it to me. (Matthew 25:35–40)

For centuries the Christian tradition has upheld the right of dispossessed people to secure a dignified life for themselves and their families. Papal Statements, Encyclicals, and Bishops' Pastoral Letters have defended the right of people to migrate in pursuit of living a dignified life. Pope Leo XIII in the first social encyclical, *Rerum Novarum* (On the Condition of Labor, 1891), established the right of each person to work to survive and to support his or her family. In the apostolic constitution, *Exsul Familia* (On the Spiritual Care of the Migrant, 1952), Pope Pius XII reaffirmed that migrants have a right to a life of dignity and therefore a right to migrate to locations where work is available. In other words, all people have the right to conditions that are worthy of human life. Pope John XXIII in *Pacem en Terris* (Peace on Earth, 1963) reaffirmed the right of people to migrate not only within their country but also beyond its borders, if necessary. This principle was reaffirmed by Pope John Paul II in an address delivered to the New World Congress on the Pastoral Care of Immigrants in 1985. In his address, Pope John Paul II stated: "The fact that he [the migrant] is a citizen of a particular state does not deprive him of membership to the human family, nor of citizenship in the universal society, the common, world-wide fellowship of men."

Church documents, especially the directive outlined by the Catholic Bishops of Mexico and the United States in *Strangers No Longer: Together on the Journey of Hope* (2003), emphasize the belief that opportunities to live a dignified life should be provided to men and women in their own homelands, but they also acknowledge that when this is not possible, people have a right to migrate in search of means to support themselves and their families (US Catholic Bishops, 2003: 9). In cases where it is necessary for families to migrate, church teaching and the biblical tradition provide rich sources of understanding and exhortation. The Catholic Bishops of Mexico and the United States make it clear that "regardless of their legal status, migrants, like all persons, possess inherent human dignity" (US Catholic Bishops, 2003: 38). They acknowledge the right of sovereign nations to protect their borders, but above all considerations they affirm the dignity of the human beings created in God's likeness, including the right to secure dignified work and the right to travel from one place to another in search of work (US Catholic Bishops, 2003: 9).

In the biblical tradition hospitality goes beyond simply welcoming the stranger. It also dictates just treatment of the stranger. Hospitality requires not only that the stranger be welcomed into the household as a "guest," but that the "guest" become a member of the household, the community. The practice of sharing the community goods is a reminder to the community that the mistreatment and abuse suffered by their ancestors in a foreign land should never be repeated and that every man and woman must be treated justly and compassionately. "He has told you, O mortal, what is good; and what does the Lord require of you but to do justice, and to love kindness, and to walk humbly with your God?" (Micah 6:8).

The Pastoral Constitution on the Church in the Modern World of the Second Vatican Council reflects an increasing awareness of the universal dignity proper to the human person. The document is a reminder of the privileged place that human beings occupy in Creation and of the rights and duties that flow from that privileged standing (US Catholic Bishops, 2003: 26). Fundamental to Christianity is the belief that men and women are entitled to responses and conditions that enable them to live lives consistent with their standing as human beings made in the image of God. In order to accommodate these moral entitlements, the social order must be allowed to change in ways that benefit people. Social change "must be founded on truth, built on justice, and animated by love; in freedom it should grow every day toward a more humane balance" (US Catholic Bishops, 2003: 26). In practical terms, the Second Vatican Council obligates Christians everywhere to embrace a global understanding of who is one's neighbor and reminds Christians that everyone counts as a neighbor. Without exception, respect is due toward every human being.

In *Strangers No Longer*, the Catholic Church acknowledges the prerogative of sovereign nations to control their borders. Secure national borders protect the interests of each nation's citizens and in a sense promote justice and equality among a nation's citizens. At the same time, the moral rights and dignity of individual human beings figure prominently in the Catholic Church's social teaching. Sometimes financial and life exigencies require persons to migrate beyond the borders of their homeland (*Church in the Modern World*, 1965: 66). In such cases, the demands of justice and equity must be ensured without violating the rights of people who, out of severe exigency, find it necessary to immigrate. Their dignity and human rights must be respected, even if they lack documents granting them legal permission to be in the country (US Catholic Bishops, 2003: 9). In the eyes of the church, people on the move must always be treated with respect and compassion, which are the essence of Christian hospitality. The expectation that hospitality will be extended to them is based on the biblical imperative to treat the "stranger" with dignity.

The Search for Hospitality

Because of economic inequality in the world, including unequal or unjust distribution of resources and opportunities, some people are compelled to migrate in search of a better life for themselves and their families. Many migrations place human families in precarious situations, often facing woefully inadequate living conditions and the abuse of their human rights.

The inhumane treatment of migrant peoples is not abstract; it manifests itself in concrete realities. In 1996 I participated in a gathering of the Sisters of Mercy of Latin America and the Caribbean, during which I was exposed to several realities that were outside my previous context. In Panama, I accompanied a group of Sisters to a neighborhood that was originally built for single men of African descent, who came to that region to work on the railroad. The single-room dwellings without running water or bathrooms were situated in the poorest sector of the city. The men who lived there eventually brought their families over the border to join them. They gave their one-room houses more living space by building a loft-style floor midway above the entrance door. Several decades later at the time of my visit, their descendants were still living in those same deplorable dwellings. The entire community had only one water source. Daily, even now, mothers and children draw water from that single source for all their living needs. Bathroom facilities located in a central station serve everyone in the neighborhood. The unsanitary conditions seriously compromise the health of the inhabitants, especially the elderly and children. Enticed to immigrate, the men and their families had been "welcomed" only for their economic contribution. The "hospitality" they received did not include incorporating them into a just and adequate system of settlement. Their treatment was base and inhumane.

On another trip, I had the opportunity to visit with other migrant workers, this time within the United States. This immersion trip introduced me to women field workers. The sights, sounds, and odors of their deplorable working conditions remain with me even now. These migrant women harvested crops that would later be transported to neighborhood supermarkets and eventually to family tables. They told stories of how the very act of picking crops covered with pesticides exposed them to chemicals that jeopardized their health. As they labored over the crops, liquid pesticide ran down their hands and arms, leaving a thick coating of strong chemicals. Later, eating their lunch with unwashed hands, they unwittingly ingested toxic residue. The water they were given to drink was also polluted. When they refused to drink it, they incurred the owner's rage. The labor of the immigrant workers served the interests of the American consumers, but the rights and dignity of those workers were violated by the system that exploited their labor.

The challenges that migrant women face in the United States are not unique. Mexican women on the US–Mexican border are an ideal labor force for transnational industries. But the same industries exhibit little concern to provide them with just wages, secure their occupational safety, or mitigate environmental hazards. The women are welcomed for the labor they provide, but their health and safety are routinely jeopardized.

As the two examples of women workers illustrate, economic inequality places impoverished workers and their families in precarious situations. Poor women especially become a resource to be used and exploited for their contribution to the workforce. The resources, skills, and creativity that they could have offered to their children, families, and communities become instead the resources for increasing someone else's wealth.

Seeking out sources of work or revenue, poor women sometimes feel compelled to leave their homelands. They often migrate from rural environments to border towns or urban centers. Their desperate search for economic security exposes them to great danger. Horrific examples of the dangers these migrant women experience have been documented in Juarez, Mexico. Since 1993 more than 350 young women have been abducted, raped, and murdered in that Mexican border city. Most of these young women have been employed in *maquiladoras* (enormous assembly plants), where they have been "welcomed" to work in US-owned factories on 12-hour shifts for $4–8 dollars a day. The families of the missing women have searched to find out what happened to their young women, but their efforts usually bear no fruit. Regrettably, the number of disappearances continues to increase.

The workers who I encountered not only in Panama but in the southwestern United States and along the Mexican border are tragic examples of how people on the move are often forced to take on jobs that place them in precarious situations. As migrants desperately seeking work to sustain their families and themselves, they are "welcomed" into factories, industries, and fields for the cheap labor they provide, but are denied the genuine hospitality of just social structures and systems worthy of their dignity as human beings created in the image of God.

The Catholic Church emphatically teaches that justice and equity require that people who work, thereby contributing to the economic advancement of a nation or region, must be treated in a dignified manner. Minimal hospitality, such as opening up of one's home, is not sufficient; genuine hospitality requires that they be given fair wages and safe working conditions (*Church in the Modern World*, 1965: 66). Moreover, those who hire immigrants must provide the means for them to function in society. *Erga Migrantes Caritas Christi* (*The Love of Christ towards the Migrants*), issued by the Pontifical Council for the Pastoral Care of Migrants and Itinerants in 2004, states:

> [I]t is important that communities do not think that they have completed their duty to migrants simply by performing acts of fraternal assistance or even by supporting legislation aimed at giving them their due place in society while respecting their identity as foreigners. Christians must in fact promote an authentic culture of welcome capable of accepting the truly human values of the immigrants over and above any difficulties caused by living together with persons who are different. (*Love of Christ towards the Migrants*, 2004: 39)

Hospitality to Strangers

Those who themselves have migrated from homelands understand the difficulties of adapting to a new land. My father came to the United States from El Salvador to pursue certification in accounting. The poverty of his childhood taught him to value education. He understood that education provided a pathway to a better future, and he wanted to provide our family with such a future. Sometimes he would talk about how, with few resources, he immigrated to the United States from El Salvador. Carrying with him an address on a slip of paper, he looked for an acquaintance from El Salvador, only to find that the person he sought had moved. I never asked him how he managed, but he must have been given lodging and hospitality by someone, because throughout his life, he often expressed deep gratitude for the many blessings he received from God's loving care. My father never forgot the challenges he experienced in his new homeland. Indeed, his vivid memories of being a "stranger" moved him and my mother to extend kindness to others.

Many of my childhood memories are of my father and mother reaching out with hospitality to our extended family, friends, and strangers. One of my earliest memories

(I believe I was about four years old) was of an event that took place when we lived in a crowded apartment complex, not far from a laundry service run by a Chinese family. Occasionally, my father would go to the laundry, and in time all of us came to know the family. One night as I slept in the bedroom that I shared with my sister, I was awakened by a knock on the front door. Hearing my father get up and answer the door, I too got up to see what was happening and discovered the daughter of the owner of the laundry service standing in our living room. Distressed and crying, she explained to my parents that because she had not made curfew, her father had locked her out of the family home. My parents listened to her and then prepared the living room sofa for her to sleep on that night. In the morning, they returned the young women to her father and assured him that she had spent the night safely in our family home.

In that same apartment building lived a woman from the Soviet Union whom other neighbors treated with suspicion. My parents, however, included her in our family, treating her with affection and respect. Further down the street, Mrs. Anderson, an elderly woman, lived alone. As children we were encouraged to visit her, keep her company, and run small errands for her. Our parents did not teach in words only, but modeled practical Christian hospitality.

The Love of Christ towards the Migrants instructs Christians to give special attention to migrants, "whose language or culture is different from those of the host country," and to ensure that migrant communities are able to contribute to the church and to society (*Love of Christ towards the Migrants*, 2004: 89). The expression "special attention" includes not only attending to the immediate needs of daily living, but also promoting programs that will affect the long-term integration and self-sufficiency of immigrants. In order to facilitate immigrants' participation in their host society, the document calls for a commitment to work for family unification, education of children, housing, work associations, and civil rights. The document also emphasizes that it is important not only to give attention to immediate needs (food, clothing, shelter), but to develop long-range and all-encompassing programs that will effect beneficial social and institutional changes. The document also calls for a commitment to assure complete participation in the host society.

In the case of my own family, as we grew, what had begun as a temporary sojourn in the United States eventually became permanent. My father first and then my mother became citizens of the United States. Both of them felt a burden to assist other immigrants. Over many decades of living in the United States, my father and mother sponsored many family members to immigrate to the United States. While my parents opened our home to relatives and friends, they went beyond basic hospitality, making sure that the newcomers had the means to function in the society of the country they had chosen as their new home. My father introduced them to the new and unusual – "alien" – dimensions of life in the United States. He translated for them, assisted them in finding jobs and housing, accompanied them as they sought to enroll their children in school, and helped them secure the skills they needed to make their way in their new homeland. Indeed, both of my parents worked hard to link family hospitality to the larger process of introducing newcomers (members of their extended family and friends) to the practices and institutions of life in the United States, thus providing them with an invaluable orientation to our home and country. In practical terms, my parents not only welcomed guests into our home, but also welcomed them effectively to the society of the host country. In doing so, they taught us – their children – that hospitality must be linked to justice.

For Christians, hospitality is an ancient practice that defines and shapes what it means to be Christian. In Jesus's words:

> Hear, O Israel: The Lord our God, the Lord is one; and you shall love the Lord your God with all your heart, and with all your soul, and with all your mind, and with all your strength. The second is that, "You shall love your neighbor as yourself." (Mark 12:28–34)

For Christians, these are the greatest commandments, and it is the neighbor near and far who we are asked to love. In particular, it is the most vulnerable people within the universal family who Christians are required to love, respect, and protect. While this imperative lies at the heart of Christianity, the obligation to love one's neighbor, the stranger, and the most vulnerable in society extends beyond the bounds of the Christian faith community and is fundamental to many other religious traditions and cultures. Here are some examples.

Hospitality in the Māori Culture

Manaakitanga is a key word in the Māori culture in New Zealand.[2] Loosely translated into English as "hospitality," it is a deeply rooted concept. *Manaakitanga*, or hospitality, is the reassurance that visitors and members of the community will have their needs taken care of with generosity.

An expression of *Manaakitanga* is traditionally seen in the practice of gift giving. Traditionally, a visiting group would bring a gift, *koha*, to the hosts. In the setting of the visit, the gift given to the hosts would often be a food not readily accessible to the hosts. For example, a tribe that lived by the sea might bring seafood, and a tribe from inland forested areas might bring birds, roots, or vegetables.

The act of presenting and receiving a gift represented a contribution to the life and well-being of guest and host alike. It was essential that the gift express *tapu*, the sacredness of all things, and that it reflect the prestige of both those who bestowed the gift and those who received it. Or, as it might be understood, the gift acknowledges and celebrates the value of communities, guests, and hosts.

The act of *koha* is expressed in ceremonial ritual. In a welcoming ceremony called the *powhiri*, after a formal greeting is sung, the gift, *koha*, is presented to the host, in a dignified ceremony. The host displays great humility by keeping eyes focused on the giver and not the gift. The ceremony ends with a physical greeting exchanged between the host and visitor(s) in the gesture of pressing noses.

In contemporary Māori society, the ancient practice of gift giving has changed to meet current realities. Today the commercial transportation of goods and the availability of a wider selection of food in supermarkets make it more appropriate for travelers to give money to the host communities. There is no set amount; the only expectation is that it be given from the heart. Gifts can be as widely divergent as song, food, carvings, canoes, money, or the offering of a personal talent or skill. It is essential that the *koha* reverence the sacred essence of all things, the *tapu*. The acknowledgment of the *tapu* in the other is to perceive the reality of sacred humanity.

The system and practice of gift giving are intrinsically linked to the concept of hospitality (*manaakitanga*). Māoris expect to fulfill visitors' needs with abundant generosity. Each one will be treated justly and given what is necessary to live in a respectful and dignified way. When the Māori community comes together on significant occasions, such as the funeral of a loved one, the practice of gift giving (the *koha* system) not only makes it possible for the receiving community to provide for the housing and nourishment of all visitors, it also assures that no one will be left with massive debts. The reciprocal nature of the *koha* system enables those needing hospitality in the future to count on it. Over time and circumstances, the roles of guest and host are reversible and interchangeable.

Hospitality among Pacific Northwest Coast Indigenous Peoples

Among the indigenous peoples of the Pacific northwest coast of the United States and Canada, the festive ceremony of *potlatch* or gift giving with singing and dancing, carried out in traditional native garb, embodies yet another expression of hospitality. In this ceremony, a family or hereditary leader invites guests to a gathering for a gift-giving feast in the family home. The gifts may be food, woven blankets, copper, other precious goods, and even money. While the *potlatch* ceremony may vary among the different indigenous communities of the Pacific northwest, the primary purpose of the ritual is to redistribute wealth. The *potlatch* is thus a practical embodiment of distributive justice in which the riches of the community are shared equally by all. Before the arrival of European colonizers with their missionaries, indigenous peoples used the *potlatch* system as a means of sharing and distributing wealth in the form of the many items necessary for life. Distribution of wealth, ceremonial dances, and music indicated the status of clans, villages, and nations. The status, however, of each family depended not strictly on the resources they possessed, but rather on the way in which they actually distributed their resources to others.

In some cases, in order to assure a proportional exchange of gifts between guests and hosts, "extra" goods could be either destroyed or given away. The practice of *potlatch* ensured just provision for all members of the community. Long- and short-term gift exchanges ensured economic support to individuals, families, and sometimes entire villages, particularly in times of scarcity.

As cultural practices, the ceremonial rituals that accompanied *potlatch*, the exchange of gifts and sometimes the destruction of goods, were not well understood by Europeans or by missionaries eager to convert indigenous people to Christianity. Government officials and missionaries alike often saw such distribution of goods not only as unproductive but also as a waste of resources. By the late nineteenth century, *potlatch* was banned altogether in Canada and the United States. Anyone found to be engaging in the practice of *potlatch* as organizer of the celebration or participant could be charged with a misdemeanor and risked imprisonment. Persistent attempts by indigenous people to reclaim their ancestral right to practice *potlatch* eventually led to its restoration in 1951.

Hospitality in the Southern Andes

Hospitality customs among the Aymara people of the Southern Andes offer another perspective on cultural practices of hospitality.[3] When family, friends, or visitors arrive at a simple adobe home, the host sends for a woven blanket or warm shawl on which the guests can comfortably sit. The blanket is placed on an earthen bench built up from the ground against one of the outside walls of the home and within the family compound. Not to provide a comfortable sitting place for guests would be a sign of disrespect. This simple gesture of hospitality conveys a warm and respectful welcome.

The host may also offer guests something to drink or eat. Even simple offerings, when they are the best the hosts can offer, express the deep regard in which guests are held. No one is turned away. This common practice characterizes small gatherings where everyone provides for the good of the whole. Underlying both the family and the community expressions of hospitality is recognition of the respect due to each person. Every individual is included in the sharing of the riches of the community.

At community gatherings, Aymara women employ their carrying shawls and spread them together in the center of the gathering, creating a space where food brought by each woman is placed for a common meal. Wrapped in the women's shawls, cold potatoes, chili sauce, fava beans, fried bread, and occasional bits of meat are carried to the gathering. Each family contributes its part to the common meal, and no one is ever excluded from the meal. When the meal concludes, the women gather up the leftovers in their shawls and distribute them equally to those in attendance. This practice of sharing characterizes small gatherings where everyone provides for the good of the whole.

Periodically throughout the agricultural and religious year, various families in turn serve as hosts (*alferados*) for community celebrations. Host families save for an entire year in order to provide food, drink, and music for the communal celebration. People coming to the celebration may give voluntary offerings of money or goods towards the overall expense of the occasion and through this gesture ease the cost of the celebration for the host family. The sharing of expenses among community members guarantees that the *alferados* will not be left with a debt. While the celebration is held at the home of the *alferados* or at some other traditional location – for example fields for Carnival, hilltop for the Feast of the Holy Cross – relatives and neighbors help in the preparation of the food. A festival meal for perhaps a couple of hundred people would typically consist of a salad made with lettuce, onion, lemon juice; roasted pig or sheep; boiled potatoes with onion greens; fava beans; and a soup of quinoa, potatoes, onions, and meat broth. The custom of having a volunteer host family not only distributes and balances the riches of the community, but also enables the community to gather joyfully in celebrating cultural events and religious ceremonies in a way that neither excludes nor impoverishes anyone.

Furthermore, each gathering begins with a ritual of forgiveness in which those gathered ask for pardon from each other for transgressions committed. The act of mutual forgiveness restores the unity of the community and enfolds those who have been "on the outs" to community solidarity, thus obviating the condition of "outsider" or "stranger." There follows always a reverential offering to "Mother Earth," the *Pacha Mama,* and a prayer asking for blessings to be bestowed on those gathered. In a gesture of equality, everyone sits at the celebration without special rank.

Contemporary practices of hospitality among the Aymara people are rooted in pre-colonial, pre-Christian times. Providing for the community is a core practice that ensures that goods will be shared and distributed throughout the year for small or larger occasions. The opportunity to come together in feasting with music and dancing adds to everyone's joy, often in the midst of difficult daily challenges. The hospitality embraces not only all community members but visitors (including strangers) as well, and contributes to the health and welfare of everyone, strengthening the bonds of kinship and communal survival.

Conclusion

The hospitality practices of the Māori of New Zealand, the indigenous people of the American Pacific northwest coast, and the Aymara of the South American Andes are complex. Further study would reveal the cultural and theological richness of these diverse cultural groups.[4] The Māori people demonstrate that hospitality expressed as gift giving can bind people together and nurture a sense of community. Through the practice of the *potlatch*, the indigenous people of the American Pacific northwest help us understand that hospitality can function as a way of redistributing community resources, thus mitigating the negative effects of social stratification. The Aymara of the South American Andes demonstrate another way in which hospitality, practiced widely and as a community ethos, can both strengthen community ties and also redistribute community resources for the good of all.

Likewise, the ancient Hebrew and Christian practices of extending hospitality to the weak and vulnerable are no less relevant in today's global community than they were in ancient times. There are reminders everywhere of people on the move, displaced, and made vulnerable by natural disasters, political upheaval, and economic chaos. Across the globe, in places like Darfur, Congo, Ethiopia, Rwanda, Haiti, Indonesia, and the Middle East, the desperate plight of vulnerable fellow human beings – our neighbors – is evident. Our hospitable response to them has the capacity to relieve much distress and injustice.

From ancient times to the present, the practice of hospitality has held a privileged, even sacred, place in many cultures and religions. Among some peoples, extending hospitality to those in need, especially to the most fragile members of society, has even been understood as a moral imperative. Diverse religious and cultural traditions express hospitality in a variety of ways, but it would seem that there are certain core values that permeate their distinct practices. Hospitality is concerned not only with extending a welcome, but gives attention to the immediate needs of the stranger, the poor, and the most vulnerable. It thus aims to protect the dignity and moral rights of all men and women and to provide each person with those things that are necessary to realize his or her full human potential.

Notes

1. Public release article from the University of Haifa, Most ancient Hebrew biblical inscription deciphered, January 7, 2010.
2. Cadigan, R.S.M. and Tui, H.L., January 2010, Information on practices of hospitality of the Māori people. Personal document from a woman of the Māori community.
3. Thuesen, Lourdes, January 2010. Information on practices of hospitality of the Aymara people. Personal interview with a woman who lived and worked among the Aymara people for 11 years.
4. European colonizers and their missionaries, however, opposed indigenous practices, such as the *potlatch*, and in doing so weakened or dismantled the cultural and religious systems that maintained just relationships both within and among tribes. Colonizing and proselytizing native peoples dispossessed them of much of their cultural, economic, and religious identities. As a consequence, the fundamental rights of indigenous people were undermined, often reducing these people to the status of strangers in their own lands.

Reference

US Catholic Bishops of the United States and the Catholic Bishops of Mexico (2003) *Strangers No Longer: Together on the Journey of Hope*, US Catholic Conference, Washington, DC.

Bibliography

Bass, Dorothy (ed.) (2010) *Practicing Our Faith*, 2nd edn, Jossey-Bass, San Francisco.

Kerwin, Donald and Gerschutz, Jill Marie (eds) (2009) *And You Welcomed Me: Migration and Catholic Social Teaching*, Lexington Books, Lanham, MD.

Newman, Elizabeth (2007) *Untamed Hospitality: Welcoming God and Other Strangers*, Brazos Press, Grand Rapids.

O'Brien, David J. and Shannon, Thomas A. (eds.) (1995) *Catholic Social Thought: The Documentary Heritage*, Orbis Books, Maryknoll, New York.

Oden, Amy G. (2001) *And You Welcomed Me: A Sourcebook on Hospitality in Early Christianity*, Abingdon Press, Nashville, TN.

Ogletree, Thomas (1985) *Hospitality to the Stranger: Dimensions of Moral Understanding*, Augsburg Fortress, Minneapolis.

Pohl, Christine D. (1999) *Making Room: Recovering Hospitality as a Christian Tradition*, Eerdmans, Grand Rapids.

CHAPTER 21

Zakat

Faith and Giving in Muslim Contexts

Azim Nanji

The Qur'an emphasizes the ethic of giving and articulates, through a variety of terms such as *zakat*, a very textured and multivalent concept of charitable giving. While inclusive of the notion of acts directed to the needs of the poor, the Qur'anic concept extends the significance of charitable giving to encompass the ideals of compassion, sharing, strengthening, and social justice. Such an ethic aims to be socially corrective and beneficial and to reflect the moral and spiritual value connected with the qualitative uses that are attached to wealth, property, resources, and voluntary effort for the welfare of individuals, communities, and society as a whole.

The perspective of the Qur'an on the sharing of wealth and individual resources through acts of giving can be said to be rooted in certain ideals:

- It is important to find balance and complementarity between the spiritual and material dimensions of human life.
- Wealth, if used responsibly and shared with those in need, is a blessing and a trust rather than an evil and a burden.
- The concept of trusteeship of wealth and other resources carries accountability for the way in which they are earned and expended.

These ethical ideals, among others in the Qur'an, established the basis both for what came to be conceived as a form of giving in Islam and for the values that underpinned its institutionalization.

As the community expanded, through conversion and conquest, Muslim rulers and scholars looked to these values for guidance on implementing such ideals. Though the world of Islam was to encompass in time considerable human, geographical, and cultural diversity, a common pattern of legal and civic virtues ensured the translation of

---

The Wiley Blackwell Companion to Religion and Social Justice, First Edition. Edited by Michael D. Palmer and Stanley M. Burgess.
© 2012 John Wiley & Sons Ltd. Published 2020 by John Wiley & Sons Ltd.

such principles into the social life of diverse communities. In this way, questions of giving, ethics, and law became connected within evolving Muslim practices and writings, and included in time the institutionalizing of procedures for the collection and distribution of what was offered as charity.

The Prophet, his successors, the community, its leaders, and even the state were seen as trustees through whom the moral and spiritual vision of the Qur'an was fulfilled in personal and community life. They were thus accountable for how they used their resources and their wealth, and they earned religious merit by utilizing these in a socially beneficial way. While recognizing that individuals were differently endowed with abilities, resources, and property, the Qur'an emphasized the ideal of social solidarity, and enjoined justice and generosity (Qur'an 16:90). In particular, while condemning the hoarders of wealth (Qur'an 3:180), it upheld as truly virtuous those who spent from their resources to assist others (Qur'an 57:17).

The specific notions of setting aside a portion for others or of recognizing the necessity and value of giving are articulated in the Qur'an through a number of terms that are often used interchangeably or whose meanings are integrated. The most significant of these terms are *zakat* and *sadaqa*.

Zakat

The Qur'an links the word *zakat* explicitly to other primary acts of belief and practice of the faith:

> Virtue does not lie merely in turning your faces to the East or to the West. Rather, it encompasses faith in God, the End, the Angels, the Book, the Prophets and to give of what you have, out of love for Him, to your relatives, to the orphaned, the needy, the traveler, to those who ask for assistance, and for the enslaved. It is also the keeping of prayer and the giving of zakat. (Qur'an 2:177)

The term *zakat* suggests the idea of growth to emphasize that the giving of one's resources is simultaneously an act that cleanses oneself and one's property and, through sharing, enhances the capacity of others. More specifically, this kind of giving is considered analogous in the Qur'an to a fertile garden, whose yield is increased by abundant rain (Qur'an 2:265). It is this multiple connotation of *zakat* that is reflected in subsequent interpretations and institutionalization of the principle in Muslim thought and practice.

The centrality of *zakat* is underlined by the number of times it is coupled with the commandment of prayer. The "right religion" according to the Qur'an is summed up in service to God, sincere obedience, virtue, prayer, and *zakat* (Qur'an 98:5). *Zakat* is deemed to be integral to the practice of Abraham, other prophets, and their communities (Qur'an 21:73). Jesus, too, is said to have ordained *zakat* (Qur'an 19:31).

Its significance in Muslim practice was further enhanced by incorporating the duty as part of the observance of the two major Muslim festivals established by the Prophet: Id al-Fitr, marking the end of Ramadan (the month of fasting), and Id al-Adha (when

Muslims celebrate the culmination of the pilgrimage, the Hajj). In both instances, the acts of giving, while purifying the individual's wealth, are also part of the wider dimension of purification undergone during the ritual performance of fasting and the pilgrimage.

Over time, *zakat* came to be distinguished by Muslim jurists from *sadaqa* and conceived as obligatory almsgiving, with very specific purposes and limits. This restrictive sense is not immediately apparent in the Qur'an, where the term is often used interchangeably with *sadaqa* (e.g. Qur'an 9:66) to connote giving. Prophetic practice provided indications for the more specific institutionalization and modes of collection of *zakat*. Such dues were also deemed to be liable on wealth that was gained from trade, farming, and livestock. Muslim commentaries of the Qur'anic verse 2:267, for example, are virtually unanimous that *zakat* was ordained also from such wealth as was accumulated from farming, and that one was to give from the best part of it and not that which had spoiled or rotted. In general, one was to give according to one's capacity, based on what had been generated from resources that were in one's possession. Generosity was to be coupled by a sense of moderation and attention to family as well as personal needs.

Another context in which giving is associated with reward from God is in Qur'an 2:245, where individuals are urged to offer God "a beautiful loan," which through God's bounty would be multiplied many times over. Since God is deemed to be the ultimate giver, such offerings are interpreted merely as acts of returning to God what is ultimately due to His generosity.

Sadaqa

Although the terms *zakat* and *sadaqa* are often used interchangeably in the Qur'an, *sadaqa* and its various forms came to be interpreted in subsequent Muslim religious and legal texts to connote a more restricted notion of voluntary rather than obligatory giving. In its original context, *sadaqa* reflects the idea of righteousness or truth, endowing the act with moral agency. In Arabic lexicological literature, the word sustains its multiple meanings, and elsewhere in the Qur'an, its derivatives, such as *al-siddiq* (Qur'an 12:46), used to describe Joseph, or *sadiq* (Qur'an 24:61), used to described a trusted friend, extend this notion of moral excellence and virtue.

The application of the term in its various contexts in the Qur'an develops some of the key themes that articulate the ideal of giving. Qur'an 9:104–105 links God's acceptance of repentance with *sadaqa*, thus suggesting its value as an act of expiation. Such a theme is further extended by recommending fasting and *sadaqa* (Qur'an 2:196) as ways of compensating for the obligation of the pilgrimage, if for some justifiable reason one is not able to undertake it. Not every *sadaqa* needs to be a gift of material value. It can also consist of voluntary effort freely given and other nonmaterial acts of compassion, which are not to be devalued (Qur'an 9:79).

It is better to give discreetly to those in need rather than for the purpose of public acknowledgement (Qur'an 2:271). Furthermore, the Qur'an is critical of those who give in order to offer the appearance of generosity or who engage in ostentatious public displays of generosity, both of which are self-serving (Qur'an 2:264). *Sadaqa*, when it is only self-seeking or conceived in purely materialistic terms, undermines the moral worth of the practice. According to the Qur'an, words of kindness and compassion are better than *sadaqa* offered to a recipient in a demeaning manner (Qur'an 2:263).

An interesting use of *sadaqa* occurs in the context of what has come to be called in the literature of Qur'anic commentary the "verse of audience" (*ayat al najwa*, Qur'an 58:12), which has been interpreted as *sadaqa* offered to the Prophet before an audience with him. This practice suggests both a context of expiation and a mark of respect and recognition of the values embodied by the Prophet as intercessor and model of conduct for the rest of the followers of Islam. In elaborating the uses to which *sadaqa* may be put, Qur'an 9:60 specifies the types of recipient who ought to benefit from it: those afflicted by poverty; those in need and incapable of assisting themselves; those who act, sometimes in a voluntary capacity, as collection stewards and custodians to ensure the collection and appropriate uses for which the dues are intended; those whose hearts are favorably inclined toward Islam and others who fall into circumstances from which they might be redeemed, such as the enslaved or captives in battle, those in debt, in travel or transit; and finally those active on God's path (*fi sabil li llah*), including those involved in the defense of life and property.

While all these categories came to be more formally defined by subsequent Muslim schools of thought and these uses of *sadaqa* were assimilated into the definition and elaboration of *zakat* to reflect a more obligatory characterization of giving, it is clear from verse 58:12 that the Qur'an envisaged a broadly encompassing framework for those who might benefit from the more formalized practice that was evolving in the early Muslim community (Umma) and for the fiscal support of the community's needy and poor. Moreover, with the growth of the Umma and its transition to a more institutionalized setting in Medina, almsgiving served as a resource to benefit and assist those who had migrated from Mecca with the Prophet to encourage others to join the Muslim community and to support the Muslims in the ensuing conflict against Mecca. Qur'an 2:273 suggests that these broader uses were to assist the poor, and also others who during this period of transition did not visibly exhibit need but who nonetheless required assistance to enhance their livelihood or to be directed toward new occupations and economic opportunities. While one aspect of giving in the Qur'an was clearly projected toward charitable acts for the poor and the needy, the practice also encompassed the wider goal of applying the donations to improve the general condition and economic well-being of other recipients and constituencies in the growing Umma. The fact that in due course the Prophet organized collection and distribution of resources suggests that the moral emphasis on giving was receiving specific institutional forms and being channeled to the broader purpose of supporting all elements in society.

The Institutionalization of Qur'anic Values

The mode of systematizing procedures for the collection and distribution of *sadaqa* and *zakat* was elaborated within the interconnected political, moral, and social order that was evolving. In an essay exploring the use of the Qur'anic term *haqq* (the real or the true), Clifford Geertz notes that the *right* and the *real* are importantly linked, even identified, at all levels of Islamic application, including the legal and moral. This linkage occurs not just abstractly as tone and mood, but concretely as deliberation and procedure (Geertz, 1983: 189).[1]

The formative Muslim community marked the initial step in creating a moral environment and an institutional fabric to advocate a framework and infrastructure for the common good that went beyond the constraints of tribal and ethnic boundaries. It validated obligations and urged corrective action to better the conditions of specific populations such as the hungry, orphaned children, widows, and those in need of support at all levels of society. The shift in early Muslim society from Mecca to Medina marked a radical change in social empowerment. The Prophet and many of his followers migrated to Medina, establishing a community that had the power and capacity to develop and build institutions to support Islam's moral vision. From a comparative perspective, the Prophet's leadership and engagement with day-to-day affairs, which assured the continuing development and security of the growing Muslim community and others in Medina, suggests a very concrete way in which faith inspired the growth and direction of the nascent Muslim society, including its economic life.

It is apparent that by the time of the Prophet's death in 632, a framework of practices that governed the collection and distribution of the *sadaqa* and *zakat* contributions had developed. Though much of the formalized, juristic pattern forming the institutionalization of this framework occurred later, some direction had emerged from the experience of the early community as well as the period of the first four Caliphs (heads of state). The record of this period suggests that they oversaw and directed the assessment, collection, and distribution of the dues, appointed collectors, and entrusted them and other followers to safeguard and apportion them for the intended recipients. It is significant that the ideals attached to giving and its underlying values were not left simply at the level of voluntary action, but that already in the Prophet's time, there were attempts to structure patterns whereby such practices could evolve institutional forms.

According to the Qur'an, various Bedouin groups who converted to Islam displayed considerable ambivalence and remonstrated against the giving of *zakat* (Qur'an 9:54–59). Al-Bukhari, the compiler of Prophetic tradition, cites a *hadith* (a narrative) in which the Prophet sends a representative to Yemen, inviting groups to become Muslim and, as part of their obligations, urging them to pay *zakat*. On the Prophet's death, after the assumption of the nascent community's leadership by the first Caliph, Abu Bakr, a number of such groups refused to forward collections of *zakat* because they felt that the death of the Prophet absolved them of contractual obligations undertaken solely with him. Their actions were perceived as a rebellion against the new authority in Medina. The new leadership felt that these revolts had to be suppressed and the practice of collection formally restored. Abu Bakr's zeal in establishing the religious obligatoriness of such practices for the emerging Muslim polity suggests that, based on his understanding of Prophetic practice, he perceived *zakat* to be obligatory. Moreover, he held that its imposition was necessary to uphold the religious obligation and to develop and sustain donations in a centralized manner to support economic and social activities within the community. Writings from across the spectrum of Muslim intellectual traditions underline the custodial role of leadership in assuring the welfare of Muslims. Over time, some scholars and religious schools of thought favored the voluntary nature of the act, believing that imposition could lead irresponsible rulers to use collections for purposes that were incompatible with the spirit of *zakat*. Sources from Shia legal works attributed to Ali and the early Imams reflect teachings that emphasize the need to entrust *zakat* to the rightful authorities in order to assure that the funds were disbursed appropriately.

This effort to create a fiscal framework for the use of donations by appropriating Qur'anic notions and values is articulated more elaborately in the juristic literature produced by succeeding generations of Muslim scholars and jurists. Such works, modern critical scholarship has argued, were attempts to make existing practice routine and to link it retrospectively with the practice of the Prophet and the early community. What is of significance is that a form of consensus had developed that such practices were believed to be grounded in Qur'anic precedent and Prophetic example. In these juristic elaborations, *zakat* became a pillar of the faith, believed to be an obligatory contribution, while *sadaqa* came to be regarded as supererogatory. *Zakat* was to be paid to the appropriate authorities and centralized within the Bayt al-Mal (the Treasury), an institution that was developed more fully under the early Caliphs. It is worth noting that over time different legal traditions developed a variety of approaches to articulate methodologies and principles for sustaining these early practices.

The Model of the Prophet

Early Muslim scholars devoted a great deal of effort to recapturing as complete a picture of the Prophet's life as they could authenticate on the basis of the *hadith* accounts of his words and actions that were transmitted by his wives, family, companions, and others from the first and succeeding generation of Muslims. Crafting the record of his life into a paradigmatic concept (Sunna) enabled these scholars to create reference points that would subsequently inform and inspire their interpretation and formalize practices they believed to be in accord with Qur'anic values and commands. The *hadith* accounts that contextualize the Qur'anic injunctions on almsgiving and extend their meaning and purpose serve as an important resource for reconstructing how the life of the Prophet served as a common referent and template for the ethical, legal, and theological aspects of community expression and identity.

Sadaqa in some of the Prophetic narratives encompasses every good deed, all kinds of assistance, even removing an obstacle from the road that could hinder travelers, and actions such as the planting of trees from which human beings, birds, and animals might benefit in the future. Some of the Prophet's sayings on almsgiving emphasize the nonmonetary and nonmaterial value of the act, so that a poor man's offering of a small amount is deemed to have as much if not more merit than a rich person's donation of a large sum. It is evident from these accounts that the recollection of the Prophet's own behavior enabled believers to assimilate a wide range of good deeds, valued more for the intentions behind them than for their material worth, and encouraged a wider culture of civic values to be developed in Muslim societies.

Emerging Legal Consensus and Patterns of Institutionalization

In defining *zakat* and *sadaqa*, Muslim scholars set their interpretation and practice within specific judicial, doctrinal, and historical formations. This process of normalizing personal and community *zakat* and *sadaqa* as part of a larger framework of obligations and responsibilities is best expressed in the Muslim literature of *fiqh* (jurisprudence). This legal science led to the elaboration and codification of norms and statutes that gave concrete form to the Qur'anic prescriptions associated with almsgiving and their distribution. The work of the jurist Abu Yusuf during the rule of the Abbasid Caliph, Harun al Rashid (786–809 CE), is an instructive example of collaboration between jurists and rulers to appropriate and extend such practices as part of the fiscal working of the state. These practices included other forms of taxation that emerged within the economic organization of the state. Thus Qur'anic obligations were elaborated and articulated parallel to the other taxes imposed by the state, but differentiated because their basis could not always be rationalized on religious grounds. In his *Muqaddimah*, the fourteenth-century historian Ibn Khaldun argues that in the early history of Islam, only those dues stipulated by Qur'anic sanction and Prophetic practice were levied, and these fixed obligations, though small, yielded large assessments. In his view, however, as dynasties grew and the state's economy became more complex, additional burdens in the form of taxes were imposed beyond the limits of equity. This caused people to lose hope in their enterprise. As a consequence, they generated fewer taxes, causing the economy to shrink. Ibn Khaludin's account underscores how dues that in earlier times appealed to a moral value tied to the notions of virtue and sharing were eventually supplanted by a more secularized notion of taxation that undermined the spirit in which people gave.

The jurist al-Shafi'i (d. 820), one of the most important scholars of the Sunni legal tradition, provides an illustration of how attempts were made to systematize and rationalize existing practice and balance newer practices of the state within the moral framework they had inherited. One of the concepts that emerged to allow continuity with past values was that of *maslaha* (the public good), by which rulers and scholars could appeal to the need to take account of the welfare of the community as a whole.

Such works, in general, built on the values of *zakat* and *sadaqa* in the Qur'an and specified in greater detail who should pay, on what kinds of property, possessions, and wealth, including that generated from farming of all kinds, when the amount should be paid and to whom, and also the minimum amounts in each category for which *zakat* was due. It is interesting to note that the principle of *zakat* was also extended to include minerals and other resources underground, as well as treasure troves. The pattern that emerges in these juristic works illustrates clearly an extension of the earlier practices of almsgiving into a more formalized obligation that was beginning to take on the character of a well-defined form of taxation, interpreted within the context of the faith but adapted to the changing needs of the state and evolving economic needs. It is important to draw attention to the fact that many of the sources that exemplify the evolution of these practices continued to emphasize the moral agency of the act, linking its obligatory character to religious merit and reward. Moreover, they often pointed to the upholding of *sadaqa* and other good acts, which had come to be interpreted as voluntary, and which in addition to *zakat* were a means of seeking God's pleasure and the reward of the afterlife. In addition to the state, civil society also became a vehicle for perpetuating traditions of giving and welfare and often compensated for the state's failure to live up to moral expectations.

In distinguishing between *zakat* and *sadaqa*, jurists pointed out that while the former had limits attached to it and its uses were specified, *sadaqa* could be unlimited. The Shia Imam, Jafar al Sadiq (d. 765), is said to have emphasized that *sadaqa* spent in the way of God included a variety of good works and thus provided a broader context for the charitable use of collected funds. Moreover, there were no constraints on to whom it was given. For instance, donations could be made to institutions, such as mosques, educational institutions, and hospitals. *Sadaqa* could also be given to those in distress or in need to improve their quality of life, even though strictly speaking they might not be impoverished. Jurists often cite the Qur'anic narrative of Joseph (Qur'an 12:88), in which his brothers, unaware of his true identity, ask him for charity to help the family in their time of temporary distress.

Based again on Qur'anic precedents and Prophetic practice, aspects of charitable giving were also translated into gifts given through endowments called *waqf* and established to last in perpetuity. In most instances, the juristic tradition specified how such gifts were to be formalized, ratified, and regulated. Jurisitic literature thus mirrors the widespread practice of almsgiving and its diversity among Muslim societies.

The turn toward systematization and formalization did not preclude acts of voluntary, personal philanthropy. Among the institutions that developed out of Prophetic precedent were those that expressed the Qur'anic value of gifting to God a beautiful loan (Qur'an 2:357). A narrative recounts how when the Prophet wished to purchase land, they gave it to the Prophet for the "sake of God." Such acts of giving, which converted resources and land into perpetual trusts for charitable uses, became an important feature of Muslim practice and were used to endow mosques, schools, hospitals, water fountains, and other conveniences for the benefit of the public. Notable Muslims, descendants of the Prophet, and many women played noteworthy roles in generating such philanthropic works.

Muslims were not the only beneficiaries of charitable acts by Muslims. There are narratives of the Prophet's life illustrating certain Qur'anic verses that indicate that non-Muslims could be beneficiaries. *Waqf* documents reveal the broad goals of giving alms and establishing charitable works to benefit the communities of which they were a part, without regard to religious affiliation.

Modern Contexts

As modern Muslim nation-states and communities that span the globe seek to relate, in varying degrees, issues of their heritage to questions of self-identification and development, practices such as those of *zakat* and *sadaqa* have offered opportunities to rethink the relevance of social welfare and charitable practices in contemporary Muslim social and economic life. The majority of Muslims live in what is considered the less developed world, and issues of social justice and equitable distribution of resources figure prominently in discussions of the relevance of Qur'anic injunctions to translate social conscience into policies and philanthropic actions for the distribution and sharing of wealth to generate economic and social justice.

Some Muslim theorists have advocated integrating *zakat* into tax policy in Muslim countries in order to develop further the ideal of a social welfare state. The rationale for such choices is said to be an integration of the moral basis of *zakat* with the principles of modern economic policy so as to meet the needs of all members of society. In recent times, some Muslim states have adopted specific policies to include *zakat* in their fiscal framework. Sudan and Pakistan offer two examples. In the case of Pakistan, a *zakat* fund was created in 1979 and since then funds have been disbursed through a centralized state bureaucracy for a variety of causes, such as ameliorating social conditions, providing scholarships for needy students, and funding welfare projects. Many Muslim countries and their citizens, endowed with greater wealth or natural resources, have also implemented policies of providing assistance, in the context of *zakat*, to poorer Muslim countries and societies.

Among institutions that have been developed to reflect ethical and socially responsible ways of dealing with financial resources are the so-called Islamic banks. While there is no consensus among Muslim scholars on the utility and value of such banks, they have achieved widespread status across the Muslim world. These banks are regulated to reflect use and distribution of funds that take account of religious prescriptions such as the censure against financial instruments bearing interest.

It is, however, within the framework of voluntary giving that the most innovative and sustainable adaptations of the Qur'anic spirit have occurred. Many Muslims, individually or as a community, have developed extensive networks to translate Qur'anic philanthropic values into active vehicles for assistance to a wide variety of constituencies. In some cases, these have developed into voluntary associations and charitable organizations to help the poor and the needy in many parts of the world. The most effective and developed of such organizations are beginning to operate globally, in collaboration with other groups, agencies, and foundations, to promote development across society as a whole. Excellent examples of such initiatives are modern Muslim foundations that are based on Muslim as well as broadly humanistic values of compassion and service. In particular, such approaches target the most vulnerable groups in Muslim societies: women and children, the poor, the unemployed, and, increasingly in recent times, refugees and victims of war and violence. Another recent development is the emergence of microfinance institutions, which focus their efforts toward the rural poor and those unable to access banks or other financial institutions. In some cases, quite dramatic success has been achieved by microfinance institutions, as in the case of Bangladesh. In this instance, an initiative founded by Mohammed Yunus, called the Grameen Bank, gave small loans to women to enable them to become independent businesswomen. Because of the program's success in improving the quality of life of rural communities, the founder was recognized by being awarded a Nobel Prize.

Conclusion

Muslim philosophers and ethicists of the past underlined the necessity for the state and society to be mindful of the needs of the poor and the disadvantaged. They insisted that resources be directed toward their needs and taught the moral significance of such acts.

Among the ethical writings of the Muslim philosopher al-Farabi (d. 970), there is a work entitled *On the Perfect State*, often regarded as a reflection inspired by Plato's *Republic* and other Greek writings on the nature of politics and society. Plato's teachings on the moral and political foundations of society refer to the harmony between parts of the soul and that of the citizens of the polis. In similar fashion, al-Farabi argues for a balance that can be achieved by society when human conduct is guided by the pursuit of moral excellence and the ruler of the state embodies in his character and action wisdom and custodial responsibility for the welfare of all citizens. For al-Farabi, issues of human happiness and proper social governance have multiple civil, political, social, and religious dimensions. He envisions them as an integrated whole, in which moral excellence must be pursued in every realm of society. Only then might the conditions of the excellent city be realized. It is perhaps against this context that the values of *zakat* and related notions of giving in Islam can play an important role in addressing the compelling issues of poverty and social injustice in our time.

Note

1 Much the same point has been made by other western scholars of Muslim civilization, such as the late Marshall Hodgson in *The Venture of Islam* (1974).

References

Al-Farabi (1985) *On the Perfect State*, Richard Walzer (ed. and trans.), Clarendon, Oxford.

Geertz, Clifford (1983) *Local Knowledge: Further Essays in Interpretive Anthropology*, Basic Books, New York.

Hodgson, Marshall (1974) *The Venture of Islam*, 3 vols, University of Chicago Press, Chicago.

Ibn Khaldun, Abd al-Rahman (1958) *The Muqaddimah: An Introduction to History*, Franz Rosenthal (trans.), Routledge & Kegan Paul, London.

The Holy Qur'an (1924) Cairo Edition.

Bibliography

Ahmed, Ajaz and Miller, Isabel (2010) *The Influence of Faith on Islamic Microfinance*, Islamic Relief Worldwide, Birmingham.

Al-Shafi'i, Muhammad Ibn Idris (1961) *Islamic Jurisprudence: Shafi'i's Risala*, Majid Khadduri (trans.), John Hopkins University Press, Baltimore.

Ali, Yusuf (1946) *The Koran: Text, Translation, and Commentary*, Muhammad, Lahore.

Amanat, Abbas and Griffel, Frank (2007) *Shari'a: Islamic Law in Contemporary Context*, Stanford University Press, Stanford.

Hallaq, Wael (2001) *Authority, Continuity and Change in Islamic Law*, Cambridge University Press, Cambridge.

Nanji, Azim (2001) Almsgiving, in *The Encyclopaedia of the Qur'an, Vol. 1*, Jane Dammen McAuliffe (ed.), Brill Academic Publishers, Boston.

Nanji, Azim (2007) Islam, in *Ethical Issues in Six Religious Traditions*, Peggy Morgan and Clive Lawton (eds.), Edinburgh University Press, Edinburgh, pp. 283–333.

Rahman, F. (1986) *Islam and Modernity: Transformation of an Intellectual Tradition*, University of Chicago Press, Chicago.

Sajoo, Amyn (2004) *Muslim Ethics: New Vistas*, I.B. Taurus, London.

Taji-Farouki, S. (ed.) (2004) *Modern Muslim Intellectuals and the Quran*, Oxford University Press, Oxford.

Vogel, Frank and Hayes, Samuel (1998) *Islamic Law and Finance: Religion, Risk, and Return*, Kluwer Law International, The Hague.

CHAPTER 22
Ecumenical and Interreligious Dialogue

Barbara Brown Zikmund

For centuries in many parts of the world, adherents of various religions have lived side by side. Informal engagement in and respect for diverse tribal and cultural religious practices often thrived without conflict. In many premodern societies religious identity was not something chosen, it was determined by birth and location. Religious diversity, when encountered, was accepted as a given and differences tolerated and respected.

Religions can be clustered into two types:

1 Religions linked to a specific culture and ethnic tradition. Tribal religions, Judaism, Hinduism, and Shinto view religious identity as inherited. They do not attempt to proselytize.
2 Missionary religions (such as Buddhism, Christianity, and Islam) are eager (even required) to share their religious views and practices through formal and informal missionary efforts.

In the modern era, as individuals and societies have diversified, religious commitment increasingly has been considered a choice rather than a status related to birth and location. Missionary religions and sects have grown and spread throughout the world generating a culture of competition. It might be said that missionary efforts "to convert" have resulted in new forms of tension, which in turn have led to the development of efforts to reunite splinter groups within various religions and to build bridges between people in different religions. Over time, efforts to live with religious diversity have led people to become self-conscious about lifestyle differences, explore different beliefs and practices, and share common concerns about social and political issues.

The Wiley Blackwell Companion to Religion and Social Justice, First Edition. Edited by Michael D. Palmer and Stanley M. Burgess.
© 2012 John Wiley & Sons Ltd. Published 2020 by John Wiley & Sons Ltd.

The Search for Christian Unity and the Development of Interreligious Dialogue

The development of formal interreligious dialogue in the twentieth century is directly related to the Christian missionary movement and the growth of Christian concern to heal historical differences among Christians. During the nineteenth and twentieth centuries, building on the global expansion of European colonial powers, Christians of many traditions sent missionaries around the world to "take the Gospel (good news) of Jesus Christ to the whole inhabited earth." European and North American Christians were leaders in this movement, and their zeal for mission enlivened their churches, creating many missionary orders and mission organizations. Christians insisted that they had truth and that the future of the world was at stake. Furthermore, as missionary activity reached out to non-Christians in Asia, Africa, and Latin America, everyone became acutely aware of the divisions and disagreements *between* Christians.

By the end of the nineteenth century, widespread knowledge of the tensions and petty arguments among Christians was considered an embarrassment and a scandal. Missionaries argued that the fragmentation within Christianity was limiting the success of Christian mission work. People new to Christianity could not understand why there were so many ecclesiastical arguments and divisions, when everyone was supposedly spreading a gospel of love and sharing a common loyalty to Jesus Christ. In spite of the fact that missionaries were sponsored by a wide spectrum of competing (even antagonistic) Christian denominations, missionaries argued that it was foolish for Christians to compete with each other in the mission field. What Christians had in common was far more important than the differences that divided them. Furthermore, the mission of the church to share the good news about Jesus was urgent.

In the late nineteenth century, prodded by reports from missionaries, chided by the redundancy of Christian diversity, and challenged by youth who felt a pressing call to evangelize, Protestants launched a global movement to overcome Christian competition and affirm Christian unity. The movement took the word "ecumenical" (from the Greek word *oikumene*, meaning the whole inhabited earth). The word asserted the responsibility of Christianity to engage the whole world. The resulting "ecumenical movement" insisted that beyond historical, doctrinal, and practical differences, there is only one church, one faith, and one baptism (http://www.oikoumene.org/en/who-are-we.html).

The beginning of the modern Christian ecumenical movement is usually dated from a World Missionary Conference held in 1910 in Edinburgh, Scotland. At that conference, over 1200 Protestant delegates from many European and North American mission societies (not churches) gathered, eager to overcome the divisions of Christianity. After Edinburgh the ecumenical movement (still predominantly Protestant) expanded in three directions. First, the mission agencies that had sent representatives to Edinburgh continued to work together and to think together about the future of missions. After 1910 they formed an ongoing International Missionary Council. Second, there was a desire to get churches to address social issues together and to explore what was sometimes called "applied Christianity." Many Protestants were already working in urban settlement houses and engaged in writing and preaching about the "social gospel." They argued that interchurch collaboration on social issues should take precedence over coordinating mission or the search for church unity. Known as the "Life and Work" movement, these Christians proclaimed that "doctrine divides and service unites." The first international gathering of Life and Work advocates took place in Stockholm, Sweden in 1925. Third, some of the missionaries who had attended Edinburgh pushed beyond the goal of mission cooperation and applied Christianity. They began planning another global meeting, dedicated to exploring the underlying differences in doctrine and church order that thwarted Christian unity. In 1927, their hope was realized when 400 people gathered in Lausanne, Switzerland, for the first World Conference on Faith and Order.

The twentieth-century ecumenical movement has a complex history. After two world wars and an economic depression, in 1948 the "Life and Work" and "Faith and Order" movements came together to form a "World Council of Churches (WCC)." In 1961, the still predominantly Protestant WCC expanded to include the International Missionary Council and most of the Eastern Orthodox churches. In 1971, another group, the World Council of Christian Education, also aligned itself with the WCC. Not all Christians were comfortable with these ecumenical organizations. Conservative Christian Fundamentalists and Evangelical Protestants remained skeptical and wary that "ecumenism" compromised doctrinal purity and biblical authority. They focused on the mission of all Christians to "convert" and "save" the entire world. Evangelical Christian organizations, spearheaded by celebrity evangelists such as Billy Graham, insisted that the mission to spread Christianity was central and refused to relate to various ecumenical organizations like the WCC. Nevertheless, by the end of the twentieth century many of them were working together and with non-Christian religious organizations to alleviate human misery. In 2010, Fuller Theological Seminary, a flagship Christian Evangelical Seminary in California, launched a new journal, *Evangelical Interfaith Dialogue*. Its founders stated that it is important to hold evangelism and dialogue together, to relate to others with conviction and civility, and to provide a place where committed Christians can exchange ideas about how to bear witness to Jesus in the midst of religious pluralism (http://www.fuller.edu/news-and-events/news/interfaith-dialogue-journal-launch.aspx).

Roman Catholic mission efforts from the seventeenth to the twentieth century were never as fragmented as Protestant mission work. Yet, as European religious wars ended and North American religious pluralism and hospitality expanded, Roman Catholics and Protestants became more tolerant of each other and more aware of many common ecumenical and interreligious challenges. Prior to the Second Vatican Council, Roman Catholics remained on the edges of most formal ecumenical ventures, but after the 1960s Roman Catholic initiatives and participation in ecumenical and interfaith relationships expanded.

Religious Pluralism, Ecumenism, and Interreligious or Interfaith Dialogue

The story of Christian ecumenical efforts to reclaim the unity of the Christian church has its own integrity. However, this story also laid a foundation for the development of what is now called interreligious or interfaith dialogue. During the twentieth century, cultivating relationships between world religions, not simply overcoming divisions *within* Christianity, became increasingly important to Christians. At the beginning of the ecumenical movement, Christians formed councils of churches, collaborated on biblical translations, and shared local, regional, and national projects. By the early twenty-first century, many metropolitan and regional Councils of Churches in North America and Europe expanded their membership and mission, becoming "Interfaith or Interreligious Councils." Their passion for Christian unity was tempered and stretched by new challenges in the face of growing religious pluralism.

Totally new organizations were created to link interreligious hospitality and dialogue to social justice. From the 1920s and into the 1950s, many of these were Christian-Jewish organizations, such as (in the United States) the National Conference of Christians and Jews (NCCJ). The NCCJ was organized in 1927 in response to an anti-Catholic campaign against Al Smith (a Roman Catholic who ran unsuccessfully as the Democratic Party presidential candidate in 1928). Its founders were dedicated to bringing diverse people together to deal with interfaith divisions. By the 1950s, when sociologist Will Herberg described the American religious landscape in terms of "Protestant, Catholic and Jew," many religious leaders embraced this ecumenical and interreligious description. Several decades later, when the NCCJ expanded its mission and identity to include all religions, recasting its acronym to stand for the National Council for Community and Justice, it recommitted itself to a full spectrum of social justice issues around race, class, gender equity, sexual orientation, and the rights of people with different abilities (http://www.nccjctwma.org/whoweare/history.html).

The Christian ecumenical movement grew dramatically in the twentieth century. In 1948 there were 147 member churches. By 2006, the 9th WCC General Assembly, with the theme "God in Your Grace Transform the World," brought together over 4000 participants from ecumenical organizations and groups, delegates from 348 member churches, and interfaith observers and visitors from all around the world. The mature Christian ecumenical movement modeled ways whereby people from all religions might build interreligious bridges of understanding and engage the problems of the world. In the final decades of the twentieth century, religious leaders of non-Christian religions also began exploring ways in which their traditions could strengthen interreligious dialogue. The work of the Dalai Lama is a good example.

Religious pluralism is not a modern phenomenon. Centuries ago, Buddhism emerged from within Hinduism, spreading throughout Asia to challenge the indigenous religious traditions of China and Japan. Later, Judaism gave witness to monotheism in the religiously pluralistic Roman Empire. Christianity initially had to distinguish itself from Judaism, then overcome the polytheism of Rome, and still later respond to challenges from Islam and indigenous religious traditions. Now, in the twenty-first century, as global communication and travel have stretched religious awareness, views of pluralism are changing. Current discussions about religious pluralism have moved beyond protecting religious purity, avoiding syncretism, or even tolerating diversity. Increasingly, people view religious pluralism not as a problem, but a challenge and even an opportunity to build positive relationships, respect differences, and work together to make the world a better place.

Religious communities are constantly changing, prodded by personal and communal efforts to find meaning. New religious groups split off from major religions: Sikhism in India, Baháʼí in Iran, Mormons in the United States. It is impossible to deny, ignore, or stop the growth of religious pluralism. In rare instances there are small religious communities that persist as isolated enclaves or spiritual islands, but most contemporary religious leaders know that they must find constructive and respectful ways to thrive amid religious pluralism.

Attitudes that Limit and Nourish Interreligious Dialogue

Interreligious dialogue or engagement begins first with awareness. If someone grows up in a closed religious community or for some reason has no contact with other religions, dialogue seems irrelevant. When adherents of one religion refuse to acknowledge the existence of other religious communities and traditions, dialogue is impossible. So the first step in interreligious dialogue is for everyone to "see" each other.

A second issue in interreligious dialogue or engagement is the rationale for dialogue itself. Why do it? If one is happy and grounded in a particular religious tradition, why become involved in interreligious dialogue at all? There are several motivations behind this question: fear that exposure to another religion will weaken personal understanding and devotion to one's own religion; concern that any appreciation for aspects of another religion might lead to error, mixing, or "syncretism"; apprehension that interreligious engagement will undermine the purity of religious doctrine or community; and finally that it is simply a waste of time. Who needs it?

One rationale for becoming involved in interreligious dialogue or engagement is highly suspect, especially when it involves adherents of religions that proselytize. Someone from one of these religions might decide to be involved in interreligious dialogue by thinking, "I need to cultivate relationships with the followers of another religion so that I will know how to argue against their religion and convert them to my true religion." Therefore, interreligious initiatives that are closely connected with missionary work are suspect, because this rationale or motivation to become involved in interreligious dialogue is dishonest. It does not cultivate authentic interreligious dialogue or engagement. Indeed, for religious people it is "offensive" in both meanings of that word, because it is deceptive, has ulterior motives, uses dialogue as espionage, and lacks respect.

Three valid reasons for participating in interreligious dialogue are often given. First, interreligious dialogue will enrich and deepen my faith and practice so that I can defend myself and interpret my beliefs and practices more effectively. This type of thinking is a good beginning. In one sense such dialogue is "defensive," because through dialogue people get answers to their own religious questions and clarify their own understandings to defend their religion. Instead of weakening religious convictions through exposure to others, many times participants in interreligious dialogue emerge stronger in their devotion to their tradition.

A second valid rationale for seeking out interreligious dialogue or engagement is that it will enrich and deepen my understanding of others so that I can be a better neighbor and friend. This type of thinking acknowledges the need to learn about other religions, to get beyond bigotry and stereotypes. In our increasingly complex religious landscape, generalizations are no longer accurate. People need to cultivate personal friendships and let others tell them who they are and how they want to be understood. This type of dialogue is "expansive," because in dialogue people learn what is important to others – what they share in common and how they are different. As a result, religious life for all is enriched and expanded.

A third valid rationale for taking time for interreligious dialogue and engagement is that when religious people come together to discover common concerns and challenges, they not only are blessed with new friendships and knowledge about themselves and about others, they are able to pool knowledge and resources to deal more creatively and effectively with social problems and political challenges. Interreligious dialogue, like ecumenical relationships, becomes a tool for social change. By understanding others and sharing common concerns, everyone is able to make a difference in the world.

There are other reasons for building bridges between religious people, but these three reasons are basic: to strengthen one's own religious commitment, to understand the commitments of other religious people, and to make a more effective impact on the problems of the world.

Forms of Dialogue

In the 1960s, the Roman Catholic Church did several significant things related to ecumenical and interreligious issues. During the Second Vatican Council, in 1965, a lengthy *Declaration on the Relation of the Church with Non-Christian Religions (Nostra Aetate* – Latin "in our age") was promulgated. The Roman Catholic Church established a new structure to deal with interreligious relations: the Secretariat for Non-Christians. In 1984 that Secretariat was renamed the Pontifical Council for Interreligious Dialogue (PCID). Also in 1984, the PCID issued an important document called *The Attitude of the Church towards the Followers of Other Religions, Reflections and Orientations on Dialogue and Mission* (usually referred to as *Dialogue and Mission*).

The *Dialogue and Mission* document summarized the teachings of the Roman Catholic Church on interreligious dialogue. In that document, Roman Catholic scholars offer a helpful typology describing four separate forms of interreligious dialogue. This four-fold typology has become widely used by people from many religions to describe and explain interreligious dialogue since the 1980s: the dialogue of life; the dialogue of action; the dialogue of theological exchange; and the dialogue of religious experience. A brief summary of these four forms appeared a few years later in a 1991 Roman Catholic document (http://www.vatican.va/roman_curia/pontifical_councils/interelg/documents/rc_pc_interelg_doc_19051991_dialogue-and-proclamatio_en.html, para. 42):

> The *dialogue of life*, where people strive to live in an open and neighborly spirit, sharing their joys and sorrows, their human problems, and preoccupations.

The *dialogue of action*, in which Christians and others collaborate for the integral development and liberation of people.

The *dialogue of theological exchange*, where specialists seek to deepen their understanding of their respective religious heritage and to appreciate each other's spiritual values.

The *dialogue of religious experience*, where persons rooted in their own religious traditions share their spiritual riches, for instance with regard to prayer and contemplation, faith, and ways of searching for God or the Absolute.

Not all interreligious dialogue relates to social action. For example, although the dialogue of theological exchange and the dialogue of religious experience are what most people think of when they hear the words "interreligious dialogue," these two forms of dialogue rarely connect to social issues. Scholarly discourse between knowledgeable leaders clarifies differences and builds relationships. Dialogue efforts to appreciate religious experience (such as prayer habits), or explore common practices (such as monasticism), also bridge distances and cultivate understandings, but they do not have much direct impact on social action. In fact, some people consider them escapist.

On the other hand, the dialogue of life and the dialogue of action are often directly related to social action. The dialogue of life occurs when relationships move beyond passive coexistence. Words like neighborliness and friendship come to mind. The dialogue of life takes place when people mix and support each other in the midst of the ups and downs of daily life; when people honor and accept diverse habits of dress or lifestyle; or when people find ways to share religious life-cycle celebrations and rituals surrounding birth, coming of age, marriage, and death.

In many situations the dialogue of life is unselfconscious. It involves simple acts of hospitality: eating together, learning about foods and patterns of fasting and feasting, encouraging children to play together, appreciating heroism and sacrifice. The dialogue of life takes place in maternity wards, at water wells, within government centers, and during funerals. It may be extending a handshake, sharing grief, rebuilding schools, comforting a child, befriending a refugee, protecting crops, or binding up wounds. The more people engage in the dialogue of life, the better prospects we have of mitigating violence and pain in the world.

The dialogue of action highlights special needs and is more intentional. This form of interreligious dialogue is self-conscious. Out of a growing awareness of religious pluralism, the dialogue of action insists that conversation is not enough and that even sharing the ups and downs of life is not sufficient. The dialogue of action echoes the voices of Christians in the late nineteenth century when they nurtured a "Life and Work" movement and insisted that "doctrine divides, service unites." People engaged in this form of dialogue have a heightened awareness and a self-conscious commitment to overcome the injustices of the world. They are very deliberate about doing things that enable communities and individuals to move beyond ordinary hospitality and community. The dialogue of action focuses on concrete actions to correct injustice and cultivate freedoms.

The 1991 Roman Catholic description of dialogue of action emphasizes the importance of interreligious dialogue for integral development, social justice, and human liberation. It states that in the dialogue of action, people "stand up for human rights, proclaim the demands of justice and denounce injustice not only when their own members are victimized, but independently of the religious allegiance of victims" (*Dialogue and Proclamation*, 1991: para. 44). Through interreligious dialogue, people from many different religious traditions come together to stand up for human rights.

Interreligious dialogue is intimately connected with religious pluralism, and it takes many forms: in life, action, discourse, and religious practices. It occurs when there are positive and constructive interreligious relations between individuals and communities of various religions or faiths directed (as the Roman Catholics put it) "at mutual understanding and enrichment in obedience to truth and respect for freedom" (*Dialogue and Proclamation*, 1991: para. 9).

The Interreligious Dialogue of Action

There have been many efforts to explain how interreligious dialogue and issues of social and political justice intertwine. In 1991, the Interfaith Relations Commission of the National Council of Churches of Christ in the USA developed a policy statement, "Interfaith Relations and the Churches," to help the 39 member churches or denominations that belong to the NCC think and act more intentionally about their interreligious responsibilities. The preamble to the statement declared,

> We speak out of a changing experience of religious diversity in our country. Events in the United States and across the world have made us more aware of the significance of the world's religions and their influence on politics, economics, and cultures. We speak out of what we have been learning in our shared ecumenical life. At home and abroad, the work of building Christian unity and our efforts for peace and human development are increasingly intertwined with questions regarding our relationships with those of religious traditions outside the historic Christian church. (http://www.ncccusa.org/interfaith/ifr.html, para. 3)

Almost 100 years earlier, in 1893 an international Parliament of the World's Religions was held in Chicago, bringing together representatives of many world religions for the first time. The 1893 Parliament was a watershed event in interreligious history, giving North Americans a first-hand encounter with religious traditions and leaders, especially from Asia and the Middle East. In 1993, the centennial year of the first Parliament, an anniversary Parliament was convened in Chicago, to build on the past and to go beyond earlier understandings of dialogue. Sponsors of the 1993 Parliament challenged participants to discuss and explore how peace, diversity, and sustainability could be strengthened through interreligious understanding and cooperation. Since 1993 Parliaments have been held every five years – in Cape Town, South Africa; Barcelona, Spain; Melbourne, Australia; and Brussels, Belgium – where adherents of many religions explore how to nurture "a just, peaceful and harmonious society . . . by engaging worldwide religious, spiritual, secular, environmental, business and educational leaders to seek commitment and practical solutions" (http://www.parliamentofreligions.org/index.cfm?n=8&sn=12).

Initiatives for dialogue in action are not always grand, multireligious international events. Sometimes they involve only two or three religious traditions. For example, in 2007, 138 Muslim scholars from all over the world issued an invitation to encourage more intentional interreligious dialogue between Muslims and Christians. In a document entitled *A Common Word between Us and You*, they shared their concern for peace and human development, calling for new efforts to deal with the problems of the world (www.acommonword.com). *A Common Word* begins, "Muslims and Christians together make up well over half of the world's population. Without peace and justice between these two religious communities, there can be no meaningful peace in the world. The future of the world depends on peace between Muslims and Christians." It continues, "The basis for this peace and understanding already exists. It is part of the very foundational principles of both faiths: love of the One God, and love of the neighbour" (*A Common Word*: para. 1, 2). The text quotes extensively from the holy books of Christianity and Islam, arguing that common ground between Muslims and Christians can no longer be simply a matter of polite dialogue between select leaders. Rather, the letter concludes,

> Let our differences not cause hatred and strife between us. Let us vie with each other only in righteousness and good works. Let us respect each other, be fair, just and kind to another and live in sincere peace, harmony and mutual goodwill. (*A Common Word*: final para.)

Increasingly, contemporary interreligious dialogue is focusing on the dialogue of action. Hollow words and elite conversations are not enough. Conversation is needed, but discourse alone does not serve the wider needs of humanity. Interreligious dialogue, understood as dialogue in action, is becoming a new way for responsible faithful communities to make a difference in the world.

The Marks of Effective Interreligious Dialogue

People from very diverse religions respond positively to this approach to interreligious dialogue. Yet, engagement with people from other religions is difficult, especially if the goal is to get beyond historical arguments, misunderstandings, and differences. What are the marks of effective interreligious dialogue that can lead to effective dialogue in action?

In 1981, the British Council of Churches came up with four principles:

1. Dialogue begins when people meet each other.
2. Dialogue depends upon mutual understanding and mutual trust.
3. Dialogue makes it possible to share in service to the community.
4. Dialogue becomes the medium of authentic witness. (http://www.ctbi.org.uk/CDA/110)

The NCC-USA "Interfaith Relations Policy Statement" (mentioned earlier) lists six marks of faithful interfaith dialogue:

1 *All relationship begins with meeting.* As people meet and form relationships with men and women of other religious traditions, the encounter may bring back bitter memories. Yet, people must not "disengage from trying to build bridges of understanding and cooperation throughout the human family."
2 *True relationship involves risk.* When people approach others with an open heart, they may be hurt. When people encounter others with an open mind, they may have to change positions or give up certainty, but they also may gain new insights.
3 *True relationship respects the other's identity.* When people meet others as they are, in their particular hopes, ideas, struggles and joys, there are new possibilities.
4 *True relationship is based on integrity.* When people meet others, everyone must accept their right to determine and define their own identity. Interreligious dialogue does not ask anyone to betray their religious commitments.
5 *True relationship is rooted in accountability and respect.* When people approach others in humility, not arrogance, they are able to discover and cultivate mutual accountability.
6 *True relationship offers an opportunity to serve.* When people embrace the dialogue of action, they are able to find opportunities through advocacy, education, direct services, and community development to respond to the realities of a world in need.

Hundreds of local ecumenical, interfaith, and interreligious organizations have developed their own guidelines and rules for ecumenical and interreligious engagement. In all cases, participants are charged to remain open to real differences and actively to listen to each other. They are also pressed to "do something" to promote and uphold justice.

Peacemaking as Dialogue in Action

Religions for Peace (RFP) came into being in 1961 "when a handful of senior leaders from the world's major faith traditions began exploring the idea of organizing a 'religious summit' to enable believers around the world to take action toward achieving peace." In 1970, the first World Conference of Religions for Peace convened in Kyoto, Japan. By the beginning of the twenty-first century, Religions for Peace had grown into the largest international coalition of representatives from the world's great religions dedicated to promoting peace – a global agency with an international secretariat in New York, links to the United Nations, regional conferences in Europe and Asia, over 75 national affiliates, and numerous local units. Religions for Peace is active in many of the most troubled areas of the world, creating multireligious partnerships, claiming allegiances across race, class, and national divides, while staying focused on stopping war, ending poverty, and protecting the earth. The agency enables religious communities to unleash their enormous potential for common action to promote conflict resolution, disarmament, advocacy on behalf of women and children, programs to overcome poverty, refugee services, accessible healthcare, attention to climate change, and more intentional collaboration among high-level decision makers to strengthen global commitments to peace. In the twenty-first century, Religions for Peace is working with 45 religious, interfaith, and value-based organizations to establish a "United Nations Decade for Inter-religious and Intercultural Dialogue, Understanding, and Cooperation for Peace" from 2011–2020 (http://www.religionsforpeace.org/about/).

Interreligious peacemaking also leads to interreligious partnerships focused on regional conflict and violence. For example, in 2003, 33 prominent Christian, Jewish, and Muslim leaders in the United States launched a collaborative effort to mobilize broad public support for active, fair, and firm US leadership in pursuit of Arab–Israeli–Palestinian peace. Known as the National Interreligious Leadership Initiative for Peace in the Middle East (NILI), it affirms seven "Principles of Cooperation": emphasizing the importance of their shared religious teachings, mutual recognition of common bonds, rejection of violence, commitment to a two-state solution, optimism that Israelis and Palestinians can make peace agreements acceptable to majorities on both sides, conviction that US leadership can make a difference, and an ongoing commitment to learn from each other in order to build bridges leading to peace (http://www.nili-mideast-peace.org/). For the NILI this initiative is a dialogue of action that uses political pressure and words of hope: "As religious leaders in the United States, we have prayed for peace, made public statements, met with public officials, and stood in solidarity with religious leaders in Israel, the Palestinian Territories and throughout the region." NILI leaders insist that "the path to peace shuns violence and embraces dialogue [and] demands reciprocal steps that build confidence" (quotes from a September 2010 statement, "New Hope for the Peace of Jerusalem," posted on the website of the National Conference of Catholic Bishops, http://www.usccb.org/comm/archives/2010/10-172.shtml).

Responding to Bigotry as Dialogue in Action

One of the most cherished stories highlighting the ways in which the dialogue of action expands understandings of interreligious dialogue took place in the town of Billings, Montana, in 1993. During the 1980s, five states in the western United States (Idaho, Montana, Oregon, Washington, and Wyoming) were targeted as "a White homeland" by so-called Christian, white supremacist, neo-Nazi, and Ku Klux Klan groups. These groups intimidated Jews, blacks, interracial couples, Muslims, gays, lesbians, and other minorities, spreading fear through harassment, assault, and even murder. Billings, Montana had already experienced several incidents of racial and religious intolerance, when in 1993 a bigoted extremist threw a rock through the window of a Jewish home. The people of Billings responded in what might be called a grassroots dialogue of action.

Each year during the holiday of Hanukah, Jewish families are encouraged to light candles and put them in their windows to remember an ancient story of how God kept temple lights burning for eight days when there was only enough oil for one day. In 1993, when the Menorah candle holder in a Jewish home was attacked and a window broken, the police suggested that the family remove the Menorah for their own protection. The Jewish parents resisted; they were reluctant to hide this important symbol of their faith. The Director of the Montana Association of Churches understood. She remembered how during the Second World War, when the Nazis ordered all of the Jews in Denmark to wear a yellow Star of David to identify themselves, the King and other non-Jews started wearing yellow stars. Suddenly, there was no way to know who was Jewish. She suggested that the community could stand in solidarity with their Jewish neighbors if everyone placed Menorahs, or pictures of Menorahs, in their windows. The *Billings Gazette* published a full-page image of a Menorah in the newspaper, and by the end of the week 6000–10 000 homes throughout Billings had Menorahs in their windows. The thwarted bigots did not withdraw quietly, however. Some cars and windows of non-Jewish families were vandalized, but Billings people did not flinch. They organized a vigil outside the synagogue to protect the Jewish community when it gathered to worship. They embraced their dialogue of action, displaying signs saying "Not in our town! No hate. No violence. Peace on Earth" (http://www.religioustolerance.org/menorah.htm).

Hate crimes violating religious freedom and undermining personal liberties continue to plague many parts of the world. Since the September 11, 2001 terrorist attacks on the World Trade Center in New York City and the Pentagon in Washington, DC, Muslims in the United States and in Europe have felt increased discrimination and fear. In solidarity, many formal and informal interreligious groups have been created. They have held vigils and marches to emphasize the importance of religious freedom and to promote legal policies that condemn and punish hate crimes.

One very successful expression of dialogue of action that seeks to overcome bigotry through social justice work is the Interfaith Youth Core (IYC). Founded in 1998 by an American Muslim who recognized how religious extremists all over the world are recruiting frustrated young people into radical movements, the IYC seeks to "build mutual respect and pluralism among young people from different religious traditions by empowering them to work together to serve others." It is called a "Core" (not a Corps) because it sees itself at the core of a movement of people throughout the world who are willing actively to embrace and promote religious pluralism. It inspires young adults to think differently and to "imagine a world where people from different religious backgrounds can come together to create understanding by serving their communities" (http://www.ifyc.org/about-movement).

Seeking Environmental Justice as Dialogue in Action

Environmental issues naturally link religious faith and practice. Out of respect for nature and building on religious understandings of creation, most religious people share a widespread commitment to preserving the earth. With greater awareness of climate change, common concerns to preserve clean air and water, and increasing sensitivity to connections between the environment, health, hunger, and homelessness, interreligious dialogue in action dedicated to "environmental justice" is growing. Faith leaders are actively seeking to redress the inequitable distribution of environmental burdens such as pollution, industrial facilities, and crime, alongside their commitment to change policies to protect the earth. One good example is the Faith Leaders for

Environmental Justice Collaborative in New York City. It brings together more than 100 faith leaders representing Christian, Jewish, Muslim, and Buddhist faith congregations to work with environmental agencies on three issues affecting the city: food justice (seeking to make healthy food more readily available to underserved neighborhoods); climate justice (raising awareness that the impact of climate change hits poor communities of color first and hardest); and energy consumption (motivating congregations to become self-conscious about energy consumption and to live out their stewardship sensitive to their shared environment) (http://www.weact.org/Coalitions/FaithLeadersforEnvironmentalJustice/tabid/360/Default.aspx).

Throughout the United States this third goal has been enhanced by the growth of an organization known as Interfaith Power and Light (IPL), which helps people of faith organize and promote positive environmental change around energy and global warming. IPL began in 1998 with Episcopal Power and Light in San Francisco. Since then, it has been working to establish interreligious IPL programs in every state. IPL's work

> includes educating congregations and helping them buy energy efficient lights and appliances, providing energy audits and implementing the recommendations, encouraging people to buy more fuel efficient vehicles and to drive less, supporting renewable energy development through "greentags," working on large-scale renewable energy installation projects such as rooftop solar, and advocating for sensible energy and global warming policy. (http://interfaithpowerandlight.org/about/mission-history/)

The Charter for Compassion

In 2009, Karen Armstrong, a highly respected international scholar of world religions, challenged religious people all around the world to create and affirm what has come to be known as the *Charter of Compassion*. The Charter asserts that the principle of compassion lies at the heart of all religious, ethical, and spiritual traditions, and it calls everyone to treat others as we wish to be treated ourselves. It asks people to acknowledge their common failure to live compassionately. The final two paragraphs of the Charter are a fitting summary of the ways in which shared interreligious commitments have and continue to nurture and undergird social justice:

> *We therefore call upon all men and women* – to restore compassion to the centre of morality and religion – to return to the ancient principle that any interpretation of scripture that breeds violence, hatred or disdain is illegitimate – to ensure that youth are given accurate and respectful information about other traditions, religions and cultures – to encourage a positive appreciation of cultural and religious diversity – to cultivate an informed empathy with the suffering of all human beings – even those regarded as enemies.
>
> *We urgently need* to make compassion a clear, luminous and dynamic force in our polarized world. Rooted in a principled determination to transcend selfishness, compassion can break down political, dogmatic, ideological and religious boundaries. Born of our deep interdependence, compassion is essential to human relationships and to a fulfilled human-

ity. It is the path to enlightenment, and indispensible to the creation of a just economy and a peaceful global community. (http://charterforcompassion.org/)

Bibliography

Charter for Compassion (n.d.) http://charterforcompassion.org/ (accessed April 20, 2011).

Churches Together in Britain and Ireland (formerly British Council of Churches) (n.d.) Background, http://www.ctbi.org.uk/CDA/110 (accessed April 20, 2011).

Dupuis, Jacques (1999) *Toward a Christian Theology of Religious Pluralism*, Orbis Books, Maryknoll, NY.

Ecumenical Interfaith Dialogue (n.d.) Mission statement, http://evangelicalinterfaith.blogspot.com/ (accessed April 20, 2011).

Interfaith Power and Light (n.d.) http://interfaithpowerandlight.org/ (accessed April 20, 2011).

Interfaith Relations Commission of the National Council of Churches in the USA (n.d.) Interfaith Relations and the Churches, http://www.ncccusa.org/interfaith/ifr.html (accessed April 20, 2011).

Interfaith Youth Core (n.d.) http://www.ifyc.org/ (accessed April 20, 2011).

National Conference for Community and Justice (n.d.) http://www.nccjctwma.org/ (accessed April 20, 2011).

Parliament of World Religions (n.d.) http://www.parliamentofreligions.org (accessed April 20, 2011).

Pontifical Council for Inter-Religious Dialogue (1991) The Attitude of the Church towards the Followers of Other Religions: Reflections and Orientations on Interreligious Dialogue and the Proclamation of the Gospel of Jesus Christ, http://www.vatican.va/roman_curia/pontifical_councils/interelg/documents/rc_pc_interelg_doc_19051991_dialogue-and-proclamatio_en.html (accessed April 20, 2011).

Religions for Peace (n.d.) http://www.religionsforpeace.org/ (accessed April 20, 2011).

Robinson, B.A. (n.d.) Menorahs in December: How the People of Billings, MT Rejected Religious Hatred in 1993, http://www.religioustolerance.org/menorah.htm (accessed April 20, 2011).

Sacks, Jonathan (2003) *The Dignity of Difference: How to Avoid the Clash of Civilizations*, Continuum, New York.

United States Conference of Catholic Bishops (2010) In Message to White House, Religious Leaders Say Peace Is Possible, September 28, http://old.usccb.org/comm/archives/2010/10-172.shtml (accessed September 28, 2011).

WE ACT (n.d.) Faith Leaders for Environmental Justice, http://www.weact.org/Coalitions/FaithLeadersforEnvironmentalJustice/tabid/360/Default.aspx (accessed April 20, 2011).

World Council of Churches (n.d.) http://www.oikoumene.org/ (accessed April 20, 2011).

Wuthnow, Robert (2007) *America and the Challenges of Religious Diversity*, Princeton University Press, Princeton.

PART III
Indigenous People

Introduction

Essays in Part III explore the approaches to social justice of eight indigenous peoples, each located in a distinct geographical region of the world: Central America, West Africa, Australia, Southern Asia, Europe, North America, New Zealand, and the Middle East. The expression *indigenous* is intended to identify peoples (usually relatively small in population) who have traditionally occupied specific regions of the world. As used here, it refers primarily to people whose underlying organizational principle is a social relationship such as family, clan, band, tribe, or other social structure, rather than the religion or sacred belief system to which they subscribe. The essays in Part III provide historical, cultural, and geographical information, but their primary purpose is to elucidate how the sacred beliefs, experiences, narratives, and social arrangements of the people in question inform their beliefs and practices in relation to social justice.

In one way or another, most of the essays in Part III show how the religious beliefs and practices of an indigenous people help sustain that people's culture. Religious beliefs and practices have social justice implications when the results or outcomes affect the well-being of the community. Thus, as Robert Baum points out in his essay on the Diola people of West Africa, "Diola concepts of social justice focus on economic equality, gender complementarity, respect for the elderly, generosity, hard work, and cooperation" (this volume: 353). Self-centered behavior was believed to undermine a complex, spiritually informed ethos, without which the Diola's basically acephalous society would cease to function.

Gregory Gagnon points out a similar sacred ethos of care for others among the Ojibwe people of the upper Midwest in North America:

> The ideal Ojibwe was generous, reciprocal with other Chippewa, and supportive of *bemadiziwin* [balance equaling a good life] . . . Ojibwe leaders were expected to care for others and to be poorer than the rest of the community . . . Ojibwe men and women were lauded for

helping the poor, the old, and those who were victims of disaster. The group was more important than the individual. (This volume: 430)

Gagnon's last comment about the group being more important than the individual resembles language that Baum used earlier about the Diola people. But the Ojibwe seem to have taken a rather different direction than the Diola on the matter of the prerogatives of the individual. For according to Gagnon, they valued and preserved the right of individuals to pursue what was best for themselves. They valued what Gagnon (citing Ross) calls "the ethic of non-interference," a principle that diminishes the tension between community responsibility and individual freedom.

Clearly, religious beliefs and practices among indigenous people help them sustain their culture by establishing principles and rules as well as myths, dramas, and rituals. They sometimes even help establish formal procedures by means of which people can invoke the aid of their neighbors during times of need, call on leaders to adjudicate disputes, or lay claim to other kinds of assistance or protection when necessary. But religious beliefs sustain culture in other important ways as well. For example, they can provide a bulwark against dominant, often oppressive or acquisitive, external cultures that threaten the social fabric of the indigenous culture. In instances like these, indigenous religions become essentially religions of resistance against external social forces that would destroy (or absorb) a people and their way of life. We see this use of religion or sacred belief systems among the Aborigines of Australia and the Gonds of central India.

We see religious resistance in a different way among the Roma people of eastern Europe. According to Maria Roth and Sorin Gog, the Roma have historically been marginalized by the dominant people – including religious people – wherever they have lived in Europe. Considered fortune tellers, magicians, and unclean, they were not allowed to enter churches, intermarry, or follow certain occupations. But in recent decades, Pentecostalism, an expressive branch of Christianity, has given them a home. The new-found religion has emphasized both personal and corporate accountability. With accountability has (gradually) come respectability and opportunity.

In some cases, religions of resistance become religions of revolution, actively challenging the status quo of the dominant culture through some militant or defiant behavior. At various times in their history, the Māori people of New Zealand exemplified religion of this sort as they sought to redress the loss of their land. Readers of American history will recognize the same pattern among certain Native Americans of the nineteenth century, such as the Sioux of the Great Plains, who practiced the Sun Dance, which military officials of the time perceived as a threatening ceremony.

Sometimes the external threat comes not from a political or economic force, but from another religion. Christine Kray explores this phenomenon in her essay on the Yucatec Maya. The expression "Yucatec Maya" refers both to an indigenous language and to a people. The language is spoken by about a million people in southern Mexico and western Belize; the people are descendants of those who created the ancient Maya civilization. Today most Yucatec Mayas practice a form of Roman Catholic Christianity that, as Kray puts it, "is culturally distinctive, with its own sense of social justice," emphasizing "equality and cooperation" (this volume: 353). The external threat comes from a missionary-minded protestant church that seeks to proselytize the Yucatec Maya. According to Kray, "What emerged [among the Yucatec Maya] is a particularly strong religious sense of justice that stresses equality and cooperation within the community as protection against outside encroachment" (this volume: 387).

The essays in this volume illustrate a feature not uncommon to indigenous people in the contemporary world. Small in numbers, they often struggle to maintain economic, social, and religious viability in the presence of a dominant culture. In some cases the dominant culture was once an external colonizing force. In circumstances like these, it is tempting to idealize the life of the indigenous people during the time before they were affected negatively by colonizers. But of course, while there is no doubt that many indigenous peoples have suffered great injustices at the hands of colonizers, it is also true that life among indigenous people prior to colonization rarely, if ever, achieved the ideals held forth by those people. Poverty, conflict, power ploys, exploitation of women and nonnatives were ever-present possibilities. Moreover, with the decline of major colonial empires, it is an open question whether the core values of indigenous peoples will prove robust enough to overcome the corrosive and debilitating forces of colonialism, and rich and compelling enough to claim the allegiance of new generations of people. It is one thing to talk about the sustaining role that religious beliefs and practices have played in the past. It is quite another for those beliefs and practices to play a guiding role for future generations.

Rich in detail, the eight essays on indigenous people present a number of issues for reflection and discussion at the intersection of religion and social justice.

CHAPTER 23

Africa

Religion and Social Justice among the Diola of Senegal, Gambia, and Guinea-Bissau

Robert M. Baum

In examining a concept such as "social justice" in other cultures, it is important to point out that there may not be a direct cognate term and approximating terms may have different histories within their languages and religious traditions. Among the Diola (Jola) of West Africa, the closest term to western ideas of social justice would be *cashumaye*, a term that means all things good, a correct relationship with the Supreme Being known as Emitai, and as a result a peaceful and harmonious life. It could also be translated as Emitai's peace and, in that sense, parallels the Arabic term *salaam* and the Hebrew *shalom*. In the greetings that one performs whenever one encounters an acquaintance for the first time in a day, one wishes on the other *cashumaye*, the peace of Emitai, and the other person responds with *cashumaye baleh* (or *kep*, in northern dialects), only the peace of Emitai. Throughout the day, at the foundation of all social interaction is the quest for this harmonious relationship with Emitai, lesser spirits, the land, one's neighbors, and one's family. This ideal forms the basis of all social critiques, and is the concept most closely associated with what people in the English-speaking world conceive of as "social justice."

The Diola number approximately 600 000 people and are a significant minority population in southern Senegal and Gambia and northwestern Guinea-Bissau. Often described as the best wet rice farmers in West Africa, rural Diola still focus on rice production as their staple crop. Although there appear to be brief periods in early Diola history when they may have been organized in small kingdoms, Diola are usually characterized as acephalous (stateless) communities, which rely heavily on local assemblies and councils of ritual elders as their primary means of deliberating on community issues and formulating township-wide policies. In the late nineteenth century, French, Portuguese, and British colonizers found the Diola particularly difficult to pacify and

---

The Wiley Blackwell Companion to Religion and Social Justice, First Edition. Edited by Michael D. Palmer and Stanley M. Burgess.
© 2012 John Wiley & Sons Ltd. Published 2020 by John Wiley & Sons Ltd.

incorporate into their colonial systems. Even after the conquest, Diola persisted in their opposition under the guise of tax resistance and a persistent refusal to succumb to forced labor or to be conscripted into colonial militaries, which continued until Senegalese independence in 1960. Colonial officials from all three nations complained bitterly about the Diola's love of independence and their determined resistance to colonial administration. Diola involvement in the Casamance secessionist movement, which has persisted since the early 1980s, is a further indication of the Diola's deep commitment to self-governance without centralized authority.

The Diola include the largest number of adherents of a traditional African religion in the Senegambia region. Since the late nineteenth century, however, large numbers of northern Diola have converted to Islam, a smaller number to Roman Catholic Christianity, and the number of adherents of Diola traditional religion, the *awasena* path, has steadily declined. Still, some northern Diola spirit shrines continue to be consulted, male initiation rituals are still conducted, and women's fertility rituals continue to command significant support. Since the Second World War, women prophets, claiming direct revelation from the Diola Supreme Being, Emitai, have become influential among the northern Diola of Boulouf. In contrast, among the southern Diola, conversion to Islam remains uncommon, though many people have become Roman Catholics. Still, the *awasena* path remains important among the Diola, south of the Casamance River and into Guinea-Bissau. Southern Diola retain a long-standing tradition of prophets claiming direct revelation from the Supreme Being that has continued into the twenty-first century.

In my historical studies of Diola religion, I have stressed the broad access of both Diola men and women to ritual authority through a large number of different spirit shrines, as well as a tradition of divine revelation from the Supreme Being, Emitai, throughout Diola history, that have provided it with a capacity for innovation that defies the ways in which western scholars have often viewed "traditional" societies. Closely related to these innovative qualities is a deep suspicion of the concentration of religious or political authority in the hands of any small group of people and of a sense that social injustice in the forms of consolidating power or wealth or mistreatment of the poor results in ecological hardships such as drought or insect infestations, the loss of political autonomy, and other forms of social disruption. In a Diola system of thought, just social practice is essential for there to be the adequate rainfall and bountiful crops that are required for the Diola to survive as autonomous communities.

In this essay I will focus on Diola *awasena* views of social justice and discuss Diola Muslim and Christian views only in so far as they reflect influences that stem from Diola religion. This discussion will focus on attitudes toward economic inequality, access to knowledge and power, cooperative labor relations, and the continued quest for local control over local resources and over the major issues of rural township life. Diola concerns about social justice focus on issues surrounding the concentration of political or economic power and concerns about any sense of elite entitlement. Added to this are expectations that people will be generous with their own goods and with their time, helping their neighbors and their community when called on for assistance. Lurking in the background are the means of controlling those who would challenge this prevailing social ethic, including people who are shunned for violating social norms, mocked by songs about their refusal to meet community expectations, or accused of witchcraft because they are seen as persistent transgressors of everything that is held to be "right" and ethical in Diola society. But the Diola account of social justice also carries over into concepts of spiritual sanctions enforced by the various cults or spirit shrines (*ukine*), a Diola concept of judgment by Emitai, and a Diola theory of history in which the world has been created and destroyed many times. I shall conclude with a discussion of Diola prophets, claiming direct revelation from Emitai, who outline a cohesive view of a just society of Diola communities living on Diola land.

Diola Ethical Categories

Diola concepts of social justice arrange moral behavior along a spectrum ranging from things that are absolutely forbidden (*gnigne*) to those that are absolutely required of members of the Diola community. Violations of the obligations imposed by various spirit shrines – including the penetration of sacred forests or other spirit shrine sites that one has no right to attend; violations of behavioral norms associated with gender roles (e.g., menstrual avoidances, male avoidance of maternity houses, and female avoidance of cemeteries); the taking of life outside of war; most cases of theft; witchcraft and sorcery – are all considered absolutely forbidden and are subject to spiritual sanctions by the spirit shrines or by the Supreme Being, Emitai. The spirit shrines afflict wrongdoers with specific diseases, such as leprosy, which is associated with theft, but could afflict not only the thief, but anyone in his or her family who benefited from the theft. The Supreme Being judges the moral worth of individuals when they die and determines the nature of their afterlife.

Underlying Diola concepts of justice is a collective sense of responsibility, reward, and benefit. In a very literal sense, in Diola society, one is one's brother's keeper. Anyone who benefits from the wrongdoing of his or her kin could be subject to sanctions. In most cases, Diola communities do not take direct action to punish the violator of these prohibitions. In the one case of an accusation of theft that I witnessed in the township in which I lived, the father of the accused boy (both of whom were Christians) offered full restitution to the Peulh Muslim storekeeper, as well as a live goat in compensation, in an effort to ward off any spiritual chastisement for his son or their family. The boy who stole found it difficult for years to find a wife, since no woman wanted to marry someone known as a thief. Furthermore, it was thought that Emitai would take it into account at the time of judgment after death, when the Supreme Being determined if the individual led a good enough life to become an ancestor or would be punished as a phantom and exiled to the forest areas that surround the township.

For Diola, actions related to witchcraft and activities involving souls that attack the spiritual essences of other people, crops, or food are also considered forbidden. Invariably, Emitai condemns witches to become phantoms for a long period of time before being reborn; the worst of them are eventually reborn as highly vulnerable cattle, vulnerable because their horns point downward.

Other actions are considered bad (*diakoute*), but do not warrant spiritual sanction in this life. They include temporary moral lapses or errors of judgment, such as drunkenness, shirking work obligations, and selfishness, which are subject to criticism by family, friends, and neighbors, but do not require sanctions imposed by various types of spirits. Most actions are considered morally neutral. Certain actions are obligatory, such as fulfilling one's ritual obligations at the spirit shrines, or conducting funeral rituals for one's relatives; failure to perform them could lead to spiritual sanctions. Finally, there are recommended acts, which exhibit central Diola values of courage, generosity, hard work, and cooperativeness; failure to perform them could lead to social criticism but not spiritual sanction.

All of these actions are categorized by a sense that socially destructive consequences follow from the violation of prohibitions or the neglect of positive obligations. These are not mere "taboos," only forbidden because the Supreme Being or lesser spirits prohibit them. For example, men and women, though so distantly related that they could not name a common ancestor, cannot marry one another if they were born in the same extended compound. Such a marriage, if it eventually dissolved – and many Diola marriages do end in divorce – would lead to members of the compound taking sides in the marital dispute, which would threaten the stability of the most basic social units of Diola society. Similarly, theft of rice threatened a whole system of Diola agriculture, which relied on the security of the rice fields, the piles of harvested rice awaiting transportation back to the township, and its security within their granaries. Such violations not only release a polluting, life-destructive force, which must be removed through ritual sacrifice, but they also disrupt the fundamental social and economic ties of Diola communal life.

There is also a sense that the fullest moral community among the Diola is confined to the extended family (*hank*), which is headed by the oldest man of the compound. As one moves beyond the family to the subquarter, both positive ethical obligations and forbidden actions lose some of their comprehensive force. The sense of obligation weakens still further at the level of the township quarter, the township, and among the Diola subgroup (e.g., the Esulalu or Buluf). Possibilities of violence and other socially disruptive actions increase with the degree of social distance, and the sense of positive obligations to work cooperatively or share scarce resources diminishes as one moves further and further from the extended family network.

Envisioning Social Justice

Diola concepts of social justice focus on economic equality, gender complementarity, respect for the elderly, generosity, hard work, and cooperation. People who hoard wealth, who transgress the proper relationships between men and women, who fail to respect their elders, who are stingy with what they have, who shirk hard work, or who are uncooperative in group settings all fundamentally challenge what it means to be a good human being. Their self-centered and unjust behavior challenges a complex ethos that simultaneously stresses the importance of the individual and of conformity to collective norms, without which their basically acephalous society would cease to function. Despite some economic disparities, people are obligated to share. Despite a system of male hegemony, men must respect women, and those who abuse women are seized with devastating illnesses associated with the women's fertility shrine, *Ehugna*. Young people must address those old enough to be their parents as father or mother and should be both deferential and attentive to their elders. People who shirk their work obligations, on both community and family projects, increase the burden of work on others. Uncooperative people threaten the unity of the community, which is tenuously embodied in the priest-king (*oeyi*) and which has often broken down into violent conflicts between village quarters or neighborhoods.

Historically, Diola measured their most significant material wealth in terms of the ownership of rice paddies, the fullness of their rice granaries, and the number of cattle that they control. Diola societies are unusual in that they combine intensive farming of the limited areas that flood sufficiently to allow the cultivation of swamp rice, the absence of landless people, and a highly diffuse form of political organization, often labeled as "stateless" or acephalous. In many societies when arable land is in short supply, a landless group hires itself out as laborers and creates some form of state that regulates and maintains a social system that grants unequal access to agricultural resources. Diola concepts of social justice run directly counter to this more common mode of socially stratified intensive agriculture and to the view that land can be bought and sold. Those who seek to gain control of too much land are often accused of being witches, who use their nefarious powers to gain more than their share of community resources. Thus, witchcraft accusations serve as a powerful check against the violation of a Diola ideal of universal access to arable land.

To be poor in Diola society, an *assoukatene*, is to be without cattle. Diola households require cattle to be sacrificed when an adult dies, when a boy is initiated in the circumcision ritual known as *Bukut*, when one is "seized" to become a priest of an important spirit shrine, or when one has committed a major violation of community norms. During the era of the Atlantic slave trade, six or seven cattle were a required ransom to purchase the freedom of one's family members who had been seized in warfare or raiding. Those without cattle sold some of their rice paddies for cattle in order to raise the ransom required for the liberation of their kin. To be without cattle was to be utterly without spiritual resources to ensure the safe journey of the dead to the place of the ancestors, to protect one's sons in the dangerous rigors of male initiation, to be able to protect one's family against the horrors of slavery, and to purify oneself and one's house from the polluting effects of grievous wrongdoing.

Unfortunately, there were other kinds of poverty. When the rains failed or other misfortunes struck individual farmers, they could be without rice. According to Diola traditions, when someone was without rice (cooked rice is also the term for a meal) he approached a neighbor, relative, or friend at dusk, and told him of his situation. The person who had rice was obligated to share with the hungry person and could not reveal the name of that person to anyone, not even to his or her spouse. A refusal to provide rice when one was able to do so or shaming someone without rice by naming them would eventually lead to a reversal of fortunes. The person with rice would become a supplicant to the person who initially had no rice.

This sense of obligation to one's neighbor carries over into obligations to share in a public context. One of the terms for a rich person, *oussanome*, means literally "give me some" in the imperative. People with wealth are obligated to share it. Wealth should not be hoarded but kept in constant circulation or it could be lost. Given that the primary indicators of wealth, besides rice paddies, were cattle and the quantity of rice in one's granary, wealth was highly perishable and was seen as a transient phenomenon. It was subject to attacks by witches (*musaye*), who could eat the spiritual essence of cattle, causing their death, a common occurrence in an area where animal forms of African sleeping sickness remained frequent. Witches might eat the kernels of rice within their husk, leaving only the appearance of whole rice in a granary, again a common occurrence when termites and rodents often penetrate the granaries. Furthermore, people who had wealth but failed to distribute it have often been accused of being witches themselves, with the suggestion that it was membership in a society of witches that gave them more than their share of a relatively finite quantity of community wealth.

I have witnessed a discrete form of sharing whenever my Diola adopted family had an unusually lavish meal. Small bowls of the dish, with or without the accompanying rice, were sent to relatives, neighbors, and friends. Similarly, when there was a major animal sacrifice at a shrine that did not have elaborate restrictions, small portions of the meat of the sacrifice were distributed to relatives, neighbors, and friends. In both cases, the family's obligation to share its bounty was explained in practical terms: when one had no food, one's neighbor would provide.

During the era of the Atlantic slave trade, when the relative status of rich and poor became far more pronounced, some slave traders were accused of being witches, whose success in their nefarious activity was linked to this antisocial role, particularly when the targets of their slave raiding were children from their own community. Their activities were often seen as directly parallel to the nocturnal attacks of witches who drank their victims' life force, which resided in the blood. Slave raiders who sold children from their own communities attacked their township's life force, their future, which resided in their children.

In an effort to deflect these types of accusations, an emerging slave-trading elite introduced new types of religious cults. These cults emphasized wealth as a means of access to priestly office and emphasized the sacrifice of many animals, which were distributed with palm wine and rice to those who did not benefit from slave-raiding activities. In turn, the spirit shrines (*ukine*) were believed to provide spiritual protection to those engaged in slave trading and warfare, while legitimating their role as powerful individuals who protected and provided for the community. Such transformations occurred in the basic family cult, known as *Hupila*; the town council shrine, known as *Hutendookai*; the male circumcision shrine, known as *Bukut*; and the shrine of the elders, known as *Hoohaney*. This generosity of an emerging, wealthy elite forestalled the types of witchcraft accusations that plagued others who hoarded wealth. A woman prophet of the Supreme Being, known as Alinesitoué Diatta, challenged this emphasis on wealth as a means of access to spiritual power and, during the Second World War, opened Diola religious offices to the poor, to young people, and to women in greater numbers.

Another central value in Diola society is an emphasis on cooperative labor. When a boy about to marry begins the laborious task of constructing a house, his age mates come and help him create a level and hard foundation for the building. Each growing season is accompanied by obligations to maintain a portion of the fence that keeps livestock out of the rice paddies. Young men and women hire themselves out in labor societies, to help with planting or harvesting, and the proceeds of their labor are contributed to the youth organizations of their neighborhood or to a social group of friends who celebrate various holidays together. There is a Diola proverb that draws attention to this obligation: "You cannot thatch a roof with a single piece of straw." For those who fail to meet such obligations, there is a warning proverb that says, "A person with a dry [stingy] hand, will be buried in a single cloth." This proverb suggests that no one would voluntarily bring a cloth to wrap the body of the deceased. Only the family of a stingy man, who had no choice in the matter, would do so. There was also an enforcement aspect to such a requirement. A group known as the *kumachala* forms a kind of township police and enforces the collective obligations from fence maintenance to wage and price controls levied by elders of the town council shrine of *Hutendookai*. The *kumachala* can break into the granaries of men who refuse to maintain their fences, help themselves to rice, and leave the rest for animals to graze on, just as the negligent farmers allowed livestock to graze in the township's rice paddies.

In the system of government that the Diola developed before the colonial occupation, there was a profound concern about the concentration of power in the hands of any one or any small group of individuals. Although authority for community decisions was concentrated in the hands of Diola elders, and young people had relatively little authority, there was an elaborate system of checks and balances to ensure that no one could reach that level of authority in more than one of the most powerful councils of elders of the most powerful spirit shrines. In the township of Kadjinol, where I have lived intermittently since 1974, the three most powerful shrine clusters involved the *oeyi* or priest-king, blacksmiths, and women who have given birth to children. The first two shrine clusters were exclusively for men; the last was restricted to married women, including widows and divorcees, who had given birth. All three exercised jurisdiction over the entire community, though in different areas of community concern. The men who controlled the blacksmith shrines were from the various blacksmith clans, while the shrines of the priest-kings were predominantly from other families. A blacksmith was involved in the inner council of the priest-king's shrine but did not serve a similar role among the blacksmiths. In all three cases, councils of elders controlled the actions of the powerful priests who performed the rituals, thereby checking any proclivities the priests might have had to abuse power. The esoteric knowledge of the various spirit shrines in Diola society provided individuals with power and influence and, before receiving such knowledge, they had to demonstrate their ability to handle this power responsibly and without abusing their authority. No one was allowed access to this restricted level of knowledge at all spirit shrines, because the temptation to abuse the authority that such access would provide would be too tempting.

Diola concepts of social justice were also expressed through their antithesis, the social conduct of witches. In Diola societies, witches (*kusaye*) were said to travel in the night, as disembodied souls, which consumed the souls of other human beings or the spiritual essences of some of their body parts, or rice and other foodstuffs, or engaged in other antisocial behaviors. According to several elders, witches organized themselves into secret clubs that met at night to disinter the spiritual essences of the people they killed. In sharp contrast to ordinary members of Diola society, they organized themselves in a strict hierarchy, and no one who did not contribute dead people to their communal feasts was allowed to participate. In contrast to ordinary Diola, Diola witches conspicuously displayed their wealth in human and animal meats. European witches who attended these gatherings were said to arrive in "spirit" Mercedes-Benzes that could navigate the marshy areas where the witches held their gatherings, and the cases of liquor and perfume that they brought to the gatherings could be seen by those with special "eyes" or special powers of the "head" who could detect the activities of witches. At these witches' gatherings they also had sexual orgies, focused on the very old partnering with the very young and the healthy of body partnering with lepers and others who were forbidden or considered odious. In a society where public displays of affection were sharply criticized and where any direct contact with lepers must be limited to spiritually powerful blacksmiths, these were extraordinary departures from ordinary Diola life. They represented the nightmare of Diola existence, pointing by negative example to the boundaries of acceptable behavior and providing vivid warnings to those who seek to contravene fundamental concepts of social justice.

Diola concepts of history also reflect fundamental ideas of social justice and ethical behavior. At the beginning of time, according to Diola creation accounts, there was a single couple, who regularly sought the advice of the Supreme Being on a wide range of issues in their daily lives, from the nature of their relationship to the origins of life. As the number of people grew, however, and human life grew more complex, they consulted Emitai less and less and began to engage in destructive behaviors, such as witchcraft. Eventually, things became so bad that Emitai decided to destroy the world. This act of destruction has occurred many times in the past and will occur many times in the future. Each time, a couple survives and begins the process all over again, reflecting a cyclical view of history. Consistently, according to Diola historians, the world is in the midst of a downward cycle, reflecting both Diola engagement in the Atlantic slave trade and the growing incidence of witchcraft. The socially corrosive impact of the slave trade, the threat to the autonomy of Diola institutions during the colonial and postcolonial eras, and the growing disruption of family life throughout these eras suggest that we are headed toward another destructive event, which will be followed by the rejuvenation of the world. In that sense, ethical lives and appeals to social justice diminish the precipitous decline of the world, delaying its destruction and persuading Emitai to wait a little longer to see whether people are able to alter the course of human history.

Prophetic Visions of Social Justice

In the twentieth and twenty-first centuries, a new form of Diola prophets, literally people "whom Emitai has sent," mostly women but also some men, began to teach what Emitai commanded them to teach, introducing a series of rain shrines and an ethical critique of the colonial and postcolonial situation of the Diola. The most famous of these prophets was Alinesitoué Diatta, who began to have revelations in 1941, was arrested by the French administration in 1943, and exiled to Timbuctou, where she died of scurvy within a year. At a time when Vichy French officials imposed military conscription and forced labor, while demanding significant quantities of rice and cattle for an isolated colonial administration, French agricultural planners sought to force Diola farmers to grow peanuts (groundnuts) as a cash crop and to use Asian rice seeds that offered higher yields but were more vulnerable to drought, disease, and insects. In the late 1930s and in 1941, devastating droughts caused crop failures on Diola lands. Migration to urban areas by young people and married men led to increasing economic differentiation and new indices of wealth, even in rural Diola communities. In 1939, Catholic missionaries renewed their efforts to convert Diola to Christianity, through the appointment of the first bishop of the Casamance. Islam continued to grow among northern Diola and in the regional capital of Ziguinchor.

In the midst of all these challenges, Alinesitoué had her first visionary experiences. In the midst of a crowded city market in Dakar, she heard the voice of Emitai, who commanded her to go down to the sea and dig a hole in the sand. Water filled the hole, which she understood to mean that Emitai wanted her to bring rain to the Casamance and to end the drought, by offering a new vision of Diola society. She insisted that the drought and the loss of political, economic, social, and cultural autonomy were all linked together. In order to alleviate the hardships confronting them, Diola had to reaffirm the fundamental tenets of a Diola vision of a just society. She introduced a new spirit shrine, *Kasila*, that would be used to ask Emitai directly for life-giving rain. In response to the growing social inequality of Diola society, however, priests would be chosen by divination. Women and men, rich and poor, young and old – all could be chosen through a divining ritual, in which a chicken was sacrificed to choose a new priest. This new way of choosing priests opened up a key new ritual to both sexes, to the young, and to the poor. The black cattle sacrificed at the shrine were provided by those who had them, but they earned no special place in the ritual and no access to any kind of restricted knowledge. Alinesitoué challenged an emphasis on age and wealth that had been growing in importance since the era of the Atlantic slave trade.

In response to the French administration's emphasis on new crops, she emphasized the importance of families farming together, with men and women both performing their proper tasks in the cultivation of rice. She rejected the spread of peanut farming, because it had already led many northern Diola men to abandon rice farming to their wives and daughters in order to concentrate exclusively on peanuts as a cash crop. She argued that Diola were created by Emitai to grow rice, that the proceeds of the peanut crop would be used to buy rice imported by the French from Indochina, and that peanut cultivation could only be done on forest land that was needed to harvest palm products, fruits, medicines, and game animals. She also cautioned against adopting foreign rice seed to the exclusion of the varieties of African rice (*oryza glaberimma*) that were first domesticated in the Casamance, Gambia, and Niger river valleys. The autonomy of Diola agriculture played a central role in her vision of a revitalized Diola nation.

Finally, Alinesitoué sought to restore the moral community of the Diola township. Her ritual of *Kasila* emphasized sharing of meals for an entire week. People ate together in the public square and were forbidden to take any food into their homes. They sang songs of their ancestors and spent the night sleeping in the public square. No implements of European origin could be used in the rituals, a restriction that both reaffirmed the importance of Diola local craftsmanship and rejected the new emphasis on western goods being brought back by migrant youth and men. She insisted that all Diola, regardless of whether or not they had embraced Christianity or Islam, had an obligation to participate in these rituals seeking Emitai's mercy and the gift of rain. Everyone also had to observe the Diola day of rest, every sixth day, on which farming the rice paddies was prohibited, though other forms of work could proceed. Finally, in an effort to retain the vitality of Diola youth, Alinesitoué opposed French military conscription, forced labor, and taxation, which undermined the vitality of the local township.

In her brief, two-year career as a prophet, Alinesitoué offered a vision of social justice based on universal ritual participation focused on the Supreme Being, in which anyone could be chosen by Emitai to be Its priest (Diola do not consider the Supreme Being to be gendered). She emphasized the equality of all people in Diola townships, the obligation to share with everyone, and the ending of privileges based on wealth, age, or gender. She emphasized the common task of Diola people to grow rice and raise cattle, without external interference or distraction. Finally, though she did not reject the new religions of Christianity and Islam, she insisted that Christian and Muslim Diola still had to fulfill their duty to their families and communities, to procure rain from Emitai, by respecting Its day of rest and participating in the rituals of *Kasila*.

After her exile, other people came forward offering critiques of the Diola's increasing integration into a colonial or postcolonial economy. After independence, these prophets engaged in similar critiques of an independent Senegal's agricultural schemes. They did so in the name of Alinesitoué, offering her view of a Diola moral community that could sustain itself and its traditions. This vision has also been embraced by the leaders of the Casamance secessionist movement (Mouvement des Forces Democratiques Senénégalaises) since 1982, claiming that Alinesitoué was the Diola Joan of Arc. Given that the secessionist movement was led by a Catholic priest, however, they played down her role as a prophet and her critique of religious hierarchies and focused on her desire for continued Diola autonomy. The leadership secularized her teachings just enough that both Muslim and Catholic leaders could identify with her. At the local level, particularly in areas where Diola religion remains strong, the people accepted no such separation. For them, the revival of Diola traditional religion was absolutely central to Alinesitoué's vision of a social justice, on Diola land, in autonomous Diola communities.

Conclusion

Diola imagined a world at the beginning of the cycle of human history, in which people lived in harmony with Emitai and with one another. The distractions of family life, the desire to provide for children, and the growing complexity of human relationships led people to neglect their relationships with the Supreme Being, to act selfishly, and to work against the world of *cashumaye*, the peace of Emitai. They began to neglect communal work obligations and their responsibility to share food and other goods for the welfare of the community, and they sought to increase their own portion of available wealth through the nocturnal activities of witches and their antisocial societies. According to Diola views of history, Emitai became so discouraged by the state of the world that It eventually destroyed this world and began the process again, with one couple who enjoyed the relationship of *cashumaye* with Emitai. This has happened many times in the history of the universe and Diola historians strongly suggest that we are headed in that direction again, as a direct result of the Atlantic slave trade, colonization, and postcolonial integration in a global economy.

Yet, throughout the twentieth century, in direct response to the European occupation of their lands, Diola prophets emerged who called people back to social ideals embodied in a correct relationship with the Supreme Being. They established spirit shrines for the direct invocation of the Supreme Being (Emitai) to provide them with life-giving rain, which was seen as a direct manifestation of Emitai. They reaffirmed the importance of community in performing these rituals, stressing the collective and egalitarian nature of correct ritual performance, emphasizing universal access to the special knowledge associated with the cult, the eating of meals together in the public square, and the absence of hierarchies. Prophets challenged the embracing of the new religions of Christianity and Islam, but only to the extent that they rejected people's obligations to Diola religious communities. They rejected the practices of migrant labor, forced labor, and military conscription, which disrupted the community. Finally, they rejected the emphasis on foreign cash crops, most notably peanuts, which distracted men from their basic obligations to grow rice and dramatically increased women's work in the cultivation of this staple crop. Their vision of social justice was one of Diola autonomy in Diola territories; an egalitarian social life with minimal senses of hierarchy in terms of age, wealth, or gender; and a strong emphasis on collective action on behalf of the community. Their ideal of *cashumaye*, which has deep roots in Diola history, has become the Diola ideal of social justice at the dawn of the twenty-first century.

Bibliography

Baum, Robert M. (1999) *Shrines of the Slave Trade: Diola Religion and Society in Precolonial Senegambia*, Oxford University Press, New York.

Baum, Robert M. (2001) Alinesitoué: A West African woman prophet, in *Unspoken Worlds: Women's Religious Lives*, 3rd edn, Nancy Falk and Rita Gross (eds.), Wadsworth, Belmont, CA, pp. 179–195.

Diatta, Christian Sina (1995) *Parlons Jola: Langue et Culture des Diolas*, L'Harmattan, Paris.

Girard, Jean (1969) *Genese du Pouvoir Charismatique en Basse Casamance (Senegal)*, IFAN, Dakar.

Journet-Diallo, Odile (2007) *Les Creances de la Terre: Chronique du Pays Jamaat (Joola du Guinee-Bissau)*, Brepols, Brussels.

Linares, Olga (1992) *Power, Prayer, and Production: The Jola of Casamance, Senegal*, Cambridge University Press, Cambridge.

Snyder, Francis (1981) *Capitalism and Legal Change: An African Transformation*, Academic Press, New York.

Thomas, Louis Vincent (1959–1960) *Les Diola: Essai d'Analyse Fonctionelle sur une Population du Basse Casamance*, IFAN, Dakar.

Waldman, Marilyn R. and Baum, Robert M. (1992) Innovation as renovation: The "prophet" as an agent of change, in *Innovation in Religious Traditions*, Michael S. Williams, Collett Cox, and Martin S. Jaffeel (eds.), Mouton de Gruyter, Berlin.

CHAPTER 24

Australia

Religion and Social Justice in a Continent of Hunter-Gatherers

Robert Tonkinson

Today, some 500 000 Australians identify themselves as Aboriginal; of these, approximately 80% live in urban areas. This figure excludes an unknown number, estimated to be many thousands, of people of Aboriginal descent, who have "disappeared" into the population at large, as a result mainly of historically severe and protracted assimilatory pressures plus high levels of racism directed against their people. The contemporary status of an "Aboriginal" person rests on two major criteria: self-definition via an individual proclaiming this identity; and recognition of this claim by a vaguely defined "Aboriginal community." Much has indeed changed dramatically since 1788, when the British established a penal colony near where Sydney now stands.[1] Yet the frontier of first contact with the invaders lasted almost 200 years, ending as the last groups of previously undisturbed Aborigines left their Western Desert homelands in the 1960s. Early in the colonial period, churches were established and soon after came missions, to serve Aborigines who were displaced from their traditional hunting lands and soon had no alternative but to beg on the fringes of white society. These institutions were motivated much less by any ideas about social justice than evangelization and charity work. Since then, however, many of the churches changed their stance and extended their concern for social justice to Aborigines.

It is important to make very clear at the outset that the spectrum of Aboriginal experience in Australia today is vast, covering at one extreme highly assimilated, well-educated bureaucrats and professionals occupying senior positions, and at the other those people in remote regions who speak English as a second language and in some cases have experienced first contact with whites in their lifetimes. Generalizing from such massive diversity is a risky but not impossible endeavor, since the identifiable Aboriginal population is statistically disadvantaged in terms of *all* major socioeconomic indicators. The 1960s saw a notable increase in both forms and levels of protest by Aboriginal people against adverse government policies and their often deplorable

---

The Wiley Blackwell Companion to Religion and Social Justice, First Edition. Edited by Michael D. Palmer and Stanley M. Burgess.
© 2012 John Wiley & Sons Ltd. Published 2020 by John Wiley & Sons Ltd.

situation in comparison with the rest of society, which had prospered considerably in the years after the Second World War. In recognition of historical discrimination and exclusionary law and practice, and of the Aborigines' prior occupation of the continent, a number of laws have been passed in recent decades. Notable legislation has been enacted having specific application to Indigenous Australians, for example the *Aboriginal Land Rights (Northern Territory) 1976* and the *Native Title Act (1993)*. Nationally, under Australian law as it stands, all citizens, including indigenous Australians, are subject to the same rights and obligations.

Much of this essay looks back to salient characteristics of religious systems characterizing Aboriginal societies at the time of initial contact with Europeans, with the intent to explore the relationship between religion and issues surrounding "social justice." Aboriginal Australian societies represent what is possibly the longest continuous hunter-gatherer adaptation in the world.[2] In the course of their 60 000 or more years of tenure, Aborigines successfully peopled the world's driest continent, undeterred by the absence of domesticable plants and animals (even the late-arriving dingo was semi-feral), metal tools, written languages, and so on. Given this extraordinary time frame, significant climatic and topographical variations, the small scale of these societies, the necessity for dispersal precluding large or protracted aggregations, and considerable linguistic diversity (over 200 different languages were spoken), it is not surprising that Aboriginal identity was notably localized and moral boundaries were accordingly circumscribed, though never absent.

Available evidence suggests that the first Australians enjoyed many millennia of isolation in the world's oldest and geologically most stable continent, which afforded them ample time to adapt to such phenomena as climatic and sea-level changes, and significant floral and faunal extinctions. The Aborigines are a genetically distinct group with considerable internal diversity and no close relationships outside Australia. These characteristics suggest that they had been spared periodic intrusions of new ideas, dogmas, and technologies.[3] Once the continent was peopled, however, it was inevitable that regional differences in material culture, population densities, extractive activities, and subsistence patterns would develop. Strong continuities and continent-wide uniformities nevertheless persisted in fundamental structural and cultural forms. Everywhere, surface variation in beliefs, behaviors, social groupings and categories, and language was underlain by these widely shared cultural elements. These were undoubtedly related to the homogenizing and cohesive power of webs of kinship and gift exchange and the continual generation and circulation of religious lore. Viewed in global perspective, Aboriginal Australian societies and cultures shared many features with other hunter-gatherers, suggesting that particular modes of adaptation impose similar kinds of limitations. In the Australian case, there is sharp contrast between minimal but functional material technologies and the extraordinary richness and complexity of social and religious forms, into which the Aborigines must have directed an enormous amount of energy.

The Aboriginal social fabric was so thoroughly permeated by religion that nomadism itself is construed as a religious act, carried out in emulation of the activities of ancestral creative beings. Much of this essay therefore focuses on religion as essential to any discussion of Aboriginal values and institutions, and thus to "social justice." This notion, which is associated with many things, notably a liberal philosophy and Catholic social teaching, appears at first glance to have no equivalent in Aboriginal thought. In this essay, then, I attempt to identify some comparable structures, ways of thinking, and behaviors that may offer points of similarity to notions of social justice. I also discuss the extent to which Aborigines conceive of the individual having rights vis-à-vis society, or of human rights more generally. To understand how ideas of social justice relate to a continent of nomadic hunter-gatherers, it is necessary to consider a number of related factors: Aboriginal religion permeates worldviews, and the place of the individual cannot be understood apart from kinship, notions of personhood, and issues of social control, for example. First, I set the scene by outlining issues surrounding societal scale and polity, and draw ethnographic examples largely from the Mardu people with whom I have enjoyed a long association. They live in the Western Desert, which is a culturally homogeneous region covering one sixth of the continent.[4]

Scale and Polity

Hunter-gatherer societies are typically small in scale, kinship based, and politically "headless." Local concerns tend to dominate in the absence of centralized institutions. Most had neither chiefs nor headmen, and kinship statuses framed almost all social interaction. The rhythm of life in these familistic societies oscillated between dispersal and aggregation, with the "normal" situation necessarily one of dispersal, so as to maximize each small group's access to food and other resources. The dominant ethos of these societies was strongly egalitarian, but in most there were clear status differences that favored initiated men. Leadership was muted and situational, changing according to the task or ritual at hand. In most contexts, men led by example and quiet persuasion rather than by ordering others to do things. Age (or seniority) and gender were the most important criteria for differentiating people. Wisdom, and accordingly respect, grew with age. In Australia, certainly, the concerns of mature males took precedence over those of the rest of society, since men openly proclaimed responsibility for both production and cultural reproduction. In most hunter-gatherer societies, women provided the bulk of the diet, but in Australia men claim that food is made available for women to gather only because of men's ritual activities, and women did not openly challenged such assertions of hegemony. Beyond relationships based on kinship, the most important statuses in much of Australia were those of male and female ritual hierarchies. However, although religiously these institutions were seen as vital, they were largely irrelevant to the everyday necessity of getting a living from hunting and gathering.

Aborigines are notable among the world's hunter-gatherers because their nomadism existed along with deeply felt, multiple attachments to one or more homelands; individuals and small descent-based groups hold the responsibility for key sites in those homelands. Dialects or languages were directly linked to areas of land, with language and people sharing connections to a given stretch of territory. Larger gatherings, based largely on kinship, affinity, language, and ritual ties, would take place when resources permitted, in order to conduct ritual and social business. However, the most visible, on-the-ground, social grouping was the "band." In the Western Desert, for example, this face-to-face familial and economic unit typically contained about 15–30 members, usually closely related. It varied in size, sometimes swelled by greater numbers when neighboring bands met up, and when food and water resources permitted. Western Desert people would have spent about 95% of their time in bands. The circuit normally covered by a band was its "range," which overlapped with those of its various neighbors. The band, however, was in no way coterminous with "society." Powerful bonds of kinship, marriage, shared dialect or language, exchange, shared religious responsibilities, and so on continually focused its members' attention outward, to a larger body of related people sharing much in common.

The large, temporary aggregations, often called "big meetings" in much of remote Aboriginal Australia, served vital functions, including dispute settlement, initiation ceremonies, exchange of rituals, items of material culture and other lore, arrangement of betrothals, planning for future meetings and their ritual programs, not to mention information transfer, formal introductions to previously unmet kin, and the excitement and heightened emotions that accompanied ritual performances. Issues that could perhaps be considered as relating to social justice beyond the level of the band were likely to be most visible during the disputes' settlement process integral to such gatherings. In the Western Desert, at least, rituals could not succeed in their aims if participants were upset, so it was essential that all differences be aired and dealt with to the satisfaction of the assembly before ritual activities began; from that point, conflict was strictly forbidden. These gatherings evidence widely shared moral values and worldviews, and the existence of a coherent "society" well beyond the bounds of the local landholding group.

Religion

Orderly social life throughout most of the continent was based on obedience to the dictates of a body of rules said to have been instituted by ancestral beings in the creative epoch of the Dreaming.[5] Today, in many remote areas, Aborigines most commonly use another English term, "the Law," in reference to this blueprint for life. The Law can be described as a body of jural rules and moral evaluations of customary and socially sanctioned behavior patterns attributable to the dictates of the founding beings. It is thus all-encompassing, and issues concerning justice, punishment, and retribution are embedded within it.[6] Broadly, the Dreaming explains how things came to be as they are, and the Law specifies how life is to be lived. The Dreaming is a complex notion, a timeless "everywhen" (in Stanner's apt designation) that embraces past, present, and future and remains relevant for remote-dwelling Aboriginal people. Traditionally, not a day could pass without people being cognizant in some way of its presence, since they were constantly surrounded by visible "proofs" of the Dreaming: the features of the landscape in daylight and celestial bodies at night.

Aborigines believe that their landscapes were created eons ago, when the ancestral creative beings came ashore and began to spread across what was then a featureless land. As they traveled, their many exploits, accidental and intentional, created the features of the landscape, leaving "tracks" that would be indelibly imprinted on every adult's mental map of their country. More importantly, they hunted, gathered, fought, and exchanged religious objects, rituals, and knowledge. Some, but not all, of their behaviors would become templates for human institutions. Notable or distinctive shapes and features in the landscape, as well as human happenings therein, were undoubtedly the inspiration for much of the mythology that evolved.

Eventually exhausted by their superhuman efforts and the weight of the sacred paraphernalia that they wore and carried, the creative beings lay down and "died," having completed their earthly tasks. They then transformed into stones, other natural features, or celestial bodies, before withdrawing forever, as spirits, into the spiritual realm somewhere "out there." What remained, though, was the powerful "life essence" contained in their bodies and in everything they possessed, touched, or left behind on earth. Aborigines believe that its power was undiminished, constantly animating all life forms, and remaining available to human actors through ritual. They and their associated spirits, some of which act as messengers between the spiritual and human realms, were believed to maintain a continuing interest in the human realm. Earthly life could be understood as a kind of contract: as long as humans followed the rules laid down by the creative beings, particularly with regard to ritual responsibilities, the flow of enabling power from the spiritual realm into the world would continue, ensuring natural and cultural reproduction.

The Law-abiding person, by dutifully following the founding design, was conforming to the terms of life laid down in the Dreaming, and submitting to what Stanner calls "a sacred purpose." By acting in this way, people reaped the benefits of reciprocity; namely, the continued fertility of living things and the maintenance of a long-term ecological and social status quo. Because society and culture were so firmly grounded in religion, the changes that inevitably occurred were interpreted and absorbed within a pervasive ideology of non-change: the "blueprint" or life design laid down by the ancestral beings was to be faithfully followed for all time. In its unquestioning acceptance of the terms of a life already fixed and immutable, the dominant human disposition would be assent and obedience rather than the pursuit of progress or revolution.

How, then, do Aborigines learn their Dreaming heritage? Their deep understanding is acquired from early childhood, largely through having landscape features and their mythological significance repeatedly shown and explained to them, but also through the media of myths, rituals, song lines, and objects of many kinds. All the notable marvels of the Dreaming are embodied in one or more of these elements. Creative and world-ordering acts of the first beings are narrated in myths, acted out in dance, condensed into song, and "proven" both by landforms that bear the indelible imprint of these founding dramas and portable sacred objects intimately connected to the beings themselves. Landforms weld the Dreaming solidly to territory by mediating between the creative era and the human realm. Song, dance, and storytelling are the means through which communication with the spiritual realm is enhanced and reciprocity is guaranteed. Myths reveal the nature of the founding design and of its creators; and totemic beliefs forge vital, life-sustaining links between individuals, groups, specific sites, and ancestral beings. For Aborigines, the spiritual realm and that of humans and nature were essentially one intricately interconnected unity.

Stanner stresses that the essence of Aboriginal religions lies in its essential life-mindedness: it magnifies the worth of the individual, as both flesh and spirit; and most spirits, particularly those associated with one's own territory, look after their human relatives. Aborigines also naturalized the human innovatory component in their cultural development by treating creative individuals as conduits for, rather than originators of, new knowledge entering society. As Maddock (1982: 119) notes:

> Aborigines claim credit only for fidelity to tradition or, as they put it, for "following up the Dreaming". It is the powers alone who are conceived of as creative, men being passive recipients of unmotivated gifts. As men deny the creativity which is truly theirs, they account for their culture only by positing that to create is to be other than human. To be human is to reproduce forms.

New knowledge emanated from the withdrawn spiritual powers of the Dreaming, largely during altered states of consciousness, particularly dreams, and was rapidly absorbed into the timeless, unbounded Dreaming realm. There were times and circumstances of altered consciousness when Aborigines could briefly transcend their humanity and tap this reservoir, as for example during dance, dreams, and heightened emotional and ritual states. Yet Aboriginal religion is neither deeply mystical nor preoccupied with the occult. These societies collectively evolved a conception of history as cosmic rather than chronological, with religious conceptions of causation, being, and purpose given primary and unchallenged status. While it is true that people could not claim credit for independent creativity, they were not denied their individuality.

Morality

Although in western societies there is a tendency to take for granted an intimate connection between religion and moral systems, elsewhere in the world, especially in small-scale societies, the relationship may be tenuous or virtually nonexistent. Aboriginal myths may describe acts that were neither moral nor acceptable, in terms of the sociocultural master plan said to have been bequeathed by the creative beings to their human descendants. At times the ancestral heroes were neither measured nor just in their actions, which could be unpredictable and perverse. The lives of Dreaming beings were somewhat similar to those of humans, with the same potential for altruistic or antisocial acts. If bad things happen but are unpunished in a myth, it may end with a statement affirming that what has transpired belongs only to the Dreaming. Should the event involve instituting something that is to endure for ever, one of the characters may say so. Mardu mythology seems at least to suggest a moral element in much Dreaming behavior, particularly through its concern for the instituting of, and demanding adherence to, a Lawful way of life by the living descendants. It may be that immoral acts are safely locked into the world of mythology to serve as bad examples, harmlessly accentuating the forbidden to highlight what is acceptable morally.

Aboriginal societies displayed neither an explicit religious ethic nor any kind of religious creed. Stanner concluded that Aborigines attributed only a vague moral-ethical authority to the creative beings, because three vital preconditions for their development were absent: a tradition of intellectual detachment; a body of interpreters charged with the task of codifying basic tenets or principles; and an external challenge that would have called morals and beliefs into question. He identified two complementary emphases in the doctrine of the Dreaming: the instituting of things in an enduring form, and, simultaneously, the endowing of those things, including humanity, with their good and/or bad properties. While Aboriginal mythology may reveal considerable moral ambiguity, Stanner believed that evidence for the operation of moral principles is clear in rituals. He noted structural parallels between certain myths and rituals: a steady rise to a tense crisis that has a distinct moral quality, and, in the case of initiation rituals, that brings about in the initiates a transformation that is at once physical, moral, and spiritual. In his view, these rituals are disciplines that shape the young, uncompleted male and transform him into a being of higher worth, both socially and spiritually.

Their Law told Aborigines which Dreaming behaviors were to be emulated or avoided. As if fully aware of human imperfections, the ancestral creators instituted informal but effective socialization processes to inculcate notions of right and wrong. Yet, if someone breaks the Law, as is bound to happen at times, it must be people and not the withdrawn Dreaming beings who punish the offender. The spiritual powers do not exist to uphold the laws of society by punishing transgressors, having long since withdrawn into their own realm. Once they leave behind a set of rules for the lawful functioning of human life, they rely on individuals to regulate their own behavior; failing this, a system of kin-based obligations generally works well in preventing offenders from threatening the status quo. Even where spiritual sanctions exist, human agents are in most cases essential for their execution, and such sanctions are limited to specific ritual infringements. The great power or life essence believed to reside in sacred objects and in certain songs, dances, and localities is extremely dangerous for some sections of society. For example, in the Western Desert region men believe that, should women somehow see such objects or trespass into men's sacred areas, they would soon sicken and die. This belief is nonetheless supplemented by human action: such offenders should be killed if discovered, because of the grave nature of their offense.

Kinship

The key integrating institution in virtually all the world's small-scale societies is kinship, and this takes us close to the heart of concepts very similar to those entailed in social justice. Although age and gender largely determine a person's social status, neither is sufficient to regulate behavior. Principles akin to social justice lie within the framework for interpersonal behavior constituted by principles of "classificatory" kinship.[7] Everyone is born into a universe of kin that defines one's obligations and responsibilities to all others within its bounds. Although children do not have to abide by its dictates, they internalize both the ideal and actual patterning of social relationships while growing up. "Strangers" cannot be interacted with until their precise kinship connection to a given person is established by older relatives who can identify it.

In familistic societies, kinship frames virtually every relationship of dominance, deference, obligation, or equality. Everyone with whom one interacts is classified and known by a particular kin term, and adult social interaction is modeled on a set of behaviors that ideally characterize the kin relationship involved. People constantly use kin terms in addressing and referring to others, and the system offers them a ready-made, mutually understood interactional code. Because a kin term is simultaneously a status term, it encodes a great deal of information useful for framing social interaction. Regardless of whether some other person is loved or hated, admired or envied, patterned kin behavior allows both actors a measure of predictability in their encounters. Most westerners would find such systems confusing and unnecessarily restrictive, but not so people in small-scale societies such as those of hunter-gatherers. The relatively restricted and patterned behavioral field that is created by kinship has advantages: it provides a good measure of predictability in behavior and enhances each individual's sense of self and of belonging. A strong sense of security and well-being stems from being enveloped in a cocoon of kin, with every one of whom some feeling of mutual obligation and responsibility ideally exists.

The notion that absolutely everyone in one's social field throughout the life cycle is a "relative" means that there is no room at all for such abstract ideas as "nationhood" or "the citizen isolate." These were unthinkable notions in Aboriginal societies, a fact that renders problematic the very idea of "social justice" as generally understood.[8] As I noted above, this is not to say that individuality in its many expressions was frowned on, or unduly constricted, or that it functions in ways that preclude individuals being held responsible for their own behavior. In all small-scale societies, though, self-regulation is enormously important in everyday life and egotism finds no favor whatsoever. As Stanner (1979) makes clear, Aboriginal religion places a high value on the individual as both flesh and spirit. In fact, to live in a universe of kin is essentially to live in a moral universe, and the strong bias in favor of inclusion that is fundamental to kinship ensures that fair and just behaviors toward others will obtain under normal circumstances.

Worldview

Can elements akin to those associated with social justice be easily located in Aboriginal worldviews? Individual males were socialized to develop strong convictions about their collective responsibility for world maintenance, via the correct performance of rituals at the appropriate times. To ensure a continual outpouring of power or life force from the withdrawn spiritual powers, each generation was charged with the regular and proper performance of rituals and obedience to the Law. In all Aboriginal societies, the relationship between humans and nature is a close one, expressed and affirmed in their totemic beliefs, a fundamental element of people's worldviews. In both its individual and group forms, totemism implies that there is a unity of substance or flesh between people, plants, animals and the rest of the natural environment. Individuals are linked to the Dreaming powers through enduring, indissoluble, and multiple totemic associations. The existence of an intimate connection between humans and animals is also reflected in people's conceptions of the creative beings: almost all had the ability to assume either human or animal form and behavior when the occasion demanded. The Mardu may be emphatic about the essential "humanness" of Marlu the Kangaroo, for instance, yet in relating the exploits of this major creative being, a person will use the verb "hop" to describe Marlu's mode of locomotion.

Given the vagaries of climate and rainfall in much of the continent, it may seem surprising that Aboriginal worldviews typically manifested an attitude of security and confidence. This is undoubtedly because they were grounded not only in an encyclopedic environmental knowledge, but also because their religion tells them that the omnipotent spiritual beings make available to those who obey the Law a huge reservoir of life-giving and life-sustaining powers. Until relatively recently, scholars have tended to dwell on the shortcomings and disadvantages of hunter-gatherer technology and economy, and therefore to allot great importance to ecological imperatives as limiting hunter-gatherer possibilities. From this perspective, these societies appear to be dangerously fragile, poised constantly not far from the brink of starvation or thirst. In reality, the Aborigines took their great skills in exploiting the environment very much for granted, as knowledge gained almost incidentally in the normal process of maturation. Yet they placed a heavy cultural stress on the necessity to behave lawfully: survival skills are useless if people neglect the Law, thus provoking the spiritual powers to refuse reciprocity, with the result that no rain falls and the land becomes infertile. Everywhere, Aboriginal worldviews dwelt on spiritual rather than ecological imperatives as guaranteeing the good life.

Personhood

Tensions between the individual ego and the needs and wishes of the group are a human universal, and every society needs to achieve a workable balance if it is to remain stable. Of interest in the Aboriginal case is that, traditionally, children were given virtually free rein to test the limits of their environment and display all their emotions (including temper tantrums among small children) without fear of intervention, chastisement, or physical punishment from their elders. Yet by the time young people reached social adulthood, they were typically tractable and obedient, and assumed their multiple obligations and responsibilities to others without complaint or rebelliousness. A deeply imbued sense of what the Mardu call *kunta*, "shame, embarrassment," lay at the heart of individual self-control in Aboriginal societies. In times of conflict or tension, both men and women were given to intense verbal and, less commonly, physical exchanges using fists or weapons. Other kin would quickly intervene in such interpersonal clashes, their role depending on their particular kinship link to the protagonists, who typically calmed down rapidly, and let go of their anger rather than continue to bear grudges. Verbal shaming was often sufficient to subdue high emotions. People might break rules and be punished, or have grievances that need to be settled, and there were mechanisms by which these outcomes could be achieved. The absence of codified laws did not mean an absence of justice or a free-for-all.

Social Justice

Applying the term "social justice" to small-scale, kin-based, strongly egalitarian societies presents major challenges. Throughout this essay, the great contrasts between hunter-gatherer and western-type societies have been implied rather than dwelt on, since they are quite obvious in terms of scale and polity, for a start. The concept of social justice probably originated in, and has been drawn from, hierarchical societies, most likely those that were large-scale, class- or caste-based polities. In these, an individual's life can be sustained in the midst of strangers, and an inevitably unequal distribution of power and influence exposes people in the lower orders to the threat or reality of discrimination and the worsening of inequalities. As I have endeavored to show, hunter-gatherer societies lie at the opposite end of the spectrum of human possibilities. Their members live in a world of biographies, and strangers exist only beyond the limits of one's society. True, men have more rights than women and their responsibility for key elements of social reproduction is not challenged, but in everyday social life the ethos of egalitarianism is strongly held, and much male rhetoric about their superiority to women takes place in men-only groups.

Most kin relationships carry with them a degree of permissible variation in their behavioral content and say nothing about the emotional closeness or distance between the two interacting individuals. Yet these status relationships cannot be abandoned, and it is difficult to ignore them and negotiate very different relationships. There is no absoluteness of individuality in the eyes of the Law; all is relational, and embedded, and the relative kinship positions are concretized. There is, then, no social space for people to develop a consideration of "social justice" in the abstract. Rather, how they treat every other individual adult (children are universally indulged to a degree unheard of in most western societies) is significantly determined by kinship. For every punisher, there is a protector (in different situations, key kin, such as a male's elder brother or female's elder sister, can be both), for every critic, a defender, and so on.

Most Aboriginal societies possess some form of social category system. These groupings are activated for certain purposes, most often during ritual and in association with major rites of passage for males. However, such divisions are essentially balanced, and the content of their interactions is often joking and ribaldry, between those who are wife givers and those who are wife receivers, for example. The kind of domination that might engender a desire or necessity for social justice is absent from Aboriginal social formations. It is not that there may be no unhappiness on the part of individuals frustrated by society's strictures, but that those individuals do not then constitute some enduring subset of society. Such resentments tend to be situational and temporary. Strains toward significant inequalities have certainly been identified in different parts of Aboriginal Australia, but by and large these are contested and fluid, and countervailing forces work against the hardening of inequality into something resembling caste or class. In any case, the scale of these societies is all wrong for such development, and the stakes would be quite low, given the mode of production and the status of individuals as mediums rather than innovators.

Although it is arguable that there was no obvious equivalent of the concept in indigenous cultures, in Australia today social justice is often invoked by the indigenous minorities, as well as non-indigenous Australians on their behalf. The colonial past and its legacies of dispossession, racism, marginalization, and so on have left the vast majority of indigenous people patently disadvantaged – and this in a society that espouses liberal democratic principles. Most talk of social justice concerns Australia's responsibility to ensure that all its citizens enjoy the same basic rights, versus the reality of serious and persisting inequalities in the case of its indigenous minorities (see note 8). There is much still to do before social justice is achieved, particularly in terms of equality of outcomes. The Indigenous Affairs policy of the current Labor Federal Government aims to close an alarmingly and persistently wide gap between indigenous and non-indigenous Australians, according to all major social indicators. Significantly, most of the nation's mainline churches are actively involved, to varying degrees, in bridging efforts, and in exerting moral pressure on governments, state and federal, to do more. Missions, with their decidedly checkered history, are no more, but the churches continue to provide practical and material assistance in addition to more directly religious pursuits.

Notes

1   Scholarly estimates of the total Aboriginal population at that time vary wildly, between about 300 000 and over 1 million.
2   This paper concerns Australia's larger indigenous minority only, since there are significant cultural differences between Aborigines and the much less numerous Torres Strait Islanders, and space limitations preclude discussion of both peoples. The latter population is heavily concentrated in north coastal Queensland.
3   Their isolation was broken along parts of the northern coastline when Makassan traders (from what is now southern Indonesia) began making seasonal visits to harvest bêche-de-mer some 150 years before British settlement. Their influence on Aboriginal societies did not appear to have spread very far (see Mulvaney, 1989).
4   I have worked with the Mardu (aka Martu) since 1963 and have written two monographs (and numerous articles) about them: *The Jigalong Mob* (1974) and *The Mardu Aborigines* (1978/1991)
5   See Stanner (1979). The creative epoch is also known as "the Dreamtime," but inappropriately so because it is timeless, embracing past, present, and future dimensions.
6   This follows the definition proposed by J. Wilson (1961) and K. Wilson (1961) and also their example in using the capitalized word "Law" to distinguish the Aboriginal concept from that of English speakers. However, in employing the English term, Aboriginal people are evidently making a conceptual equation of the two social systems, emphasizing the existence of rules, formal behaviors, and social control in both.
7   In this kind of system, kinship terms used between blood relatives are also applied to more distantly related, or unrelated, people. These classifying systems rest on two major principles: first, in reckoning kin relationships, siblings of the same sex are classed as equivalent (e.g., one's father's brothers are classed with one's father and called by the same term; likewise, one's mother's sisters are also called "mother"). Secondly, the classifying principle can be expanded to embrace a theoretically infinite number of people.
8   Today, however, the Australian Human Rights Commission has an Aboriginal and Torres Strait Islander Social Justice Commissioner, whose annual report on the enjoyment and

exercise of indigenous human rights and recommendations to government for addressing issues in these areas has become a major reference work. It is published electronically at http://www.humanrights.gov.au/social_justice/sj_report/sjreport08/ (accessed September 28, 2011).

References

Maddock, K. (1982) *The Australian Aborigines: A portrait of their society*, 2nd edn, Penguin, Melbourne.

Mulvaney, D. John (1989) *Encounters in Place: Outsiders and Aboriginal Australians, 1606–1985*, University of Queensland Press, St Lucia.

Stanner, W.E.H. (1979) *White Man Got No Dreaming: Essays 1938–1973*, Australian National University Press, Canberra.

Wilson, John (1961) Authority and leadership in a "new style" Australian Aboriginal Community, Pindan, Western Australia, unpublished MA thesis, University of Western Australia.

Wilson, Katrin (1961) The allocation of sex roles in social and economic affairs in a "new style" Australian Aboriginal Community, Pindan, Western Australia, unpublished MSc thesis, University of Western Australia.

Bibliography

Bern, J. (1979) Ideology and domination: Toward a reconstruction of Australian Aboriginal social formation, *Oceania* 50: 118–132.

Berndt, R.M. and Berndt, C.H. (1988) *The World of the First Australians*, rev. edn, Aboriginal Studies Press, Canberra.

Burridge, K.O.L. (1973) *Encountering Aborigines: A Case Study – Anthropology and the Australian Aboriginal*, Pergamon, New York.

Keen, I. (1996) *Knowledge and Secrecy in an Aboriginal Religion*, Oxford University Press, Oxford.

Stanner, W.E.H. (1989) *On Aboriginal Religion*, Oceania Monograph 36, University of Sydney, Sydney.

Tonkinson, R. (1988) Ideology and domination in Aboriginal Australia: A Western Desert test case, in *Hunters and Gatherers, Volume 1: Property, Power and Ideology*, T. Ingold, D. Riches, and J. Woodburn (eds.), Berg, Oxford, pp. 170–184.

Tonkinson, R. (1991) *The Mardu Aborigines: Living the Dream in Australia's Desert*, 2nd edn, Holt, Rinehart and Winston, Fort Worth.

Tonkinson, R. (2004) Resolving conflict within the law: The Mardu Aborigines of Australia, in *Keeping the Peace: Conflict Resolution and Peaceful Societies around the World*, G. Kemp and D.P. Fry (eds.), Routledge, London, pp. 89–104.

CHAPTER 25

Central America

A God for the Poor – Folk Catholicism and Social Justice among the Yucatec Maya

Christine A. Kray

Yucatec Maya is an indigenous language spoken by about a million people in southern Mexico and western Belize, and Yucatec Maya speakers are some of the descendants of those who created the ancient Maya civilization. Very little of the ancient religion(s) survives to the present. Instead, beginning in the sixteenth century, Spanish colonizers converted the Maya to Roman Catholicism. Nonetheless, the version of Catholicism practiced in Yucatec Maya towns and villages today is culturally distinctive, with its own sense of social justice. While all cultures have their own take on what is "just," "right," and "fair," the Maya emphasize equality and cooperation. This folk version of justice reflects the region's history of colonialism and of modern-day economic exploitation within global capitalism, and has found new voice in discourses of liberation theology.

This essay explores the social and economic conditions (colonial and present-day) that have created fertile ground for religious ideals of equality and cooperation. It explores the various strands of folk Catholicism among the Yucatec Maya, including formal doctrines and practices introduced by the priests, folk rituals that have been created by villagers themselves, and the latest doctrines of liberation theology introduced by missionary nuns, noting throughout the unifying themes of equality and cooperation.

The southern Mexican state of Yucatán comprises a few large towns, where the Spanish language dominates, and hundreds of smaller villages of Maya speakers. Village layouts radiate outward from a central square, each with a town hall and Catholic church, part of the heritage of Spanish colonialism. This unique geographical pairing of government and church derives from Spanish policies of colonialism and is mirrored in a modern-day cultural linkage between church and social justice.

The Wiley Blackwell Companion to Religion and Social Justice, First Edition. Edited by Michael D. Palmer and Stanley M. Burgess.
© 2012 John Wiley & Sons Ltd. Published 2020 by John Wiley & Sons Ltd.

The prehispanic (pre-Conquest) Maya world of southern Mexico, Guatemala, Belize, and northern Honduras was characterized by hierarchy and dispersal, not by equality nor, probably, village solidarity. During the Classic era (ca. 250–900 CE), nobles and divine kings united tens of thousands of people around ornate cities famed for their works of art and architecture, hieroglyphic writing, mathematics and astronomy, and long-distance trade. In the late Post-Classic era (through 1500 CE) in Yucatán, the population was concentrated along the coasts, facilitating trade routes connecting central Mexico and Central America. On the eve of the Spanish conquest, the Yucatán peninsula was divided into some 16 provinces, each dominated by a noble lineage, and most headed by a *jalach winik* or "'true man." The towns were governed by *batabs* plus a local council, deputies, and heads of wards. Three separate classes of people comprised Maya society, including the nobility (*almejens*), commoners (*yalba winik*), and slaves, who were primarily captives of war (Roys, 1957: 3–10). How the ancient Maya spread themselves over the land reflected the larger social complexity. There were lands corresponding to provinces, towns, neighborhoods, lineages, the nobility, and individual households (Villa Rojas, 1961). While some cities boasted dense populations, other regions had a more dispersed settlement pattern in which towns bled into one another, and still other regions were characterized by the isolated hamlets of agricultural homesteads (Kurjack and Garza, 1981: 298–300; Robles Castellanos and Andrews, 1985: 68–70). Into this complex political world Spaniards set foot in the early sixteenth century.

In general, Spanish colonial administration made Yucatecan society more homogenous and localized. The friars were concerned that the "Indians" be protected from the degenerative influence of the Spanish settlers, and so a policy of *reducción* or reduction corralled Indians into discrete, compact villages. The result of this settlement reorganization was that throughout the colonial period, Spaniards and *mestizos*, mixed European and indigenous, generally lived in the towns, and Indians in villages in the countryside (Farriss, 1978, 1984). Prehispanic political connections between local settlements were severed. The polities of the *jalach winiks* were dismantled. In addition to being the unit of settlement, the village became the political unit of the colony as well. A *gobernador* served as the head of the town council (*cabildo*) (Farriss, 1984: 232). Indian villages were granted common lands (*ejidos*), of which villagers had rights to farm. In fact, all lands within village limits that were not owned by individuals belonged to the village as a whole, and these lands were protected under Spanish colonial law (Farriss, 1984: 208).

The Indian village was also made the basic unit of the colonial economy. Villages were subjected to a series of mandatory tributes, taxes, and labor drafts. In the *encomienda* system, villages were granted to individual conquistadors in a gesture of gratitude by the Crown for their participation in the conquest. The Indians owed the *encomenderos* or encomienda recipients (and subsequently, their offspring) regular tribute in cash or in kind. Another set of taxes was levied by church and civil officials. These taxes were exacted of individuals, but typically collected by the *cabildo*. These various taxes included mandatory alms, fees for baptisms, confirmations, weddings, burials, and catechism. Civil taxes included a tax to support the court system and a community tax for village expenses (Farriss, 1984: 39–56; Patch, 1993: 26–32).

Finally, the Indians participated in a series of forced labor drafts, also organized at the village level. *Servicio personal* or personal service was compulsory service in the homes of the Spaniards in the towns for one week per year. Corvée labor teams built roads, churches, and public buildings, and transported people and goods. In addition, Indians worked one day per week attending to village tasks (Farriss, 1984: 47–56; Patch, 1993: 29). Village officials were charged with collecting the taxes and organizing the forced labor drafts, reinforcing a sense of shared responsibility within the village.

Spanish evangelization took place within parish subunits called *visitas*, which corresponded to the villages, effectively making the village the locus of colonial religion. As in other parts of the colonies, the aspect of Christianity that the Indians of Yucatán adopted most enthusiastically was the cult of the saints. Each village was dedicated to and named after a patron saint. Under missionary guidance, village *cofradías* or confraternities were established for the organization of *fiestas* in veneration of the patron saint on the saint's designated day in the Catholic calendar. In exchange for this veneration, the saint was to ensure the health and welfare of the villagers for the coming year. Certain village lands were set aside as *cofradía* lands for agricultural fields or cattle ranches worked by collective labor drafts; the products of the *cofradía* lands went toward the annual fiestas or as a mutual aid fund for the emergency needs of villagers (Farriss, 1984: 262–272). The patron saint thus became yet another Spanish colonial institution that reinforced a sense of shared responsibility and cooperation among co-villagers.

If Spanish colonial administration solidified local settlements as units of the political economy and religion, Indians responded favorably, and the *kaj* or village became the locus of group identity. As Restall concludes:

> Whether or not some Mayas felt a sense of macroregional loyalty and identity before the Conquest, it is clear that after the imposition of Spanish colonial government Maya self-identity, definition, pride, and loyalty focused on the cah [*kaj*]. (Restall, 1997: 18)

Even though the *ejidos* and colonial village administrative systems were dismantled in the nineteenth century following independence, *ejidos* were restored in most Yucatecan villages in the mid-twentieth century following the Mexican Revolution, reviving a sense of shared rights and responsibilities. Meanwhile, the village layout, centered on the pairing of town hall and church, and the continued devotion to the patron saint provided continuity between the corporate colonial community and the present.

My ethnographic work on Yucatec Maya religion was conducted throughout the 1990s in the village of Balankaj (pseudonym). Although village affairs are not always peaceful and the village is divided between political factions, there is a strong sentiment that the village should be united and should cooperate. Cultural values of equality and cooperation can first of all be seen in practices of food sharing. Food is shared between households on a daily basis. Sisters-in-law, neighbors, *comadres* (women linked by godparenthood), sisters, and cousins all regularly bring each other little pots of food. If someone buys a small treat at the store, it will soon all be divided up among the friends, relatives, and *compadres* with whom one is sitting. A visitor to a house will always be offered a little something to eat, if only a piece of fruit from a tree in the yard. A saying goes that you should always give a visitor "at least a little water," because you never know if that visitor is not Jesus Christ himself. A vocabulary distinction is made between *ts'aik*, "giving," and *sijik*, "gifting" or "giving as a gift." Food is always "gifted," indicating that the giving involves the giving of both the food itself and the goodwill of the giver, necessarily linking the giver and receiver in a relationship of goodwill. Moreover, it is important that you sit and eat the food together with its giver. Sitting and eating together, especially sharing the same plate, draws people together in a very special way.

Ritualized redistribution of food is a central element in all ceremonies, religious and civil. The importance of food sharing is seen at the harvest celebration of *pibil nal*, oven-roasted corn, on the first Sunday in October. At this time, the corn harvest is in full swing, and spirits are high. During the rest of the year, corn is dried for storage. However, the fresh corn on the cob and tortillas and corn gruel made from fresh corn are especially delicious. On the preceding night, farmers and their families dig an underground oven (*pib*) in the field or in the backyard and roast corn cobs in it overnight. Throughout the next morning, gifts of roasted corn cobs and little pots of corn gruel will be taken to one's relatives, neighbors, and *compadres*, or they will be invited to the house to eat. As much corn and gruel as is gifted away is also gifted back from the harvests of the same relatives, neighbors, and *compadres*. The day is a joyous one, as everyone stuffs themselves with the fresh corn tastes for which they have been waiting with great anticipation. What is significant about this harvest celebration is that although all the households are preparing exactly the same foods, they each offer gifts of their own to others. *Pibil nal* is at the same time a celebration of the harvest and a ritual orchestration of sharing.

All village Catholic ceremonies involve a *t'ox* or distribution of food, gifted by the ritual sponsors. An announcement of a ritual event is often followed with the question, "What is going to be distributed [to eat]?" The focus on the gifting and eating of food reflects the high value that is placed on commensality; the gifting of food and the eating together unite giver and all the receivers in a state of communion. In a *t'ox* of food, all portions are supposed to be exactly the same. The elders are served first, and then everyone else in order by seating arrangement.

Catholic ceremonies in Balankaj can be seen as occasions that oblige co-villagers to come together, act as equals, and cooperate by sharing goods and efforts for the perceived common good. First, most elements of Catholic practice orchestrated by church officials (the priest and the visiting nuns) reinforce a sense of equality and sameness. For example, the mass, the recitation of the rosary, and the novena (a prayer service, often repeated over nine nights) all oblige parishioners to stand, sit, kneel, and recite the same phrases at the same time. In these activities, the parish acts as one. For each of the sacraments of baptism, confirmation, first communion, and marriage, the children and the parents become ritually tied to another couple through the practice of godparenthood (*compadrazgo*), which creates lifelong bonds of fraternity and obligation between *compadres* (the parents of the child and the godparents).

Since the 1980s, Protestant missionaries of the Church of God of Prophecy (CGP) have made inroads into the village (Kray, 2002) and Protestant converts now account for 8% of the village population, while 92% remain Catholic. The ways in which Catholic practices reinforce equality and cooperation can be seen most clearly if they are contrasted with those of the CGP. In general, the discourses and rituals of the Catholic church project a "corporate" personhood, in both senses of the word. The person is configured as "corporate" as in corporal, material, physical. The person is also "corporate" as in connected to others, collective, and communal. In contrast, the CGP stresses the salvation of the independent, individual soul.

The CGP focuses on an interior, spiritual element in the individual person. Salvation is considered dependent on the concerted mental efforts of the individual in the private space of the mind/heart/soul. The *creyente* "believer" makes a conscious, agentive decision to "accept Christ as his or her personal savior." Faith, not works, is of utmost importance. One works toward salvation by establishing a direct relationship with God through personal prayer that originates in the mind/heart/soul of the individual believer. The CGP stresses that the person should read the Bible daily and contemplate its message; another individual, mental practice. As part of the emphasis on the individual mind and soul, the CGP convert rejects the physical body, which is thought subject to all kinds of physical temptations. Converts similarly emphasize the spiritual nature of the deity (the Holy Spirit) rather than the incarnate Christ, and the Lord's Supper is seen as a symbolic communion with God rather than the physical ingestion of his body and blood. The CGP also distances its members from the larger society: the CGP God is a transcendent God, and the convert rejects this earthly life and looks forward to the Second Coming of Christ and a life beyond this one.

In contrast, village Catholicism privileges connections and obligations between people. The ideal person is necessarily linked to the social world of family and community, and the body is the necessary vehicle for salvation, as bodies labor, produce offerings, and genuflect in community rituals. Salvation of the individual is ultimately dependent on one's postures and gestures within the social and physical world, rather than a mental, spiritual, direct relationship with God. Rather than faith, what is stressed are one's actions within the social world and one's participation in embodied collective rituals, rather than individualized prayer. The Catholic church does not reject the body, but rather celebrates the carnal aspect of God in the example of Christ who became flesh and whose body and blood are ingested in the Eucharist. The Catholic church does not reject society as an evil and corrupt "world," but expresses a desire for a true community of a unified church on this earth in this lifetime. Details and examples will illustrate this contrast.

The interior soul of the person is not ignored in village Catholic discourse, but simply deemphasized. A faith in God is taken for granted and not discussed. CGP converts often refer to themselves as *kreyeenteso'ob*, "believers" (from *creyentes*); Catholics, too, often refer to converts as *kreyeenteso'ob*, as they recognize the CGP emphasis on belief. For village Catholics, belief and faith are beside the point – of course one believes, but the real issue is what one does. For example, the priest's homilies generally explore how the principles of the scripture readings can be applied in one's daily social interactions. The Catholic emphasis on action relies on a scriptural basis: "Even so faith, if it hath not works, is dead, being alone" (James 3:17).

Village Catholic discourse emphasizes social obligations. The "social doctrine of the church" implies that one be respectful and loving toward all humans. This is a common theme of the priest's homilies, of the nuns' informal talks, and of villagers' discussions about God's will. Many Catholic songs envision a world united in one church under God. The popularity of these songs is attested to by the fact in the absence of the priest and nuns, the catechists often choose these songs to sing, and the parishioners have memorized the words and sing them loudly. In one popular song, "Together Like Brothers," the parishioners walk together:

> Together like brothers
> members of a church,
> we go walking
> toward an encounter with our Lord. . . .
> United at prayer, united
> in song,
> we will live our faith
> with the help of the Lord.
> The church is in march.
> To a new world we are going,
> where love will reign,
> where peace will reign. (EDISEPA, n.d.: 24; all translations in this essay are my own)

Similarly, in "We Go Together" the parishioners go together to the altar where they eat from the "table of unity":

> We go together
> singing to the Lord,
> and at his altar we arrive
> with songs of love.
> . . .
> As the swift rivers
> join together in the sea,
> so do we Christians run
> all together to the front of the altar.
> We are a people redeemed
> that arrives tired at your altar,
> and we all want to eat together
> from this table of unity. (EDISEPA, n.d.: 30)

In contrast to CGP discourse, which rejects society as an evil and corrupting "world," the Catholic church envisions a united religious community on this earth.

Village Catholics are also considered responsible for one another's spiritual development and salvation. After death, unless the soul is free of sin, it goes to purgatory, where it must suffer in fires "until all the sins are burned away," after which it passes on to heaven. The family bears the responsibility of saying a series of prayer services called *reesas* (from *rezar*, prayer) at set anniversaries of the death to pray that the soul of the deceased be sped on its way from purgatory to heaven. These prayer services are performed after three days, one week, three weeks, thirty days, seven months, and on every anniversary of the date of death. Additionally, one can light a candle and say a prayer to a saint for the spiritual rectitude of a family member while he or she is alive. In contrast, CGP converts insist that the salvation of the individual is completely in his or her own hands. One cannot pray for another's spiritual health, and once a person dies, there is no purgatory to pass through; one goes directly to heaven or hell.

In the Catholic church, the corporeal aspects of person and deity – the ties to the real, physical world – are not rejected, but are often stressed. While the CGP God is transcendent, the Catholic God is immanent. While CGP converts spiritually commune with God through individual prayer and individual Bible study, Catholics physically commune with God through the Offering and the Eucharist. In the Offering, parishioners give the "fruits" of their physical labor; with this money are purchased the wine and bread that are transformed in the Eucharist. Regarding the Lord's Supper, CGP converts say that it provides for symbolic (not real) union with God. In the Catholic church, however, the Eucharist is not merely a symbol, but is the actual body and blood of Christ transubstantiated in the mass, and parishioners commune with God by physically ingesting him in the communion wafer. Similarly, a nun described the line to receive the communion wafer as a "pilgrimage" in which the church as a whole meets to commune with God, and she stressed that when parishioners partake of the wafer, they commune both with God and with the community of the church. The church's communion with Christ and with the community of the church in the Eucharist are themes in another common song, "The Lord Invites Us Now":

> Today the family of God
> that breaks the bread on the altar,
> eats the body of the Lord,
> and coexists in the union.
>
> This holy communion
> is brotherly food;
> it is a testament of love,
> it is a family banquet. (EDISEPA, n.d.: 85)

Human labor, fruits of the earth, and the body and blood of Christ are united in the chalice and ingested in unison, instantiating the family of God.

Folk Catholicism

Beyond the official church activities organized by the priests and visiting nuns, there is another powerful strand of village Catholicism, which we can call "folk Catholicism," consisting of the rituals organized by the parishioners themselves. Like the official Catholic activities, the folk Catholic activities encode and reinforce ideas and patterns of equality and cooperation within the village. First, the *cha'an* is a fiesta in honor of the patron saint of the village. Balankaj's patron is Saint Andrew, and in years past, a nine-day *cha'an* was held in his honor, including nine nights of novenas, bullfights, *jarana* dancing, fireworks, and a *relleno* (turkey, pork, and chicken in a blackened chili stew) feast. A married couple would take on the burden of sponsoring the *cha'an*. Labors and goods would be pooled together with the help of the couple's families, *compadres*, and neighbors – and ideally the entire village – to create the *cha'an*. Since the costs of a true *cha'an* are now seen as too burdensome, rituals in honor of the saints now take the form of a *gremio*. A *gremio* can be offered in devotion to any saint in the calendar year, and is completed within 48 hours. Like a *cha'an*, a married couple takes on ritual sponsorship, with the help of family, *compadres*, and neighbors. A *gremio* includes a *relleno* feast for all villagers, two nights of the novena, a procession of the saint, and a concluding mass in the saint's honor.

The village Catholic calendar is a never-ending cycle of activities. Between *gremios* for different saints nearly every month and the ceaseless round of baptisms, confirmations, first communions, and weddings in the village, there is always some ritual activity for which one is preparing, is participating in, or is cleaning up from. In a concrete and a figurative sense, the church is the center of the community, as it is located in the physical center of the village and it is the most common social meeting space. To illustrate how folk Catholic rituals orchestrate cooperation and a sense of a shared future, I describe one set of *gremios*, those for the Christ Child (*Niño Dios*). On December 16, the nearly three weeks of festivities surrounding Christmas begin. This is the most festive time of the year, a time when the entire village (except for the Protestants) is united for an extended period in worship, feasting, and entertainment.

The Christmas season begins with *posadas* or lodgings performed in honor of Saint Joseph from December 16–24. These *posadas* reenact Joseph and Mary's search for lodging in Bethlehem the night Christ was born. Each night, a different family volunteers to grant lodging to the Holy Couple. The service begins in the church, where, behind the altar, sits a crèche made of palm fronds covered with electric Christmas lights, in which are placed the images of Mary and Joseph. The congregation performs a special novena with Christmas carols. Afterward, one of the four elderly men who serve as *padrinos* or godfathers (caretakers) of the saints takes up a staff with an image of the cross, and leads a procession out of the church. The couple that is granting *posada* carries the images of Mary and Joseph, and behind them follow the catechists and parishioners, holding candles and singing Christmas carols. The procession goes to three houses in turn; at the first two houses, the Holy Couple is denied lodging, but at the third house, they are allowed to enter. The host family has constructed a crèche for the Holy Couple, where they are placed to rest for the night. Before the saints are placed bowls of corn gruel or another hot drink so that they may eat. The house is crowded with devotees for a novena, with children and men spilling out into the dark roads; a *t'ox* distribution of food follows, as always. These activities are repeated over nine nights.

On December 24, the celebrations for the Christ Child begin. Village women spend the day in the time-consuming task of preparing huge pots of steamed tamales; some are eaten for dinner and two from each house are taken to the church to be distributed later that night. In the afternoon, the Dance of Abraham and Isaac begins, and winds its way throughout the whole village. The two primary dancers are configured as brothers, and are known as "Our Grandfathers," the grandfathers of the village. They wear wooden masks and long dark blue robes with hoods. A third dancer, the Devil, wears a leather mask in the shape of a horse's head and a set of green army fatigues. (The association of evil with the horse probably dates back to the conquistadors, who introduced horses to the New World.) The Dance of the Grandfathers is a dance-drama: the Devil knows that the Christ Child will be born that night, and he wants to steal the baby, while the Grandfathers try to protect it.

The Devil is a prankster character who goes around the village disrespecting property, people, and polite behavior. He runs into people's yards and steals buckets and brooms; steals fruit from people's trees and sits spread-legged in the middle of the road to shove it in his snout; runs after and scares children; picks people's flowers and offers them unabashedly to teenage girls; and rides off on people's bicycles chasing after dogs, sheep, and goats. The Grandfathers chase after the Devil, trying to stop his antics, but often trip over themselves and each other.

At 10 p.m., the village Catholics are assembled at church for a mass. Everyone then moves to the courtyard to watch and join in the theatrics of the Grandfathers and the Devil, who dance a comic version of the *jarana*. The Grandfathers grab the Devil, throw him to the ground, and pretend to butcher him; the men gathered around make bids for the different cuts of meat. At midnight, the women and girls go back inside the church for the final novena for Saint Joseph. The Grandfathers change into white robes, signifying the arrival of the new year. The mock fighting between the Grandfathers and the Devil continues, and teenage boys join in the fun, spinning the Devil around and tossing him around in a circle. By this time, the women and girls have finished the novena, and stand with lit candles at the door to the church, singing carols, blocking the Devil from entering the church as the mock battles continue in the courtyard. Everyone has a role to play in protecting the Christ Child from the Devil so that he may be born. At 1 a.m. everyone reenters the church, singing carols. The four godfathers of the saints add the image of the Christ Child in a little crib into the crèche scene, symbolizing his birth. All of the tamales brought by the women earlier in the day are then distributed in a *t'ox*. The significance of the meal is not in sharing different kinds of food, since the tamales are generally made following the same recipe. Rather, the significance is that everyone should give with *ki'imak óolal*, "gladness of the soul," and nourish one another.

Early the morning of December 25, the godfathers of the saints lead an all-day procession of the Christ Child in his crib around the entire village. The entourage – including the godfathers, the three masked dancers, the catechists, and assorted kids – stops at each Catholic house in turn. The members of the household pay their respects by praying to the Christ Child and offering small gifts. Many houses will offer a novena and a *t'ox*, so that the procession around the village proceeds until the early hours of the following morning.

On the morning of December 26, the godfathers of the saints carry the Holy Family to the house of the sponsors of the first of three *gremios*. Every Catholic household will offer help in terms of money, ingredients for the feast, and labor to one of the *gremios*. The preparation of the *relleno* stew, a feast for about 700 people, is well underway. A *jarana* band accompanies a procession around the village to gather up the *ramillete* decorations made by volunteers. The *ramilletes* are collections of colored tissue-paper flags cut into designs representing flowers and placed on wooden sticks, bundled together to make tall, colorful bushes. They are taken to the church as offerings to the Holy Family, and the band then returns to the sponsors' house, to play while the

Grandfathers and Devil dance a comic *jarana*. At 7 p.m., the sponsors lead their helpers in a procession with the band to the house of the couple that has accepted the burden of the *gremio* sponsorship for the following year. Ritualized handshakes and sharing of cigarettes and shots of rum mark the transfer of the burden. The procession returns to the sponsors' house for a novena in honor of the Christ Child. At 10 p.m., the *vaquería* (the first night of a *jarana* dance) begins in the village center and all villagers are welcome, to dance or be entertained.

The morning of December 27, the *relleno* stew is finished and almost the entire village comes to feast and dance the *jarana*. A final novena is offered and the Holy Family is returned in a procession to the church. The sponsoring couple pays for a special mass and, finally, the flowers of the *ramilletes* are distributed to parishioners. From December 28–29, a second couple sponsors a second *gremio*, with *relleno* feast, novenas, processions, *ramilletes*, *jarana* dancing, and a mass. A third *gremio* closes the Christmas season on January 5–6 (for the Epiphany).

The festivities for the Christ Child solidify a sense of commonality and shared responsibilities within the village. The Grandfathers are "Our Grandfathers," at once the protectors of the Christ Child and the ancestors who unite the village in one ritual kin group. Several elements of the ritual activities signal to ritual participants that they belong to one group with a shared future, including the collective food preparation and commensality of the *relleno* feasts and *t'ox* distributions, the coordinated action of the novenas and masses, and the way in which the processions of the *posadas*, the masked dancers, and then the Christ Child wind through the entire village, marking the space as a unified Catholic space. As part of their participation in the celebrations, people in fact reproduce the patterns of cooperation lauded in public discourse. The rituals require that they come together, nourish one another, and coordinate their offerings and their efforts over the course of three weeks, to bring honor to their common God. Regardless of anger or resentments that might have built up in their interpersonal relationships, the three weeks of ritual activities for the Holy Family ensure a continuity of cooperation within the village year after year. Then, too, it is only a month before the rituals of the Lenten season begin, with a new round of village-wide ritual cooperation.

Liberation Theology

New elements of Catholic theology and practice have been readily embraced in recent years in the village, specifically those of liberation theology. The doctrines resonate strongly with cultural values of equality and cooperation. They also resonate strongly with a sense of ethnic and class injustice, which, while rooted in a long history of colonialism and its heritage, is fueled by more recent experiences of villagers within global capitalism.

The people in Balankaj, as elsewhere in Yucatán, are shifting from subsistence agriculture to participation in the larger global capitalist economy. Before the 1970s, nearly all men in the village earned their living through swidden agriculture (supplemented with cattle husbandry, apiculture, and hunting) and women tended backyard gardens and smaller domestic animals. However, eroded soils, population pressure on the land, and a precipitous decline in the market value of corn and beans (generated by competition from US farmers under "free trade") are making agriculture an untenable pursuit, and villagers are drawn to the cash income promised by new economic opportunities. These most notably include offshore manufacturing, in which villagers work in textile factories sewing clothes for export markets and the burgeoning international tourist industry. Villagers have turned their underground natural pool (*cenote*) into a tourist attraction where they charge admission and sell food and handicrafts, while many others work in Cancún for periods of time and bring money home to their families.

Although people of Maya descent elsewhere in the Yucatán peninsula call themselves "Maya" or "mestizo" ("mixed") (cf. Castañeda, 2004), people in Balankaj seem to prefer to frame their relations with outsiders within a class idiom. They use terms that date back at least to the colonial period: *masewal* or commoner for themselves and *ts'ul* or lord for Spanish-speaking townspeople and light-skinned foreigners. The terms have special import today in relation to recent economic transformations. Fully incorporated into regional and global markets, Maya villagers are vulnerable, most significantly to people who hold a distinct advantage in this economy, including both Spanish-speaking city dwellers and wealthy international tourists and factory owners. In competition with city dwellers, villagers fare poorly. The Spanish speakers are the inheritors of the wealth, both material and symbolic, of the colonial period. If a villager seeks a job, he is generally employed by a Spanish-speaking city dweller, as they are the ones who own the businesses and large ranches, and are the managers of the factories in the industrial park. They are the engineers who control construction projects and hire villagers as day laborers, and they are the teachers who offer the education and Spanish-language skills needed for the pursuit of a profession. The villagers' lower levels of education and Spanish language skills (themselves the legacy of historical inequities) leave them at a disadvantage in direct competition; consequently, on entering the cash economy, they are at a working-class level.

The sense of exploitation is fierce, as villagers are daily confronted by the wealth of visiting tourists that they know they can never achieve. They know that the daily wage for an agricultural laborer or factory worker (about US $4) is equivalent to what a tourist pays for a margarita, and that a tourist will typically have several along with his steak fajitas dinner while they are eating tortillas and beans. They know that the $100 a month that they earn in a textile factory is equivalent to what a tourist pays for a hotel room for one night. They know that the retail mark-up in US stores of the textiles they sew is hundreds of times what they earn for their labor. They rail against the fact that while a woman may earn a profit of less than $2 for a week's delicate work of making a hand-embroidered dress, tourists will still try to bargain for a lower price. It would seem that the more vulnerable that villagers become economically, the more salient are identity labels, such as *masewal* and *ts'ul*, which underscore their disadvantage. Indeed, as often as villagers refer to themselves as commoners (*masewalo'ob*), they refer to themselves as *óotsil máako'ob* or poor people. There is a sense of limits – an upper limit to what they have been allowed to achieve.

Given their intensified consciousness of economic inequalities, it is not surprising that liberation theology, which proclaims the special love of God for the poor and the need for social justice, falls on eager ears. While villagers might feel the pain of economic inferiority in their daily lives, liberation theology assures them of a certain moral superiority. It refers to an expansive, fluid set of theological discourses and evangelical practices that arose in post-Vatican II Latin America. It seeks to liberate people from oppressive conditions at the same time as it liberates their souls. Liberation theologians speak out against dictatorship, human rights abuses, ethnic discrimination, and especially endemic poverty. Their social message is derived from a particular interpretation of scripture. Liberation theologians have declared that the church should have a "preferential option for the poor," meaning that the church itself should renounce material wealth, that it should actively seek to improve the material conditions of the poor, and that the major thrust of evangelization should be with the poor. Liberation theology expresses a "preferential option for the poor" for three different reasons. First, poverty is seen as evil: "the result of the oppression of some people by others" – and Christian duty calls for eradicating this evil on earth. Second, poverty is associated with the freedom from material goods that is necessary for communion with God. Finally, the church should be poor so that it can feel compassion for and solidarity with the poor (Berryman, 1987: 31–33).

The Second General Conference of Latin American Bishops in Medellín in 1968 produced a "Document on the Poverty of the Church," in which they recognized and affirmed a growing commitment among the Latin American clergy to the poor (Hennelly, 1990: 114–119). These sentiments were supported and elaborated in the final document, "A Preferential Option for the Poor," of the Third General Conference of the Latin American Bishops in Puebla in 1979. The bishops write:

> [T]he evangelical commitment of the church . . . should be a commitment to those most in need . . . [T]he poor merit preferential attention . . . Made in the image and likeness of God . . . [when subjected to poverty] this image is dimmed and even defiled. That is why God takes on their defense and loves them . . . That is why the poor are the first ones to whom Jesus' mission is directed . . . and why the evangelization of the poor is the supreme sign and proof of his mission. ("A Preferential Option for the Poor": 254–255)

Theologian Jon Sobrino, former colleague of the assassinated Archbishop Oscar Romero, echoes these sentiments when he writes: "Wealth and poverty are contrary and mutually exclusive realities . . . the former condemnatory and the latter salvific. The true church, therefore, ought to be shaped by poverty and by an opposition to wealth" (Sobrino, 1993: 83). In his interpretation of the Spiritual Exercises of St. Ignatius of Loyola he writes:

> Wealth leads to the vain honors of this world, which leads to pride, which in turn leads to every other vice. Poverty leads to being disgraced and scorned, which leads to humility, which in turn leads to every other virtue. (Sobrine, 1993: 84)

These ideas about the moral corrosiveness of wealth and the moral superiority of poverty echo Yucatecan ideas about the inverse relationship between wealth and morality.

In Balankaj, the missionary nuns of Las Madres de la Luz have been preaching liberation theology since the late 1980s. In sermons, songs, and community activities, poverty and humility are reclaimed from a disparaged position and reinterpreted as virtuous. The messages about the worthiness of the poor and of humble, hard work have had a great impact on the villagers, who in turn use these maxims to provide an interpretive framework for their interaction with *ts'uls*.

In homilies and more informal talks, the nuns remind the parishioners that Jesus himself was poor. Born in a manger, the son of a carpenter, he lived as a mendicant wandering preacher without the luxury of a home, was sold for 30 coins of silver, was put to death as a criminal, and was laid to rest in a borrowed tomb. The nuns frequently recite biblical passages that find virtue in poverty and evil in wealth, including:

> And again I say unto you, It is easier for a camel to go through the eye of a needle, than for a rich man to enter into the kingdom of God. (Matthew 19:24)
>
> But many that are first shall be last; and the last shall be first. (Matthew 19:30)
>
> [Christ] Who, being in the form of God, thought it not robbery to be equal with God: But made himself of no reputation, and took upon him the form of a servant, and was made in the likeness of men: And being found in fashion as a man, he humbled himself, and became obedient unto death, even the death of the cross. Wherefore God also hath highly exalted him, and given him a name which is above every name. (Philippians 2:6–9)
>
> Let the brother of low degree rejoice in that he is exalted: But the rich, in that he is made low: because as the flower of the grass he shall pass away. For the sun is no sooner risen with a burning heat, but it withereth the grass, and the flower thereof falleth, and the grace of the fashion of it perisheth: so also shall the rich man fade away in his ways. (James 1:9–11)
>
> Hearken, my beloved brethren, Hath not God chosen the poor of this world rich in faith, and heirs of the kingdom which he hath promised to them that love him? (James 2:5)

Songs introduced by the nuns that have become favorites in church services are ones that exalt poverty, humility, and hard work. In "You Are the God of the Poor," which is part of the *Nicaraguan Peasants' Mass* composed by Carlos Mejía Godoy in 1975, God is "human and simple," doing manual labor in the fields and the city:

> You are the God of the poor,
> The human and simple God;
> The God that sweats in the street,
> The God with sunburned face.
> For this reason I call on you,
> As do my people;
> Because you are the laborer God,
> The Christ who works hard. (Ministerio de Música, n.d.: 30)

In another popular song, "Mother of the Poor," the Virgin Mary is praised for her humility, simplicity, and freedom from material desires:

> Mother of the poor
> The humble and simple,

Of the sad and the children
Who always trust in God.
You, the most poor
Because you never expected anything;
You, persecuted, fleeing from Bethlehem.
You, who offered a manger
To the King of Heaven:
He was your only treasure.
You, who in His hands,
You gave yourself up without fear,
You, who accepted
Being the slave of the Lord,
You sing a poem of gladness:
"Sing, my soul,
Because God has exalted you."
You, who have lived through pain
And poverty,
You, who have suffered
At night without a home;
You who are the mother
Of the poor and forgotten. (EDISEPA, n.d.: 299–300)

The theological messages about the virtues of the poor have had a great impact in Balankaj, and are used to render judgment in daily life. For example, when complaining about the low price a *ts'ul* buyer at the market gave him for his beef, Don Porfirio said, "When the time comes, salvation will come to the person who suffers the most." On three separate occasions, inserted into critiques about *ts'ul* behaviors, I heard the biblical parable of the rich man, who did not tend to Lazarus as he lay dying of leprosy at his mansion gate; yet after death, Lazarus ascended to heaven, and the rich man descended to hell. On several occasions, I heard: "It is easier for a camel to go through the eye of a needle, than for a rich man to enter into the kingdom of God." Finally, when Don Juan was complaining about how *ts'ul* ranchers pay the minimum wage of 12 pesos (US $4) to an agricultural laborer for a full day's grueling labor in the burning sun, he noted that it is "contrary to the will of God." Liberation theology provides new discursive tools for social critique.

Conclusion

There have been strong continuities in religious practice in Yucatán from the colonial period to the present, but there are few continuities of ancient practices. Rather, the beliefs and practices that have persisted over the years are those that protect and preserve community solidarity and cooperation against outsider exploitation. Spanish colonial policies corralled "Indians" into compact villages centered on town hall and church, gave them shared rights (to collective lands), shared privileges (the protection of a patron saint), and shared responsibilities (the collection of taxes and tributes). Additionally, Catholic doctrine preached over the centuries has stressed good works within the community and responsibility for one another, while practices within the church orchestrate unity of action. Correspondingly, folk rituals also celebrate community ties and require cooperation for the common good throughout the calendar year. In recent years, as incorporation within the global capitalist economy has intensified a sense of structural inequality, liberation theology, with its strong critiques of inequality and exploitation, has added yet another layer to an already strong religious system that promotes and protects the village community.

Christianity is a system of beliefs and practices that has shown itself malleable to different interpretations, leading to a multiplicity of local Christian varieties. Over time in Yucatán, Catholic discourses and practices have evolved within a context of colonial and modern-day exploitation. What has emerged is a particularly strong religious sense of justice that stresses equality and cooperation within the community as protection against outside encroachment.

References

Berryman, Phillip (1987) *Liberation Theology: The Essential Facts about the Revolutionary Movement in Latin American and Beyond*, Pantheon Books, New York.

Castañeda, Quetzil E. (2004) "We are not indigenous!": The Maya identity of Yucatan, an introduction, *Journal of Latin American Anthropology* 9(1): 36–63.

EDISEPA (n.d.) *1852 cantos para evangelizar cantando*, Ediciones Servidores de la Palabra, Mexico.

Farriss, Nancy M. (1978) Nucleation versus dispersal: The dynamics of population movement in colonial Yucatan, *Hispanic American Historical Review* 58(2): 187–216.

Farriss, Nancy M. (1984) *Maya Society under Colonial Rule: The Collective Enterprise of Survival*, Princeton University Press, Princeton.

Hennelly, Alfred T., SJ (ed.) (1990) *Liberation Theology: A Documentary History*, Orbis Books, Maryknoll, NY.

Kray, Christine A. (2002) The Pentecostal reformation of self: Opting for orthodoxy in Yucatán, *Ethos* 29(4): 395–429.

Kurjack, Edward B. and Garza T. de González, Silvia (1981) Pre-Columbian community form and distribution in the Northern Maya area, in *Lowland Maya Settlement Patterns*, Wendy Ashmore (ed.), University of New Mexico Press, Albuquerque, pp. 287–309.

Ministerio de Música (n.d.) *Cancionero de las CEBs*, Arquidiócesis de Salta, Salta, Argentina, http://www.cebs.com.ar (accessed June 27, 2011).

Patch, Robert W. (1993) *Maya and Spaniard in Yucatan, 1648–1812*, Stanford University Press, Stanford.

Restall, Matthew (1997) *The Maya World: Yucatec Culture and Society, 1550–1850*, Stanford University Press, Stanford.

Robles Castellanos, Fernando and Andrews, Anthony P. (1985) A review and synthesis of recent postclassic archaeology in Northern Yucatan, in *Late Lowland Maya Civilization: Classic to Postclassic*, Jeremy A. Sabloff and E. Wyllys Andrews (eds.), University of New Mexico Press, Albuquerque, pp. 53–98.

Roys, Ralph L. (1957) *The Political Geography of the Yucatan Maya*, Carnegie Institution Publication #613, Carnegie Institution of Washington, Washington, DC.

Sobrino, Jon, SJ (1993) The economics of ecclesia: A poor church is a church rich in compassion, in *New Visions for the Americas: Religious Engagement and Social Transformation*, David Batstone (ed. and trans.), Fortress Press, Minneapolis, pp. 83–120.

Villa Rojas, Alfonso (1961) Notas sobre la tenencia de la tierra entre los mayas de la antigüedad, *Estudios de Cultura Maya* 1: 21–46.

CHAPTER 26

Europe

The Roma People of Romania

Sorin Gog and Maria Roth

Historical Overview

The word "Rom," meaning man or male in the Romani language, is the origin of the preferred name of the minority that in the last decade became aware of its rights, as opposed to the name "Gypsies," which originated in the Byzantine Empire, and was associated with a blamed and oppressed identity.[1] According to Petrova (2003) they refer to themselves as Roma, which correlates to *people* in the plural masculine gender, with a connotation of *us* as opposed to *them*, to differentiate all others referred to by the term *gadje*. Gypsies were considered a heretical sect and called *atzinganoi* (unclean), due in part to their having been regarded as Muslims in a Christian empire. This explains the names Zigeuner (German), Gitens (French), Tsigan (Czech), Cigáni (Slovakian), Cigány (Hungarian), and Tigan (Romanian). According to Helmut Samer (2001), the Athingani were mentioned in Byzantine documents in the eighth century. They were considered fortune tellers, magicians, and unclean and were not allowed to enter churches, intermarry, or follow certain occupations.

The Roma minority, Europe's most oppressed ethnicity, lived for centuries in slavery in many parts of western, central, and eastern Europe. Today they are spread throughout many different communities all over Europe and central Asia. Most historians believe that Roma people immigrated from northwestern India. From there they went to the Persian Empire, then further to Armenia, then to the Byzantine Empire, and from there either in the Balkans, and to central and eastern Europe, or to western Europe (Alinčová, 2002; Hübschmannová, 2002).

The origins of migration of the Roma people are often explained by myths (Grigore, 2001). According to one traditional religious myth, the Roma people were the craftsmen who made the nails used to crucify Christ, an act that damned them to eternal penitence. According to another myth, they were Egyptians, who were condemned to nomadic life because they refused to host the Holy family during its flight from Herod. The Roma people often presented themselves as pilgrims from "Little Egypt," sentenced by the pope to years of wandering as punishment for betraying the Christian faith following an alleged Muslim conquest (Petrova, 2003).

The welcoming of Roma in western Europe did not last for long. Though in the Byzantine Empire they were skilled laborers – artisans, craftsmen, metal workers, musicians – many local civil authorities, church leaders, and community leaders believed that they were trespassers and social parasites. As a result, Roma were routinely banned from entering towns and villages, excommunicated from churches, or deported from regions and countries.

During the late Middle Ages, the status of the Roma worsened. Many western and central European countries banned Roma travelers from entering their territories and enforced these interdictions with extreme cruelty, including hanging, mutilation, forced labor, and imprisonment. A.I. Gonta (1997) researched historical archives and found evidence dating back to the eleventh century in Hungary, Poland, and the Romanian regions of the existence of enslaved Roma (along with Tatars and other nomadic people). These people, enslaved when kings or other rulers conquered territories, were bought and sold or given as gifts to landlords and religious leaders.

According to Hancock (1987), in those turbulent times, with Mongol attacks, soldiers moving around, and crusades, Roma as well as other nomadic tribes were subjected to slavery as a means to supply a cheap labor force for the Roman empire. Gonta (1997) believes slavery to be grounded in three factors: the pope's decision to enslave all nomadic people who transgressed the borders of the state; the custom of repaying warriors for taking part in the wars; and a desire to render the enemy powerless.

In Romanian Orthodox mythology, subjugating the Roma was linked to the idea that Gypsies are alleged to be followers of Ham, the son of Noah who was damned because he mocked Noah. Myths of this sort allowed the Orthodox Church, which preached equality of all people before God, to justify depriving the Roma of their freedom and imposing on them all manner of harsh practices and regulations. For example, their lords imposed arbitrary decisions in matters concerning work and all aspects of family life, including marriage and selling off family members. Those who resisted the will of the lords suffered severe punishment, sometimes death. Death itself was not an equalizer. Even for Roma who converted to the Orthodox Church, separate cemeteries were created (Gonta, 1997). A similar range of treatment was applied to Roma in Serbia and Hungary and other eastern European countries. Enslavement continued until the nineteenth century, when modern European opinion began to swing against this degrading practice (Hancock, 1987).

From medieval times onward, many political authorities have tried to force the Roma to assimilate into their cultures and to convert to Islam or Christianity. According to Petrova (2003), during Ottoman rule (sixteenth to eighteenth centuries), much of the population of Albania and Bosnia (along with other peoples in other parts of the Balkans, including Roma) converted to Islam.

Methods used to "civilize" the Roma during the Enlightenment (seventeenth and eighteenth centuries) in Spain and in the Austrian-Hungarian Empire set the stage for harsh practices and arbitrary rules. Roma were forbidden to use the Romani language, and they were compelled to adopt the clothing and the language of the people in or near whose villages they settled. As a way of restricting their travel, Roma were prevented from using horses and wagons. Children were separated from their parents, women were segregated from men in the workhouses, and in some instances Roma were forced to marry non-Roma.

Throughout central and eastern Europe, the Roma people are still strongly discriminated against and are the object of various exclusion practices. In terms of social equality, the discrimination against the Roma people means that they are becoming one of the most marginalized and underprivileged ethnic groups and that they are excluded from the main structures of opportunities, including education, job markets, and healthcare. The mass media have played an important role in generalizing stereotypes and ethno-nationalistic feelings toward the Roma community, which are materialized in beatings, scapegoating, and local pogroms (Gheorghe, 1999).[2]

The experience of social and economical marginality is a constant theme within the social world of Roma communities from central and eastern Europe. The demand for social justice is not only a political discourse by nongovernmental organizations (NGOs) and different political groups concerned with this issue, it is also a current topic of concern in the everyday life of Roma. Disempowerment, social exclusion, discrimination, and the pervasive violation of ethnic rights are the main concerns of the Roma agenda to attain social justice and equality in their home countries.

Western European countries were seen by many Roma from central and eastern Europe as a safe havens where they could benefit from the same social rights and justice and become equal members within society. Massive unemployment among the Roma community and the absence of social safety nets prompted waves of migration to Germany and other European Union countries. These migrations in turn triggered widespread anti-Roma sentiments in western European countries where the Roma settled, which resulted in intergovernmental agreements to deport the Roma to their countries of origin. Finding out that they were marginalized and treated with contempt both in their counties of origin and in western European countries ended the dreams of many Roma to be integrated into societies where social justice and equality are publicly promulgated.

Religion has always played a prominent role in the struggle for social justice in eastern and central Europe. Thus it is not surprising that religious communities were seen by the Roma as instruments to integrate themselves into mainstream society and to become respectable members of the community. For this reason, the Roma have tended to adopt the religion of the majority populations where they have settled and to reproduce the confessional structures of the dominant religious groups. Thus, most Roma in central and eastern Europe are members of the Orthodox Church and the Roman Catholic Church. There are also small Muslim Roma communities in countries such as Bulgaria, Bosnia-Herzegovina, Kosovo, and Croatia. For the majority of Roma, affiliation with one of the historical churches was viewed as a means toward social inclusion and as a way to gain acceptance by the dominant group.

Religiosity and Exclusion Practices

The Roma from all around the world are known for being a syncretistic religious community with a genuine inclination for the magical realm. Various pollution taboos, purification rituals, and specific holy days are still practiced among some of the Roma. Some of these beliefs might be related to the ancient Hindu cultural traditions that Roma are believed to have brought with them from India and preserved during their long migration and wandering (Gall and Hobby, 2009: 397). But some of them, such as witchcraft and palm reading, are, despite popular stereotypes, only recent cultural acquisitions that in fact constitute strategies to capitalize on western spiritual concerns and to make money. Most of the Roma do not actually believe in such practices (Okely, 2007).

Within traditional institutional religious settings, the Roma people encountered throughout central and eastern Europe the same issues that they met in daily life: exclusion and marginalization by the majority. The source of this treatment has not been religious dogma or an ethno-phobic clergy, but the larger community of believers, the same people who in everyday life harbor deep-seated prejudices against the Roma and deny them access to education, healthcare, and economic resources.

This exclusion is not peculiar to a specific religious tradition but is encountered in both Christian and Muslim communities (Crowe, 2000). A common claim by mainstream believers is that Roma adherence to mainstream religion is mere formality; that Roma still practice magic and do not really adhere to the values embodied by institutionalized religion. Some funeral customs, for example, are still performed in ways that violate mainstream religious practices. Roma are tolerated by local priests because they are considered outsiders and religiously unteachable (Foszto, 2006). The fact that the Catholic Church recently adopted official guidelines for the pastoral care of Gypsies proves that Roma are treated as marginal members of local churches and that they have not yet been fully assimilated into the mainstream church.

The same patterns of exclusion are encountered in the other main European religion, Orthodox Christianity. Most of the Roma from Romania belong to the Orthodox Church or to the Hungarian Reformed Church (in Transylvania), depending on the dominant religion of the community. In both of these historic churches, the Roma are formally attached to the mainstream church, but are not integrated into the daily life of the religious community and attend church services only rarely. This pattern is particularly evident in rural areas, where Roma are strongly discriminated against and are usually restricted to living on the outskirts of the villages (Gog, 2008). A vivid expression of this religious marginality is evident in the way in which cemeteries are organized in the rural part of Romania (and in certain places in other central and eastern European countries as well). The cemeteries are divided by religious and ethnic borders that reproduce the social spaces of interaction of everyday life, but although Roma have the same religion as the majority, they have to be buried in a separate section of the cemetery.

In the postsocialist period (after 1989), Roma religious identity has undergone an important change due to the resurgence of the evangelical movement among them.

The massive postsocialist conversion to neo-Protestant movements is a widespread phenomenon throughout central and eastern Europe. In Romania the neo-Protestant communities are the fastest growing religious organizations, and nowhere are they more successful than among the Roma.[3] The Roma are particularly drawn to Pentecostalism, and the majority of neo-Protestant Roma belong to this religious movement.

What makes Pentecostalism so interesting is that it establishes, through the symbolic mechanisms of religious conversion and the networks of the local church, a specific way of dealing with the social and ethnic exclusion of the Roma people. It facilitates the means for this marginalized community to create its own structures and narratives of identity. The Pentecostal movement provides the institutional means for the creation of micro-communities that are highly capable of imagining ethnic narratives that can mobilize Roma as a unique and distinct social group.

Religious and Ethnic Identities of Roma during the Communist Period

The conversion of Roma to Pentecostalism has two different genealogies in Romanian society: the communist period, which led to a multiethnic, unified religious community, and the postsocialist period, which led to the emergence of ethnically distinct Roma Pentecostal churches. The overwhelming majority of the Roma churches (almost 90%) have appeared in the last two decades, and so they are a specific phenomenon of the postsocialist period.

The Pentecostal movement started in Romania in the interwar period (1919–1939), during which Pentecostals were recurrently outlawed by the government and declared a sect (Cuctuc, 2001: 78, 81–82). They were finally recognized as a legal religious association by the Religious Law of 1948. Under the strict supervision of state authorities, they were allowed to establish new churches and to organize themselves as a public religious community.

The various evangelical movements started evangelizing the Roma only in the 1970s. This project was carried out by international religious organizations such as the Society for the Reformation of Gypsies or the British Gypsy Gospel Mission, which took it upon themselves to preach the Gospel to Roma people. The Pentecostal movement for the Gypsies originated in France. Within three decades, it claimed to have converted over 70 000 Gypsies, mostly in western Europe, and to have ordained over 400 pastors and 1600 preachers (Fraser, 1992).

Eastern Europe became only belatedly a mission region, accompanied by an increasing awareness of the need to bring the Gospel to the destitute Gypsies from this area, especially Yugoslavia, Bulgaria, Macedonia, Hungary, Romania, Czechoslovakia, Poland, and later Russia (Ridholls, 1986: 104–109). In all of these countries, including Romania, all Gypsy Pentecostal groups that were established were quickly dismantled by state authorities and their religious leaders imprisoned (Ridholls, 1986: 108).

Mainly this happened because the communists allowed religion to function only in institutionalized forms, with public and fixed hours for meetings and supervised by a state representative. Popular and mystical movements that spread unattended and unapproved by the state could not be controlled, and they were outlawed and penalized by state authorities. As a result of communist regulations, Roma were never able to establish a Pentecostal church of their own, and the Roma converts were for a long time members of the same churches as Romanian Pentecostals (Ridholls, 1986: 106).

During the communist period, not only was religion controlled by state authorities (especially conversion to neo-Protestant movements), but the expression of ethnic identity was also tightly controlled. Throughout eastern Europe the communist regimes tried to find a way to deal with the "Gypsy problem" (Barany, 2000: 424–430). According to the prevailing political dogma of the time, ethnic identities were expected to disappear when proletarian class ideals were internalized and when the "new society" was established, in which identities would not be defined according to ethnic criteria but according to social position within the triumphant labor force.

In this "new society," Gypsies were always considered a pariah social group with a deviant lifestyle that had to be the object of specific state policies (Barany, 2002: 112–116). The only avenue of salvation envisaged for them was through organized labor. This ideological conviction set in motion different strategies of "converting" Gypsies into good citizens and disciplined workers (Stewart, 1997: 97–111).

In order to achieve this social transformation, Gypsies were strongly encouraged to participate in a much needed industrial labor force, which required minimal education or job skills. In most of the eastern European countries, Romania included, the communists set out to accomplish the "conversion" of the Gypsies by means of a Sedentarization Act (prohibition of nomadism and the obligation to have a clearly defined permanent location). As a result, their social condition (housing, welfare, healthcare) generally improved, and they gradually acquired certain basic social rights throughout eastern Europe (Kligman, 2005: 64).

In some countries, Gypsies were forbidden to speak Romani in public or to observe their traditional holy days (Barany, 2002: 112–154). Cultural and social Roma associations, newspapers and publications in their native language, and theaters that catered to Gypsies were all shut down by the communists in hopes that within a few generations Gypsies would be completely integrated into mainstream society. In Romania, as throughout eastern Europe, communist authorities established very quickly the legal apparatus to deal with the Gypsy community (Barany, 2000: 425–427). The aim of all of these actions was to annihilate their ethnic identity and to set in motion clearly defined assimilation polices (Barany, 2000).

As a result of the policies of control and assimilation in Romania and elsewhere, the Roma community was unable to retain and perpetuate its distinct Romani identity, autonomous organizations, and the leadership required for sustained ethnic mobilization (Barany, 2002: 143). During the communist period, virtually no ethnic mobilization occurred among the Gypsies (Barany, 2002), and most of the achievements in the realm of ethno-politics[4] obtained during the interwar period were leveled by the socialist party and its national ideology.

After the fall of communism these political constraints disappeared, and the Roma community was able to reorganize itself and affirm its distinct ethnic and cultural identity. The increasing conversion of Roma to Pentecostalism has to be understood as an overt attempt to institutionalize a new type of social narrative regarding what it means to be a "true" Roma, and to create the symbolic and institutional resources for a new management of ethnic identity that could not be established during the communist period.

The emergence of a "new heavenly citizenship" grounded on an ethical orientation to life and of a renewed religious-ethnic community committed to overcoming the strong traditional kin fragmentation of Roma has to be understood as an overt strategy for ethno-genesis. In order to comprehend how this new social structure functions, it is necessary to understand two related but distinct phenomena:

1. The symbolic architecture of the Pentecostal conversion and how the religious moralization of conduct (ethical transformation of the everyday life according to a religious worldview) is employed as a demarginalization strategy.
2. The emerging religious community that aims at integrating the Roma converts, a process that leads to the attenuation of exclusion and marginalization.

Pentecostalism among the Roma

A distinct feature of Pentecostalism is its emphasis on mystical experiences and supernatural events that the common believer can experience personally (Lange, 2003: 32–46). Unlike the Orthodox and Catholic religious traditions that control and validate religious experiences through their institutional structures, the Pentecostal religious tradition enables a religious discourse that affirms the possibility of a personal experience of "the gifts of the Spirit" through mystical prayer that can sometimes lead to miracles and supernatural healings. Encountering the spiritual realm individually and directly, without any clerical mediation, becomes in the Pentecostal tradition an integrative symbolic mode of imagining the religious community.

Interviews with Roma Pentecostal converts (Gog, 2008) revealed that religious conversion is claimed to have taken place after the person experienced or witnessed a miracle (e.g., a supernatural healing). Experiencing or witnessing miracles endows their particular individual biography with meaning and a sense of being divinely elected. The Pentecostal religious experience completely restructures the lives of the converted Roma. They give up morally and socially questionable behavior (e.g., stealing, cheating on their spouse, drinking alcohol, and smoking) and adopt strong moral codes that express the "new way" they have found. Through religious conversion, a new conceptualization of the self emerges that is embodied in a new set of social practices.

Assuming a puritan ideal of life, the converted Roma embrace a powerful dichotomy between the spiritual (mystical) realm and the everyday (mundane) realm and strive to create a new type of religious community in which there is no place for "worldly" pleasures such as dancing, parties, and hanging out in bars. The new faith revolves around church life and living daily as witnesses of God, particularly to the unconverted Roma, so that converts are able to engage in practices that constitute markers of a new social and cultural identity and that set them apart from nonconverted Roma.

Another central aspect of the religious conversion of Roma to Pentecostalism is the importance given to reading the Scripture. The Roma have relied for long time on an oral transmission of culture. Being a marginalized and disempowered community, the Roma lacked the means necessary to generate an intellectual stratum. But Pentecostalism is able to create just such a stratum, because conversion to it usually leads to increased literacy. Reading and interpreting the Bible is an important part of the daily devotional time. As a consequence, Pentecostal Roma families emphasize the need to educate their children.

For Pentecostal Roma, the Bible is considered the new authoritative resource that addresses key problems and issues of daily life and establishes a metric for social relations. As a result, all Roma traditional culture, rituals, and ways of life are filtered through the scriptures and are abandoned if found to be explicitly or implicitly at odds with them. Religious conversion leads to a radical change of values and to different practices of self. The final products of this religious reinterpretation of the self are a strong ethical justification for conduct and a new cultural code. Roma abandon their traditional customs and holidays and subject their traditional leaders and social practices to careful scrutiny. This approach often leads to conflict within the Roma community, and Roma Pentecostals are perceived by some of their Roma fellows as traitors to Roma culture.

The moralization of conduct enables Roma converts to present themselves as different from how they appear in popular stereotypical portraits. In other words, the moralization of conduct is a religiously communicative mechanism that allows converts to distance themselves from the nonconverted Roma who have a bad reputation. Converts make use of semantic dichotomies to reinforce the idea that they are completely different from how the majority stereotypes them: Roma are stereotyped by others as lazy, but Pentecostal Roma describe themselves as hard working; others view them as cheaters and liars, but they describe themselves as honorable and honest; alcoholics as against sober; unspiritual (immoral), spiritual (moral); given to magical syncretism, religiously literate; dirty, clean; and so on. For Pentecostal Roma, Gypsiness is something to be proud of.

These rhetorical devices often have the intended outcome. Local authorities are happy about the Penticostalization of Roma because their personal and social transformation leads to lower crime rates; teachers appreciate the fact that in Roma Pentecostal familics that placc a high value on education the children tend to drop out of school less often than other Roma children; non-Roma villagers enjoy having access to a cheap and reliable workforce.

This religiously motivated ethic is institutionalized among the Roma through the emergence of local churches. Most of these churches, built within the confines of their segregated communities, serve as gathering places for religious and nonreligious events. The religious meetings are compulsory for church members and are meant to nurture a religious environment in which they can strengthen their faith and employ the religious knowledge they acquire in their own life. Community life is valued and encouraged by Pentecostals, and this fact contributes to a reaffirmation of the social identity of the Roma converts.

The ecclesial structure is defined by local Roma people who are advanced in their religious experience and who can lead the community of faith through sermons, counseling, basic education, and pastoral care. A literate, religious leadership emerges wherever a neo-Protestant community is created. The leadership – pastors, elders, and deacons of local churches – constitutes the legitimate clerical hierarchy of the emerging communities. In the traditional churches (Roman Catholic, Orthodox), Roma people do not occupy such positions. Among Pentecostals, the local church provides the Roma with an institution of their own that enables them to express their own lifestyle and cultural identity. It is precisely this institutional framework and local empowerment that mainstream society refuses them in everyday life.

The local religious community is an important factor for the establishment of strong networks of trust. The community of believers is religiously transformed into an extended family and the entire kinship structure is redefined and restructured according to the new religious values they have adopted. The "brothers" and "sisters" commit themselves to sustain each other not only spiritually but in daily life struggles as well. The emerging community based on religious fellowship is an egalitarian one in which traditional kinship and status are leveled. Being part of a strong community is an important resource for reducing social anomie. Strong faith communities counteract marginalization practices against all Roma and provide the Roma with social cohesion, which they need but which mainstream society refuses to give them.

Pentecostalism and the New Ethnic Imagination

For the Roma community, the postsocialist transitions meant in general a worsening of their social and economical condition. This reality increased their awareness that their emerging marginality could be dealt with only in political terms of ethnic mobilization of a very fragmented and disempowered community.

During the postsocialist period, the need to imagine an overarching and integrating ethnic identity became increasingly urgent (Gheorghe, 1999). The fact that Roma did not constitute a territorial ethnic group, did not have a kin state to support them (McGarry, 2009: 107), and lacked the necessary human and technical resources (Barany, 2002) were only a few of the impediments to attaining this goal. The principal impediment, however, was the overall fragmentation of the Roma community and its traditional kinship structures. The Roma from eastern Europe are strongly divided into kin groups and traditional professional groups that are dominated by conflicts, feuds, and symbolic battles over which members of the group are the true Roma.

Because of this fragmentation during the postsocialist period, a new ethno-political discourse emerged that aimed at an international level to recognize the Roma as a stateless nation and nonterritorial ethnic group, and at a local level to reconstruct Gypsiness so that it could overcome the general kin fragmentation. The new imagined community narrative included replacing the term "Gypsy" with "Roma," promoting a common language (Romani), and constructing a united transnational ethnic group that was both European and Indian.

This new way of imagining what it means to be a Gypsy was intended to provide a platform for different political and social projects aimed at demarginalizing Gypsies (Barany, 2002: 65–67) and simultaneously promoting the construction of a symbolic community capable of overcoming the general kin fragmentation. These initiatives have been undertaken largely by international activists who use the language of human rights and establish networks to lobby supra-state organizations such as the United Nations and the Council of Europe. These activists use political parties and NGOs to promote the new Roma identity at the local level throughout the countries of eastern Europe.

However, the proliferation of Roma organization and ethno-politics has not led to a general consolidation of Roma identity at the grassroots level, as had been expected. The traditional way of identifying Gypsiness according to kin groups fractured many of the organizations and none of them has been able to gain widespread support.[5]

Two decades of ethnic mobilization among the Roma and concerted attempts to construct a new ideology of Gypsiness have yielded few positive results.[6] Few of the initiatives have had an impact on the daily lives of Roma (McGarry, 2009: 109). Moreover, the Roma people have perceived ethno-genesis strategies as elitist initiatives. This negative response from the Roma people has generally delegitimized all of the political attempts to represent the Roma community in the public sphere (Barany, 2002: 204). In stark contrast, Pentecostalism has emerged as a popular movement that is able, through the creation of a religious community, to articulate a distinct way of conceptualizing Gypsiness.

A common explanation for Roma converting to Pentecostalism relates to the local strategies of a phenomenon known as auto-assimilation to the dominant group. Pentecostal religious brotherhood, it is argued, establishes a common language and social space in which ethnic identity is absorbed through the establishment of an ethnically mixed religious community. According to this thesis, Roma should become part of and integrated into the majority ethnic group (Romanians) through a stress on their ethnic Roma features.

Ethnographic data reveal a completely different picture. Pentecostalism does not lead to the ethnic and social integration of Roma. According to most of the Roma Pentecostal converts, the same practices of exclusion that exist in the Romanian Orthodox Church and the Hungarian Reformed Church are reproduced within the Romanian Pentecostal Church as well. The Roma feel marginalized and treated with contempt by other Romanian Pentecostals.

These perceptions explain why in the past two decades a new type of organization has emerged among the Roma; namely, Roma Pentecostal churches. These churches emerged partly in response to Roma desire to have a religious community of their own where they could manifest themselves as Roma. (Curiously, all the religious services are conducted in the Romanian language, not the traditional Roma language.) Roma converts have managed to organize themselves as local churches, provide training for future Roma pastors, and form a legal association that enables them to function as a state-recognized religious community.

In the past two decades, the conversion of Roma to neo-Protestant movements has resulted in the creation of hundreds of distinct Roma Pentecostal churches. Almost all of these churches – Roma Pentecostal leaders say 90% – have been established during the postsocialist period. All of these churches have been located in predominantly Roma communities, and the clergy have been recruited from among their own people.

It is within these Pentecostal communities that a new type of ethnic community is being built. The conversion to Pentecostalism has been accompanied by a growing awareness that Roma as an ethnic group have an important religious calling (Fraser,

1992) and that there is a genuine "religious essence" of the Roma soul to which Pentecostalism is able to give expression. More accurately, the new religious narrative that is being institutionalized among Roma converts to Pentecostalism produces Roma as a distinct ethnic group in a way that far exceeds the successes of the international political activists. The "new heavenly citizenship" provides through the local church not only salvation for the wretched soul, but also the common understanding of a proud ethnic identity and a strategy to achieve social demarginalization through the moralization of conduct.

Gypsiness is seen by Roma Pentecostal believers as something very special. Indeed, it is regarded as a gift from God. Congregational meetings commonly include narratives of religious revival. The narratives have recurrent themes: Roma are low and marginal, but God has chosen them to do great things and to show His power through them. Narratives of this sort – narratives that call attention to Roma social marginality and capitalizing on their religious calling to achieve great spiritual things – generate hope among Roma Pentecostals.

Where other approaches have failed, the Pentecostal movement, by emphasizing the unity of converted Roma as members of the body of Christ, has succeeded in overcoming the traditional fragmentation based on kinship relationships (Gay y Blasco, 1999). Roma Pentecostals have succeeded in establishing new local public spaces of interaction (local churches) and networks of trust among their marginalized and fragmented community (Fraser, 1992). In these ways it has been able to attenuate the consequences of social discrimination to which Roma are subjected by the majority population. Local Pentecostal churches provide them with the symbolic and social capital that permits them coherently to modulate a new social, cultural, and (most importantly) ethnic identity. The religious language of Pentecostalism provides a medium for forging such identities, and this language has been popularized at the lower socioeconomic level among the masses.

In this respect, Pentecostalism is transformed into something more than a religious community that strives for other-worldly salvation. Roma Pentecostals have an explicit social project that aims at generating a shared ethnic identity and social demarginalization. Just as Romanian Pentecostals invest considerable effort into establishing a religious alternative educational system that enables them to religiously socialize their children away from the secularizing tendencies of western culture, so too the Roma find in Pentecostalism the symbolic and social resources to mobilize themselves as an ethnic group. Throughout eastern Europe the systematic outcome of Roma converting to Pentecostalism is the establishment of Roma local churches and the emergence of Roma religious leaders, which play an important role in generating both a new imagined ethnic community and social networks that supply the Roma with the symbolic capital necessary for demarginalization.

The secular model of Gypsiness considers this approach much too puritanical, narrow, and uncompromising. Nevertheless, the identity model promoted by mainstream leaders and hundreds of NGOs – a model that emphasizes the ethnic unity of all Roma/Gypsies, calls attention to a Roma/Gypsy common history, and promotes the constitution of an international diaspora that originated in India – has on a local level less and less social currency. Indeed, it is increasingly perceived by local Roma communities as corrupt and as little more than a strategy to use public money for self-interested gains.

The new "heavenly citizenship" model of identity has gained credibility within the Roma community by generating social cohesion and mitigating the effects of the exclusion and discrimination practices to which they are subjected. The new religious language and practices through which they are able to express their Gypsiness enable them to find ways to resist marginalization through the moralization of conduct. The local Pentecostal church empowers a destitute and marginalized community to find its own voice and provides the resources to mobilize its members socially and politically as an ethnic minority. In the past two decades, Pentecostalism has emerged as an important cultural factor in reconstructing Gypsiness.

Notes

1 Some scholars argue that the term "Roma" is a distinct way to essentialize the Gypsy community and refers to an ideological project, linked to the Romani International Movement, that aims at mobilizing a diverse and fragmented marginal social group (Gay y Blasco, 2008). For this reason, many Roma people from Romania reject this term and insist on being called Gypsies. However, the term "Gypsy" has also been used by some people in a derogatory way. Throughout this essay, I use both terms in order to refer to the different politics of managing social and ethnic identities. My purpose is to express respect for the diversity of ethnic conceptualization that this community is using in everyday life.
2 In a recent nationwide poll, 32% of people living in urban parts of Romania and 36% of people living in rural parts stated that they would not want to have a Roma/Gypsy as a neighbor. Only homosexuals are perceived as negatively as the Roma community (The Barometer of Inclusion of Roma, Soros Foundation, 2006).
3 See the table below.

Table 26.1 The denominational structure of the major ethnic groups existing in Romanian society, according to the 1992 and 2002 National Census (%).

	Orthodox	Roman Catholic	Greek Catholic	Reformed	Lutheran Evangelical	Unitarian	Neo-Protestant	Without religion/ Atheist
Romanian, 1992	94.68	1.77	0.94	0.08	0.03	0.01	1.99	0.12
Romanian, 2002	94.08	1.78	0.83	0.09	0.02	0.01	2.59	0.07
Hungarian, 1992	1.71	41.20	1.44	47.10	1.23	4.56	1.72	0.24
Hungarian, 2002	1.98	41.00	1.37	46.47	1.15	4.54	2.07	0.23
Roma, 1992	*85.30*	4.81	0.89	4.39	0.07	0.23	2.85	0.86
Roma, 2002	*81.88*	3.80	1.15	3.06	0.06	0.13	8.57	0.35

Source: 1992 and 2002 Census of Population and Dwellings, National Institute for Statistics, Romania.

4 Throughout this essay we assume a constructivist approach to ethnic identity (Anderson, 2006). By management of ethnic identity we understand a conscious and active process that aims at developing a socially constructed ethno-cultural narrative that is shared by a specific community. This involves such things as popularizing a common history, a common language, and a common origin. These in turn require ethnic activists (a national intelligentsia) that are able to articulate at grassroots levels integrated "imagined communities" (Anderson, 2006: 4–7). The expression "imagining an ethno-national community" refers to a modern social and cultural process by which nation-states are able to affirm their sovereignties by inventing a shared identity for the people of their nation. Terms such as "ethno-politics," "ethnic mobilization," and "ethno-genesis strategy" that I use throughout this essay refer to this active social process of constructing ethnic identities.

5 For instance, in Romania at the beginning of the 1990s there were at least seven Roma parties, each of which was based on a different traditional kin group of Gypsies. The absence of a clear Roma ethnic narrative resulted in a great deal of political fragmentation among the Roma and internal fights (McGarry, 2009: 14). Nor was the Romanian experience unique. As a result of "unmodernized" identity narratives that relied on kinship groups, the same pattern of fragmentation and infighting unfolded in almost every eastern European country.

6 Several factors explain why this political attempt at imagining an overarching ethnic Roma identity has failed: the low number of intellectual elites that sometimes favored a quick process of assimilation rather than one of cultural affirmation (Barany, 2001: 1–3); a wide cultural and social gap between postsocialist Roma intelligentsia and Roma traditional groups (Barany, 2004: 205); an "ambiguous nationalism" (McGarry, 2009: 116); and the lack of resources necessary for a coherent ethnic mobilization.

References

Alinčová, M. (2002) Byzantium, *ROMBASE*, http://ling.uni-graz.at/~rombase/cgi-bin/art.cgi?src=data/hist/origin/byzanz.en.xml (accessed February 15, 2010).

Anderson, B.R.O.G. (2006) *Imagined Communities: Reflections on the Origin and Spread of Nationalism*, Verso, LondonBarany, Z. (2000) Politics and the Roma in state-socialist eastern Europe, *Communist and Post-Communist Studies* 33(4): 421–437.

Barany, Z. (2002) *The East European Gypsies: Regime Change, Marginality, and Ethnopolitics*, Cambridge University Press, Cambridge.

Crowe, D.M. (2000) Muslim Roma in the Balkans, *Nationalities Papers: The Journal of Nationalism and Ethnicity* 28(1): 93–128.

Cuctuc, C. (2001) *Religii care au fost interzise in Romania*, Editura Gnosis, Bucharest.

Foszto, L. (2006) Mono-ethnic churches, the "undertaker parish," and rural civility in post-socialist Romania, in *The Postsocialist Religious Question: Faith and Power in Central Asia and East-Central Europe*, Chris Hann (ed.), LIT, Munster, pp. 269–292.

Fraser, A. (1992) *The Gypsies*, Blackwell, Oxford.

Gall, T.L. and Hobby, J. (2009) *Worldmark Encyclopedia of Cultures and Daily Life*, Gale, Farmington Hills, MI.

Gay y Blasco, P. (1999) *Gypsies in Madrid: Sex, Gender and the Performance of Identity*, Berg, Oxford.

Gay y Blasco, P. (2008) Picturing "gypsies": Interdisciplinary approaches to Roma representation, *Third Text* 22(3): 297–303.

Gheorghe, N. (1999) The social construction of Romani identity, in *Gypsy Politics and*

Traveler Identity, Thomas E. Acton (ed.), University of Hertfordshire Press, Hatfield, pp. 153–171.

Gog, Sorin (2008) Post-socialist religious pluralism: How do religious conversions of Roma fit into the wider landscape? From global to local perspectives, *Transitions* 48(2): 92–101.

Gonta, A.I. (1997) Robii tigani si tatari in satul moldovenesc din evul mediu [The Roma and Tatar slaves in the Moldovian village in the Middle Ages], *Romathan: Studii despre romi* 1(1): 69–86.

Grigore, D. (2001) *Curs de Antropologie si folclor rrom: Introducere in studiul elementelor de cultura traditionala ale identitatii contemporane [Anthropology and Roma Folklore Course: Introduction to the Study of Traditional Culture and Contemporary Identity]*, Credis, Bucharest.

Hancock, I. (1987) *Pariah Syndrome. An Account of Gypsy Slavery and Persecution*, Karoma Publishers, Ann Arbor, MI.

Hübschmannová, M. (2002) Origin of Roma, *ROMBASE*, http://romani.kfunigraz.ac.at/rombase/cgi-bin/art.cgi?src=data/hist/origin/origin.en.xml (accessed September 29, 2011).

Kligman, G. (2005) On the social construction of "otherness": Identifying "the Roma" in post-socialist communities, *Review of Sociology* 7(2): 61–78.

Lange, B.R. (2003) *Holy Brotherhood: Romani Music in a Hungarian Pentecostal Church*, Oxford University Press, Oxford.

McGarry, A. (2009) Ambiguous nationalism? Explaining the parliamentary under-representation of Roma in Hungary and Romania, *Romani Studies* 19(2): 103–124.

National Institute for Statistics, Romania (1992, 2002) Census of Population and Dwellings, http://www.insse.ro/cms/rw/pages/index.ro.do (accessed April 18, 2011).

Okely, J. (2007) *Own or Other Culture*, Routledge, London.

Petrova, D. (2003) The Roma: Between a myth and the future, *Social Research* 70(1): 11–161.

Ridholls, J. (1986) *Traveling Home: God's Work of Revival among Gypsy Folk*, Marshall Pickering, Basingstoke.

Samer, H. (Helmut. 2001) Maria Theresia and Joseph II: Policies of assimilation in the age of enlightened absolutism, *ROMBASE*, http://ling.uni-graz.at/~rombase/cgi-bin/art.cgi?src=data/hist/modern/maria.en.xml (accessed April 18, 2011).

Stewart, M. (1997) *The Time of the Gypsies*, Westview Press, Boulder, CO.

CHAPTER 27

Middle East

The Kurds – Religion and Social Justice of a Stateless Nation

Charles G. MacDonald

The aftermath of the first Gulf War in early 1991 saw the Iraqi Kurds rise up and seize control of the Kurdish region in Iraq. The Kurdish leadership was out of the area at the time. Saddam Hussein's forces, which had previously attempted to exterminate the Kurds in the Anfal Campaign after the Iran–Iraq War in 1988, moved to put down the Kurdish uprising. This was done brutally. More than 2 million Kurds fled through the snow and bitter cold into Turkey. Another 700 000 Kurdish refugees escaped into Iran. Many Kurds, especially children, died of the cold on the mountainsides as they fled Iraq. They lacked food and water. The western media seemed to focus on the death of the children. In one interview, a Kurdish leader was asked about the death of so many children. The western journalist was shocked when the leader said that it was better the children died than the older Kurds. He went on to explain that you can make more children, but it was only with the older Kurds that you have tradition. He feared the death of a nation.

It is sometimes difficult to understand peoples' contrasting values. The Kurds are a people with a complicated mix of traditional values arising from their historical experience, culture, religion, and political aspirations, juxtaposed with emergent values from an ever-changing world of technology, social networking, democratic ideals, and economic well-being. In February 2011, revolutionary mass protests, "the Arab Spring," spanned the Middle East, especially after apparent successes in Tunisia and Egypt. Kurds also rose up in the stable and peaceful Kurdish region of northern Iraq. They challenged Masoud Barzani, the President of the Kurdistan Regional Government. Elsewhere, the democratically elected government of Iraq was also targeted by protesters' demands. The Kurdish demonstrations underscore the change that is coming from young Kurds caught up, in part, in the new technological revolution that pursues social justice.

This essay examines the modern development of the Kurdish people as they have struggled in the Middle East, facing discrimination, conflict, social injustice, human

---

The Wiley Blackwell Companion to Religion and Social Justice, First Edition. Edited by Michael D. Palmer and Stanley M. Burgess.
© 2012 John Wiley & Sons Ltd. Published 2020 by John Wiley & Sons Ltd.

rights violations, and genocide. Kurds have responded to their tragic experience with the realization that "life goes on." This Kurdish experience – or experiences, as the case may be – must be placed in the specific Middle East context from which Kurds have emerged as victims of social injustice. The legacy of imperialism and the manipulation by outside powers, together with the domination of the Kurds by other national or ethnic groups (the Turks, Arabs, and Persians in particular), have accelerated the push for Kurdish nationalism within the Kurdish political experience. This, in turn, has generated or legitimized the concept of national self-determination, as well as the concept of armed struggle whenever Kurds have been denied their anticipated political rights and aspirations. The Kurds' historical drive for political status has been a fight for social justice.

To realize social justice, Kurds have pursued different political rights and aspirations based on the political context of the different parts of fragmented historic Greater Kurdistan. Greater Kurdistan was partitioned by the artificial boundaries created by the European powers and by Fortuna or the effects of fortuitous circumstance. An essential factor in this political context is the legacy of the millet system, by which empires have ruled the area's mosaic of religious communities or millets. Peoples were not identified by their national experience or ethnicity,[1] but by their religion. The existence of these millets, these religious nations, has become the basis for group identities and has complicated the establishment of the European state system in the Middle East. The apparent result, as one scholar put it, was "stateless nations" (such as the Kurds) and "nation-less states" (Helms, 1990). Thus, the relationship between religion and politics in the Middle East has been in sharp contrast with the European experience of the separation of church and state. Europe saw the rise of nationalism and the nation-state. Religious affiliation determined how Middle Eastern groups were viewed and defined, rather than nationality or ethnicity.

Kurdish People, a Nation Divided

The Kurds are arguably the third largest national group in the Middle East behind the Arabs and the Turks. The Kurds, an Indo-European people, are descendants of the ancient Medes. The Kurdish language is an Indo-European language on the Iranian tree of languages, as is Farsi. The Kurds are the predominant population in an irregular, boomerang-shaped area of land extending from southeastern Turkey and the northeastern edge of Syria through northern Iraq and eastern Iran to parts of Armenia and Azerbaijan. "Greater Kurdistan" was known to the Kurds as the "Kurdistan of Five Parts" and included Turkey, Syria, Iraq, Iran, and the Soviet Union. The divisions of Kurdistan grew to six parts following the fragmentation of the former Soviet Union and resulted in separate national development for Kurds in each of their host states.

The effect of the historical division of Kurdistan is threefold. First, the Kurds have found themselves within the borders of a state that spoke a different language or languages. The Kurds thus have no commonly used language. The Kurds spoke dialects of Kurdish in their respective communities, but were forced to learn, inter alia, Turkish, Arabic, Farsi, and Russian, according to the policies of their host states. Even the alphabets used often varied between states. The denial of the right to study one's own language has had a far-reaching impact on any potential national unification. Second, the political development of the Kurds in each instance has been limited to the state in which they exist. The Kurdish communities in each state have had a unique national experience and different political goals. Third, ethnically "different" from the people who control the state, the Kurds have often become pawns for outside powers who sought to use them against the host governments. Kurds subjected to manipulation, often found themselves on opposite political sides from Kurds across the border. For example, Iran has used Iraqi Kurds against the Iraqi government, and Iraq has used Iranian Kurds against the Iranian government.

Religion

In the Middle East religion becomes a backdrop for politics. The millet system historically established boundaries between religious groups. There was an aspiration of unity within the religious groupings, but the reality was one of diversity. The diversity too often prompted intolerance toward the other, both within a specific religion and between different religions. The Kurds, known formerly as non-Arab Bedouins, were usually associated with tribal values. They were a part of the Islamic world, but were not known for a zealous approach to religion. Generally speaking, Kurds in the Middle East are Sunni Muslims, especially in Turkey, Syria, Iraq, and northern Iran (the northern part of historic Kurdistan). In southern Iran and in Iran's Kurdistan Province, some Kurds are exceptions and are Shi'a. Abdul Rahman Qasemlou, a former leader of the Kurdistan Democratic Party of Iran (today known as the Democratic Party of Iranian Kurdistan or PDKI), indicated that about 25% of the Kurds in Iran were Shi'a, with 75% being Sunni (Qasemlou, 1980: 110). Some Kurds in southern Kurdistan follow the "twelver" sect of Shi'sim. Also in the south, Ali Ilahis are linked to the "sevener" sect of Shi'ism (Van Bruinessen, 1978: 31–33). Although the Kurdish communities are small, the Kurds in Armenia and Azerbaijan are also identified as predominantly Shi'a.

The Yezidis in Iraq's Mosul province represent a different case (Fuccaro, 1999). The Yezidi Kurds have been tied to the "sevener" sect, but also represent an ancient heterodox religious sect linked to Zoroastrianism and Sufism. While Yezidi religious practice has elements associated with other religions, the Yezidis speak Kurdish and essentially have a Kurdish culture. Yezidi Kurds have existed in a multicultural environment, but their religion has not been recognized as legitimate. The Yezidis were not granted the status of a recognized millet. Not being so protected, they have been persecuted by various groups. The Yezidi Kurds are also present in Armenia.

Even the Sunni Kurds stand apart from Arab and Turkish Sunnis. The Sunni Kurds follow the Shafi'i school of Islamic thought, as distinct from the Hanifi school. In Iran, the Sunni Kurds have essentially been treated as a religious minority and subject to discrimination. A firm move against the Kurdish Sunni beliefs was apparent in the revision of the original draft constitution of the Islamic Republic of Iran. For example, Article 13 recognized the Shi'a Ja'fari school of thought, which was followed by most Iranians, but provided for other schools of thought, such as the Shafi'i, to be applied locally in areas where they were followed by the majority (MacDonald, 1989: 61–62). This provision was removed in the final constitution. The provision for the guarantee of equal rights for ethnic groups (such as the Kurds), found in Article 5, was also removed. This was in accord with Ayatollah Khomeini's vision of world order in which no ethnic minorities or national groups existed, since there was no place for them in a unified Islamic community. According to Khomeini, the national groups and the separation of Islamic peoples into states was a "great trick of the West to undermine Islam" (Radio Tehran, December 17, 1979).

The dramatic increase of Sunni-Shi'a sectarian violence in Iraq in 2007, sparked in part as an effort to undermine the United States presence, brought religious violence and civil war in Iraq into the international limelight. It also has had a significant impact on the future of Sunni–Shi'a relations throughout the Middle East. It further complicated the already complex relationship between Shi'a and Sunni communities and the degree to which they could be influenced by outside powers. In other words, religious differences were exacerbated by interstate rivalries and conflict, as they had been so many times before in the Middle East. In Iran, the United States came to support the opposition to the Islamic government, such as Sunni Muslims and other minorities. Thus, it became more difficult to distinguish whether the Iranian Kurds were persecuted or discriminated against by the Iranian government because they were a religious minority or an ethnic minority. The result was ever-present social injustice for innocent peoples targeted because of their religion or ethnicity.

Social Justice

The experience of social injustice has been a catalyst for the pursuit of freedom or independence from tyranny, whether such injustice came from a local ruler or a colonial or imperial power. This effort to acquire power and to be free of the unjust rule of others is ageless and is a function of politics. Woodrow Wilson took his concept of self-determination to the Paris Peace Conference in the aftermath of the First World War with the essential belief that peoples should rule themselves. This set the modern stage for the pursuit of national self-determination by national or ethnic groups the world over. The Kurds have Ehmed-i Xani's *Mem U Zin*, in which Kurds desired a Kurdish ruler for Kurds as early as the seventeenth century. This Kurdish desire to have a Kurdish state with a Kurdish ruler has eluded Kurdish nationalists. The social injustice the Kurds have experienced has resulted in the pursuit of social justice by various means. Perhaps the most significant are armed struggle, the political process, and the rule of law. Each of the three has had varied success, and they are not mutually exclusive. Each has been a function of the context in which the Kurds find themselves within each host state. Thus, the pursuit of social justice is transitory as Kurdish life goes on, but some changes linked to new technologies have changed the process in the twenty-first century.

In all parts of historic Greater Kurdistan, Kurds continue to suffer social injustice in various forms, ranging from discrimination and persecution to repression, torture, and death. Traditionally, the spectrum of Kurdish goals has extended from cultural survival to various degrees of autonomy and self-rule to independence. The means were often political and military organizations that sought to bring the government or state in question to justice.

Kurdistan in Iraq

Kurdish organizations that have sometimes been outlawed often had their roots in the anticolonial period after the Second World War and sought some form of self-determination. In Iraq, Kurds sought the goals of autonomy and democracy. The Kurdistan Democratic Party fought civil wars with the central government. In 1970, when a ceasefire was reached to work out an autonomy agreement, the involvement of the United States had a major impact. The United States encouraged Mustafa Barzani not to accept the agreement and to take up arms again against Iraq's central government. The Iraqi Kurdish armed struggle continued. The United States, Israel, and Iran supported the Kurdish effort by providing assistance through Iran. The Kurds were abandoned abruptly, however, when the Shah signed the 1975 Algiers Accord with Iraq's Saddam Hussein. Iran received long-wanted concessions on the Shatt-al-Arab river boundary in return for cutting off assistance to the Kurds. Following the Iran–Iraq War (1980–1988), Iraqi Kurds were targeted by Iraq's forces. The tragic Anfal Campaign (February–September 1988) saw tens of thousands of Kurds killed. Iraq's attack on the Kurdish town of Halabja brought the horrors of chemical warfare to the world's attention. After the United States and coalition forces forced Saddam Hussein's forces out of Kuwait in 1991, the United States encouraged the Kurds to rise up against the Iraqi government. When the Kurds did, the United States failed to support the Kurds and as many as 3 million Kurds were forced to flee into Turkey and Iran. This Kurdish tragedy set the stage for Operation Provide Comfort and the creation of what was to become a de facto Kurdish state in the north of Iraq.

Members of the two major Iraqi Kurdish organizations (the Kurdistan Democratic Party, KDP, and the Patriotic Union of Kurdistan, PUK), inter alia, came to play active roles in the Iraqi political process under the US administration of Iraq following the removal of Saddam Hussein. Jalal Talabani of the PUK became the President of Iraq and Masoud Barzani of the KDP became the President of the Kurdistan Regional Government. The Kurds have established a significant military capability in their region after Saddam. The realization of the Kurdish political goals of autonomy and democracy, however, has come about through a determined Kurdish participation in the political process in Iraq.

Kurdistan in Turkey

In Turkey, the Kurdish struggle against social injustice and for self-determination is a complex one, with many examples of the horrors of ethnic conflict. The Turkish denial of the very existence of ethnic Kurds was an extreme example of nation building following the break-up of the Ottoman Empire. Turkish nationalist leader Mustafa Kemal

Ataturk wanted to unify the new Turkish state. One of Ataturk's "six arrows" of Kemalism (his reform program) was "populism," which asserted that all citizens had equal rights as Turks. Kurds were granted equal rights as "Mountain Turks," but were denied their own language. Even the use of the work "Kurd" was punishable by imprisonment. It was in this environment that the principal Kurdish nationalist organization, the Kurdistan Workers Party (PKK), in Turkey came to seek independence through armed struggle. Formed by Abdullah Ocalan in 1978, the PKK was set up as a communist organization linked to the doctrines of Stalin. The PKK's armed struggle with the Turkish military and security forces has reportedly resulted in upwards of 40 000 lives lost. The armed struggle saw various iterations of the PKK, whose names have included KADEK and Konga-Gel. The Kurdish goal of armed struggle has seen a number of declared ceasefires and changes in the goal of self-determination from independence to federalism. The capture of Ocalan on February 15, 1999, brought changes to Ocalan's stated goals and was a watershed in the PKK's struggle.

Apart from the PKK, Kurds in Turkey also sought social justice through the Turkish political process. Kurds have participated in numerous political parties and as independents to pursue Kurdish interest. The political process has seen numerous pro-Kurdish political parties participate. Many of these parties were subsequently declared illegal and disbanded, only to be replaced by others. The most recent pro-Kurdish party is the Peace and Democracy Party (BDP). The BDP followed other such parties that included the Democratic Society Party (DTP), the Democratic People's Party (DEHAP), the People's Democratic Party (HADEP), the Democracy Party (DEP), and the People's Labor Party (HEP), among others.

While the stated goal of the PKK was initially an independent Kurdish state, the PKK moved toward a form of federation. The PKK wanted to follow the success of the Palestine Liberation Organization, which achieved legitimacy in the Arab–Israeli conflict. The PKK offered ceasefires and an acknowledgment of the laws of armed conflict in an effort to influence not only Turkey, but also the United States. Although the PKK was unsuccessful, the United States did suggest to the Turkish government the idea of a political solution for the Kurdish problem in place of a military solution. Turkey responded by requiring US citizens to have a visa to enter Turkey. Turkey was not willing to negotiate the Kurdish issue with an outside party.

The current Justice and Development Party (AKP) has offered a new approach to the Kurdish problem referred to as the "Democratic Opening" or "Democratic Initiative." AKP seeks to solve the Kurdish problem through democratic reforms. The creation of a civil society where there is no governmental injustice toward any ethnic group would not be a simple move, but a long and difficult process based on the rule of law.

In addition to the participation of Kurds in the Turkish political system, the London-based Kurdish Human Rights Project (KHRP) has sought to fight injustice and human rights violations through the rule of law. Turkey has been brought before the European Court of Human Rights to respond to human rights cases. The process has used law to redress social injustice, with both Turkey and the Kurds seeking justice through the rule of law.

Kurdistan in Iran

In Iran, as in Iraq, Kurds have traditionally sought "autonomy and democracy." The central government of Iran has not hesitated to use force against Iranian Kurds to deny their political goals. Kurds have been mistreated, and many have been killed, including Kurdish leaders. Qazi Mohammed and his Kurdistan Democratic Party of Iran were able to establish a de facto autonomy following the Second World War when there was a Soviet military presence in Iran. His effort to have the Iranian government accept a de jure autonomy and democracy within Iran failed. Qazi Mohammed was hanged by the Iranian military following the departure of Soviet forces. His death was apparently the result of a personal vendetta. The US Embassy in Tehran had been told that Qazi Mohammed would not be harmed. Following the Iranian revolution, the Kurds again seized control of Iranian Kurdistan. Dr. Qasemlou, the KDPI leader, assured Ayatollah Khomeini that the Kurds did not wish to secede from Iran, but sought only self-rule in a democratic Iran. Khomeini sent Iranian airpower to bomb the Kurdish cities, which had no effective air defense. The KDPI was forced to flee. Qasemlou was assassinated in Vienna in July 1989 as he held negotiations with Iran's Islamic government. Iran was implicated in his death. Qasemlou was preparing to come to Washington, DC at the time. Qasemlou's successor, Dr. Sadegh Sharafkandi, was assassinated on September 17, 1992, in Berlin.

The current Secretary General of KDPI is Mustafa Hejri. Iranian Kurds have not become an integral part of the Iranian political process. They did support the reformist government of former Iranian President Mohammed Hatemi, but continue to suffer human rights violations under the government of President Ahmadinejad. Human rights organizations and other opposition groups do use the current legal structure in Iran to pursue social justice, but the judiciary remains a staunch supporter of the current government. In addition, the Kurdish Human Rights Project (KHRP) cannot bring Iran to an international court for human rights violations, but it can call on Iran to honor its own laws that support social justice.

Other parts of historic Kurdistan

The Kurds in Syria continue to struggle for cultural survival. Syria has denied Kurds the right to practice their culture and religion. This was made brutally clear in the 2009 Human Rights Report, *Repression of Kurdish Culture and Human Rights in Syria*. A 2010 United Nations Human Rights Council criticized Syria in its report on the right to food. The report targeted Syria for its discrimination against as many as 250 000 to 300 000 stateless Kurds who lacked access to public food. The Kurdish Human Rights Project also has taken Syria to task, especially concerning the citizenship rights of Kurds. It has criticized the revoking of Syrian citizenship rights of Kurds during the 1960s. The stateless Kurds in Syria have also suffered mistreatment and torture. Kurdish organizations in and out of Syria continue to call attention to the denial of Kurdish culture and persecution of the Kurds in Syria.

The Kurds in Armenia and Azerbaijan, parts of the former Soviet Union, face various types of human rights violations. The Kurdistan Human Rights Project (KHRP) has supported claims against Armenia in the European Court of Human Rights pertaining to freedom of expression. KHRP has also taken Armenia and Azerbaijan to task for failing to honor their Organization of Security and Cooperation in Europe obligations in the area of human rights. Some Kurds have attempted to foster Kurdish organizations within the Kurdish areas of Armenia and Azerbaijan, but have been frustrated in their efforts. Nevertheless, outside organizations, like KHRP, have continued to play a human rights watchdog role.

Changes and the Next Generation

Kurds interact within the various settings in which they find themselves while facing a complex identity that is both tribal and modern, religious and secular, and Kurdish or assimilated into the various cultures of Turkey, Iraq, Iran, Syria, Armenia, and Azerbaijan. Young Kurds who use the internet, Facebook, YouTube, and other social networking sites have become part of a new generation of globalization. Their values and use of technology are creating a new world, not readily understood by the older generations. The effects of the "Arab Spring" demonstrations have ushered in a new era of instant news sent by iPhone video cameras. The Iranian revolution was fueled by audio cassettes identifying social injustice. The excesses of Saddam Hussein's Republican Guards attacking hapless Kurds were sent around the world via fax machines. Now the internet not only provides a description of social injustice in the Middle East, but videos can be instantly sent to YouTube via iPhones. Hiding genocide and human rights violations is no longer possible. The ability of states to deny atrocities has been destroyed. All states must deal with the immediacy of truth in the public's eye around the world. Kurdish political organizations and news services are also taking advantage of Facebook and other social networking internet sites to establish virtual communities of Kurdish nationalists that transcend borders and use multiple languages.

Another technological advancement that transcends borders is satellite television. Kurdish satellite television received its first license in 1994 and began to transmit in 1995.[2] Called "Kurdistan in the Sky" or "sovereignty in the sky," Med TV marked a new era in which access to Kurdish language would no longer be blocked by borders or controlled by host states. The world of Med TV was repeatedly challenged by Turkish authorities. The studios in London and Denderleeuw, Belgium gave way to studios elsewhere. Med TV was eventually closed, as was its successor, Medya TV. Roj TV opened in Denmark and transmits a new Kurdish reality that builds a sense of Kurdish appreciation. Other Kurdish television stations have followed suit, such as KTC of Iraq's Kurdistan Democratic Party.

The next generation of Kurds understands the ongoing discrimination against Kurds throughout the various parts of historic Kurdistan. The situations in Syria, Iran, Armenia, and Azerbaijan offer little more than opportunities to challenge human rights violations and to attempt to keep the Kurdish culture alive. The situations in Turkey and Iraq are more promising, as Kurds are playing a more immediate role by promoting social justice through participation in the political system. In Turkey, the ruling AKP is an Islamic Party, but it exists within Turkey's democratic political system. The pro-Kurdish Peace and Democracy Party (BDP) is also working within the system to promote social justice for the Kurds. In Iraq, the KDP and the PUK are both playing significant roles in the Iraqi democracy. Such political participation, along with the use of law to pursue social justice, does not stop social injustice. It does, however, contribute to a move toward civil society.

While technology has given young people the opportunity to support social justice, another dimension of the Kurds' search for social justice has been realized within the Kurdish region of Iraq. The United States Department of State, Bureau of Democracy, Human Rights, and Labor releases country reports on human rights each year. The Iraq Country Report identified Kurdish human rights violations against other ethnic groups. The Kurdish authorities are realizing that they also must be circumspect when it comes to social justice. The youth are not inhibited by tradition and in the "Arab Spring" have not hesitated to protest against the corruption of both the KDP and the PUK. This also signals that social justice has an economic dimension. The denial of social justice, if not addressed, can induce the young to resort to violence, as has been the case in the past.

The traditional values of the Kurds promise to preserve the Kurdish nation, but some traditional practices also must be addressed. A pioneer of women's rights in Kurdistan, Dr. Nazand Begikhani, launched Kurdish Women: Action Against Honor Killing (KWAHK) in 2000. It was broadened to other women's issues under the name of Kurdish Women's Rights Watch in 2004. Some would argue that it would be easier for a Kurdish nationalist leader like Masoud Barzani to fight Saddam Hussein than it would to deal with the issue of the treatment of women in Kurdistan. Nevertheless, the Kurdish Regional Government has taken up the challenge and has established an Honor Killing Monitoring Commission in 2007, headed by its Minister for Human Rights. The pursuit of social justice continues.

Notes

1 Professor Richard N. Frye of Harvard asserted that there was no concept of ethnicity in the Middle East prior to the twentieth century. When I asked in a 1983 National Endowment for the Humanities class session how he could say that, he indicated that there was no word for ethnicity in the Middle Eastern languages.
2 I happened to be at the offices of the Kurdish Parliament in Exile on Avenue Louise in Brussels when the first scheduled transmission took place. The Kurdish leaders from Turkey had tears of joy in their eyes. It was such a success. "The Three Little Pigs" in Kurdish represented the beginning of access to the Kurdish language by children throughout Kurdistan. News in Turkish and Kurdish represented a new opportunity for Kurds to avoid censorship.

References

Fuccaro, Nelida (1999) Communalism and the state in Iraq: The Yazidi Kurds, c. 1869–1940, *Middle East Studies* 35(April): 1–26.

Helms, Christine M. (1990) *Arabism and Islam: Stateless Nations and Nationless States*, US Government Printing Office, Washington, DC.

MacDonald, Charles G. (1989) The Kurdish challenge and revolutionary Iran, *Journal of South Asian and Middle Eastern Studies* 8(Fall/Winter): 52–68.

Qasemlou, Abdul Rahman (1980) Kurdistan in Iran, in *People without a Country*, Gerard Chaliand (ed.), Zed Books, London, pp. 95–121.

Van Bruinessen, Martin (1978) *Agha, Shaikh, and State: On the Social and Political Organization of Kurdistan*, Luzoc, London.

Bibliography

Ahmed, Mohammed M.A. and Gunter, Michael M. (2000) *The Kurdish Question and International Law: An Analysis of the Legal Rights of the Kurdish People*, Ahmed Foundation for Kurdish Studies, Oakton, VA.

Entessar, Nader (1992) *Kurdish Ethnonationalism*, Lynne Rienner, Boulder, CO.

Hassanpour, Amir (1992) *Nationalism and Language in Kurdistan, 1918–1985*, Mellen Research University Press, San Francisco, CA.

Heper, Metin (2007) *The State and Kurds in Turkey: The Question of Assimilation*, Palgrave Macmillan, New York.

Imset, Ismet G. (1992) *The PKK: A Report on Separatist Violence in Turkey, 1973–1992*, Turkish Daily News Publications, Istanbul.

Kirisci, Kemal and Winrow, Gareth M. (1997) *The Kurdish Question and Turkey: An Example of a Trans-state Ethnic Conflict*, Frank Cass, London.

Limbert, John (1968) The origins and appearance of the Kurds in pre-Islamic Iran, *Iranian Studies* 1(Spring): 41–51.

MacDonald, Charles G. and O'Leary, Carole A. (eds.) (2007) *Kurdish Identity: Human Rights and Political Status*, University Press of Florida, Gainesville, FL.

Markus, Aliza (2009) *Blood and Belief: The PKK and the Kurdish Fight for Independence*, New York University Press, New York.

McDowall, David (1996) *A Modern History of the Kurds*, I.B. Tauris, New York.

Olson, Robert (ed.) (1989) *The Emergence of Kurdish Nationalism and the Sheikh Sa'id Rebellion, 1889–1925*, University of Texas Press, Austin.

Van Bruinessen, Martin (2000) *Mullas, Sufis, and Heretics: The Role of Religion in Kurdish Society*, ISIS, Istanbul.

Watts, Nicole F. (2010) *Activists in Office: Kurdish Politics and Protest in Turkey*, University of Washington Press, Seattle.

White, Paul (2000) *Primitive Rebels or Revolutionary Modernizers? The Kurdish National Movement in Turkey*, Zed Books, London.

Yildiz, Kerim and Muller, Mark, QC (2008) *The European Union and Turkish Accession: Human Rights and the Kurds*, Pluto Press, London.

Yildiz, Kerim and Breau, Susan (2010) *The Kurdish Conflict: International Humanitarian Law and Post-Conflict Mechanisms*, Routledge, London.

CHAPTER 28
New Zealand
The Māori People

Rawinia Higgins

"Me mate au, me mate mō te whenua" (If I Am to Die, Let Me Die for the Land)

Land is one of the key elements to Māori identity. It embodies the histories, genealogies, and spiritual connections to the past, present, and future. Religious beliefs emanate from the land, Papatūānuku, which is the embodiment of the primal earth mother. Papatūānuku is in turn guarded by Ranginui, the sky father. The creation narrative, for Māori, begins with these two ancestors, and political and social struggles continue to be centered on the protection and maintenance of the land. The proverb (*whakataukī*) quoted above was exclaimed during a battle between two tribes, Ngāti Whakaue and Ngāti Hauā, at Ohinemutu (Mead and Grove, 1996: 33). This proverbial saying summarizes the content of this essay, which examines how the Māori people vehemently protected their land against the increasing influx of European settlers (Pākehā). Māori did not view land as an asset for ownership, but as part of their cultural identity and spiritual beliefs, and yet despite the introduction of new forms of technology and ideology, Māori continued to fight against the European acquisition of land. This brief political history outlines two of the key areas that were severely affected by the onslaught of the new culture, and the impact it had on Māori perceptions of land, power (*mana*), and identity. As part of this struggle we see the emergence of significant Māori political and religious groups in an effort to reclaim their land (*whenua*) as a means of maintaining their power (*mana*) and identity as people.

The Treaty of Waitangi is the founding document of New Zealand and was signed by some 40 Māori chiefs on February 6, 1840. Using aspects of their distinctive tattoo (*moko*) designs, most chiefs signed the Māori version, thereby consenting to the terms of the Treaty of Waitangi as they understood them. The most important note here is to understand that Māori did not cede sovereignty. The contentious issues surrounding

---

The Wiley Blackwell Companion to Religion and Social Justice, First Edition. Edited by Michael D. Palmer and Stanley M. Burgess.
© 2012 John Wiley & Sons Ltd. Published 2020 by John Wiley & Sons Ltd.

this Treaty will not be explored in detail. Nevertheless, they need to be established before examining the issues pertaining to land and settlement, as they provide a frame for the interface between Māori and Europeans and how subsequent disputations arose despite having a Treaty.

The Treaty of Waitangi came about as a result of the impending European settlement. For the British Government, the Treaty of Waitangi was a means of guaranteeing the Māori's welfare (Sinclair, 1957: 20) by guaranteeing them their lands and other valued resources under Article II of the Treaty. However, land soon became a point of dispute between Māori and the incoming settlers, who desired possession of the vast land resource of the Māori. Whereas Māori viewed land as sacred (*tapu*), settlers regarded such values as merely "idle objections to the sale of land" and considered the Māori perspective to be illegitimate (*Taranaki Herald*, June 20, 1857, cited in Sinclair, 1957: 6). Europeans sought the land for themselves, in order to convert it into English-style farms and to develop New Zealand as a colony of Britain. Māori were determined not to relinquish all their lands so easily to settlers. As Sinclair (1957: 4) observes, "[t]his contest for dominion lay beneath the relations of the two races through most of the nineteenth century, and no compromise seemed possible." Antagonism started to build between Māori and Europeans as a result of the latter not understanding the culture or the values of the people of the land (*tangata whenua*). This antagonism was intensified when Māori participated and succeeded in economic trading with Europeans. "Living among a numerous population of 'savages,' and conscious of the superiority of their own culture, the settlers came both to fear and despise their neighbours" (Sinclair 1957: 10).

> The word "Maori" conjured up in the settlers' minds a stereotype based on experience in other colonies. This stereotypical Maori bore little resemblance to the actual Maori, though to the settlers daily misunderstandings seemed to lend validity to this picture. It was the stereotypical Maori as much as the actual one that influenced the behavior of European settlers. When the wars broke out it was this fictitious Maori whom they thought they were fighting. (Sinclair, 1957: 10)

The influence of the Christian missionaries allowed Māori to begin to understand European culture and values. Their work predated the contact between settlers and Māori, and they were instrumental in transforming Māori philosophical, spiritual, and cultural belief systems. The tireless work of the missionaries and their Māori converts saw other Māori questioning their sacred beliefs and fundamental customary concepts. The influence of the missionaries prompted Māori to accept European settlers. Despite the fact that the Māori accepted the newcomers (albeit on terms established by the Europeans), the settlers still believed that they were superior to the "savages" and continued to demand more land from the government. The Governor, George Grey, agreed that it was a profitable time to benefit from the land-hungry settlers and subsequently created land-purchase policies that were designed to advance European settlement (Sinclair 1957: 44).

The settlers' desire for land, regardless of Māori ownership/occupation (*ahi kā*) rights, and the Māori's growing reluctance to sell their land gradually escalated tensions and resulted not only in bloodshed but also in profound cultural changes in Māori families (*whānau*), clans (*hapū*), and tribes (*iwi*). Keith Sinclair (1957: 61) believes that Māori nationalism developed over a period of time from 1800 to 1858 as a result of the changing Māori reaction to Europeans. During the initial contact period (1800–1840), Māori were relatively willing to accept the new culture. From 1840–1848 there appears to have been some unorganised Māori resistance to the settlers, principally those Europeans who associated themselves with the New Zealand Company settlements. Not until the decade from 1848 to 1858 did more organized structures of resistance come to the fore to prevent sales and to protect the *whenua*. More significantly, however, Sinclair (1957: 61) locates the foundation of a "national organisation" from 1848. Civil war broke out between sections of tribes that opposed selling land and those that supported land sales. During this period the King Movement (Kīngitanga) was also established as an expression of Māori nationalism. (This movement will be discussed later in the essay.) Tensions between the growing number of settlers and the decreasing Māori population intensified after 1853 and by 1860 the Unification (Kotahitanga) movement had gained prominence.

These political developments demonstrate the effects of European culture on Māori customary practices (*tikanga*). Māori believed that land could not be gifted or disposed of without the consent of the whole tribe and if these occurred it had to be beneficial for that respective tribe. Interclan or intertribal fighting had long been a feature of traditional Māori society, not just for the acquisition of lands, but often more about how individual people exerted power over others. The influence of the new culture was instrumental in breaking down the spiritual connection that the Māori had with their land.

To puku! Horo tangata, horo whenua!
"Your belly! O man-eaters, O land-gobblers." (Mead and Grove, 1996: 173)

This proverb expresses the pressure that settlers exerted to get Māori to sell their land. The pressure by settlers to acquire land is evident through the unification of many Māori as tribes to take a national stance in order to protect their *whenua*.

"Kua maoa te taewa" (The Potato has been Cooked)

Te Whiti o Rongomai, the Taranaki prophet and leader from Parihaka, is the source for this prophecy. As Mead and Grove (1994: 161) explain,

> The potato was a metaphor for the Maori people being overcome by European arms and land confiscations. He [Te Whiti] meant that being so cooked meant the potato could be eaten without further action.

Te Whiti o Rongomai's prophetic saying expresses the lengths to which the people of Taranaki went in order to maintain their connection with their land.
It is important to begin by referring to the Waitara Purchase (1859–1860) as an example of how Māori belief in "collective responsibility" toward land had broken down

among those people in Te Ati Awa (a tribal group located on the west coast of the North Island) as a result of the influence that Pākehā culture had over Māori at this time. Prior to the Waitara Purchase, the Land Purchase Department had to adhere "to the traditional Maori custom of communal rights to land. This meant no Maori could sell his own individual piece ... without the consent of the whole of the owners" (Sinclair, 1975: 145–146). Wiremu Kīngi Te Rangitake, chief (*rangatira*) of Te Ati Awa, ardently opposed the Waitara purchase, and wrote to the colonial government continually during the terms of office of three Governors (Fitzroy, Grey, and Gore Browne), asserting that his people would not sell Waitara (Sinclair, 1957: 117). Speaking to all the Governors, he said, "Waitara shall not be given up" (Sinclair, 1957: 117). When Kīngi Te Rangitake wrote to Fitzroy, he tried to appeal to the Governor's sense of spiritual connection to land by asking the Governor, "Friend Governor, do you not love your land England – the land of your fathers? As we also love our land at Waitara?" (*AJHR*, 1881: E-1.19, cited in Sinclair, 1957: 117). Drawing on Māori ideology, Kīngi Te Rangitake petitioned the Governors to understand the importance of land to Māori by drawing a comparison to land in England. It is evident that Kīngi Te Rangitake used the reference to genealogy (*whakapapa*) to indicate the spiritual significance of the land to Māori in his appeal to the Governors. Subsequent actions that took place suggest that Pākehā did not have the same spiritual affinity to the land as Māori.

Te Teira (also from Te Ati Awa) offered to sell land in Waitara to Governor Thomas Gore Browne in March 1859. The Governor, interested in the offer, explained to Te Teira that he would have to prove his title to the land. "Teira then laid a *parawai*, or bordered mat, at the Governor's feet, as a symbol that he placed his land in the Governor's hands" (Sinclair, 1957: 137). Te Teira, without consulting the chief Kīngi Te Rangitake, offered Waitara as a means of revenge (*utu*) against Kīngi Te Rangitake for another issue. Te Teira offered the land as a means of slighting the power and authority of his chief without considering the outcomes that the sale would have for the community. The ability of an individual to offer tribal lands for sale is an example of the influence that European culture had in breaking down Māori social beliefs. The extreme actions of Te Teira in seeking retribution against Kīngi Te Rangitake for his own personal issue appeared to be more important to the former than any consideration of the implications for the people. As a result, there was a shift away from a cultural belief in the primacy of community prerogatives in favor of the individual's preferences and choices.

> There is no doubt that within a Pakeha worldview a concept of individual responsibility is dominant, and likewise that within a Maori worldview a concept of collective responsibility is dominant. (Patterson, 1992: 142)

Te Teira did not prioritize the "collective responsibility" of ensuring the protection of Waitara. Rather, he saw the prerogatives of individuals as outweighing those of the collective. Not only would he obtain retribution against the Kīngi Te Rangitake, but also attain more power and authority from the government by being acknowledged as the landowner of Waitara. The animosity between Kīngi Te Rangitake and Te Teira reflected the government's policy of divide and rule in order to acquire more lands without being delayed by obtaining tribal agreement.

> The government, in spite of denials, had been considering for some time a policy of buying up the claims of small groups as they came forward, rather than waiting for all claimants to agree on a sale. This was seen as the only way to break the "deadlock" in Taranaki.
> (Parsonson, 1991: 263–264)

Te Teira's revenge was acknowledged when the colonial government "officially" judged Wiremu Kīngi Te Rangitake as having no rights to the lands in Waitara and, therefore, allowed the purchase to go forward (Parsonson, 1991: 264). "This celebrated 'purchase' was the root of the war in Taranaki and ultimately of the war in Waikato" (Ballara, 1998: 263). Belich (1986) supports this interpretation, though he believes that there were other reasons behind these wars:

> the widespread desire for the imposition of British administration, law, and civilization on the Maoris was so important that it should rank with land-hunger as a cause of war. (Belich, 1986: 77)

This "civilizing" of Māori by the British was instrumental in undermining Māori cultural practices. To "civilize" means to reclaim from a savage state; to introduce order and organization; to refine and enlighten. To speak of civilizing the Māori implies that they lacked social practices that maintained order among their people. But the Māori surely did not lack such practices and customs, nor did they live in a "savage state" as the Europeans supposed. Europeans – many of whom did not understand the Māori world (*te ao* Māori) – dismissed Māori culture as having little value. In time, the unenlightened view of the European came to adversely affect the way Māori themselves viewed their cultural practices and beliefs.

After the Waitara Purchase, Kīngi Te Rangitake interfered and resisted the Crown's surveyors by removing the surveying pegs, in order both to assert his power and authority and to protect the community's lands. Kīngi Te Rangitake and his people set up their fortified settlement (*pā*) at Te Kohia. European troops were sent in and told Kīngi Te Rangitake to surrender. "When they refused to do so, the troops opened fire" (Waitangi Tribunal, 1996: 18–19). This was the commencement of the long wars in Aotearoa/ New Zealand.

The *New Zealand Settlement Act 1863* gave the colonial government the right to confiscate vast amounts of land if Māori were seen to be rebelling against the Crown.

> The New Zealand Settlements Act was directed to national security, and the rationale was stated in the statute itself: its purpose was to achieve law and order by establishing "a sufficient number of settlers able to protect themselves and to preserve the peace." (Waitangi Tribunal, 1996: 2)

In addition to the *New Zealand Settlement Act 1863*, the Colonial Parliament introduced the *Suppression of Rebellion Act 1863*, which was designed to forcibly arrest and kill suspected rebels without a trial (Sinclair, 1975: 147). Taranaki Māori were forced to accept the individualization of land titles, which disbanded communal ownership. "The penalty for non-compliance was to be the forfeiture of their lands" (Sinclair, 1975:

146). The initial reasons for the land wars were overshadowed by the eventual outcome of these wars, where the colonial government confiscated vast amounts of Māori land. In 1865, in Taranaki alone, nearly 1 199 622 acres of prime land were confiscated (Waitangi Tribunal, 1996: 1). Evicted from their homelands, the Māori felt alienated from the land, which in turn profoundly affected their identity as a people.

Ko Ngāruawāhia tōku tūrangawaewae (Ngāruawāhia is My Standing Place)

For Waikato tribes this utterance by King Tāwhiao (the second Māori king) signified the importance of Ngāruawāhia as the base for the King Movement (Kīngitanga). The King Movement is considered the most notable expression of Māori nationalism in New Zealand history. However, it also became one of the real reasons behind colonial confiscations of land. The pressure that Europeans applied to individuals within tribal or clan groups to sell land was a catalyst for the debasement of Māori customary practices. The sudden rise of nationalism amongst Māori proved an effective means of raising the fears of early settlers. In 1861, Governor Grey believed that the King Movement, its people, and their own governing bodies were becoming a significant threat to his colonial authority (McKinnon, 1997: 38).

Some tribes saw the benefit of uniting in light of the European pressure to sell land. At a meeting at Pūkawa in 1856, the notion of a Māori king was discussed among chiefs from various tribes and Potatau Te Wherowhero of Waikato was nominated as the best candidate. Wiremu Tamihana Tarapipipi Te Waharoa, also known as the "king maker," supported Potatau's nomination and lobbied with tribes of the Waikato area for their support of the "king" as a means of producing laws that would protect people and their lands (Oliver, 1991: 312).

> Tamihana spoke strongly to express his concern for the establishment and maintenance of law and order within the tribes. He hoped that a Maori kingship would provide effective order and laws, unlike the Pakeha government, which allowed Maori to kill each other and only involved itself when Pakeha were killed. (Stokes, 1991: 292–293)

Eventually, Potatau agreed to assume the mantle of king and was inaugurated at Ngāruawāhia in 1858. Potatau stated at the ceremony: *"Kotahi te kohao o te ngira ekuhuna ai te miro mā, te miro pango, te miro whero."* (There is but a single eye of the needle through which white, black, and red threads must pass.) This statement symbolized the ideology of unity among the people, including Europeans. Potatau Te Wherowhero did not see himself as being in conflict with Queen Victoria's sovereignty and, prior to his ascension to king, he was consulted by the Governors of the time for the Māori position on various matters.

> However, after his acceptance of the kingship he was increasingly estranged from the governor's confidence. As land disputes increased in number and severity Te Wherowhero was in many cases forced into a position of opposition to government policy. (Oliver, 1991: 312)

Potatau's reign as king was short lived; after two years in the position he died and was succeeded by his son, Tāwhiao Tukaroto Matutaera Potatau Te Wherowhero. Tāwhiao's reign as king coincided with arguably the most tumultuous period in the relationship between Europeans and Māori, with the wars of Taranaki and Waikato, and resulting confiscations that left Tāwhiao and his people landless. British forces invaded the Waikato in 1863. They supposedly believed that the Waikato were preparing themselves for an assault on Auckland. "Tawhiao and his people lost over a million acres to the settler government and subsequently to the settlers themselves" (Mahuta, 1994: 146).

Left to live like refugees, Tāwhiao and his people retreated into Ngāti Maniapoto lands, now known as the King Country, and contemplated the future of his people. It was at this time that Tāwhiao was said to have developed his prophetic visionary sayings (*tongi*), which reminded his people that they needed to adhere to the ideologies of the King Movement (Mahuta, 1994: 146). Tāwhiao also adopted the Pai Mārire religion and this is still followed by the people of the movement today. During this period the king (till then known by his forename, Matutaera) received the name Tāwhiao from Te Ua Haumēne, the founder of the Pai Mārire religion (Head, 1991: 285).

Tāwhiao tried to push the government to agree to some reconciliation for the Waikato confiscations, but little was agreed on. Frustrated by the lack of progress, Tāwhiao decided to petition Queen Victoria, in a bid for the Treaty of Waitangi to be honoured (Mahuta, 1994: 148).

> The petition proposed a separate Maori parliament, the appointment of a special commissioner as intermediary between Pakeha and Maori parliaments, and an independent commission of inquiry into land confiscations. (Mahuta, 1994: 148)

However, the Queen's representative, Lord Derby, informed Tāwhiao that he would have to consult with the New Zealand government. The latter claimed that there had not been any injustices caused to Māori and that the Treaty of Waitangi had not been breached. As a result, Tāwhiao's proposals were dismissed. Tāwhiao, however, continued to work toward a distinctive parliament and within Waikato he instigated gatherings known as the *poukai*, which allowed for people under the Kīngitanga to have direct consultation with the king, while ensuring that everyone was well catered for with food and other goods. Later, Tāwhiao established his own parliament (*Te Kauhanganui*), in which all tribes were invited to participate (Mahuta, 1994: 148).

During Tāwhiao's reign he was assisted by Manga Rewi Maniapoto (a chief of Ngāti Maniapoto), who orchestrated many assaults on behalf of the King Movement. He expelled John Gorst from Otawhao and removed the magistrate from Waikato, because he believed that they were undermining the power and authority of the king (Henare, 1991: 40). Prior to this, however, Maniapoto assisted Wiremu Kīngi Te Rangitake during the Taranaki wars. Based on this experience, he believed that the government was trying to incapacitate Māori authority, especially in regard to land issues. "Rewi's realistic outlook led him to conclude that the British intended to invade Waikato unless the King movement was abandoned" (Henare, 1991: 40). Under orders from Governor Grey, Lieutenant General Duncan Cameron invaded Waikato on July 8, 1863.

The major battles of the Waikato region between 1863 and 1864 (between Māori and Pākehā) took place at Ngāruawāhia (as discussed earlier), Rangiriri in November 1863, and Pāterangi-Orākau in January–April 1864. Military action was extended to Pukehinahina in April 1864 to ensure that no members of the Kīngitanga could take refuge in the Western Bay of Plenty area. The Waikato wars were considered the most successful Pākehā military operations of the time. "It [the campaign] had clear goals, military victory accompanied by the withdrawal of the inhabitants from the occupied area" (McKinnon, 1997: 38).

Māori resisted the Pākehā attacks on the Waikato. Such participation in the conflict and the association with the King Movement were seen as means of resistance and rebellion against the Crown. To Māori, such participation was merely a defense of their rights to land. George Grey argued that the amount of land confiscated had to be equivalent to the "degree of guilt" under the *New Zealand Settlement Act 1863* (McKinnon, 1997: 39). However, those tribes of the King Movement who participated in the defense of the land during the European invasion received differing levels of punishment when the lands were confiscated. "Ngāti Hauā lost about one-third of their lands; Waikato almost all, Ngāti Maniapoto whose land had not been occupied by British forces, virtually none" (McKinnon, 1997: 39). These tribes and others suffered the injustice of having their land taken from them for allegedly rebellious acts. However, it appears that Māori who owned valuable lands were targeted most severely in both the Taranaki and Waikato cases. Land confiscations were inconsistent when they were executed, as those who had the best land, had the most taken away regardless of the level of their participation in the "rebellious" acts. The invasion and subsequent confiscation of land were hypocritical under the *New Zealand Settlement Act 1863*. This Act purported to ensure that peace was maintained in the country; however, the European soldiers who entered into the Waikato had very suspicious motives for their raids. The primary motive of the Waikato invasion was to disband the King Movement, as it had become a threat to Europeans. The Waikato had 1 202 172 acres of land confiscated from them.

The Influence of Māori Religious Leaders

While European culture was instrumental in the disempowerment of tribes, some Māori used the new culture as a mechanism to overcome and reclaim their power and authority. The establishment of the King Movement was an example of Māori implementing ways to reclaim their power and authority by uniting at a national level. Māori society had never been based on a monarchy system, as signified by using the word Kīngitanga, a transliteration based on the word "king." During the same period of discontent (1848–1858), other Māori came to prominence in the form of Māori religious leaders, including Te Whiti o Rongomai (Te Whiti), Tohu Kākahi (Tohu) (both from Parihaka), Titokowaru (from Southern Taranaki), Te Ua Haumēne (Te Ua) (also from Taranaki) and Te Kooti Rikirangi Te Turuki (Te Kooti) (from Rongowhakaata). Apart from Titokowaru, the aforementioned were the founders of Māori religious groups that provided the basis for a renewed stand by Māori against the actions of the

Crown. Their combined resistance to the pressure of the Crown for land sales saw important relationships being forged among these men.

Te Whiti o Rongomai and Tohu Kākahi, both learned in the Bible, used their knowledge of the scriptures as the basis of the *He Tikanga Hou* (a new doctrine) religion (Keenan, 1994: 190). These two men were noted for their prophetic sayings, but they were best known for their passive resistance to the confiscation of land. Their resistance to armed constabulary forces in Taranaki frustrated the government of the time and prompted it to imprison Te Whiti and Tohu in the South Island. Once they were released, they continued their passive resistance against land sales and the eventual confiscation of lands in Taranaki (Keenan, 1994: 193).

The numerous accounts of Titokowaru suggest that he moved between acts of peace and war. A well-known warrior, Titokowaru appeared to the Crown be a notorious Māori "rebel." His ability in warfare earned him a reputation as a feared warrior and rebel. Titokowaru also assumed the mantle of Te Ua Haumēne on the latter's death and established Te Ngutu o te manu as his base. Subsequently, he sought reconciliation between Māori and the Crown (Belich, 1991: 322).

Te Ua Haumēne's views were similar to those of the other three men. In 1862, Te Ua established the Pai Mārire religion, also known as Hauhau, which is considered "the first organised expression of an independent Maori Christianity" (Head, 1991: 283).

> Te Ua associated with leaders of the anti-land-selling movement in Taranaki, driven into political action by the purchase of the Waitara block under terms which contravened Maori customary law. He became a supporter of the King movement, and in 1860 fought against the government, acting also as chaplain to the Maori soldiers. (Head, 1991: 283)

Te Ua was also considered a prophet of the time, and he used his prophetic visions, the Old Testament, and traditional Māori theologies as the basis for his religion. For many years the Pai Mārire were thought to be murderous and belligerent. This reputation prompted Europeans to believe that all Māori resistance movements were inhumane and barbaric (Belich, 1986: 204).

Te Kooti Rikirangi Te Turuki adapted aspects of the Pai Mārire faith to establish his Ringatū religion. The upraised hand is the sign used by this faith and "it was emphasized by Te Kooti himself that the holding up of the hand was not for the purpose of warding off bullets, but as an act of homage to God" (Greenwood, 1942: 21).

In addition to being a noted prophet, Te Kooti had become notorious for his ability in warfare. His actions frustrated the government, whose representatives pursued him throughout the countryside in the hope that they would be able to punish him. However, Te Kooti enjoyed the support of both Tūhoe (a tribe located in Te Urewera) and the King Movement, which allowed him to evade arrest. *Te Whai a Te Motu* (the pursuit around the island), signifying Te Kooti's ability to evade Pākehā, was commemorated by Tūhoe when they established the meeting house (*wharenui*) at Ruatahuna. This house is named after this event and as an expression of resistance against the Crown. The Crown desperately tried to capture Te Kooti to prevent his stirring up Māori to resist European efforts. Te Kooti stated, "Although you go in pursuit of me, even with the Governor, I will not be captured by you, nor will I be killed by you, and it will be simply through accident that I shall die" (Binney, 1991: 198). Despite the "pursuit around the country," Te Kooti continued his teachings and became famous for his prophetic sayings, which became an important element of the Ringatū faith. One such saying was:

> Ko te waka hei hoehoenga mo koutou i muri i ahau ko te Ture, ma te ture ano te Ture e aki
> The canoe for you to paddle after me is the Law, only the Law will correct the Law.
> (Binney, 1995: 490)

This proverb expresses Te Kooti's vision that the way to regain autonomy was to use European culture, expressed here as "the Law," against itself. If Māori were going to become disempowered through these laws, then Te Kooti believed that the only way Māori would reclaim their autonomy would be to use European law against itself. It is this insight by Te Kooti and other prophets of the time that also influenced a change in culture, from an initially tribally based culture to a more pan-tribal orientation. The adoption of European culture resulted from the pressure that had been placed on Māori to sell their land and the subsequent land confiscations. This adaptation by Māori culture did not mean that Māori lost sight of their ultimate aim of maintaining their rights to be self-determining and autonomous under the Treaty of Waitangi.

The different layers of Māori religious and political movements resulting from land loss show a common bond among Māori people as a result of the turmoil introduced by British settlers and the government of the time. Toward the end of the 1800s it became obvious to Māori that their resistance initiatives were not producing the outcomes they desired and that the government was still trying to drive them from their land base. All of the Māori resistance groups not only shared the common suffering of the loss of their land, but all remained committed to maintaining their distinctive Māori identity. This discouraging period for Māori, near the end of the nineteenth century, was darkened further by renewed epidemics of diseases and the government's continued attempts to assimilate the Māori.

Protecting Mana or Acts of Rebellion?

The injustices suffered by Māori, and in this case those of Taranaki and Waikato, were so immense that the Europeans left these tribes stripped not only of their land but also their self-worth. Māori protests against surveyors and the military continued as a means of protecting their power and authority. The acts that were inflicted on the Māori of both Waikato and Taranaki were intended to disempower these tribes. Europeans believed that they had the ability to determine Māori cultural practices, especially in respect to land, ultimately breaking down the ideology of collective responsibility toward land. Despite the government's desire to disempower the Māori and gain control of their power base (their land), the Māori resisted the government, although at a huge expense to themselves.

The relationship that the Māori had with Europeans prior to the Treaty of Waitangi was amicable, and Māori maintained their own autonomy as tribal groups on their lands. However, in the decades following the Treaty of Waitangi, the relationship deteriorated as European culture and customs began to influence Māori. The pressure placed on Māori to sell their land often left smaller tribes exposed and vulnerable to their demands. Without the strength of numbers to continue to protect their lands, the resistance by these tribes often proved futile. Governments had failed to honor their obligations under Article II of the Treaty of Waitangi, which guaranteed Māori their land, possessions, and treasures (*taonga*). These failings brought about a change in Māori customs, in which tribes felt compelled to unite in order to ensure that the autonomy of each tribe remained intact. Establishing the King Movement united many tribes, but doing so raised fear and trepidation in the colonial governmental officials, who saw this movement as rebellious. Establishing the King Movement provided the government of the time with the rationale it needed to confiscate the Waikato lands. Kīngi Te Rangitake's stand against the surveyors at Waitara was meant to demonstrate that, by not seeking the approval of the entire Māori community, the government had purchased the land illegally. The Waitangi Tribunal found that in respect of the Taranaki claim, the Crown failed to acknowledge the sovereignty of this tribe to determine its own domestic affairs and, more importantly, those related to its lands.

> It is the right of peoples to determine themselves such domestic matters as their own membership, leadership, and land entitlements. Remarkably, it was presumed that the Government could determine matters of Maori custom and polity better than Maori and that it should have the exclusive right to rule on what Maori custom meant. (Waitangi Tribunal, 1996: 5; O'Malley, 1998: 11)

The presumption that European people in government fully understood Māori customary practices and so could make decisions on behalf of Māori is farcical. If Europeans of the time had fully understood Māori customs, they would have acknowledged Kīngi Te Rangitake's efforts to resist the Waitara purchase.

> The result was not only the distortion of Maori custom by those who did not understand it but the introduction of a profoundly wrong process. The process, which still applies today, is one where decisions particular to Maori are made not by Maori but on their behalf, even in the administration of their land or in the application of their traditions. (Waitangi Tribunal, 1996: 5; O'Malley, 1998: 11)

Conclusion

The Māori proverbial saying (*whakataukī*) cited at the outset of this essay – "*Me mate au, me mate mō taku whenua*" (If I die, let me die for my land) – has resounded throughout the colonial history of Aotearoa/New Zealand and reveals the passion that Māori have for their land. More than simply a belief or a value, it gives voice to ancestral connections to the land that date to a time before the arrival of the Europeans. This essay has examined how Māori perceptions of land changed with the arrival of Europeans and explored how, when threatened with a loss of land, Māori fought to protect their autonomy over the land.

Prior to the signing of the Treaty of Waitangi in 1840, the relationships between Māori and new settlers were amicable; however, no sooner had the ink of the signatures dried than the relationship disintegrated. The new culture began to influence Māori customs, especially those related to land, as a means of disempowering the people. Europeans wanted the land and not all Māori wanted to sell. The tensions between the two cultures increased, with Māori seeking to protect their land and Europeans striving to acquire more land. Furthermore, the government believed that Māori needed to be civilized as a means of introducing order into the country. This belief led officials to look down on Māori cultural practice and to dismiss its importance in maintaining social order among Māori.

The influence of European culture was responsible for the change in traditional Māori social practices. Their traditional sense of collective communal ownership was replaced with a sense of individual ownership. Furthermore, the integration of European values affected the social order within many tribes. This change in social order forced Māori to develop their own strategies to deal with the pressure to sell their land. Māori advanced the notions of nationalism through both political and religious movements. These movements included aspects of European culture and ideology in their created dogma as a mechanism to reclaim power and authority. The government was threatened by these movements and sent in armed forces to prevent a Māori uprising. Māori stood against the government to protect their lands to the death. Article II of the Treaty of Waitangi guaranteed Māori their lands and their treasures, yet European settlers ignored this obligation. Māori were left to defend the autonomy of their people and their land. This essay has focused on historical developments in Taranaki and Waikato, in order to illustrate the lengths to which Māori would go to protect their land. Despite the efforts of the Māori, the New Zealand Settlement Act in 1863 provided the government with the right to confiscate Māori land for any acts of rebellion or resistance to land purchases. Millions of acres were subsequently confiscated from Māori. Ultimately, Māori were left alienated from their land, their connection to their ancestors (including their primordial parents Ranginui and Papatūānuku), their autonomy, and ultimately their identity. However, Māori continued and still continue to struggle to overcome the injustices that their ancestors incurred, because without land there can be no identity as a people.

References

Ballara, Angela (1998) *Iwi: The Dynamics of Māori Tribal Organisation from c. 1769 to c. 1945*, Victoria University Press, Wellington.

Belich, James (1986) *The New Zealand Wars and the Victorian Interpretation of Racial Conflict*, Penguin, Auckland.

Belich, James (1991) Titokowaru, Riwha? – 1888, in *The People of Many Peaks: The Māori Biographies from the Dictionary of New Zealand Biography, Vol. 1 (1769–1869)*, Claudia Orange (ed.), Department of Internal Affairs/Bridget Williams Books, Wellington, pp. 320–326.

Binney, Judith (1991) Te Kooti Arikirangi Te Turuki, in *The People of Many Peaks: The Māori Biographies from the Dictionary of New Zealand Biography, Vol. 1 (1769–1869)*, Claudia Orange (ed.), Department of Internal Affairs/Bridget Williams Books, Wellington, pp. 194–201.

Binney, Judith (1995) *Redemption Songs: The Life of Te Kooti Arikirangi Te Turuki*, Auckland University Press, Auckland.

Greenwood, William (1942) *The Uppraised Hand or The Spiritual Significance of the Rise of the Ringatu Faith*, Polynesian Society, Wellington.

Head, Lyndsay (1991) Te Ua Haumene ? – 1866, in *The People of Many Peaks: The Māori Biographies from the Dictionary of New Zealand Biography, Vol. 1 (1769–1869)*, Claudia Orange (ed.), Department of Internal Affairs/ Bridget Williams Books, Wellington, pp. 283–286.

Henare, Manuka (1991) Maniapoto, Rewi Manga? – 1894, in *The People of Many Peaks: The Māori Biographies from the Dictionary of New Zealand Biography, Vol. 1 (1769–1869)*, Claudia Orange (ed.), Department of Internal Affairs/Bridget Williams Books, Wellington, pp. 39–41.

Higgins, Rawinia (2004) He Tānga Ngutu, He Tūhoetanga. Te Mana Motuhake o te Tā Moko Wahine: The Identity Politics of Moko Kauae, PhD dissertation, University of Otago.

Keenan, Danny (1994) Te Whiti-o-Rongomai III, Erueti? – 1907, in *The Turbulent Years 1870–1900: The Māori Biographies from the Dictionary of New Zealand Biographies, Vol. 2*, Department of Internal Affairs/Bridget Williams Books, Wellington, pp. 189–194.

Mahuta, R.T. (1994) Tawhiao, Tukaroto Matutaera Potatau Te Wherowhero? – 1894, in *The Turbulent Years 1870–1900: The Māori Biographies from the Dictionary of New Zealand Biographies, Vol. 2*, Department of Internal Affairs/Bridget Williams Books, Wellington, pp. 145–149.

McKinnon, Malcolm (ed.) (1997) *New Zealand Historical Atlas*, David Bateman, Auckland.

Mead, H. Moko and Grove, Neil (1994) *Nga Pepeha a Nga Tūpuna – Te Wahanga 3*, Department of Maori Studies, Victoria University of Wellington, Wellington.

Mead, H. Moko and Grove, Neil (1996) *Nga Pepeha a Nga Tūpuna – Te Wahanga 4*, Department of Maori Studies, Victoria University of Wellington, Wellington.

Oliver, Steven (1991) Te Wherowhero, Potatau? – 1860, in *The People of Many Peaks: The Māori Biographies from the Dictionary of New Zealand Biography, Vol. 1 (1769–1869)*, Claudia Orange (ed.), Department of Internal Affairs/Bridget Williams Books, Wellington, pp. 310–326.

O'Malley, Vincent (1998) *Agents of Autonomy: Maori Committees in the Nineteenth Century*, Huia, Wellington.

Parsonson, Anne (1991) Te Rangitake, Wiremu Kingi? – 1882, in *The People of Many Peaks: The Māori Biographies from the Dictionary of New Zealand Biography, Vol. 1 (1769–1869)*, Claudia Orange (ed.), Department of Internal Affairs/Bridget Williams Books, Wellington, pp. 261–266.

Patterson, John (1992) *Exploring Maori Values*, Dunmore Press, Palmerston North.

Sinclair, Douglas (1975) Land: Maori view and European responses, in *Te Ao Hurihuri: Aspects of Maoritanga*, Michael King (ed.), Hicks Smith, Wellington, pp. 115–140.

Sinclair, Keith (1957) *The Origins of the Maori Wars*, New Zealand University Press, Wellington.

Stokes, Evelyn (1991) Te Waharoa, Wiremu Tamihana Tarapipipi? – 1866, in *The People of Many Peaks: The Māori Biographies from the Dictionary of New Zealand Biography, Vol. 1 (1769–1869)*, Claudia Orange (ed.), Department of Internal Affairs/Bridget Williams Books, Wellington, pp. 290–295.

Waitangi Tribunal (1996) *The Taranaki Report: Kaupapa Tuatahi* (WAI 143 – Muru me te raupatu. The Muru and Raupatu of the Taranaki Land and People), G.P. Publications, Wellington.

CHAPTER 29
North America
Ojibwe Culture

Gregory O. Gagnon

Ojibwe culture, developed in the misty past, provided a complete understanding of the world, of social relationships, and of societal norms. Although its values were given to the Ojibwe by supernatural beings and were augmented by dreams, human agency was a prerequisite to maintaining the Ojibwe world. Kinship was the core organizing principle of Ojibwe society in traditional times and remains crucial. Although individuals were autonomous, they derived their worth from being good relatives supportive of the supernatural and human community. "We are all relatives" begins many prayers and formal speeches by Ojibwe. *Bemadiziwin*,[1] balance equaling a good life, was the ultimate goal of all Ojibwe.

This essay focuses on Ojibwe traditional culture as it was formed in time immemorial and explores the means by which social justice was created, conceptually, and practiced. Most traditional values and their expressions persist in the twenty-first century. The descriptions in this chapter are a synthesis of the Ojibwe paradigm, a model of the world that has constantly changed throughout time while remaining faithful to *bemadiziwin*. Ojibwe culture was and is the same and different, simultaneously. It has always been and has always fluctuated.

Social justice was almost entirely a function of kinship. The extended family and/or clan had responsibilities for elaborating and maintaining societal norms. Any who suffered from disease or from misfortunes could expect the whole community of relatives to provide support. Hunger, for instance, was a constant threat in the winter and all were expected to share equally. Orphans were not possible in Ojibwe culture, because the family readily took children into their community, and all clan members were considered kin. Individuals who violated norms were managed by the family-community in order to restore balance within the world.

The Wiley Blackwell Companion to Religion and Social Justice, First Edition. Edited by Michael D. Palmer and Stanley M. Burgess.
© 2012 John Wiley & Sons Ltd. Published 2020 by John Wiley & Sons Ltd.

The Ojibwe Context

The Ojibwe culture is among hundreds indigenous to North America.[2] Currently, the Ojibwe, part of the Algonquian language–culture complex, are scattered throughout their aboriginal homeland on 22 reservations within the United States and in 125 Canadian band reserves. Independent polities unified only by cultural consciousness have characterized the Chippewa since their beginnings. The Anishinabe core homeland stretches from Sault St. Marie, where lakes Superior, Michigan, and Huron join, to both sides of the Red River of the north. Additional Ojibwe communities extend into Saskatchewan and Montana. Most scholars conclude that the Chippewa were about 30 000 in 1600, around 25 000 in 1764, about 32 000 in 1885, and in 1910, the nadir of Indian populations in North America, about 46 000 Chippewa were within the two countries. The twenty-first-century Ojibwe population exceeds 150 000 in the United States and over 94 000 in Canada. More than half of Ojibwe do not live on reservations.

Ojibwe religion is a fluid mixture of collective ceremonies, personal relationships with the supernatural, and a syncretic blend of the two. Many Chippewa describe the difference between their religion and Christianity as the difference between their spiritualism and institutionalized churches. Chippewa religion is shamanistic, but also has religious societies that have particular functions within the culture. The Midewiwin Society, the Big Drum Society, and Sun Dance ceremonies are ingredients in the religious lives of traditional Ojibwe. Sweat lodges, dreams, revelations, community thanksgiving observances, and specific prayers are also included. Chippewa people partake of those ingredients that are needed at particular times in community and individual lives.

Contemporary Ojibwe are subject to the strictures imposed by incorporation within the United States and Canada, but social justice within the communities still resembles traditional control systems, particularly on the isolated Canadian reserves (Ross, 1992). Values derived from traditional foundations, leavened by larger society influences, continue to inform Ojibwe behavior. Although many have acculturated to a large degree, traditional ceremonial expressions remain vital in Ojiwe communities. In the traditional revitalization continuing today, the Midewiwin Society dominates. This healing society incorporates various aspects of most other aboriginal and borrowed ceremonial practices and their supernatural intentions. Some include prophecies that are derived from the misty past and contain apocalyptic warnings about environmental degradation that must be addressed by a return to traditional *bemadiziwn* and must be embraced by the dominant society.

Traditional religious expressions are often combined with those of the Native American Church (also known as the Peyote religion), Catholic, Presbyterian, Methodist, Baptist churches, and even the Bahá'í faith. Chippewa appear to have been always willing to blend effective ceremonies from other cultures within their own belief systems. For instance, the Big Drum ceremonial complex originated among the Dakota in the late nineteenth century and was transmitted to Ojibwe communities by Dakota leaders.[3] Individual Ojibwe see no contradiction in being Catholic and Mide at the same time, for instance.

Ojibwe Belief System

Chippewa understanding of the world is conveyed through its creation narrative. The narrative begins nearly all extended ceremonies in the Midewiwin Society and is often described in truncated versions on various solemn occasions. The powers of supernatural persons-other-than-human, manitous, created the milieu for Ojibwe existence in a world where *bemadiziwin* is the ideal. Nanabozho (the most dominant primordial manitou) created the earth after the great flood and gave the Anishinabeg their world. Nanabozho bestowed morality, values, ceremonies, laws, cultural practices, and everything necessary to be Ojibwe. Socially responsible behavior in everyday life is necessary in order that oneself and one's family, friends, and neighbors may achieve *pibadiziwin* (Vecsey, 1977: 153).[4]

But Nanabozho is also a coward, a braggart, a violator of the most basic prohibitions like incest, and a loner. He is a classic trickster who is also a classic culture hero. The dualism of good and evil, admirable and despicable, benign and evil is a common characteristic of manitous. Thunderbirds protect the Ojibwe against bad manitous, but they also bring destruction. Mishebeshu, the Underwater Manitou, is a threat to Ojibwe, but he protects the game and allows Ojibwe to hunt them. This dualism of character is sometimes an obstacle to western scholars' understanding of Ojibwe culture. There are other difficulties in intercultural understanding.

All versions of the Chippewa origin tradition include basic events: Nanabozho's birth as a manitou[5] and rearing by Nokomis; Nanabozho's revenge quest against his father, the West Wind; the killing of Nanabozho's wolf brother by Mishebozho, who is an underwater monster-manitou; Nanabozho's retaliation against Mishebozho, flooding of the earth; Muskrat's success in diving for soil from which Nanbozho (re)creates the earth; Nanabozho's creation of humans (not in all versions) and Anishinabe culture; and the continued existence of myriad manitous.

But Ojibwe religion does not have a canon. At least 48 transcriptions of the origin narrative exist (Smith, 1995: 159), and they vary widely. Some even incorporate a creation narrative that includes Sky Woman, thus resembling the Iroquoian origin tradition; others start from a dark void, followed by Gitchee Manitou (the Great Spirit) conceiving the earth and providing means to populate it with every living thing. Others do not concern themselves with an origin of the world. Instead, they just leap directly to the genesis of Ojibwe culture as created by Nanabozho (Johnston, 1995; Peacock and Wisuri, 2002).

Variations are attributable to the geographical distribution of Ojibwe communities, different dialects, the poetic license of narrators, and the passage of time. Approximately 200 other narratives elaborate and define the world of the Ojibwe (Vecsey, 1977: 94). Further complications stem from interpretations by the several scholars who have imposed their theoretical models on Ojibwe traditions (Barnouw, 1977; Vecsey, 1977; Johnston, 1995; Smith, 1995; Warren, 2009, etc.).

All nonhuman beings, including some seen as inanimate by western cultures such as rocks and grasses, are persons, often described as "persons-other-than-humans." For Ojibwe, all human persons and persons-other-than-humans are sacred, of equal worth, and entitled to respect. Wanton destruction of any of them earns consequences for all living things. Thus, for example, one does not slaughter for sport because this is disrespectful. The special role of humans is to harmonize the world through ritual and behavior.[6]

Perhaps the only completely evil "persons" in Ojibwe culture are the *wendigos*. *Wendigos* are monster cannibals that emerge during the starving times of deep winter. Not only are they cannibals, they can turn human beings into *wendigos*. They can be killed by humans, who are taught the method through dreams. Many Ojibwe stories describe the terror of communities suffering from *wendigo* depradations and the dangers of traveling alone in the winter. *Wendigos* can be controlled by manitous or by humans shown the way by manitous.[7]

Other obstacles to understanding Ojibwe culture are the scarcity of analytic narratives, changes over time, syncretism, the ethnocentrism of most observers, and the problem of using analogies and similes. It is tempting to describe the Midewiwin Society as a religion, to characterize Gitchee Manitou as like the Christian God, and to see similarities between personal manitous (*pawhagun*), given in dreams, and Catholic guardian angels. The danger lies in converting similes into synonymous terms. Despite these impediments, a composite Chippewa culture based on commonalities is discernable.

Manitous, animals, plants, and even what western culture defines as inanimate objects like rocks, soil, and water have power, and power can be projected by them. The Ojibwe extension of "person" to all things translates into an Ojibwe recognition that there are social relationships among persons as well as among most persons-other-than-humans. Fundamentally, Ojibwe people are expected to respect all things. Failure to do so has repercussions. By the same measure, respect for persons and persons-other-than-humans is meritorious.

In Ojibwe culture, manitous must be respected and propitiated. There is a hierarchy of manitous that includes personal guardians-helpers; animal manitous, sometimes called owners, who govern the behaviors of animal persons; manitous who control particularly important sites; freelance manitous' and a few extremely powerful manitous. These dominant manitous include Gitchee Manitou,[8] also known as the Controller of Life, The Four Winds, The Thunderbirds, and Mishebozho (the primary underwater manitou). Ojibwe think "of their world as a kind of a drama in which actors of unequal power relate to each other through patterns of blessing and reciprocal obligation" (Overholt and Callicott, 1982: 161). Ultimately, the manitous are responsible for Ojibwe life and whatever befalls the Anishinabeg (human beings).

Anishinabeg have the responsibility to assure that *bemadiziwin* is maintained by observance of the protocols and ceremonies given by Nanabozho. These observances are modifiable through dreams that provide prophetic instructions for new or modified ritualization. Ojibwe societies include individuals, both men and women, who have special inspired relationships with manitous. *Djessakids*, seers or prophets, learn through the Shaking Tent ceremony and are empowered through dreams. *Wabenos* are "Men of the Dawn," who also are dependent on dreams for their power to affect the world and its people. *Mide* priests heal in the Midewiwin ceremonies. Contemporary Ojibwe describe the Midewiwin as "their" religion. Anthropologists call these spiritually empowered males and females shamans. Shamans provide special access to the supernatural.

These gifted Ojibwe have the power to do good or evil just as the manitous do, because they can draw on manitou powers. Ojibwe society is intensely aware that power exercised can have both positive and negative effects. Shamans were feared because of their potential to harm. Medicine people protect against witchcraft by other shamans and offer beneficial spells. However, the main purpose of these supernaturally endowed people is to heal – to provide a means to redress deviations from *bemadiziwin*.

Individuals or even an entire family could draw on the ritual knowledge of shamans to provide protection against witchcraft, to generate power to acquire desired results, and to mark the stages of life. Dreaming is a key ceremony because dreams are real expressions of the future, courses of action, and means of conveying sacred knowledge from manitous to persons. During the pre-reservation days, extended families spent much of the year away from other Ojibwe because they dispersed for trapping and to survive the winters. Family life reinforced traditional values and provided the variety of interpretations of culture that characterize Ojibwe. Family-kinship is the core of Ojibwe society. (Wilson, 2009: xxix).

Ojibwe were given numerous ceremonies that ritualize the maintenance of *bemadiziwin*. Most ceremonies begin with the sweat lodge, where guided prayer provides purification of the individual and offers the chance to appeal to manitous. Other ceremonies include naming, fasting to obtain a personal manitou (*pawahgun*), puberty ceremonies for women, Midewiwin ritual, dances of power, Big Drum ceremonies, and Feasts for the Dead. Community-wide ceremonies of thanksgiving marked each major cycle in the Ojibwe year: spring fishing, wild rice harvests, maple sugar tapping, and harvests of the corn, beans, and squash.

Storytelling, *minawajimo*, is one of the most important ceremonies of Ojibwe culture.[9] Stories offer the opportunity to provide continuous reinforcement of values and convey the sacred beliefs of Ojibwe culture. Grandparents were nominal heads of families and were revered for their knowledge. As repositories of cultural knowledge, grandparents or elders narrated sacred stories, entertaining anecdotes, and the history of the group. Storytelling was interactive but guided by the elders. Louise Erdrich describes stories as "renewal for the soul." Kimberly Blaeser indicates that Ojibwe stories have "a sacred center from which ripples of power and connection emanate" (quoted in Wilson, 2009: xlix l). There were storytellers for each community and, of course, adults often used stories to instruct children about specific behaviors as the need arose. Ojibwe life was replete with enculturating stories.

Composite traditional values can be derived from the origin narratives, over 200 ancillary stories, and conclusions drawn from ethnographies. Ojibwe composite values are respect, generosity, courage, wisdom, kinship, consensus and the overarching *bemadiziwin*. If the values are attained, then the good life is assured and the world will behave as it should. Persons and persons-other-than-humans will live in a world of harmony. Stories reinforced and explicated these values. Stories, like Ojibwe culture as a whole, stressed the individual's responsibility to the whole, but also indicated the importance of individual choice. Many stories of Nanabozho, the Trickster, demonstrated that he sometimes produced good despite violating norms. Individuals needed to draw their own conclusions about proper action. Children and adults were expected to apply the general principles of stories to their own lives.

Ojibwe Cultural Practice

The ideal Ojibwe was generous, reciprocal with other Chippewa, and supportive of *bemadiziwin*. Many commentators noted that Ojibwe leaders were expected to care for others and to be poorer than the rest of the community. Leaders were expected to epitomize generosity. Chippewa culture recognized that life could be capricious. Ojibwe men and women were lauded for helping the poor, the old, and those who were victims of disaster. The group was more important than the individual. At the same time, Ojibwe valued the right of individuals to pursue what was best for them. Rupert Ross's study of contemporary First Nations led him to distill "the rules of traditional times." He calls them "the ethic of non-interference, the ethic that anger not be shown, the ethic respecting praise and gratitude, the conservation-withdrawal tactic, and the notion that time must be right" (Ross, 1992). Each of these behavioral rules focuses on tempering the tension between community responsibility and individual freedom.

Not unexpectedly, Ojibwe did transgress against the laws taught in the oral traditions despite cultural pressures. Violations of the sacred law invoked the wrath of manitous. Sanctions against transgressors nearly always focused on convincing deviants to eschew violations of norms and to return to the community. In the absence of governments with coercive powers, sanctions emanated from the community and manitous. Vecsey points out that violations of norms "were unethical acts against persons, and thus they offended the manitos, the ultimate upholders of morality" (Vecsay, 1977: 174). Manitous utilized disease to punish transgression. Diseases could punish individuals or whole societies. Curing disease required restoring morality through proper ceremony conducted by one of the priests (shamans). Avoiding disease "required leading proper, ethical lives" (Vecsey, 1977: 174). Origin traditions also described what should not be done. Punishment was dispensed in this life. There was no reckoning after death.

Kinship groups, families and clans, dealt with acts against persons or against the interrelated community. Ojibwe government did not have coercive power; rather, it existed through tradition, was defined by the narratives, and reflected the consensus of Ojibwe communities. Extended families made domestic decisions (marriage, inheritance, crimes against persons, etc.) in conjunction with other families. Generally, the eldest male was the leader of a family, but he "ruled" through consensus. Groups of families created bands centered on particular locations like LaPointe, Sault St. Marie, Mackinac, Sandy Lake, Leech Lake, and Mille Lacs. Bands were led by *ogima* (leaders, often translated into English as chiefs). *Ogima* and other prominent offices like *oshkabewis* (messenger or spokesman) were often hereditary in a family, but those who did not lead well were replaceable by the consensus of the community. Ojibwe bands did not have unpopular leaders because leaders had to be supported by the people; support could be withdrawn easily and quickly.

Decisions for the band were made through consensus, particularly by those who were most knowledgeable. For instance, *ogimag* did not direct ceremonies – those who were qualified by knowledge and community recognition led ceremonial life. For instance, some bands selected what came to be called "Wild Rice Chiefs" who made decisions about the harvest. As interaction with Europeans and Americans required one spokesperson for each band, bands would appoint them, but they had to reflect consensus. Political decisions were the purview of the experienced, recognized elders, with the *ogima* having particular influence, but all could express themselves. War decisions fell to war leaders, who did have quite a bit of power while an expedition was progressing, but these, like Cincinnatis, returned to nonauthoritative roles immediately after hostilities. *Ogimag* gradually acquired more power in the nineteenth century as a response to American expansion. However, consensus remains the ideal for decision making throughout Chippewa country, even when tribal governments are elected.

No Ojibwe tribal-level decision making institution ever existed, even in origin narratives. In any but the cultural sense, the expression "Chippewa tribe" is a misnomer. The tribe consisted of multiple polities bound together by a common cultural paradigm that was widely shared, though quite varied in practice. Historically, families coalesced with others into bands, particularly in the summer months. Several bands gathered into communities at important sites for hunting, fishing, ceremonies, forming war expeditions, and discussing possible unified actions. Boweting (an area near Sault St. Marie) remained an important center for Ojibwe bands from the inception of Ojibwe culture until the late nineteenth century. Lapointe or Madeline Island (within northern Wisconsin) was considered by western migrating Ojibwe to be the epicenter of Ojibwe culture until the 1860s. Leech Lake, Mille Lacs, Winnipeg, and Pembina (within Minnesota, Manitoba, and North Dakota) were other major foci into the 1870s. Bands intermarried, joined expeditions with one another, conducted ceremonies together, and even gathered at fur trading posts. These activities provided a sense of cultural identity but not political centralization.

Ojibwe Social Justice System

Although a formal, institutionalized Ojibwe justice system is an oxymoron, a pattern of ordering social justice is discernible. An Ojibwe's first consideration when confronted with deviant actions was to ascertain what caused them and how to restore *bemadiziwin*. Was it disrespect of a manitou? If so, then the prescription was to work with a shaman to restore balance. Was it witchcraft? If so, then the response was to bring a shaman into the picture because he, sometimes she, could counter the witchcraft.

If someone offended a family member, then the family would decide what to do. Depending on the infraction, the offender's family would be brought into the discussion or even the whole community might be included. In serious cases, like homicide, retribution was the option of the family. Retaliation was sanctioned by the origin narrative. Nanabozho killed the Underwater Manitou who had killed his brother, the wolf. In some versions, Nanabozho also killed his Father, the West Wind, to avenge the death of his mother. If the homicide were unintentional or there were mitigating circumstances, the family would be urged to accept compensation. Compensation, not revenge, restored the community harmony. Why lose two members of a community and further damage the community? Sometimes the exchange of vengeful acts continued through several generations, but communities tried to convince the injured families to accept compensation for the good of the community. Extreme cases of cycles of retribution were uncommon. The pressure of community wellness mitigated against feuds and violent retaliations.

Accusations of witchcraft were common. Shamans' control of power could wreak havoc and many, particularly the *wabeno* priests, were feared. Responses to curses included providing presents to a powerful shaman who could punish the witch and counter spells. Sometimes shamans were killed, as were those accused of using witchcraft.

Ojibwe culture was generally quite tolerant. One of the rules of behavior was not to interfere with others. If an individual or a family decided that they did not fit into the community, they were free to leave. Interband mobility was common. When Christian missionaries appeared, the Ojibwe approach was to listen respectfully and indicate that Christian beliefs were for Christians, not for Ojibwe. However, Ojibwe who chose to become Christian were not ostracized. In short, despite the emphasis on community importance, individuals were free to believe as they wished.

Perhaps the most prevalent means to enforce norms was the institution of ridicule. It was directed at those who neglected their families, abused their wives, bragged, were not generous, did not respect their elders, or committed other antisocial actions. Accounts indicate the effectiveness of ridicule as a control mechanism (Kohl, 1985[1860]: 268). Chippewa communities were small, even when several coalesced in the late spring and early summer, so community pressure was generally effective.

Ojibwe Life Cycle

The basic pattern of Chippewa life began in the early spring. Small extended family groups (usually 10–20 per group) left their winter homes and moved to their maple groves (sugar bushes) to tap the trees. Several intermarried extended families convened at the sugar bushes. After making sugar, the families generally moved to one of the major sites of Ojibwe fishing like Sault St. Marie, Madeline Island, Leech Lake, and Fond du Lac. These larger villages were the focus of band membership. Communities were governed by clan leaders guided by tradition. Marriages, military expeditions, feasts of the dead, midewiwin ceremonies, and trade were common activities in these larger villages, sometimes numbering about 3000 people. These conglomerate communities often were separated into distinct villages located near one another so that the basic pattern of small community size was maintained.

As fall approached, extended families, perhaps enhanced by new spouses and relatives from other communities, moved to wild rice lake camps. Fall fruits were harvested along with the wild rice and the last major hunting expeditions were launched. With the approach of winter around late November, the large families broke into component parts, with each moving to winter quarters. Trapping, survival, and enculturation were the dominant activities during the winter. Although stories were told throughout the year, the continuing creation narratives (*atisokanag*) were told only when the dangerous snakes, toads, and frogs were not around to take umbrage. In the winter encampments, girls and boys learned the teachings of Nanabozho and the wisdom gleaned from dreams. Although the *atisokanag* were told by elders usually, other adults and even children reinforced the veracity of the tales and often called for elaboration through the introduction of other well-known parts of the origin narrative. All were regaled with the good that befalls the group when norms are followed and all were warned of consequences when norms were violated.

This cyclical pattern of life and social routine was modified as conditions changed. European expansion to North America accelerated change. Even before extensive contact, mid-seventeenth-century French market researchers arrived in the Sault St. Marie area, offering new products to Indians long accustomed to commerce. Jesuits followed. Refugees from the Iroquois Wars of the seventeenth century also had an impact on settlement patterns. Disease spread along the trade routes with decimating results. New religious ideas arrived not only with the French Jesuits but with other Indians as well. Trapping for the fur trade required men to stay in winter camps longer. Preparing pemmican and furs in huge quantities required alteration in women's roles. Intra-tribal warfare intensified and the search for new markets stimulated migration of the Chippewa westward from their initial homeland around Sault St. Marie (Michigan and Canada).

Ojibwe Responses to European and American Commercial and Political Expansion

Europeans and Americans introduced challenges to Ojibwe understanding of justice. Changes in societal patterns required changes in the origin narrative. Chippewa epistemology was configured not only by the gifts of Nanabozho and other manitous, but also by dreams. Dreams introduced new explanations and new stories. Diseases were caused by manitous so, at first, the Frenchmen who brought viral diseases were expected to intervene with their manitous. Many Ojibwe accepted Christian baptism as a means of combating disease and this led to the introduction of the concepts of sin, redemption, and intolerance.

The fur trade required new stories to explain the wealth it provided. One story is about the woman who married a beaver who supplied all of her needs. Another story described the beaver as the source of new houses, guns, food, blankets, and beads. Of course, the beaver manitou had to be respected and propitiated. The existence of white people was incorporated as being prophesied and some Ojibwe even modified the creation part of the origin narrative to include the creation of whites, then blacks, then Asians.

American and Canadian imperialism took nearly all Ojibwe land by the 1870s. Their colonial policies challenged Ojibwe epistemology by forcefully changing all of the conditions for existence within Chippewa country. In the early nineteenth century, Chippewa responded to American encroachments by turning to prophets. Many Chippewa listened to the Shawnee Prophet who inspired a nativist response in the Northwest Territory of the United States. Eventually some Chippewa would fight with the Prophet's brother, Tecumseh, against the United States.

As American missionaries spread with American settlers and Chippewas faced the greater and greater constriction of their country, Ojibwe adapted. By 1870 only miniscule portions of the land Nanabozho had created remained for his people. Resources were taken or controlled by colonial governments. Some narratives even include the death of Nanabozho – but prophesized his return when the Ojibwe returned to traditional teachings. Americans applied sanctions to Ojibwe for trespassing and other American crimes.

One particular problem was alcohol abuse. Chippewa use of alcohol began with the French traders and continued with the British and Americans. Since people lost their sensibilities when drunk, Ojibwe tended to try to restrain the destructive behavior of drunks, but did not subject them to the usual sanctions applied to sapient individuals. As Americans imposed their laws, Chippewa came to accept the use of jails and fines for alcohol abuse. The social problem tended to get worse as American control removed Chippewa independence and group cohesion. However, the idea of restoring society by treating the individual was retained.

United States policy altered Chippewa approaches to social justice by forcing them into locations and rules that were not part of traditional life. For example, the United States and Canada imposed a grinding poverty that affected the ability of Ojibwe to provide social justice for their own people. The intended goal of both Canadian and American policies was to assimilate all American Indians, destroying tribalism. Many Chippewa see this approach as cultural genocide. Chippewa were forced to send their children to schools that denigrated Ojibwe culture and treated traditional knowledge patronizingly or as superstition. Christian churches officially considered themselves as the only "true" religion. However, many missionaries displayed sympathy for Ojibwe culture and humanity. Government policies deliberately privileged Christianity. Until the 1960s in the United States and somewhat later in Canada, the national government sought to control every aspect of Ojibwe life.

Ojibwe were incorporated into the legal and social systems of the dominant countries. As a result, they were not allowed to utilize the sanctions of retaliation or compensation for miscreants. Instead, crown/federal courts imposed Anglo legal sanctions. As a result, Indians went to jail, learned to deal with the adversarial system of the dominant societies, and adopted a more legalistic framework for understanding the world. Although Ojibwe clung tenaciously to their core values of family and generosity, they found it difficult, if not illegal, to practice the ceremonies. Both Canada and the United States outlawed traditional religion and punished *djassakids* (shamans) and the priests of the Midewiwin. Despite the pressures, however, traditional religion was not obliterated.

Dominant-society social services replaced community power to define and administer social justice. State welfare, rations, annuities, and domestic laws replaced clan and family responsibilities. Dysfunctions were concomitant with the assault on traditional values, sanctions, and Ojibwe control. Divorce, suicide, disease, and anomie became features of reservation life. Regulation was no longer the purview of Ojibwe elders guided by manitos. Reserves and reservations became the sites for alcohol abuse, family disruption, crime, and violence. Neither the Canadian nor the American government replaced what it had destroyed in the Ojibwe culture. Nearly all Ojibwe communities became examples of what happens when balance no longer exists. *Bemadiziwin* became increasingly difficult to achieve.

Since the 1960s, the intensive control of daily life by the dominant societies has been relaxed. The United States and Canada have both allowed tribal culture, particularly the religious aspects, to be reasserted. Holy people are once again revered and the traditional stories are told publicly. Schools even offer courses in traditional culture. The result is a renaissance of emphasis on traditional values and efforts to realize these values within the framework of reservation life. Some reservations have established peace courts to mimic the traditional means of social justice. Peace courts can be equated with mediation, making it understandable and acceptable to the dominant societies. Tribal courts, at least in the United States, are able to apply traditional knowledge to their decisions.

Social welfare systems are now generally administered by tribal governments, which mitigates the problems of an imposed system. At the same time, Chippewa polities are still required to conform to American/Canadian norms and laws. For instance, all felonies must be tried in federal court in the United States, rendering tribal values moot. Eligibility for social services depends on the guidelines created by the larger society.

Conclusion

Ojibwe culture remains an enduring, vibrant, evolving organism. Since its inception in the misty past when Nanabozho created the world and brought values to the Anishinabeg, core values have been maintained. Social justice in the Ojiwe world was required by the manitous and continuously reinforced with sanctions. Humans were expected to provide for the weak and unfortunate, share generously, respect individuals, whether humans or persons-other than- humans, and utilize social sanctions to address deviants. Even after the challenges of Christianity and incorporation into the Canadian and American states, these values remain. Ojibwe people seek *bemadiziwin* as they always have.

Notes

1 Objibwemowin, the Chippewa language, is difficult to translate. I have parsed *bemadiziwin* to encompass the concept of balance in the universe combined with the idea of an ideal Ojibwe life – to live in a good way is to live in and maintain balance in the natural and supernatural world.

2 The ethnonym Ojibwe is only one of many that denominate this aboriginal woodlands and subarctic culture. Ojibwa, Ojibway, Chippewa, Anishinabeg, Anisnaabeg, Anishinabe, Saulteurs, Mississaugas, and many other variations are essentially synonymous. Similar variation occurs in the spelling of many Ojibwemowin words. For instance, the Culture Hero-Creator-Trickster in the origin narrative is rendered variously as Nanabozho/Nanabooshoo/Nanapush/The Great Hare-Gitchee Wabooz/Wenabozhoo, etc. Chippewa is the term adopted by the Bureau of Ethnology and the United States government, while Ojibwe is predominantly used within Lake Superior Chippewa bands. Anishinabe (original

man, first man, plural = Anishinabeg) is preferred in many contexts. I use the three interchangeably unless quoting from a source that uses a different name.

3   There is no essential reason for being concerned with the sources of Anishinabe ceremonies or beliefs, as these are embedded in the culture and are seen as a whole. For instance, it is enough to note that Christianity borrowed from other religions, but this does not negate descriptions of Christian belief systems. Similarly, Ojibwe culture may well have created a Great Mystery (Gitchee Manitou) – a supreme God – because of Christian influences, but the nature of Gitchee Manitou remains true to aboriginal tradition. In practice, there are many major manitous with none supreme; monotheism is not really aboriginal Ojibwe, but it is contemporary.

4   *Pemadiziwin* is a dialectical variation of *bemadiziwin*. Spelling of Ojibwe words varies considerably.

5   Manitou is usually translated as spirit or supernatural being. No manitou was supreme, but they did interact with Anishinabeg constantly. Manitous demanded respect, punished disrespect, and could provide assistance to individuals and communities. A vital part of Ojibwe religion was propitiating manitous. For instance, if men did not offer tobacco to deer manitou, deer would not be found by hunters. Thunderbirds were manitious, as were the underwater monsters known as Mishebozo. Visions brought to a fasting Ojibwe identified personal manitous that would protect and guide individuals.

6   This concept of care against disrespect, common to all American Indian cultures, is the origin of the anachronism that Indians were the first ecologists. It was part of the human–manitou covenant that if one showed respect, then resources would be abundant. This agreement between animals and humans precluded the need for the concept of humans maintaining the environment.

7   Well-known *wendigo* stories include the girl who broke the *wendigo* into little pieces (mosquitos), the baby who became a *wendigo* by showing disrespect for manitous, and the little girl who grew to be a giant and killed the *wendigo*. Most Ojibwe storytellers have a repertoire of *wendigo* stories.

8   Gitchee Manitou is almost certainly a postcontact concept used by Chippewa to demonstrate that they have monotheism of a sort. This "Great Spirit" becomes analogous to the Creator in contemporary times, but it is a synecdoche for the several creators that make up part of the Ojibwe creation story.

9   Traditional Ojibwe culture forbade the teaching of the sacred narratives of origin (*atisokanag*) at any time other than when snakes, toads, and frogs were hibernating, because these were likely to take umbrage and punish humans. During the winter, these dormant persons could not hear. In this essay, I have followed a practice with which I am comfortable and which many others do also. I tell only stories that are published and therefore available in all seasons. If this offends, please remember that I am trying to behave in a good way, with respect.

References

Barnouw, V. (1977) *Wisconsin Chippewa Myths and Tales and Their Relation to Chippewa Life*, University of Wisconsin Press, Madison.

Johnston, B. (1995) *The Manitous: The Spiritual World of the Ojibway*, HarperCollins, New York.

Kohl, J.G. (1985[1860]) *Kitchi-Gami: Life among the Lake Superior Ojibway*, Minnesota Historical Society Press, St. Paul.

Overholt, T.W. and Callicott, J.B. with Ojibway Texts by William Jones (1982) *Clothed-in-Fur and Other Tales: An Introduction to an Ojibwa World View*, University Press of America, Lanham, MD.

Peacock, T. and Wisuri, M. (2002) *Ojibwe: Waasa Inaabidaa – We Look in All Directions*, Afton Historical Press, Afton, MN.

Ross, R. (1992) *Dancing with a Ghost: Exploring Indian Reality*, Reed Books, Toronto.

Smith, T.S. (1995) *The Island of the Anishnaabeg: Thunderers and Water Monsters in the Traditional Ojibwe Life-World*, University of Idaho Press, Moscow.

Vecsey, C.T. (1977) *Traditional Ojibwa Religion and Its Historical Changes*, University Microfilms International, Ann Arbor, MI.

Warren, W.W. (2009[1885]) *History of the Ojibway People*, 2nd edn, Theresa Schenck (ed.), Minnesota Historical Society, St. Paul.

Wilson, M. (2009) *Rainy River Lives: Stories Told by Maggie Wilson*, Sallie Cole (ed.), University of Nebraska Press, Lincoln.

Bibliography

Benton-Banai, E. (1979) *The Mishomis Book: The Voice of the Ojibway*, Indian Country Press, St. Paul, MN.

Bieder, R.E. (1995) *Native American Communities in Wisconsin 1600–1960*, University of Wisconsin Press, Madison.

Chute, J.E. (1998) *The Legacy of Shingwaukonse: A Century of Native Leadership*, University of Toronto Press, Toronto.

Cleland, C.E. (2001) *The Place of the Pike (Gnoozbekaaning): A History of the Bay Mills Indian Community*, University of Michigan Press, Ann Arbor.

Danziger, E.J. (1979) *The Chippewas of Lake Superior*, University of Oklahoma Press, Norman.

Danziger, E.J. (2009) *Great Lakes Indian Accommodation: Resistance During the Early Reservation Years, 1850–1900*, University of Michigan Press, Ann Arbor.

Hilger, M.I. (1992[1951]) *Chippewa Child Life and Its Cultural Background*, Minnesota Historical Society, St. Paul.

Hoffman, W.J. (1891) The Mide Wiwin or "Grand Medicine Society" of the Ojibwa, *Annual Report of the Bureau of Ethnology 1885–86*, Government Printing Office, Washington, DC.

Peers, L. and Brown, J.S.H. (2000) "There is no end to relationship among the Indians": Ojibwa families and kinship in historical perspective, *The History of the Family: An International Quarterly* 4: 529–555.

Valliere, L., Jr. (2004) *Memories of Lac du Flambeau Elders with a Brief History of Waaswaagoning Ojibweg*, E.M. Tornes (ed.), University of Wisconsin Press, Madison.

Vennum, T. (2009) *The Ojibwa Dance Drum: Its History and Construction*, Minnesota Historical Press, St. Paul.

CHAPTER 30

Southern Asia
The Gonds of India – A Search for Identity and Justice

Sushma Yadav

In the early written history and mythology of the Indian nation, there are descriptions of aboriginals or primitive nonagrarian communities domiciled on Indian land, mostly under forest cover or along the foothills of mountainous ranges and subsisting on hunting and naturally grown food grains and other edible substances like fruits, roots and so on. Prehistoric inscriptions and our mythological texts abound in the descriptions of their conflicts with those emerging as new agrarian societies, invading the aboriginals, seizing their homelands, and weeding out the forest cover to harness land for their cooperative agricultural practices, with a social distribution system of sharing their agricultural products, called *Yagya*, and developing agricultural technologies with phases of time. The striving of those aboriginals to safeguard their homeland, forest cover, and their typical nature-dependent, close-knit way of living, against those strongly influencing and comparatively more developed agrarian people, has been variously inscribed in the ancient texts, beginning from as early as Rigveda itself. It will be seen later in this essay that such conflicts presented a close interaction between the inhabitants of the tribal homelands and the surrounding mainland.

In contemporary India, such communities are referred to as primitive or scheduled tribes and are described in multiple ways: Aboriginals or Adivasi, meaning original owners of the country; Girijans, meaning hill tribes; Vanavasi or Atavikasi, meaning forest tribes or folk; wilder aboriginals; animists; primitive tribes; backward Hindus; submerged humanity; and other names as well (Das, 2000: 1). The term indigenous is not used in the Indian context.

Historically, these communities were characterized by a lifestyle distinct from agrarian communities. They subsisted on different combinations of shifting cultivation, hunting, and gathering of forest products: all activities closely linked with forests. Their nature-oriented cultures celebrated and fostered this close bond with nature, while also emphasizing communal ownership and consumption, closely knit kinship structures,

---

The Wiley Blackwell Companion to Religion and Social Justice, First Edition. Edited by Michael D. Palmer and Stanley M. Burgess.
© 2012 John Wiley & Sons Ltd. Published 2020 by John Wiley & Sons Ltd.

and minimal hierarchies. The evolution of civilization also influenced their religious tenets and practices, worldview, culture, and the egalitarian character of the community, which make the issue of social justice relevant in their context.

Social justice in the context of this essay refers to the concept of a society in which justice is achieved in terms of ensuring just and fair treatment and a just share of the benefits to individuals and groups (Miller, 1976). It can also refer to the distribution of advantages and disadvantages within a society with preferential and differential treatment and policies largely at the level of the state (Rawls, 1971). However, in certain primitive and conventional communities in India, religion also plays an important role in determining the attitude and means of ensuring social justice in terms of safeguarding their typical way of living, tenets, and practices; defending their ownership rights on their holdings; and preserving specific areas of their habitat against encroachments of expanding urbanization, immigrants, builders and traders.

The Constitutional Context

The government of India refers to these communities as Scheduled Tribes. It has been argued that the "original inhabitant" contention is based on a dubious claim and that the adivasi–non-adivasi divide is artificial. Although the word tribe is nowhere defined in the Constitution of India, its Article 366 (25) defines Scheduled Tribes, translated in Hindi as Anusoochit Janajatis, as "such tribes or tribal communities or part of or groups within such tribes or tribal communities as are deemed under Article 342 to be the scheduled Tribes (STs) for the purposes of this Constitution" (Verma, 1990: 10–11; Chaudhary, 2009: 14–27). The Article also prescribes the procedure to be followed for specification of a scheduled tribe. However, it does not contain the criterion for the specification of any community as a scheduled tribe. An often-used criterion is based on attributes such as: geographical isolation; backwardness; distinctive culture, language, and religion; and shyness of contact. Interestingly, the new Tribal Policy Document, issued by the Government of India in 2006, acknowledges the redundancy of the criterion (Chaudhary, 2009: 25).

These tribes are a curious mix, reflecting the paradox of majority–minority, isolation–integration, and tradition–modernity at the same time. Religion, in terms of animistic and totemic beliefs, continues to hold sway, but ideas of equality, justice, development, entitlement, and empowerment are also not completely wished away. Therefore, an attempt is made to understand all these and other related issues like growth, nationhood, and identity by making an in-depth study of the Gonds of Bastar (Chhattisgarh) in central India, infected with development deficit, tribal discontent, crisis of governance, and Naxal violence.

The Gonds of Bastar

The people we call Gonds are spread over a vast region, speak several languages and dialects, and even display cultural differences. They, along with some 40 allied tribes who refer to themselves as Gonds, are among the largest tribal groups (about 5 million according to the 2001 census) in south Asia and possibly the world. More than 20% of the Gonds in Chhattisgarh live in the Bastar region only. The Bastar district has been described as a "melting pot of races" and, consequently, of cultures, predominantly due to its early encounters with the Mughals and British.

Prior to 1947 when it was merged with the Indian union, Bastar was one of the many hundred princely states of India. Despite its large size (39 114 sq. km.), larger than Belgium, Bastar was relatively unknown to people outside it. Glasfurd, a colonial administrator, described it as

> interminable forest, with the exception of a small cultivated tract around Jagdalpore, intersected by high mountain ranges, the inhabitants are composed of rude, uncivilized tribes of Gonds; in some parts almost savages, who shun contacts with strangers, have but few wants which they cannot supply themselves; honest and interesting but a race who prefer the solitude of forests to the bustle of towns, and the freedom of the savage to all the allurements and comforts of civilization. (Glasfurd, 1862: para 175)

Similarly, in 1938, Grigson, a former administrator of Bastar and its first major anthropologist, painted the region as follows: "this remains a land of savages, seeking still for human victims to sacrifice to their fetishes, skilled in herbs and simples, and potent practitioners of magic and witchcraft" (Grigson, 1991: 3). Interestingly, most of the recent immigrants to Bastar (state servants, traders, or shopkeepers) describe them as "poor but carefree," "lazy," "backward," "alcoholic," and "promiscuous."

The Bastar Gonds are distinguished by a number of names: Halbas, Bhatras, Dhurwas (formerly Parjas), Dorlas, Abujhmaria (Hill Maria), Ghotul Muria, Jhoria Muria, Damdami (Bison-horn) Maria, and Raja Muria. Many of them have become traditional agriculturalists. Nonetheless, some practice the shifting cultivation of primitive times even today, besides collecting forest produce, fishing, and hunting. A part of the community has specialized in forging metal goods in cottage industries and other primary-sector activities. They also have a special skill, the knowledge of the medicinal plants, herbs, and animal products that they still use for curing various ailments.

Remarkably, the Gonds are also the only Indian tribe to have set up a kingdom with 52 garhs, formerly known as Gondwana or the country of Gonds (Mishra, 2007), and they ruled the greater part of central India from about the fourteenth century (or earlier) to the eighteenth century. The contemporary social composition of the tribe ranges from royals, members of Parliament, members of the State Legislature, senior bureaucrats, judges, and social activists to the poor villager who lives at subsistence level. Over the years, they have developed a system of social hierarchy like the mainstream Hindus, which does not conform to the usual image of tribal egalitarianism.

Almost all the Gonds, practicing settled cultivation, recognize individual rights of ownership over land. But group or community ownership over land also exists among those who still practice shifting cultivation, like the Hill Marias of Bastar (Sundar, 1999: 55–59). Normally, the right over movable and immovable property passes through a male lineage; that is, from a father to his sons, each getting an equal share. The daughters have no right over any property as such. The Hindu Succession Act is not applicable to the Scheduled Tribes. They are governed by their own customary laws. The traditional *panchayats* among the Gonds still exercise a lot of influence and continue to settle social, economic, and petty crimes.

Gond religion and culture

The majority of Gonds practice Hinduism with a special orientation toward nature and animal-gods. Their religious beliefs vary by lineages and are typically nature based. The sacred status of certain animals and plants, such as monkeys, cows, peacocks, cobras (*nagas*), elephants, *peepul* (sacred fig), *tulsi* (holy basil), and neem, has held totemic importance for them and there are stories attached with each of these (Elwin, 2009: 213–262).

Their religious practices, tenets, beliefs, totems, and rituals have influenced Hindu society from ancient times. The animal gods like Hanuman and Ganesha as well as the use of coconut and banana leaves in rituals are believed to be drawn on in the tribal culture. Linguistic influence and borrowings from their dialects into Sanskrit and modern Indian languages are also significant – *maatanga* (elephant), *anganaa* (woman), *alaabu* (bottle-gourd), *unduru* (rat), *kadali* (banana), *karpaas* (cotton), *taamboola* (betel), *maricha* (pepper), *sarshapa* (mustard), and *laangala* (plow), to name a few, may be mentioned here (Burrow, 1955: 378–379).

The evolution of the Gond settlements is narrated in folk songs and stories, which tell about old days when

> people lived in small groups, sometimes even one or two houses to a village, scattered in the clearings of the forest. And then a group of men, with no fixed abode, would come hunting and see the lone and distant fire burning in the night and ask for fire. Daughters (of the community) would go in marriage (with them) and the newcomers would be shown where they too could harness land. And so the villages grew . . . On the slopes of hills, men and women cut down the trees and cleared the land and sowed seeds that had been consecrated by the *Perma*. Sometimes the harvest was like gold; sometimes they find the crop ruined by wild beasts presumably because the spirits of the forest had not been appeased. Too good or too bad a harvest, sickness and death, a pot falling unexpectedly were all signs of the Earth mother's unwillingness to give them a place, signs that it was time to move on. (Sundar, 1999)

Thus, there is a direct connect between well-being and the pleasure of the deities, of which there are three main categories in Bastar. These must be propitiated: the Earth, the Mother Goddess, and the deity of each lineage or clan. The Earth is generally referred to as *jaga*, or sometimes simply old man *(murtak)* or old woman *(murtal)*. The Earth is also called *bhum* or *mati*. The Earth includes the spirits of the forest and rivers, who must be separately appeased, or else they are said to appear as tigers and cobras and bite humans. All the major agricultural festivals (e.g., the seed-sowing ceremony or the new-mango-eating festival) are celebrated at the shrine of the Earth.

The original object of worship is generally only a stone or a tree, but when taken elsewhere, the Matas (Mother Goddesses) are represented by a flag and umbrella. Matas perform the function of warding off sickness and calamities, and accordingly *jatras* and *mandais*, which are festivals intended for these purposes, are celebrated in the Mata shrines of the hamlet/village and *pargana* (subdivision) respectively.

The relation between humans and their Gods is an intimate one, as this extract from a prayer to mark the end of the threshing season reveals. The speaker addresses himself to all the gods concerned:

> I have cleaned my teeth and bathed, I have prostrated.
> On cattle, goats, fruits, flower and grain
> Kali Mai *Phiranta* roams with *Rahat Kali*
> Causing the eruption of poxes inside and outside
> Peacefully take it away, take the road, take it away
> When you are used to roam so much, don't sit here
> any longer . . .
> Rice and incense are living, a chicken too is alive
> Bananas are alive – you will get all these definitely
> *Sukhrau, Munnarau* (spirits of the forest) – they will be given
> separately, from now on don't cause bad dreams at night . . . (Sundar, 1999: 26–27)

Thus, the Devi (Goddess) is asked to take away the illness she has brought and promised the blood of living beings in return, with assurance that she will have enough for herself. The *pujari* (priest) continues, invoking all the gods of field and forest. He names the mountains (Badal) and the rivers (Malangier and Talpeir), and calls the ancestors (Boda Dhur, Koklu Dhur, Sargi Dhur, and Dangdi Dhur):

> Turn one house into two houses, one seed into two seeds
> One basket into two baskets
> Even after this [offering], if you don't do this
> Man's soul will be angry
> Don't prevaricate, there is rice for you here is the witness [reads the rice omens] (Sundar, 1999: 27)

The sacrificial chicken refuses to eat the rice, which would indicate that the Devi has not accepted the offering or answered whatever request the *pujari* put. He gets angry:

> After all this, you stall my words and prevaricate
> After all this, you don't listen, but caw like a crow
> roar like a tiger.
> Why do you do this? Be happy with this much . . . (Sundar, 1999: 27)

During the old days, the Gonds say that the world was dangerous and difficult, but their ancestors had power and could argue with their gods. The Mata was powerful and capricious, yet she could be reasoned with. Colonial rule brought new gods – revenue officials and forest rangers, the police and soldiers – in front of whom the villagers lost their ability to speak. This reinforced the colonial perception of them as inarticulate "children" (Sundar, 1999; Elwin, 2009).

Gonds believe in sorcery practices and witchcraft. They believe that evil spirits and the gods' displeasure cause most diseases and misfortunes. They ask soothsayers and diviners to find out the cause of problems and to suggest remedies. Sometimes, *ojhas* (witch doctors/sorcerers) and shamans (healers) can provide this advice. They use special rites and rituals to control the actions of a deity or spirit that is causing a particular affliction. Shamans fall into a trance and give voice to the demands of an offended god or spirit.

The Gonds typically choose their marriage mates, and a tribal council approves the matches. The father of a groom pays a bride price, which is opposite to the social evil of dowry in urban or so-called civilized India. Newlyweds live with the groom's family until it is possible for them to move into a house of their own. Sometimes Gond matches are made when a groom and bride elope. These marriages must be approved later by relatives and the village council. A woman's consent is important for marriage. The council also can approve divorces, displaying easier justice and the least litigation.

Ghotul *or dormitory living*

Ghotul or dormitory living is unique but popular and is the most important institution of the social life of the Maria and Muria Gonds of Bastar. It was the central focus of Muria life, coming down to modern times from Lingo, the heroic ancestor of the tribe, who founded it.

> The first ghotul is described as being as beautiful as the horns of bison, beautiful as a horse's throat. Its central pillar was a python, its poles were cobras. The frame of the roof was made of kraits tied together with vipers and covered with the tails of peacocks. The roof of the veranda was made of bulbul feathers. The walls were of fish-bones, the door was fashioned of crimson flowers, the doorframes were the bones of ogres. The floor was plastered with pulse. The seats were crocodiles. The lord of the house wore a turban like a white gourd-flower; his dhoti was coloured silk; his shirt shone in the sun; his clogs were made of sandalwood, his stockings of mongoose fur, his belt was a long thin snake; as he walked he sparkled. In his hand he carried the eighteen instruments of music, heavy with the charms of love. (Elwin, 2009)

For the Murias, the *ghotul* was the center of social and religious life. An independent autonomous children's republic, it had an all-pervading influence on the adults, who could not manage any social function without its help. All the unmarried boys and girls of the tribe had to be members of the *ghotul*. This membership was elaborately organized; after a period of probation, boys and girls were initiated and given special titles, which carried with them graded ranks and social duties. Leaders were appointed to lead and discipline the society; the boys' leader was often called the *Sirdar*. The girls' leader was the *Belosa*. Boy members were known as *cheliks* and girls as *motiaris*.

The *cheliks* and *motiaris* had important duties to perform on all social occasions. The boys acted as acolytes at festivals, the girls as bridesmaids at weddings. They danced together before the clan-gods and at great fairs. They formed a choir at the funerals of important people. Their games and dances enlivened and enriched village life and redeemed it from that crushing monotony that was its normal characteristic in other parts of India.

It was natural that the *ghotul* fostered every kind of art, for here the boys and girls were all the time on their toes to attract one another and to make life what they believed it should be: beautiful, lively and interesting. And so the boys made and decorated charming little combs for their girls, and elaborate tobacco boxes for themselves; the girls made necklaces, pendants, and belts of beads and cowries. The boys caved the pillars and doors of their *ghotul* building, which was often the finest house in a village. They made exciting toys and masks. And above all they danced:

> To witness this dance could be an unforgettable experience and these people, for all their poverty, found in the supreme ecstatic rhythm to their dance a way of life that raised them above mediocrity into a kind of splendor. (Elwin, 2009)

There were two types of *ghotul*. In the first, and probably the oldest, which was sometimes called the "yoking" *ghotul*, the rule was fidelity to a single partner during the whole of the premarital period. Each *chelik* was paired off with a *motiari*; he was formally "married" to her and she took the feminine form of his title as her own. Divorce was allowed, though infidelity was punished.

In the second type of *ghotul*, which was probably a later development of the classic model, any kind of lasting attachment between *chelik* and *motiari* was forbidden. No one could say that such and such a *motiari* was *his* girl; his attachment was rationed to three days at a time.

In both types, the *ghotul* was like a little school where the children were taught lessons of cleanliness, discipline, and hard work that remained with them throughout their lives. They were taught to take a pride in their appearance, to respect themselves and their elders; above all, they were taught the spirit of service. These boys and girls worked very hard indeed for the public good. They were immediately available for the service of state officials or for labor on the roads. They had to be ready to work at a wedding or a funeral. They had to attend to the drudgery of festivals. They would be punished for not attending to *ghotul* duties.

There were no signs of corruption or excess; these bright-eyed, merryfaced boys and girls did not give you the impression of being the victims of debasing lust. Adultery was very rare, and was visited with supernatural punishment when it did occur. One of the reasons could be that the *ghotul* system discouraged the custom of child-marriage, which was rapidly spreading through tribal India. The *ghotul* boys and girls were almost completely free from many modern vices. Prostitution was unknown. No *motiari* would ever give her body for money.

Lately, some elements who claim to be progressive oppose the continuation of the *ghotul* institution as harmful to the development of tribal youth, particularly their health and education. However, the Traditional Leaders (TLs) treat *ghotul* as part of tribal culture and society, which should be preserved and developed with modern facilities. There are others who feel that message of the *ghotul* – that youth must be served, that freedom and happiness are more to be treasured than any material gain, that friendliness and sympathy, hospitality, and unity are to be fostered – is of great importance for all societies (Elwin, 2009).

At the time of any type of necessity, harvesting, house building, or any ceremonial occasion, any tribal/villager may ask for the help of the *ghotul* members; and they gladly meet those in return for certain remuneration, which is, in most cases, a feast. Thus in many different aspects of Muria life, *ghotul* forms an essential organization of social security and social well-being.

The outside world viewed the Gonds as uncivilized. Earlier colonial administrators and later Abu'l Fazl's comments on the Gonds fall into this category:

> These people live in forested regions and spend their time in fending for themselves and procreating. It is a race of very low status and the people of Hindustan look down upon them, considering them outcastes who do not accept their religion or laws. (Abu'l Fazl, 2010[1902–1939]: 323)

However, the self-image of the Gonds, reflected in their folk songs and traditions, is different and portrays an image of people who were poor but free and happy, with the quality of enthusiasm and zest in their lives. Their dances were among some of the finest in India, which brought rhythm and beauty to their otherwise hard lives.

Constitutional provisions and development

The Indian constitution was formed keeping in view this plurality, diversity, and the social problems associated with them. It included special provisions for the rights of these groups. The provisions in the Constitution make it incumbent on the state to "take care" of the STs and to safeguard their interests. In addition, a number of laws have been enacted by the central government (such as the *Protection of Civil Rights Act 1955*, the *Scheduled Castes and Scheduled Tribes [Prevention of Atrocities)] Act 1996*, the *Scheduled Tribes and Other Traditional Forest Dwellers [Recognition of Forest Rights Act, 2006]*, and the *Debt Relief Act, 2007*), as well as by the state governments (particularly those relating to prevention of alienation and restoration of tribal land, restriction on cutting of trees, money lending, and reservations). Furthermore, a National Tribal Policy is on the central anvil (Singh, 2007: 760).

The planned development brought with it the specter of roads, dams, mines, and industries on tribal lands. With these came the concomitant processes of displacement, both literal and metaphorical, as tribal institutions and practices were forced into uneasy existence or gave way to market or formal state institutions. The Gonds, like many other tribes, found themselves at a profound disadvantage due to the influx of better-equipped outsiders into tribal areas. The repercussions on the basis of their already fragile socioeconomic livelihood were devastating, ranging from loss of livelihood, to land alienation on a vast scale, to pauperization and hereditary bondage. They responded occasionally with anger and assertion, but often also in anomie and despair, as the forests were more than a means of livelihood for them.

Contemporary Social Challenges

The Gonds face problems typical of tribal peoples throughout South Asia and much of the world. They suffer exploitation and discrimination, and often are forced by the wrong or partial or selfish execution of inappropriate official policies and market forces to live on less productive lands in remote areas (Roy, 2010). They are experiencing increasing pressure on their land, a rise in the number of displaced and migrant landless laborers, and high levels of poverty (Chauhan, 2010). Lack of education and low levels of literacy further reduce economic opportunity, so much so that the recent Multidimensional Poverty Index (MPI) developed by Oxford University noted that the STs in India have the highest MPI (0.482), almost the same as Mozambique, and a headcount of 81% (Suroor, 2010).

Land

Most of the Gonds were concentrated in heavily forested areas that combine inaccessibility with limited political or economic significance. In the early twentieth century, however, large areas fell into the hands of nontribals, on account of improved transportation, communications, and commercialization. The Gonds, however, viewed land as a common or community resource, free to whomever needed it. By the time they accepted the necessity of obtaining formal land titles, they had lost the opportunity to lay claim to lands that might rightfully have been theirs. The ruling elite belatedly realized the necessity of protecting tribes from the predations of outsiders and prohibited the sale of tribal lands (Sharma, 1980).

The Gonds lost title to their lands in many ways: lease, forfeiture from debts, or bribery of land registry officials. Regions that had been the exclusive domain of tribes came to have an increasingly mixed population of tribals and nontribals. Postliberalization, tribal alienation and displacement have escalated fast. According to a member of the National Advisory Council, nearly 8.539 million tribals have been displaced since 1990 (Chauhan, 2010).

They were cheated of their valuable timber wealth and minor forest produce by the forest contractors and the liquor vendors robbed them of their meager earnings. Moneylenders kept them in debt bondage. The all-round exploitation of the Gonds resulted in a number of tribal revolts. The most notable of them were the Bastar Rebellions of 1859 and 1911 and the Gond Rebellion of 1940 (Singh, 1982).

In fact, the forest regulations ran counter to the fundamental needs and sentiments of the tribesmen. As admitted by a Forest Officer, "Our laws are of such a kind that every villager breaks one forest law every day of his life," which also meant that the villager in relation to Government perpetually suffered from a bad conscience, became both timid and obsequious, and it was almost impossible to develop in his mind a sense of citizenship, for he no longer felt at home in his own country (Elwin, 2009).

The Gonds resorted to litigation, which placed a great burden on them, besides the physical distress and exhaustion of long journeys to the distant courts, the demoralizing contact with lawyers, lawyers' touts and petition writers, and the bewilderment of dealing with laws that they did not understand and that often ran counter to their own traditions. Often in a fairly simple registration case, the applicant and four witnesses had to travel an aggregate of 3700 miles before their business was finished.

Similarly, there are stories of how the tribals were duped by the outsiders. Elwin quotes one thus:

> A merchant bought a couple of hundred rupees' worth of grain from a fairly well-to-do Gond and paid for it with two hundred-rupee notes. The "notes" were coloured factory labels removed from bales of cloth. The Gond, who could not read, accepted them with pleasure, thinking he had a bargain, and only discovered the fraud when he took the notes to a police station – not to complain but to get change. (Elwin, 2009)

Fairs: A mix of religion, culture, and politics

How religion, culture, and ambitions of sociopolitical justice get reflected, one can see in the fairs, of which the Gonds are fond. One such annual religious and cultural gathering is the Dussehra or Muria/Maria Durbar, which was started with the intention of training the king in administration and addressing the complaints of his subjects. It is an occasion when the tribes are told of the noble intentions of the state, exhorted to conserve forests and engage in improved agricultural practices, and if they behave well and cooperate, are promised the fruits of development, at times symbolized by the graduation from loincloths to "full pants." It is an occasion for the profession and rewarding of loyalty.

Dussehra, which has been celebrated for the last 586 years, worships the goddess Danteshwari, who is the Bastar symbol of power. Tribals of Bastar pray to the goddess and submit their gratefulness for bestowing on them plenty of crops and for receiving her blessings for a prosperous life full of food, liquor, money, and peace in life.

During the Dussehra festival, a galaxy of central and state ministers and senior government officials are usually present on the dais, but tribal people and their traditional leaders, such as *pargana* Manjhis and Patels, exclusively touch the feet of the member of the royal family, demonstrating the emotional attachment and respect toward them.

Behind the intimate relationship between ruler and ruled is a unique system of governance developed by the kings of Bastar. It is unique in the sense that tribal self-governance institutions like *pargana* Panchayats, under the leadership of Manjhis, and tribal village Panchayats, under the leadership of Patels, were given full autonomy of functioning and royal patronage in their respective areas by the king of Bastar.

Thus, where modern institutions of justice are still beyond the reach of tribals due to their complex and formal mode of functioning, the Traditional Panchayats (TPs) are easily accessible to the people and are best suited to the tribal ethos of justice. They report crimes to the police and at community level, and help the victims of tragic incidents on humanitarian grounds. They collect money and food grain and give it to the family of the victims. Crime against women is viewed very seriously by the tribals and heavy fines are imposed on the culprits.

The Darbar or tribal court provides a unique linkage between tradition and modernity for the Gonds. The tribals and the traditional chiefs of hilly and remote areas were invited to present their problems before the rulers to receive remedial measures to mitigate the hardship of tribal life. In contemporary Bastar, in the presence of top leaders and officials of civil and police administration, tribal chiefs put forth the problems of their areas. They demand from the government various facilities for development related to agricultural development, irrigation, electricity, road, transportation, educational and medical facilities, loans and so on. They also demand better facilities for celebrating the Dussehra festival. Thus, the Dussehra is a great source of operational linkages between traditional and new leaders, who cooperate and coordinate to make this annual event successful as a matter of community pride, tribal identity, and the continuity of their cultural heritage.

The traditional leaders mainly listen to people's sufferings and grievances; settle marriage disputes among the village community; control illicit relationships in the community; settle community disputes by consensus; punish thieves and minimize robbery; help the poor by cash and kind, particularly at the time of marriage and distressful economic conditions; help disabled people in getting assistance from the community as well as from the government; look after the peace and security of the village community; help in cases of serious illness; accompany the tribesmen to government offices for solving their problems; help the family of the victim in a case of unnatural death in a village; organize cultural programs of dance, music, and singing at auspicious occasions of festivals and the arrival of new crops; and manage the *ghotul* and the annual cultural fairs of their communities.

From the perspective of activists, Bastar needs to be protected against exploitation and degradation, as the innocent tribals living in harmonious village communities in symbiosis with each other and with nature are now in the process of being smashed and fragmented by the monolith of the repressive state. However, participation in larger political and economic processes has been a feature for much longer and the people of Bastar have resisted and maneuvered their way through this history, rather than being passive victims or heroic rebels. They love the forest with a passionate devotion. It is to them "the forest of joy," "the forest of sweet desire." It is the scene of the early romances of their childhood, and the arena in which they engage on their most heroic struggles with nature.

The reservation of vast tracts of forests, inevitable as it was, was therefore a very serious blow to tribespeople. They were forbidden to practice their traditional methods of cultivation. They were ordered to remain in one village and not to wander from place to place. If they had cattle they were kept in a state of continual anxiety in case they strayed over the boundary and rendered them liable to what were for them heavy fines. If they were forest villagers, they became liable at any moment to be called to work for the Forest Department. If they lived elsewhere, they were forced to obtain a license for almost every kind of forest produce. At every turn, the Forest Laws cut across their life, limiting, frustrating, and destroying their self-confidence.

The Gonds of Bastar even today survive on forest produce and other living creatures, except poisonous snakes. Nontribals, particularly the higher-caste population in tribal areas, on the other hand, are quite well off. They seem to have taken the lion's share of development opportunities while the masses of Gonds are still living in semi-naked conditions, without even two square meals a day. They can hardly afford the basic necessities of life and mere survival is their greatest challenge. They have become subservient or subalterns in their own places due to the exploitation of powerful vested interests. Their only relief is the still functional traditional Panchayats and elders, who work hard to coordinate with the New Panchayati Raj Leaders so that community consensus and the wider participation of the community in governance can be ensured.

Religion for the Gonds is life saving and a continuous discourse with nature, but it also now appears to be a change agent, linking them with newer ways of life and civilization. Their primitive ways of ensuring equity and social justice are losing ground and giving way to the adoption of a lifestyle that is suffocating, modernizing, and dehumanizing at the same time. They must create a past, present, and future, a history and an identity for themselves with respect and dignity – an entire discourse – all at once.

Acknowledgment

I thankfully acknowledge my discussions with Professor O.P. Dwivedi, Fellow, Royal Society of Canada, Shri B.S. Baswan, IAS (Retd.), Director, IIPA, and Sh.K.K. Sethi, IAS (Retd.). The research support from Dr. Nidhi Yadav, research officer, Dr. Ambedkar, Chair, and the typing assistance from Mr. Sunny Arora is also acknowledged. I wish to gratefully acknowledge the financial support from the Dr. Ambedkar Foundation, facilitating field visits for this essay. Above all, I owe the completion of this essay to one of the editors of this volume, Professor Michael Palmer. Without his patience and trust, the essay would not be part of this book.

References

Abu'l Fazl (2010) *Akbarnama*. Vol. 2. Translated by H. Beveridge. Low Price Publications, Delhi. Originally published 1902–1939.

Burrow, T. (1955) *The Sanskrit Language*, London: Faber.

Chaudhary, S. N., ed. (2009) *Tribal Development since Independence*, Concept Publishing Company, New Delhi.

Chauhan, Chetan (2010) NAC member trashes Centre's tribal policy, *Hindustan Times*, August 19: 18.

Das, S. T. (2000) *Lifestyle: Indian Tribes*, New Delhi, Gyan Publishing House.

Elwin, Varrier (2009) *The Oxford India Elwin: Selected Writings*, Oxford University Press, New Delhi.

Glasfurd, Capt., C. L. R. (1862) Report on the Dependency of Bastar, Jagdalpur Record Room, District Collectorate, Bastar.

Miller, David (1976) *Social Justice*. Clarendon Press, Oxford.

Mishra, Suresh (2007) *Tribal Ascendancy in Central India: The Gond Kingdom of Garha*, New Delhi: Manak Publications.

Rawls, John (1971) *A Theory of Justice*, Harvard University Press, Cambridge, MA.

Roy, Arundhati (2010) A Convergence of Interests. *Hindustan Times*. http://www.hindustantimes.com/A-convergence-of-interests/Article1-587339.aspx. Accessed April 20, 2011.

Sharma, B. D. (1980) *Brief Review on Tribal Development*, Ministry of Home Affairs, Government of India, Series No.28.

Singh, Indrajit (1982) *The Gondwana and the Gonds*, Universal Publishers, Lucknow.

Singh, Bhupiner (2007) Tribal Scenario in the Context of Economic Liberalization and

Globalization. *Indian Journal of Public Administrationi* LIII (4): 759–766.

Sundar, Nandini (1999) *Subalterns and Sovereigns: An Anthropological History of Bastar (1854–1996)*, Oxford University Press, Delhi.

Suroor, H. (2010) Media Hype and the Reality of New India. *The Hindu*, July 20.

Verma, R. C. (1990) *Indian Tribes through the Ages*. New Delhi: Publications Division, Ministry of Information and Broadcasting.

Bibliography

Banerjee, B.G. and Bhatia, Kiran (1988) *Tribal Demography of Gonds*, Gian Publishing House, Delhi.

Baruah, Sanjib K. (2010) Angst writ large in tribal land, *Hindustan Times*, August 16: 11.

Bijoy, C.R. (2003) The Adivasis of India – A history of discrimination, conflict, and resistance, *PUCL Bulletin*, http://www.pucl.org/Topics/Dalit-tribal/2003/adivasi.htm (accessed April 18, 2011).

Fuchs, Stephen (1974) *The Aboriginal Tribes of India*, Macmillan, Delhi.

von Furer-Haimendorf, Christoph (1985) *Tribes of India: The Struggle for Survival*, Oxford University Press, Delhi.

Ghurye, Govind Sadashiv (1980) *The Scheduled Tribes of India*, Transaction Publishers, New Delhi.

Grigson, W.V. (1993[1944]) *The Aboriginal Problem in the Central Provinces and Berar*, Vanya Prakashan, Bhopal.

Krishnan, P.S. (2007) *Empowering Dalits for Empowering India – A Road Map*, First Dr. Ambedkar Memorial Lecture, Manak Publications, New Delhi.

Lund, Brian (2002) *Understanding State Welfare: Social Justice or Social Exclusion?* Sage, London.

Maurya, R.D. (2009) *Tribals and Panchayats of Central India*, B.R. Publishing Corporation, Delhi.

Mehta, B.H. (1984) *Gonds of the Central Indian Highlands: A Study of the Dynamics of Gonds Society*, Concept, New Delhi.

Miller, David (1999) *Principles of Justice*, Harvard University Press, Cambridge, MA.

Pallavi, Aparna (2006) Gonds nourish aspirations at annual fair, http://www.indiatogether.org/2006/feb/soc-gonds.htm (accessed April 18, 2011).

Parida, Jayanta (2006) *Tribals: Development, Displacement, and Rehabilitation*, Classical Publishing Company, New Delhi.

Pfeffer, Georg and Behera, Deepak Kumar (2009) *Contemporary Society: Tribal Studies*, Concept, New Delhi.

Pingle, Urmila and von Furer-Haimendorf, Christoph (1987) *Gonds and Their Neighbours: A Study in Genetic Diversity*, Ethnographic and Folk Culture Society, Lucknow.

Raj, Aditya and Raj, Papia (2004) *Linguistic Deculturation and the Importance of Popular Education among the Gonds in India*, Adult Education and Development, New Delhi.

Rath, Govinda Chandra (2006) *Tribal Development in India: The Contemporary Debate*, Sage, New Delhi.

Sharma, Anima (2005) *Tribe in Transition: A Study of Thakur Gonds*, Mittal Publications, Delhi.

Shelagh, Weir and Lal, Hira (1973) *The Gonds of Central India: The Material Culture of Gonds of Chhindwara District*, British Museum, London.

Varghese, K.G. and Chauhan, Chetan (2010) The law catches up with Vedanta, *Hindustan Times*, http://www.hindustantimes.com/rssfeed/newdelhi/The-law-catches-up-with-Vedanta/Article1-591306.aspx (accessed April 20, 2011).

Yadav, Sushma (2006) *Social Justice: Ambedkar's Vision*, Indian Institute of Public Administration, New Delhi.

PART IV
Social Justice Issues

Introduction

Essays in Part IV deal with issues that have social justice implications and that religions address, but that are not unique to any single religion. The topics were chosen because of their importance in the contemporary conversation about social justice. The purpose of the essays is not to resolve the debates, but to deepen our understanding of the issues and to show how some (not all) religions deal with the issues in question.

Two essays – Andrew Lustig's "Beginning of Life" and Courtney Campbell's "Death and Dying" – help us understand how some religions deal with issues of life and death: control of fertility, abortion, assisted reproductive technologies, human nonreproductive cloning, the meaning of death and dying, and stewardship in the cost of dying.

Four essays deal with themes that arise from specific issues in the continent of Africa. In "Colonialism," Brigid Sackey helps us understand the history and bitter legacy of colonialism and the role played by religion. In "Abundant Life or Abundant Poverty? The Challenge for African Christianity," John Padwick discusses both the opportunity and the profound challenge that poverty and wealth present to a religion like Christianity. Afe Adogame takes on one of the most intractable medical, social, and political issues of our time: Acquired Immune Deficiency Syndrome (AIDS). In "AIDS, Religion, and the Politics of Social Justice in sub-Saharan Africa," Adogame tries to ascertain whether the politics of engagement (and indifference) by African religions in combating AIDS becomes a matter of social justice. "What," he asks, "do the various religions understand as social justice? Do they perceive AIDS as a social justice issue?" (this volume: 483). Finally, Glenda Wildschut, in "Human Rights: The South African Experience," explains the process of the Truth and Reconciliation Commission and the role of religious leaders and institutions in securing reconciliation in the aftermath of a long and truly tragic chapter – that of apartheid – in South Africa's national story.

We have devoted much attention to issues in Africa for two main reasons. First, the most important and controversial features of Africa's story/stories – colonialism,

---

The Wiley Blackwell Companion to Religion and Social Justice, First Edition. Edited by Michael D. Palmer and Stanley M. Burgess.
© 2012 John Wiley & Sons Ltd. Published 2020 by John Wiley & Sons Ltd.

profound economic stratification, HIV/AIDS, racial issues – are important in their own right. We cannot understand Africa and its people unless we understand these issues. But also, these important and controversial features are not unique to Africa. Thus, to study them in their African context is to prepare the way to study them in other parts of the globe.

Some of the essays relate directly to the American context. Paul Harvey's "Religion, Civil Rights, and Social Justice," for example, emerges directly from the American scene, as does Louis Gallien's "The 'Double-Conscious' Nature of American Evangelicalism's Struggle over Civil Rights during the Progressive Era."

There is an important reason why the expression *human rights* appears in the title of Glenda Wildschut's essay on South Africa and the expression *civil rights* appears in the essays by Harvey and Gallien. A right is an individual's entitlement to something. If an entitlement derives from a legal system, then the entitlement is a "legal right" or a "civil right." The American civil rights movement of the 1950s and 1960s was predicated on the principle that the rights (the entitlements) those involved sought were already guaranteed by the Constitution of the United States of America. In South Africa, those who sought to overthrow the apartheid system of government could make no such constitutional appeal. They therefore appealed instead to another kind of entitlement, one deriving from a system of moral standards independently of any particular legal system. This kind of entitlement is called a "moral right" or a "human right." According to those who claim them, human rights are based on moral norms and principles that specify that all human beings are empowered to do or entitled to have certain things. They also claim that human rights are universal. If anyone possesses them, everyone possesses them. Finally, and very importantly for the South African context, human rights are not limited to a particular jurisdiction.

Justice issues centering on gender and sexuality have been in the public eye in western countries since at least the nineteenth century. It is also true that until recent decades they have not received the same level of attention and response from scholars, politicians, and church leaders as have issues of race. In "Gender and Sexuality in the Context of Religion and Social Justice," Mary Hunt explores the changing language and categories of gender and sexuality as religious people attempt to be faithful to their own religious traditions but also adapt to the social landscape they inhabit.

Ruth Burgess confronts one of the big questions of modern social justice facing religious people: How should we respond to people with disabilities? The question is complicated, in part because the language of disability is not morally neutral. The descriptions and categorizations of disabled people often carried with them overt or implied moral evaluations. Also, religions have inconsistent histories in their dealings with the disabled. Their practices often do not line up with their theologies, and their theologies of disability sometimes fail to align with other facets of their moral teachings. Burgess believes that beneficial changes for people with disabilities began to occur when religiously motivated people abandoned superstitious explanations in favor of scientific explanations. In her view, this transition marked the path toward fair and beneficial treatment for people with disabilities.

Laurel Kearns provides the only essay dealing with ecological concerns. "Ecology and the Environment" explores how religion, justice, and environmental concerns come together in a concept that she calls "eco-justice." Her conversation partners are primarily in the Christian tradition, mainly because the discussion over environmental issues is now decades strong in that tradition. But she also shows how other religious traditions embrace environmental concerns.

Many of the essays in Part IV deal with profound issues that at times seem intractable, even overwhelming. The final two essays offer the prospect of a more hopeful way. *Hopeful* does not imply naive idealism. In "Christianity and Non-Violent Resistance," Celia Cook-Huffman examines an approach toward social justice that, far from being Pollyannaish, is best described as the "disruptive, defiant, unruly face of religion" (this volume: 607), which stands as the nonviolent alternative for social change. In "Building Peace in the Pursuit of Social Justice," Mohammed Abu-Nimer offers an aspirational alternative. In cases involving deep-rooted conflict (including clashes among people with different religious identities), Abu-Nimer describes peace building as a transformative process that attempts to replace old perspectives and values that fueled the conflict with new concepts and values of equality, dignity, and human rights. The new concepts and values offset what he describes as "the dehumanization that commonly accompanies violent conflict, as sometimes occurs when religious identities are mobilized" (this volume: 623). It is important to conclude with the sober thought that Abu-Nimer does not present peace building as a panacea to problems of social justice. Rather, it is a process that involves much hard work and makes no promise of success. In the end, it only offers the hope of a more rational and just way to resolve conflict and build a better future for all concerned.

CHAPTER 31
Colonialism

Brigid M. Sackey

Colonialism has been a universal phenomenon, but Africa has experienced its most devastating and enduring effects, as indeed it is believed that the continent is still suffering under its scourge. From the eighteenth century and lasting until the twentieth century, Europeans colonized virtually the whole of Africa and most of these colonies regained their sovereignty after the Second World War. This essay looks at how religion (Christianity) informed the delivery of social justice under colonialism in Africa. It discusses the interconnectedness of colonialism, Christianity, and social justice and their lasting impact on African peoples.

What Is Colonialism?

Colonialism is a system of domination whereby an external, sovereign country willfully and forcefully occupies another, independent country in order to exploit the latter's human and natural resources. In the process, the intruder country imposes its system of governance, laws, cultures, religion, language, education, and economics on the hitherto free indigenous citizens, thereby curtailing their freedom and rights. For example, forced labor was used in European colonies in Africa in order to extract huge volumes of agricultural and mineral resources, and many Africans were also drafted into armies of the colonizing powers, where they served in various capacities (Kellar, 1995: 158).

Colonialism cannot be viewed in isolation, as it was facilitated particularly by European Christian missionary enterprises in Africa in the early 1400s and again in the 1800s. Colonialism has a Christian background because the colonial administrators were Christians; they were Portuguese, French, Belgian, Italian, Spaniard (Catholic), British (Anglican), and German (Presbyterian, Evangelical, Calvinist). Indeed, like

---

The Wiley Blackwell Companion to Religion and Social Justice, First Edition. Edited by Michael D. Palmer and Stanley M. Burgess.
© 2012 John Wiley & Sons Ltd. Published 2020 by John Wiley & Sons Ltd.

Christianity, European colonialism was concerned with social justice embedded in the idea of a "civilizing mission." Accordingly, social justice is a plane on which Christianity and colonialism share common concepts such as conformity with European values, individual rights, and domination, as well as the belief in racial superiority and inferiority. In addition, Christianity is concerned with the dignity and equality of the human being and being mindful of the poor and vulnerable.

Social Justice

The term "social justice" is a common, universal concept that revolves around the ideas of a just society, equal opportunities, and the general well-being and freedom of human beings. In Africa, most of these ideas about social justice are embedded in the religious beliefs and practices of the people. Most of the religious beliefs and practices existing in precolonial and colonial times continue to operate today. Prior to the inception of colonialism, Africans believed (and still believe) in two distinct, interdependent, and constantly interacting worlds, the physical and the spiritual worlds.[1] The spiritual world comprises a belief in one God, a host of deities that inhabit natural phenomena, ancestral spirits, as well as good and evil spirits that together keep the society in equilibrium. Social justice in traditional Africa aims primarily at contributing to social stability and harmonious relationships within ethnic groups (Shorter, 1977).[2]

African traditional society places a collective and equitable value on human life and conduct, as the individual exists only because others exist, as captured in the saying "I am because we are, and since we are, therefore I am,"[3] a philosophy that is also embedded in the South African (Nguni) concept of *ubuntu*. *Ubuntu* refers to a sense and practice of community as well as a readiness for reconciliation and friendship. Thus, actions that promote the peace and stability of the community are viewed as just and encouraged, while actions that destroy the equilibrium in society are not. It is believed that the spiritual world rewards good human conduct with abundant rain, harvests, children, and general prosperity, and punishes adverse conduct with drought, famine, infertility, and misfortune. It is said that in the olden days the deities were the "policemen" of society because they could detect and punish any crime committed by human beings. These traditional African social justice ideals, which are unwritten but transmitted orally from generation to generation, came into conflict with those of Christianity during colonialism.[4]

Some of the offenses in the unwritten code of justice included murder, suicide, sexual offenses, treason, witchcraft, cursing a chief (traditional ruler), and abusing the authority of the chief and elders. These grievous offenses were generally prosecuted by customary law in the chief's court or at the shrine of a deity and incurred severe punishment. Other offenses such as domestic quarrels, insults, disrespect, and neglect of familial obligations were usually dealt with privately by elders within the family. Taboos and other prohibitions on all aspects of life were put in place to check human conduct. Thus, it is evident that the administration of justice was the duty of both spiritual entities (deities) and human entities (chiefs and family elders).

In the colonial era, traditional beliefs were condemned by Christian missionaries and colonial administrators, who also took over the responsibility of delivering justice from their European perspectives. For example, Africans were taught to disregard the authority of their chiefs and to consider themselves as a separate community under the authority of the European missionary, as evidenced by the following: "I now go to church. I am not under the chief. The priest says we must not do them or it is against the law of the church" (Mobley, 1970: 76). This new teaching was not only a rejection of traditional African culture, philosophy, and ideas of social justice, but also represented a gross defiance of the chief who was (is) both the spiritual and political head of the society and by extension the custodian and administrator of justice.

Why Did Colonialism Take Place?

According to Schweizer (2000: 5), some Europeans began to see the slave trade as a social injustice and became morally convinced that the colossal wrongs of the slave trade ought to be rectified. To Christian missionaries, this conviction was understood as God's call to elevate the "uneducated heathen" from their state of ignorance and idolatry to a European level of religiosity. Beginning with the abolitionist act of 1772, slavery was banned first in Great Britain and almost a century later in other parts of the world. In pursuit of their agenda, some Europeans established a number of small but permanent colonies along the coasts of Africa to facilitate trade, to resettle slaves seized from illegal slavers, and to establish plantations. These colonies, in such places as the Lower Senegal River, Sierra Leone, the Gold Coast, Nigeria, and Gabon, eventually became toeholds for the colonization of the whole of the continent (Keim, 1995: 124). The industrial revolution and capitalism, both of which spawned European expansionism, also facilitated colonialism. By encouraging demand for African raw materials such as agricultural and mineral resources to boost burgeoning industries back in Europe, they facilitated a shift away from the slave trade to the exchange of nonhuman goods. Furthermore, the prevailing European evolutionary ideas of the period – that culture generally evolved in a uniform, unilinear progression, with Africans at the lowest level of the ladder and Europeans at the apex – were also used to justify colonialism in the sense that European colonizers saw Africans as their "burden" (the "white man's burden") and considered it their obligation to elevate them to their level. Hence, they needed to colonize them through what they called the "civilizing mission," which manifested itself in colonialism.

For example, one of the policies used in the French and Portuguese colonies was called "assimilation." Assimilation was a policy that purported political and cultural equality, a strategy to make Africans think and behave like Europeans. Ironically, the application of a European idea of equality created more social injustices, as the attempts by both colonizers and religious groups to redress the wrongs of the slave trade gave rise to another form of inequality, namely colonialism.

Colonization in Africa began in earnest in 1885 as an outcome of the Bond of 1884, signed at the Berlin Conference in Germany. This meeting legitimized the "scramble for Africa" by formally sanctioning the partitioning of the continent among European powers, notably the British, French, Portuguese, and Germans (Gellar, 1995: 135). Families, communities, and ethnic groups were separated without due consideration of their kinship relations, religions, cultures, and even languages. Thus, African peoples became Anglophone, Francophone, and Lusophone. This artificial and nontraditional separation has prevailed to date. Attempts by African leaders to change these borders through expansion and secession have failed, as in the case of Nigeria, which led to the Biafran war in the 1960s and the Katanga wars in Zaire (now Democratic Republic of Congo). In West Africa, for example, part of the Akan people of Ghana now reside in the Ivory Coast; part of the Ewe people of Togo live in Ghana and part in Benin (formerly Dahomey). Paradoxically, Berlin itself, where Africa's border destiny was decided in 1884, suffered a similar fate by becoming a divided city after the Second World War under the protection of allies of the Soviet Union, France, Britain, and the United States. Fortunately for the Germans, the fall of the Berlin Wall in 1989 reunited the German people, who brought this state of affairs on themselves by causing the world war. In contrast, Africans, who suffered colonial injustice through no fault of their own, are still separated from one another by artificial national boundaries.[5]

Christianity in Africa

Christianity entered North Africa as early as in the first century CE and spread to Ethiopia and areas around Nubia (Sudan) by the sixth century. However, it did not take root beyond these areas due to the Islamic invasion, which swept across West Africa in the seventh century. In the fifteenth century, a Papal Bull commissioned Portuguese explorers and sent with them Catholic priests to convert Africans. They arrived in Ghana (Gold Coast) in 1471 and settled in Elmina, where they were enchanted by the immense deposits of gold and turned their attention to trade (Debrunner, 1967). The gold trade developed into the slave trade, bringing competition and rivalry among Europeans such as the Dutch, British, French, Germans, and Danes on the Ghanaian coast.

As the slave trade intensified, the evangelizing activity in Elmina declined sharply, because the priests had been attracted to trade (Debrunner, 1967). The persistent interest and involvement of the clergy in this trading venture seem to suggest that the economic interests of the missionaries, rather than providence, was the principal motivation driving evangelization (Amin, 1989: 72–73). In any case, it was not until the late nineteenth century, when colonialism was firmly advancing, that Christianity began to gain firm roots. In this regard, Christianity and colonialism, both of which had European roots, can rightly be described as complementary. In Ghana, Protestant missionary attempts to revive the evangelization process started by Portuguese Catholics were renewed in the mid-1700s. The Protestant missionary enterprise was reportedly successful because it included missionaries of African descent, particularly from the West Indies. Behind this seemingly laudable inclusion was an ulterior motive; namely, that the Europeans included these Africans because they could not cope with the prevailing climatic conditions, to which Africans were more accustomed. In a sense, both sides benefited from the arrangement, but the motivation of the Europeans was hardly praiseworthy.

Colonialism, Christianity, and Social Justice

Colonialism and Christianity depended on each other to survive. The colonizers often settled on lands forcibly seized from non-Westerners, whom they described as "primitive," "savages," and "heathens." In this context, religion played a crucial role in legitimizing their action. The Calvinist Dutch settlers, first known as Boers and then as Afrikaners, believed that they were predestined by God to claim the land, water, people, and other resources of the Cape Colony of South Africa. As they spread, they decimated the Khoikhoi people whom they encountered (Keim, 1995: 128). The subsequent British claim to the Cape Colony and eventual colonization gave way to the notorious policy of apartheid, which lasted until the early 1990s; the role of the Dutch Reformed Church in consolidating apartheid is well known. Under these circumstances, life, freedom, and development among Africans were profoundly disrupted. For example, New British settlers in the Cape Colony of South Africa in the nineteenth century used biblical imagery to advance the view that the Lord had brought them there to occupy the African lands and to push them away, as God did to the Philistines by permitting Israel to take their land (Stuart, 2002).

Christian missionaries and colonial administrators collaborated to make colonialism effective. Africans were conscripted into the two world wars through the teamwork of the colonial and Christian powers. For example, in a three-way conversation among French Prime Minister Georges Clemenceau, French President Raymond Poincaré, and the Vicar Apostolic of French Sudan (now Mali), the President reportedly said to the Vicar, "My Bishop, France needs all its children [for the war]. You only can organize and direct this campaign," to which the Bishop replied, "I am your man" (Sundkler and Steed, 2000: 612). Similarly, in Burkina Faso Africans were forcibly recruited with the help of Bishop Lemaitre. Arguably, the French colonialists supported a policy of inclusion when they felt that their lives and livelihood were threatened. In this case, they drafted Africans for self-interested purposes. But when a policy was perceived as serving the advantage of the Africans, they elected to exclude Africans. Lawrence (2009) cites examples of how Africans' quest for political equality in the French system and access to political power were challenged.[6]

In Uganda, the Christian era was closely tied to the imperial takeover in 1893, which restructured the political framework. During this time, the Ganda regime at regional and local levels, identical with the new Christian parties, flourished under these changed conditions and Christian ruling classes were established across the country (Sundkler and Steed, 2000: 582). Such classes were also formed by the elite, who followed the Christian and colonial ideas of social justice such as individualism and feelings of superiority, to the detriment of their own cultural ideals.

The convergence of colonialism, religion, and social justice can be further seen in the historical legacy of the European colonial edifices (castles and forts), used as conduits for the slave trade along the coasts of Africa in addition to being places of residence for European slave traders and the chaplains, who also fraternized together in the castles. The convergence of religion and social justice is evident in the Cape Coast Castle in Ghana. The male slave dungeon is situated directly below the Castle's Catholic chapel. In this environment priests said Mass, recited "Our Father," and prayed for mercy for the traders.[7] Colonized Ghanaians were convinced that the missionaries and the colonialists were one and the same people. It is alleged that during the colonial era, when a converted African en route to church on Sunday met a white man, the African would return home because he had already encountered God. The white man was regarded as God himself. The Ghanaian image of European Christians and colonial officials can be summed up in these words: "If you see a Christian, you've seen a colonial master; if you see a colonial master, you've seen a Christian." Indeed, "in 1906 Mensah Sarbah warned the missionary to beware of their identification with other Europeans ('trademan' or 'governor-man') lest his image become distorted" (quoted in Mobley, 1970: 74). This conviction that all Europeans were like-minded people was supported by the relationship and cooperation that existed between the two groups. The colonialists were Christians belonging to different denominations, but they overlooked their doctrinal differences as Methodist, Presbyterian, Anglican, and Catholic, and cooperated in their mistreatment of Africans.

African peoples have suffered denigration, resulting in the decimation of their populations through the slave trade, systematic racism, and rejection of their cultures, as colonialism and Christianity created new identities for them. Imposing foreign systems of law, governance, education, clothing, agriculture, and belief on Africans, they usurped the power and authority of traditional rulers and consequently introduced confusion into Africans' traditional indigenous cultures. These identities, which were alien and sometimes negative, implied a sense of inferiority, which was internalized by colonized Africans and continues even to the present day. Internalizing identities created by others makes a people lose not only their self-esteem and cultural values, including their views of social justice, but also their history and legal systems. African legal systems were (and still are) flexible and geared toward restorative and reconciliatory justice. In fact, the current court practice in Ghana, called Alternative Dispute Resolution, was modeled on indigenous Ghanaian legal understanding.

From the foregoing, we can infer that in the African context colonialism, religion, and social justice complemented one another, in as much as Christian missionaries' ideas of social justice harmonized with the "civilizing" agenda of European expansionists. As a result, Christianity has been described as a major facilitator of European colonialism (Mobley, 1970; Sanneh, 1983). The missionaries allowed their theology of justice to be occluded by the way they cooperated with the colonialists. It has also been convincingly argued that on occasion Christian missionaries, often in unintentional and unanticipated ways, transformed the consciousness of indigenous peoples in a manner that foreshadowed and facilitated colonial domination (Stuart, 2002: 67).

Colonialism, Christianity, and Social Change

Both the colonialists and the Christians condemned indigenous African religions, which were closely interwoven with the indigenous peoples' concept of justice, as indeed were their customs, ethics, and entire social structure and organization. As already stated, African religion is the basis of African life, so that the condemnation of religion affects other aspects of life. In the African worldview, religion must be able to provide the daily, existential needs of life, as well as regulate people's conduct by punishing and rewarding adverse and good conduct respectively. But during the colonial era, the African worldview was (at least partially) replaced with Christian and European worldviews, and this interference with African views and customs not only weakened the social justice delivery system, but introduced contradictions and confusion into key aspects of the beliefs, practices, and social arrangements of their indigenous cultures.

One social institution that was significantly transformed by colonialism and Christianity and affected the religious worldview was the family, which in Africa comprises the living, the dead, and those yet unborn. When Europeans sought to replace the existing extended African family system with the one that was familiar to them, they introduced confusion. The European family system is basically nuclear and monogamous, while the traditional African family is based on an extended social system that is also generally polygynous. (Polygyny is a marriage system in which a man marries several women.) Among Africans, marriage is an obligation from which no one should be left out. It is also an integral part of the human life cycle that, together with birth, puberty, and death, makes the transitions from one stage in life to the other smooth and complete. With women outnumbering men in almost every society, polygyny makes it possible for every woman to marry and also endows every woman with certain rights and privileges that enable her to assume her rightful position in society. When Europeans tried to impose on Africans a nuclear family structure, they caused significant transformations that created much social confusion.

From a European perspective, polygyny was a source of social injustice because young girls were made to marry older men. This means that baby girls who were betrothed to older men were made to consummate the marriage as soon as the girls had undergone puberty rites. The perceived injustice was that, whereas young girls were not permitted to choose and marry their male peers, men, even in their old age, were free to marry much younger girls. Colonial rulers and Christian missionaries also saw puberty rites, especially those that entailed female circumcision (or female genital mutilation), as a social injustice and opposed the practice. Marriage payments, called bride wealth, also conflicted with European norms. On the other hand, Africans considered certain rites of passage – ceremonies that accompany birth, puberty, marriage, and death – as central to their way of life because they had religious significance and also because they ensured equality. Puberty rites, for example, provided formal traditional education for young people and prepared them for marriage, a prerequisite for procreation and the perpetuation of human life.[8]

This clash of cultures set the stage for social conflict, and the attendant injustices of Christianity and colonialism collaborated as a double-edged sword to cut polygyny on both sides: the church condemned polygyny as abhorrent and heathen, and the colonial administration enacted laws that made monogamy a *sine qua non* for becoming civilized and Christian. Converted polygynists were obliged to divorce extra wives before they could partake in the Lord's Supper. They were (and continue to be) viewed as second-class Christians with fewer rights and privileges. The rejection of this marriage system is one of the reasons for the emergence of African independent churches, which admitted Christian polygynists without prejudice.[9]

Again, family cohesion was disturbed through European education, which also became bait for conversion and segregated Africans from their families of origin into new "families" or settlements, called "salem." This segregation served both religious and political purposes. It served as a means to prevent Christian converts from reverting to their African religious beliefs and practices so as to avoid "contamination" with nonconverts. The western education that the children of the converts received while in seclusion made it possible for colonial administrators to exercise complete authority over the "natives." Colonialists expected that these children would succeed their parents as guardians of the Africans in their own group. Also, they would grow up, for example, as British subjects and take jobs in the colonial administration. The non-Christian Africans who did not avail themselves of education remained on the lowest rung of the educational ladder. This education stratification led to the creation of class identification among Africans: educated European Christians were considered superior to illiterate, pagan Africans. In Ghana, the establishment of segregated Christian communities resulted in "the converts considering themselves above the true national life and made them look down with disgust and contempt on certain features and characteristics of the people" (Mobley, 1970: 77).

Other forms of injustice perpetrated by the Europeans took the form of segregation of residential areas. The Europeans lived in separate quarters of the town (white man's town) with separate hospitals. No Africans were accepted in these areas. One would have thought that converted Africans would be equal to the European Christians, but not only did discrimination become discernible, it was actually authorized. In Ghana, the "Mosquito Ordinance" (CAP 75) in the colonial statutes prescribed spraying against mosquitoes only in areas inhabited by Europeans. Areas inhabited by Africans were excluded.

Colonialism, Christianity, and Chieftaincy

Prior to foreign intrusion into Africa, most Africans lived in sovereign, independent states, some of which were ruled by their own elected rulers according to their traditional customs. These rulers had both political and religious functions that reflected the African belief in physical and spiritual worlds. Traditional African rulers, sometimes females, were political figures whose authority was rooted in religion. They exercised executive, legislative, and judicial powers and also presided over religious events, festivals, and sacrifices to the deities and ancestors.[10] Because the authority of the chief was both political and spiritual, he functioned as a link between the living and the dead. Among the Akan people in southern Ghana, the Ohenma (a female monarch, also referred to as queen or queen mother, who was either the mother or sister of the Ohene or ruler) was responsible for nominating and installing the ruler through performing certain customary rituals. Nominations and installations that did not involve the queen mother were null and void. Through installation rituals, the ruler, who was democratically elected, was brought into close contact with his ancestors and became a legitimate, sacred intermediary between the living and the ancestors, without whose protection and aid misfortune would befall the community.

The new ruler publically took an oath to uphold the contract thus formed between the dead and the living.[11]

The British colonialists recognized the strength of traditional rulers and tried to use them to their advantage. Traditional rulers had their specific titles, such as Ohene, Mantse (Ghana), Oba, Eikwei (Nigeria), and Kabaka (Uganda), but under colonialism these heterogeneously titled individuals became homogenized under the generic name of "chiefs." The authority and power of African rulers changed dramatically under British colonialism through the introduction of "indirect rule." Indirect rule served as a buffer between the colonizers and the local people, as the traditional rulers carried out colonial objectives and thus consolidated European rule over the people. The colonialists superimposed the British legal system on the chiefs through Ordinances, a series of legislations, and as a result curtailed the chief's authority and power. Thus, the source of the chief's power came to be derived from British colonial authorities and not from the people he ruled as custom demanded. For example, through the Native Jurisdiction Ordinance (NJO) of 1883 and the Chief's Ordinance (CO) of 1904, governors had the power to suspend, depose, or exile chiefs as well as to install their own chiefs without regard to the prevailing traditional customs. Sometimes they installed and published the names of people who did not belong to the rightful royal lineage. The authority and functions of the female monarch were also disregarded by the colonial administrators. As the people did not recognize these chiefs, they contested these installations, which caused disaffection from the legitimate line of chiefs and generated many injustices that led to rivalries and conflicts, some of which have persisted until today.[12] In areas where no traditional rulers existed, the British created "warrant chiefs" to enforce their system of governance. In Eastern Nigeria this practice contributed to the Aba women's riots, when the people rejected this category of chiefs (Isichei, 1983).

In sum, the legitimacy of an African ruler was subjected to the authority of the colonial governor as the traditional authority of the chief, the customs and traditions of the people, and the oath of office no longer mattered. The usurpation of the chief's power particularly affected the oath that he took during his installation, the breach of which was a legitimate ground for the people to unseat the chief. Also, the oath, as mentioned earlier, was significant because it is a contract between the chief, the living, and the dead. In effect, colonial rule not only affected the dignity of the traditional ruler, but put him in a situation that involuntarily caused him to renege on his oath, an offense that amounted to infringement of contract and attracted both social and spiritual sanctions.

Christianity also attacked African political institutions by preventing Christian converts from becoming traditional rulers, because they regarded the rituals that legitimized them as chiefs to be heathen practices. To them the chief himself was a symbol of paganism, because he was the custodian of the ancestral stool[13] and presided over pagan rituals. For example, Christians condemned libation, a form of sacrifice involving pouring a liquid (usually water or alcohol) on the ground to invoke the ancestors and deities for intercession in human activities. A Christian therefore could not be a chief in the colonial era. Currently, there is still a divided opinion about Christianity and chieftaincy. While some Ghanaian Christians share the sentiments of unity and continuity expressed in the ritual of chiefship, others question the spiritual role of the chief and refuse to participate in the rituals, which they consider idolatrous.

Revisiting African Social Justice

African social justice is based on equality and human rights. It is exemplified by African humanism, which is rooted in lived dependencies and reciprocities shaped by traditional values of mutual respect for one's fellow kinsman and a sense of position and place in the larger order of things. Traditional African social justice seeks first and primarily the well-being of the larger community, expressed in the notion of "another's needs" or *ubuntu* (Bell, 2002: 40, 89). Consequently, on achieving political independence from colonial rulers, many African leaders reverted to the form of social justice that was familiar to them and their people. Two such leaders were Kwame Nkrumah (the first president of Ghana) and Julius Nyerere (the first president of Tanzania).[14] After liberating their own countries, they pursued a struggle for the total liberation of Africa by providing shelter in Ghana and Tanzania and even money for freedom fighters to overthrow European domination in their respective countries. On the eve of Ghana's Independence Day, March 5, 1957, at the Accra Polo Ground, Nkrumah declared that the independence of Ghana was meaningless unless it was linked with the total liberation of Africa. These leaders believed that although formal, political colonialism had ended, it had not completely disappeared but was transformed into neo-colonialism, a new form of colonialism. According to Nkrumah (1965: 1), after colonial powers "gave" their colonies independence they continued to oppress them by giving them "aid" for development (original quotation marks).

> Under such phrases, however, it devises innumerable ways to accomplish objectives formerly achieved by naked colonialism. It is the sum total of these modern attempts to perpetuate colonialism while at the same time talking about "freedom," which has come to be known as neo-colonialism. (Nkrumah 1965: 1)

To redress colonial injustice, Nkrumah swiftly began to reduce the inequality and uneven development of north and south Ghana; establish free education at all levels; expand healthcare; develop industries; and improve infrastructure. In the religious sphere, he encouraged equality by supporting the syncretization or putting together as one religion the three major prevailing faiths in Ghana: African Traditional religions, Islam, and Christianity. Nkrumah's recognition of African religions attracted strong criticism from Christians, which led to the deportation of some expatriate clerics (Pobee, 1991).

Nyerere's fight for social justice earned him great respect and honor, as the Catholic Church has recently (in the postcolonial era) started proceedings for his beatification as a holy person (*The Catholic Standard*, 2009:3). In his Arusha Declaration of 1967, Nyerere used the concept of *ujamma* (family-hood) and equality to rebuild his nation. He described *ujamma* as a strategy to build a society in which all members have equal rights and equal opportunities; in which all can live in peace with their neighbors without suffering or imposing injustice, being exploited, or exploiting; and in which all have a gradually increasing basic level of material welfare before any individual lives in luxury.

However, it seems that social justice sometimes goes hand in hand with social injustice. By attempting to focus on rural development, Tanzanians were encouraged, and sometimes forced, to live and work on a cooperative basis in organized villages. Nearly ten million peasants were relocated, and many were effectively forced to give up their land, which they resisted. Nyerere's strategy of *ujamma* defeated its own objective of eradicating exploitation, as people were prevented from using their land in the way they wanted. Also, the strategy had a negative impact on the African family system, which is consanguineous (based on blood relations), as families became separated during the relocations. In short, the strategy of *ujamma* seems to have fared no better than the Christian concept of *salems*, which in an earlier time also fragmented families.

African Independent Churches

African Independent Churches were founded by African women and men at the end of the nineteenth century. They emerged, in part, in response to several factors: they suffered racial discrimination by European colonialists; they were deprived of leadership positions in colonial administration and in the Christian churches; they were alienated from their land and language by the Europeans; and they experienced political and cultural domination by the Europeans. African Independent Churches usually combine African and Christian cultural elements into a distinct religious phenomenon. They claim that through the power of the Holy Spirit they heal, prophesy about impending dangers or misfortunes, interpret dreams, and help alleviate societal problems so as to effect a positive change in a person's life. They express joyful worship through loud music and vigorous dance. African Independent Churches generally do not view polygyny as a sin and usually do not discourage its practice. They also do not regard chieftaincy and Christianity as incompatible. In fact, some of them model their church organizations alongside traditional structures of chieftaincy. Through these African-initiated churches, Africans have returned to leadership positions and are able to have a new religion that is more compatible with their traditional culture.

Conclusion

The real impact of the shared civilizing ideology of European Christians and colonialists is that the liberties of free African people – their social structures, governance systems, and economies – were substantially changed or destroyed. Prejudice and the use of force in the colonial and Christian missionary enterprises are some of the factors that brought about some historical exclusions, which in turn encouraged nationalist aspirations and innovations that allowed Africans to reinvent their familiar forms of social justice.

Notes

1. Contemporary Africans still believe in the material and spiritual worlds. Indeed, belief in these two realms forms the basis of most cultural practices and human conduct, even after the colonial experience. This means that there are threads of continuity with the past and, therefore, it is difficult to write about most beliefs and practices in the past tense, which is why I sometimes write about the past using the present tense.
2. See Shorter (1977).
3. Mbiti, quoted in Shorter (1977).
4. For more on the differences between Christian and traditional African values, see Mobley (1970); Sanneh (1983); and Isichei (1983).
5. Some of the protracted effects of the colonial division of people were manifested recently during the African Nations Football competition held in Angola in January 2010. A separatist group in Cabinda called FLEC attacked and killed some members of the Togolese football team even before the tournament had begun.
6. See Lawrence (2009).
7. The castle is a piece of evidence of the slave trade and the role of Christianity in it (active or passive) that is difficult to reconcile, and the visit of the American president, Barack Obama, and his family to the Cape Coast Castle in July 2009 resonated similar sentiments.
8. These rites are still performed in contemporary times, though the practice has reduced considerably. However, there are increasing public debates about whether to return to some of these rites as an African approach to development.
9. Currently, monogamy and polygyny exist side by side. The incumbent South African president, Jacob Zuma, is in a polygynous relationship, being married to three women at the same time.
10. Ancestors are spirits of dead family members believed to be alive in the spiritual world. They have a keen interest in the affairs of the living and keep vigilance on their conduct. Ancestral beliefs are still prevalent among many Africans.
11. The traditional chieftaincy institution could not be entirely destroyed by colonialism and Christianity. It has been revived, though it has been greatly transformed.
12. As recently as 2010, the installment of a chief in Ghana (Wenchi chief) has been declared null and void because it was "without the participation of the Queen and the procedure adopted did not conform to the customary practice of the Wenchi Paramount Stool" (Fynn, 2010: 17).
13. A stool (usually a wooden seat) is a symbol of the traditional ruler's authority. It is also a symbol of the presence of the ancestors.
14. Tanzania was formed by the amalgamation of two East African nations, Tanganyika and Zanzibar, in 1964.

References

Amin, S. (1989) *Eurocentrism*, Monthly Review, New York.

Bell, R. (2002) *Understanding African Philosophy*, Routledge, New York.

Chief's Ordinance (CO) (1904) Public Records and Archives Administration Department (PRAAD), ADM 4/1/124, Accra, Ghana.

Debrunner, H. (1967) *A History of Christianity in Ghana*, Waterville Publishing House, Accra.

Fynn, D. (2010) Instalment of Wenchi Chief declared null and void, Daily Graphic, 10 July: 17.

Gellar, S. (1995) The colonial era, in Africa, P.M. Martin and P. O'Meara (eds.), 3rd edn, Indiana University Press, Bloomington, pp. 135–154.

Isichei, E. (1983) *A History of Nigeria*, Longman, London.

Keim, C.A. (1995) Africa and Europe before 1900, in *Africa*, P.M. Martin and P. O'Meara (eds.), 3rd edn, Indiana University Press, Bloomington, pp. 115–134.

Kellar, E.J. (1995) Decolonization, independence, and the failure of politics, in *Africa*, P.M. Martin and P. O'Meara (eds.), 3rd edn, Indiana University Press, Bloomington, pp. 156–171.

Lawrence, A. (2009) Political equality and nationalist opposition in the French colonial empire, paper prepared for the Comparative Politics Workshop on September 29, Department of Political Science, Yale University.

Mobley, H. (1970) *The Ghanaian Image of the Missionary*, E.J. Brill, Leiden.

Mosquitoes Ordinance (Cap 75) (1911) Public Records and Archives Administration Department (PRAAD), ADM 4/1/254, Accra, Ghana.

Native Jurisdiction Ordinance (NJO) (1883) Public Records and Archives Administration Department (PRAAD), ADM 4/1/125, Accra, Ghana.

Nkrumah, K. (1965) Neo-colonialism, http://www.marxists.org/subject/africa/nkrumah/neo-colonialism/ch01.htm (accessed April 19, 2011).

Nyerere, J. (1968) *Ujamma: Essays on Socialism*, Oxford University Press, London.

Pobee, J.S. (1991) *Religion and Politics in Ghana*, Asempa Publishers, Accra.

Sanneh, L. (1983) *West African Christianity*, Maryknoll, New York.

Schweizer, P. (2000) *Survivors on the Gold Coast: The Basel Missionaries in Colonial Ghana*, Smart Line Publishers, Accra.

Shorter, A. (1977) Concepts of social justice in traditional Africa, http://www.afrikaworld.net/afrel/atr-socjustice.htm (accessed April 19, 2011).

Stuart, D. (2002) Converts or convicts? in *Christian Missionaries and the State in the Third World*, H.B. Hansen and M. Twaddle (eds.), James Currey, Oxford, pp. 66–75.

Sundkler, B. and Steed, C. (2000) *A History of the Church in Africa*, Cambridge University Press, Cambridge.

The Catholic Standard (Accra, Ghana) (2009) November 29–December 7: 3.

Bibliography

Martin, P.M. and O'Meara, P. (eds) (1995) *Africa*, 3rd edn, Indiana University Press, Bloomington.

Native Administration (Colony) Ordinance (NAO) (1927) Public Records and Archives Administration Department (PRAAD), ADM 4/1/132, Accra, Ghana.

Odotei, I. and Awedoba, A. (eds) (2006) *Chieftaincy in Ghana*, Sub-Saharan Publishers, Accra.

Sackey, B.M. (2006) *New Directions in Gender and Religion: The Changing Status of Women in African Independent Churches*, Lexington Books, Lanham, MD.

CHAPTER 32

Abundant Life or Abundant Poverty?

The Challenge for African Christianity

T. John Padwick

Africa is a continent rich in human, natural, and mineral resources. Despite this, African countries continue to remain in a more or less solid block at the bottom of the UNDP (United Nations Development Programme) Human Development Indices. This contrast between the potential natural and human riches of the continent, the reality of acute poverty for hundreds of millions, and the unfulfilled promises of "abundant life" in African religions has led its religious leaders in recent decades into a prolonged search for solutions. This chapter examines, largely from an historical perspective, the background and continuing influence of traditional African religions, and the struggles – spiritual, theological, organizational and political – of leaders and members of the African Christian churches to bring their faith into a more effective engagement with the challenge of poverty. I assume that religions evolve through engaging with the challenges that arise at specific times and in specific cultures. I shall pay attention to African perceptions of poverty and its causes, in order to appreciate the nature of the responses from African religions. I write from a committed perspective, as both an "outsider" and an "insider": British and white, I have lived most of my life in Kenya as a Christian missionary, development worker, and theologian working with African Independent Churches, and latterly as a member of one of these churches. The focus of this essay is on sub-Saharan Africa, and I restrict my use of the term "African" to the people of this region.

The Genesis of African Poverty

Poverty is a social construct, and has meaning only within specific contexts. Across the world in many earlier societies a lack of material possessions was not in itself shameful. Rahnema (2001: 3) calls this "customary poverty." During the precolonial period (up to ca. 1890), in African states, kingdoms, chieftaincies, and in acephalous societies of semi-autonomous clans, poverty and affluence were present side by side. The lack of historical records and the diversity of physical environments and types of society (hunter-gatherer, pastoral, agricultural, urban based) make any broad description of poverty in this period very difficult (Iliffe, 1987: 64). In such societies, material poverty as a long-term and debilitating condition was unacceptable, and various customs ensured that a poor man was assisted to lift himself and his family out of poverty (he might be given some land and lent a cow, for example). What was truly stigmatizing was not the lack of material goods but that of significant relationships. Without relatives, friends, age-mates, and patrons, without support in crisis or disability, and the human dignity that comes from social acceptance, a fully human life could not be enjoyed.

The traditional economies and social life of many African communities were deeply disrupted by the slave trade and then by colonialism. In the colonial period, African economies became distorted. Africans were encouraged to grow what they did not consume and to consume what they did not produce (Boahen, 1990: 102). The enforced isolation imposed by colonialism – the disruption of unmediated relations between Africa and the rest of the world – was a major factor in slowing Africa's growth. In the postcolonial period, most African nations embarked on a process of industrialization. Following dramatic rises in the price of oil in the 1970s, and aggressive lending by northern banks, African countries became heavily indebted. In the late 1980s and early 1990s, Structural Adjustment Programs (SAPs) were imposed by the World Bank and International Monetary Fund, primarily to ensure that African nations remained within the global finance system. SAPs caused a widespread collapse of public services, or their restriction to those who could pay (Taiwo, 2010: 261 ff.). Global structures of trade and finance remained dominated by northern interests. Meanwhile, the continuing rise in corruption in most African countries (abetted or ignored by many northern governments and corporations) restricted both economic growth and the development of democratic institutions. As a result, during the 1990s the poor in general became poorer.

In the 2010 UNDP Human Development Report, the 20 countries with the world's lowest human development were all – except for one – African. This does not mean that there has been no progress – economic growth rates have risen significantly in a number of African countries over the decade 2001–2010, the democratization of the 1990s is still bearing fruit, and there has been substantial public and private investment in education. As yet, however, public health has not fully recovered from SAPs, and in a number of countries the impact of HIV remains critical. Social, political, and ethnic tensions (frequently exacerbated by clientelism in politics) continue to boil over into open conflict. The economic gains that have been made are only slowly – if at all – affecting the lives of the poorest half of the population. Income disparity in Africa as a whole is high, and in some countries extremely high.[1] Rapid urbanization means that the locus of poverty is shifting toward the city and its informal settlements. The privatization of land (in many societies held in precolonial days by the ancestors in the name of the community) continues to expropriate the poor. More recently, the sale or lease of large blocks of land to Middle East and Asian nations lacking agricultural resources of their own threatens a further loss of African control over the continent's resources. Moreover, climate change and environmental degradation are already destabilizing the economies of particular regions.

Largely as a result of the rise of the capitalist economy, the customary poverty of traditional African societies is rapidly being overtaken by what Rahnema (2001) terms "modernized poverty." This is the lack of socially constructed needs and the resources to meet those needs. Television stations nightly broadcast images into the shanty towns of the good life unreachable by the poor. The majority of the poor are not destitute, partly because they possess the human resources and social networks that help them to survive: access to land, the support of social networks, the transmission of the traditional knowledge that enables communities to live in harsh conditions, and forms of religion that are owned by communities at the grass roots. However, the growth of the free market and rapid urbanization threaten the survival of these social resources and steadily erode the concept and practice of small-scale human community. Addressing a similar situation, the Camerounian theologian Mveng (1994) proposes the concept of "anthropological poverty," "when persons are bereft of their identity, their dignity, their freedom, their thought, their history, their language, their faith universe, and their basic creativity, deprived of all their rights, their hopes, their ambitions." It is precisely in these areas of social and spiritual capital, however, where the strength and the capacity for response of African religions are to be found.

Traditional African Religions and Their Continuing Influence

I use here a definition of religion proposed by ter Haar (2009: 1) for the African context: "a widespread belief in an invisible world, inhabited by spiritual forces or entities that are deemed to have effective powers over the material world." This definition has the merit of incorporating nonjudgmentally people's use of spiritual powers. Elsewhere this use is often dismissed as "witchcraft," "animism," "magic," or in other prejudicial terms. I also refer to precolonial African religions, and their persistence into the present, as "traditional African religions" in the plural. Traditional religions have close relationships with particular ethnic communities – they rarely seek to evangelize outside their own ethnic group – and they exhibit considerable variety. The contrasts are particularly strong between the traditional religions of West Africa and those of East, Central and Southern Africa. It is also important to recognize that traditional African religions – as human constructs developed to deal with existential challenges of particular contexts – have been evolving since they emerged. They continue to provide a common African language of religion that influences contemporary African Christianity and Islam and the responses of these global faiths to poverty and related challenges.

Across this diversity are many common themes: the belief in a spiritual world, parallel to and interlocking with the material world; the existence of human and spiritual beings with mystical powers that can influence events in the material world; the understanding that a good life must be lived in harmony with other human beings, living and dead, and with other spiritual forces, including those located in the natural world.[2] The normal state of humankind is assumed to be that of well-being, or abundance of life

(Magesa, 1997). Failure to maintain harmonious relations with humans and other beings leads to the blocking of blessings from the creator God, and the exercise of mystical sanctions by offended beings. As a result, people's well-being is diminished. They fall sick, lose political power or employment, and become impoverished. Often the effect extends beyond the individual to "dis-ease" experienced by the extended family and the wider community. In Africa there is no sin that is private, for all sins have an impact on the well-being of the community, present and future. The concept of *ubuntu* (literally, "humanness") defines the essence of being human as participation in this community: "I am because we are; because we are I am."

In traditional African religions spiritual and material power are strongly linked, and the perception that "all power has its *ultimate* origins in the spirit world" remains common today (Ellis and ter Haar, 2004: 4). Consequently, intervention by human beings in the spiritual realm to influence events in the physical world is a major concern of all African religions, through the use of what ter Haar (2009: 5, 11) calls "spiritual technology." Possession by spirits, ancestral or divine – and in the Christian tradition, by the filling of the Holy Spirit – is believed to give insight into spiritual realities and guidance in tackling life's problems. This is particularly true in the realm of healing (understood holistically as the restoration of well-being). Evil forces are constantly active, however, and the spiritual world is dangerous. African traditional diviners, the prophets of African Independent Churches (AICs), and Pentecostal pastors take on the battle with such forces for the benefit of the community. Dealing with issues like unemployment, sickness, failure to be promoted, infertility, and loss of vitality (both spiritual and physical) requires confronting the powers of witchcraft, the evil eye, sorcery, evil spirits, curses, and Satan. "One who is called by the spirit . . . takes on a social responsibility comparable to that of the Old Testament prophets." (ter Haar, 2009: 46).

It has become almost an article of faith among African scholars that there was "generally greater accountability and greater commitment to the social welfare in traditional Africa" (Olupona, 2009: xiii). As a result, for both scholars and politicians, the conscious revival of positive aspects of African tradition is seen as a key both to long-term poverty eradication and the struggle for a wider liberation. If *ubuntu* is for many commentators the foundation of African philosophy, *ujamaa* (literally "family-hood"; politically, "African socialism") is the political working out of the principles of *ubuntu*. As a political philosophy, *ujamaa* was developed by President Nyerere of Tanzania as an African alternative to the western capitalist model of development. It contains a strong ethical element, for which the social teaching of Nyerere's Catholic faith, and also the *undugu* (brotherhood) of Islam were other sources. For Nyerere, participation in the community even becomes an epistemological principle – knowledge is analyzed in relation to society, not to the individual (Nyerere, 1973; Frostin, 1988: 27–83, 61–20). Both *ubuntu* and *ujamaa* continue to influence African Christian theologians today and are beacons of alternative African philosophies and politics.[3]

Contemporary responses to African poverty, then, draw on traditional African religions in three ways. At the popular level, "spiritual technology" and moral reformation are employed to handle problems in the material world. National days of prayer and repentance are called to deal with corruption or natural disasters. Also at the grass roots, the local community serves as a strong social support system to protect and rescue the vulnerable. At the level of national politics, there have been various attempts to recover values of *ubuntu* and related concepts as counterpoint values to those of western capitalism and the free market, and to assert the possibility of a more egalitarian African society.

Christian Missionaries, the Colonial Project and Models of Development

The practice of development in Africa derived originally from colonial practice and theory. The philosophical concept of "development," which emerged in the twentieth century from the idea of "progress," has its roots in the Hebrew and Christian visions of a future perfect world and was strongly shaped by the eighteenth-century European Enlightenment. Enlightenment thinking assumes that progress can be achieved through rational investigation of problems, which can be described "objectively," and which can form the basis of appropriate interventions to achieve progress (Hettne, 2009: 1, 8–14; ter Haar, 2009: 17, 74–78). Enlightenment thinking and Christian faith both lay behind the birth of the western Christian missionary movement in the late eighteenth century, and the related antislave-trade campaign. These marked the beginnings of a long and continuing series of western interventions to consciously "improve" the state of Africa. Already, however, a disjuncture was developing in the West between the Christian vision and secular concepts of progress, a disjuncture that continues to have implications for contemporary western perceptions of the relationship between development and religion.

Development is generally linked to modernity and modernization. Taiwo (2010: 8) finds the essence of modernity in "modes of being," specifically subjectivity, reason, and progress. He argues that African appropriation of such modes of being was promoted by early nineteenth-century Christian missionaries in West Africa. These missionaries consciously sought to propagate Christianity, civilization, and commerce through the promotion of trade, literacy, and formal education, and the growth of professions like architecture, printing, and medicine. As a result, a modernizing African elite began to develop, committed to the progress of their own communities. This elite adopted and adapted aspects of modernity that they found useful – they were on their way to creating a specific African modernity. Taiwo characterizes this early model of missionary engagement as one of "autonomy"; that is, building the *agency* of Africans, often through the self-conscious creation of a middle class.

This process was interrupted by the subsequent imposition of the structures of formal European empires, which lasted from the last third of the nineteenth century until the eventual achievement of political freedom in the late 1950s and 1960s. Formal empire trumpeted the importance of modernizing, and the provision of education, health facilities, and improved agriculture. On the other hand, it denied Africans the rights of democratic citizenship, participation in modern legal systems, and new forms of social consciousness and organization – all natural workings out of modern modes of being. Influenced by a popular form of social Darwinism, the colonial project and the contemporaneous Christian missionary movement by and large regarded

Africans as a lower category of human beings, and, critically, rejected their agency. As a result, Taiwo (2010) argues, Africans were prevented from engaging naturally and critically with modernity and with their own traditions. The long-term consequence has been the failure of Africa's democratic institutions and legal systems.

African Independent or Instituted Churches

In protest at missionary paternalism and the denial of civic and political rights, missionary-educated Africans took matters into their own hands, and from the late 1890s founded the so-called Ethiopian or nationalist churches. This early form of African Independent or Instituted Churches (usually referred to as AICs) became the forerunners of African nationalism.[4] Strong in Nigeria, South Africa, and Kenya, the Ethiopian churches regarded the struggle against colonialism as a divine calling. In Kenya, the Independent churches of the Mount Kenya region (a term used by the churches themselves) emerged from an initiative to set up schools free from missionary control that would teach African values as well as formal education and skills in social organization. Such churches asserted their right as agents to select what was useful and appropriate from the missionary and colonial models of development.

Another African Christian response to the colonial situation was derived more directly from the spirituality of traditional African religions. Spiritual churches, the second wave of AICs, emerged after the First World War, and were based on an appropriation of the Christian gospel from within a traditional African worldview. These African Christians discerned within the colonial and missionary enterprise the seeds of secularism and individualism. Frustrated by missionary incomprehension of the concept of spiritual power, they founded their own churches, rooted in African culture and known as Aladura ("praying") churches in West Africa, Zionist and Apostolic churches in Southern Africa, and Roho ("Spirit") and Akurinu churches in East Africa. In Kenya, for example, the missionary encouragement of nuclear families and of an educated and upwardly mobile middle class able to benefit from contacts with colonial authorities was regarded as destructive of communal values, and therefore as "against the Holy Spirit." These Kenyan churches continue to be suspicious of the dominant model of development, stressing community building and the redistribution of surplus resources among the poor of the community of faith (Padwick, 2003: 335–342).

After the achievement of political independence in most countries in sub-Saharan Africa in the late 1960s and early 1970s, the missionary-educated African elite, now leaders of the new governments, found these popular religious movements and churches difficult to understand and handle. In 1964, almost immediately after political independence, the Zambian government's suppression of the Lumpa Church of Alice Lenshina was achieved only through violent confrontation. Expressive and loosely structured movements like the majority of the AICs were of little use to government leaders intent on the modernization of the nation (Padwick, 2003: 248). (A notable exception was the very large Kimbanguist church in the Democratic Republic of the Congo, which had very well-structured programs for building schools and clinics.[5]) In contrast, the mission-founded churches (now largely under African control) were coopted by the new governments as agents for and partners in development programs. Indeed, by the 1970s a common requirement for government recognition of new churches was a commitment to some kind of development program. More recently, however, the capacity of the Spiritual churches to build communities at the grass roots in both the rural villages and in the rapidly expanding informal urban settlements has become apparent.

The Christian Churches and Development in the Postindependence Era

After political independence, the "mainline" Christian churches (i.e., those founded by missionaries and enjoying significant overseas connections and support) continued to run development programs: schools and hospitals, as in the colonial period; and new activities such as agricultural and health extension programs in the villages; HIV prevention, care, and support from the 1990s; and micro-enterprise projects. These churches also became increasingly involved in civic and political education at election periods.

From the 1980s, however, increasing external funding began to go to nongovernmental development organizations (NGOs) with roots in secular Enlightenment thinking. Such NGOs frequently considered religion to be a hindrance to modernization, and simply ignored the practice of religion in the communities with which they worked. Only since the mid-1990s, with the emergence of such concepts as "spiritual capital" (ter Haar, 2009: 75, 78) and faith-based initiatives (FBIs) (Olupona, 2009: xvi–xvii), has the role of religion in development begun again to be given its proper place by western governments and world bodies. In Africa, the key event marking this shift in perception came in 2000, when the Council of Anglican Provinces of Africa invited other African churches to meet with the World Bank to discuss development cooperation (Belshaw et al., 2001: 3). Even so, much of this meeting was focused on what has been called an "instrumentalist" understanding of the relationship. In this, development agencies use the structures of faith bodies from the village level upward to gain access to people, while making little effort to engage with the content of faith (in which they generally lack knowledge or skills). "Spiritual capital" in this context means merely the social capital of religious bodies. In contrast, to engage with faith as motivation for, and goal setting in, development programs (in a similar manner to the early nineteenth-century missionaries) would require agencies to adopt long-term "critical solidarity" with faith bodies and their faith – which even some of the largest western Christian development agencies have been reluctant to do.

Abundant Life and African Christian Theology

After the high hopes for progress of the initial postindependence era had been dashed, the search for "abundant life" rapidly became the broad concern of African Christian theology. This term embraces the theologies of the Catholic and Protestant churches, the latter under the umbrella of the All Africa Conference of Churches (AACC). In that they seek to improve the condition of Africa, these theologies are all "practical theologies," and can be roughly grouped into three: theologies of inculturation, liberation, and reconstruction.

Inculturation theology, the first of these movements, engaged with traditional African culture and religion in order to develop an African understanding of community and personhood and a truly African Christian faith and identity. Key proponents of this school are Kwame Bediako, John Mbiti, Charles Nyamiti, Laurenti Magesa, Bolaji Idowu, and Kwesi Dickson, among many others. This theology emerged as an attempt to set right the missionary and colonial disparagement of African culture, and to overcome the strong sense of cultural alienation that many educated African Christians felt in the immediate postindependence period (roughly, the 1960s and 1970s). One criticism of this school is that its stress on African community leads to a reliance on consensus as the preferred methodology for social change. If, however, as many commentators maintain, the main cause of Africa's poverty is understood to be unjust economic and political structures, then the theologian must adopt a form of social analysis that uncovers the structures of power (global and local) before moving to conflict as a necessary part of the solution. However, such critical social analysis has rarely been welcomed by church leaders (Frostin, 1988: 70).

In contrast, in the 1970s and 1980s, African liberation theology – while not abandoning the cultural issue – took struggle very seriously as a source for theology and a methodology of action. The Camerounian Ela argues:

> We need to go back to actual history, and locate the most profound symbols of African culture in a broader context, a context that bears the marks of domination and conflict. (Ela, 1988: 175)

Frostin (1988: 6–10) notes five characteristics of this liberation theology:

- It is the poor who are the "interlocutors" of the theology (i.e., those raising the questions that theology should address).[6]
- It asks: "whose side is God on – that of the oppressed or the oppressor?"
- It is conflictual in methodology, starting with the conflict between rich and poor.
- It practices social analysis.
- It sees the doing of theology as "a second act," dependent on a prior involvement in concrete experience and engagement in the social struggle ("praxis").

A key strand in African liberation theology is South African black theology. Drawing on the experience of black South Africans under apartheid, and the struggle for black power, it may be said to have come of age after the death of Steve Biko in 1977. In this theology, blackness describes the condition of oppression – of which "being black" under apartheid was the most concrete and universal experience. To Allan Boesak (1977: 1–2), black consciousness is an *alternative* consciousness – a rejection of dominant modes of thought that are imposed on black people. It asserts the right of the oppressed to define their own realities and to struggle for their own liberation. The best-known production of this school is the "Kairos Document" of 1985, a searing critique of South African "state" and "church" theologies for their support of or connivance in the injustice of apartheid. The document led to widespread public debate.

After the end of the Cold War in the early 1990s, the theology of reconstruction sought to bring the two strands of inculturation and liberation together in a new African political environment of multiparty democracies and a (hoped-for) economic revival (Dedji, 2003). In 1991, at a symposium of the AACC, the Kenyan Jesse Mugambi proposed reconstruction as the new theological paradigm, with accompanying social transformation. Mugambi (1995) takes the theme from the book of Nehemiah of rebuilding the nation of Israel after its return from exile. His program is multidisciplinary and ecumenical. In South Africa after the achievement of majority rule, Villa-Vicencio (1992), continuing the critical social analysis tradition of liberation theology but also recognizing the need for cultural empowerment, sought to lay out the groundwork of a theology of nation building. Both Mugambi and Villa-Vicencio urged a move away from struggle toward reconciliation, consensus, and peace building in the African tradition. The Congolese-born Kä Mana (1992; see Dedji, 2003) rejects the earlier search for an African identity based on cultural ethnicity as fundamentally flawed in a broken Africa that first needs social transformation. For him, the African crisis is due to the lack of appropriate engagement between the spiritual values of African culture and western modernity. It is the transcendent and utopian promise of the Christian gospel that can create a dynamic for change, and the role of the church is to enable Africans to engage critically with the contemporary world.

In a survey of recent African theological writing, the South African commentator Maluleke (2002) observes a trend toward theological engagement with popular forms of African religion and struggle (AICs, the working class and peasantry, and women's groups). He highlights an emerging focus on the agency of ordinary Africans, struggling to survive, surviving, and creating new discourses reflecting on God's interventions in their history. Similarly, the Ugandan Katongole (2005) urges the need for a prophetic theology that will offer a new "social imagination," rooted in the experiences of ordinary people, and based on an understanding of the church as the social institution that can give critique, vision, and direction in social transformation. Quite independently of these academic theologians but moving in a somewhat similar direction, the umbrella body of AICs, the Organization of African Instituted Churches (OAIC), is working on enabling AICs to articulate and reflect on their popular oral faith ("founding visions"), so that these churches can relate their Christian faith more effectively to contemporary challenges in their struggle to build "just communities."

Arguably, the greatest success of African Christian theology in the last 25 years has been its role in the struggle for human, civil, and political rights, particularly in the achievement of majority rule in South Africa and the democratization of regimes elsewhere. This is an area where the language of the Enlightenment coincides with popular political concerns. But despite the recent initiatives mentioned above, these academic theologies have not yet engaged successfully with popular religious discourse – a necessity for any genuine social transformation that is to involve the grass roots. In fact, it is in the grassroots theologies of the Spiritual AICs, and especially those of the indigenous Pentecostals, both rooted in the African traditions of spiritual conflict with the forces of evil, that the future of African Christianity probably lies. Even the historical "mainline" churches are ineluctably being drawn toward Pentecostalism in their preaching and practice – if not yet in their formal theology – lest they lose their members, and particularly their youth.

African Pentecostalism

African Pentecostalism is the "cutting edge" of contemporary African Christianity, and the latest stage in Africa's search for power and the recovery of identity (Kalu, 2008: 4). In 2006, according to the World Christian Database, members of Pentecostal denominations numbered 12% (107 million), while Pentecostal members of other denominations, including AICs, numbered 5% (40 million) of Africa's 870 million people (Pew Forum, 2006). This truly remarkable growth from nothing in 1900 is primarily attributable to the fact that Pentecostalism and traditional African religions share the same language of spiritual power. Indigenous Pentecostalism emerged first through traditional African prophets influenced by Christian teaching, then through Christian prophetic movements that foreshadowed the AICs (Prophet Harris in the Ivory Coast, for example, whose key ministry was from 1913–1915), and subsequently through the Spiritual AICs (Kalu, 2008: 35–39). Contemporaneously with these indigenous manifestations, Pentecostal missionaries from the North began to arrive – the fruit of the 1906 Azusa Street revival in Los Angeles. Revival next began to affect some of the "mainline" churches, as in the East African Revival of the 1930s. Starting from the 1960s, Pentecostal crusades, mainly from North America, often accompanied by training sessions for evangelists, have become a common phenomenon across the continent. Their effect was primarily to stimulate the emergence of tens of thousands of indigenous Pentecostal pastors. Next, the North American-led "Fire Convention" of 1984 in Harare introduced teachings of deliverance and prosperity. The latest phase of this rapidly changing movement has seen a new critique of prosperity teaching, an occupation of the public space with Pentecostals standing for political office, and a renewed charismatization of the mainline churches (Kalu, 2008: 3–22).

This brief history serves to correct the widespread tendency to see African Pentecostalism as a merely a branch of North American Pentecostalism, or as an aspect of globalization operating only in the interests of the global North. Certainly, North American influence has been strong since the 1980s, but the flow of influence has not been only one way. Secondly, it sees African Pentecostalism as drawing significantly on African cultural and religious roots. Ter Haar (2009: 59), indeed, claims that its current growth and spread across all denominations reflects a "decolonization of the mind." Some writers (Paul Gifford [2004] is a good example) argue that African Pentecostalism is reintroducing magic to handle issues of poverty and disease that can better be dealt with scientifically, and that a focus on the miraculous obscures rationality and the ethic of hard work. In these writers' view, the role of the African church is to promote effective engagement with modernity and the globalizing world economy. Such criticisms need to be nuanced. Spiritual technology remains an African approach to existential problems; but it is normally balanced in everyday life by practical effort as well. Many

Pentecostal churches offer practical assistance to members to start small businesses, or offer advice on investment. It is better to say that African Pentecostalism draws out the fears and hopes of ordinary people, addresses them in an idiom that they can understand, and seeks to empower them with hopes of a radically new future. At the same time, it gives them a sense of global citizenship, and the support of a strong community of faith. It promotes both consciously and unconsciously key entrepreneurial skills in a way that the older Spiritual AICs focused on *ubuntu* values still find difficult.

Conclusion

Traditional African religions characteristically sought to deal with poverty in the context of community, by the means of both spiritual technology and practical means. After the arrival of western missionaries to sub-Saharan Africa, the Protestant missionary project of introducing modernity and progress to Africans was interrupted and distorted by formal colonialism. AICs emerged in protest, practicing a measure of autonomy. Ethiopian AICs embraced modernity as a means of recovering political freedom and the return of lost lands. The Spiritual AICs rejected much of the colonial and missionary form of development, and claimed a spiritual freedom to revert to a spiritual and practical communalism. In this, the poor were full and equal members of the community of faith, and spiritual technology was employed against the powers of evil. The missionary-founded churches benefited from modernity, and embraced "development" on the western model, in alliance with colonial and postcolonial African governments. However, African theologians from these churches have subsequently been haunted by the loss of African identity and values. For all its conscious engagement in political, economic, and social issues affecting the state of Africa, the formal academic discourse of these theologians has rarely succeeded in engaging the masses. In contrast, Pentecostalism has reached back into the roots of traditional African religion, taken spiritual technology into contemporary life, and taught a new self-confidence in the future that is open to all social groups and classes. The western development model has been taken to its logical and secular conclusion by the intervention of numerous NGOs, but the continual flourishing of religion in Africa and elsewhere is forcing these secular agencies to imagine the possibility of other narratives in which religion once again is a key aspect of a full and abundant human life.

Notes

1 "Very high" in Kenya, Uganda, Nigeria, and Botswana and "extremely high" in Namibia, South Africa, and Zambia. Based on the comparison of Gini coefficients in UN-HABITAT, 2010: 26.
2 The emphasis on harmony with the natural world has led to recent engagement with traditional African religions for ecological purposes (Daneel, 2001).
3 One such program, *Ubudehe,* is a current Rwandan government program offering support to community projects organized by village cooperatives. It takes its name from traditional communal work groups in the village. See Olupona (2009: xv).

4   For a general survey of AICs, see Allan Anderson (2001); Ogbu Kalu (2009: 22–39, 65–83).
5   The full title of this church is "The Church of Jesus Christ on Earth through the Prophet Simon Kimbangu."
6   In Roman Catholic Liberation Theology this principle is expressed in the phrase "preferential option for the poor."

References

Anderson, Allan H. (2001) *African Reformation: African Initiated Christianity in the 20th Century*, Africa World Press, Trenton, NJ.

Belshaw, Deryke, Calderisi, Robert, and Sugden, Chris (2001) *Faith in Development: Partnership between the World Bank and the Churches of Africa*, World Bank/Regnum Books International, Oxford.

Boahen, A. Adu (1990) *African Perspectives on Colonialism*, Johns Hopkins University Press, Baltimore.

Boesak, Allan (1977) *Farewell to Innocence: A Socio-Ethical Study on Black Theology and Power*, Orbis Books, Maryknoll, NY.

Daneel, Marthinus L. (2001) *African Earthkeepers: Wholistic Interfaith Mission*, Orbis Books, Maryknoll, NY.

Dedji, Valentin (2003) *Reconstruction and Renewal in African Christian Theology*, Acton Publishers, Nairobi.

Ela, Jean-Marc (1988) *My Faith as an African*, Orbis Books, Maryknoll, NY.

Ellis, Stephen and ter Haar, Gerrie (2004) *Worlds of Power: Religious Thought and Political Practice in Africa*, Hurst, London.

Frostin, Per W.E. (1988) *Liberation Theology in Tanzania and South Africa: A First World Interpretation*, Department of Theology, Lund University, Malmo, Sweden.

Gifford, Paul (2004) *Ghana's New Christianity: Pentecostalism in a Globalizing African Economy*, Indiana University Press, Bloomington.

Hettne, Björne (2009) *Thinking about Development*, Zed Books, London.

Iliffe, John (1987) *The African Poor: A History*, Cambridge University Press, Cambridge.

Kä Mana (1992) *Foi Africaine, Crise Africaine et Reconstruction de l'Afrique*, HAHO/CETA (Conférence des Eglises de Toute l'Afrique), Lomé, Togo.

Kalu, Ogbu (2008) *African Pentecostalism: An Introduction*, Oxford University Press, Oxford.

Katongole, Emmanuel (2005) *A Future for Africa: Critical Essays in Christian Social Imagination*, University of Scranton Press, Scranton, PA.

Magesa, Laurenti (1997) *African Religion: The Moral Traditions of Abundant Life*, Orbis Books, Maryknoll, NY.

Maluleke, Tinyiko Sam (2002) The rediscovery of the agency of Africans: An emerging paradigm of post-Cold War and post-apartheid black and African theology, in *African Theology Today*, Emmanuel M. Katongole (ed.), University of Scranton Press, Scranton, PA, pp. 147–169.

Mugambi, J.N.K. (1995) *From Liberation to Reconstruction: African Christian Theology after the Cold War*, East African Educational Publishers, Nairobi.

Mveng, Engelbert (1994) Impoverishment and liberation: A theological approach for Africa and the Third World, in *Paths of African Theology*, R. Gibellini (ed.), Orbis Books, Maryknoll, NY, pp. 144–165.

Nyerere, Julius K. (1973) *Freedom and Development/Uhuru na Maendeleo*, Oxford University Press, Dar es Salaam.

Olupona, Jacob K. (2009) Foreword: Understanding poverty and its alleviation in Africa and the African Diaspora – an interdisciplinary approach, in *Religion and Poverty: Pan-African Perspectives*, Peter J. Paris (ed.), Duke University Press, Durham, NC, pp. ix–xx.

Padwick, Timothy John (2003) Spirit, desire, and the world: Roho churches of Western

Kenya in the era of globalization, PhD dissertation, University of Birmingham.
Pew Forum (2006) Overview: Pentecostalism in Africa, http://www.pewforum.org/Christian/Evangelical-Protestant-Churches/Overview-Pentecostalism-in-Africa.aspx (accessed February 20, 2011).
Rahnema, Majid (2001) Poverty, http://www.pudel.uni-bremen.de/pdf/majid2.pdf (accessed February 20, 2011).
Taiwo, Olufemi (2010) *How Colonialism Preempted Modernity in Africa*, Indiana University Press, Bloomington.
Ter Haar, Gerrie (2009) *How God Became African: African Spirituality and Western Secular Thought*, University of Pennsylvania Press, Philadelphia.
Thomas, Douglas E. (2005) *African Traditional Religion in the Modern World*, McFarland, Jefferson, NC.
UN-HABITAT (2010) *The State of African Cities 2010: Governance, Inequality, and Urban Land Markets*, UN-HABITAT, Nairobi, http://www.unhabitat.org/pmss/listItemDetails.aspx?publicationID=3034 (accessed April 18, 2010).
Villa-Vicencio, Charles (1992) *A Theology of Reconstruction*, Cambridge University Press, Cambridge.

CHAPTER 33
AIDS, Religion, and the Politics of Social Justice in Sub-Saharan Africa

Afe Adogame

From the outbreak of the first major AIDS epidemic in parts of Africa in the 1980s, the pandemic has remained one crisis that has shot the continent into the global limelight. While HIV/AIDS is a global emergency, its epidemiology in sub-Saharan Africa is profound and fundamentally different from the rest of the world. The prevalence rates, the infected and the affected, and the death rates from AIDS vary between African countries, though they are highest in southern and eastern Africa. While figures are mostly speculative estimates and projections, Africa ranks first as a context most heavily affected by HIV/AIDS than any other world region. A one-time Ugandan chief epidemiologist encapsulates the short, devastating history of AIDS in Africa as he enthuses: "It all started as a rumour... Then we found we were dealing with a disease. Then we realised that it was an epidemic. And, now we have accepted it as a tragedy" (Iliffe, 2004: 25).

The epidemic is acknowledged as the foremost development issue facing many African countries and the greatest threat to the survival of its teeming population (World Bank, 2000). The demographic impact of HIV/AIDS is gradually attaining breath-taking proportions, leading to social disruption, systematic slump in growth rates, reduction in life expectancy, and modification of population structures. It is having an adverse impact on fertility rates and mortality patterns, as well as altering the nature and composition of families. Though the risks of contracting HIV are especially high for young people, its impact transcends all strata of society, regardless of age, gender, class, or religion.

The history of HIV/AIDS is rather controversial, in light of the politicization of the AIDS etiology in Africa. Some scholars have situated this historiography within a conspiracy theory, with very compelling narratives of historical and contemporary traits of global exploitation, expropriation, and social injustice. Susan Hunter (2003) weaves

The Wiley Blackwell Companion to Religion and Social Justice, First Edition. Edited by Michael D. Palmer and Stanley M. Burgess.
© 2012 John Wiley & Sons Ltd. Published 2020 by John Wiley & Sons Ltd.

together the history of colonialism in Africa, and demonstrates how a history of the exploitation of developing nations by the West is directly responsible for the spread of disease in developing nations and the AIDS pandemic in Africa. Her striking example of the reluctance of drug companies to provide cheap, affordable medication and vaccines in poor countries is illuminating. Tony Barnett and Alan Whiteside (2002) aptly argue that both prevention and impact mitigation responses have been half-hearted and inadequate. In dealing with the social and economic impacts of HIV/AIDS, they link its growth to national and global inequalities (Irwin et al., 2003).

In the face of this looming crisis, Africa is becoming increasingly vulnerable and thus faces serious challenges in providing sustainable healthcare, antiretroviral treatment, and support to a teeming population of people infected with and affected by HIV-related illnesses. Another challenge is to mitigate the toll of new HIV infections. Coping with the impact of AIDS deaths on orphans, community and national development is crucial. De Cock et al. (2002) caution that a uniform global approach might not be suited to the extreme geographical and epidemiological heterogeneity of the pandemic. They contend that "the emphasis on human rights in HIV/AIDS prevention has reduced the importance of public health and social justice, which offer a framework for preventive efforts in Africa that might be more relevant to people's daily lives and more likely to be effective" (De Cock et al., 2002: 67).

In spite of the common rhetoric on and about AIDS at local/global levels, prevention and impact mitigation responses have been largely sporadic, hypocritical, and inadequate. To date, the scourge seems to have defied any discernible medical therapeusis and curative measures, thus leaving it gradually to erode the fabric of African societies. In the absence of massively expanded prevention, treatment, and care efforts, the AIDS death toll is expected to continue to rise.

It is against this backdrop that the denial and abysmal neglect of, indiscriminate response to, and fractured engagement with HIV/AIDS in local and global domains can be examined as a social justice issue. This essay explores to what extent the politics of engagement and/or indifference by African religions in combating AIDS becomes a matter of social justice. What do the various religions understand as social justice? Do they perceive AIDS as a social justice issue? I shall argue that their engagement, or lack of it, is largely contingent on local/global response trajectories. The fluid attitudes and negotiation patterns of African religious traditions toward AIDs partly mirror perceptions and responses by local/global players such as the United Nations, the World Bank, the World Health Organization (WHO), national governments, nongovernmental organizations (NGOs), faith-based organizations (FBOs), and other stakeholders. I shall briefly highlight this nexus and then explore whether and how practitioners of indigenous African religions and new African Christianities conceptualize AIDs as a social justice issue. First, I briefly review the enigmatic concept of social justice.

Social Justice

There is hardly any universally accepted definition of social justice. In *A Theory of Justice*, John Rawls proposes:

> Each person possesses an inviolability founded on justice that even the welfare of society as a whole cannot override. For this reason justice denies that the loss of freedom for some is made right by a greater good shared by others. (Rawls, 1971: 3)

Social justice is both an ideological and a political construct. Even when meanings are proffered, they are hardly fixed, eternal entities, but are susceptible to change and redefinition over time. In considerations of what social justice stands for, the basic requirement of respecting human responsibility is always presupposed. Social justice has to do with the application of the concept of justice on a social scale. The concept is also employed to describe the movement toward a socially just world. This process in itself appears vague and meaningless, except when located within a specific local context. In each context, the way in which social justice is framed hinges on the concepts of human rights and equality.

The claim to an objective standard of social justice has been widely criticized as utopian and idealistic. While some commentators accept as the basic principle of social justice the idea that all human beings have a right to life, they may disagree with the conclusions that follow from various definitions. Critics of social justice have also rejected the concept as meaningless, religious, self-contradictory, and ideological, believing that to realize any degree of social justice is unfeasible and that the attempt to do so undermines liberty. Friedrich Hayek has leveled one of the most vehement critiques of the concept of social justice:

> There can be no test by which we can discover what is "socially unjust" because there is no subject by which such an injustice can be committed . . . [Social justice] does not belong to the category of error but to that of nonsense, like the term "a moral stone." (Hayek, 1973)

Despite such criticisms, the concept of social justice continues to gain currency within academic or public discourses. In relation to public health and AIDS, De Cock et al. (2002: 67) define social justice as "the fair distribution of society's benefits, burdens, and their consequences, including the benefits and burdens of public health action or lack thereof." Ideally, all people are entitled equally to key ends such as health protection or minimum standards of income. The global reality and enthusiasm for combating AIDS are a far cry from these ideals of social justice. The rest of the essay will explore African religious definitions of, discourses on, and responses to AIDS, partly as a mirror reflection and a direct consequence of global politics on AIDS and social justice.

The Global Politics of AIDS and Social Justice in Relation to Africa

Global dynamics and impact

As the AIDS epidemic enters its fourth decade, the global discourse on and response to the pandemic has evolved through ambivalent trajectories of silence, denial, scepticism, lukewarmness, indifference, abysmal neglect, discrimination, stigmatization, systemic proactivity, and sporadic disease-specific interventions. In fact, HIV/AIDS is one of the few global themes that has received the most profound attention from a plethora of academics, thus resulting in an avalanche of literature within a relatively short time. Ironically, it appears that the "actual talk, writing about it," competing discourses evidenced in the burgeoning literature on AIDS obviously caricature the "actual doing something about it," local–global responses and actions by stakeholders.

In the case of Africa, Gill Seidel (1993) identifies the major discourses on HIV/AIDS (medical, medico-moral, developmental, legal, ethical, and rights discourses of groups living with HIV/AIDS and of African pressure groups) circulating within sub-Saharan Africa and how these distinctive yet overlapping discourses contend for hegemony. He demonstrates how the dominant discourses – medical and medico-moral – have shaped the AIDS agenda. He also subsumes all discourses under two categories: discourses of control and exclusion; and discourses of rights and empowerment. In fact, the dichotomization and prioritization of discourses by stakeholders have much to do with the politics of social justice in Africa.

Recognition of the epidemic in parts of Africa and of the potential for it to spread internationally came in the mid-1980s and led to the first global response: the creation by the WHO of the Special (later the Global) Programme on AIDS (De Cock *et al.*, 2002: 68). In the late 1980s, the language of human rights became part of the discussion around HIV/AIDS (Gostin and Lazzarini, 1997; UNAIDS 2000).

Since 1987, WHO's Global Programme on AIDS has provided support and guidance for AIDS projects in over 150 countries. Nevertheless, WHO was rather slow and skeptical in responding to the HIV/AIDS epidemic in Africa, as it contended that it was not the region's primary healthcare concern (Carael, 2006). In 1985, Halfdan Mahler, WHO's Director-General, said: "AIDS is not spreading like bush fire in Africa. It is malaria and other tropical diseases that are killing millions of children every day." Realizing the statement's inaccuracy, Mahler quickly admitted that "[e]verything is getting worse and worse in AIDS and all of us have been underestimating it, and I in particular" (*Times of Zambia*, September 11, 1985). The WHO Global Programme for the Fight against AIDS was swiftly put into action and aimed at raising $1.5 billion a year by the end of the decade to help in prevention and educational efforts, with priority to Africa (Altman, 1986; Carael, 2006: 33). In 1987, Jonathon Mann, the director of the Global Programme, estimated that between one and several million Africans may already have been infected with HIV (Sabatier, 1987).

Together with five other UN agencies, WHO set up the new joint UN Programme on HIV/AIDS (UNAIDS) in 1995 (WHO Fact Sheet, 1996). The initiative was quickly embroiled with the politics of accessibility of AIDS drugs, negotiating price reductions of patented AIDS drugs to Africa. Practical issues, the weak healthcare infrastructure, and the physical delivery of drugs to remote parts, which were of concern, were often politicized and in some cases polemicized against the backdrop of wider western skepticism regarding the feasibility of rolling out antiretroviral treatment to those living with HIV in Africa. The erroneous perception of patients' inability to adhere to treatment, such as not taking the drugs at the correct time, led in 2001 to infamous remarks by USAID boss Andrew Natsios: "[Africans] do not know what watches and clocks are.

They do not use western means for telling time. They use the sun" (WHO, 2006). Joep Lange, the President of the International AIDS Society, was too optimistic when he said, "If we can get cold Coca Cola and beer to every remote corner of Africa, it should not be impossible to do the same with drugs" (2002).

The inherent politics about the feasibility of providing AIDS drugs to Africa was partly silenced by the so-called "3 by 5" initiative, unveiled by WHO and UNAIDS in 2003. The overtly ambitious program was a global initiative to provide antiretroviral therapy to 3 million people with HIV/AIDS in developing countries by the end of 2005. Although the "3 by 5" target was hardly realized, the campaign managed to ensure a substantial increase in the number of people on treatment in Africa and to raise political support and financial commitment for HIV/AIDS in resource-poor countries. Earlier, in 2001, the Global Fund to Fight AIDS, Tuberculosis and Malaria was created, to finance a scaling up of resources for interventions against all three diseases. Two years later, US President George Bush announced the President's Emergency Plan for AIDS Relief (PEPFAR).

Despite the politics of social (in)justice that envelops them, these global initiatives were augmented by increases in funding by private, national, and international stakeholders. As Jennifer Ruger (2004) notes, together these efforts represent one of the most important trends in global health. The movement for increased funding for HIV/AIDS in developing countries brought attention to the issue and initiated a process of responding to it. Ruger's critique of the process has cogent social justice implications and ramifications. According to her,

> Combating HIV/AIDS in low and middle income countries requires more than prevention and treatment – important as this two pronged strategy is. It requires improving the conditions under which people are free to choose safer life strategies and conditions for themselves and future generations. (Ruger, 2004: 121)

This viewpoint requires people to be empowered to act on their own terms and an appeal to a particular vision of the "good life." It also recognizes the interrelatedness of health and other valuable social ends, such as education, social justice, employment, and civic rights, while also emphasizing the importance of individual agency or freedom.

Ruger (2004) remarks that combating HIV/AIDS in developing countries requires more than disease-specific interventions; it must also include a country's broader development strategies. Earlier, De Cock *et al.* (2002: 67) proposed to demystify HIV/AIDS, address it with adequate resources, and define it as a public health issue rather than as a moral problem. They contended that some approaches to HIV/AIDS are poorly adapted to the crisis in Africa, because the issue has not been defined and addressed as an infectious disease emergency. They asserted:

> How an issue is defined strongly affects how it is addressed. Portrayal of HIV/AIDS against a background of either human rights, poverty, gender, or public health elicits different responses, but the measure of each response must be its ability to curtail the epidemic, and at what social cost. (De Cock *et al.*, 2002: 68–69)

Local impulses and imprints

It is within the purview of these global dynamics that the response trajectories of African governments, NGOs/FBOs, and religious organizations to the AIDS crisis can be better discerned. Iliffe (2004) weaves the historiography of governments' responses to the AIDS crisis through three phases:

1. Phase one involves denial, discrimination, and stigmatization.
2. In the second phase official responses were restricted to the health sector.
3. The third phase was characterized by a multisectorial approach to managing HIV/AIDS.

These phases are not mutually exclusive. The earliest phase, from the mid-1980s, was generally an era in which AIDS was redefined jocularly in public circles as an American Initiative to Discourage Sex – a disease of "white people" and "homosexuals." The decade of the 1980s was mostly characterized by insufficient government responses to AIDS in Africa (Carael, 2006: 31). The capacities and priorities of government focused on immediate economic concerns, war, or political crises at the expense of the looming epidemic.

Nonetheless, some strategies focus on prevention efforts, such as education about sexual behavior, sexual abstinence, faithfulness to one partner (or having fewer partners), or the ABC methodology (abstinence, be faithful, condomize). Some prevention strategies met with opposition from religious authorities, as some Muslim and Christian entrepreneurs found prevention campaigns such as condom promotion difficult to reconcile with their religious teachings. UNAIDS reported:

> The fear of offending powerful religious constituencies ... created gridlock in some national governments, and for good reason. Conservative lobbies have shown that they can obstruct everything from family life and education to condom promotion if they choose. (UNAIDS, 2000)

Many senior politicians were reluctant to admit to a generalized HIV/AIDS epidemic in their countries for fear of creating panic or discouraging tourism. Clearly, this initial indifference and impassivity by religious and political entrepreneurs had social justice implications: people badly in need of compassion, fair consideration, spiritual support, and medical treatment received little if any of these.

The tone and attitude of some politicians changed with time. In 1987, Zambian President Kenneth Kaunda announced to the world that his son, Masuzyo, had died of AIDS. When announcing the death of his son from AIDS in 2005, Nelson Mandela told the BBC: "Let us give publicity to HIV/AIDS and not hide it, because [that is] the only way to make it appear like a normal illness."

The recent phase, from 2000, saw the conscious inauguration of national action committees on AIDS; proliferation of HIV/AIDS emergency and strategic action plans; and partnerships with NGOs, FBOs, PLWHAS, and international bodies such as WHO,

UNAIDS, World Bank, and PEPFAR. Government activities include prevention campaigns adopting the ABC strategy, dispensation of antiretrovirals to PLWHAs at subsidized rates, campaigning for the prevention of mother-to-child HIV transmission, improvement of blood screening procedures, and development of facilities to eradicate HIV transmission via blood transfusion.

The Religious Ferment in AIDS as a Social Justice Discourse

In the ensuing robust, competing discourses on HIV/AIDS in Africa, social science, development, and biomedical scholarship largely ignored and until recently undermined the place of religion – indigenous religions, Christianity, Islam, and religious NGOs/FBOs – as change agents/agencies. In tackling health, illness, and disease, these scholarly perspectives neglected the religious doctrines and faith central to the worldviews and praxis of religious groups, both of which are quintessential for religious groups and individuals affected by HIV/AIDS. In the indigenous religious conceptualization of disease, healing is central to understanding responses and measures to combat HIV/AIDS. Specifically, religious organizations and their developmental roles, or the lack thereof, have assumed significance in an era in which several African societies continue to experience unprecedented socioeconomic crises, political uncertainties, ecological disasters, war, and health crises such as the HIV/AIDS scourge.

While national governments, NGOs, and international agencies have adopted measures to mitigate the impact of the disease, the role and impact of religious groups have not been conspicuous. At the same time, literature on the interconnectedness of religion and HIV/AIDS in Africa is burgeoning (Mahlangu-Ngcobo, 2001; Adeboye, 2007; Adogame, 2007; Prince *et al.*, 2009). In thought and praxis, religious traditions have simultaneously succeeded and failed to address AIDS as a social justice issue. In what follows, I draw instances from perceptions, strategies, and responses of practitioners of indigenous African religions and new expressions of African Christianities.

Indigenous Religious Practitioners as Stakeholders

Consideration of indigenous religious practitioners' conceptualization of AIDS as a social justice issue and of their strategies and roles in combating AIDS in Africa requires a caveat. Africa is socially and culturally fragmented, to the extent that generalizations on social justice might simply be speculative. Alyward Shorter notes:

> While there is no single concept of social justice which can be called universally African, there are a number of differing experiences which have a relatively wide currency. These experiences relate to different social levels: the family, community and the political structure; and to the different styles of life dictated by the various environments and cultural traditions. (Shorter, 1977: 1)

In spite of the plurality that prevails in Africa, it is possible to discern certain affinities and regularities. Thus, the burden of exploring the concept of social justice in Africa lies in its complex historical and cultural heterogeneity. This fact may be relevant for unearthing indigenous religious responses to HIV/AIDS. A certain novelty is discerned when indigenous societies, whose epistemologies and indigenous vocabularies have no space for AIDS, simply delineate it as "a strange disease without a name."

The experiences of society as clearly bounded groups strongly outweigh the experience of ego-centered networks of personal relationships. In such situations, the stability and continued existence of the group are much more important considerations than the rights of the individual.

> Social justice in traditional Africa, was also intended to contribute to social stability, and harmonious relationships within the ethnic group, and the lesser groupings of which it was composed. The expectations of the individual were largely dictated by structures, relationship patterns and roles. Social justice, therefore, implied conformity to these things. (Shorter 1977: 2)

The quest for social well-being is founded on the equilibrium of good relationship and trust between the individual, community, and supersensible cosmos, vertically and horizontally. Social well-being is understood in terms of social justice, by which the community flourishes through the benevolence of spiritual entities. The absence of social justice angers the benevolent spiritual forces, which bring epidemics and natural disasters to the community. The search for the "good life" is imbued with concerns to achieve a socially just society. However, such spiritual etiologies of AIDS must coexist with social ecologies and other determinants of the epidemic as social phenomena.

The pursuit, attainment, and retention of social cohesion, social justice, and cosmic equilibrium loom large in African religious worldviews. The negotiation of these socioreligious ideals privileges religious specialists as arbiters in the intricate interactions between the spiritual and mundane worlds and entities. Indigenous healers, diviners, shrine priests, medicine-men, spirit mediums, and other functionaries serve as spiritual reservoirs of the local communities in which they are located.

> African traditional healers mirror the great variety of cultures and belief systems existing on the continent, and possess equally heterogeneous experience, training and educational backgrounds. (King and Homsy, 1997: S218)

When a crisis or calamity, such as spiritual, health, psychological, or natural disaster, is impending or strikes, the onus lies on these human–spiritual agencies to proffer and provide ritual remedies, prevention, cure, and healing for individuals, communities, and groups in order to recoup social cohesion, justice, and cosmic harmony. Indigenous health providers are often (though not always) motivated by concerns to ensure and maintain a socially just society.

Traditional healers are well known within the local communities where they work for their expertise in treating many sexually transmitted diseases (STDs) and AIDS (Green, 1994; UNAIDS, 2002; Amzat and Abdullahi, 2008). Sexually transmitted infections (STIs) often lead people to visit traditional healers in South Africa (Peltzer *et al.*, 2006). By a large majority, they remain the preferred and universally accessible care providers in Africa (King and Homsy, 1997, S223).

> Traditional healers have remarkable knowledge about HIV symptoms, causes, transmission routes and their own prevention and curative methods. The operational plan for comprehensive HIV and AIDS care, management and treatment for South Africa recognizes the role and function of traditional healers in the continuum of care, compliance, adherence, adverse event reporting, referral system and ensuring safe traditional health practices. (Department of Health, 2004)

Most healers have treated STD for generations, but their explanations of STD and AIDS vary considerably with regard to the nature, causes, and modes of transmission of these diseases.

However, the concepts underlying these explanations appear remarkably similar across national/cultural boundaries (King and Homsy, 1997: S218).

> Beliefs related to the prevention of STD or AIDS follow the logic of transmission and causation, and therefore include limiting the number of sexual partners, wearing protective charms or tattoos, having "strong blood", using condoms to reduce the risk of pollution or undergoing a "traditional vaccination" consisting of introducing herbs in skin incisions.
>   The wide use of traditional medicine in developing countries in Africa is mostly attributable to its accessibility, acceptability, and affordability. (Amzat and Abdullahi, 2008: 156)

The individual and collective initiatives by indigenous healers and diviners toward tackling and combating STD/AIDS were and continue to be largely contested and rebuffed by biomedical practitioners, media vendors, global health players, policy makers, NGOs, and other stakeholders. Traditional health personnel and their medical recipes were often demonized as primitive, retrogressive, and unhealthy. Considerable prejudice remains ingrained among western health practitioners about the justification, validity, and integrity of traditional medical practices (King and Homsy, 1997: S217). This rejection and stigmatization of traditional health personnel are a form of social injustice in what should be a collective quest for a panacea to the AIDS epidemic. Africans become estranged from a holistic health agency and praxis that are very much ingrained in their cosmologies.

Undoubtedly, and ironically, it is primarily because of the unprecedented shock that AIDS dealt to the developed world and to modern medicine that a renewed interest has emerged in supporting collaborations with traditional healers in the hope of finding new, more effective ways to fight and prevent this disease. In several African countries, advocacy for traditional medicine and attempts to involve healers in primary healthcare predate the newer resolve in the face of the AIDS epidemic (King and Homsy, 1997: S222; Amzat and Abdullahi, 2008: 153–154). New initiatives spurred collaboration between traditional healers and biomedical practitioners for HIV/AIDS protection, prevention, and care. Experiences and research results indicate that modern and traditional belief systems are neither incompatible nor mutually exclusive, but rather complementary (King and Homsy, 1997; UNAIDS, 2002). As King and Homsy note,

> the bridge between alternative and biomedical health care is generally built by the client rather than the provider, as has been the case for AIDS. The multiple use of different

medical systems by AIDS patients, whether symptomatic or not, has forced the interest of the biomedical sector in potentially valid alternatives. (King and Homsy, 1997: S223)

Initially, several projects attempted to assess the value of traditional herbal remedies for the treatment of illnesses associated with AIDS (King and Homsy, 1997: S217). As Amzat and Abdullahi observe, "In the light of the problems associated with the modern health care delivery system, non-governmental institutions have intensified efforts in seeing the role of the traditional healers in the areas of HIV prevention and treatment" (Amzat and Abdullahi, 2008: 156). The most important milestone in support and interest in research and development in traditional medicine and HIV/AIDS was the establishment of an East and Southern Africa Regional Task Force on Traditional Medicine and HIV/AIDS (Gemma et al., 2000).

The WHO has advocated the inclusion of traditional healers in national AIDS programmes since the early 1990s (UNAIDS, 2000).

> WHO recommendations are based on the premise shared by many researchers that, as a highly respected, widely distributed and often consulted group of health practitioners, recognized traditional healers have the cultural knowledge and skills to make an impact on disease prevention, health promotion and care including AIDS. Indeed, the African healer is often consulted as a marriage counselor, social worker, religious and spiritual guide, and legal and political advisor. (King and Homsy, 1997: S217). In 2002, the WHO launched its first comprehensive traditional medicine strategy to assist efforts to promote affordable, effective, and safe use of traditional medicine and complementary alternative medicine (UNAIDS, 2002).

These collaborative initiatives are hardly homespun and may not have emanated from the traditional healers themselves, but were driven primarily by western health entrepreneurs and agencies. Traditional health personnel are not motivated by any underlying plan or theoretical concern; their resilience as the preferred and most accessible care providers has social justice implications for Africa. The participation of indigenous healers in projects encourages them to empower and provide emotional support to clients living with HIV/AIDS. They generally contribute to ensuring social stability. However, they also sometimes promote instability, such as when charlatans posing as healers may instill awe and fear in AIDS victims, actions that further stigmatize indigenous healers as witches.

I shall now examine whether and how versions of African Christianities define AIDS as a social justice issue; and explore their strategies and methodology for combating AIDS.

Engaging Christianities in HIV/AIDS and Social Justice Discourses

The diverseness of African Christianities makes generalizations about their engagement with AIDS suspect. Responses, or the lack thereof, to HIV/AIDS will vary based on institutional stature, doctrinal emphases, mission goals, operational strategies, and civic/social roles. Social justice is implied in the ways in which some churches (whether as a matter of purposeful social strategy or for other reasons) engage AIDS, while others do not. I will highlight some general religious attempts at dealing with AIDS on a comparative basis, but will also focus on a specific example to tease out how a Pentecostal Christian church thinks about and combats HIV/AIDS.

Ruth Prince et al. (2009) explore ways in which Christianity is becoming a very influential factor in the engagement of AIDS in some African countries. They offer insight on the interrelationships of Christianity, AIDS, and society through three themes: ways people deal with illness and death, treatment and care for the sick, and questions of morality, kinship, gender relations, and sexuality; the place of religion in the public sphere, in relation to civil society and government, development, and public health; and transformations within Christian practices and worldviews in Africa (Prince et al., 2009: v). They failed, however, to unravel how Christianity seems to have negated principles of social justice with its previous indifference to and stigmatization of those infected and affected by AIDS.

Earlier, Adeboye (2007) illustrated religious NGO/FBOs' commitment to the prevention and management of the epidemic, and demonstrated how their response to HIV/AIDS has been more spontaneous than that of national governments. She remarks that the churches' current response was preceded by denial, which transformed to stigmatization and later softened to concern. As Adeboye notes, the change of perception resulted from three primary factors: realization that the epidemic has gained inroads into the church; the campaign by governments and NGOs against stigmatization; and media criticism of churches' lukewarm response and attitude toward those infected with HIV.

Christian intervention came from church congregations, FBOs, and faith-based NGOs. Adeboye (2007) outlines three main strategies: prevention campaigns; treatment and care; and mitigation of impact. The first involves reducing stigma and breaking silence, generating awareness, and promoting behavioral change. Treatment and care involve voluntary counseling and testing; post-test counseling and pastoral care; medical care and treatment; and promotion of mental health and restoration of hope to PLWHAs. The last strategy involves developing techniques to mitigate the impact of AIDS: caring for widows; establishing orphanages; providing nutritional assistance (food donations), counseling, and free medical treatment for children and their caregivers; and combating poverty. All of these initiatives have been given prominence by and within different religious and faith-based constituencies in Africa. They indicate how some churches in Africa are now, more than ever, motivated by conscious planning to achieve a socially just outcome in combating AIDS.

Adogame (2007) explores how African-led Pentecostal churches such as the Redeemed Christian Church of God (RCCG) contextualize HIV/AIDS, cope with the epidemic, and join other stakeholders in combating the pandemic. RCCG exemplifies how indigenous churches have spread globally from Nigeria to over 75 countries within Africa, North America, Europe, Asia, Australia, and Middle East.

Indigenous religious epistemologies make sense in African-Pentecostal ritual sensibilities. Basically, they share a similar mentality in their belief tradition, employing an indigenous hermeneutic of spiritual power, but casting it within new conceptual frames of reference. Metaphorically, the RCCG refers to HIV/AIDS as a demonic spirit and those afflicted by the illness as victims of spiritual demonic attack. Their conceptualization of disease and healing is quintessential in grasping the combined strategies adopted in coping with HIV/AIDS. Such understandings of disease and healing are located within wider realms of personhood, society, life, and thought. Healing takes on a holistic modality encompassing the physical, psychological, spiritual, mental, emotional, and material dimensions.

The quest for spiritual fervor led to the personification of certain illnesses as the outright manifestation of the devil. There are frequent references to spirits of disease, illness, HIV/AIDS, barrenness, death, and poverty. RCCG's liturgical tradition involves highly expressive actions characterized by a heavy dose of rituals to resolve existential problems. Rituals are packaged to handle spiritual attacks such as sickness, HIV/AIDS, and virtually all life's vicissitudes. Ritual practices have an overt connection to ensuring social justice, although certain ritual enactments may raise questions of social injustice.

RCCG adopted a useful medium for "breaking the silence" on HIV/AIDS. They engage theotherapy (spiritual healing), providing spiritual succor, moral advocacy activities, and medical help with the provision of drugs, facilities, and funds to the infected and the affected. African Missions (AM) was initiated in 1996 to "support the RCCG in reaching its vision for Africa in fulfillment of its end time mission of saving souls, particularly the oppressed and under-privileged . . . to educate and reduce the spread of the AIDS epidemic in many African countries." AM has expanded its activities to Europe and the United States, and launched projects to raise awareness and financial assistance for AIDS victims in Africa. In 2003, AM North America in collaboration with CitiHope International donated HIV/AIDS drugs valued at $1.5 million to Nigeria for use in treating HIV/AIDS-related complications (Adogame, 2007: 480).

As part of an underlying strategy toward achieving a socially just outcome, RCCG operates an office, the Redeemed AIDS Programme Action Committee (RAPAC), to deal with HIV/AIDS from both spiritual and medical angles. RAPAC is a religious NGO that defines itself as "an FBO with primary focus on creating awareness, educating on prevention, provision of spiritual support and counselling for People Living with HIV/AIDS, People Affected by AIDS (PABA)." RAPAC also promotes sex education and reproductive health programs for youths/adults through training to improve the quality of life within the church by the provision of spiritual support and counseling for PABA.

RCCG's strategies have been both precautionary and therapeutic, utilizing both spiritual and medical means. On the spiritual level, HIV/AIDS becomes personified as one of several demonic spirits that populate the cosmos and that is dealt with through theotherapy or spiritual healing. On a more pragmatic level, RCCG has launched other programs to combat AIDS. Funds have been generated locally and internationally for procuring AIDS-related drugs. It evolves programs that engage young people in AIDS prevention and encourage creative activities that divert young people away from practices that lead to acquiring the HIV virus. In this way, RCCG's public role becomes visible and its extra-religious functions complementary in social contexts where efforts by local and international agencies have proved insufficient to combat the spread and impact of HIV/AIDS. RCCG initiatives can thus be considered as strategies of social justice in the collective quest to combat HIV/AIDS.

Conclusion

The nexus between AIDS, religion, and social justice is an intricate one, although the religion matrix has been relatively marginal in AIDS discourses, scholarship, and social activism in most African countries. The epidemic is simultaneously a social justice, human rights, public health, and political issue that deserves thoughtful and committed responses. Equity and social justice are of paramount concern in responding to the HIV/AIDS pandemic. There is an urgency to tackle the sociopolitical, economic inequities that drive the epidemic and restrict access to information, treatment, and care. Local and global players share accountability in the face of overwhelming social and economic inequalities and disparities. An important element in negotiating AIDS is the prevention of new HIV infections. Stakeholders can be proactive, dealing with structural conditions of the epidemic that would prevent achieving satisfactory results for HIV infected and affected persons. For example, successful HIV prevention campaigns within African countries need to be highlighted and repeated. Another challenge is to provide treatment and care that will allow people living with HIV to live longer and healthier lives. Tackling the AIDS crisis in Africa is a long-term task that requires sustained effort and planning – both within Africa and across the global community.

This essay has highlighted how religious groups in Africa may provide moral leadership, social capital, and institutional resources dedicated to social justice and equality. The social-religious aspects of the epidemic are as important as the biomedical ones. Religious beliefs, attitudes, and practice can either enhance or stifle the pursuit of social justice.

References

Adeboye, O. (2007) *Dispensing Spiritual Capital: Faith-Based Response to the HIV/AIDS Epidemic in Nigeria*, Faculty of Arts, University of Lagos, Lagos.

Adogame, A. (2007) HIV/AIDS support and African Pentecostalism: The case of the Redeemed Christian Church of God, *Journal of Health Psychology* 12(3): 475–484.

Altman, Lawrence K. (1986) Global program aims to combat AIDS "disaster." *New York Times*, November 21.

Amzat, J. and Abdullahi, A.A. (2008) Roles of traditional healers in the fight against HIV/AIDS, *Ethno-Med* 2(2): 153–159.

Barnett, T. and Whiteside, A. (2002) *AIDS in the Twenty-first Century: Disease and Globalization*, Palgrave Macmillan, New York.

Carael, M. (2006) Twenty years of intervention and controversy, in *The HIV/AIDS Epidemic in Sub-Saharan Africa in a Historical Perspective*, Philippe Denis and Charles Becker (eds.), Academia-Bruylant, Louvain-la-Neuve, http://www.refer.sn/rds/IMG/pdf/01TITRE.pdf (accessed April 19, 2011).

De Cock, K.M., Mbori-Ngacha, D., and Marum, E. (2002) Shadow on the continent: Public health and HIV/AIDS in Africa in the 21st century, AIDS in Africa V, *The Lancet* 359 (June 8): 67–72.

Department of Health (South Africa) (2004) *Operational Plan for Comprehensive HIV and AIDS Care, Management and Treatment for South Africa*, Department of Health, Pretoria.

Gemma, B., Gerard, B., Donna, K., Barbara, G., and Ernet, R. (2000) Traditional medicine and HIV/AIDS in Africa: A report from the International Medicine and Local Communities in Africa, Conference of the Parties to the Convention on Biological Diversity, Nairobi, Kenya.

Green, E. (1994) *AIDS and STDs in Africa: Bridging the Gap between Traditional Healers and Modern Medicine*, Westview Press, Boulder, CO.

Gostin, L.O. and Lazzarini, Z. (1997) *Human Rights and Public Health in the AIDS Pandemic*, Oxford University Press, New York.

Hayek, F.A. (1973) *Law, Legislation and Liberty: The Mirage of Social Justice, Vol. 2*, Routledge, London.

Hunter, S. (2003) *Black Death: AIDS in Africa*, Palgrave Macmillan, New York.

Iliffe, J. (2004) *A History of the African AIDS Epidemic*, James Currey, Oxford.

Irwin, A., Millen, J., and Fallows, D. (2003) *Global AIDS: Myths and Facts – Tools for Fighting the AIDS Pandemic*, South End Press, Cambridge.

King, R. and Homsy, J. (1997) Involving traditional healers in AIDS education and counselling in sub-Saharan Africa: A review, *AIDS* 11(Suppl. A): S217–225.

Lange, Joep (2002) Speech by the President of the International AIDS Society. XIV International AIDS Conference, Closing Ceremony, Barcelona July 12.

Mahlangu-Ngcobo, M. (2001) *AIDS in Africa: An African and Prophetic Perspective*, Gateway Press, Baltimore, MD.

Peltzer, K., Mngqundaniso, N., and Petros, G. (2006) HIV/AIDS/STI/TB knowledge, beliefs and practices of traditional healers in KwaZulu-Natal, South Africa, *AIDS Care* 18(6): 608–613.

Prince, R., Denis, P., and van Dijk, R. (eds.) (2009) Special issue: Christianity and HIV/AIDS in East and Southern Africa, *Africa Today* 56(1).

Rawls, J. (1971) *A Theory of Justice*, Belknap Press, Cambridge, MA.

Ruger, J.P. (2004) Combating HIV/AIDS in developing countries, *British Medical Journal* 329: 121–122.

Sabatier, R. (1987) AIDS in the developing world, *International Family Planning Perspectives* 13(3): 96–103.

Seidel, G. (1993) The competing discourses of HIV/AIDS in sub-Saharan Africa: Discourses of rights and empowerment vs. discourses of control and exclusion, *Social Science and Medicine* 36(3): 175–194.

Shorter, A. (1977) Concepts of social justice in traditional Africa, *Pro Dialogo Bulletin* 12: 32–51.

UNAIDS (2000) *Collaboration with Traditional Healers in HIV/AIDS Prevention and Care in Sub-Saharan Africa: A Literature Review*, UNAIDS Best Practice Collection, Geneva.

UNAIDS (2002) *Ancient Remedies, New Disease: Increasing Access to AIDS Prevention and Care in Collaboration with Traditional Healers*, UNAIDS Best Practice Collection, Geneva.

World Bank (2000) *Intensifying Action against HIV/AIDS in Africa: Responding to a Development Crisis*, World Bank, Washington, DC.

World Health Organization (2006) Global access to HIV therapy tripled in past two years, but significant challenges remain, http://www.who.int/mediacentre/news/releases/2006/pr13/en/index.html (accessed April 19, 2011).

Bibliography

McNeil, Donald G., Jr. (2000) Companies to cut cost of AIDS drugs for poor nations, *New York Times*, May 12.

CHAPTER 34
Religion, Civil Rights, and Social Justice

Paul Harvey

From the colonization of the Americas to the twentieth century, race and religion were joined in the project of civilization and subjugation. Christianizing others involved civilizing them. Sometimes this involved brutally stripping colonial subjects, especially enslaved Africans and Native Americans, of the garments of their own civilizations, including language, religious belief, and cultural practice. At other times, the joining of Christianization and civilization underwrote idealistic crusades of bringing formerly enslaved peoples into American civilization, as in the abolitionist movement and, later, in the creation of black schools and colleges during Reconstruction. In other instances, the intertwining of Christianity, civilization, and whiteness justified the complete exclusion of peoples from the American Republic.

Yet if the dominant form of religion in America – Christianity, especially Protestantism – has fostered the racialization and subjugation of peoples, it also has undermined this legacy of oppression, largely through a reenvisioning of the Christian tradition empowered by the ideas of the subjugated and their allies. Christian myths and stories were central to the project of creating racial categories in the modern world. But the central text of Christianity, the Bible, was also amenable to more universalist visions, and in that sense could never be a fully reliable ally for theorists of racial hierarchy. Social injustice in American history was created in part through a religious rhetoric of possession and subjugation; social justice in American history came about in part through a reimagining of that same tradition to encompass notions of human equality, civil rights, and social justice.

The transformation of religious thought and practice from subjugator to liberator has been one of the most dramatic stories of American history. That transformation came about largely through a deconstruction and then reconstruction of religious texts by those who historically had been oppressed by them. This essay will focus especially on the role of African American Christianity in that transformation.

The Wiley Blackwell Companion to Religion and Social Justice, First Edition. Edited by Michael D. Palmer and Stanley M. Burgess.
© 2012 John Wiley & Sons Ltd. Published 2020 by John Wiley & Sons Ltd.

In the twentieth century, especially in the civil rights movement of mid-century, Christian thought helped to undermine the white supremacist racial system that had governed America for centuries. Black Christians, who formed the rank and file of the civil rights movement, demolished the political structures of segregation, and with them some of the folklore of blackness as inferiority that had enslaved so many Americans for so many centuries. In the 1950s and 1960s, black civil rights activists in groups such as the Congress of Racial Equality, the Southern Christian Leadership Conference, and the Student Nonviolent Coordinating Committee emerged from black churches and finally penetrated the walls of segregation, still guarded by conservative white churchmen and opportunistic politicians. The civil rights revolution in American history was, to a considerable degree, a religious revolution, one whose social and spiritual impact inspired numerous other movements around the world.

Colonial and Antebellum Era

Getting from the religious justification for conquering lands, dispossessing peoples, and enslaving "others" to the religious roots of social justice and civil rights was a centuries-long saga. One sees some of the earliest roots of this saga in eighteenth-century Virginia. There, Anglican missionaries complained that planters resisted slave Christianization because, as one put it, "it often makes them [slaves] proud, and not so good servants." There were substantial reasons for this suspicion, for Christianized slaves sued for freedom and pointed out the contradiction of Christianity and slaveholding. In one case in 1723, a group of Christian slaves, of mixed-race parentage, pled their case for freedom in a letter to a newly installed bishop who oversaw Anglican affairs in the colonies. They were, they wrote, "Baptised and brouaht up in a way of the Christian faith and followes the wayes and Rulles of the chrch of England." They complained about laws "which keeps and makes them and there seed Slaves forever." The hardness of their masters kept them from following the Sabbath: "wee doo hardly know when it comes for our task mastrs are has hard with us as the Egyptians was with the Chilldann of Issarall." Their letter concluded with an explanation of why they did not sign their names, "for freare of our masters for if they knew that wee have Sent home to your honour wee Should goo neare to Swing upon the Gallass [gallows] tree." These slaves retained an older, more radical view of Christian conversion: their religious status gave them rights to freedom and respect, for which they were willing to fight. They spoke the language of power precisely because they knew the language of power – in courtrooms, in letters to imperial officials, and, as a last resort, in rebellions (Ingersoll, 1994: 780).

In the mid-eighteenth century, the nascent antislavery movement largely was confined to religious radicals, especially Quakers, and various fringe groups. By the time of the Declaration of Independence and the struggle for independence, it was clear that America was to be a white man's country. Civil rights would be nonexistent for Indians and the enslaved, and tenuous at best for a small free black population. And yet, the religious roots of social justice movements already were evident, even if largely underground. Fledgling evangelical antislavery movements resulted in manumissions in parts of the South, and a rejection of slaveholding as an institution in parts of the North. Yet civil rights remained a distant dream for nonwhites, and even white allies of Indians and slaves typically held few notions of incorporating them fully into the American Republic.

In the first part of the nineteenth century, an era dubbed the "democratization of American Christianity" (Hatch, 1989), democratic politics and the rapid rise of populist Christian sects created a new context for American ideas of freedom, a kind of Methodist millennium. From the underside of that millennium, however, American ideas of freedom promised universalist visions, but delivered a republic based on universalist premises, although in practice racially exclusivist and white supremacist. That paradox lay at the heart of Native and African American thought and practice. Just as the Declaration of Independence became a touchstone for African American thought, both as a positive and a negative reference point, and as white idealists and missionaries took their Christianity to Indian tribes whom they defended against governmentally imposed removal and repression schemes, the universalist language of democratic Christianity provided a base for alternative visions of a pluralist Republic that respected the civil rights of all.

Antebellum northern black thinkers in particular enthusiastically participated in the rhetoric, language, and concepts of their place and time, including ideas of America's chosen mission. At the same time, nationalism fused with religio-messianic ideals increasingly informed black thought as the antebellum era progressed. Enlightenment universalism and black nationalism often merged, for both spoke to profound and deep aspirations of African Americans as a people, and both as well were consonant with Afro-American religious traditions. Forms of rhetoric often understood to be antithetical, or competing brands of black thought, merged into each other. One the one hand, African American writers and orators repeated many of the same phrases about the divinely appointed destiny of America as did their white contemporaries. This did not mean that they spared America from biting critiques for its racist oppression, but that they saw the true American ideals as within the ultimate design of God. Black thinkers and writers trusted in God's providence, but warned Americans of their ultimate fate for ignoring the course of history. As the fiery free black antislavery writer David Walker put it in his cri de coeur *Appeal of the Colored Peoples of the World*, "Unless you speedily alter your course, *you* and your *Country are gone!!!!!* For God Almighty will tear up the very face of the earth!!!" (Newman *et al.*, 2001: 271).

While the monumental figure of Frederick Douglass consistently articulated universalist ideals of black integration into the American republic and resistance to all forms of separatism or colonization, black nationalists such as the well-known antebellum black ministers Henry Highland Garnet and Martin Delany pressed the case for resistance and separate black institutions. Their debate in the antebellum era forecast long-lived controversies among African Americans who were in, but evidently never could be of, the American Republic. As Delany put it, the "determined aim of the whites" was to "crush the colored races wherever found," with the Anglo-Saxon taking the lead in "this work of universal subjugation" (Newman *et al.*, 2001: 235). Delany and others came from a generation as inspired by the possibilities of the spread of civilization worldwide as they were resistant to American racism. Their answer was a sort of intellectualized form of what became a mass movement in the twentieth century with the advent of Marcus Garvey and the African Orthodox Church. Delany and Alexander Crummell were two of the best-known spokesmen for black nationalist thought in the nineteenth century. Both placed African Americans within the movement of history – not as a people without history, as Hegel said of Africa, but as a people who would carry history forward on their shoulders. Twentieth-century black prophets and thinkers, from W.E.B. DuBois to Elijah Muhammad, Malcolm X, and James Cone, carried forward diverse varieties of black nationalism that arose from this nineteenth-century context (Blum, 2007).

After Freedom

After the Civil War, newly organized black churches and independent black denominations, freed from the constraints of slavery, organized vigorously among the freed people. Through this era, African Americans expressed a "divine discontent" with a republic that remained beholden to white supremacy, thus betraying the egalitarian promises of the Declaration of Independence, of the Protestantism that dominated the national religious culture, and of the black men who had fought for the Union during the Civil War.

Since the King years, as historian Taylor Branch refers to the period from the Montgomery bus boycott of 1955–1956 to the Selma march (in Alabama) of 1965, black churches and ministers have stood as iconic emblems of the civil rights struggle. And black church leaders have cultivated that view of their own history, for it is a narrative that places black churches at the center of one of the most important moments of American history. And it was church activists – most visibly Martin Luther King, Jr., but also black Baptist leaders such as Fred Shuttlesworth, John Lewis, and Fannie Lou Hamer – who infused the struggle with their religious passion and steely commitment. This view is captured best by Vincent Harding's *There Is a River*, a work that places the beginnings of the civil rights movement with rebellions aboard slave ships and moves forward from there. In this telling, activism in freedom struggles moved like a river current through black history. The recent historiographical move to stress the "long history of the civil rights movement" follows that river current through the longue durée of black history, part of a larger project to reperiodize our concept of the civil rights movement away from the "Montgomery to Memphis" paradigm (Harding, 1993; Hall, 2005).

Activists in the 1960s held a more chastened view, and others looking for church leadership against segregationism also ran into historical obstacles. If Vincent Harding's *There Is a River* traced an unbroken stream of black religious activism and radicalism from the earliest days of slavery through to the civil rights movement, Gayraud Wilmore's *Black Religion and Black Radicalism* showed the disjunctures in this history. For Wilmore, black religion through the Civil War and Reconstruction era provided both consolation for suffering slaves but also power for those seeking to break the shackles of bondage. The central role of black churches during Reconstruction, moreover, showed how the subterranean power of African American religious practices in the invisible institution could become visible and very public when African Americans were given the opportunity for a public life.

Nowhere was this more the case than in the low country of Georgia in January 1865, when Baptist minister Garrison Frazier led a delegation of black Georgians in a colloquy with General William Tecumseh Sherman and Oliver O. Howard, soon to be head of the Freedmen's Bureau. In January of 1865, African American ministers from Savannah and the Georgia low country advised Union war officers on assisting the refugees set free by Sherman's march. Longtime Baptist pastor Garrison Frazier counseled federal officials that "the way we can best take care of ourselves is to have land and turn it and till it by our own labor . . . and we can soon maintain ourselves and have something to spare." Frazier also expressed a decided preference to "live by ourselves" rather than "scattered among the whites," over the objections of the Methodist James B. Lynch, who took the view that ex-slaves and southern whites "should not be separated." Sherman set aside for black war refugees lands in the Georgia and South Carolina low country and Sea Islands, a decision soon transformed in the prevailing folklore ("forty acres and a mule") as a governmental promise to provide land for the freed people (Billingsley, 1998: 30–34; Hahn, 2003: 145). Throughout the South, black religious leaders followed Houston's lead, actively shaping African American life under freedom, and realizing the implicit social power of the newly visible black church.

Scholarship on Reconstruction emphasizes the power of the black church; scholarship focusing on the Jim Crow era has tended to emphasize its impotence, highlighting instead the "constricted social spaces" described by scholar Curtis Evans (Evans, 2008). Scholars searching for an activist tradition in black church politics hardly could hide their dismay at the role of the church during the long and dismal interregnum between the demise of Reconstruction and the advent of the civil rights movement. What was the role of the church in the rural South during Jim Crow? For many students of the subject, it appeared to be little, at least measured by the standards of public activism during Reconstruction. Black religious practices appeared to be "compensatory," allowing for emotional enthusiasms that "compensated" for the lack of any real social agency in this world. Black religion had been depoliticized or "deradicalized" (Wilmore, 1998). *The Negro's God*, to quote the title of Benjamin Mays's study of the subject, seemed to be a psychic projection of a fantasy from another world, an alternative universe in which black southerners could exercise some control over their own lives (Mays, 1969[1938]). Allowed to worship such a God on Sundays, the Negro then returned to his labors the next morning, with spiritual consolation to withstand another week of humiliation.

Historically, the religion of southern folk appeared to be apolitical. Critics called it "otherworldy" or "compensatory," and to some extent doubtless it was. But W.E.B. DuBois pointed out that while religion might be seen as "mere symbolism," to the freed people "God was real. They knew him. They had met Him personally in many a wild orgy of religious frenzy or in the black stillness of the night" (DuBois, 1935: 124). As a scholar and social scientist, DuBois was often critical of the black church as an institution for its increasing insularity, its focus in the twentieth century on internal growth and power politicking, and its inability before the civil rights movement to utilize its enormous resources effectively on behalf of African American people (Blum, 2007).

At the same time, however, DuBois as a poet and sensitive essayist understood the kind of powerful work going on in the rituals and the ostensibly "otherworldly" preaching emanating from black pulpits.

As DuBois's work suggests, the implicit potential of southern folk religion – what contemporary scholars might call the "hidden transcript" contained in religious behavior – bears close scrutiny. The historian Robin D.G. Kelley has argued:

> we need to recognize that the sacred and the spirit world were also often understood and invoked by African Americans as weapons to protect themselves or to attack others . . . Can a sign from above, a conversation with a ghost, a spell cast by an enemy, or talking in tongues unveil the hidden transcript? (Kelley, 1993: 88)

To Kelly's question one might add, can one's private and communal prayer when facing down racist sheriffs, voting registrars, or snakes thrown on one's front porch embolden resistance and serve as the antidote to the opiate of the people fed by Jim Crow's spokesmen? In Mississippi and Alabama and other places in the 1950s and 1960s, the "hidden transcript" came to the surface (Kelley 1993).

Black Christians had a history to which they could appeal, especially the history of black religio-political activism in the era of Reconstruction. But black Christians in America also had a complex history, one in which constricted social spaces restricted social activism. To borrow Harding's imagery, the river sometimes flowed in a torrent, and sometimes – very often, in fact – was dammed up by the powerful forces of white supremacy and by the divisive internal politicking that substituted for power struggles that would matter in the larger world. The historical relationship between religion, civil rights, and social justice was thus a complicated one.

Religion and African American Civil Rights in the Twentieth Century

It is sometimes said that the civil rights movement of the mid-twentieth century, from the Second World War through the 1960s, emerged from "the black church," a falsely singular term for what was in fact a multifarious set of beliefs and institutions. Historians cite evidence such as the number of ministers in the struggle and churches that served as gathering points for mass meetings. At the same time, movement leaders constantly contended with the fact that "the black church" actually was not, by and large, behind the movement. Whether because of indifference, fear, theological conservatism, or coercion and terrorism, many congregations simply avoided involvement. Thus, the relationship between religion, race, and rights during the 1960s is considerably more complicated than often portrayed, particularly in the recent deification and consequent oversimplification of Martin Luther King's life and work. Still, a movement based on secular ends – the extension of citizenship rights in the American nation-state – drew its sustenance from spiritual understandings, language, and motivations. It was a fundamentally Protestant imagery – of Exodus, redemption, salvation – that inspired the revivalistic fervor of the movement. And it was ministers and church activists who lent their moral passion and steely commitment to the quest for freedom.

Leaders of the freedom struggle knew first hand of the numerous congregations that closed their doors to movement meetings. "The preachers, number one, they didn't have nothing to do with it," two local activists recalled of the movement in Mississippi. "Teachers number two, they didn't have nothing to do with it. Until things got when they could tell they wasn't gon' kill 'em, and then they went to comin' in." In Holmes County, a Mississippi civil rights worker reported, "we got turned down a lot of times from the black minister . . . He mostly was afraid because they [whites] whooped a few of 'em and bombed a few churches. The preacher didn't want his church burned down, and them old members was right along in his corner" (McLeod, 1991: 54). There was good reason, of course, for this fear. In the early summer of 1964, 41 black churches in Mississippi, of various denominations and geographical locations, went up in flames. The long-time South Carolina NAACP organizer Septima Clark understood that the tenure of local black ministers often depended on the approval of whites. Even with their congregations' support, they could be "run out of town if the white power structure decided they ought to go." Ministers who shied away from involvement were not necessarily opposed to the movement but might have been "just afraid to join it openly. It's simply a contradiction: so many preachers support the Movement that we can say it was based in churches, yet many preachers couldn't take sides with it because they thought they had too much to lose" (Harris, 1999: 88).

Still, in spite of the fear, coercion, and terrorism instilled through the structures of the history of American racism and the practices of the segregated South, black Christians who formed the rank and file of the civil rights movement managed to demolish the political structures of segregation. Key to their work was a transformation of Protestant thought in ways that deftly combined the social gospel and black church traditions, infused with Gandhian notions of active resistance and "soul force," as well as secular ideas of hardheaded political organizing and the kinds of legal maneuverings that led to the seminal 1954 court case of *Brown v. Board*.

The civil rights movement had legislative aims; it was, to that extent, a political movement. But it was more than that as well. It was a religious movement, sustained by the deeply Protestant religious imagery and fervor of southern black churches. The historically racist grounding of whiteness as dominant, blackness as inferior was radically overturned in part through a reimagination of the same Christian thought that was part of creating it in the first place. As one female sharecropper and civil rights activist in Mississippi explained in regard to her conversion to the movement, "Something hit me like a new religion" (Harvey, 2005).

In the 1950s and 1960s, the "silent South" spoke, black Protestants loudest of all. As he took over his Baptist pulpit in Montgomery, Martin Luther King, Jr. had no idea of the history that was about to overtake him, but long-time community activists quickly recognized the usefulness of the young doctoral candidate. The story in elaborate detail has been told most fully, and for a popular audience, in Taylor Branch's trilogy (1989). David Garrow's *Bearing the Cross* (1999) provides a landmark scholarly biography that places King firmly in the context both of his southern religious roots as well as his northern theological training and his connections with political organizers outside the church world, such as the pacifist radical Bayard Rustin. Garrow places much emphasis on King's visionary spiritual experience in the mid-1950s, a second conversion experience that steeled him for the numerous attempts on his life and the constant internecine struggles within movement organizations.

The connection between religion, civil rights, and social justice in everyday life found an especially powerful connection in the "local people," who did much of the actual work of the civil rights movement. Aldon D. Morris's *The Origins of the Civil Rights Movement: Black Communities Organizing for Change* (1986) begins not with Montgomery but with an earlier boycott led by black Baptist pastor T.D. Jemison in Baton Rouge, Louisiana in 1953, an action that set the stage for mass mobilizations to come. Morris refers to the Southern Christian Leadership Conference (SCLC) as the "decentralized arm of the black church." Morris argues strongly for the central role of churches in organizing and carrying out the black freedom struggle, noting that only an indigenous organization such as the church could have served so effectively as an agent of mass mobilization.

The argument advanced by Morris is furthered by Andrew Manis's memorable biography of Fred Shuttlesworth, *A Fire You Can't Put Out* (Manis, 1999), which shows the longtime Baptist pastor in Birmingham at the forefront of civil rights crusades in this most brutally racist of southern cities, long before the more well-known names from SCLC showed up in 1963. No one represented the movement's fire more than the Reverend Fred Shuttlesworth, who served in Birmingham during fateful crusades in the infamously tough industrial town. Shuttlesworth gradually made his name locally first in Selma, and later in Birmingham, as a willful preacher with a "combative spirituality." Electrified by the *Brown v. Board* decision and his sense of God's hand moving in history, Shuttlesworth's civil rights career blossomed in the 1950s. He felt divinely inspired to defy a response to the banning of the NAACP in Alabama imposed by the state authorities. Resisting more senior ministers who urged moderation, Shuttlesworth and his followers organized the Alabama Christian Movement for Human Rights (ACMHR). He saw the new group as part of a "worldwide revolution which is a divine struggle for the exaltation of the human race." Repeated attempts on his life only enhanced his personal authority and charisma. In 1957, white terrorists exploded dynamite at his home, nearly killing his wife and children. Shuttlesworth emerged from the severely damaged building uninjured (Manis, 1999: 24–27, 79, 97, 112).

Civil rights activists such as Shuttlesworth mixed the language of evangelicalism with the tenets of American civil religion. In their minds, both the Bible and American history were full of freedom struggles. They were also inseparable in the mind of Fannie Lou Hamer, who personified the fortitude and vibrant religious imagery of the movement. Daughter of a sharecropper in Ruleville, Mississippi, she experienced sexual abuse and later sadistic torture at the hands of local policemen. Hamer rose to prominence in the 1960s as a liaison between "local people" and national civil rights leaders. With her wicked sense of humor, spirited singing voice, and uncompromising stance on justice, Hamer articulated a liberation theology that sustained her through years of struggle and turmoil. "She compares herself frequently to Job . . . without a trace of self pity or some warped sense of pride," wrote one northern admirer serving in Mississippi. "Her faith in God is pervasive and in a sense dominates her life . . . There is a prophetic, messianic sense about her — an awareness, an electricity, a sense of mission which is very rarely absent."

As a girl, Hamer had joined the Strangers Home Baptist Church in her home town. She quoted the Bible expertly and led congregational song, skills that served her admirably in the 1960s. In 1962, at an SNCC meeting in a rural church, Hamer and a few others volunteered to register for voting. This serious act of political defiance against the state regime earned them a beating in the county jail. After their release, they experienced economic and verbal harassment. For example, the mayor of Ruleville canceled the tax-exempt status of Williams Chapel Missionary Baptist Church, Hamer's congregation, reasoning that by welcoming in SNCC field secretaries the congregation had been using the building for "purposes other than worship services." Hamer eventually won a seat in the Mississippi Freedom Democratic Party's delegation, originally sent as a protest against the all-white official state delegation, to the Democratic national convention of 1964. Hamer incited Lyndon Baines Johnson's special ire as she delivered an impromptu national address explaining why the Freedom Democratic Party would not settle for the compromise of taking two seats on the official state delegation. Queried by reporters, Hamer responded with an extemporized narration of black Mississippians who had risked their lives simply for trying to exercise citizenship rights. Hamer led the participants in her favorite freedom song, "This Little Light of Mine," a tune known by Sunday schoolers everywhere (Jackall, 1967; Dittmer, 1995: 137; Lee, 2000).

Hamer's political stance required spiritual sustenance. "Before 1962," as she later wrote, "I would have been afraid to have spoken before more than six people. Since that time I have had to speak before thousands in the fight for freedom, and I believe that God gave me the strength to be able to speak in this cause." She used her knowledge of the Bible in public rebukes of the timid. As she told one group of black Mississippians, "we are tired of being mistreated. God wants us to take a stand. We can stand by registering to vote – go to the court to register to vote." Christ would side with the sharecroppers in Mississippi during their struggle. Answering the inevitable charges that civil rights workers were agitators and communists, she retorted, "if Christ were here today, he would be branded a radical, a militant, and would probably be branded as 'red.'" Christ was a "revolutionary person, out there where it was happening. That's what God is all about, and that's where I get my strength." Summing up her life's work, she explained, "we can't separate Christ from freedom, and freedom from Christ." She criticized southern churches for doing "too much pretending and not enough actual working, the white ministers and the black ministers standing behind a podium and preaching a lie on Sunday." It was "long *past* time for the churches to wake up" and address fundamental issues of justice. Ephesians 6:11–12 provided sufficient evidence for the spiritual basis of the freedom struggle: "Put on the whole armor of God, that ye may be able to stand against the wiles of the devil. For we wrestle not against flesh and blood, but against principalities, against powers, against the rulers of the darkness of this world, against spiritual wickedness in high places." Women such as Fannie Lou Hamer "placed Jesus where his experiences, as passed through the traditions of the Black church, could be used in the freedom struggle" (Hamer, 1968: 168; Hobson, 1999: 17).

Both Shuttlesworth and Fannie Lou Hamer came out of very specific church traditions; and both recognized that their traditions were there not only to be used, but also when necessary to be rebuked, or simply to be overcome, gotten over. Hamer was not shy about issuing ultimatums to her pastors and congregants when they shied away from involvement in the movement; and Shuttlesworth was not hesitant to do the same to his own congregants. Both saw the church as an instrument of liberation, but they had to overcome much of their own training in the church to do so. History was their ally, but only if a version of that history that separated churches from everyday struggles was bypassed in favor of a vision of churches that was consistent with their earlier role in Reconstruction. They were successful to the degree that the churches and black ministers became iconic symbols of the civil rights struggle. They were also successful to the degree that the church's liberationist potential could become another heavy burden.

Religion and Civil Rights in a "Postracial" America

Studying the history of the black church in American public life presents a paradox. On the one hand, thinking of the role of black churches during the Civil War and Reconstruction, during the progressive era, or in the civil rights movement suggests that the African American church historically has taken an activist and progressive role in the public realm. Yet in all the cases cited above, only a minority of churches and clergymen were ever involved, with the majority of churches remaining relatively quiescent or content to minister to internal spiritual or local communal needs and stay at some remove from the realm of public policy. Thus, despite the great collective power of African American churches, they have remained, in the words of James Melvin Washington, a "frustrated fellowship" (Washington, 1986). A recent important collection of case studies of the role of African American churches in contemporary public life suggests a similar conclusion. As editor R. Drew Smith writes, "a consistent refrain is that there is a potential for – or at least an expectation of – black church public policy influence that has been, to this point, largely unfilled." Admittedly, this is a significant burden to put on churches that are often situated within beleaguered communities, but "it is one that they inherited as a result of their civil rights movement involvements" (Smith, 2004: 3).

In the post–civil rights era, some have suggested that America has moved into a "postracial" era, despite the overwhelming statistics documenting racial inequality in American society. Thus, activists who have mined the connection between religion, civil rights, and social justice will have plenty of work to do in the future. The struggle continues, and Frederick Douglass's words remain true today: "without the struggle, there is no progress." Religion will remain central to that struggle, even though religious institutions are not always well adapted to carrying on the struggle. Social justice and civil rights today centrally involve issues of economic justice, problems for which the moral declarations in which religions specialize have less pertinence or direct power to effect change.

References

Billingsley, Andrew (1998) *Mighty Like a River: The Black Church and Social Reform*, Oxford University Press, New York.

Blum, Edward J. (2007) *W. E. B. Dubois, American Prophet*, University of Pennsylvania Press, Philadelphia.

Branch, Taylor (1989) *Parting the Waters: America in the King Years, 1954–1963*, Simon & Schuster, New York.

Dittmer, John (1995) *Local People: The Struggle for Civil Rights in Mississippi*, University of Illinois Press, Urbana.

DuBois, W.E.B. (1935) *Black Reconstruction: An Essay toward a History of the Part which Black Folk Played in the Attempt to Reconstruct Democracy in America, 1860–1880*, Scribner, New York.

Evans, Curtis (2008) *The Burden of Black Religion*, Oxford University Press, New York.

Garrow, David (1999[1987]) *Bearing the Cross: Martin Luther King, Jr., and the Southern Christian Leadership Conference*, Harper Perennial, New York.

Hahn, Steven (2003) *A Nation under Our Feet: Black Political Struggles in the Rural South from Slavery to the Great Migration*, Harvard University Press, Cambridge, MA.

Hall, Jacquelyn Dowd (2005) The long history of the civil rights movement and the political uses of the past, *Journal of American History* 91: 1233–1263.

Hamer, Fannie Lou (1968) Sick and tired of being sick and tired, *Katallagete* 26.

Harding, Vincent (1993[1981]) *There Is a River: The Black Struggle for Freedom in America*, Houghton Mifflin Harcourt, New York.

Harris, Frederick (1999) *Something Within: Religion in African American Political Activism*, Oxford University Press, New York.

Harvey, Paul (2005) *Freedom's Coming: Religious Cultures and the Shaping of the South from the Civil War through the Civil Rights Era*, University of North Carolina Press, Chapel Hill.

Hatch, Nathan (1989) *The Democratization of American Christianity*, Yale University Press, New Haven.

Hobson, Fred (1999) *But Now I See: The White Southern Racial Conversion Narrative*, Louisiana State University Press, Baton Rouge.

Ingersoll, Thomas (1994) "Releese us out of this cruell bondegg": An appeal from Virginia in 1723, *William and Mary Quarterly 3rd ser.*, 51(4): 777–782.

Jackall, Robert (1967) Diary entry for May 25 and 26, in Robert Jackall Papers, Wisconsin Historical Society, Madison.

Kelley, Robin D.G. (1993) "We are not what we seem": Rethinking black working-class opposition in the Jim Crow South, *Journal of American History* 80: 75–112.

Lee, Chana Kai (2000) *For Freedom's Sake: The Life of Fannie Lou Hamer*, University of Illinois Press, Urbana.

Manis, Andrew (1999) *A Fire You Can't Put Out: The Civil Rights Life of Birmingham's Reverend Fred Shuttlesworth*, University of Alabama Press, Tuscaloosa.

Mays, Benjamin (1969[1938]) *The Negro's God as Reflected in His Literature*, Atheneum, New York.

McLeod, Jay (ed.) (1991) *Minds Stayed on Freedom: The Civil Rights Struggle in the Rural South, An Oral History*, Westview Press, Boulder, CO.

Montgomery, William (1993) *Under Their Own Vine and Fig Tree: The African American Church in the South, 1865–1900*, Louisiana State University Press, Baton Rouge.

Morris, Aldon (1986) *The Origins of the Civil Rights Movement: Black Communities Organizing for Change*, Free Press, New York.

Newman, Richard, Rael, Patrick, and Lapsansky, Phillip (eds.) (2001) *Pamphlets of Protest: An Anthology of Early African American Protest Literature, 1790–1860*, Routledge, New York.

Smith, R. Drew (ed.) (2004) *Long March Ahead: African American Churches and Public Policy in Post–Civil Rights America*, Duke University Press, Durham, NC.

Washington, James Melvin (1986) *Frustrated Fellowship: The Black Baptist Quest for Social Power*, Mercer University Press, Macon, GA.

Wilmore, Gayraud (1998[1973]) *Black Religion and Black Radicalism: An Interpretation of the Religious History of African Americans*, Orbis Books, Maryknoll, NY.

CHAPTER 35

Human Rights

The South African Experience

Glenda Wildschut

Within the South African context, faith has always been in the forefront of social discourse, whether it be to defend the apartheid regime, with its horrendous atrocities, or to oppose it. The lines between the private religious and public secular have always been blurred in a country whose foundations are rooted in the Judeo-Christian paradigm. It is therefore not surprising that human rights and gross human rights violations in South Africa have been viewed through lenses of religious discourse. It is within this context that the Truth and Reconciliation Commission was born. Not unexpectedly, the Commission was headed up by a prominent religious figure. In this essay I explore the work of the South African Truth and Reconciliation Commission as an instrument to deal with human rights abuse, how the amnesty process worked, the work of the Human Rights Violations Committee and the Repatriation and Rehabilitation Committee, and finally the role of the faith communities in the ongoing work of nation building.

South Africa, like so many other countries, was faced with a past devastated by gross violations of human rights that had occurred during many years of racism and oppression. During the transition from apartheid to democracy, the country had to grapple with the vexing legacy of the past in order to create the possibility of a future in which human rights abuses would not be repeated.

In moving from repression to democracy, fundamental principles such as the rule of law should be established that will distinguish the old regime from the new. While there may be strong political pressure for "victor's justice" in dealing with those who served the repressive regime and harsh retribution against a large number of individuals, these sentiments need to be balanced with the need for political stability.

Many countries have had to deal with the past and rid their society of its legacy. If, however, the process is not dealt with correctly, such actions may deepen rather than

---

The Wiley Blackwell Companion to Religion and Social Justice, First Edition. Edited by Michael D. Palmer and Stanley M. Burgess.
© 2012 John Wiley & Sons Ltd. Published 2020 by John Wiley & Sons Ltd.

heal the divisions within the nation. The real test is to ensure that dealing with the past is as important as the democratization process. These were the considerations in South Africa as it grappled with the legacy of apartheid, since it affected all aspects of life for the majority of its people. Some felt that leaders of the previous regime who were responsible for apartheid abuses needed to be prosecuted. Prosecution, they argued, was not only essential to achieve some degree of justice, but a public airing and censure of their crimes was the best way to draw a line between old and new government, lest the public perceive the new authorities as simply more of the same. Others claimed that to prosecute leaders of the apartheid regime would simply be an exercise in show trials, unsuitable in a democracy, and that they would merely be manifestations of victors' justice. They further felt that the best way to rebuild and reconcile the nation was to close the chapter on the past by granting a blanket amnesty to all perpetrators of gross human rights violations.

This debate arose during the peace negotiations in South Africa. Members of the ruling party were adamant that amnesty should be granted to security personnel. The liberation movement, on the other hand, insisted that both knowledge and acknowledgment of gross violations of human rights was essential for the country to move forward.

Convinced that accountability was a prerequisite for establishing a culture of human rights in a new democracy, the South African Parliament came up with a compromise, which would reveal and acknowledge the past, but would promote reconciliation and offer amnesty to perpetrators in return for full disclosure of the truth. The *Promotion of National Unity and Reconciliation Act of 1995* was promulgated to establish the Truth and Reconciliation Commission (TRC). Anglican Archbishop Desmond Mpilo Tutu was appointed Chairperson of the Commission. Following a rigorous selection process, the President appointed 17 commissioners.

The TRC was created through political negotiations between the National Party and the African National Congress. The TRC was charged with uncovering as much as possible of what transpired in the country from the time of the Sharpville massacre in 1960[1] to the inauguration of Nelson Mandela as the first democratically elected president in May 1994. The Minister of Justice, Dullah Omar, articulated the vision for the TRC in the following words:

> Instead of revenge
> There will be reconciliation,
> Instead of forgetfulness there will be knowledge and acknowledgment
> Instead of rejection there will be acceptance by a compassionate state
> Instead of violations of human rights there will be the restoration of the moral order and respect for the rule of law. (Botman and Peterson, 1997)

The Objectives of the TRC were clearly set out in the *Promotion of National Unity and Reconciliation Act* (Act 95-34, 26 July 1995):

a) Establishing as complete a picture of the causes, nature and extent of the gross violations of human rights which were committed . . . including . . . the perspectives of the victims and the motives and perspectives of the persons responsible for the commission of the violation, by conducting investigations and holding hearings;

b) Facilitating the granting of amnesty to persons who make full disclosure of all the relevant facts . . . ;

c) Establishing and making known the fate or whereabouts of victims . . . ;

d) Compiling a report providing as comprehensive an account as possible of the activities and findings of the commission . . . which contains recommendations of measures to prevent the future violations of human rights. (Truth and Reconciliation Commission, 1998)

Under the watchwords "Truth, the Road to Reconciliation," the TRC spent three and a half years taking statements and conducting numerous public hearings listening to accounts of human rights violations, both from victims and from those directly or indirectly responsible for human rights violations. More than 26 000 witnesses appeared before the Commission. As a Commissioner, I felt that this was a painful examination of the past, yet it provided a genuine catharsis for the entire society. For the first time victims testified publicly before the whole country about the suffering they had endured. Also for the first time, perpetrators publicly confessed the crimes they had committed.

The historical importance of the TRC's work, both for the future of South Africa and for the ethical challenges it raised, is significant. What is important to note is that the commission launched not only an inquiry into what happened but also a process intended to promote reconciliation. Other truth commissions, such those established in Latin America,[2] only sought information to support prosecutions. These commissions held their hearings in private, with very limited public involvement. The information uncovered by the TRC may lead to prosecutions in the future, but the central purpose, enhanced by its power to grant amnesty, moved away from prosecutions toward the ideal of restorative justice. Restorative justice can be described as an approach that encourages those who have committed wrongdoing to take responsibility for their actions. Jim Consedine describes restorative justice as moving away from a punitive, condemnatory stance to one in which an attempt is made to repair the emotional and material damage of crime (Consedine, 1995: 7).

How the Amnesty Process Worked

Any person could voluntarily apply for amnesty provided that he or she completed the prescribed form. These applications were scrutinized for completeness and formal compliance and thereafter captured on a central database. The application was then passed on to the investigation unit. Once the investigations were completed, the committee members evaluated whether the application should be heard in chambers – that is, behind closed doors – or in public.

Members of the Amnesty Committee generally sat in panels of three, with a High Court Judge as the chairperson. The applicant was entitled to legal representation that presented their case to the committee. They could be cross-examined by the victims or their representatives.

Often, when victims were unable to add to the factual nature of the evidence being presented, they would make a statement rather than testify per se. Such statements related to how they felt about what had happened or provided background to the events or people affected by the actions of the applicants. These statements often contributed to a sense of catharsis and closure for the victims. Occasionally, we witnessed spontaneous, heart-warming reconciliatory encounters between the parties. The parties sometimes called for private sessions at which to explore the reconciliation process further.

Reconciliation and Truth

The TRC's governing act is the *Promotion of National Unity and Reconciliation Act*. As something to be promoted, it is self-evident that reconciliation is not an event, but a process and often a long and painful journey. Differing from person to person, this journey sometimes ended abruptly and sometimes lasted for years. Archbishop Tutu, speaking of reconciliation, said, "Reconciliation is not about being cozy; it is not about pretending that things were other than they were. Reconciliation based on falsehood . . . is not true reconciliation and will not last." He went on to say, "it is only on the basis of truth that true reconciliation can take place" (Truth and Reconciliation Commission, 1998: Vol. 1, Ch. 5, 106–110, Vol. 5, Ch. 9, 350–435). I believe that seeking out the truth was the basis of the work of the TRC.

Jürgen Habermas states that the notion of truth comprises three essential elements. First, it should correspond to the facts. In other words, it must involve an accurate description of the instance, including the context and background. Second, it should comply with a normative system, in the sense that both those who make a statement (of facts) and those who receive it are able to make a judgment. Thus, it must appear to be a "fair" conclusion, in language that is accessible, and it must confirm to "normal" practices. Third, the statement should be sincere, in the sense that it must have integrity. In other words, it should be the result of a process that is credible and that involves credible and committed adjudication (Bronkhorst, 1995: 145–146).

If the process and resultant "truth" conform to these criteria, they are more likely to contribute to reconciliation. In the context of the TRC, reconciliation can be understood at different levels of complexity.

Individual reconciliation

Coming to terms with the facts is necessary to lead to reconciliation; for example, in some instances, the family of a victim who had disappeared may have to accept that their loved one has in fact been killed. An individual's reconciliation with the facts in turn facilitates closure. However, sometimes this revelation can lead to denial and the need for revenge. Remarkably, we saw very little of this during the TRC. We are not aware of any revenge attacks during the work of the TRC, despite revelations of horrific abuses. Of course, even though there were some people who were not satisfied with the process, it does appear that most testifiers were satisfied with finding out the truth of what happened. Perpetrators, on the other hand, often found it hard to come to terms with their guilt or to accept moral responsibility for their actions. In the amnesty process, remorse was not a requirement.

Reconciliation between victims and perpetrators

Many victims expressed the need to know the truth in order to forgive. This same need is evident in victims in other settings. Victims need to know whom and what to forgive. They also need to know that they are hearing the full truth. If they remain unconvinced, they are unlikely to be prepared to reconcile with the perpetrator.

Reconciliation at a community level

It is important to remember that the nature of the conflict led to deep divisions in communities. These divisions occurred at various levels, between young and old, men and women, neighbors and even within families, as well as between ethnic and racial groups. To some extent, the Commission was able to facilitate reconciliation meetings where such elements found common ground. Often, truth telling led people to see each other in a different light, as they were able to understand or relate to the motives and the context described by the applicants as a basis for their actions. Another important cultural factor that is of relevance in this context is *ubuntu*, a traditional African concept that refers to our interconnectedness and a strong belief that identity is expressed through community. In some sense, the notion of *ubuntu* assisted communities to find healing by acknowledging their commitment to a shared sense of community.

Reconciliation at a national level

The work of the Commission highlighted the different understandings that people have of this notion of national healing. It also focused attention on the differences between individual responses, often rooted in personal and religious notions of reconciliation, and those that have a political or ideological application to a society in transition. In this sense, some observers believed that the difficulties of truth telling and truth finding, which had a robust legalistic process, were not ideally suited to facilitating reconciliation. Nevertheless, the Commission and the amnesty committee conducted themselves in a manner that would facilitate evenhandedness on the part of all parties and generally allowed the parties a measure of latitude to come together and possibly reconcile (Doxtader and Vicencio, 2004: 230–231).

In *A Country Unmasked*, Alex Boraine spells out the work of the Commission and how it understood the distinctions between four kinds of truths. The first is objective or factual truth. The task here is to reach findings based on facts and information collected and received or placed before it. The second kind of truth is personal or narrative truth. Through the telling of their stories from their perspective, victims and perpetrators have given meaning to the varied and textured South African story. Through print and electronic media, these stories were communicated to a broader audience and made a significant contribution to the cathartic process. These narratives came to the commission not as legal arguments, but rather as painful personal accounts. The third kind of truth is social or dialogic truth, which is established through discussion, debate, and experience. Here the Commission engaged the larger South African community in various discussions. Academics, nongovernmental organizations (NGOs), faith communities, the media, the health sector, and political parties made representations to the commission. Alex Boraine reminds us that the acquisition of information was as important as the process of establishing it. The fourth type of truth is healing or restorative truth. This type aims at gathering knowledge that contributes to the healing of the nation and the restoration of the dignity of victims and survivors by acknowledging their contributions to the task of attaining democracy (Boraine, 2000).

The Commission not only listened to the evidence of individuals, but invited various sectors of society to make presentations. Here, leaders from the business sector, healthcare, the legal system, and the religious community were able to explain how these sectors were complicit in human rights violations and, on the other hand, opposed the apartheid system through activism. These hearings afforded leaders in some instances the opportunity to make public apologies, which had the potential for reconciliation. These gestures, coupled with the restoration of dignity that acknowledgment of victims represents, were fundamental to ensuring that people begin to embrace the new culture of democracy and human rights and restoring credibility to state institutions.

The public and inclusive nature of the Commission may have further contributed to the process of national unity. Public hearings were conducted in every part of the country: large cities, small towns, and rural hamlets. The Commission went to these places, conducting hearings in all manner of buildings, from large, imposing city halls to small, unassuming churches and school halls.

The major challenge, though, was whether these activities ensured that the vast majority of the people who were victims of apartheid would benefit from the new order. In this regard, South Africa still struggles with gross disparities and structural inequalities. Consistent with the terms of its mandate, the Commission resolved that it would focus its inquiries on gross violations of human rights and that it therefore would not (could not) investigate the broader effects of apartheid. This decision gave rise to much criticism. Many critics of the Commission argued that the TRC missed the opportunity to address the social injustice brought about by apartheid. A commonly held definition of social justice refers to the justice and equality found in all aspects of a fair and harmonious society. Apartheid, on the other hand, was designed to deprive the majority of South Africans of their right to equal opportunities. For the vast majority of South Africans, human rights abuses were pervasive:

> the system itself was evil, inhumane and degrading . . . amongst its many crimes, perhaps its greatest was the power to humiliate, to denigrate and to remove the self – confidence, self esteem and dignity of victims. (Truth and Reconciliation Commission, 1998)

Apartheid was a grim reality for every black South African. For many it meant expulsion, forced migration, bulldozing and gutting of their homes, the requirement to carry passes, forced removal to ghettos, and increased poverty and desperation. Forced into "independent homelands" (Bantustans) without jobs, communities experienced powerlessness, vulnerability, fear, and injustice.

Many of the killings and torture documented by the Commission occurred because of the resistance of ordinary people who protested against their material conditions brought about by apartheid. Many were severely beaten by police for merely speaking out and demanding a better education. While the Commission, as stated before, did not focus on the social and economic inequalities, these narratives formed the vital context within which it fulfilled its mandate.

To demonstrate examples of the kinds of cases brought before the Human Rights Violations and Amnesty Committees, I recount two cases, which illustrate the complex nature of the process and its ramifications, not only for the victims, but for their families, friends, and communities. They also demonstrate the multilayered nature of reconciliation.

Case 1: The Charismatic Youth Leader

Siphiwo Mtimkulu was a charismatic leader of the Congress of South African Students (COSAS) in Port Elizabeth in the period 1979 to 1981. He was detained without trial in May 1981 and released five months later. Immediately following his release, he felt gravely ill, vomiting and in constant pain. He was admitted to a large tertiary care hospital in Cape Town, where his hair began to fall out. Doctors struggled to keep him alive. He was diagnosed as suffering from thallium poisoning, a toxin that was very difficult to acquire in South Africa. When Siphiwo was released from hospital, he was confined to a wheelchair. In April 1982, he sued the Minister of Police and his commissioner for his detention, torture, and poisoning. Two weeks later he disappeared and was never seen or heard of again.

In 1990, during a specially established commission, the Harms Commission, the deaths of Siphiwo and his comrade Topsy Madaka were investigated. The security police were accused of their murders. The police, in turn, accused Topy and Siphiwo of being dangerous youth, inciting others and instigating the youth to violence and distributing ANC (African National Congress) pamphlets. Topsy Madaka had recruited youngsters for MK (the military wing of the ANC), they argued. The members of the security police, Colonel Nieuwoudt and Colonel Du Plessis, both denied that they had poisoned Siphiwo or knew who did it. Professor Frances Ames of the University of Cape Town testified that she had examined Siphiwo and found that he was poisoned with thallium. Although it was difficult to get the poison in South Africa, the security police were known to be experimenting with it.

During the last week of May 1996, Siphiwo's parents prepared to take their story to the Human Rights Violations Committee hearing of the TRC in Port Elizabeth. During their first appearance at the TRC, a court order was served to the Commission preventing the parents from testifying. The two implicated policemen had managed in this instance to silence the family.

Two weeks later, however, Joyce Mtimkulu was able to testify and tell of the poisoning of her son. After years of denying that they knew what had happened or knew of the disappearance of Siphiwo Mtimkulu and Topsy Madaka, Nieuwoudt and du Plessis applied for amnesty for their deaths. In September 1997, the Amnesty Committee hearing took place. Joyce Mtimkulu said that it was a great day for her and the family, because at last they were going to hear what happened to their son.

The amnesty hearing revealed that du Plessis and Nieuwoudt had proposed that Siphiwo be eliminated. The policemen testified that they concluded that killing the two activists would be the only solution to the problem of the young leaders. However, the TRC evidence suggested another possible motive: Mtimkulu had sued the state for his detention and poisoning at the time of the decision to kill him. The policemen admitted that the ensuing court case would have been very embarrassing.

At the amnesty hearings, Nieuwoudt testified that he gave Madaka and Mtimkulu sleeping pills in their coffee, and then he and his colleague shot them. The policemen described in detail how they burnt the bodies and disposed of the ashes in the Fish River. They left Mtimkulu's car at the Lesotho border post to create the impression that he had left the country.

Case 2: The Brave Commander

Phila Nadandwe left South Africa illegally to join the military wing of the African National Congress, Umkhonto we Siswe (MK). After she left school, she did her basic military training in Angola in 1985, which was provided by MK. The name given to her was Zandi. Her comrades remember her at the time as exemplary, highly intelligent, committed, and hardworking.

After her training, she was sent to Swaziland where she conducted several operations into KwaZulu Natal. Her dedication impressed her commanders, and soon she was promoted to commander. One of her comrades, Richard Jones, remembered her as a strong and powerful personality with a strong and powerful body to match.

Her unit was very successful, and Phila grew in confidence and stature within the military wing.

Phila and her partner, Bheki Mabuza, started living together in Manzini, Swaziland and had a baby named Thabang. In October 1998, Phila mysteriously disappeared after meeting with some comrades in KwaZulu Natal. Her disappearance caused consternation among her unit members. She was a key person in the structures operating in the region and knew what was happening in the high command of the military wing. They knew something was wrong, as she was still breastfeeding Thabang and had left him with a childminder without a word.

The longer she stayed away, the stronger the rumor became that Phila had become an askari. (Askaris were former liberation fighters who joined the apartheid government's security police and were used to kill anti-apartheid activists. They often became askaris after being captured and tortured by security police.) These rumors brought shame on Phila's and Bheki's families.

In 1997, the TRC investigators visited Phila's father with news that Phila was dead and that she was not an askari. She had been killed by the South Africa Police. The truth about her death came from the very men who killed her: six policemen who applied for amnesty from the TRC for her murder. Hendrik Botha, Salman DuPreez, and Jacobus Vorster were heard.

Phila was killed because the police were worried about the effectiveness of her unit and wanted to neutralize her. They decided to abduct her from Swaziland and then to persuade her to switch sides and work against MK. In October 1998, the men went to Swaziland using false passports, accompanied by two askaris. The askaris set up a meeting with Phila in Manzizni. Her colleague, Richard Jones, drove her to the meeting. She told him she would see him later, then got into the car with the askaris. (She, of course, did not know that they were askaris.) According to the police, she was forced to cross the border fence with them.

Back in South Africa, Phila was severely tortured and interrogated, but she refused to become a turncoat and police collaborator. She told them that she would never cooperate with them. The police concluded that she was "a tough nut to crack" and that she should be killed. A hole was dug near the house where she was questioned. She was blindfolded and led to the shallow grave, where she was killed and buried.

Phila's father, stepmother, and sister were in the room when the evidence was given before the Amnesty Committee. Nathan Ndwendwe's eyes filled up with tears as he listened to how his daughter was killed. He quietly shook his head from side to side as the tears rolled down his face.

Another relative jumped up and angrily called out to the applicants that she wanted to know everything about Phila's death. Richard Jones was also in the public gallery and was deeply moved to find out how brave his former commander had been. "Now everyone knows that Phila was the bravest commander," he said afterward. "Even these policemen grudgingly admit that she was a brave woman."

The amnesty applicants took the TRC investigators to the farmhouse where Phila's grave was. When her skeleton was laid bare, it showed the gunshot wound in her skull that probably killed her. When her body was uncovered, a blue plastic bag was found wrapped around her waist. The policemen told the commission that they put the plastic bag over her to try to maintain some sense of her female dignity.

The Amnesty Committee granted amnesty to the policemen because they had a political motive, acted under instruction from their superiors, and made a full disclosure.

The two cases recounted here not only ilustrate the types of violations brought before the Commission, but also point to the challenge of developing a reparation and rehabilitation policy.

The Importance of Reparation and Reconstruction

Several questions emerge when one considers the issue of reparation and rehabilitation for human rights violations. How does one repair the damage caused by a violation? How do we compensate for the grief and emotional trauma of the abuse? How are grief and suffering quantified? How do we place a monetary value on the grief suffered by the loss of a loved one in order to establish appropriate compensation? These were some of the questions referred to the Reparation and Rehabilitation Committee (RRC) of the

TRC in meetings held with testifiers in preparation for public hearings before the Commission. Many were uncomfortable with the concept of granting amnesty to perpetrators and were uncertain about how reparations would be implemented. While there was anger about amnesty, there was also understanding about the need to overcome the bitterness of the past. There was considerable mistrust, but also a willingness to face the harsh realities of the need to find a way to rebuild and repair the damage inflicted on many. While initially there was no request for financial compensation, nor any indication that people would only testify on condition that compensation would be granted, the Commission was painfully aware that most victims were desperately in need of financial and other social compensation as a direct result of the violations perpetrated against them. While the Commission was empowered to grant amnesty, it did not have the authority to grant reparation. The Reparations Committee in the Commission was mandated to make a recommendation to the President on a reparations policy. This inequality was a bitter pill to swallow and equally hard to deal with because, apart from urgent interim relief, we were only able to make recommendations at the end of the process. However, the Committee paid attention to the moral and legal basis for granting reparations. The report states:

> It is generally accepted that victims and survivors of terrible atrocities of the past deserve reparation and rehabilitation. The state, as well as the community, owes it to them that adequate measures should be taken to restore their dignity and self-respect. Comprehensive measures should also be taken to restore their physical and mental wellbeing. Without adequate reparation and rehabilitation measures, there can be no reconciliation either on an individual or community level. . . .
>
> The responsibility for reparation lies with the present government which is morally obligated to carry the debt of its predecessors, and has accepted this. It is, however, equally imperative that the whole community especially those who benefited most from the unjust system of the past should accept its co-responsibility for the reparation and rehabilitation of the victims of the conflict of the past. (Truth and Reconciliation Commission, 1998)

What the Commission could not ignore in the development of the reparation policy is whether such a policy could serve all citizens. Could a comprehensive policy address the broader socioeconomic and social injustices that formed the basis for human rights violations; and could the policy address the need for institutional reform to ensure fundamental change toward a culture of human rights in society? The success of reparation must take into account individual and collective interests. They require dedication to change in the face of scarce resources. The monetary aspect of reparation – that is, compensation – must go alongside measures to rebuild a better future and thus have an impact on the poor economic and social conditions that have so dehumanized many. It should ensure that the real beneficiaries are acknowledged and that the process does not replace one set of beneficiaries with another. The power in the policy lies in its ability to inspire a willingness and an attitude to ensure that the historical deprivations and inequalities are eradicated. Symbolic reparation must involve participants in decisions about memorials and monuments. Otherwise, these will become meaningless artifacts that do not contribute to reconciliation but rather further alienate communities.

The Reparation and Rehabilitation Committee looked carefully at examples of reparations policies elsewhere in the world. Experience in other countries showed that if not dealt with wisely, the issues lead to major difficulties in the future. After decades, for example, new governments in Latin America had to deal with public pressure for mechanisms to redress the past. All sectors of society have a role to play in contributing to reparations. Large corporations and individual citizens could do a great deal to indicate their willingness to contribute to making up for the wrongs of the past. Similarly, the churches and other faith-based institutions can play an important part in facilitating healing processes.

The Role of Faith-Based Institutions

As part of the sectoral hearings, the Commission heard testimony from some of the major faith communities in South Africa. All testified to the fact that some of the churches, particularly the Dutch Reformed Church, gave their blessing to the system of apartheid and provided the theological rationale for the separation of racial groups. The apartheid system was regarded as stemming from the mission of these churches. Other churches gave the apartheid state tacit support, regarding it as a guarantor of Christian civilization.

On the other hand, religious communities also suffered under apartheid – their activities were disrupted and their leaders imprisoned. Motivated by strong values and a powerful sense of justice, many church and other religious leaders became powerful opponents of apartheid, calling for its end and for a dispensation free of injustice. Many of those who testified recognized the necessity for religious communities to participate in the national healing and reconciliation process.

Forty-one faith communities appeared before the Commission, representing a wide range of traditions, such as the Baptist Union of South Africa, the Jamiatul Ulama (Muslim), the South African Council of Churches, the Anglican Church, the Hindu Faith, and the African Traditional Religion. Both the Chief Rabbi and the Hindu Sabha sent representatives and written statements to the Commission.

Despite their claim to loyalties that transcend the state, South African churches implicitly or as a matter of policy allowed themselves to be structured along racial lines. This is still evident in many churches today.

The TRC report notes the following with regard to propagating "State Theology":

The term State Theology is derived from the Kairos document and refers to the theology that gave legitimacy to the Apartheid State. The effects of State Theology were to "bless injustice, canonize the will of the powerful and reduce the poor to passivity, obedience and apathy." Few churches did not allow a distinction between black and white members at Sunday worship. The most obvious example of a faith community propagating state theology was the Dutch Reformed Church, although it never (even its submission to the commission) confessed to actually bowing down to the monster that Apartheid disclosed itself to be. Right wing Christian groups also promulgated State Theology and acted as arms of the state, infiltrating especially evangelical and Pentecostal denominations. This became particularly evident in investigations into the information scandal of the late 1970s when it was disclosed that government was funding groups such as the Christian League – the fore-runner of the Gospel Defense League. (Truth and Reconciliation Commission, 1998: Vol. 4, 69–70)

Many observers of the TRC's faith community hearings, like Genevieve Jacques of the World Council of Churches, noted the importance of the role of the religious sector in admitting to their complicity in violations of human rights and to committing to assist in correcting the wrongs of the past. Facilitating processes of redress, forgiveness, and restoring human dignity is, after all, intimately connected to the mission of most faiths. The task of bringing communities and individuals together jointly to rebuild a wounded nation can be achieved through the involvement of the religious community. We have witnessed this active participation of some churches in land restitution, for example, and in efforts to restore the dignity of victims and perpetrators alike through mediation and accompaniment.

There is still much work to be done. Reconciliation, healing, and reparation take time and cannot be rushed. The process of achieving these is part of the struggle for justice that is an important agenda in South Africa, as it continues to seek to address the wounds of the past.

Notes

1. The Sharpville massacre took place on March 21, 1960. Since the 1920s, the movement of black South Africans had been controlled by a law passed by the white Nationalist Government to enforce greater segregation. This law served as an instrument of state harassment of its political opponents. The African National Congress decided to launch a campaign of protest against these laws on March 31, 1960. The rival Pan Africanist Congress preempted this launch by organizing its own campaign of resistance on March 21. It was at this protest that the South African police opened fire, killing 69 people. This event became known as the Sharpville Massacre in deference to the town where the protest took place.
2. See, for example, Minow (1998); Jacques (2000).

References

Boraine, A. (2000) *A Country Unmasked: Inside South Africa's Truth and Reconciliation Commission*, Oxford University Press, Oxford.

Botman, H. Russel and Petersen, Robin M. (eds.) (1997) *To Remember and To Heal*, Human and Rousseau, Pretoria.

Bronkhorst, D. (1995) *Obstacles and Opportunities for Human Rights*, Amnesty International, Amsterdam.

Consedine, J. (1995) *Restorative Justice: Healing the Effects of Crime*, Ploughshares Publication, New Zealand.

Doxtader, Erik and Vicencio, Charles Villa (eds.) (2004) *To Repair the Irreparable*, David Philip Publishers, Claremont, South Africa.

Jacques, Genevieve (2000) *Beyond Impunity*, WCC Publications, Geneva.

Minow, Martha (1998) *Beyond Vengeance and Forgiveness*, Beacon Press, Boston.

Truth and Reconciliation Commission, South Africa (1998) Final Report, 7 Vols, http://www.justice.gov.za/trc/report/index.htm (accessed April 20, 2011).

CHAPTER 36

The "Double-Conscious" Nature of American Evangelicalism's Struggle over Civil Rights during the Progressive Era

L.B. Gallien, Jr.

In 1903, W.E.B. DuBois, the first African American to earn a doctorate in sociology at Harvard University, penned the term "double consciousness" in his first book, titled *The Souls of Black Folks*, germane to the conflicted nature of black people's attitudes toward themselves as a proud and accomplished racial group, contrasted to their "second-class" conditions under Jim Crow codes. These accompanying codes and laws severely restricted their civil rights in a segregated America among the people who had enslaved them in the previous century. In his book, DuBois highlighted the degree of ambivalence that African Americans felt toward their status in America: a newly freed people with unlimited and unlocked potential who remained socially, economically, politically, and culturally chained to an apartheid country and subservient to a majority culture that remained ambivalent about their claims to racial equality (DuBois, 2007).

Double consciousness is also an apt term to describe American evangelicalism, an important Protestant religious movement that was prominent at the time of the publication of DuBois's book. This religious and cultural movement held an equally conflicted "double-conscious" attitude toward civil rights and equality, even though pioneer members of this movement, like college presidents and evangelists Charles Finney (Oberlin) and Jonathan Blanchard (Wheaton), had led the struggle against slavery and for the civil rights of African Americans long before it gained ground with other antebellum abolitionist efforts in the Midwest (Marsden, 1991).[1] However, in what the late historian Timothy Smith coined as the "great reversal," many American evangelicals during the progressive era actually reversed their stands on issues of social justice and civil rights, and some evolved as fundamentalists as a reaction against the universal secular theories (e.g., Darwin, Marx, Freud, higher criticism) that were capturing the minds of the American and European academies and filtering down to religious institutions. During this same time, fundamentalist and evangelical groups' adoption of dispensational theology and premillennial eschatology contributed greatly to this "great reversal." Added to these religious factors were the legalization and social acquiescence of Jim Crow codes across the country, particularly in the South (Smith, 1977). However, by the middle of the twentieth century, the level of uneasiness that evangelicals felt was greatly magnified when they examined Scripture from a cultural context, along with the "testifying" and prophetic fortitude of African American peoples.[2] This feeling of unease about race and civil rights remains among current evangelical groups.

Purpose

It is the intent of this essay to show how the inherent contradictory tributaries (not unlike DuBois's idea of "double consciousness") of thought among emerging white fundamentalist leaders like D.L. Moody (whose attitudes toward race and civil rights never matched those of early evangelical leader Charles Finney) drove the nineteenth-century evangelical movement toward a more fundamentalist and racial segregationist twentieth-century mindset that still exists among its members. Indeed, the emerging fundamentalist movement caused many Christian institutions to grow increasingly silent (and, later, even belligerent) on issues of civil rights in the twentieth century (Dorsett, 1997; Hart, 2003). With the exception of Quaker institutions like Swarthmore, Haverford, Earlham, Guilford, and Bryn Mawr, this "great reversal" of American evangelical Christian colleges and churches on issues of race and social justice also drove them intellectually "underground," because of their unwillingness to seriously examine with their students or parishioners (nor debate with their peers) the rising secular theories as evidenced in the works of the aforementioned theorists. Neither would they engage in debates that centered on the fundamental equality of African Americans to whites, especially in the area of racial integration along with the inherent rights of African Americans to vote, hold office, integrate churches and neighborhoods, and run for public office, as guaranteed by the Constitution (Marsden, 1980). Few evangelicals debated or engineered a movement against Jim Crow laws.

These pejorative attitudes were particularly evident at fundamentalist institutions like Wheaton and other "bible-believing" churches, which moved from a radical abolitionist position (thoroughly engaged with the political and social issues of the day) in the antebellum period to fundamentalist beacons that proclaimed involvement in progressive social issues as "worldly" behavior at the turn of the nineteenth century. The notable evangelical exception to Wheaton's fundamentalist metamorphosis at this time was Oberlin College, which transitioned slowly and surely into a progressively social and politically prophetic college where the issue of civil rights became de rigueur and the gospel of individual salvation was translated into the social gospel. However, both Oberlin and Wheaton lost important parts of their historical missions as they became more singularly focused on either the social gospel (Oberlin) or personal salvation

(Wheaton). The other important and growing aberration to typical evangelical responses on race was the Los Angeles Azusa Street Revival of 1906, which was one of a very few recorded racially integrated revivals led by black preachers in far western California, which, in turn, birthed the twentieth-century Pentecostal-Charismatic movement (Barnard, 1969; Bartleman, 2000).[3]

In this essay, I identify several key issues as central to understanding the growing ambivalence that those evangelical leaders felt toward issues of civil rights and social justice; as a result, they forfeited their previous prophetic voice to the mainline Protestant denominations of the twentieth century. These beliefs were left relatively fixed until many seminary professors began to challenge the literal nature of the apostle Paul's writings during the civil rights movement of the 1960s – tenets that evangelicals were slow to embrace. (Some still refuse to believe that Scripture takes a firm position on racial equality.) The following issues significantly retarded evangelicals' view on civil rights during the progressive era:

- The legalization of Jim Crow codes and the embrace of the Supreme Court decision of *Plessey v. Ferguson* (1897) of separate but equal.
- Pre-millennial eschatology, or the belief that the world would grow increasingly evil until the second coming or the imminent Rapture of the Church by Jesus Christ; therefore, involvement in issues of social justice was a waste of time and paled in significance to spreading the Gospel.
- Dispensational theology, a wooden and literal hermeneutic that viewed Scripture in distinct epochs that were fixed over time; as a result, slavery and inequality were accepted aspects of each epoch and could not be successfully resisted.
- Racism, the belief that African Americans were fundamentally unequal to whites in almost every area of life.

Significantly, a few decades ago there was recognition on the part of church historians and theologians that the scholarship of Donald W. Dayton, a preeminent Wesleyan scholar, made us aware of a revisionist narrative on a significant number of American evangelical leaders and movements in the antebellum period of the nineteenth century. In his groundbreaking book titled *Discovering an Evangelical Heritage* (1976), Dayton recounted the history of a small band of radical evangelical leaders who ignited the abolitionist movement and fueled the drive to end fundamental inequalities based on race, class, and gender. It was this book that ignited a small groundswell of research among other Wesleyan, Holiness, and Pentecostal scholars in the little known or understood history of Wesleyans and other evangelical churches such as Congregationalists in America. During this period (the 1970s) the charismatic holiness movement broke out among many "bible-believing" churches across America (emblematic of the Jesus Movement) and spread quickly across mainline and other independent churches as well. This also led to an appreciation for the inclusive manner in which Pentecostal and charismatic populations began to navigate the weighty waters of racial integration on Sunday mornings. As a result, scholars representing the antebellum periods of evangelical radicalism on issues of race and gender began reinvestigating the role of radical evangelicals in the nineteenth century on the issue of civil rights, and found that some of their leaders, at least in their sermons and in some of their practices, believed that both blacks and women had equal access to both their rights under our government and the throne of God (Dayton, 1976; Synan, 2001).

Antebellum Evangelical Civil Rights "Prophets"

> I am now quite certain that the crimes of this guilty, land: will never be purged away; but with Blood. (John Brown, December 2, 1859, Charlestown, Virginia)

With the notable exceptions of black leaders like Harriett Tubman, Sojourner Truth, and Frederick Douglass during the antebellum era of slavery, other prominent leaders of either color were few and far between, especially those who advocated full emancipation and equal rights for black slaves (Bordewich, 2005). Dayton rightfully points to Charles Finney as one of the early evangelical revivalist leaders who stood boldly against slavery during his revivalist crusades across the Midwest and Eastern Seaboard. Finney's revivals drew tremendous crowds in all the areas he preached, from the Midwest to New York City. He not only advocated for the abolition of slavery but, during his presidency of Oberlin College – the first college in the United States to admit blacks and women together with white men in 1833 – he approved of the ordination of women. With the assistance of the wealthy Tappan brothers of New York (the founders of modern-day Dun and Bradstreet), Oberlin and other radical reformatory institutions trained people for social change. Institutions like Oberlin, Knox, Berea, and Wheaton were as much about social, political, and religious causes as they were about the formal education of young people. Their graduates became social change agents in a variety of fields, including the ministry and missions. However, for some radical leaders like the Tappan brothers and John Brown, neither Finney nor many New England abolitionists went far enough to free black people from their political and social chains. For them, the end of slavery was only the beginning of the journey for full civil rights and racial equality. Few scholars locate these early fervent and radical evangelicals within the wider religious evangelical movement of that period.

David Reynolds's definitive biography on John Brown traces his fervent Calvinist roots to his passion for evangelicalism and the freedom of African Americans. Brown can be considered a preacher in line with Harriett Tubman. Like Tubman, his beliefs in the equality of African Americans were firmly rooted in his evangelical interpretation of Scripture. He not only lived out those beliefs; he insisted that his entire family be willing to die for them as well (Reynolds, 2005).[4] He raised his children to believe that God had chosen them to free enslaved blacks in America, and it clearly became their life mission.

Brown grew up in a progressively social and religious family in Connecticut and Ohio. His father, Owen, was on the Oberlin College Board of Trustees and was founder of the Western Reserve Anti-Slavery Society in 1833. In Hudson, Ohio he became involved in the Underground Railroad and his barn became the tenth stop on the railway system in Ohio. John also learned earlier that Indians had been marginalized and dispossessed from the government and that their rights were central to a just society as well. But his father's main concern was the righteousness of his family. Having had a few children die before adolescence, Owens's main concern was whether they had "died in Christ" (Reynolds, 2005: 22). Though a strict Calvinist, he carried the burden for the souls of his children to his grave – a lesson not lost on his son John, who took the Christian commitment that his father instilled in him a step further to radical social and political action.

John Brown taught his sons to model their lives after the biblical patriarchs. From the Old Testament, Brown learned of a judgmental and stern God who commanded people to fight for justice and their freedom. In the New Testament, he read of a God who insisted that Christians assist those who were oppressed and in bondage. For Brown, there was no contradiction in holding a gun in one hand and the Bible in the other: they were inseparable. So, it cannot be considered strange when Huey Newton, a leader of the Black Panther Party, declared 100 years later that the only white man in America who did anything good for black folks was John Brown, because "he gave us guns" (Bordewich, 2005: 398).[5]

Brown always considered himself an itinerant preacher; if there were no licensed preachers in the area, he would often preach in a local barn or schoolhouse. As a tanner, he insisted that all his employees attend church every Sunday and family worship each morning. When either his family members or employees disregarded a biblical tenet, Brown had no trouble whipping them or dismissing employees who could not live up to his understanding of biblical standards of living.

As Brown's plans for guerilla warfare in and among the hills and mountains of the Virginias and other Southern outposts became widely known after his death, one can only speculate how successful he might have been if he had obtained a substantial amount of abolitionist money from the evangelical philanthropist Tappan brothers. Like Nat Turner's rebellion only a few decades earlier, the idea of Brown and freed slaves roaming around the South engaged in guerilla warfare could only spark panic in the hearts of slave owners. And when his raid on Harper's Ferry, Virginia failed to produce the revolution Brown had hoped for in 1859, he had to face the capital consequences of being convicted as a federal "terrorist." His biblical-like sojourn presages the bipolar reaction from his country: the hatred emanating from the South and the sainthood ascribed to Brown from the abolitionist North, after a trial and execution that were infamously covered in *Harper's Weekly* and became a nationwide event that spawned songs, sonnets, and recriminations that have endured in American folklore. But more importantly, it was the signal event that assisted in launching Lincoln's invasion of the South a year later.

Lewis and Arthur Tappan: Radical Evangelical Philanthropists

Though from a different class background than John Brown, Lewis Tappan was one of the influential Tappan New England brothers, whose silk business would eventually evolve into Dun and Bradstreet, a multimillion-dollar New York stock exchange credit reporting service. The Tappan Brothers bankrolled much of the antiabolitionist movement across New England and the Midwest, including the influential American Anti-Slavery Society.

Like Brown, the Tappans were born into a strict Calvinist home, where they personally experienced and were transformed by the Second Great Awakening, a widespread religious revival that began on the Eastern Seaboard and eventuated into personal decisions for Christ for both brothers. The brothers began to be more alarmed at the widespread institution of slavery and Lewis personally financed the defense of the African defendants in the infamous *Amistad* incident of 1839, in which a group of African slaves from Sierra Leone had been captured by Spaniards and sent on to Cuba, where they later mutinied on their way to the United States. Their civil case eventually landed before the US Supreme Court, where former President, John Quincy Adams, argued successfully for the defendants (Linder, 2008).

It can be safely concluded that the Tappan brothers, outside the collective contributions of churches, were the main philanthropic contributors to the antislavery cause. The movement was undergirded by gifted ministers like Theodore Weld, Lyman Beecher, Harriett Tubman, Sojourner Truth, Charles Finney, and Charles Stowe (whose sister Harriett's book *Uncle Tom's Cabin* became an inflammatory, bestselling, antislavery narrative). These men and women, aided by Tappan money, presaged the eventual triumph of the abolitionists and turned slavery into a moral cause akin to retaining the Union – which animated more men's service to the Union than the overthrow of slavery (Wyatt-Brown, 1969: 102).

Again, if the various groups financed by the Tappans had coalesced with other fugitive groups like the Underground Railroad, and John Brown's guerilla-like tactics combined with the Anti-Slavery Society, the Civil War might have been averted and a master plan for guerilla warfare might have been more successful than an outright military invasion, which took hundreds of thousands of lives. Mark Noll and other contemporary historians make it clear that most Northerners fought for the preservation of the Union, and it was only after Garrison lobbied Lincoln mercilessly during the war that he finally agreed to make the abolition of slavery the centerpiece of the war with the signing of the Emancipation Proclamation. Thus, most evangelical groups were satisfied with the co-joining of the preservation of the Union on one end and the abolition of slavery on the other. However, very few evangelicals were willing to fight for the eradication of an inherited racism that was deeply embedded in America's psyche after the Civil War; even evangelicals leading the fight against slavery could not and would not wed the two causes in the Reconstruction era (Noll, 2008).

Jim Crow Era

It was during the era of Jim Crow laws in the South that evangelicals mirrored the rest of the country on issues of civil rights and race. The Supreme Court case of *Plessy v. Ferguson* (1896) codified segregation in America and there were few evangelical groups or leaders who spoke out against this apartheid system.[6] Indeed, most evangelicals believed that the separation of the races was in agreement with much of what they read in the Old Testament. Did not Scripture enjoin the Israelites to "come apart and be ye separate" from other racial, ethnic, and religious tribes in order to maintain both their genetic and spiritual purity? Therefore, it did not take much convincing from demagogue-like preachers to convince evangelicals that they did not need to crusade for a race of people who were now legally free. As a result, neither the ubiquitous specter of racism nor uniform civil rights was needed, especially after such a costly war that astonished the world over its carnage.

As we view the genesis of the progressive era, we find that evangelicals were much more concerned with (what they would term) *worldly* behavior by an increasingly post-Victorian society than they were with the social, economical, and political realities of black people.[7] By the time Christian fundamentalist leaders coalesced at a convention in 1919 at Niagara, New York in order to unify their call to arms against the modernist intellectual forces of Marx, Freud, Darwin, and higher criticism of Scripture (along with an increasingly socially liberal society), evangelicals had long felt that these issues were more important to confront than the issues of racism and bigotry, the legacy of slavery.[8] They then ceded much of their "Christian" voices to fundamentalist groups and doctrine.

Another divisive issue was and is the cultural divide over how whites and blacks worshiped on any given Sunday. Even during the Civil War, many Southern black churches worshiped very differently from white audiences, especially if there were house churches on the plantations. Many of their rituals had a cultural base in Africa, and not many resembled the formal liturgy and services of mainline Protestant churches. (Some exceptions to this norm were those slaves who worshiped in the same church as their masters.) Indigenous slave services were filled with spontaneous shouts, testifying, spirituals, and call-and-response sermons that lasted well into the afternoon.[9] Contrasted to this were and are European-centered services with precise liturgy, music, prayers, announcements, and sermons that lasted to noon. To this present century, this divide has not been successfully broken except by mega-church preachers such as T.D. Jakes, Joel Osteen, Tony Evans, and Charles Stanley, whose churches are located in urban areas that have been integrated since the 1970s. However, few black preachers experience white audiences as a majority of their church members and vice versa.

Lost Evangelicals: The Rise of Fundamentalist Doctrines

Doctrinal purity or biblical "right thinking" has been an obsession with many American religious moral crusaders since the days of the American Puritans. For abolitionists like Charles Finney and other biblical students and scholars, the eschatological doctrine of postmillennialism fueled their passion against slavery and for civil rights for African Americans.

Eschatology involves the study of future events in the life of the church that will eventuate in the second coming of Christ and the apocalyptic events that center on the end of the world as we know it, accompanying an eventual new Heaven and Earth and the demise of Satan and his demonic forces. Christian scholars studied the mystical narrative of St. John along with the Old Testament Book of Daniel for hermeneutical clues to Christ's second coming over many millennia. And the range of beliefs is as varied as the number of Protestant denominations in the United States.

Many evangelical leaders from the nineteenth century believed that they were living in a period when their collective righteous acts would hasten the thousand-year reign of Christ on Earth. They believed that the world would progressively become better and that good would triumph over evil, to the extent that Jesus Christ would return to Earth to set up His thousand-year reign as suggested in Revelation. As a result, the eradication of slavery and the crusade to make the United States a Christian nation were fueled by the belief that their moral and civil actions would result in Christ's return and eventual earthly reign (Mathison, 1999).

However, by the progressive era, and certainly by the end of the First World War, there were few preachers and scholars who held such a view. With such destructive forces occurring between European revolutions, America's Civil War, and the First World War, most evangelical Christians could not maintain with very much moral force that the world was getting better. Also, the writings of John Nelson Darby, a Brethren preacher, gained much ground among emerging twentieth-century fundamentalists.[10] And many of his tenets were codified in their doctrinal statements.

Darby wedded dispensational theology to premillennial eschatology in a biblically progressive hermeneutic that was both attractive and more easily understood among common people. It became a sensible pedagogical method that took such highly abstract and symbolic imagery in Daniel and Revelation and translated it into a visible diagram that was codified by fundamentalist churches for most of the twentieth century.

In brief, Darby divided human history from Adam and Eve to the Church age into specific "dispensations" or biblical eras, in which God made covenants with his people Israel and later, the Church as described in the Book of Acts. The nation of Israel is viewed as God's people, and Yahweh's promise to make them a great nation involves the Church's protection of the modern-day Jewish state of Israel. Thus, this theology weds Old Testament doctrines (God's promise to Israel) with New Testament doctrines (Christ's second coming). In doing so it animated fundamentalists and made strange bedfellows of Orthodox Jews and fundamentalist Christians, especially over the issue of Israeli self-determination.[11]

The eschatological doctrine of premillennialism holds that the forces of Satan will become more powerful and that the world will degenerate to the extent that its only obvious hope for salvation rests in the belief that Jesus Christ will rescue humans from their inward and outward decay by setting up his kingdom on earth. However, their teaching specifically states that eternal security is reserved solely for those who have been saved from their sins through the atoning blood of Jesus Christ, God's Son – his provision for their sins.

Premillenialists believe, unlike postmillennialists, that the Church will be raptured (or supernaturally taken from this Earth) until Christ wages his final war against Satan and sets up a new Heaven and new Earth that will be designed for eternity. This doctrine, when combined with dispensational theology, had much to do with the "great reversal" of evangelicals from their earlier commitments to civil rights and equality.

The Ramifications of Dispensational Theology and Premillennial Eschatology on Evangelicals' Attitudes toward Civil Rights

If Charles Finney represents the postmillennial ideal of a radical American revivalist evangelical, then D.L. Moody is a contrasting counterpart to Finney's postmillennial beliefs and emphasis on civil rights. He is also a key transitional figure in American church history, especially as it relates to America's emerging Christian fundamentalist movement as well.

D.L. Moody was born in Northfield, Massachusetts in 1837 to pious New England parents and was soon admitted to the Unitarian Church. However, his association with the evangelical movement began in 1856, about which he stated, "I was born of the flesh in 1837. I was born in the Spirit in 1856" (Dorsett, 1997: 32). The many revivals and prayer meetings led by holiness ministers like Phoebe Palmer and others convinced many Protestant Christians that their infant baptism was not enough to persevere through this life, but that they needed the power of the Holy Spirit to be fully sanctified and empowered to live an overcoming Christian life (White, 1986). In short, they needed a second baptism, experience, or crisis brought on by the Holy Spirit in order for them to understand their need for a holiness-Pentecostal embedded sanctifying spirit. Moody's revivalist career was fueled by a passion for souls and sanctification. His moral, social, and political beliefs were always subordinate to his spiritual beliefs and, unlike Finney, he rarely melded the aforementioned causes into his sermons or revivals. It would be unfair, however, to ignore his social work in the city of Chicago or his keen interest in the progressive education of men and women.[12]

When contrasted to Finney's activism, Moody's revivalist influence during the rise of fundamentalism was enormous. The increase in social and political activism among the mainline denominational churches, contrasted with the revivalist nature of the increasing nondenominational churches, marked their differences more sharply, especially when coupled with their differences in statements of faith. Clearly, they were a threat to those denominations that were attempting to reconcile their doctrines with the competing theories of Darwin, modern psychology, and higher criticism of Scripture. Bible churches proclaimed loudly and clearly through the sermons, messages, tracts, and works of evangelists like Moody, Mordecai Ham, and Billy Sunday that their adherents needed to be revived spiritually and that the "world was not their home."[13] Also, Mark Noll clearly delineates this period of American evangelicalism as one where their churches, associations, missionary groups, and institutions went intellectually underground as well (Noll, 1994; Emerson and Smith, 2007: 39).[14]

Unfortunately for the emerging fundamentalist movement, its institutions spurned control or structural ecclesiology and tended, as Mark Noll and others have demonstrated over time, to split again and again over doctrinal rightness and social purity. Indeed, it was not uncommon to witness church congregations divide and build structures within physical sight of the other, with families and friends rigidly split over doctrinal and social code differences.

This era also witnessed the rise of bible colleges and institutes like the one D.L. Moody and Emma Dryer established before the turn of the century called the Moody Bible

Institute, built on the same physical campus as Moody Church, a large "bible-believing" church consistent with Moody's fundamentalist beliefs.

About 25 miles west of Moody's campus was and is Wheaton College, an academically reputable liberal arts college founded by radical abolitionist Jonathan Blanchard in 1860 and a close cousin to Oberlin College. Blanchard maintained an Underground Railroad stop within the basement of Main Hall and personally boarded black students in his house close to campus. He also later sponsored the initial ministry of one of his first female seminary graduates in 1876, Rev. Frances Townsley (Gallien, 1998). In many ways, Wheaton was also emblematic of the "great reversal." Blanchard's son, Charles, became his father's successor at the end of the nineteenth century, and he was enormously influenced by Moody's magnetic assistant, Emma Dryer, who was a staunch premillennial dispensationalist. It was Dryer more than any other man who successful challenged Charles to reverse his father's stands on postmillennialist eschatology and he signed on with the fundamentalists during this same period. As a result, Wheaton College, an institution that was once considered to be a replication of Oberlin College, became a fundamentalist beacon for bible and independent institutions and moved into Moody's sphere of influence.[15] It took years before Wheaton forged its own identity as an academically rigorous, widely evangelical, liberal arts institution that could be compared favorably to institutions like Oberlin (Hamilton, 1994).

The Doctrinal Impact of Fundamentalist Doctrines on Evangelicalism

Within the context of the United States' acceptance of *de jure* segregation coupled with general apathy toward the issue of civil rights, the widespread doctrinal acceptance of premillennial dispensationalism buried any hope of evangelicals' involvement with black leaders like W.E.B. DuBois or Booker T. Washington over the issue of their civil rights.

Dispensationalists believed in a wooden and literal translation and application of the Old Testament and St. Paul's writings to the Church. Therefore, the seeming validation of Paul's writings on slavery and adherence to the principles and laws reserved for the Israelis during the Old Testament periods were proclaimed to be relevant to Christians in the twentieth century. As a result, these tenets not only retarded any crusade-forming coalition with black leaders, it actively discouraged such cooperative ventures by preachers who informed their congregations that African Americans were not equal to them, as *seemingly* evidenced by the Hamitic curse in the Old Testament and Paul's justification of slavery in the New Testament (Webb, 2001; Haynes, 2007).

Premillennialists believed fervently in the imminent return of Jesus Christ and, therefore, their primary responsibility to that end was to "save souls." Any activism in the realms of politics, social change, economics, and even participation in an imminent war (the First World War) were secondary to pressing their friends and neighbors to make "a decision for Christ." The idea that Christ could return "any minute" caused another retreat from civil rights. Under Christ's reign, all would be equal, but not until he set up his earthly kingdom. So, before one joined a protest march or lobby for others' earthly rights, one needed to consider that one would be wasting one's time if their souls were going to hell.[16]

These doctrines taken together as a fundamentalist package for independent churches signaled the end of the original nineteenth-century evangelical movement's emphasis on the equality of women and African Americans. And, even though there was a rise in attendance at women's colleges, bible colleges, and historically black colleges and universities, and from immigrant and middle-class groups, their educational impact had little effect on evangelicals' attitudes toward race, because most of these institutions mirrored the same attitudes to women and blacks during this era. Historically black colleges and universities (HBCUs) educated their own race and therefore, because of their numerical minority status among collegiate institutions, their central messages of self-determination only reached a certain percentage of their race (Watkins, 2001).

Evangelicals' Failure to Confront Racism

Evangelicals' retreat from civil rights is partly explainable in terms of their recognition of Jim Crow laws, their adoption of fundamentalist doctrines, and their general apathy in the aftermath of the Civil War. But the overriding reason for their failure to complete their moral crusade was simply their refusal to confront their own racism.

Since the genesis of America's colonial past, there have been at least three stages or levels of racism that many evangelical families can identify in their histories: religious–civil, dysconscious, and unconscious.

Type I: Religious–civil racism

Evangelicals believed in a fundamental or systemic racial inequality that had been promoted by the US government since slavery and was codified under laws like Dred Scott that affirmed what many believed: black people were property and had no claim to civil rights. Their churches taught the veracity and wider implications of the Hamitic curse and justified slavery through a literal interpretation of Paul's writings to the Church. The stereotypes of black people were composed from what psychologists call "self-fulfilling prophecies." That is, if black Americans behaved in ways that white people believed about them, then they would be left alone. Some of these monikers were: ignorant, lazy, shiftless, sexually charged, loyal, passive, contented in their state of subservience, and a people who borrowed spiritualities from white men and Africa.

Type II: Dysconscious racism – white privilege

Evangelicals intellectually and spiritually believed that black people were equal to whites. Yet because of the pernicious stereotypes and prejudices that were rooted in slavery and perpetuated during the segregationist era of American history, they could not break free from their conviction that blacks are inferior to whites. And while many evangelicals became more widely educated after the Second World War, they struggled with the feelings (reinforced by a myriad of cultural clues) that somehow black people were really not on the same cultural and social ladder and held on to some deeply seeded suspicions of African American culture. Finally, they expected that their pervasively evangelical culture would be *the* ethical, moral, religious, and political framework that would unilaterally inform the United States and all other cultures, including African American; and that all should be subordinate to their belief system, especially since many of them believed that their value base was and is the epistemological framework of the Founding Fathers.[17]

Type III: Unconscious racism

Modern-day evangelicals like Jim Wallis and Tony Campolo would in all likelihood place themselves in this category: rejecting most, if not all, racist stereotypes, they admittedly struggle with culturally pervasive and pejorative images of black people in the television, radio, movie, magazine, and music industries that continually revive stereotypes and misconceptions of black Americans. As a result, many of their unconscious images are filled with fear; and fear is one of the paralyzing and debilitating conditions of racism. Accordingly, it is nearly impossible for almost any person to be free of America's "original sin" of white racism (Wallis, 1984; Campolo, 2008).

Double Consciousness Revisited

The double-conscious nature of American evangelicals centers on the same book (Bible) that they have used both to defend slavery (Southern plantation owners) and to rise up to abolish it (John Brown). As a result of these conflicting tributaries and interpretive teachings on race, American evangelicals remain ambivalent about civil rights. On one hand, they believe that Christ's and Paul's teachings on equality are clear. They have few problems believing that African Americans can be "brothers and sisters in Christ." However, issues of equality and systemic racism remain in their churches.

Yet, there are other religious groups, like Anabaptists, whose voices have consistently been raised against racism and other social ills and whose doctrinal system is not far from many evangelicals. Institutions like Goshen College and Eastern Mennonite University remain in the larger evangelical Consortium of Christian Colleges and Universities and their stances on racism have been clear; however, they hold to an evangelical statement of faith. Also, other voices among modern-day evangelical leaders, like Jim Wallis, Tony Campolo, Jim Sire, Phillip Yancey, and the editors of *Christianity Today*, have made issues of race central to their ministries and publications.

However, as a religious group, their ambivalence toward matters of race remains problematic, as many of them have stayed silent and hold clearly conflicting views on racial leadership (e.g., Barack Obama). Clearly, as DuBois suggested about his own race over a century ago, their consciousness has not been raised to the point where they have clear and consistent measures of racial equality.

Notes

1 I use the term *evangelicalism* in the following context: evangelicalism was and is a movement of American religious Protestants who believed that for a person to be eternally secure in their faith in Jesus Christ and to gain eternity with Him, they must verbally confess their sins, request forgiveness for their sins, and ask for Jesus Christ to reside in their hearts, or in their spiritual being. This was and is called a personal and spiritual "born again" experience. Many of the adherents to evangelicalism believe that this verbal confession is the sole way to eternal existence with God. So, the people I refer to in this essay all had this "born again" experience. Protestants used Christ's New Testament scriptural admonition, "You must be born again," to justify such a spiritual mandate.

2 Indeed, eminent historian Bertram Wyatt-Brown (1969: 60) concluded: "In spite of the outward simplicity of the evangelical movement, it was a crusade of peculiar contradictions. Its advocates claimed to be "profoundly serious," not "solemn triflers," and yet they appealed to an anti-intellectual emotionalism."

3 Pentecostal churches later claimed that their emphasis on the Holy Spirit's "power to overcome" produced an implicit egalitarianism among the races in America. Their claim can be confirmed by the inordinate number of Pentecostal churches in the United States that are racially integrated.

4 This fact was no small oath, since Brown had fathered 20 children by two wives and some of them later died at Harper's Ferry, West Virginia. As Reynolds (2005: 40) notes: "The clan raised by John Brown was the only white family in pre-Civil War America willing both to live with black people and to die for them."

5 Huey Newton's comment, made in a speech on the University of Michigan campus when I was in high school in 1968, echoed Frederick Douglass's evaluation of Brown: "though a white gentleman, [Brown] is in sympathy a black man and is deeply interested in our cause, as though his own soul had been pierced with the iron of slavery." Newton's quote represents the degree of ambivalence many black radicals felt toward liberal white civil rights activists.

6 Jim Crow laws were local and state laws and codes enacted between 1876 and 1965 that codified racial inequality, thus *de jure* racial segregation became legalized. Also, the Supreme Court decision of *Plessy v. Ferguson* (1896) sanctioned these codes and laws of separate but equal.

7 It was during this period that the Holiness Movement among evangelical groups became popular among many constituents. This movement emphasized the role of the Holy Spirit in the sanctification of the believer. Adherents were urged to concentrate more on their spiritual lives than their physical, since their physical natures were temporal. The "worldly" moniker was one to avoid, as it suggested behaviors that were copied by society (Dayton, 1985).

8 The World Christian Fundamentalist Association began in Niagara, New York in 1919 both as a reaction against the secular theories of the period and a response to their

conviction that the mainline denominations (e.g., Episcopalian, Unitarian, Congregational) were becoming liberal. As an outgrowth of the convention, many of their churches became independent, bible churches that birthed new Protestant and holiness denominations like the Christian Missionary Alliance, Evangelical Free, Nazarene, and many other independent churches (Marsden, 1991).

9 The obvious exceptions to these societal norms are people who possess the same phenotype, but for whatever reason, culturally identify with a group of people who are not their skin color. Servants in the North before and during the war attended church services with their owners, and as a result, many of them joined the mainline denominations or founded hybrid substitutes like the African Methodist Episcopal Church. See, for example, *The Most Segregated Hour* (2005) and Battle (2006).

10 See Boyer (1994). One of the bestselling American authors of the twentieth and twenty-first centuries is a popular Christian premillennialist, Tim LaHaye. His books have earned him millions of dollars all over the world and these proceeds have financed many fundamentalist causes. See for example LaHaye and Jenkins (1995).

11 Indeed, evangelist and entrepreneur Pat Robertson has been viewed as a Christian Zionist because of his avid and fervent support for the state of Israel via his writings and television broadcasts on the 700 Club/Christian Broadcasting Network, Virginia Beach, Virginia.

12 Moody was on the board of trustees of Wellesley College during the time the founding Durant family was in control of the college. He also founded boys' (Mount Herman, 1881) and girls' schools (Northfield Academy, 1879) near his birthplace of Northfield, MA. And of course, the Moody Bible Institute also survives near the historic nondenominational Moody Church in downtown Chicago, IL. Edward Blum also acknowledges Moody's ambivalence for the social gospel in his *Reforging the White Republic* (2007).

13 As Emerson and Smith (2007: 41) note, all three evangelists held segregated revivals all over the South. None challenged the prevailing codes until the advent of Billy Graham's crusades of the 1950s, when he insisted that all his revivals were to be integrated.

14 Emerson and Smith (2007) claim that over 85% of Protestants in America were evangelical Christians during this period. An increasing number of white Northerners' attitudes toward race mirrored their Southern counterparts. Between Jim Crow laws and segregated churches, evangelicals had abandoned much of their antebellum civil rights rhetoric and agenda.

15 Indeed, beyond the Blanchard-Fisher family's governance of the college, Moody's adherents have also played a large part in the spiritual development of the college. Rev. Joseph Stowell, the former pastor of Moody Church, and Duane Litfin, the former President of Wheaton College, attended the same seminary and became Presidents of their respective colleges during the 1990s. Stowell is a current member of the Wheaton College Board of Trustees.

16 An emerging Protestant movement that was inviting social change was the Holiness-Pentecostal movement, begun in Azusa Street in Los Angeles during this same period. The fact that such a large revival was racially integrated and led by a black preacher caused immediate attention. But for many, California was already viewed as a futuristic state in America (Bartleman, 2000).

17 For a comprehensive examination of the way in which many conservative evangelicals and fundamentalists view the founding of America, see Marshall and Manuel (2009).

References

Barnard, John (1969) *From Evangelicalism to Progressivism at Oberlin College, 1866–1917*, Ohio State Press, Columbus.

Bartleman, Frank (2000[1925]) *Azusa Street*, Whitaker House, New Kensington, PA.

Battle, Michael (2006) *The Black Church in America: African American Spirituality*, Blackwell, Malden, MA.

Blum, Edward (2007) *Reforging the White Republic: Race, Religion and American Nationalism, 1865–1898*, LSU Press, Baton Rouge, LA.

Bordewich, Fergus (2005) *Bound for Canaan: The Underground Railroad and the War for the Soul of America*, Amistad Publishing, New York.

Boyer, Paul (1994) *When Time Shall Be No More: Prophecy Belief in Modern American Culture*, Belknap Publishing, Cambridge, MA.

Campolo, Tony (2008) *It's Friday but Sunday's Comin'*, Nelson Publishers, Nashville.

Dayton, Donald W. (1976) *Discovering an Evangelical Heritage*, Harper and Row, New York.

Dayton, Donald W. (1985) *The Late 19th Century Revivalist Teachings on the Holy Spirit*, Taylor and Francis, London.

Dorsett, Lyle (1997) *A Passion for Souls: The Life of D. L. Moody*, Moody Publishers, Chicago.

DuBois, W.E.B. (2007[1903]) *The Souls of Black Folks*, Cosimo Classics, New York.

Emerson, Michael and Smith, Christian (2007) *Divided by Faith: Evangelical Religion and the Problem of Race in America*, Oxford University Press, Oxford.

Gallien, Louis (1998) *A Daughter of the King: The Life and Ministry of Rev. Frances Townsley During the Progressive Era*, Women in Baptist Life Collection, Mercer University Archives, Savannah, GA.

Hamilton, Michael (1994) The Fundamentalist Harvard: Wheaton College and the Continuing Vitality of American Evangelism, 1919–1965. PhD dissertation, Notre Dame University.

Hart, D.G. (2003) *Defending the Faith: J. Gresham Machen and the Crisis of Conservative Protestantism in Modern America*, P&R Publishing, Phillipsburg, PA.

Haynes, Stephen (2007) *Noah's Curse: The Biblical Justification for Slavery*, Oxford University Press, Oxford.

LaHaye, Tim and Jenkins, Phil (1995) *Left Behind*, Tyndale House Publishers, Carol Stream, IL.

Linder, Douglas (2008) Stamped with glory: Lewis Tappan and the Africans of the Amistad, *Social Science Abstract*, http://www.ssrn.com/abstract=1109114 (accessed April 19, 2011).

Marsden, George (1980) *Fundamentalism and American Culture*, Oxford University Press, London.

Marsden, George (1991) *Understanding Fundamentalism and Evangelicalism*, Eerdmans, Grand Rapids.

Marshall, Peter and Manuel, David (2009) *The Light and the Glory: God's Plan for America*, 3rd edn, Revell, Grand Rapids, MI.

Mathison, Keith (1999) *Postmillennialism: Eschatology of Hope*, P&R Publishing, Phillipsburg, PA.

Noll, Mark (2008) *God and Race in American Politics: A Short History*, Princeton University Press, Princeton.

Noll, Mark (1994) *The Scandal of the Evangelical Mind*, Eerdmans, Grand Rapids, IL.

Reynolds, David (2005) *John Brown, Abolitionist: The Man Who Killed Slavery, Sparked the Civil War and Seeded Civil Rights*, Knopf, New York.

Smith, Timothy (1977) *Revivalism and Social Reform in Mid-Nineteenth Century America*, Johns Hopkins University Press, Baltimore.

Synan, Vinson (2001) *The Century of the Holy Spirit: 100 Years of Pentecostal and Charismatic Renewal*, Thomas Nelson, Nashville.

The Most Segregated Hour (2005) Documentary, Forever Young Productions.

Wallis, Jim (1984) *Agenda for Biblical People*, HarperCollins, New York.

Watkins, William (2001) *The White Architects of Black Education: Ideology and Power in*

America, 1865–1954, Teachers College Press, New York.

Webb, William (2001) *Slaves, Women, and Homosexuals: Exploring the Hermeneutic of Cultural Analysis*, IVP Press, Downers Grove, IL.

White, Charles E. (1986) *The Beauty of Holiness: Phoebe Palmer as Theologian, Revivalist, Feminist, and Humanitarian*, Zondervan, Grand Rapids, IL.

Wyatt-Brown, Bertram (1969) *Lewis Tappan and the Evangelical War against Slavery*, LSU Press, Baton Rouge, LA.

CHAPTER 37
Gender and Sexuality in the Context of Religion and Social Justice

Mary E. Hunt

Gender and sexuality used to be considered given and fixed. A man was a man, a woman a woman, a heterosexual was straight, a lesbian or gay person was gay. Now, after decades of pain, discussion, research, and legislation, gender and sexuality are changing and contested categories in US society and around the world. In the balance are laws governing marriage and inheritance, what it means to be a person, and how to behave morally. Religion is one of the primary sources shaping culture. So it is no surprise that religions are the locus of struggles and debates as these social justice issues unfold.

An overview of the US religious landscape in this regard necessarily focuses on Christianity and Judaism because they are the largest groups having the most social influence. But there is also ferment in Islam and Buddhism as well as among pagan and native groups. This account will focus on the two large groups, since they seem to have the most influence in the culture, but the changes are broadly based.

Many public discussions, including those in Congress, over matters like the Equal Rights Amendment and the Employment Non-Discrimination Act are informed by religious concepts. Arguments, both progressive pro-sex and conservative sex-negative ones, are sometimes espoused by people who are not even adherents of the traditions from which the arguments come, a clue that religious teachings are powerful shapers of culture. This consideration of gender and sexuality as social justice issues reflects contemporary and ongoing religious concerns that are a well-established part of the cultural landscape.

Gender

Gender as a category of analysis emerged in US society in the debates over women's right to vote in the nineteenth century. Prior to that time, it was assumed that women and men were different and that women were subordinate and men were in charge of everything but the daily household chores. This notion was based on Christian and Jewish scriptural passages, including the creation accounts in Genesis 1:1–2:3 (the seven days of creation, which include the creation of human beings) and 2:4–25 (God formed a male and from the male's rib, a female), and several Pauline texts including admonitions for women to be submissive to their husbands in Ephesians 5:25.

That view held sway well into the twentieth century. It was reflected in laws and customs. For example, women were not able to secure their own credit cards without a husband's approval; certain jobs were advertised for women and others for men. Even though changes in the understanding of gender have been enormous, remnants of the earlier views can still be found. Those who take the Bible literally, for instance, and those who claim that "natural law" dictates social life live as if the earlier worldview were still operative.

Nineteenth-century suffrage leaders Elizabeth Cady Stanton and Susan B. Anthony realized that until and unless women were understood as full persons in a religious sense, they would not be treated as such under civil law. So, in addition to their work on legislation, they took on the interpretation of the Bible as a source of cultural information about women. Stanton formed the Revising Committee, a group of Christian women, most without specialized training in theology, to read and comment on the passages in the Bible that deal with women. They published their results in a volume entitled *The Woman's Bible* in 1895. It was an effort to interpret those verses in which women were featured and to offer alternative explanations to the ways in which the texts were preached in most churches. The book was by all accounts an innovative and unique approach that helped to change minds about the place of women in society. It went out of print quickly but was revived in 1974 during the second wave of feminism when feminist theology began in earnest.

Women eventually got the right to vote in 1920, thanks in small part to religious support from progressive groups such as the Unitarians, whose buildings were sometimes the sites of organizing meetings. By that time, some Protestant denominations, notably the United Church of Christ (1853), ordained women to ministry. Some Protestant women were circuit-riding preachers, and some Catholic sisters were busy founding schools and hospitals. They functioned as proof positive that women could do what men could do, thus eroding some of the gender difference arguments. Other women took on roles that had previously belonged to men, for example factory work and administration, while the men fought in the two world wars. This, too, helped to change people's minds about gender.

After the Second World War, civil rights for African American people emerged as the premier social justice issue. Religious groups, especially progressive Protestants, Catholics, including many nuns and priests, and many Jews, were in the vanguard of those calling for full legal rights for all Americans. Many clergy and religious leaders, including the Rev. Dr. Martin Luther King, Jr., brought the weight of their respective traditions to bear on public arguments in favor of (and also, disgracefully, in opposition to) the legislation. Similar religious participation in the antiwar movement during the Vietnam era in the 1960s was a factor in shifting consciousness. Opposition to the war was inspired and fueled by religious commitments to peace and justice.

This track record of religious involvement in US social life, despite the constitutional separation of church and state – better, of religion and politics – meant that subsequent movements, including the women's movement and the gay movement, would also involve religious thinking at the heart of the debate. Religious leaders would play key roles in bringing about social justice on these fronts.

In 1960, theologian Valerie Saiving wrote an article entitled "The human situation: A feminine view" (Saiving, 1960). She argued that men's and women's experiences are so different that they even sin differently. While men tend to sin through acts of pride and power, women tend to sin by being distracted and diffuse, allowing others to define them; in short, the opposite of men's ways of sinning. Saiving reasoned that if this were the case, then the solutions that religions offer, for example in the case of Christianity self-sacrificial love, would be detrimental to women if they were helpful to men. She paved the way for considering religion to be gendered activity.

The specifics of Saiving's argument did not persuade huge numbers of people, but the underlying concept that women and men are so different as to be different religiously opened up decades of feminist work. Since 1960, virtually every aspect of religion is scrutinized through a gender lens: church history is reread to see where women were obscured or ignored; the scriptures of many traditions are reanalyzed as if gender matters; ministry and liturgical life are reexamined and renewed to reflect gender-inclusive language and imagery for the divine as well as for humanity; ethics and moral theology are rethought from a gender-sensitive starting point as if women's experiences were unique and heterosexism were a sin. Of course there has been virulent opposition to these efforts – everything from declaring their proponents to be heretics to defunding organizations and religious agencies that purport them. But even the opposition proves that religion and gender are intimately related. It is now taken as a given in the field as well as in society at large that issues of gender have a religious component.

Mary Daly, a Catholic feminist theologian-turned-philosopher, observed that "If God is man, then man is God" (Daly, 1973: 19). Her work was met with the deep recognition that a fundamental problem, a neuralgic issue, had been named. Ascribing male human characteristics to the divine both reflects masculine power and allows, encourages, and confirms it in society. Those with the power to name the divine surely possess other powers as well.

The idea that women, too, reflect the divine fully and without reservation was a revolutionary idea in the 1970s. It flew in the face of historical church teachings about women, such as Tertullian's view that women were "the devil's gateway" or Thomas Aquinas's idea that women were "misbegotten males." Some scholars rejected all anthropomorphic imagery for the divine. Others suggested focusing on Goddesses. It was conversation that had public impact insofar as it helped women to see that they were not second-class members of creation or society.

Mary Daly and other feminist theologians insisted that the language and imagery of the divine were integrally related to the ways in which women and men acquitted themselves in society. Scholar/activists such as Anne McGrew Bennett added that, in like manner, racial and bellicose images of God had a negative impact on society. The default whiteness of the Christian God, for example, and the images of God as lord, ruler, and king, serve to solidify the power of those who hold sway in a society. Religion was also understood to be racialized and to reflect class stratification.

Debates over these matters in religious circles were heated and difficult. Some groups rejected all social scientific data, claiming instead that revelation was from God alone. But by the late 1970s, virtually all Protestant denominations and many Jews were grappling with gender issues. Catholics came a little later, but no less passionately, to the discussions. In churches and rabbinic circles, the ordination of women was decisive. After all, if the ministry and leadership positions of religious communities were reserved for men only, then it was no wonder that government officials, judges, and ordinary citizens assumed that women were not capable of being heads of households, taking loans without a male co-signer, going to certain schools, or being members of clubs without being adjunct to their husbands who were members. Religious claims about justice and equality now had to include justice and equality for women.

While religious changes took place at their own pace, it is interesting to note how they unfolded hand-in-hand with the advent of legal, accessible birth control, the legalization of abortion in 1973, and the ultimately unsuccessful but vigorous efforts to ratify the Equal Rights Amendment. Some refer to these struggles as the gender wars. Perhaps a less bellicose image is more fitting to the efforts, but in any case, the struggles changed the face of society. How women and men live together in daily life – as friends, spouses, colleagues – has changed significantly from gender-stratified and gender-determined roles to far more egalitarian ways of being, thanks in part to religious efforts.

Jewish women formed the National Council of Jewish Women (1893) and Hadassah (1912), which laid the groundwork for their leadership in the wider community. The first woman rabbi ordained was Regina Jonas in Germany in 1935. In the United States, the first woman ordained was Sally Priesand in the Reform movement in 1972. The Reconstructionist movement followed by ordaining its first woman in 1974, with the Conservative movement allowing women on the *bima* (altar) in 1985. Orthodox Jews still do not generally ordain women, though a few have received ordination from their teachers. Blu Greenberg and other Orthodox Jewish women insist that there is no *halakhic* (legal) reason not to ordain women. While Betty Robbins was first appointed a cantor in 1995, it was not until 1975 that Barbara Ostfeld-Horowitz was ordained a cantor. Women professors of Judaic studies eventually took their places in academia. Each step along the way represents both a religious change and a social change.

Women priests were ordained in the Lutheran Church in 1970 and in the Episcopal Church in 1974. In Roman Catholicism, debates over the ordination of women to the priesthood raged for decades. Thus far, they have not led to ordination by the institutional church. A variety of Catholic feminist ministers, including both those ordained by groups like the Roman Catholic Womenpriests and those ordained by small communities, as well as many women who are not ordained, are becoming increasingly common. There is also in Catholicism a general referendum on the hierarchical structure of the institutional church and deep questioning of the very notion of a caste set aside – even including women – for priesthood.

Among Muslim women, similar challenges to traditional notions of wife and mother, covering of the female body, and marriage laws were part of twentieth-century life. In the twenty-first century the matter of women imams – that is, women who lead congregations in *salat* or prayer – is under consideration. This is already done in three of the four Sunni schools and in the Shia schools when women worship with other women. However, neither Sunni nor Shia, with few exceptions, permit women to lead mixed groups. Scholarship on this matter is underway. It can be speculated that in time Muslim women, like their Jewish and Christian counterparts, will probably be allowed to function fully as spiritual leaders. This shows the reciprocal ways in which religion and the larger culture influence one another.

Buddhist women experience similar changes. Some Zen Buddhist women have been ordained priests. Others are fully ordained nuns, such as Venerable Bhikkhuni Kusuma in Sri Lanka, who has international influence. Wiccan and Pagan groups have long been led by women. Goddess religions have a majority of women in leadership.

These groups are smaller, so their impact on the larger society has not matched that of the more numerous Christian and Jewish ones. Nevertheless, the near unanimity of religious ferment and progress on seeing women as full human beings capable of decision making and religious agency has been decisive in bringing about social justice for women. At the same time, the opposition to women's religious equality has mirrored the opposition to women's civil equality. Concrete accomplishments in the religious sphere helped to bring about the social equality of women and men because they provided deeply rooted reasons for rejecting the old models and embracing new, egalitarian ones.

Abortion rights have long been the locus of social wrangling over gender. Since the Supreme Court ruling in *Roe v. Wade* in 1973, women's right to privacy assures that women with their doctors, not the church or state, will make reproductive decisions. This has become a lightning rod for social struggle, since it is one of the most obvious examples of how the culture has changed. Legal abortion is one of the key issues named by those who seek equality around the world, for example the United Nations, as part of larger development strategies. The Vatican and some largely Muslim countries have attempted to block consensus at UN meetings on women's rights.

Those who oppose legal abortion base many of their arguments on the idea that the fetus is a person who deserves to live. Those who support legal abortion begin with the idea that women are moral agents who can and must decide what happens to their own bodies. The beliefs are deeply held on both sides and seemingly with little middle ground. People have killed one another over these ideas; doctors who perform abortions have been murdered by people who rely on religiously founded beliefs. The matter is far from settled, but religious arguments are central to the social justice work at hand.

This brief overview of some of the issues raised by new understandings of gender shows that the implications are far-reaching. It takes only a look at family photos to see how one's grandparents lived and dressed, how one's parents conducted their family life, and how even today's adults live differently than they did in their youth. Equality of men and women is largely, though by no means universally, assumed. Disparities in pay and promotion are but one example of the ongoing problem. But most religions have acknowledged the theoretical point that being treated equally, regardless of gender, is a human right. The full practice of that insight remains elusive. Equality becomes even more important as changes in the understanding of sexuality take place.

Sexuality

Sexuality is equally, if not more, contentious than gender in religious circles. Heterosexuality, like the early gender concepts, was simply taken as normative until the mid-nineteenth century, when the word "homosexual" began to appear as a description of a same-sex-loving person. Until the mid-twentieth century, homosexuality, if acknowledged, was generally seen as aberrant, illegal, and immoral conduct. The notion that there were people whose default sexual preference was for those of the same gender was still a new idea in the 1960s at the beginning of the so-called gay liberation movement (it included lesbians and transgender people, but the word "gay" was used generically). Bisexual people's claims came later, with transgendered people's experiences now functioning as a challenge to all previously understood concepts of sexuality. The unfolding of the issues is a primer on the role of religion in the accomplishment of social justice.

Religious arguments raged on all sides of the questions. Traditional Christian and Jewish understandings of women and men led to the conclusion that heterosexual coupling and marriage were the normative human experiences. In the 1960s, as women's roles expanded and men took on more domestic responsibilities, the possibility of living well and with social recognition outside of heterosexual marriage became a real option for significant numbers of people. Previously, of course, there had been same-sex-loving people, but they tended to be isolated and/or to live in small social groups. Some were wealthy and/or bohemian enough to live outside of social conventions, but others simply suffered under the limits of normative heterosexuality.

Persons who preferred same-sex to opposite-sex partners for intimate relationships began to make their lives public as part of the general sexual ferment of post–Second World War society. Men who had served in the military and women who had lived in communities that were predominantly female because men were at war gradually grew accustomed to the reality of same-sex-loving people. The Kinsey Reports (1948 and 1953) opened the conversation about sexual orientation, making clear that perhaps up to 10% of the population is oriented toward same-sex loving. The Mattachine Society (1950), a men's group dedicated to protecting and improving gay rights, and the Daughters of Bilitis (1955), a lesbian social and support group, were early efforts to offer community and fellowship to same-sex-loving people who were rejected by many sectors of society. The American Psychiatric Association removed homosexuality from its list of diagnostic categories in 1973.

Eventually, same-sex-loving people demanded the legal right not to be arrested for same-sex conduct. They fought for social rights, including the right to serve honorably and honestly in the military and to have access without prejudice to housing and jobs. And they expected religious rights; namely, to be seen as healthy, good, and natural human beings doing their best to love others. The paradigmatic event of the struggle occurred in June 1969, when same-sex-loving people fought back against the police who raided the Stonewall bar in New York City to arrest the patrons. Since then, the Lesbian, Gay, Bisexual, Transgender (often abbreviated LGBT) rights movement has been in full swing.

If the so-called gender wars were hard fought religiously, efforts to bring about same-sex rights are even more difficult in religious circles. Like abortion, same-sex love is seen as a defining social issue because the implications of it are so far-reaching. Just as abortion rights are opposed by some who feel that women are only carriers of divinely generated human persons from the moment of conception, those who oppose lesbian, gay, bisexual, and transgender love consider heterosexuality to be divinely given for all human beings. Religious challenges to that way of thinking are among the most powerful motors of change.

Jewish and Christian scriptural verses are cited to argue that homosexuality is morally wrong. For example, Genesis 19:1–5 (the story of the men of Sodom), Leviticus 18:22 (lying with a man as if with a woman), Leviticus 20:13 (punishment of death for men who lie with other men), and Deuteronomy 23:17 (another mention of sodomy) are the most often cited in the Hebrew scriptures. I Corinthians 6:9–10 (homosexuals among those who will not inherit the reign of God); 1 Timothy 1:9–10 (reference to male prostitutes); and Romans 1:21–31(the question of what is natural/unnatural sexually) are among the most widely referred to in the Christian testament. All of these texts have been subject to serious scholarly revision. These texts have grounded so many other ways of thinking about sexuality beyond the religious. For example, in the absence of other sources, early psychological ways of seeing same-sex love were influenced by biblical texts.

Just as feminist theology emerged to deal with the fundamental issues of gender and the implications of a gendered reading of religion, so, too, has lesbian, gay, bisexual, transgender theology emerged as a source for rethinking the fundamental issues of sexuality. It is sometimes called queer theology. LGBT scholars and activists deal with the religious dimensions of heterosexism; that is, the normativity of heterosexuality to the exclusion of the legal, moral, and social rights of same-sex-loving people. Of course, there are also many scholars who oppose this work, but they are not known by any particular overarching name.

This theological work is occasioned by a watershed in culture, one that the writers of the scriptures never imagined; namely, a time when same-sex love would be seen by many people, including those in religion, as one more way of loving. It is a product both of the expanding gender roles and of the social sciences. Psychology led the way by erasing homosexuality from its diagnostic categories of mental illness. Sociology contributed endless studies of the lives and loves, families and communities, of same-sex-loving people. Economics contributed more data about the reality of same-sex-loving people in terms of their family and work lives.

As more and more information became available, and as more and more queer people "came out" to tell their own stories, it became obvious that homosexuality, far from being an abnormal, immoral practice, is simply another variant on human loving. This view is not shared by everyone, though even opponents admit that there is a growing cultural consensus in the West. Nonetheless, discrimination against LGBT people still exists. In employment, for example, the Employment Non-Discrimination Act is pending legislation to counter this situation. Same-sex-loving people have been barred from serving openly in the US military. The repeal of the "Don't Ask, Don't Tell" policy in 2011 was a hard-fought change. One of the major issues involved remains how military chaplains will deal with a fully open and inclusive force, a clue that religions remain one of the major shaping forces in social justice.

Religions are primary resources for understanding marriage, divorce, sexual practices, and the bearing and rearing of children. Both religious traditions and religious communities change on the basis of social input, just as society changes on the basis of religious input. Suggestions that religions are immutable are hard to substantiate. Slavery is the best example of how even traditions that supported the practice and provided a scriptural basis for it gradually found other religious social justice arguments that trumped those teachings.

Scholars of religion, pastors, and activists faced the evolving nature of sexuality head on from the beginning. In the 1960s, even before the Stonewall uprising, there were gay and lesbian religious groups. For example, what is now the Universal Fellowship of Metropolitan Community Churches (MCC) was founded by the Rev. Troy Perry, who gathered a small group of lesbian and gay people for a religious service in his living room in 1968. There are now more than 300 MCC congregations in 22 countries. Dignity, a Catholic LGBTQ (lesbian, gay, bisexual, transgender, queer/questioning) group, started in 1969 when a small group gathered for mass. Today, Dignity has dozens of chapters all over the United States.

Early on, queer people, like the suffragists before them, realized that social changes were intimately linked with changes in religion. So they went to the source of the problem, their respective faith traditions, which they also considered the font of some of the solution. In their faith groups they could meet and worship as LGBT people, and challenge and ultimately transform the teachings of their religions. That work continues, as the laws and customs needed to make same-sex-loving people full citizens with all human rights are still in process.

Scholarship about religion as well as worship and fellowship shape culture. Historian John Boswell wrote *Christianity, Homosexuality and Social Tolerance* (1980), a landmark text in which he made the case that same-sex love has long been at the heart of the Christian tradition. Jesuit priest John McNeill offered the first Catholic treatment of the issues in *The Church and the Homosexual*, in which he claimed the pastoral importance of inclusive loving. Bernadette Brooten, a scholar of religion, laid out the particular issues for women in her book *Love between Women* (1996). She argued that, in the early Christian period, the taboo was not simply because the two people were women, but because lesbian relationships tended to be equalitarian. The normative male–male pattern was teacher–student, master–slave, older man–younger man in the Greek and Roman world. So women broke two taboos at once: that against same-sex loving and that against egalitarian partnerships.

These scholarly works and many that followed developed in tandem with a growing movement of religious LGBT people to find community among those of their own faith traditions. They were living proof that being gay or lesbian, bisexual or transgender was not incompatible with being religious. Jewish congregations like Bet Mispaha in Washington, DC and Bet Simchat Torah in New York City became popular places for worship and socializing. Virtually all of the Protestant denominations had their own support and action groups, including Integrity for the Episcopalians, the United Church Coalition for LGBT Concerns, and Lutherans Concerned, to name just a few. Most of these groups existed alongside the denominational structures, not within them. But eventually some denominations, notably the Unitarian Universalist Association and United Church of Christ, set up offices as part of their formal structures to deal with LGBT issues.

Jewish groups flourished as well. The World Congress of Gay, Lesbian, and Bisexual Jewish Organizations with more than 50 members reflects the variety and reach of LGBT people throughout the Jewish community. Some Orthodox Jews worked to reconcile their faith with their sexuality, despite strong opposition in their circles. Muslim groups have been equally diverse and active, ranging from those that condemn homosexuality to those that support same-sex marriage. They are a growing part of the interreligious LGBT community.

Pagan and Wiccan groups have long included queer people among their ranks. The Radical Faeries are a loosely held coalition of gay men who seek spirituality together. The Gay Buddhist Sangha is a queer-friendly community, and the Gay Buddhist Fellowship is a men's group that supports its members in the practice of their tradition.

The National Religious Leadership Roundtable, under the auspices of the National Gay and Lesbian Task Force, is a coalition of many of these groups. The Roundtable meets annually, functions as a clearinghouse for information, and serves as a locus of public activity to bring about religiously informed social change.

Ordination once again became a contested matter in terms of sexuality. If publicly sanctioned religious leaders included LGBT people, then it would be hard to teach against same-sex love. Moreover, since clergy and religious leaders enjoy a certain privileged place in society, their support and affirmation for same-sex-loving people is crucial.

The United Church of Christ ordained William Johnson in 1972 in what is considered the first ordination of an openly gay person in a US Christian denomination. The first openly gay Orthodox rabbi was Steven Greenberg, who was ordained in 1983 and came out in 1999. In 1977, Ellen Barrett was the first openly lesbian/gay person ordained in the Episcopal Church. But the pitched battles to accept or deny same-sex-loving candidates for ordination are the stuff of twentieth-century religious history.

A famous Presbyterian case involved the Rev. Jane Adams Spahr, who was called to minister in 1974 at the Downtown Presbyterian Church in Rochester, New York. In an unusual move, the local presbytery blocked her appointment. The congregation and other supporters helped Jane Spahr develop another ministry, That All May Freely Serve. TAMS became a well-organized, ecclesial change group in Presbyterian circles, as well as a source of ministry. In 2010, that denomination voted at the national level to affirm a single standard of ordination for all candidates. Previously, LGBT people were expected to be single and celibate. The decision remains to be ratified by the local presbyteries but signals the direction in which that church seems to be going.

All of these religious struggles ensue while society as a whole grapples with the reality of same-sex couples and increasing numbers of families made up of two people of the same gender and children. Because religious arguments are cited on both sides of the fence, it is increasingly important for religious leaders to understand and articulate their traditions' theologies. Same-sex marriage presents a test case for how much things have or have not changed.

Marriage is widely considered one of the pillars of society. For many people it is the locus of family and the context in which children are raised. Marriage is a way of giving those who make such covenants benefits, like access to one another's social security benefits on death and the right to file joint tax returns, and reciprocal responsibilities such as assuming one another's debts.

In many societies, marriages are performed in the civil arena, in the courts or with a justice of the peace, while weddings happen in religious settings, with the minister or rabbi officiating in the name of the community. In the United States, despite the alleged formal lines between church and state, custom allows clergy and religious leaders to preside at weddings, which are also the occasions during which the marriage actually takes place. Instead of separating the two functions, the priest or rabbi, for example, acts in the place of a state or local official to sign the marriage certificate (the legally binding contract) as well as to confer the blessings of the religious tradition. Thus, as the possibility of same-sex marriage makes its way through the courts and legislatures, the ballot boxes and town halls, religious issues are inevitably bundled into the package.

Some religious groups, notably the Quakers and the Unitarian Universalists, have permitted ceremonies for same-sex couples for years. But others, including the Roman Catholics and Southern Baptists among the largest denominations, continue to stand foursquare against any such moves. The institutional Roman Catholic Church made common cause with the Mormons in California in 2008 to pass Proposition 8, the California Marriage Protection Act, a ballot proposition and constitutional amendment that declared marriage legal only between a man and a woman. Religious arguments and religious leaders were prominent in the social struggle. Same-sex marriage, at this writing legal in Massachusetts, Iowa, Washington, DC, Vermont, and New Hampshire, remains the most contested social justice matter on the sexuality agenda.

Bisexual people have been involved in virtually all of the same struggles. While the word "bisexual" is included in the umbrella term LGBT, there has been much less analysis about its meaning. Still, some people claim it as their sexual identity and use it as a springboard for their spirituality.

A strong challenge to all understandings of gender *and* sexuality has come from transgender (often called trans) people, who have upended all of the assumptions about human embodiment. Trans people have many experiences, including those who feel that they were born into the wrong body and wish to change their gender, those who simply prefer dressing in the clothing of the gender that is the opposite of theirs (sometimes called cross-dressing), people who were born with genitals that conflict with their chromosomes, and so forth. As the biological matters are being sorted out by scientists, theologians have taken up the religious issues, since personhood is so widely predicated on gender and sexuality.

The challenge of trans people is twofold. The first is how people who live as one gender can change to another with the minimum of legal, medical, and social hurdles. For example, in some states a diagnosis of gender dysphoria and a bilateral mastectomy is enough to warrant a change from female to male gender on a driver's license. Serious concerns about the medical industry's treatment of trans people are among the religious issues being raised. Are people treated fairly, are prices for treatments too high, is too much influence given to doctors when the issues related to trans experience are far more pervasive in the human person than simply the medical? Nevertheless, changes are in process.

The second challenge is to the very notion of gender. If some people can change their gender, perhaps in midlife, what does that mean about others? Are all people fluid and changeable in their gender, just as many seem to be in terms of sexuality? These questions remain to be answered, but they surely have religious overtones and implications, since religions are so formative in human self-understanding. Wisdom from Jewish, Muslim, Wiccan, and Pagan sources is just beginning to emerge. If same-sex love has been a new reality for religious groups to understand according to their teachings, transgender people pose an even greater challenge, since they force consideration of something basic about human experience.

Virginia Ramey Mollenkott, an evangelical feminist, wrote the book *Omnigender: A Trans-Religious Approach* (2001), in which she spelled out the experiences of trans people and reflected on them in light of Christian scriptures. For example, she suggested that the Pauline text Galatians 1:28, "neither male nor female," might be read literally to mean that genders are not so important. Other traditions will reread their texts in light of this developing understanding of human sexuality. Religions that teach that all human beings are creatures of the same God, or that each human person is worthy of dignity, will have little trouble incorporating trans people into their theologies and communities. The difficulties come in dealing with the challenge to fundamental anthropological understandings of what it means to be human for everyone.

Christine Gudorf, a Catholic theologian, made the case for profound changes in religious understanding in her landmark article, "The erosion of sexual dimorphism: Challenges to religion and religious ethics." She argued that the reality of transgender experience points out that "we should recognize that both sex and gender are socially constructed categories; both sex and gender must be interpreted" (Gudorf, 2001). She concluded that sexual polymorphism is complex. Whether religions like it or not, that is the reality with which they need to deal on moral and spiritual issues.

Laws and social customs regarding transgender people are just beginning to change. Many people have never met a trans person, or at least not known if they have. Workplace issues are beginning to arise when the old canard about which rest room to use comes forth. But if same-sex love is any measure, progress will be steady as people meet and come to know their neighbors who are trans people and the human race will continue apace, albeit with a greater measure of social justice.

Future Struggles

Sexuality and gender are still live and contested issues in the world's religions. They are sites of struggle and evidence of power shifting within some US religious groups. Just as slavery changed from something that religions condoned to something they condemned, so too will religious claims to love, justice, equality, and mutuality be useful components in the many-pronged strategies to assure social justice on sexuality and gender.

References

Boswell, John (1980) *Christianity, Social Tolerance, and Homosexuality: Gay People in Western Europe from the Beginning of the Christian Era to the Fourteenth Century*, University of Chicago Press, Chicago.

Brooten, Bernadette J. (1996) *Love between Women: Early Christian Responses to Female Homoeroticism*, University of Chicago Press, Chicago.

Daly, Mary (1973) *Beyond God the Father*, Beacon Press, Boston.

Gudorf, Christine E. (2001) The erosion of sexual dimorphism: Challenges to religion and religious ethics, *Journal of the American Academy of Religion* 69(4): 863–891.

McNeill, John (1993) *The Church and the Homosexual*, Beacon Press, Boston.

Mollenkott, Virginia Ramey (2001) *Omnigender: A Trans-Religious Approach*, Pilgrim Press, Cleveland, OH.

Saiving, Valerie (1960) The human situation: A feminine view, *Journal of Religion* 40: 100–112.

Bibliography

Christ, Carol P. and Plaskow, Judith (eds.) (1979) *Womanspirit Rising: A Feminist Reader in Religion*, Harper & Row, San Francisco.

Comstock, Gary David and Henking, Susan E. (eds.) (1997) *Que(e)rying Religion: A Critical Anthology*, Continuum, New York.

Ellison, Marvin M. and Plaskow, Judith (2007) *Heterosexism in Contemporary World Religion: Problem and Prospect*, Pilgrim Press, Cleveland, OH.

Ellison, Marvin M. and Thorson-Smith, Sylvia (eds.) (2003) *Body and Soul: Rethinking Sexuality as Justice-Love*, Pilgrim Press, Cleveland, OH.

Jung, Patricia Beattie, Hunt, Mary E., and Balakrishnan, Radhika (eds.) (2001) *Good Sex: Feminist Perspectives from the World's Religions*, Rutgers University Press, New Brunswick, NJ.

Jung, Patricia Beattie and Smith, Ralph F. (1993) *Heterosexism: An Ethical Challenge*, SUNY Press, Albany, NY.

Kolodny, Debra R. (2000) *Blessed Bi Spirit: Bisexual People of Faith*, Continuum, New York.

Plaskow, Judith (2005) *The Coming of Lilith: Essays on Feminism, Judaism, and Sexual Ethics, 1972–2003*, Beacon Press, Boston.

Plaskow, Judith (1990) *Standing Again at Sinai: Judaism from a Feminist Perspective*, Harper & Row, San Francisco.

Ruether, Rosemary Radford (1993) *Sexism and God-Talk: Toward a Feminist Theology*, Beacon Press, Boston.

Scanzoni, Letha, and Mollenkott, Virginia Ramey (1978) *Is the Homosexual My Neighbor? Another Christian View*, Harper & Row, San Francisco.

Schüssler Fiorenza, Elisabeth (1983) *In Memory of Her: A Feminist Theological Reconstruction of Christian Origins*, Crossroad, New York.

Tanis, Justin (2003) *Trans-Gendered: Theology, Ministry, and Communities of Faith*, Pilgrim Press, Cleveland, OH.

Wilcox, Melissa M. (2003) *Coming Out in Christianity: Religion, Identity, and Community*, Indiana University Press, Bloomington.

CHAPTER 38
Beginning of Life

Andrew Lustig

Religious and ethical issues at the beginning of life are posed by a range of reproductive choices, techniques, and practices. These include the control of fertility; abortion; various assisted reproductive technologies; the use of embryos, embryonic stem cells, and fetal tissue in research and therapy; and the prospects of reproductive and nonreproductive cloning. The foregoing issues have all been discussed by authorities and commentators in the Abrahamic faiths of Judaism, Christianity, and Islam. These traditions reflect a variety of views, and their similarities and differences provide the focus of this essay.

Control of Fertility

Although birth control is not, literally, an issue posed by the beginning of life, but by actions to *prevent* conception, the issues are clearly linked. Judaism is a strongly pronatalist religion, with the injunction of Genesis 1:28, "Be fruitful and multiply," viewed as a fundamental mandate. The only explicit textual reference to birth control in Hebrew Scripture is found in Genesis 38:9–10, where Onan's choice to "spill his seed on the ground" (*coitus interruptus*) was viewed as "evil in the sight of the Lord," with death as Onan's punishment. In the Jewish Talmudic commentaries on these passages, Orthodox Jewish opinion therefore forbids the use of contraceptive methods that would "waste male seed" (e.g., *coitus interruptus*) and restricts the use of female contraceptives to reasons of maternal health. Conservative, Reform, and Reconstructionist perspectives tend to emphasize the good of conjugal intimacy between spouses as an independent value. They therefore include broader social and economic factors as reasons that justify contraception and affirm the right of couples to make such decisions in less restrictive fashion (Feldman, 2004).

In early Christianity, gnostic influences denied any fundamental value of procreation, while certain libertine sects stressed the separation of intercourse from the end of procreation. In reaction to such dualism, the Patristic tradition tended to emphasize procreation as the sole lawful purpose for marital intercourse. Augustine, even more negatively, viewed all sexual intercourse to involve concupiscence, and justified marital relations solely by their goal of procreation. At the Fourth Lateran Council in 1215, Pope Gregory IX pronounced the first universal papal ban against contraception, largely in response to the dualist heresy of Catharism. However, as Noonan argues, the long-standing ban can be interpreted in more positive terms as a defense of marital fidelity, because contraceptive use was very often associated with extramarital relations or fornication (Noonan, 1986: 124).

In official Roman Catholic teaching, the traditional ban on contraception remains in place, reflecting the central influence of natural law methodology in Catholic casuistry. Official teaching on all procreative issues is based on the so-called inseparability principle; viz., that the goods of conjugal intimacy and openness to procreation should not be separated in any act of marital intercourse. In that light, artificial contraception is judged to be an illicit separation of conjugal intimacy from its procreative potential. In the wake of *Humane Vitae*, Paul VI's 1968 reaffirmation of the traditional ban, many Catholic moral theologians have challenged the Church's official stance (e.g., Curran, 1978; McCormick, 1981: 209–237). They argue that, while conjugal intimacy and procreative potential are obvious marital goods, both need not be a feature of each marital act of intercourse, but rather of the marriage as a whole. Moreover, for these commentators and most non-Catholic Christians, the "artificiality" of some forms of contraception (in contrast to so-called natural family planning) fails to constitute, in itself, a morally decisive feature in choices about responsible parenting.

Unlike the Catholic tradition, the Eastern Orthodox Church does not discern a moral difference between artificial or natural birth control methods. Orthodox commentators, citing Patristic writings, do not limit marital intercourse to the end of procreation, but also celebrate it as an expression of mutuality and love. While Orthodoxy bans permanent sterilization, no official Orthodox statements forbid the use of artificial contraceptives, so long as they are not abortifacients, and so long as the marital relationship as a whole remains open to the good of children (Harakas, 1991: Section 21).

Until the 1930s, Protestant Christian denominations rejected the use of contraceptives, largely in the spirit of a general commitment to the values of marital fidelity (because contraception was often associated with extramarital sex) and hospitality toward offspring. The Lambeth Conference of the Church of England in 1930 marked the first departure from this unanimous prohibition; at that time, the use of artificial contraception was sanctioned as an appropriate exercise of responsible parenting. Most major Protestant traditions followed suit, and by 1961, the National Council of Churches affirmed the moral appropriateness of contraceptive use in marriage, subject to mutual consent between couples. In general, current Protestant teaching on contraception reflects the post-Lambeth consensus regarding the legitimacy of contraceptive use by married couples. That significant shift in thinking reflects two key factors: an increased knowledge of the biology of reproduction; and greater recognition of the many cultural variables, especially modern socioeconomic circumstances, that are relevant factors in responsible family planning (Noonan, 1986: 125).

In Islam, most Muslim scholars conclude that contraception is allowed. As Hathout observes, "[a]ny contraceptive method is acceptable, provided that it is not harmful and that it does not act by causing abortion" (Hathout, 1991: 104). There is no prohibition of birth control in the Qur'an. Moreover, a *hadith* (saying of the Prophet) allows *coitus interruptus* (*'azl*), the only contraceptive method known at the time. With the spread of modern methods, all contraceptives that are not abortifacients are deemed acceptable. Islam remains, however, a strongly pronatalist tradition. As with Judaism and most non-Catholic Christian perspectives that allow artificial contraception, Islam affirms procreation as a religious duty and rejects outright, or markedly restricts, voluntary childlessness as a legitimate choice of couples otherwise fertile.

Abortion

Perhaps no issue among the Abrahamic faiths reflects a greater divergence of views than that of abortion, with a spectrum of views about the moral status of the embryo and fetus.

The Jewish discussion of the status of the fetus reflects a rich tradition of rabbinical discussion and the application of case-based reasoning as a central moral method (Zoloth, 2004). While Jewish thinkers affirm the significant value of fetal life, Judaism does not ascribe the fetus the full status of a person (*nefesh*) until the head emerges at the time of birth. The major textual precedent for that judgment derives from a passage in Exodus 21:22–23, which describes a situation where a pregnant woman is harmed as the bystander to a fight between two men. If her fetus is lost, judges determine an appropriate payment (in that patriarchal setting, a spontaneously aborted fetus was considered the father's lost property), but do not view fetal death as the loss of a human life. That text is amplified by a later passage in the Mishneh (200 CE) that directly addresses situations in which pregnancy poses a danger to the pregnant woman. In this text, the woman's life takes precedence over that of the fetus; hence, the fetus may be dismembered and extracted until such time as the "greater part" of the fetus has emerged; after that point, the fetus is considered a *nefesh* and its life is of equal value. In the twelfth century, Maimonides, while appearing to accord the fetus personal status, justified abortion when the woman's life is threatened by analogizing the fetus to a pursuer (*Rodef*) who may be killed in her defense. Later rabbinical discussions found analogous ways to extend possible reasons for justifying abortion to include threats to the woman's health as well as her life. In the modern era, significant rabbinical opinion has expanded threats to the woman's health to include threats to mental health and well-being. For example, the abortion of a severely affected fetus (such as a fetus diagnosed with Tay-Sachs) is justified by appealing to the distress and suffering caused the mother rather than for the affected fetus's own sake (Mackler, 2003: 136–139).

Roman Catholic teaching on abortion is far more restrictive than Jewish perspectives because of the official Catholic position on the moral status of embryonic and fetal life. However, Catholic teaching has evolved over time. While abortion has always been viewed as a serious sin, judgments about its gravity earlier in the tradition were based on the Greek Septuagint translation of the Exodus 21:22–23 passage that added a distinction, based on Aristotelian categories, between the "unformed" and "formed" fetus, with only the abortion of the formed or ensouled fetus viewed as homicide. Debates continued until the nineteenth century, when Pius IX forbade all direct abortions in 1869. The only exceptions allowed in the tradition involve cases of so-called indirect abortion (for example, removal of a cancerous uterus in a pregnant woman), where abortion is a foreseen but not directly intended result of surgery (Cahill, 2004).

Discussion continues among many Catholic moral theologians in response to the magisterium (e.g., Shannon and Wolter, 1990). These commentators note that until the formation of the so-called primitive streak (at about 14 days), the possibility exists for either spontaneous twinning or the formation of one chimerical individual from two distinct embryonic masses. On those grounds, appealing to earlier Catholic discussion of the differences between the "unformed" and "formed" fetus, these critics question whether a distinct individual can be assumed to exist from the time of conception (which, as they also point out, is a process rather than a discrete moment).

In Protestant Christianity, as Beverly Wildung Harrison observes, explicit texts concerning abortion are rarely found prior to the twentieth century, although John Calvin clearly expressed his opposition to abortion in his commentary on Exodus 21:22. Nonetheless, the issue of abortion has emerged as a major topic in recent Protestant statements, with positions that range from what may be described as conservative to moderate (Harrison, 2004). There are two general points worth noting here. First, despite the highly charged nature of the political discussion of abortion, it is inaccurate to try to capture the moral sentiments at work in Protestant documents in terms of the simplistic rhetoric often central to the secular debate. While only Roman Catholic, Orthodox Christian, and some evangelical Protestant groups view all direct abortions as unjustified, it is inaccurate to characterize moderate Protestant voices as "pro-choice" in the secular sense of that phrase. As Cole-Turner observes, while Protestants have, in recent decades, been "generally supportive of the right of women to choose an abortion, . . . they [have] adopted a cautious approach of limiting to the most serious reasons the circumstances under which this right could be exercised" (Cole-Turner, 2004: 736). Even those traditions that emphasize individual freedom and discernment do not equate those capacities with the simple exercise of choice. For example, recent Lutheran statements limit the "sound reasons" for a morally justified abortion to circumstances of clear threat to the pregnant woman's life, "involuntary or non-voluntary intercourse," and severe fetal abnormality (Nelson, 1997: 158). A recent widely cited Reformed discussion limits morally justified abortions to "what are often called the 'hard cases,' which probably amount to only a small percentage of abortions actually performed" (Bouma *et al.*, 1989: 226). After careful attention to the theological nuances of particular traditions, a general conclusion can be offered to summarize Protestant perspectives on the *moral* choice of abortion: while not viewed as homicide or morally proscribed in all cases, abortion is morally serious because early human life, while not seen as fully personal, is deserving of respect. This general sense thus distinguishes what might be called the "Protestant consensus" from the tenor of much of the secular discussion, which focuses almost exclusively on reproductive autonomy.

As a second point, however, that "Protestant consensus" refers primarily to the *morality* of abortion as a personal choice, rather than to its legality in the context of social pluralism. Except for those perspectives like Roman Catholicism that equate abortion with homicide (and perhaps even for them), questions of morality and legality warrant separate consideration. One important issue, especially in light of recent developments in early abortifacients such as RU-486, is to consider the most appropriate forms of moral discourse for religious communities to adopt on deeply divisive issues like abortion. In contrast to Catholic and some evangelical Protestant perspectives, most Protestant statements tend to limit the factors that morally justify abortion, even as they express support for a pluralistic public policy that respects individual choice.

Abortion has also been a prominent topic among Muslim theologians during the past several decades. The tradition draws on Chapter 23:12–14 of the Qur'an concerning the origin of human life, with an accompanying *hadith* that describes a tripartite process of fetal development resulting in ensoulment at the 120th day. Some Islamic jurists forbid abortion in all cases. Other schools allow abortion for a range of factors included under the rubric of "health." A third group allows unconditional abortion prior to the time of quickening (Serour, 1997: 177). During a recent Cairo international conference on "Bioethics in Human Reproduction," a consensus emerged that, in light of modern scientific knowledge, "we now know that human life in utero can be recognized at a much earlier stage." As a result, because abortion involves the "termination of human life," it should be restricted to cases involving threats to maternal life or health or to prevent serious fetal anomalies (Serour, 1997: 177–178; Bakar, 2004).

Assisted Reproductive Technologies

Assisted reproductive technologies (ARTs) include artificial insemination (AI), in-vitro fertilization (IVF), techniques of gamete and embryo transfer within the body, and the practice of surrogate motherhood. Their emergence has occurred against the backdrop of rising infertility for an increasing number of couples during recent decades. The technical development of ARTs has been paralleled by significant recent discussion by religious communities.

Religious discussions of ARTS raise many issues, but seven themes are especially prominent:

1. ARTs sever the intrinsic link between marital intimacy and procreative potential in marital intercourse.
2. ARTs introduce third parties into the marital relationship.
3. ARTs pose significant possible risks to resulting offspring, including the confusion of lineage.
4. IVF often involves the destruction of unimplanted embryos.
5. ARTs reflect attitudes and values that tend to dehumanize reproduction.
6. Some ARTs, especially surrogate motherhood, involve commercialization and potential exploitation (Brody, 1990: 46–47).

7. ARTs raise questions of distributive justice, in light of more pressing basic healthcare needs for many people.

We will proceed thematically here, drawing on representative examples of shared concerns among the Abrahamic faiths, while selectively highlighting emphases from particular perspectives.

As we have seen, official Roman Catholic teaching is unique among Christian, Jewish, and Muslim perspectives in its act-centered analysis of the goods of marriage. As with contraception, the "inseparability principle" leads to negative judgments regarding most new reproductive technologies because they sever the unity of marital goods. In several statements, Pius XII forbade artificial insemination even by the husband, in part because sperm is obtained by masturbation, viewed as an act "against" nature, and because (like artificial contraception) artificial insemination separates procreative activity from marital intimacy (Pius XII, 1949). On the same basis, in its 1987 *Instruction on Respect for Human Life and Its Origins and on the Dignity of Procreation*, the Vatican concluded that IVF, even with gametes from the spouses, is an illicit separation of marital intimacy and conception (Congregation, 1987). In the same document, however, technical means that serve to facilitate either natural reproduction (e.g., ovular stimulation or drugs to enhance sperm volume or motility) or conception within a woman's body (e.g., gamete intrafallopian transfer) are deemed appropriate. In a more recent statement, the Vatican, again emphasizing the inseparability principle, also rejects intracytoplasmic sperm injection, which effects conception outside the body (Congregation, 2008). Numerous Catholic moral theologians have criticized the church's ban on artificial insemination or in-vitro fertilization using gametes from husband and wife. As with contraception, these critics propose as an alternative to the traditional act-centered analysis a broader "relationship-oriented" approach to the goods of marriage. Richard McCormick, for example, observes that official church teaching emphasizes the "natural perfection" of sexual intercourse as it occurs normally. He focuses instead on the typical case of infertility between spouses that involves the lack of such perfection. McCormick argues that an aesthetic standard is here being confused or conflated with a moral norm. He calls, instead, for a broader understanding of the intention of IVF, not as a substitution for sexual intimacy but as a kind of prolongation of it, and thus not involving the total severance of the unitive and procreative goods of marriage (McCormick, 1989: 348).

Eastern orthodox Christianity, Judaism, and Islam, as we have seen, view marital intercourse as having the intrinsic value of uniting husband and wife in a bond of mutual love and commitment. Unlike official Catholic teaching, however, all other Christian denominations, all branches of Judaism, and all schools of Islam view the goods of marriage in relational rather than act-centered terms. Consequently, ARTs are assessed within the context of the marriage relationship as a whole.

Virtually all Abrahamic faiths voice concerns about the involvement of third parties in reproduction, with judgments ranging from condemnation to caution. Official Roman Catholic teaching condemns such involvement as a violation of the dignity of marriage and of the right of the child to be born of the sacramental union of spouses (Congregation, 1987). Orthodox Christianity views such involvement to be "tantamount to adultery" (Brody, 1990: 55). Both traditions reject all third-party involvement, including gamete donation and surrogacy. Jewish opinions on third-party involvement vary. Orthodox Jewish opinion generally rejects the use of donor gametes and the practice of surrogacy as either tantamount to adultery or as a violation of the marital relationship. Some Conservative and Reform scholars are more open to the use of donor gametes. These commentators find no intrinsic prohibition of such donor usage, but recommend case-by-case judgments that weigh the possible harms to resulting offspring with the benefits of enabling some infertile couples to have children. On the other hand, despite such openness to the use of donor gametes, the preponderance of Jewish opinion expresses opposition to surrogacy, because *halakhah* (Jewish law) tends to emphasize that maternal identity is determined primarily by gestation and birth (Mackler, 2003: 174–176).

Islam, like Judaism, ascribes great religious significance to having children. Thus, Muslim scholars accept, even encourage, a range of infertility treatments and accept the separation of reproduction from conjugal relations in choices about both contraception and reproduction. However, the religious importance of tracing one's lineage is central to Islamic understanding. For that reason, official adoption is not practiced by Muslims, and on the same grounds, all third-party involvement in reproduction is banned. The use of donor gametes and the practice of surrogate parenting are both viewed as violations of that central Islamic norm.

Protestant opinion on the use of donor gametes is somewhat more mixed. The majority of Protestant statements approve of artificial insemination and in-vitro fertilization using gametes from the married couple. However, differences emerge concerning the use of donor gametes, with some groups viewing such donation as quasi-adulterous, others finding it morally acceptable with the consent of the spouses. However, most recent Protestant statements express strong disapproval of surrogacy on two grounds: for its tendency to commodify reproduction, and for its reliance on the alienation in the gestational mother of ordinary maternal attitudes of spiritual and psychosocial bonding.

As we have seen, religious assessments of ARTs involve different perspectives on the moral status of embryos. Official Roman Catholic teaching has direct implications for IVF because the procedure ordinarily produces extra embryos, which are often then destroyed, in direct violation of respect for life from the moment of conception. The latter judgment also informs the Vatican's ban on the use of any form of prenatal genetic diagnosis that involves the selective destruction of embryos before implantation, and also the practice of so-called selective fetal reduction in cases when multiple embryos have been implanted and abortion of one or more fetuses increases the odds of survival for those remaining. All forms of embryo research, including embryonic stem cell research, are rejected on the same grounds. Still other techniques, including cryopreservation and certain forms of embryonic manipulation, even if not involving destruction of the embryo, subject it to unjustified risk and constitute offenses against the respect owed persons from conception onward (Congregation, 2008).

The official position of Orthodox Christianity shares the Catholic judgment regarding embryonic life; on that basis, it also rejects practices that involve the destruction of embryonic life. However, unlike Roman Catholicism, Orthodox Christianity appears to allow IVF using gametes from the married couple so long as all fertilized ova are implanted (Harakas, 1982).

What appears as a fairly moderate perspective in the Protestant writings can be found on the question of the status and disposition of extra zygotes. Among evangelical Protestants, exemplified by the Southern Baptist Convention, the destruction of embryos is condemned as the taking of innocent human life. For other denominations, including the Episcopal Church and much of the Reformed tradition, concern about embryonic destruction appears to be outweighed by the good of aiding the infertile couple (Granbois and Smith, 1993: 89–96; Cole-Turner, 2004).

As we have seen, neither Judaism nor Islam ascribes full personal status to the embryo. Given the pronatalist stance of both traditions, most recent opinions affirm the appropriateness of in-vitro fertilization using the couple's own gametes, and Jewish statements encourage prenatal screening and preimplantation genetic screening, in keeping with the central value they place on the duty of procreation and the future health of children (Cole-Turner, 2004).

Numerous recent statements have also discussed the actual or possible dangers of ARTs to dehumanize reproduction. That emphasis is central to recent Roman Catholic documents. The 1987 *Instruction*, for example, warns of the dangers of ARTs that tempt us to "go beyond the limits of reasonable dominion of nature" (Congregation, 1987). Two earlier influential Protestant thinkers have provided the thematic background to ongoing Protestant discussion. Paul Ramsey argued that a union between the conjugal and procreative aspects of marital sexuality follows from a covenantal understanding of Christian marriage as reflecting the unity of Christ and his Church. On that basis, Ramsey rejected both artificial insemination by donor and surrogate motherhood, although he accepted contraception and sterilization in order to prevent the transmission of serious genetic diseases (Ramsey, 1970). Joseph Fletcher, by contrast, argued that increasing mastery of reproduction and genetics evinced a greater and more radical humanity, because by deliberate choice we overcome the vagaries of nature and biology (Fletcher, 1974).

In addition to the foregoing issues, concerns about justice emerge as a central emphasis in religious discussions of issues at the beginning of life. Jewish, Christian, and Islamic discussions affirm jointly the dignity of individual persons and the necessary sociality of persons in community, thereby linking notions of liberty and community in a way that is distinct from many secular conceptions of persons and society. In contrast to individualistic theories, a fundamentally social understanding infuses Abrahamic perspectives, with the themes of justice and the common good underscoring the realities of human dependence and interdependence.

One fundamental issue of justice concerns the moral status of early human life. As we have seen, official Roman Catholic and Orthodox Christian views, as well as some evangelical Protestant perspectives, accord full personhood to the embryo; therefore, the direct taking of innocent embryonic or fetal life constitutes a direct violation of a person's right to life and cannot be outweighed by other values. In addition, virtually all Jewish, Christian, and Islamic perspectives, including those that do not accord full personal status to early human life, raise significant questions about distributive justice in relation to new reproductive technologies and practices. Distributive justice considers two questions. First, in the context of limited societal resources, which sorts of medical benefits should be viewed as elements of "basic healthcare"? Second, in setting priorities and establishing limits, how shall we fairly distribute the benefits of healthcare (including the potential benefits of reproductive technologies)?

Recent Jewish and Islamic discussions have emphasized the significance of NRTs as appropriate means to overcome infertility, though within the constraints discussed above. At the same time, concerns have been raised about the marketplace values that too often drive the current provision of infertility services. There are well-documented financial and psychological costs to women who undergo IVF procedures. There also may be larger dangers of commodifying childbearing in ways that undercut traditional understandings of parental relations and family life. Given the risks that may be posed by an unfettered marketplace, many recent discussions have included calls for significant government regulation and oversight (e.g., Tendler, 2000; Zoloth, 2001: 108; Cahill, 2005: 192–210).

In addition, there are more global questions posed by NRTs. Does it serve the common good to focus research on costly and often exotic technologies while other, more basic healthcare needs remain unmet? Will market-driven, merely technical advances in some fairly exotic forms of technology be more likely to reinforce or exacerbate current inequities between the haves and the have-nots, both nationally and globally? In secular discussions of technology, such issues are often underemphasized, if they are mentioned at all. But they figure prominently in Jewish, Christian, and Islamic discussions of new reproductive technologies, and of bioethics more broadly (e.g., Serour, 1997: 181–182; Cahill, 2005: 192–210; Zoloth, 2001).

Human Reproductive Cloning

On February 21, 1997, Dr. Ian Wilmut, a researcher at the Roslin Institute in Scotland, reported, with a fanfare of headlines, the first successful instance of mammalian cloning, with the arrival of Dolly, a sheep cloned from a specialized body cell of an adult sheep. Since that time, the prospect of human cloning has been the topic of significant secular and religious discussion.

All commentators, both secular and religious, agree that human reproductive cloning would currently pose unacceptable risks of physical harm to resulting offspring and should be banned on those grounds. However, even if further research should address such risks, there are other aspects of cloning that warrant religious scrutiny.

Jewish positions on the prospect of human reproductive cloning, unsurprisingly, are mixed. For some in the tradition, the prospect of human cloning is viewed as far removed from the framework of God's creative purposes as expressed in Genesis 1:27–28 (Lauritzen and Stewart, 2004: 462–463). For other Jewish scholars, however, cloning might be viewed in certain cases as an appropriate opportunity for partnership with God, especially in cases of male infertility when cloning offers the only possibility of continuing one's lineage or in order to avoid genetic disease in one's offspring (e.g., Tendler, 1997).

That difference in Jewish opinion reflects a broad division to be found across the Abrahamic faiths regarding the primary meaning of creation as a theological category. Those who emphasize the stewardship of creation tend to view cloning negatively, as an illicit instance of "playing God," of usurping God's ordering of creation, and as an illegitimate exercise of human pride classically termed hubris. Sometimes the religious opposition to human cloning draws on themes and values that are more broadly shared by the general public. For example, many religious critics conclude that human cloning may exacerbate an already prevalent tendency to view our progeny as products rather than as gifts, or that it would represent an effort to objectify our children in ways that demean their dignity as individuals. This broader form of opposition may also appeal to shared intuitions about the dangers of psychological harm to cloned individuals, or about threats to deeply shared societal and cultural attitudes toward the institution and practice of parenting (e.g., Meilaender, 2000).

Scholars who are more positively disposed toward the prospect of human cloning make a different set of claims. They offer scenarios that portray cloning as, in some instances, the legitimate expression of our human role as what they call "created co-creators." Rather than judging cloning to be prima facie evidence of hubris, these theologians find in human freedom and creativity, including the creative possibilities of cloning, a perhaps positive expression of our capacities as creatures who have been granted an ever-increasing dominion over nature (e.g., Sachedina, 1997). From these more optimistic voices, then, cloning represents the possibility of co-creating with God, in effect a new way to welcome children into the world. For example, Lutheran theologian Ted Peters, while not necessarily enthusiastic about human cloning, also cautions that we should reserve final judgment until more is known about its prospects (Peters, 1997).

For other religious commentators, the deliberate choice of cloning poses unacceptable threats to the psychological well-being of the resulting cloned individual. Human beings, the Abrahamic faiths profess, are made in the image of God. This language means that, as creatures, we are unitary wholes, composed of body, soul, and spirit. We are not immortal souls in bodies, as if our bodies are incidental to our essential selves. That is a pagan notion of immortality, a Greek not a Hebraic understanding. Nor are our spirits reducible to our bodies. Any form of reductionism that would reduce our spiritual nature to an epiphenomenon – that is, an apparent reality finally and fully reducible to the laws of physics and biology – is equally unacceptable. Rather, a Christian understanding of the human person views us holistically – as ensouled bodies or embodied souls.

The implications of this outlook for the prospect of human cloning are also holistic. Jewish, Christian, or Islamic perspectives do not succumb to genetic reductionism. Thus, a human clone, although a younger genetic twin, would of course not be the same person as the one replicated. Nature *and* nurture, after all, are both at work in the formation of our personalities. Any crude notion that replicating a genotype would be replicating a person would be mistaken, especially from a holistic Christian view. At the same time, such holism would not trivialize the importance of our physical selves to our well-being as people. While the clone would be a distinct individual, we know quite well that our genetic and phenotypic differences tend to reinforce our sense of distinctive identity. It seems plausible that cloned individuals would face far greater difficulties in establishing a unique sense of self. It seems equally likely that those who replicate human clones would tend to burden them with prior expectations, thus infringing on their freedom to become unique individuals.

Anglican theologian Oliver O'Donovan views reproductive cloning as a perverse expression of the tendency to objectify children as products of our own will, different in degree, if not in kind, from other forms of assisted reproduction. With cloning, we specify in advance a full human genotype; we close ourselves to the usual novelty of sexual begetting; we impose our intentions on a child in a new and revolutionary way. From this perspective, the process of cloning, then, changes the relation between parent and child. Unlike other forms of assisted reproduction, which simply facilitate the ordinary process of conception, with replication the perspective shifts. While in natural procreation, a child is begotten by virtue of what we *are*, cloning gives existence to a being not by what we are but by what we intend and design. (O'Donovan, 1984).

Human Nonreproductive Cloning

1998 witnessed the successful derivation of human embryonic stem cells. During the past decade, significant research has proceeded on nonreproductive cloning, aimed at the development of stem cells that could be used to cure or ameliorate many serious diseases and also to grow specific organs and tissues. Judgments about therapeutic cloning hinge primarily on different assessments of the moral status of the embryo, including "spare embryos" from IVF procedures and embryos that may be created expressly for research purposes. As we have seen, official Roman Catholic and Orthodox Christian teaching, as well as Southern Baptists (2001) and other evangelical Christians, condemn the destruction of embryos as the illicit killing of innocent human beings. However, most other religious perspectives, including Judaism, Islam, and much of Protestantism, express greater openness to nonreproductive or therapeutic cloning. Their willingness stems, in large measure, from their stances toward embryonic life. Judaism and Islam do not ascribe full personal status to the embryo; indeed, in Jewish thought, the unimplanted embryo has no moral standing (Dorff, 2000). Moreover, the mandate of healing is a central emphasis in Jewish thought (Tendler, 2000). Recent Islamic opinions vary, but many Muslim scholars express at least qualified support for embryonic research in light of its healing potential (e.g., Serour, 1997: 175–176; Sachedina, 2000). Among mainline Protestant statements, two themes have been especially prominent: first, that nonreproductive cloning holds the promise to "advance dramatically the quality of human health and well-being" (Peters, 2001: 137); but second, that such research should be subject to careful oversight and regulation in order to assure that its potential benefits will be justly distributed (Cole-Turner, 1997).

Conclusion

A recent survey of religious opinions regarding the possibility of human cloning finds that the Abrahamic traditions are "pluralistic in their premises, modes of argument, and conclusions" (Campbell, 1997: 39). That observation, directed at cloning, applies more broadly; it provides a useful descriptive summary of the full range of issues at the beginning of life discussed here. Among the Abrahamic traditions, several core theological themes and values are broadly shared. Life is viewed as a blessing of God as Creator. Human beings are creatures made in God's image, with the capacities to be both the stewards and transformers of God's creation. Human life is a basic value to be accorded respect and protection. Parenting and family relations are esteemed as the basic context for begetting and raising children. Finally, individual choices and actions are not viewed atomistically, but as occurring within community, with an emphasis on the requirements of justice and the common good.

However, as we have seen, those themes, while broadly embraced, are variously interpreted in Judaism, Christianity, and Islam. Different views on appropriate sources of authority and moral insight, different interpretations of revealed texts, and different understandings of tradition and ecclesiology lead to a variety of moral conclusions on particular topics. This rich pluralism is especially evident in religious judgments about issues at the beginning of life.

References

Bakar, Osman (2004) Abortion: Islamic perspectives, in *Encyclopedia of Bioethics*, Vol. 1, 3rd edn, Stephen Post (ed.), Macmillan Library Reference, New York, pp. 39–43.

Bouma, Hessel, Diekema, Douglas, Langerak, Edward, Rottman, Theodore, and Verhey, Allen (1989) *Christian Faith, Health, and Medical Practice*, Eerdmans, Grand Rapids, MI.

Brody, Baruch (1990) Current religious perspectives on the new reproductive techniques, in *Beyond Baby M: Ethical Issues in New Reproductive Techniques*, Dianne Bartels, Reinhard Priester, Dorothy E. Vawter, and Arthur Caplan (eds.), Humana Press, Clifton, NJ, pp. 45–63.

Cahill, Lisa (2004) Abortion: Roman Catholic perspectives, in *Encyclopedia of Bioethics*, Vol. 1, 3rd edn, Stephen Post (ed.), Macmillan Library Reference, New York, pp. 31–35.

Cahill, Lisa (2005) *Theological Bioethics: Participation, Justice, and Change*, Georgetown University Press, Washington, DC.

Campbell, Courtney (1997) Religious perspectives, in *Cloning Human Beings*, National Bioethics Advisory Commission, Washington, DC, pp. 39–61.

Cole-Turner, Ronald (ed.) (1997) *Human Cloning: Religious Responses*, Westminster John Knox Press, Louisville, KY.

Cole-Turner, Ronald (2004) Embryo and fetus: Religious perspectives, in *Encyclopedia of Bioethics*, Vol. 2, 3rd edn, Stephen Post (ed.), Macmillan Library Reference, New York, pp. 732–740.

Congregation for the Doctrine of the Faith (1987) Instruction on respect for human life in its origins and on the dignity of procreation, *Origins* 16(40): 698–711.

Congregation for the Doctrine of the Faith (2008) *Instruction Dignitas Personae on Certain Bioethical Questions*, http://www.vatican.va/roman_curia/congregations/cfaith/documents/rc_con_cfaith_doc_20081208_dignitas-personae_en.html (accessed October 1, 2011).

Curran, Charles (1978) Ten years later: Reflections on *Humanae Vitae*, *Commonweal* 105: 425–430.

Dorff, Elliot (2000) Testimony, *Ethical Issues in Human Stem Cell Research, Vol. III: Religious Perspectives*, National Bioethics Advisory Commission, Rockville, MD, pp. C1–C5.

Feldman, David (2004) Population ethics: Jewish perspectives, in *Encyclopedia of Bioethics*, Vol. 4, Stephen Post (ed.), Macmillan Library Reference, New York, pp. 2061–2064.

Fletcher, Joseph (1974) *The Ethics of Genetic Control*, Anchor Press, Garden City, NY.

Granbois, Judith and Smith, David (1993) The Anglican communion and bioethics, in *Bioethics Yearbook, Vol. Three: Theological Developments*, B. Andrew Lustig (ed.), Kluwer Academic, Dordrecht, pp. 83–115.

Harakas, Stanley (1982) *Contemporary Moral Issues Facing the Orthodox Christian*, Light and Life Publishing, Minneapolis.

Harakas, Stanley (1991) Eastern Orthodox bioethics, in *Bioethics Yearbook, Vol. Three: Theological Developments*, B. Andrew Lustig, ed.), Kluwer Academic, Dordrecht, pp. 117–131.

Harrison, Beverly Wildung (2004) Abortion: Protestant perspectives, in *Encycopedia of Bioethics*, Vol. 1, Stephen Post (ed.), Macmillan Library Reference, New York, pp. 35–39.

Hathout, Hassan (1991) Islamic concepts and bioethics, in *Bioethics Yearbook, Vol. One: Theological Developments*, B. Andrew Lustig (ed.), Kluwer Academic, Dordrecht, pp. 103–117.

Lauritzen, Paul and Stewart, Nathaniel (2004) Cloning: III. Religious perspectives, in Stephen G. Post (ed.), *Encyclopedia of Bioethics*, Vol. I, 3rd edn, Macmillan Reference USA, New York, pp. 462–467.

Mackler, Aaron (2003) *Introduction to Jewish and Catholic Bioethics*, Georgetown University Press, Washington, DC.

McCormick, Richard (1981) *How Brave a New World?* Doubleday, Garden City, NY.

McCormick, Richard (1989) *The Critical Calling: Reflections on Moral Dilemmas Since Vatican II*, Georgetown University Press, Washington, DC.

Meilaender, Gilbert (2000) Testimony, in *Ethical Issues in Human Stem Cell Research, Vol. III: Religious Perspectives*, National Bioethics Advisory Commission, Rockville, MD, pp. E1–E6.

Nelson, Paul (1997) Bioethics and the Lutheran Communion, in *Bioethics Yearbook, Vol. 5: Theological Developments*, B. Andrew Lustig (ed.), Kluwer Academic, Dordrecht, pp. 143–169.

Noonan, John (1986) Contraception, in *The Westminster Dictionary of Christian Ethics*, James Childress and John Macquarrie (eds.), Westminster Press, Philadelphia, pp. 124–126.

O'Donovan, Oliver (1984) *Begotten or Made?* Clarendon Press, Oxford.

Peters, Ted (1997) *Playing God? Genetic Discrimination and Human Freedom*, Routledge, New York.

Peters, Ted (2001) Embryonic stem cells and the theology of dignity, in *The Human Embryonic Stem Cell Debate*, Suzanne Holland, Karen Lebacqz, and Laurie Zoloth (eds.), MIT Press, Cambridge, MA, pp. 127–139.

Pius XII (1949) Christian norms of morality, in *Medical Ethics: Sources of Catholic Teaching*, Kevin O'Rourke and Philip Boyle (ed.), Catholic Health Association, St. Louis, MO, p. 56.

Ramsey, Paul (1970) *Fabricated Man: The Ethics of Genetic Control*, Yale University Press, New Haven, CT.

Sachedina, Abdulaziz (1997) Testimony, in Transcript of National Bioethics Advisory Commission Hearing, March 14, http://bioethics.georgetown.edu/nbac/transcripts/1997/3-14-97.pdf (accessed April 19, 2011), pp. 48–65.

Sachedina, Abdulaziz (2000) Testimony, in *Ethical Issues in Human Stem Cell Research, Vol. III: Religious Perspectives*, National Bioethics Advisory Commission, Rockville, MD, pp. G1–G6.

Serour, Gamal (1997) Islamic developments in bioethics, in *Bioethics Yearbook, Vol. Five: Theological Developments in Bioethics*, B. Andrew Lustig (ed.), Kluwer Academic, Dordrecht, pp. 171–188.

Shannon, Thomas and Wolter, Allan (1990) Reflections on the moral status of the pre-embryo, *Theological Studies* 51(4): 603–626.

Southern Baptist Convention (2001) Resolution on human cloning, http://www.sbc.net/

resolutions/amResolution.asp?ID=572 (accessed April 19, 2011).

Tendler, Rabbi Moshe (1997) Testimony, in Transcript of National Bioethics Advisory Commission Hearing, March 14, pp. 14–24, http://bioethics.georgetown.edu/nbac/transcripts/1997/3-14-97.pdf (accessed April 19, 2011).

Tendler, Rabbi Moshe (2000) Testimony before the National Bioethics Advisory Commission, *Ethical Issues in Human Stem Cell Research, Vol. III: Religious Perspectives*, National Bioethics Advisory Commission, Rockville, MD, pp. H1–H5.

Zoloth, Laurie (2001) The ethics of the eighth day: Jewish bioethics and research on human embryonic stem cells, in *The Human Embryonic Stem Cell Debate*, Suzanne Holland, Karen Lebacqz, and Laurie Zoloth (eds.), MIT Press, Cambridge, MA, pp. 95–111.

Zoloth, Laurie (2004) Abortion: Jewish perspectives, in *Encyclopedia of Bioethics*, Vol. 1, Stephen Post (ed.), Macmillan Library Reference, New York, pp. 28–31.

CHAPTER 39
Death and Dying

Courtney S. Campbell

The prospect of human mortality is one of the "ultimate questions" to which religious traditions, both classical and contemporary, respond in diverse ways with ritual, myth, teaching, doctrine, and communal practices. Embedded in this religious diversity are foundational assumptions about whether there is an ontological reality to death, whether dying can be differentiated from death, the nature of the relationship between the body and self, and ethical teachings and practices in the care of dying persons.

The postures that religious traditions and their adherents assume toward death and/or dying can have significant social justice implications. For example, a contemporary critique of western faith traditions is that they embody tendencies toward "otherworldliness"; that is, religious teachings portray death as a passage of the soul to a transcendent and qualitatively better afterlife. The transient nature of human mortality can dispose adherents to indifference toward social justice in this world on the assumption that ultimately justice will prevail in a trans-social world to come.

Other faith communities emphasize a foundational commitment to the sanctity of human life, which in some circumstances can entail an ethical imperative to utilize life-extending technologies, even at exorbitant cost and social conflict. A prominent example of this implication occurred in the religious, legal, and political controversy over Terri Schiavo, a Florida woman who died in March 2005 after over a decade in a persistent comatose condition.

This essay presents an overview of the teachings of major world religions on death and dying, including the religious meanings attributed to "death," its relationship to "dying," and the underlying concept of "self" that dies or lives on. These basic conceptual understandings inform communal practices on ethical questions regarding decisions about end-of-life care, cessation of medical treatment, and hastening death through euthanasia.

The Wiley Blackwell Companion to Religion and Social Justice, First Edition. Edited by Michael D. Palmer and Stanley M. Burgess.
© 2012 John Wiley & Sons Ltd. Published 2020 by John Wiley & Sons Ltd.

Concepts of Death and Social Justice Conflicts

The language of "death" is richly metaphorical and mythological in religious experience, but this analysis will confine itself to the biological "facts" of death. The formal philosophical conception of death affirms that "death" signifies the irreversible loss of the essentially significant characteristics of a living being. For many religious traditions, the essentially significant characteristic marked by death is the "separation" or "departure" of the soul, spirit, or animating life force from the body. It has been difficult to transfer this interpretation of metaphysical loss into feasible medical guidelines or legal policies. The medical and legal cultural consensus regarding death has focused on the complete cessation of some vital, but scientifically measurable, aspect of human biological existence, such as the irreversible cessation of cardiac, respiratory, or integrative brain functions.

Social justice issues emerge when the scientific and metaphysical standards of death conflict. For example, in November 2008, a 12-year-old boy, Motl Brody, was declared dead at Children's National Medical Center in Washington, DC due to the cessation of brain activity subsequent to brain cancer. However, his Orthodox Jewish parents sought a court order to continue life support, because their tradition does not recognize brain-oriented standards of death. While the young boy died of heart failure prior to a legal ruling, the social justice question raised is how society can ensure effective and uniform policy without imposing impediments to religious liberty.

The objections of conservative Christian traditions to withdrawing life support from patients in persistent coma also reflect in part different interpretations of death. While such patients are not dead by medical standard or legal statute, a diagnosis of irreversible traumatic brain injury implies negligible prospects for recovery of language, memory, or social interaction. Removing life support from such patients can be medically defensible, but also religiously objectionable, because the moral rationale for treatment withdrawal is attributed to judgments about quality of life, rather than commitment to the sanctity of life. Religious conservatives argue that such judgments display social bias against vulnerable, voiceless persons, insofar as living persons are treated essentially as though they were already dead, and that a quality-of-life ethos has a negative spillover effect onto other social and medical practices.

Beyond the question of what constitutes death, the central religious question is less about the biological processes of death than it is about the meaning of death and the dying experience. Death is not a problem to be solved by medical technology or philosophical inquiry as it is an ordeal that calls a religious community to respond. Religious traditions provide resources to engage the question of the significance of both death and a life lived in the shadow of mortality, as well as to embody practices of caring for the dying and the body.

Care for the Dying

Religious communities have traditionally assumed responsibility for care of the person, both body and spirit, as the end of life nears. The classical world religions – Buddhism,

Christianity, Hinduism, Islam, Judaism – care for the spiritual needs of the dying person through such rituals as prayers, readings from sacred texts, meditation, blessings from religious authorities, and community involvement. The purposes of such rituals include heightening religious consciousness, compassionate witness, reconciliation and closure in relationships, and discovery of spiritual truths.

The last four decades have witnessed increasing engagement with spirituality in dying by professional caregivers. A pioneer has been hospice care, which has been favorably received by many faith communities. The hospice movement drew on a Christian practice dating back to the fourth century CE of enacting "works of mercy" by providing a place of rest and healing for the sick, the hungry, the wounded, and the stranger. The modern hospice, initiated by Dame Cicely Saunders in 1967 in the United Kingdom, retained this emphasis on caring for the vulnerable even as it developed an alternative mode of care for dying persons. Its features include symptom relief and comfort care; holistic treatment that addresses the physical, emotional, relational, and spiritual needs of patients and their families; a view of dying as a normal process for human beings; family participation with the dying person in decision making; and permitting patients to die at home, or in a home-like setting. These commitments converge with religious values of communal presence, compassion, nonabandonment, and commitment to the socially vulnerable.

Matters of social justice are embedded in hospice care, particularly as such care is widely underutilized. A 2003 study concluded that lack of equitable access to a hospice service "constitutes a violation of justice and fairness in our society that should be rectified" (Jennings et al., 2003: S3). Religious communities that enter a collaborative partnership with the hospice movement to care for the dying must advocate for equality of access to such services.

Professional interest in the spirituality of dying was enhanced by the studies of dying patients conducted by psychologist Elisabeth Kubler-Ross (1926–2004). Kubler-Ross articulated a model of five "stages" experienced by the dying person: denial, anger, bargaining, resignation, and acceptance. She proposed that dying persons could be "teachers" to the living in matters pertaining to spiritual care, such as candid communication, meanings of hope and healing, the value of presence, and patterns of bereavement. Notably, her theory of stages of dying and bereavement was profoundly indebted to her familiarity with Asian religious teachings, especially Hinduism and Buddhism (Kubler-Ross, 1969).

Increased professional involvement in spiritual care is valued by patients: a recent study indicated that two-thirds of a patient population would be agreeable to physician inquiries about their religious or spiritual beliefs in the event of grave illness. Researchers have developed methods for physicians to make assessments of patients' spiritual needs, and some professionals advocate that a patient's medical history should include questions about belief, rituals, worship, and integration in a religious community. Understandably, other physicians find such conversations to be outside their professional competency or responsibility.

This professional controversy is an important context for justice in end-of-life care. Dying patients and their families confront many decisions about medical treatment within a framework of religious values or spirituality. When these values are not communicated to or clarified between patient and professional, the prospect of misunderstanding is high, as is the potential for violating patients' rights when they are most vulnerable.

Decisions and Values about Death's Timing and Method

The most scrutinized matter of justice in end-of-life care concerns decisions about use or cessation of life-extension technologies. While death is a biological inevitability, its timing and manner have become a burden of decision resting on patients, families, and professionals. The array of prospective decisions is intimidating, including choices about the following:

- Participating in organ donation.
- Formulating an advance directive.
- Finding a balance of pain medication that minimizes pain but preserves lucidity rather than inducing sedation.
- Providing, refusing, or withdrawing life-extending medical technology.
- Providing, refusing, or withdrawing a specific technology of great controversy, invasive tube feedings for nutrition and hydration.
- Requesting that death be hastened through physician provision of lethal medication or lethal injection.

These are matters of social justice for at least three important reasons. First, as society has provided substantial support for biomedicine to make life-extending technologies available, it has a stake in their judicious utilization. Second, society has entrusted to patients (and families as proxies) the legal (and moral) rights to make decisions about these questions, and thus has a political and ethical investment in having patient choices respected and patient dignity preserved. Third, the decisions of individual patients can create social scarcity, as exemplified in waiting lists for transplantable organs, or rationing expensive end-of-life medical treatments.

A continuum of religious argumentation on these questions extends from support of vitalism, or the provision of all necessary life support, on the most conservative side, to warrants for physician-administered euthanasia on the most liberal side. A beginning task is identifying the central values commonly invoked in religious discourse in a very fluid professional, social, and legal discussion.

Sovereignty

Religious discourse invokes the sovereignty of God over life and death or appeals to a transcendent ground of being. However, understanding divine sovereignty as a sufficient condition for choices removes the decision over life support from human responsibility. One difficulty with relying exclusively on this value is that, given the continued advances in life-prolonging medical technology, the divine will then seem arbitrarily subordinated to technological progress.

The prohibition on killing

The affirmative version of this value is the commitment to the sanctity of human life. In end-of-life care, this value typically entails the illegitimacy of voluntary killing of one's self, or suicide, or hastening patient death by medical professionals, as in euthanasia. Most religious reasoning differentiates withdrawing or refusing medical treatment from acts of suicide or euthanasia, even when the probable outcome of terminating treatment is patient death. That is, religious reasoning stresses the intent and inherent nature of the action more than its outcome.

Stewardship

Endowed with qualities of freedom and reason, stewardship entrusts persons with accountability to make decisions that promote responsible caring. Stewardship is relevant to the responsible use of resources within the community; given the high costs of end-of-life care, stewardship overlaps with the social justice problems of allocation and scarcity.

Solidarity with vulnerable persons

While religious communities seek to empower individuals in end-of-life choices and advocate for change in social structures that discriminate or inhibit personal responsibility, a realistic recognition exists that dying persons can need protection from situations of potential exploitation. Moreover, studies indicate that social inequities experienced in a lifetime due to social worth, economic status, racial and ethnic diversity, and gender may carry over to the realm of dying, further necessitating practices of solidarity with the socially marginalized.

Compassion

The core meaning of compassion entails bearing the burdens and suffering with the person who is suffering; compassion always implies human presence to the sufferer. Compassion is also enacted through providing various medications that alleviate physical pain and discomfort.

Relationship

A dying person characteristically is embedded in relationships with family, with fellow members of a religious community, with professional caregivers, and with God or a sacred source of being. The cumulative effect of these relationships should be a community of caring presence to the dying person. Significantly, in the pioneering studies of Kubler-Ross, the prospect of loss of these relationships, or a perception of abandonment, was a greater fear for the dying person than the prospect of death itself.

Liberty

The value of liberty redirects the audience of accountability for stewardship to one's conscience. It affirms a claim of noninterference in matters of end-of-life care, and thereby rejects authoritarianism from the state, ecclesiastical organizations, or the medical profession. In democratic societies, religious liberty constitutes one ground for recognizing legal rights that the state has conferred on persons to make decisions about their dying.

Dignity

Dignity refers to the inherent value of each person and the equal value of all persons. Dignity is retained by every person even as they decline physically. The moral claim of dignity is that a dying person be allowed to die according to the same values by which they have lived; dying is "a part of life" not simply biologically but in the integrity and coherence that death brings to a person's life.

These core values are not always complementary, but instead can conflict. The controversy over physician methods of hastening death, for example, is often portrayed as a conflict between commitments to the sanctity of life and to compassion and personal liberty. The teachings of any given religious tradition reflect processes of selecting and prioritizing certain values above others within the constraints of background understandings of the meaning of death, the nature of self, and the relationship of self and body. This relationship of worldview and ethical teaching permits some general comparisons between religious traditions on end-of-life issues.

Hinduism

While perspectives on death in Hindu teachings are exceptionally diverse, one influential representation is displayed in the narrative the *Bhagavad Gita* (ca. 100–400 CE) or the "Song of God." As the narrative opens, the heroic warrior Arjuna is confronted with the dilemma of engaging in war against his kin. When Arjuna expresses reticence to kill members of his family, Lord Krishna informs him that he lacks understanding of death and the nature of the self:

> Our bodies are known to end, but the embodied self is enduring, indestructible, and immeasurable; . . . It is not born, it does not die; having been, it will never not be; unborn, enduring, constant, and primordial, it is not killed when the body is killed. (*Bhagavad Gita*, 1986: 32, 33)

Meanings of death, dying, and self

Within this Hindu tradition, then, biological death occurs on separation of the eternal self, or *atman*, from the transient body. Bodily death is ultimately insignificant, for the authentic self continues to exist due to its indestructible nature. Although the eternal self is freed at death from the perishable body, *atman* remains subject to the cycles of karma, *samsara*, and reincarnation. Karma is the impersonal law of cosmic justice that entails that each person receives what he or she deserves, in this life or in a future incarnation. A person who accumulates enough merit, through paths of devotion, discipline, meditation, and so on, experiences liberation (*moksha*); union with universal consciousness (*atman-Brahman*); and the cessation of separateness of being. Insufficient merit subjects the person to endless *samsaric* cycles of death and rebirth, wherein the *atman* is reincarnated in some physical form. The human body presents obstacles to liberation, but also is the only physical form offering an opportunity for liberation.

Physical decline notwithstanding, Hindu teaching sees dying as an occasion for heightened religious awareness and diminished ignorance and illusion about reality. Moreover, Hindu traditions affirm the importance of conscious mindfulness as a person approaches death because the content of consciousness at death can produce a more favorable rebirth. Hence, the *Bhagavad Gita* is customarily read to a dying person so that its teachings can be consciously absorbed without distraction.

Implications for medical care and social justice

The core Hindu concern about the cultivation of religious consciousness as the end of life approaches has prompted discussion among Hindu scholars about whether physicians should inform a dying person and the family of impending death, lest such disclosure impede heightened religious awareness. The extent of providing pain medication is also debated, since pain relief to the point of sedation would defeat the purpose of alert consciousness at death. Sufficient medication to moderate pain in dying is appropriate so that the dying person can maintain awareness and relative lucidity.

Hindu scholars have situated questions about end-of-life care within the tradition's historical toleration of self-willed voluntary death by those who are enlightened or who seek consummation of their quest for liberation. This has been cited as a precedent for refusing or withdrawing burdensome treatment; it is disputed whether it can also serve as a precedent for physician euthanasia (Young, 1989: 93–111).

It is instructive that Krishna's instructions to Arjuna come in the context of social conflict; nearly two millennia later, the *Bhavagad Gita* would be a source of inspiration for Mahatma Gandhi (1869–1948) in his post–Second World War nonviolent campaign for Indian independence against British rule. Within Hinduism, contexts of social injustice present opportunities for learning about matters of ultimate importance.

However, a quest for ultimacy, including knowledge of reality, which lies beyond this transient world, may place social justice in the religious background.

Buddhism

Buddhism begins in an encounter with dying and death. In the narrative the "Great Renunciation," the Indian prince Siddhartha Gautama (ca. 560–480 BCE) had been sequestered in his father's palace for his first 29 years. On venturing beyond the palace walls, he encountered "four passing sights": an old person, a dying person, a corpse, and a monk (Kramer, 1988: 54). This experience motivated Siddhartha's spiritual quest to attain serenity in the face of inevitable physical diminishment and death. His quest culminated in "enlightenment," knowledge of the reality that all beings are impermanent and subject to suffering, decay, and death, and Siddhartha became known as "the Buddha" (the awakened one).

Meanings of death, dying, and self

The Buddha's insight on the impermanence of being led to rejection of the eternal self of Hinduism and his contrary posture of "no-self" (*an-atman*). Death is a corporeal manifestation of ongoing processes of change and impermanence and signifies the dissolution of the five aggregates of matter, sensations, perceptions, mental formations, and consciousness that form a temporal but not permanent self. Since the aggregates are themselves impermanent, the self is always "becoming" but has no definitive essence; moreover, death has no ontological reality. Instead, the concept of impermanence implies that death is a process in which a person continuously lives and dies in each moment.

Unenlightened beings are ignorant of this reality of continuous change through desire and attachment to the ego and sense of continuous self. In his dying discourse to his followers, the Buddha disclosed the remedy for self-delusions: the "Noble Eightfold Path" of rightness in speech, action, livelihood, concentration, effort, mindfulness, thought, and understanding. Cultivating these qualities of cognition, intent, and conduct leads to the release known as nirvana, a condition of "blowing out" or extinguishing of ignorance, desire, and suffering.

As with Hinduism, dying in Buddhism should be a time of religious learning, with mental energies and spiritual practices, including meditation, breathing, and visualization, and repetition of the mantra of the Three Refuges – the Buddha, the *dharma* (teaching) and the *sangha* (community) – devoted to Buddhist wisdom. This spiritual preparation for death cultivates mental states that will heighten the prospects for enlightenment or rebirth status. One Buddhist manual advises the dying: "Your mind state at the time you draw your last breath is crucial, for upon this hinges the subsequent direction and embodiment of the life force" (Kapleau, 1989: 140). Unlike western practices, Buddhist death rituals seek the welfare of the deceased.

Implications for medical care and social justice

The Buddha admonished his followers to avoid speculation on death as a distraction from the immediate practical tasks of overcoming suffering and cultivating compassion and wisdom. Released from preoccupation with the self and the threat of death to the ego, the Buddhist is liberated to practice compassion for others.

Subsequent Buddhist teachers have emphasized compassion in care of the dying. Buddhist teachings on the karmic consequences of rebirth entail that learning in the presence of a caring community is the most critical aspect of end-of-life care. Pain control is an expression of compassion even in circumstances when pain medication may have a secondary consequence of hastening death. However, Buddhist teachers generally prohibit euthanasia, or the intentional taking of life, as a violation of the duty of *ahimsa* (nonharm), even when motivated by compassion.

Judaism

Meanings of death, dying, and self

In the Genesis creation narrative in the Torah, the human being is formed from the earth, and animated by the divine infusion of *nefesh* or *ruah*, breath or spirit. One marker for death in the Hebraic tradition that evolved into Judaism, then, is the departure of spirit from the body and its return to Yahweh.

In the earliest forms (2000 BCE) of Hebraic tradition, this departure of spirit or return of vital life forces (breath, blood) to God did not mean a continuation of personal identity beyond death. The person formed from dust returns to dust on death and experiences a condition that Hebraic teaching portrayed as analogous to sleep. The body is a source of religious meaning and communal obligation (the community prepares the body for burial and observes a prohibition against bodily desecration). These Hebraic and proto-Jewish traditions are thus profoundly earthly or this-worldly in orientation. Immortality occurs only through one's posterity or an ongoing community of faith.

When this community of faith experienced in its later history (700–500 BCE) a crisis of identity and the rupture of community through conquest, exile, and dispersion, concepts of immortality of the soul and personal resurrection emerged. Communal differences over the significance of death and the status of a self post-mortem are present in contemporary Judaism, with Orthodox Jews affirming a self that survives death and will experience resurrection, while Reformed Jews reject immortality other than through Jewish tradition's ongoing life.

Implications for medical care and social justice

Disagreements about the nature of the body, the appropriation of medical technology, and the status of the self post-mortem generate diversity within Judaism regarding end-of-life treatment questions. Orthodox Judaism, for example, rejects the concept of brain death and some Orthodox scholars affirm a religious imperative to use life-extending technologies until a person enters the status of *goses*, which in its most restrictive terms occurs 72 hours prior to the cessation of biological life. Other Orthodox scholars do allow withdrawing life support at a much earlier stage of dying.

By contrast, some scholars within Reformed Judaism draw on values of personal liberty, dignity, and compassion, to support physician prescriptions of medication to hasten death or voluntary euthanasia, at least as a matter of individual choice free of state intervention. This position does not recognize an ethical or legal difference between refusing treatments and using medical means to hasten death. Reform scholars also affirm a social imperative of protecting vulnerable dying persons, such as those who lack adequate health insurance or family caregivers.

Jewish teaching sees the world not as an illusion (as in eastern traditions) nor as fallen through sin (as in Christian traditions), but as deliberately left incomplete by God so that human beings could fulfill responsibility for its completion: the phrase *tikkun olam* evokes a Jewish imperative to heal or perfect creation. The meanings of death found in Hebraic and Jewish thought thereby constitute a historical tradition, a communal identity, and legal teaching engaged in establishing social justice in the world.

Christianity

The good news ("gospel") of Christian tradition presupposes an understanding of the significance of death. The tradition originates in the death and resurrection of the Jewish rabbi, Jesus of Nazareth. The universal symbol of Christian faith is "the cross," a symbolic reminder of the manner of Jesus's death by crucifixion to redeem humanity from sin.

Meanings of death, dying, and self

The central Christian meaning of death is separation. Physical death, which afflicts all humanity as a consequence of disobedience and sin, signifies separation of soul and body. Moreover, the inherent human disposition to sin manifests alienation from God and represents a spiritual death. Christian teaching holds that both spiritual and physical separations are overcome through Jesus's death and resurrection. In Christian soteriology, believers receive the grace of divine presence and a post-mortem reunion of soul and body.

Christianity understands the person as an embodied self. The physical body, while an instrument of the self, is a "temple of God's spirit" (1 Corinthians 6:18) and is thus intrinsic to self-identity. The Christian meaning of the body is accentuated through rituals such as baptism and eucharist, teachings of the Church as the "body of Christ" in history, and convictions about bodily resurrection.

As represented in the *ars moriandi* (art of dying) of the fifteenth century, Christianity has often ritually structured dying as a period of reconciliation and preparation. This tradition persists in recommended rituals of prayer, confession, anointing, and pastoral ministry, as well as openness to hospice care.

Implications for medical care and social justice

Christian pluralism about the deliberate termination of life reflects divergent conceptions of a good death. Evangelical and Orthodox Christian communities generally permit refusing or withdrawing medical treatment that is futile in terms of patient recovery. In circumstances of incurably dying patients, the values of stewardship, compassion, and community support cessation of life support. However, as exemplified in teachings of the Southern Baptist Convention, the largest US Protestant denomination, some conservative Protestant traditions understand nutrition and hydration provided through feeding tubes as comfort care to be extended to all dying persons in symbolic recognition of their dignity. Feeding-tube refusal or withdrawal is thereby situated within a broader prohibition of euthanasia. This perspective, supplemented by appeals to protecting vulnerable persons, formed the basis for conservative Christian opposition to feeding-tube removal in the Terry Schiavo case.

Roman Catholic Christianity has sought to inculcate a "culture of life" to critique a "culture of death" in liberal societies that permit abortion, euthanasia, and assisted suicide. Values of stewardship, compassion, relationship, dignity, and protecting the vulnerable legitimate the forgoing of disproportionately burdensome medical treatments. While this view had generally applied to nourishment through feeding tubes, in a papal allocution in 2004 the late Pope John Paul II reaffirmed the humanity of patients in a persistent vegetative state and their rights to basic healthcare, including providing nutrition and hydration through feeding tubes. The allocation stipulated that feeding-tube removal when nourishment is provided constitutes "euthanasia by omission" because the intent is to bring about death.

Professionally responsible physicians occasionally perform "palliative sedation," typified when a physician prescribes higher doses of morphine to relieve terminal pain. However, morphine in strong enough doses can suppress respiration sufficiently to hasten death. The practice of palliative sedation appears to many to diminish pain in dying persons by methods that are practically indistinguishable from euthanasia.

Ecclesiastical teaching in Roman Catholic (and many Protestant) traditions defends palliative sedation through the principle of double effect. Papal teaching permits physicians to suppress pain by narcotics, "even at the approach of death and if one foresees that the use of narcotics will shorten life" (Sacred Congregation, 1990: 10). The death that occurs is considered an unintended and "indirect" death, a secondary or "double effect" of a primary intention of a legitimate medical action, the relief of pain. The intent distinguishes the action from euthanasia. Double-effect reasoning, while subject to criticism for its sharp distinction between intention and foresight, allows these traditions to affirm the sanctity of life and compassionate care for pain relief, while maintaining that euthanasia is incompatible with medicine's healing vocation.

For some liberal Protestant traditions, physician-performed euthanasia based on motives of compassion, love, or mercy, as well as respect for personal choice, can be legitimated. Compassion for the suffering of the irreversibly dying may be invoked as a justification for a policy of euthanasia, or as a warrant for "emergency case" euthanasia. The latter is illustrated in the case of a New Orleans physician, Anna Pou, charged with the murder of nine patients through drug injection in the wake of Hurricane Katrina. A grand jury refused to indict Dr. Pou in July 2007 because of the extreme circumstances she confronted. However, emergency euthanasia is specific to the emergency and cannot be generalized into policy.

The corporate presence of the Christian community in the world reflects foundational commitments to social justice, often conveyed through the symbol of the kingdom of God. Christian scholars contend that emulating the passion of Jesus for justice in the kingdom of God involves concrete actions in such areas as healthcare reform and ensuring access to healthcare for all persons, as well as requiring justice in health-related realms such as environmental and economic justice.

Islam

Islam, a religion of submission to the one God (Allah), is revealed in the sacred text, the Qur'an, and exemplified in the *sunnah*, the acts and sayings of Allah's final prophet, Muhammed (ca. 570–632 CE). In contrast to the Christian view that death is a consequence of human sin, the Qur'an situates death within the goodness of divine creation and human destiny of resurrection: "So blessed be God, the Best to create! After that, at length ye will die. Again, on the Day of Judgment, will ye be raised up" (Qur'an, Sura 23:14–16).

Islamic teaching designates mortal life as a time of "testing" of character to determine worthiness for eternal life with Allah: "He Who created Death and Life, that He may try which of you is best in deed" (Qur'an, Sura 67:2). Observing similar passages in the Qur'an in which "death" is rhetorically placed prior to "life," scholar A. Yusaf Ali comments, "Death, then, is (1) the state before life began, which may be non-existence or existence in some other form; (2) the state in which Life as we know it ceases, but existence does not cease" (Qur'an, note 5556).

Death is thereby a necessary passage to a post-mortal realm of existence, during which the soul takes temporary leave of the body. Muslims anticipate universal resurrection preceding a calamitous day of judgment, with human beings judged by Allah as deserving of eternal reward or punishment.

Implications for medical care and social justice

The cluster of values of sovereignty, sanctity, solidarity, and stewardship generate a presumption in Islamic teaching for employing life-extending technologies so long as they benefit the patient. However, futile medical treatments that prolong life unnecessarily can be refused or withdrawn. This permission applies to patients who are in a persistent vegetative state. In these circumstances, values of dignity and community, including public good (*maslaha*), are given priority. Islamic proscriptions against suicide and affirmations of the healing role of medicine underlie proscriptions on direct physician assistance in dying or euthanasia.

The divine creation and inevitability of death place life in its proper perspective and gives meaning to mortal acts and responsibilities. The Islamic mission in the world is to strive for an ideal social order comprised of peace and justice. In this context, medicine has an indispensable calling: Islamic medical oaths value the physician as an instrument through whom God preserves life and health. The meaning of physician practice is illuminated by Qur'anic teaching: "And if he saveth a life, he hath saved the life of all mankind" (Qu'ran, Sura 5:32).

Islamic teaching affirms that societies will be more just and peaceful to the extent that they are founded on a belief in a world to come. An other-worldly orientation infuses this-worldly actions with direction and responsibility toward securing peace and justice.

Stewardship in the Cost of Dying

The staggering costs of end-of-life care present a profound issue of social justice. Some scholars and policymakers argue that end-of-life care should be rationed, with the anticipated billions in savings redirected to persons without any health insurance, or to persons suffering from chronic but nonterminal conditions (for example diabetes, stroke). Others argue that a protracted and expensive dying process is a compelling utilitarian rationale for legalized physician assistance in suicide or euthanasia.

Religious traditions generally have not been in the forefront of advocacy of either of these two approaches. These proposals violate core values, including sanctity of life, compassion, community, liberty, and solidarity with the vulnerable. However, the social justice context of dying is a matter of stewardship of scarce resources for religious traditions. Religious communities can display responsible stewardship through advocacy of greater access and use of hospice care, death education for their adherents, endorsing planning for dying, including initiatives to complete advance directives, and encouraging the medical community to devote more research to pain control and palliative care.

References

Bhagavad-Gita (1986) B.S. Miller (trans.), Bantam Books, New York.

Holy Qur'an (1983) A. Yusaf Ali (trans.), Amana Corporation, New York.

Jennings, B., Ryndes, T., D'Onofrio, C., and Baily, M. (2003) *Access to Hospice Care*, Hastings Center, Garrison, NY.

John Paul II (2004) On life-sustaining treatments and the vegetative state, *National Catholic Bioethics Quarterly* 4(3): 573–576.

Kapleau, P. (1989) *The Wheel of Life and Death*, Anchor Books, New York.

Kramer, K. (1988) *The Sacred Art of Dying: How World Religions Understand Death*, Paulist Press, Mahwah, NJ.

Kubler-Ross, E. (1969) *On Death and Dying*, Macmillan, New York.

Sacred Congregation for the Doctrine of the Faith (1990) *Declaration on Euthanasia*, Daughters of St. Paul, Boston.

Young, K. (1989) Euthanasia: Traditional Hindu views and the contemporary debate, in *Hindu Ethics: Purity, Abortion, and Euthanasia*, H. Cowart, J. Lipner, and K. Young (eds.), SUNY Press, New York, pp. 93–111.

Bibliography

Aries, P. (1974) *Western Attitudes toward Death*, Johns Hopkins University Press, Baltimore.

Barry, V. (2007) *Philosophical Thinking about Death and Dying*, Thomson Wadsworth, Belmont, CA.

Bemporad, J. (1989) Judaic concepts of the soul, in *Death, Afterlife and the Soul*, L.E. Sullivan (ed,) Macmillan, New York, pp. 205–213.

Borg, M.J. (2003) *The Heart of Christianity*, HarperCollins, New York.

Cophenhaver, B.P. (1978) Death: Ars moriendi, *Encyclopedia of Bioethics*, W.T. Reich (ed.), Free Press, New York.

Crawford, S.C. (2003) *Hindu Bioethics for the 21st Century*, SUNY Press, New York.

Doka, K.J. and Morgan, J.D. (eds.) (1993) *Death and Spirituality*, Baywood Publishing, Amityville, NY.

Dorff, E.N. (1996) *The Jewish Tradition: Religious Beliefs and Health Care Decisions*, Park Ridge Center, Chicago.

Easwaran, E. (1996) *The Undiscovered Country: Exploring the Promise of Death*, Nilgiri Press, Tomales, CA.

Ehman, J.W. Ott, B.B., Ciampa, R.C., Short, T.H., and Hansen-Flaschen, J. (1999) Do patients want physicians to inquire about their spiritual or religious beliefs if they become gravely ill? *Archives of Internal Medicine* 159(15): 1803–1806.

Irish, D.P., Lundquist, K.F., and Nelsen, V.J. (1993) *Ethnic Variation in Dying, Death, and Grief*, Taylor and Francis, Washington, DC.

John Paul II (1995) Evangelium vitae, *Origins* 24(42): 690–730.

Kelsay, J. (1993) *Islam and War*, Westminster/John Knox Press, Louisville, KY.

Keown, D. (1998–1999) Suicide, assisted suicide and euthanasia: A Buddhist perspective, *Journal of Law and Religion* 2: 385–405.

Land, R. and Moore, L.A. (1995) *Life at Risk: The Crises in Medical Ethics*, Broadman & Holman, Nashville.

LaRue, G.A. (1996) *Playing God: Fifty Religions' Views on Your Right to Die*, Moyer Bell, London.

Numrich, P.D. (2001) *The Buddhist Tradition: Religious Beliefs and Health Care Decisions*, Park Ridge Center, Chicago.

Peppin, J.F., Cherry, M.J., and Iltis, A. (eds.) (2004) *Religious Perspectives in Bioethics*, Taylor & Francis, New York.

Rahman, F. (1989) *Health and Medicine in the Islamic Tradition*, Crossroad Publishing, New York.

Rahula, W. (1974) *What the Buddha Taught*, Grove Press, New York.

Rinpoche, S. (1994) *The Tibetan Book of Living and Dying*, Harper Collins, New York.

Saunders, D.C. (1991–1992) The evolution of the hospices, *Free Inquiry* 11: 19–23.

Shannon, T.J. and Walter, J.J. (2004) Implications of the Papal allocution on feeding tubes, *Hastings Center Report* 34(4): 18–20.

Sulmasy, D.P. (2006) Spiritual issues in the care of dying patients: It's okay between me and God, *Journal of the American Medical Association* 296: 1385–1392.

Tolstoy, L. (1981) *The Death of Ivan Ilyich*, Bantam Books, New York.

Veatch, R. (1974) *Death, Dying, and the Biological Revolution: Our Last Quest for Responsibility*, Yale University Press, Nashville, TN.

CHAPTER 40
Religion's Influence on Social Justice Practices Relating to Those with Disabilities

Ruth Vassar Burgess

Defining Basic Terms

Social justice relates to the belief and practices that a society initiates and maintains to sustain its systems. One of these systems is religious beliefs and practices. Embedded within religion is a subcategory that applies to both civil and religious practices toward those classified as disabled.

Religion, as a sociocultural phenomenon, has supported different social justice beliefs and practices since primordial times. Most religions evolved for sectarian or survival purposes. They may be inclusive, in that they clarify who can belong to their spiritual group or who may be excluded. These imply a sense of correctness, such as "We are okay; you are not okay." In this manner adherents, who qualify according to their parochial definition, may or may not partake of sacramental functions. When religion and social justice beliefs meet at the crossroads, it has an impact on those with disabilities and their caretakers. It is here that belief systems influence how groups determine truth and implement their common practices.

A broad secular definition of religion is needed if one is to understand how world religions relate to those with disabilities. For example, during the twentieth century many of the traditional duties and traditions once conducted by religious groups were given to state and national governmental agencies. Thus, the relationships between church/synagogue/temple/mosque and state became blurred as to who was responsible for providing compassionate, appropriate, and the most responsive services. The following definition has been selected for this essay: "Religion is defined as those beliefs to which one bows his head and bends his knees" (Karl Luckert, 2009). This definition can apply to traditional religious groups, and even to the civic delivery of services to those with disabilities and their caregivers.

In recent years, international attention has been directed toward those with disabilities and their caregivers. These concerns illustrate an evolving interest in social justice practices globally. It is estimated that 650 million people or 10% of the population have disabilities. The incidence would be higher if one included those disabilities related to aging. The complexity of the status quo is based on historical formative beliefs, various interpretations of civil and religious laws, and the need for social care.

Through religious teachings and moral practices, cultural standards evolve defining what constitutes a disability and its subsequent sociocultural responsibilities. The term "individuals with disabilities" refers to those who differ from the "usual or normal" cultural expectations. In western societies these differences are categorized as different mental characteristics, sensory abilities, communication skills, behavior, and emotional development, as well as physical and health issues. Services for these individuals are given or withheld according to societal systems, beliefs, and practices, including religion.

The impact of religion on individuals with disabilities becomes complex as one studies belief and practices trans-temporally and trans-spatially. As cultural expectations, access to resources, and scientific thought have evolved, so the identification and acceptance of those with disabilities have changed. Increasingly, some cultures do not have a word for disabilities. For example, in historical Arabic writing there was not a single word meaning disability. Rather, there were specific words that might be included in some categories of disabilities. Not only have societal attitudes and practices been altered, but also religions have modified their perceptions and how they related to those with disabilities over time. However, founding or former beliefs have continued to have an impact on current political and religious systems.

This essay provides a survey through a historical narrative of social justice practices toward those with disabilities. It is from these belief systems that concepts such as equality, fairness, justice, and other social constructs were adopted and practiced. Specific contributions to our current understandings are found in four religious belief systems: Vedic Hinduism, Judaism, Christianity, and Islam. These religions provided social justice practices based on historical belief systems. Vedic Hinduism provided a system that required lifelong commitments to implementing karma. This understanding influenced how one performs social justice practices in this life in order to have a better reincarnation in the next life. Judaism introduced the concept of ritual purity for those who are to offer prayers. This was something selectively bestowed but not easily attained. Certainly, those with disabilities were not seen as without blemish. While the three Abrahamic faiths (Judaism, Christianity, and Islam) reported healings from disabling conditions, Christianity extended the possibility of healing and other miracles toward those disabilities outside of ethnic boundaries. Finally, the unity of spiritual aspirations and needs cannot be separated from human desires and material needs, as seen in Islam. In the twenty-first century scholars debate the rights of disabled persons from the viewpoint of Islamic shari'a law. Islam continues to emphasize the significance of adherents obeying religious laws in all aspects of life. Discussions have included the possibility of developing a special branch of Islamic jurisprudence focusing on people with disabilities. While these four religions all admonish adherents to do "good," their admonitions vary according to cultural and historical backgrounds.

This essay is organized in three major sections. First, a historical overview presents a progression of practices toward those with disabilities based on their society's understanding of social justice. The second section is subdivided according to distinct contributions from Vedic Hinduism, Judaism, Christianity, and Islam. These religions' historical beliefs influenced their definitions and practices relating to social justice toward those with disabilities and their families. The third section provides a summary and conclusion.

Review of Historical Social Justice Practices Toward the Disabled

Oral histories and narratives from the classics record myths concerning the rejection and extermination of those with noticeable differences. Infants were left to the elements, including being placed on anthills to die and to have their bones picked clean by vultures. Imperfect children were placed on rocks for the fowls and beasts to eat. Some were burned. In east Africa, it has been reported that the oldest female relative drowned weaker infants, although the tribe felt an obligation to give the infant a funeral, sometimes using a log to represent the child. For others, the religious cultural beliefs that maladies were a result of prior incarnations or payment for the sins of the fathers drove social justice practices. The belief in evil eyes or dark spirits led frequently to physical mutilations of the mother and child. Certainly, disabilities were thought of as a mark of God's displeasure. The births of these children might also be seen as signs that bad luck or a catastrophe could be pending. The salvation of an individual was not the primary issue; the survival of the group or tribe became their preservation goal.

In primitive periods, those born with visible impairments were subjected to a harsh physical environment in which infanticide was practiced. Demons were thought to cause the disability. The disabled survivor was persecuted, neglected, and isolated. Frequently, a child born to disabled parents was killed. Superstition and the drive to survive guided the practices of exorcism and demonology. Survival of the corporate group drove the tribe's practices.

During the Greco-Roman period, a disabled child's destiny was left to the father. If the father did not hold the infant in his arms, the rejected child was usually thrown off a cliff, drowned, or exiled. Demons were thought to inhabit the infant or the mother. Hence, religion entered the intervention process as it developed different exorcism protocols. However, there were those who timidly wrote that there might be natural explanations for these human differences. Interestingly, Plato expressed concern for the "deviant." He believed that the family should care for its own.

The relationship between religion and civil authority was and continues to be blurred. Skeletons with deformities have been unearthed dating back to the Greco-Roman period. While they did not use the term "disabled," the Greeks used *teras* and the Romans wrote of a *monstrum*. These words were commonly used to describe mythological monsters. The Latin *mutus* referred both to those who could not speak and those who were thought to be stupid (Brignell, 2008). Frequently, deities bore the burden for infanticide. In addition, tribal members extended negative practices by incurring different forms of social alienation, such as occupational and marriage limitations, for families with disabled members. Though dressed in different terms, survival of the fittest took many avenues throughout the centuries.

Harsh physical treatment resulted from superstitions during the Middle Ages. While witch burning, torture, and exorcism were not uncommon, there were instances of disabled individuals receiving veneration, since their disability was viewed as an act of God. Pity and the belief that "except for the goodness of God, there go I" were common and extended into the modern era. However, the seeds of the scientific method were being planted. Natural explanations for illness and differences were sought by inquiring minds.

Many of the same practices prevailed in the sixteenth and seventeenth centuries. The courts still accepted exploitation of those with disabilities, but more examples of humane treatment were being reported. Ponce de Leon advocated for the oral instructional method rather than the manual instruction method for the deaf. Jonathan Swift wrote on the ill effects of poverty. This was to be expanded to include those with blindness in the eighteenth century. During the twentieth century, mental illness became known as a physical disease rather than a subcategory of mental retardation or of demonic possession. The movement for human treatment, institutional custodial care, and social acceptance accelerated in the nineteenth and the beginning of the twentieth centuries. The rise of scientific medicine, psychological research, mental measurements, and humanism brought changes in the treatment of those with disabilities.

At the beginning of the twentieth century, medical and psychoanalytic models became popular social practices. Asylums and "crazy houses" served as holding buildings for the disabled, who were housed away from their families and communities of heritage. Behaviorism with its external and repetitious practices followed this model. The "separate but equal" placement and services were found to be discriminatory and less effective by the courts. The anthropological model, which encouraged inclusion within the least restrictive environments, came into favor, supported by state and federal mandates. Furthermore, the validity of psychological measurements was questioned in light of cultural biases resulting from mental measurement errors. The significance of mediating environments was encouraged within different ecosystems. Therefore, families and caregivers were encouraged to take active roles in the services provided for those with disabilities. This model encouraged the provision of knowledge and services from birth through adulthood. Social justice had moved from basic survival possibilities, to "magical thinking," and then to secular policies and procedures. These were prompted by research and lobbying by secular social action groups.

However, ancient theological controversies continued to be argued over by religious pundits. These concerns may raise questions that are oblique to those with disabilities and their caregivers. Within religious conclaves, there were disagreements as to the worth of the individual as an object of creation. They posed seemingly basic questions, such as: Is there a static or dynamic relationship between one's creator and the creation? A static belief advocated that God sends or approves of disabilities to "teach humans lessons," either individually or to a group. How, then, does the creation respond to such a "heavenly gift"? Should the most appropriate or responsive spiritual, medical, vocational, and educational services be enabled? If so, who determines the types of engagement? Do practices seek minimalism or do they enable the most appropriate services and care? As an example, the Christian renewal studies theologian Yong (2007) raised the question: If healing is central to Christianity, how does the group explain the absence of healing? Then Yong makes a linguistic distinction between healing and curing. Reaching back to the writings of St. Paul in the first century, Yong (2007) and Eiesland (1994) proposed that the "weaker" and "less honorable" members are the most indispensable since they assist the "body of Christ" in fulfilling diversity, which is presented as God's plan. This is puzzling. Using pejorative language ("weaker and less honorable"), one must respond by asking: Who needed to be healed or cured – an individual, the caregivers, the group, society, or the ethereal body of Christ?

At the other end of the continuum is the dynamic approach that advocated there is an active God who created and is creating. As part of the ongoing creation, human beings are malleable. Plasticity is a characteristic of the brain. Therefore, being created in the image of God, all humans have the possibility of developing positive alternatives. These alternatives were possible through mediated encounters. A mediated approach could occur through the interpretation of traditional wisdom literature or through human mediators. The static belief supported the status quo. The dynamic approach provided an ongoing, optimistic alternative.

When looking back over these changes that have occurred in the treatment of the disabled, one can conclude either that much has changed or that little theological progress has been made. Through the centuries, social justice definitions and practices have depended on the perceived needs of society. The recent changes in services were the products of the scientific method and social activism, not religion.

Social Justice Distinctions from Four Major Religions

How sacred texts and myths are perceived varies. Some see them as direct words given by God on Mount Sinai (Judaism), the Mount of Beatitudes (Christianity), in the city of Mecca (Islam), or by the river Ganges (Hinduism). Others believe that the Holy Spirit guided the ink quills of the medieval scribes as they copiously copied the words of Jesus or the decisions given by the Muslim jurists. Modern theologians seek validity by using techniques such as cross-referencing, archeology, or biomedicine, as well as voting on the "authenticity" of ancient scripts. These historical practices supported by evolving oral traditions framed social justice practices toward the disabled.

Vedic Hinduism: A comprehensive social justice system

In India around 8000 BCE the divine was understood as a combination of cosmic law and earthly realties. In cosmic creation, dual gender energies emerged. It was understood that cosmic relations were immutable. It is significant to understand this system in relationship to those with disabilities. As Hinduism (*sanatan dharma*, meaning the "eternal law") began to be codified, communities emerged in which rules were given in order to maintain civil duties and responsibilities. Three basic elements formed the early Hindu religion: reverence, devotion, and surrender to the will of God. There was one true God with many energies emanating from Him. One word cannot define the infinite and seven concepts must be embedded in one's understanding of God: omniscience, sovereignty, power (energy), strength, vigor, splendor (glory), and righteousness. The 1108 names of the incarnate God were synonyms. Each word represented a different aspect or essence of the one God.

This loving God admonished adherents to follow two tenets. First, humans must love all and hate none. Second, humans must live in peace and harmony. We are like birds that live in one tree, which is the globe. When living according to these tenets, a person asks: "How can I make you happy? Thus you cannot think to hurt them." A person is considered disabled when he is not following his karma, his reason for existence.

Karma is the doctrine of inevitable consequences. This central idea concurred with the belief in reincarnation, or earlier life forms and experiences. How one successfully or unsuccessfully completed good karma in an earlier incarnation resulted in one's present living situation. Disabilities could be explained according to these beliefs. Negative karma could be obtained if one did not show consideration for those with disabilities. Then how one successfully completed one's appointed karma in this life would influence one's karma in later incarnations. It was hoped that one could perform sufficient positive karma to be ultimately joined with God.

The ancient beliefs of Hinduism evolved and were recorded in the religion's sacred texts. Those most frequently cited are the *Vedas*, *Upanishad*, *Vedanta*, *Itihasa*, and *Bhagavad Gita*. The texts were transmitted by *gurukuls* (residential, communal, extended family-like schools) that were taught by gurus (respected teachers). These texts do not specially address how adherents should think about and treat those with disabilities as the term is understood in the twenty-first century; rather, they provided a social system whereby caregivers provided nurturing in order to fulfill their karma. The core concept of karma offered a distinction from the three Abrahamic religions in which God provided life experiences and through faith one attained salvation, healing, and some form of afterlife. In Hinduism, one experiences a disability if one does not live up to one's karma. Those who do not live up to their karma do not thrive. They will pay later in future lives during reincarnations. So how or why is one disabled? A person is disabled by not following his or her karma. There is no innocent party if one does not fulfill one's karma. To achieve positive karma, one must show respect and seek harmony. Thus one must think and ask: "In what way can I make you happy?" This means that a person cannot think to hurt those with disabilities. (Unfortunately, among the poor there are still reports of babies or children being maimed in order for the young to earn money from begging.) An example of karma in action is the story of Maharishi Ashtavkra, a Hindu saint, who was believed to have had a disability. In referring to his bodily affliction, he mentioned that it was only temporary because of his past karma. Ashtavkra taught that others needed to care for the inner "light," since it contained the soul, whereas the whole body was built merely of earth, water, fire, and air.

In the *Sushruta Samhita* from the fourth century CE, Sushrutha, a noted Ayurvedic surgeon, listed seven categories of diseases (Kamlesh Kapur, 2010). Interestingly, these categories are comparable to recent health-related groupings. However, they do not directly address all the areas that were thought to be disabling.

1 Some disorders are genetic, which means that they are inherited from parents.
2 Some problems are caused by things going wrong during pregnancy.
3 Many diseases are caused by wrong diet and improper digestion, thus leaving undigested particles in the body.
4 Some disorders are caused by accidents such as nearness to a person suffering from disease, assaults, snakebites, or other similar accidents.
5 A few disorders are caused by variations in the seasons or due to aging.
6 Diseases are caused by epidemics.
7 Many diseases occur when we compromise our defense mechanism by wrong habits.

The holy *Vedas* required adherents to show four types of respect: respect for nature; respect for parents and elders; respect for teachers because they disseminate knowledge; respect for one's society and nation, shown through service. These four types of respect provided opportunities for engaging in good karma.

During the primordial days of Hinduism, those with disabilities were taken care of first by their extended families. A four-generational social justice model nurtured the extended family model. Even the architectural designs of homes supported intergenerational transmission of culture. In rural areas there was a central or great hall with a side bedroom leading from it. The kitchen, storage, and other rooms led off this. Where there was less available land, the extended families used a vertical plan. The oldest family members lived on the first floor. On the second floor was the father's family. On each of the higher floors were younger members of the family. There was little need for facilities for older people, because as the younger family members moved around doing daily duties they would check in with the elderly. Respect for the elderly was ingrained in this extended family model. To be dependent on others outside of the family was an indignity.

Moreover, everyone rushed to be of assistance to the oldest family members. Children kneeled at the feet of elders, requesting blessings. In the Vedic marriage vows the groom said: "I will be steadfast and fixed as stars." The bride replied: "I will be resilient as the constellations." They pledged to give inner strength, produce progeny, be a friend in every way, and look after the dependent, family, relatives, and those less fortunate.

Judaism: Purity or wholeness in religious practices

Judaism began with the patriarch Abraham, who left Mesopotamia (now Iraq) and led his clan to Israel. They brought with them existing creation stories and myths concerning divine and human relationships. Embedded in these narratives were beliefs that emphasized order and reason, dependability and mutuality. Laws emerged that were to be obeyed. This relationship between the Jewish God and his chosen people pertained to a covenant that allowed divine power to be limited by the agreement that the deity entered into with the Jewish people (Abrams, 1998: 7).

Then there were the narratives detailing enslavement in Egypt and the miracle stories of how they escaped from Pharaoh's tyranny. Egypt became a metaphor for that which was abhorrent to their unseen God. In order for the chosen to be purified from the ways of Egyptian society, these people wandered in the desert for 40 years. They survived under the guidance of their unseen God, who provided for their travels and food. Equally important was to establish order, priestly hierarchy, and rules for spiritual and physical purity. From these early experiences came the first five books of the Hebrew Bible, which were known as the Torah. Later, after the splitting of the kingdom of Israel into Judea in the south and Israel in the north, more parts of the Torah were created (Abrams, 1998: 3).

Judaism comprises Orthodox, Conservative, and Reformed groups. Each of these has additional subdivisions. The Orthodox adhere to the belief that God gave the exact words to Moses as he was writing the Torah. This contains 613 *mitzvoth* (commandments) that were binding on Jews. Both written and oral versions of the Torah were of divine origin and contained the exact imprint of God. Conservative adherents accepted the binding nature of Jewish law (*halakhah*), but believed that the law should change and adapt to aspects of the predominant culture. In the creation of the world God provided a framework. Humans were partners in completing His creation. However, Conservative Jews must remain true to Judaism's values during the process. Reformed Judaism affirmed the central tenets of Judaism. Its adherents believed that the Torah was the foundation of God's ongoing revelation that enables humans to learn from scientific methods. Their emphasis on ethics promoted social action in order to enable a better world. Judaism has and will continue to ferment, since the struggle between continuity and change was central to its ethos. Differently from most religions, Judaism encouraged open, informed discourse and probing into the rationales behind multiple perspectives.

Judaism's cult of the priesthood has direct implications for those with disabilities. Those with imperfections were not allowed to offer religious sacrifices. The inner places of worship required the purist forms of dedication. They referred to an absence of the taint of death (i.e., ritual impurity); the embodiment of perfect human life (the blemish-free priests); perfect animal life (the blemish-free sacrificial animals); and senses fully stimulated by incense, bells, loaves, and so forth that were at the heart of temple worship (Haran, 1985: 216). A proclamation of "unclean" by the priest was required when an individual had leprosy or a serious disease of the skin. Physical seclusion from the group was required. This was a legal rather than a moral mandate. If a cure occurred, a purification ritual was then required.

Sharing similar status, the disabled and prostitutes were considered unclean, similar to women during the menstrual cycle. Specific examples of uncleanness included blindness and certain eye diseases, injuries to the thigh, a deformed nose, lameness, the loss of a limb, skeletal deformation, muscle degeneration, a humped back, skin disease, and the loss of a testicle. The deaf and mute were subnormal, while the blind were considered normal. Some thought of the blind as the "walking dead." As a whole, those with disabilities were considered impure, thus disqualifying them from full participation in religious rituals (Stiker, 2007: 24). The Essenes further prohibited the disabled from entering into military combat. This temple cult formed the precedent for how to approach God in cleanliness and without blemish. Those found impure were subjected to alienation practices.

Sin was seen as the most common cause of disabilities. It is interesting that the problem usually lay with humanity not fulfilling the laws rather than God creating lameness, blindness, or illness. An exception to this belief is the story of Job. He had a plethora of misfortunes, but his story introduced the possibility that God allowed those misfortunes and that there was a requirement for social responsibility toward those who were suffering. If the afflicted were patient and steadfast in practicing God's laws, there would be a positive ending to their story.

In the Songs of the Suffering Servant in the book of Isaiah, another genre was recorded. Here we find the possibility of a single person taking the suffering for the group. The protagonist, who was innocent, was willing to take the punishment for the social inequities of the Israelites. At other times the God of Israel punished people because they did not remain true to his commandments and they began to assimilate the customs and beliefs of others. It was not until they returned to their tradition that their God would bless them and even restore their land. Here both the people and the land received positive or negative retribution.

A pericope that illustrates a modern adaptation in both Jewish and scientific thought is the theory of structural cognitive modifiability and its applications, conceptualized by Reuven Feuerstein (2006), a Romanian Jew. Early in his life Feuerstein had been acculturated by the Hassidic tradition within an Orthodox Jewish community. The Hassidic concept of *teffelin* was interpreted to mean "When one's heart goes out to others." Social justice was to be delivered based on the religious belief that all humans were created in the image of God. When differences arose, compassionate intervention was to occur through a mediator. Therefore, regardless of one's circumstances – including disabilities – humans were dynamic, evolving entities. Thus, religion influenced social justice practices toward those with disabilities and their caregivers. With the assistance of a mediator, humans could learn how to learn, allowing them to become modifiable throughout life. Humans were considered malleable, not fixed entities. After all, were they not created in the image of God?

It must be noted that Judaism provided the foundation first for Christianity and later for Islam. While remaining in a covenantal relationship with their understanding of the unseen God, the Jews formed a core and systems that did not resort to evangelism. While their ideas were often complex and abstract, they offered evolving benevolent applications. This understanding of the law provided resilience for survival, despite their many dispersions. The Jews defined what was "without blemish" and only the clean and pure priesthood could offer up the atonement sacrifices. How one integrates "purity or without blemish" with being created in the "image of God" is still under discussion, however.

Christianity: Hope through healing

Christianity emerged as a religion between 27 and 30 CE, as a sect embedded in Judaism. Under Roman persecution and Jewish Orthodox malfeasance, this fledgling religion emphasizing the triune God broke away and began to grow into a major world religion.

This monotheistic religion worshipped three persons (God the Father, God the Son, and God the Holy Spirit) in one essence.

As Christianity spread in the Roman world, it came into contact with many cultures. It did not adhere to the exclusivity found in its Jewish heritage. Thus diversity of interpretations and social justice practices became influenced by various individual and group experiences, heritages, and emerging knowledge. Later, with the advent of the age of reason and the scientific method, further formations and reformations were to influence Christianity. Eastern Christianity emphasized group identity for salvation. (For example, Emperor Constantine, who influenced the Council of Nicea where the elements of the New Testament were accepted, declared his subjects to be Christians.) Later Christians in the West encouraged individual salvation practices.

Although Judaism and Christianity had commonalties, such as the Hebrew Bible and shared traditions, there were points of distinctiveness. The Jews maintained their exclusive People of the Book covenant with God, while in Christianity salvation was possible for both Jews and Gentiles. For example, Christians proclaimed Jesus of Nazareth to be the Son of God as well as the Messiah, as prophesied in the Hebrew Old Testament. Even Jesus said that he had come to fulfill Isaiah's prophecies. This Messianic figure engendered a small following among the Jews, while others offered hatred, betrayal, and death. Jesus spoke openly about the need for reform in the religious practices of the Pharisees and Sadducees. He challenged the interpretation of the laws, placing emphasis on addressing human needs.

How, then, does Christianity view those with disabilities? Jesus's message was to fulfill the laws, but also to show compassion for those with disabilities. His philosophy extended even to those who persecuted him. Long-suffering, reconciliation, and forgiveness became seen as God-like characteristics. Followers were encouraged to emulate their Christ. They carried on Jesus's values and social justice practices, which were mainly antithetical to most religious practices in the Roman Empire.

Belief influences human roles and social justice practices. Christianity has been called the "religion of healing." It should be noted that the original idea of healing arose out of the Hebrew Bible's concept of "holy." In more recent times, the concept of completeness is frequently related to body and mind healing, rather than a more inclusive application to healing of the soul, healing of the mind, healing of the body, and healing of the community (Cox, forthcoming: 33). Richard Cox provided a comprehensive definition for a holistic goal:

> Health is the homeostasis of Mind, Body, and Spirit with the divine relationship to God. This applies whether we are speaking of emotional illness, physical illness, interpersonal conflict, domestic upsets, tribal skirmishes, or nations at war. (Cox, forthcoming)

The word "healing" may refer to different levels of meaning in the Hebrew Bible and the Christian New Testament. Some disabilities were deemed to be imparted by God (John 12:40). Other people were "blinded" by this "world," meaning the unrighteous practices of carnal society (I John 2:11). Other disabilities were considered to be the result of ancestral sins. Thus, the etiology of a disability might be understood differently. It could have been congenital (Acts 8:7, 14:10), or the disability might have developed recently (2 Samuel 4:4).

The need for healing of the nation of Israel was emphasized by the prophets (Jeremiah 3:22; Hosea 6:1). Then healing of the land was promised on the condition of repentance and return to the spirit and laws of the Torah (2 Chronicles 7:14; Hosea 14:4).

Metaphorically, the word "healing" was used when a listener did not comprehend or accept enlightenment (II Corinthians 3:14, 4:4; Ephesians 4:18; Deuteronomy 28:28; Isaiah 57:14). It was suggested that physical symptoms emerged when there were problems with the soul or in the mind. This malaise was extended even to horses, in that they might be struck with blindness (Zechariah 12: 4).

Examples of physical healing included of the blind, physical impairments, leprosy, deafness, illness, and emotional disturbances. Also the list included all manner of sickness, palsy, communication disorders, mental illnesses, and those with unclean spirits or possessed by devils (Matthew 4:24, 10:1, 12:22; Luke 5:13, 8:36).

It was recorded that Jesus even raised Lazarus from the dead (Matthew 10:8). Besides the healings of the soul, mind, and body, Jesus frequently performed miracles in places such as the temple or on holy days (Matthew 12:10, 21:14). While directly confronting the rules or laws advocated by the Pharisees and Sadducees, Jesus seemed to emphasize His concern for human need.

Why is it important to discuss healing? If healing is one of the central tenets of a religion, what are the implications when one is not healed or cured of an impairment or disability? If imperfections or differences imply problems with purity and access to God, is there no plan for redemption? Wholeness or completeness is achieved when there is a salvation or reunification of creation with the creator. It was written, "I am the Lord that healeth thee" (Exodus 15:26); "I [God] who forgiveth all thine iniquities; who healeth all thy diseases" (Psalm 103:3).

First, "healing of the soul or soul sorrow" (Psalm 41:4) enabled relief for humans from the marks of sin. Hope of divine intervention can be found in the Torah (Deuteronomy 32:39). Later, King David recognized his need for a healing of the mind (Psalm 41:4).

Healing practices evolved through the centuries. Confessions served as a healing medium in the Eastern Orthodox, Roman Catholic, and Anglican traditions. These churches also practiced the rites of reconciliation and participated in the eucharist, which was thought to bring healing. Also, anointing with oil for healing in front of a "sacred icon" or the relics of saints has been reported since the Byzantine era. Handkerchiefs anointed with oil and prayed over continue to be mediums for healing.

Healing shrines, such as the Shrine of the Katholikon at Hosios Loukas, encouraged the penitent to come and pray for healing. The shrine's relics of "Holy Luke" and "Saint Panteleimon," holy oil, and the miracle worker's mosaic portrait are located below the mosaics of Jesus and the Virgin with the Child. The power of prayer for healing is found in the words of James, the brother of Jesus: "The prayer offered in faith will save the sick man. A good man's prayer is powerful and effective" (James 5:13–16).

Anointing with oil and the laying on of hands accompanied by prayers for healing occur in many denominations. However, the therapeutic sense of touch and prayer was a recent approach in some churches. With the advent of technology, there have been healing evangelists. Early in his ministry, Oral Roberts encouraged viewers to touch television sets while he prayed so that they would receive healing. Other healing evangelists called out different illnesses or disorders from a pulpit or a television studio and commanded that the person be healed. These prayers and exorcisms usually refer to physical healings; occasionally spiritual or soul healings are mentioned. It must be noted that the evangelists seldom prayed for healings of the mind or for communities of influence. Thus, healing became an important social justice practice, emanating from Christianity, for those with either distal or proximal disabling conditions.

Islam: Allah provides social justice

Islam derived from the Arabic root "SLM." It meant that true peace and lasting purity were achieved only by submission to the will of God (Allah) and obedience to His law. Allah was and is the only eternal one and there was none equal to Him. Among His attributes were love and kindness, mercy and compassion; He was the all-knowing and the wise, as well as the judge and the peace. Allah was the most merciful and gracious, and the most loving and most concerned with the well-being of man and His creatures. Therefore, His will was one of benevolence and goodness, as seen in His laws.

The wisdom of Allah superseded all others. He created that which was best for humans, so His creations were not in vain. Disabilities, then, were lessons to be learned by the individual or for the community. The disabled provided a means to recognize the blessings Allah had provided.

A basic difference in beliefs exists between Christianity and Islam. In Christianity, man inherited Adam's sin (original sin), which was interpreted as that human were "fallen beings and should feel guilt." In contrast, Islam advocated that every person was born free from sin and possessed inherited virtue. Freedom from sin and freedom to do effective things cleared the Muslim's conscience from the idea of inherited sin.

The story of Adam and Eve provided an example of God's justice and Adam's direct responsibility to God. The story illustrated that each person must be responsible for his own actions, because no one could expiate or inherit another's sin. To assume that God was unable to forgive Adam and made others suffer for his sin, or to assume that Adam did not pray for pardon, was unlikely and contrary to God's mercy, justice, and power to forgive. Therefore, the Muslim does not accept the idea that Adam, with the whole human race, had been condemned and remained unforgiven until Jesus came to expiate their sins (Abdalati, 1977: 16).

This Islamic belief that another cannot expiate for one's sins or shortcomings has implications for those with disabilities, their caregivers, and society. Expiation cannot be blamed for one's difference or how one receives care. Rather, because God created humans, they are more likely to do good than evil. Man was neither helpless nor hopeless since God created and cared for him.

Referring to the relationship between Allah and disabilities, Professor Vardit Rispler-Chaim concluded:

> It is never proclaimed that the disease is predestined by Allah so that the ill Muslim has an opportunity to repent, or that disease is a way of punishment for certain sins. Nowhere in the Qur'an, Sunna or fiqh, is a clear causality established between Allah and the onset of a disease and or disability in a believer. (Ghaly, 2010: 42)

How have Muslims considered those with differences? By the third to the ninth centuries, important Greek sources had been translated into Arabic. These propositions advocated that physical deformities were related to one's inner spirit and character. These included the bald, the lame, the cross-eyed, beardless persons, the fair and ruddy, the hump-backed, and a person with a long nose, as well as those with a bulging forehead, leprosy, or blue eyes. However, the majority of Islamic jurists never supported these examples. "Thus people with disabilities were theoretically able to enjoy, within juristic circles, the same status as that guaranteed for human beings in general" (Ghaly, 2010: 74, 75).

Muslims claimed that those who have disabilities might have increased faith and those who suffer might attain a lofty rank in paradise or receive a bountiful reward from God. During the Middle Ages, sages proposed that Allah gave afflictions to those He loved so He would reward them later. Some of the afflictions were understood as tests of faiths. These conclusions were based on Qur'anic verses, prophetic traditions, scholars' statements, anecdotes, and poems. These multiple sources promoted the beneficial aspects of suffering and adversity. Bishr al-Hafi, a well-known mystic in the Sufi tradition, met a man afflicted with blindness, elephantiasis, madness, and epilepsy. Seeing that ants were eating the man's flesh, Bishr put his head in the man's lap and tried to speak to him. The man later reported that he wondered, "Who is this man who interferes between me and my Lord. Had He cut me into pieces, it would have been nothing but increase my love for Him" (Ghaly, 2010: 21).

The Qur'an, the Holy Bible of Muslims, accepted the exclusion of the disabled for the sanctity of the congregation or community (Sura 14.60, Sura 48). The disabled were exempt from the battle, because of their incapacity, not from spiritual pollution. The Prophet excluded etiological uncleanliness when he stated, "No reproach to the blind, no reproach to the lame, no reproach to the sick." While the crippled, the blind, and the lame were excused from military service, he, like Jesus, invited them to his banquet. Both Islam and Christianity differed from Old Testament Judaism's ritual and cultic prohibitions.

As a religion, Islam is composed of two sets of rulings: Islamic theology and Islamic jurisprudence. These are subdivided into beliefs and actions. Basic questions underlying these categories are:

> Why do disabilities exist since Allah is the Omnipotent, All-Just and All-Merciful? What are the responsibilities of the individual, caregivers, and community toward those with

disabilities? How does one keep a spiritual balance despite the existence of disabilities and other misfortunes? (Ghaly, 2010: 4)

Six major schools of law exist in Islamic jurisprudence. These schools are significant, since they interpret how believers are to implement the laws. There are four main Sunni schools: the Hanafi School, founded during the Ottoman Empire and used in Turkey, Pakistan, and India; the Maliki School, which establishes law in Morocco, Algeria, Tunisia, Libya, and some parts of Egypt; the Shafii School, used in other sections of Egypt, Iraq, Malaysia, and Indonesia; and the Hanbali School, which provides the law in the Gulf countries, especially the kingdom of Saudi Arabia. There are several schools of law in the Shii tradition. The Jafari School, the largest body, lies within Twelve Shiism. Other schools are the Isamailiyah, Zaiddiyah, Alani, and Alevi. Their major adherents reside in Iran, Lebanon, and Bahrain (Ghaly, 2010: 7). This is significant in the understanding of disabilities, because there might be different rulings relating to theology or its implementation. This includes medical treatment, rehabilitation, work, training, exemption from tax and customs duty, equality, participation, social integration, and equal opportunities. Recently, discussions have included the possibility of developing a special branch of Islamic jurisprudence focusing on people with disabilities. Islam continues to emphasize the significance of adherents obeying religious laws (Ghaly, 2010: 89, 103, 164).

Conclusion

Both the practice of religion and the existence of disabilities are universal phenomena. In their primal philosophies, religions require adherents to abide by their laws and practices. This becomes a way of maintaining their understanding of social justice. Within these, each religion struggles with basic constructs such as "same and different," "whole and broken," "pure and impure." How they interpreted these ideas continues to have profound influences on those with disabilities and their caregivers.

The following questions have been asked repeatedly in religious philosophies: How did these differences occur? Did God create imperfections in order to teach mortals lessons (God-given testing, familial guilt, moral imperfections, ancestral folly, previous life errors, blessings in disguise, tribal survival, etc.)? Religions answered by providing largely circular arguments. Changes began occurring with the rise of the scientific process and the applications of evolving social justice ideas and practices across social barriers. Laws and services were extended not only to those with physical disabilities and impairments, but to those with disorders of the mind. Community services, some integrated with religious sponsors, adopted many of the scientific insights. Nevertheless, religion maintained its emphasis on the soul and the "afterlife."

The evolution of services for those with disabilities has moved from basic survival practices, to superstitious applications, and then to outcomes of scientific thought, which provided the fodder for civil laws protecting the rights of those with disabilities. These include equal access to information; equal opportunities to demonstrate knowledge, abilities, and skills; successful participation in meaningful activities, including jobs; and providing appropriate accommodation or modifications that will enable these persons to participate successfully in society.

References

Abdalati, Hammudah (1977) *Islam in Focus*, American Trust Publications, Indianapolis.

Abrams, Judith Z. (1998) *Judaism and Disability: Portrayals in Ancient Texts from the Tanach through the Bavli*, Gallaudet University Press, Washington, DC.

Brignell, Victoria (2008) Ancient world, http://www.newstatesman.com/blogs/crips-column/2008/04/disabled-slaves-child-roman (accessed April 19, 2011).

Cox, Richard (forthcoming) Healing to Healing, unpublished manuscript.

Eiesland, Nancy L. (1994) *The Disabled God: Toward a Liberatory Theology of Disability*, Abingdon Press, Nashville.

Feuerstein, Reuven (2006) interview, Rabbi Rafi Feuerstein's home, Jerusalem, December 9.

Ghaly, Mohammed M. (2010) *Islam and Disability*, Perspectives in Theology and Jurisprudence, Routledge, London.

Haran, Menahem (1985) Temples and temple service in ancient Israel, in Judith Z. Abrams, *Judaism and Disability*, Gallaudet University Press, Washington, DC, p. 8.

Kapur, Kamlesh (2009) interview, Hindu Temple, Chesapeake, VA, December 31.

Luckert, Karl (2009) interview, Portland, OR, March 27.

Stiker, Henri-Jacques (2007) *History of Disability*, University of Michigan Press, Ann Arbor.

Yong, Amos (2007) *Theology and Down Syndrome: Reimaging Disability in Late Modernity*, Baylor University Press, Waco, TX.

Bibliography

Ahmad, Khurshid (1976) *Islam: Its Meaning and Message*, Islamic Council of Europe, London.

A'La Maududi, Sayyid (1977) *Towards Understanding Islam*, International Graphics Printing Service, Takom Park, MD.

Berry, Judy O. and Hardman, Michael L. (1998) *Lifespan Perspectives on the Family and Disability*, Allyn and Bacon, Needham Heights, MA.

Bishop, Marilyn E. (1995) *Religion and Disability: Essays in Scripture, Theology, and Ethics*, Sheed and Ward, Kansas City.

Burgess, Ruth V. (2008) *Changing Brain Structure through Cross-Cultural Learning: The Life of Reuven Feuerstein*, Mellen Press, Lewiston, New York.

Connor, Carolyn (1987) The crypt at Hosios Loukas and its frescoes, PhD dissertation, New York University.

Feuerstein, Reuven (1994) interview, Shoresh Conference, Jerusalem, June 30.

Feuerstein, Reuven, Rand, Yaacov, and Feuerstein, Rafi S. (2006) *You Love Me! . . . Don't Accept Me as I Am: Helping the Low Functioning Person Excel*, ICELP Publications, Jerusalem.

Feuerstein, Shmuel (2002) *Biblical and Talmudic Antecedents of the Mediated Learning Experience Theory: Educational and Didactic Implications for Inter-Generational Cultural Transmission*, International Center for the Enhancement of Learning Potential, Jerusalem.

Ghaly, Mohammed M. (2008) Physical and spiritual treatment of disability in Islam: Perspectives of early and modern jurists, *Journal of Religion, Disability, and Health* 12(2): 105–143.

Hardie, John B. (2000) *Social Justice in Islam*, Islamic Publications International, Oneonta, NY.

Porterfield, Amanda (2005) *Healing in the History of Christianity*, Oxford University Press, New York.

Qutb, Sayyid (2000) *Social Justice in Islam*, Islamic Publications, Oneonta, NY.

Terrell, Sandra L. and Terrell, Francis (1993) African-American cultures, in *Communication Disorders in Multicultural Populations*, Dorothy E. Battle (ed.), Butterworth-Heinemann, Newton, MA.

United Methodist Church (2009) *Social Principles of the United Methodist Church, 2009–2012*, United Methodist Publishing House, Washington, DC.

Upadhyay, Shastri Dilip (2009) interview, Hindu Temple, Chesapeake, VA, December 31.

CHAPTER 41
Ecology and the Environment

Laurel Kearns

"Who dies first? Who is sacrificed first?" Lutheran theologian Christoph Stueckelberger's (2009) haunting chapter title in *God, Creation and Climate Change: Spiritual and Ethical Perspectives* conveys the centrality of justice issues in religious responses to climate change, as he pushes Christians to wrestle with the current stalemate of the climate crisis. These are not hypothetical questions, he argues, but rather the questions that are implicitly being decided with every delay in global climate change treaties and action. In other words, inaction equals injustice. We do not want to face the questions he raises, because we do not want to admit that not acting is unjust. We are too used to seeing justice as decisions about actions, as in Stueckleberger's definition of justice: fair and just distribution of opportunities, responsibilities, and burdens. This points to the other difficult questions that lead to this inaction: Who pays, and in what ways, for proposed solutions? Who sacrifices what? Who will act first? Stueckelberger points to the issues of justice in how all these questions are answered:

> the basic ethical question confronting us today is how to distribute the limited resources between three areas – prevention, mitigation and adaptation – in order to minimize the number of victims. Climate change has become a question of global climate justice. (Stueckelberger, 2009: 48)

To begin to address these issues, he points to 14 dimensions of climate justice, some in tension with others, that make it so difficult: capability-, performance-, and needs-related justice; distributive, participatory, procedural, functional, and punitive justice; as well as transitional, restorative, transformative, and intergenerational justice (Stueckelberger, 2009: 49–51). What also makes it difficult is the enormity of the situation, for climate change affects everyone.

Obviously, there is not room in one chapter to discuss all these aspects. What I do hope to do is to give the reader a sense of how religion, justice, and environmental concerns come together in the concept of eco-justice and environmental justice. To do so, I will primarily refer to Christian efforts, as the conversation concerning environmental issues is now decades strong and has been the center of my research. But I will also try to show how other religious traditions embrace environmental concerns, for religious environmentalism is largely characterized by interfaith efforts.

The Centrality of Justice

Because of the enormity of the justice issues involved in responding to climate change, and the difficulty of making decisions regarding the mitigation of climate change, religious groups have been involved since the late 1980s in helping to frame the conversation. Religious and activist organizations are worried that the justice concerns of those with the least political clout are being ignored, while scientific issues and the economic interests of the United States, Europe, Russia, China, and India dominate the conversation. Rabbi Warren Stone, representing North American Jewish organizations, articulated why scores of religious groups would be present at the failed 2009 climate change talks in Copenhagen:

> We are called by our religious traditions to serve as a bold voice for justice. Climate change will have a dramatic impact on hundreds of millions of the poorest people on our planet, especially those who live in coastal areas. (National Religious Coalition on Creation Care, 2009)

Religious groups staged actions, organized marches, held services, and lighted candles to highlight the importance of the Copenhagen meeting and, most importantly, they went to Copenhagen to add their voices to the conversation.

Although the justice dimensions of climate change may seem obvious once you think about it, most people are not used to thinking about the justice dimensions of environmental issues. And, despite decades of religious involvement in the environmental movement, many commentators are still surprised that people of faith are involved in environmentalism. One of the chief motivations for many of these is the centrality of justice issues, the main topic of this chapter. From a religious perspective, all environmental issues have a moral aspect, but we are used to thinking about them in scientific and technocratic terms: What is the problem? Can it be fixed, and how? Scientists recognized this dimension, and in January 1990, 34 internationally renowned scientists, including Carl Sagan, sent an "Open Letter to the Religious Community," stating that "Problems of such magnitude and solutions demanding so broad a perspective must be recognized from the outset as having a religious as well as a scientific dimension."

One response to this has been to recover the sense of sacredness and intrinsic worth in the "creation" as a primary motivation for environmental concern. So the centrality of justice may come as a surprise to some who think that religious environmentalism is mainly a type of nature spirituality filled with tree huggers, star gazers, outdoor recreationists, and "pagans," who are accused of romanticizing nature (Taylor, 2002).

It is certainly true that feelings of awe, inspiration, reverence, and the sacred in nature infuse and motivate many of those involved in religious environmentalism. The shared sense of the sacred worth of the planet and all its inhabitants has indeed made religious environmentalism a primary vehicle of interfaith work. For example, the Alliance of Religions and Conservation, stemming from a gathering of world faiths in 1985 in Assisi, Italy, works with 11 faith traditions on a range of environmental issues.

But just as much, those involved are motivated by justice concerns, because justice is a central motif of most religious traditions, and because the justice dimensions of environmental issues resonate within and across religious traditions. The Joint Appeal, as the letter from scientists came to be known, led in the early 1990s to the creation of the National Religious Partnership for the Environment, formed between evangelical Christians, Jews, Roman Catholics, Christian Orthodox, and mainline Protestants in the United States. It was the justice issues of climate change that made it the environmental problem that they all readily agreed was the priority (Kearns, 2011). Theological (and political) differences meant that other topics, for instance those concerning population, did not foster the same priority and agreement. Later, a similar interfaith coalition effort would center on protecting endangered species, and the issues of justice, such as their right to exist and thrive due to the sacred worth of all species. However, as we shall see, issues concerning animals and eco-systems are not always included in environmental justice concerns.

It is not hard to understand why issues of human justice are central to a range of ecological crises facing us: climate change and the resulting unstable and changing weather patterns, environmental degradation, pollution, deforestation, and desertification. As we become more aware of the interconnectedness of planetary systems, we become aware of the repercussions of their disruption. These result in severe food shortages, drought and flooding, loss of livelihoods and fertile lands, loss of homelands (even whole countries as island nations such as Tuvalu or the Maldives are looking for other countries to accept their people since their future habitability is bleak with any rise of ocean levels), forced migrations, increased impoverishment, environmental health risks, and the resulting conflicts over land, food, and water, so that environmental refugees are on the rise globally. Hence environmentalism connects with issues of justice such as poverty and hunger, increasing economic disparity due to economic globalization, wars over resources (such as oil, coal, and water), and world health. Since women, children, the poor, and people of color often pay the biggest price for environmental degradation, environmentalism also links up with movements concerning women and children, reproductive health, racism, postcolonialism, and indigenous rights. Not only does this focus on justice enable religious environmentalism to intersect with other social movements, but the focus on justice provides a clear authoritative religious mandate for work that often is deemed suspect within some Christian, Jewish, and other religious circles because of "pagan" overtones and fear of "worshiping the creation," and within other religious circles as less important than issues of religious persecution, poverty, personal moral values, and competing group priorities.

Central to an understanding of environmentalism, and the science of ecology, is the interconnectedness of all life forms. When some bear the burden of environmental degradation disproportionately, then justice is at stake. So environmentalism is a major carrier of global connectedness, crossing religious, racial, ethnic, gender, political, and geographical boundaries, emphasizing that what happens in one place affects those far away – the consumption habits of the more industrialized and wealthy countries destroy habitat and cultures in the rest of the globe, and the pollution and waste generated in one place adversely affect those located far from the site of generation.

From a religious perspective, as the issues above clearly demonstrate, concern for right or just relations between humans is often central. For example, in the religions of the "Book," or the Abrahamic faiths of Judaism, Christianity, and Islam, issues of justice fill the pages of their scriptures, from the Hebrew scriptures' concern for Sabbath rest, debt relief, and the care of the widow, to Jesus's concern for "the least of these" and the treatment of "others" such as Samaritans, to the Prophet Muhammad's declaration that "Allah enjoineth justice and kindness" (Surah 16:90) and the core Muslim principle of *sadaqa*, understood as bearing one another's burdens. The well-known Buddhist monk Thich Nhat Hanh's Fourteen Mindfulness Trainings are filled with references to justice, including the admonition of the eleventh principle of "right livelihood," which calls Buddhists to be "aware that great violence and injustice have been done to our environment and society, we are committed not to live with a vocation that is harmful to humans and nature" (Hanh, 2003: 453). One has only to think about Gandhi to recognize the basis in Hinduism for concerns for justice. While these are only brief mentions, chapters in this volume explore the centrality of justice in these and many other religious traditions. These religious references also illustrate the tensions present within religious environmentalism: How large is the concept of justice? Does it include all of "creation" or are humans privileged and the rest of creation put there for human use?

To include other-than-humankind in issues of justice, one must first prove their religious or sacred worth, against those who argue that their religious traditions legitimate a more utilitarian (in religious language, dominion) perspective that animals and natural resources have value because of their use to humans. Going back again to central texts, Christian and Jewish environmentalists start with the message conveyed in the opening lines of Genesis – from the length and care for creation before humans arrive on the scene (the majority of the first story), to the fact that God pronounced it as very good, to what some call the eleventh commandment, "To till and keep the earth" (Genesis 2:15). Further, they remind us, the biblical mandates for the Sabbath rest laws include the just treatment of animals and rest even for the land. All three religions affirm notions of the intrinsic worth of all the creation (the Psalms and the Qur'an tell us that all creation sings praises, and in Noah, the covenant after the flood is with all of creation), independent of any utilitarian value to humans. Thus, many religious and secular environmental ethicists expand the notion of human rights to that of biotic rights – the right of all living things to a healthy ecosystem and a fair chance to thrive. They do this with the concept of eco-justice, as the common understanding of environmental justice tends to have an anthropocentric focus, as explored below.

Thus, there are often tensions between interhuman justice concerns (an anthropocentric focus) and concerns for justice for all of the planet's inhabitants (a more biocentric focus), because embracing a holistic eco-justice ethic involves difficult dilemmas of preserving species, habitats, and eco-systems, righting past injustices, and meeting an expanding human population's basic needs. These tensions can be seen in the brief history of the development of eco-justice and environmental justice concerns in the United States, as explored below.

History

As early as the 1970s, the World Council of Churches' (WCC) theme was a "Just, Participatory and Sustainable Society" that incorporated concern over the limits of and threats to the Earth's capacity to sustain current and future human life; in other words, a more utilitarian focus. Here, the justice framing is still primarily anthropocentric, yet that changed. The vision of justice is larger in the WCC theme of "Justice, Peace and the Integrity of Creation" (1983–1991). This theme made the linkage more clearly between the thriving of humans and the planet. Similarly, it was within the frame of justice that many Christians in the United States first incorporated environmental concerns, seeing environmental issues as related to issues of civil rights, toxics, farm workers, and economic justice with which they had been previously involved. The theology of eco-justice became a growing concern of much of mainline Protestantism and Catholicism as it grew in the 1980s, although the language of environmental justice also was used often, and the two terms initially were more interchangeable. The National Council of Churches Eco-Justice Working Group (NCC EJWG) used the language of both, stating"

> "Environmental Justice" is a holistic term that includes all ministries designed to heal and defend creation. Eco-Justice is an even broader term that includes efforts to assure justice for all of creation and the human beings who live in it. (NCCEJWG, n.d.)

This statement reveals a very different understanding of environmental justice, seeing it as primarily concerned with nonhuman environmental issues, and it is worth pausing a moment to understand how eco-justice and environmental justice came to be perceived as two distinct concepts, one more religious, one more secular, with an anthropocentric focus to environmental justice. In the process, a more detailed understanding of the range of justice issues in religious environmentalism will become clear.

Environmental Justice or Eco-justice?

Although most scholars (Gottlieb, 1993; Cole and Foster, 2001) trace the history of the US environmental justice movement to the 1982 Warren County, North Carolina protests (discussed below), the roots of what are now deemed environmental justice concerns within both environmentalism and US religious environmentalism can be found much earlier (Taylor, 2002). The first community effort to deal with lead paint issues, a toxicity problem that affects low-income people and people of color communities disproportionately, emerged as early as 1965. By the 1970s, dozens of groups were active, but saw themselves as part of the community empowerment movement with no connection to the environmental movement (Gottlieb, 1993: 246).

There were other factors at work that led to the lack of reception or fragmentation of the issues. As worries over the effect of pesticides on the biotic community grew as a result of Rachel Carson's *Silent Spring*, leading to the banning of DDT, there was also concern over the pesticide exposure of migrant farm workers, now primarily forgotten. Anxiety over lead paint was shifted into disquiet over leaded gasoline and thus moved away from any particular social, community context. The latter tied in with concern over clean air, but as a hazard to all in general. Many of the connections between specific hazardous materials and affected groups were viewed as occupational health issues, but with little recognition that, increasingly, the majority of those who worked in high-risk, poorly regulated industries and jobs were people of color. Little or no attention was given to the communities where the industries resided or where their waste by-products were disposed of. For a variety of reasons, including the whiteness of the main environmental movement, issues of environmental pollution as human justice issues did not become a main part of the growing environmental movement's concerns, but were seen as separate. During this same period, however, the movement of religious eco-justice was forming in an attempt to make these types of connections with environmental concerns. Further, many involved in civil rights were also making the connection. Indeed, influenced by the larger cultural climate of the civil rights and environmental movements, as early as 1970 the American Baptist Church was concerned that ecology and justice work had to be held together. In 1974, Presbyterian minister Bill Gibson, active in the civil rights movement, helped found the Eco-Justice Project at Cornell University (Gibson, 2004), which contributed to the development of the NCC Eco-Justice Working Group in 1984. The EJWG represented the cooperative efforts of the mainline, historical black, and orthodox denominations on the topic of eco-justice, under the guidance of a Director of Environmental Justice.

It was the 1982 Warren County, North Carolina campaign against the proposed placement of a PCB (polychlorinated biphenyls) landfill that brought widespread attention in the United States to the connection between environmental toxicity and race and poverty. Those organizing the campaign began to suspect that the site had been chosen not for its environmental suitability but more for the expected nonresistance by its majority of African American residents, who were seen to be undereducated, unorganized, and in need of employment. Among the more than 500 protesters arrested during the struggle were several United Church of Christ (UCC) ministers, including the Reverends Benjamin Chavis and Charles Lee, who had helped to organize the campaign as part of their work with the UCC Commission for Racial Justice. As a result of this struggle, the NCC issued a statement in 1986 called "Toxic Pollution in Minority and Low-income Communities." A year later, in 1987, the UCC Commission issued the landmark study on *Toxic Wastes and Race in the United States* and, thanks to sustained publicity efforts, garnered a great deal of attention. The study (and two subsequent ones) looked for common factors in the placement of hazardous and toxic waste sites throughout the nation and concluded that race and low income were statistically significant factors in the placement of these sites (UCC, 1987). For instance, the study found that 60% of

African Americans lived in communities with abandoned toxic-waste sites (UCC, 1987).[1] As a follow-up on their own report as well as the UCC report, the National Council of Churches and SWOP (Southwest Organizing Project) conducted public interdenominational hearings in the southwest in 1989 on "Toxic Pollution in Minority Communities" to gather further evidence and to draw attention to how little regard the major environmental organizations paid to issues in people of color communities, suggesting that it was reflective of their racial makeup (i.e., how white they were). All of this and other similar local grassroots activities aimed at fighting the tactics of polluting industries, as well as the indicting research and consciousness raising of sociologist Robert Bullard (*Dumping in Dixie* came out in 1990), led to the First People of Color Environmental Leadership Summit held in Washington, DC in October 1991, which significantly shaped what became known as the environmental justice movement.

The NCC EJWG, whether because it was primarily white and not as grassroots in makeup, or because it was explicitly Christian, was not invited to help plan the Summit. The explanation to one member – that "we don't want Christ preached" – is indicative of an artificial divide that continues to exist. (Many environmental justice scholars and activist organizations still primarily leave out participation by religious groups and religious motivations.[2]) The Summit was extremely important: 300 of the more than 650 people in attendance were delegates from primarily grassroots groups, who discovered the shared patterns to their problems and formed important networks of information and support. What was equally significant was the ratification of the "principles of environmental justice," which display a wide understanding of environmental justice: *procedural justice* through an unbiased public policy in deciding on land use, protection from hazardous/toxic wastes and nuclear testing, a safe workplace with no hazardous exposure, and the cessation of production of hazardous and toxic materials; as well as *restorative justice* in the cleanup of existing polluted sites, and the provision of healthcare and redress for those already exposed (People of Color Environmental Leadership Summit, 1991). Other principles, less evident at first but equally essential, included aspects of *participatory justice*, such as self-determination and participation in decision making, consent to all medical procedures, freedom from experimental testing on subject/dependant peoples, and the end of military occupation and exploitation, plus recognition of the special status of native/first peoples. The principles end with recognition of the intergenerational and interspecies ethical demands from the planet and future generations on our current consumptive habits.[3] Interestingly, the first principle "affirms the sacredness of the Earth" and perhaps gives one clue to why organizers did not want Christ preached: much of Christianity has not been known to recognize the sacredness of the Earth, and has historically persecuted those who do, labeling them as pagans, including some co-religionists who are seen to "worship the creation, and not the Creator" if they are involved in environmentalism. For many present, Christianity was part of the problem.

Further, despite the larger biotic vision of environmental justice, articulated in the first and third principles that affirm "the sacredness of Mother Earth, ecological unity and the *interdependence of all species*, and the right to be free from ecological destruction" as well as "the right to ethical, balanced and responsible uses of land and renewable resources in the interest of a *sustainable planet for humans and other living things*," the environmental justice movement came to be seen as secular and anthropocentric, in part as a result of the Environmental Protection Agency (EPA). Following the 1991 Summit, the EPA met with the organizers and established an Office of Environmental Equity. Activists responded that they did not want equity, or to be treated the same as everyone else (procedural justice), but rather justice as spelled out in the Principles of Environmental Justice. By Earth Day 1993, newly elected President Clinton announced an executive order on Environmental Justice, which was signed February 1994 and defined environmental justice as:

> the fair treatment and meaningful involvement of all people, regardless of race, color, national origin or income, with respect to the development, implementation and enforcement of environmental laws, regulations and policies, practices and regulations. Fair treatment means that no group of people, including a racial, ethnic, or socioeconomic group should bear a disproportionate share of the negative environmental consequences resulting from industrial, municipal, and commercial operations or the execution of federal, state, local and tribal programs and policies. (Environmental Protection Agency, 2011)

Not surprisingly, despite their prominence in the principles of environmental justice, missing are the ideas of those foundational principles of "ecological unity" and "a sustainable planet for humans and other living things." The EPA's definition was only focused on humans and the movement to a large extent reflected that definition and its founding concern over environmental racism. Further, in its critique of environmentalism, the nascent movement defined itself in terms of social justice issues. As the "Environmental Justice Timeline" from the Second People of Color Environmental Leadership Summit in 2002 states:

> There is general agreement that environmental injustice existed long before the 1991 gathering. For many, having decent and affordable housing, access to health care, quality education, safe and secure employment at a livable wage, accessible public transportation, parks and green space, clean air, safe drinking water, and healthy food are basic rights. (Second National People of Color Environmental Leadership Summit, n.d.).

But the work of religious eco-justice groups, despite focusing on the same issues plus traditional environmental concerns, was viewed as separate.

There are of course additional reasons that the environmental justice movement became primarily secular. Despite the religious grounding of many groups, such as the UCC or grassroots groups like Jesus People Against Pollution of Columbia Miss, or the Coalition Against Nuclear Trash (CANT) in northern Louisiana, organizational activists were leery of religion and churches. Additionally, people of color groups and churches were wary of environmentalists, who seemed to care only about animals and wild places or who would come in to tell them what to do instead of listening. This is why the environmental justice movement proclaimed that "the environment is where we live, work, play, and learn," in order to counter the notion that the environment to be saved was somewhere else (Cole and Foster, 2001: 16).

In addition to being presented as primarily secular, the environmental justice movement in its early days also became synonymous with environmental racism, due to its origins in the Warren County struggle and the UCC report on Toxic Wastes and RACE. More recently, activism about the environmental degradation and pollution associated with mountaintop removal of coal, which mainly affects poor whites in Appalachia, or issues surrounding CAFOs (concentrated animal feeding operations), discussed below, are broadening the term "environmental justice" to more closely fit the EPA definition.

These tensions between religious environmentalism, environmental justice, environmental racism, and the more nature-focused environmental groups has been eased only in the last decade, as churches and religious environmental organizations have worked more closely with environmental justice groups, and people of color environmental organizations, such as Sustainable South Bronx or Wild Atlanta, have flourished and broadened their sense of environmental justice to include care and appreciation of nonhuman nature.

The Contribution of Liberation Theologies

All of this activism was accompanied by significant developing conversations in the world of theology. For example, John Cobb, a well-known theologian linked to environmental concern and justice from early in his long career, asked in 1972: "Is it too late?" His concern for eco-justice, as well as a critique of economic values, was also present in other early theologians, but it was in ecofeminism that the linkages between attitudes toward nature and hierarchical forms of domination – as seen in sexism, racism, anti-Semitism, militarism, colonialism, and capitalism, and eventually heterosexism – were most fully explored from early on.

Ecofeminist liberation theologies

For ecofeminists, ecological issues must be understood alongside issues of social justice. As Catholic eco-feminist Rosemary Radford Ruether declared, "We must speak of eco-justice and not simply the domination of the earth as though that happened unrelated to social domination" (Ruether, 1992: 3). The work of Ruether reveals the history and many of the dimensions of the conversation within ecofeminism, starting with her *New Woman, New Earth* (1975). She more fully explored the intersection of systems of domination and their legitimating worldviews in *Gaia and God* (1992), and brought further attention to ecofeminists from around the globe in *Integrating Ecofeminsm, Globalization, and World Religions* (2005), in which she highlighted the voices of Ivone Gebara, Vandana Shiva, and Wangari Maathai, among other global eco-feminists who ground their work toward eco-justice in their religion and spirituality. Their work shows the breadth of ecofeminism. Vandana Shiva, a physicist by training and a prolific writer, works tirelessly in India and around the globe to raise awareness of the connections between deteriorating environments and women's health and other justice issues, such as water privatization and the struggle for fresh, potable water among the majority of the global poor, bio-piracy, the globalization and monoculturalization of agribusiness, and the large gains in corporate power through the World Trade Organization (Shiva, 1997, 2002). The work of Brazilian Catholic sister and theologian Ivone Gebara (silenced by the Vatican from 1995–1997) reached a large audience through her most ecofeminist book, translated under the title *Longing for Running Water: Ecofeminism and Liberation* (1999). In it, she illustrates the deep connection between the destruction of land and ecosystems and the lives of those whom she says are the most oppressed: urban poor women such as those in the favelas of Recife with whom she worked. Her work with the ecofeminist collective Con Spirando brings together women from throughout the Americas to explore the disproportionate burden that women, as the gatherers of firewood and water, as mothers and caretakers of the young, and as the highest gender percentage among the poor, pay for the destruction of forests, desertification, pollution of air and water, and lack of access to clean water, or to any water at all. In fact, all three work to draw attention to a growing global crisis over water, which has already caused conflict in many regions. Finally, 2004 Nobel Peace Prize winner Wangari Maathai, through the Green Belt Movement (GBM) that she helped found in 1977, organized women in her home country of Kenya and all over the globe to plant millions of trees to counter the deforestation that led to desertification, and left them walking farther and farther for firewood and water, often making them more vulnerable to attack. The GBM's mission – "to mobilize community consciousness ... for self-determination, equity, improved livelihoods and security for women, and environmental conservation" – demonstrates once again the awareness that gender justice and equity are tied with sustainability (Green Belt Movement, n.d.). Seen as a primarily secular environmental movement, Maathai discusses how her vision has been grounded in both her Kikuyu heritage and her Catholic upbringing in her most recent book, *Replenishing the Earth: Spiritual Values for Healing Ourselves and the World* (2010). These are just a few examples of visionary ecofeminist activists (ecowomanism is explored below) who demonstrate the centrality of justice issues in environmental concerns.

Latin American liberation theology

Despite the early lead by eco-feminists, well-known Latin American liberation theologians were slower to enter the conversation. Liberation theologian Leonardo Boff is perhaps the most significant, with the publication of his vision of social ecology in *Ecology and Liberation* in 1995, its Portuguese original published in 1993 on the heels of the 1992 United Nations Conference on Environment and Development (UNCED) in Rio de Janiero, Brazil. There, religious and environmental NGOs worked to criticize the dominant model of economic development, in which the clearing of land and the resultant diminishing biodiversity leads not to improvement, but to the impoverishment of people and the destruction of indigenous cultures. The model of economic development that has dominated, they pointed out, cares little for the local environment or the local people, but rather for generating income to service international debt and to facilitate the export of "natural resources" and the transfer of wealth to elites, often outside the country. Boff went on to publish the best-known liberation theology text, *Cry of the Earth, Cry of the Poor* (1997), articulating a theological/ecological holism and permanently embedding ecology as a concern for all liberation theologians.

Another side to this economic development model is the exporting of garbage and hazardous/toxic wastes not wanted at "home" or "not in my backyard" (NIMBY), as economically wealthy countries uphold their strict environmental regulations by exporting the problems to the two-thirds world. While not a Latin American theologian, Larry Rasmussen, in his widely hailed book *Earth Ethics, Earth Community* (1997), discussed the leaked 1991 memo written by Larry Summers, then chief economist of the World Bank, who suggested that the Bank should encourage the dumping of toxic wastes in "under populated countries in Africa," which he described as "UNDER-polluted" (Rasmussen, 1997: 78). Liberation theologians, ever critical of the costs of capitalism, hailed this illuminating example of what the environmental justice movement already knew: fixing environmental problems in one place can create injustice in another.

Black liberation theology

Accompanying the growth of the environmental justice movement, the early 1990s also saw the emergence of black eco-liberation theology. Theodore Walker's 1993 article "African American Resources for a more inclusive Liberation Theology" addressed head on the reluctance of black churches and theologians to incorporate environmental concerns. In an important volume, *Ecofeminism and the Sacred*, womanist Shamara Shantu Riley (1993) declared "Ecology is a sistah's issue too" and Delores Williams (1993) articulated the connections between "Sin, nature and black women's bodies." Karen Baker-Fletcher gave full voice to Christian ecowomanism in *Sisters of Dust, Sisters of Spirit: Womanist Wordings on God and Creation* (1998). James Cone, a key black liberation theologian since the 1960s, demanded in 1999 "Whose earth is it anyway?" and gave religious voice to a full vision of environmental justice, declaring in the opening sentence, "[t]he logic that led to slavery and segregation . . . and the rule of white supremacy . . . is the same one that leads to the exploitation of animals and the ravaging of nature" (Cone, 1999: 23). Equally important voices are present in indigenous liberation theologies (LaDuke 1999).

Animal Justice

Some theologians' specific inclusion of the exploitation of animals was important in connecting to the animal rights and animal welfare movements, which often are religiously grounded or motivated but seen as distinctly separate (Waldau and Patton, 2006). These movements have highlighted the terrible, filthy, inhumane conditions in care on the farm, during transport, and in the slaughter of agricultural animals. Many religious dietary certifications, such as kosher in Judaism and halal in Islam, are explicitly about the treatment of the animals being slaughtered, while other religions such as Hinduism and Jainism recognize the sacredness of some if not all animals. In the United States, animals such as chickens, cows, and pigs are kept in cages or pens with no room for natural movement in huge buildings, sometimes containing thousands of animals, often awash in their own excrement. In the case of chickens, they are confined to small cages where they cannot escape the flies and insects that swarm them, with their beaks cut off so they can't fight with each other, and animals remain where they die. For those who live near these factory farms, the water, soil, and air pollution from the animal excrement and poor care are serious issues that have broadened traditional environmental justice and religious eco-justice implications.

For many religious and secular environmentalists, concern over the unjust treatment of animals, such as that described above, and the rapid depopulation of marine species through overfishing or being "by-products" of the catch (e.g., dolphins captured in tuna netting, turtles ensnared in shrimp fishing equipment, and bottom animals caught in drag nets) is often a reason given for vegetarianism or reduced meat eating (Ruether, 1992: 225). For others, vegetarianism is motivated by a distributive justice concern over the high "costs" of meat production, whether it is the ratio of pounds of grains per pound of meat, or the ratio of water/energy per pound, to the clear cutting of vast acres of rainforests to provide grazing land for primarily exported beef that will be expended within a few years, or the deterioration of eco-systems from the presence of large numbers of grazing animals or the disposal of their excrement.

Finally, other issues of justice for nonhuman animals include a range of issues of cruelty to those with whom we share this planet: animal fighting and hunting for sport; "puppy" or breeding mills; the smuggling of exotic species to supply the pet trade; the raising or hunting of animals for fur; the use of animals for medical and pharmaceutical experimentation and research, as well as what happens to those animals when the research is done; and the illegal hunting/poaching of animals for their parts thought to have medicinal or magical properties, such as sharks, rhinos, bears, and tigers. Harder for many to see are the issues of intergenerational justice posed by the loss of habitat and sufficient breeding populations of endangered species, what environmental ethicist would call the right to thrive. Because these issues concern the just treatment of animals and our relationships with them, the various aspects of the animal welfare/rights movement are often seen as very distinct from the environmental justice movement. Yet they involve aspects of human, animal and eco-system health and well-being, inviting those who care about both into a broader ethic of eco-justice for all.

Food Justice

As already seen, animal justice issues are frequently linked to food justice issues. While for most people these are distinct movements, religious eco-justice activists are increasingly bringing them together. The food justice movement, like the environmental justice movement, is often more explicitly anthropocentric in its focus on the treatment of farm workers, such as their exposure to hazardous chemicals and pesticides due to lack of protective clothing and indiscriminate spraying while in the field. This exposure can lead to respiratory and skin illnesses, cancers, even issues of sterility and reproductive disruption, as in the case of banana workers in Central America. Farm worker injustice is further linked to the deplorable conditions in which migrant and farm workers live, as they are often undocumented or have few legal rights, and fear that employers will fire them, beat them, or turn them in if they seek redress. As has been documented in the tomato industry in Florida[4] or the chocolate/cocoa industry in Africa, many workers are living in modern slave conditions with no ability to leave or control their lives (Bowe, 2007). Food justice is also about access to affordable and healthy food.

Liberation theology's concerns for the empowerment of women and the poor and the improvement of communities through ecological restoration can all be seen in the Fair Trade movement, a central aspect of the food justice movement, which has engaged religious communities throughout the globe. By definition, Fair Trade is about the interconnectedness of people's consumption patterns and eco-systems. The principles of a fair price to workers, ecological sustainability, and democratic cooperatives in which women are also involved are central to the movement's stated values. The goal of Fair Trade is to skip the many intermediaries involved in getting a product to market that result in a minimal price and wage for the growers and workers in order to keep down the price to the final consumer. Rather, the goal is to ensure a fair wage to the laborers by guaranteeing producers a fair price in advance, while encouraging sustainable farming practices that protect the workers, consumers, and the larger eco-system.

Fair Trade cocoa, chocolate, tea, bananas, clothing, artisan products, and other items are available, but coffee is by far the largest product, in part because it is the second most traded global commodity. World Bank economic development plans encouraged vast acres of sun-grown, mechanically picked Arabica coffee in places like Brazil and Vietnam, which did not traditionally grow coffee, producing cheap coffee, but destroying both the natural eco-systems of shade-grown coffee forests and the livelihoods of more sustainable coffee producers and pickers in traditional coffee-growing places like Guatemala, Kenya, and Ethiopia. Consumers, churches, and synagogues in North America and Europe learn of the connection between environmental degradation, habitat destruction, and poverty through lessons about a "just" cup of coffee. Joking that coffee after the service is also a religious ritual, religious groups seek to add a dimension of justice to their consumption habits and challenge the changed methods of coffee production. Fair Trade certification demands economic justice in terms of a fair and predictable wage for workers and pickers, eco-justice in terms of environmentally sustainable growing practices that keep forests standing and reduce the pesticides and herbicides sprayed on plants and workers that lead to the poisoning of humans and wildlife alike, and participatory justice in the goals of education, literacy, and cooperative and democratic decision making that includes women (Kearns, 2007). Fair Trade movements, while not necessarily religious, are heavily embraced by many religious organizations, because the concept of Fair Trade demonstrates the broad concept of eco-justice introduced earlier in this essay – justice for people, wildlife, and eco-systems alike, justice for all who desire to be part of healthy, functioning, sustainable eco-systems that lead to the thriving of all living beings.

Conclusion

First and foremost, this essay has tried to demonstrate that justice concerns are central to environmental issues, in part due to the work of many religious leaders and groups. Acknowledging this, scientists and politicians have called for religious involvement to help others recognize that ecological health and well-being are moral concerns. Conversely, this essay has argued that environmental issues should be included in the religious concern for social justice. For most religious environmentalists, environmental issues should be on the agenda for all those who work for social justice. Third, environmental justice issues disproportionately affect those who are poor, powerless, and people of color, and, as such, demand full ethical consideration. Thus, this chapter has attempted to give a sense of the breadth and complexity of environmental justice issues that will involve major discussions about distributive, participatory, procedural, restorative, intergenerational, and interspecies justice. This breadth indicates that what seems just for one may not seem so from another perspective. Fourth, the essay has tried to show that the growing awareness of the interconnectedness of planetary systems and their disruption means that actions in one place can have unforeseen and unjust consequences elsewhere, as climate change so fully demonstrates.

Fifth, the chapter has argued for the concept of eco-justice, or a full vision of environmental justice that includes humans and all living creatures, so that environmental justice issues are not seen as only those involving humans, further complicating any notion of justice. Just and right relations must include all living beings. Finally, in light of the vision of eco-justice, any discussion of the justice dimension of environmental issues will involve difficult conversations about human rights versus biotic rights. Religious voices that affirm the intrinsic worth of all of creation add a crucial dimension to this discussion.

In addition to the issues described here, there are many more that cannot be covered adequately, whether it is methods of coal extraction, such as mountaintop removal in the United States; or the impact of extractive industries on indigenous groups globally; or the destruction of small-scale farming in places like India and Korea, driving farmers to suicide; or diminishing habitat for the endangered species and indigenous peoples of the North; or the "ownership" and manipulation of the DNA of plants and animals. Beyond all of these, climate change looms as one of the largest environmental justice or eco-justice concerns of all, asking us to think about the consequences of our actions on a scale few are used to, and with future generations to come in mind. The thriving of the planet is intricately linked to the thriving of humans and all living creatures, even those yet to come.

Notes

1 The "Toxic Wastes and Race at Twenty" report "revealed that racial disparities in the distribution of hazardous wastes are greater than previously reported" with "over 5.1 million people of color . . . in neighborhoods with one or more commercial hazardous waste facilities" (UCC, 2007: 4).

2 An exception is *Chronicles from the Environmental Justice Frontline* (Roberts and Toffolon-Weiss, 2001), which acknowledges the important role of the churches and faith for activists in the fight against the Louisiana uranium enrichment plant planned for Homer, LA and includes a revealing quote by an activist: "I'm telling you this in all sincerity: God led us. We had divine guidance. We tell that to everyone who interviews us, but it never ends up in print" (Roberts and Toffolon-Weiss, 2001: 80).

3 The global Earth Charter contains similar principles, aimed to "promote the transition to sustainable ways of living and a global society founded on a shared ethical framework that includes respect and care for the community of life, ecological integrity, universal human rights, respect for diversity, economic justice, democracy, and a culture of peace" (Earth Charter Initiative, 2000).
4 Religious denominations have been active in the Coalition of Immokalee Workers campaign to help workers earn one penny per pound more for the tomatoes they pick.

References

Baker-Fletcher, K. (1998) *Sisters of Dust, Sisters of Spirit: Womanist Wordings on God and Creation*, Fortress, Minneapolis.

Boff, L. (1995) *Ecology and Liberation: A New Paradigm*, John Cumming (trans.), Maryknoll Books, New York.

Boff, L. (1997) *Cry of the Earth, Cry of the Poor*, Philip Berryman (trans.), Orbis, New York.

Bowe, J. (2007) *Nobodies: Modern American Slave Labor and the Dark Side of the New Global Economy*, Random House, New York.

Bullard, R. (2000) *Dumping in Dixie: Race, Class, and Environmental Quality*, 3rd edn, Westview Press, Boulder, CO.

Cobb, J.B. (1972) *Is It Too Late? A Theology of Ecology*, Bruce, Beverly Hills, CA.

Cole, L.W. and Foster, S.R. (2001) *From the Ground Up: Environmental Racism and the Rise of the Environmental Movement*, New York University Press, New York.

Cone, J. (1999) Whose Earth is it anyway? in *Earth Habitat: Eco-Injustice and the Church's Response*, D. Hessel and L. Rasmussen (eds.), Augsburg Fortress, Minneapolis, pp. 23–32.

Earth Charter Initiative (2000) The Earth Charter, http://www.earthcharterinaction.org/content/pages/Read-the-Charter.html (accessed March 10, 2011).

Environmental Protection Agency (2011) Environmental Justice, http://www.epa.gov/environmentaljustice (accessed January 11, 2011).

Gebara, I. (1999) *Longing for Running Water: Ecofeminism and Liberation*, Fortress Press, Minneapolis.

Gibson, W.E. (2004) *Eco-Justice: The Unfinished Journey*, State University of New York Press, Albany, NY.

Gottlieb, R. (1993) *Forcing the Spring: The Transformation of the American Environmental Movement*, Island Press, Washington, DC.

Green Belt Movement (n.d.) The Green Belt Movement International, http://greenbeltmovement.org/w.php?id=21 (accessed March 12, 2011).

Hanh, T.N. (2003) The fourteen mindfulness trainings of the order of interbeing, in *Liberating Faith: Religious Voices for Justice, Peace, and Ecological Wisdom*, R.S. Gottlieb (ed.), Rowman and Littlefield, Oxford, pp. 450–455.

Kearns, L. (2007) Religion and ecology, in *Religion, Globalization, and Culture*, P. Beyer and L. Beaman (eds.), Brill Publishing, Leiden, pp. 305–334.

Kearns, L. (2011) The role of religions in activism, in *The Oxford Handbook on Climate Change and Society*, J. Dryzek, R. Norgaard, and D. Schlosberg (eds.), Oxford University Press, New York.

LaDuke, W. (1999) *All Our Relations: Native Struggles for Land and Life*, South End Press, Cambridge, MA.

Maathai, W. (2010) *Replenishing the Earth: Spiritual Values for Healing Ourselves and the World*, Doubleday, New York.

National Council of Churches Eco-Justice Working Group (n.d.) What is the Partnership? http://www.nrpe.org/whatisthepartnership/partnersIIB3_NCCC_01.htm (accessed March 24, 2011).

National Religious Coalition on Creation Care (2009) US religious groups urge strong action to reduce greenhouse gases, http://fore.research.yale.edu/news/item/u.s.-religious-groups-call-upon-delegates-to-copenhagen/ (accessed April 19, 2011).

People of Color Environmental Leadership Summit (1991) Principles of environmental justice, Environmental Justice Resource Center at Clark Atlanta University, http://www.ejrc.cau.edu/princej.html (accessed March 24, 2011).

Rasmussen, L. (1997) *Earth Community, Earth Ethics*, Orbis, New York.

Riley, S.S. (1993) Ecology is a sistah's issue too: The politics of emergent Afrocentric ecowomanism, in *Ecofeminism and the Sacred*, C.J. Adams (ed.), Continuum, New York, pp. 191–206.

Roberts, J.T. and Toffolon-Weiss, M.M. (2001) *Chronicles from the Environmental Justice Frontline*, Cambridge University Press, New York.

Ruether, R.R. (1975) *New Woman, New Earth: Sexist Ideologies and Human Liberation*, Seabury Press, New York.

Ruether, R.R. (1992) *Gaia and God: An Ecofeminist Theology of Earth Healing*, Harper San Francisco, San Francisco.

Ruether, R.R. (2005) *Integrating Ecofeminism, Globalization and World Religions*, Rowman and Littlefield, Lanham, MD.

Second National People of Color Environmental Leadership Summit (n.d.) Environmental Justice timeline – milestones, http://www.ejrc.cau.edu/summit2/%20EJTimeline.pdf (accessed March 13, 2011).

Shiva, V. (1988) *Staying Alive: Women, Ecology, and Development*, Zed Books, London.

Shiva, V. (1997) *Biopiracy: The Plunder of Nature and Knowledge*, South End Press, Cambridge, MA.

Shiva, V. (2002) *Water Wars: Privatization, Pollution, and Profit*, South End Press, Cambridge, MA.

Stueckelberger, C. (2009) Who dies first? Who is sacrificed first? Ethical aspects of climate justice, in *God, Creation and Climate Change: Spiritual and Ethical Perspectives*, K. Bloomquist (ed.), Lutheran University Press, Geneva, pp. 47–62.

Taylor, D. (2002) Race, Class, Gender, and American Environmentalism, General Technical Report PNW-GTR-534, United States Department of Agriculture, Forest Service, Pacific Northwest Research Station, Portland, OR.

United Church of Christ (1987) *Toxic Wastes and Race in the United States: A National Report on the Racial and Socioeconomic Characteristics of Communities with Hazardous Waste Sites*, United Church of Christ, New York.

United Church of Christ (2007) *Toxic Waste and Race at Twenty 1987–2007*, United Church of Christ, New York.

Waldau, P. and Patton, K. (2006) *A Communion of Subjects: Animals in Religion, Science, and Ethics*, Columbia University Press, New York.

Walker, T. (1993) African-American resources for more inclusive Liberation Theology, in *Good News For Animals? Christian Approaches to Animal Well-Being*, C. Pinches and J.B. McDaniel (eds.), Orbis Books, Maryknoll, NY, pp. 163–171.

Williams, D. (1993) Sin, nature, and black women's bodies, in *Ecofeminism and the Sacred*, C.J. Adams (ed.), Continuum, New York, pp. 24–29.

CHAPTER 42
Christianity and Nonviolent Resistance

Celia Cook-Huffman

From the beginning a basic philosophy guided the movement. This guiding principle has since been referred to variously as nonviolent resistance, noncooperation, and passive resistance. But in the first days of the protest none of these expressions was mentioned: the phrase most often heard was "Christian love." It was the Sermon on the Mount rather than a doctrine of passive resistance that initially inspired the Negroes of Montgomery to dignified social action. It was Jesus of Nazareth that stirred the Negroes to protest with the creative weapon of love. (Martin Luther King, Jr., "An experiment in love," 1958)

The civil rights movement in the United States marks one of the clearest examples of the intersection of religion and a movement striving for greater social justice using nonviolent methods. The purpose of this essay is to explore the intersection between religion and nonviolent struggles for social change. We often think of religion as a conservative force in society, and within the sociological tradition it is often portrayed as a harmonizing agent. However, throughout history it has also been a force for social change – what Christian Smith calls the "disruptive, defiant, unruly face of religion" (Smith, 1996: 1).

Even a brief survey of historical social movements reveals a wide range of movements in which religion provides both motivation and structure for social change. These movements are diverse in terms of time and place, strategies, and desired outcomes. They include the British movement to end the slave trade and the United States' nineteenth-century Abolitionist movement; struggles for just labor laws in England and America; Danish and Norwegian resistance to Nazi Germany; India's home rule movement led by Gandhi in the early 1900s; the efforts of Khan Abdul Ghaffar Khan, who organized a nonviolent "army" among the Pathans as part of the Indian independence movement; nonviolent resistance in the Palestinian Territories; Israeli Peace Movements; anti-apartheid efforts in South Africa in the 1980s; Latin American Liberation

---

The Wiley Blackwell Companion to Religion and Social Justice, First Edition. Edited by Michael D. Palmer and Stanley M. Burgess.
© 2012 John Wiley & Sons Ltd. Published 2020 by John Wiley & Sons Ltd.

Theology movements beginning in the 1960s; the United States Central American Peace Movement of the 1980s; the Polish Solidarity Movement of the 1980s; antinuclear movements; environmental movements; Burmese democracy struggles of the twentieth century; antiwar and conscientious objector movements since the inception of Christianity; Buddhist monk actions in Vietnam; New Zealand Maori independence movements in the nineteenth and twentieth centuries; Christian Peacemaker Teams accompaniment strategies; and others (Cooney and Michalowski, 1987; Lynd and Lynd, 1995; Smith, 1996; Zunes, Kurtz, and Asher, 1999; Schirch, 2006).[1]

This essay focuses primarily on Christian traditions, with the goal of illuminating the links between these spiritual traditions and nonviolent social movements. How have the teachings of these faith traditions and the call to live a Christian life been understood as a call to work for social justice that has shaped both the theory and practice of nonviolent resistance?

The Early Church

The Christian path to nonviolent resistance begins with pacifism. Scholars argue that the early Christian church, in following the teachings of Jesus, rejected war and violence. While in the New Testament Jesus does not specifically speak against participating in war, his overall message of nonresistance and the requirement to love one's enemies, taken with his own refusal to take up arms even to save himself, points to a rejection of violence as a means to address the social injustices of his time (Brock, 1981; Yoder, 2009).

The text of the Sermon on the Mount (Matthew 5–7) and the call to "overcome good with evil" (Romans 12:21) point to a consistent message of responding to violence and hate with love. This willingness to suffer and to love one's enemies provides a powerful message defining what it means to live a Christian life. The records from the early church reveal a documented pacifism that focused on the virtues of peace and the rejection of violence for self-defense and for war, and a willingness to pay the price of this stance, including persecution and martyrdom (Brock, 1981; Brown, 2003; Yoder, 2009).[2]

This pacifist stance begins to shift around the third century CE as Christianity made the transition from an illegal movement to one of many recognized religions in the Roman Empire. The fundamental shift in the pacifist stance of the early church came with the accession of Constantine as the Roman Emperor (312–337 CE). Constantine allied himself with Christians, and created a Christian empire. This change required two things to happen. First, Christians moved from being radical, persecuted outsiders to being privileged insiders. As a result, they needed an ethic for those who served in public office – those who served Caesar, so to speak. Is the ethic that guides the civil servant the same as the ethic for the Christian citizen? Many Christians said no. This answer created two worlds, one governed by the laws of God, and the other by the laws of the state, in which "God keeps one kind of peace through the emperor and creates other kinds of peace through Christians" (Yoder, 2009: 59). This dualism provided justification for agents of the state to use the sword and the "just war" tradition emerged.

This dualism also created a new framework for interpreting the scriptures. Having found a biblical and theological basis for backing the empire, the church muted its voice of resistance against the dominant ideology of the time and abandoned its global outlook. Those living outside the borders of the empire were no longer considered neighbors, but had become enemies, or at least potential enemies. By the fifth century CE the imperial army had become almost completely Christian. The pacifist stance did not reemerge until the twelfth century, and does not take a sustained form until much later, with the Anabaptist movements of the sixteenth century (the time of the Protestant Reformation) and the Religious Society of Friends in the seventeenth century (West, 1962; Brock, 1981; Brown, 2003; Yoder, 2009).

Peace Churches and the Pacifist Tradition

The groups that developed out of the pacifist movements beginning in the sixteenth century – Mennonites, Brethren, and the Religious Society of Friends (Quakers, as they are often called) – came to be known as the Historic Peace Churches, because as a basic tenet of their faith they all renounced violence. The beliefs and practices that informed these three traditions undergirded the nonviolent resistance that followed.

The Anabaptists emerged from the Protestant reformation in the sixteenth century. Several beliefs set these groups apart from others within the reformed tradition. For instance, they shared a belief in adult baptism and were thus referred to as a believer's church. They adopted Mathew 18:15–20 as the "rule of Christ," meaning that they regarded this passage as a definition of the church and took seriously the charge that the way to deal with a disagreement or accusation of misconduct was to go to the offending person and talk it out. If the situation was dealt with, then forgiveness and reconciliation would result. If the conversation was not successful, the offending person would be banned from the church (Durnbaugh, 1992; Brown, 2003; Yoder 2009).

The Anabaptists' core beliefs included a commitment to "radical discipleship, the fundamental nature of the church as a voluntary community of believers, and lifestyles characterized by loving and sharing" (Brown, 2003: 37). For these early believers the call was to be like Jesus. They aspired to live their lives in accordance with his example. For them, Jesus was normative. He did not use violence; he suffered it. Therefore, so must the believer. As a basic tenet of their faith they renounced the use of the sword, both for self-defense and for war (Yoder, 2009: 171).

> The gospel and its adherents are not to be protected by the sword, nor are they thus to protect themselves ... They do not use worldly sword or war, since all killing has ceased with them. (Conrad Grebel, circa 1525, quoted in Brock, 1981: 19)

The Quakers emerged in England in the mid-seventeenth century. George Fox, the principal founder, inspired others who came together around a number of shared beliefs and practices. At the heart of the Quaker faith was a desire to know God. One belief that set Quakers apart from other religious groups was the conviction that the "light" of God exists in every person, and that this "light," directed toward God, could bring a person into union with God. Other beliefs and practices were distinctive as well. Friends believed that all members of the community were responsible for preaching. They worshiped by waiting in silence for a member to be "moved by the spirit" to speak. They regarded truth to be a matter of conscience and thus refused to take oaths. True followers of Christ, they believed, must follow his teachings, including the calls to "turn the other cheek" and "love one another." They took seriously the high value God placed on making peace: "blessed are the peacemakers." Finally, in accordance with the so-called Golden Rule, they could not do to others those things that they would not have done to themselves. Therefore, they refused to kill either in self-defense or as soldiers (West, 1962).

> The spirit of Christ, which leads us into all Truth, will never move us to fight and war against any man with outward weapons, neither for the kingdom of Christ, nor for the kingdoms of this world. (George Fox, 1660)

Central to both Anabaptist and Quaker traditions was a commitment to live out Christ's teachings in daily interactions. For Fox, the right relationship with God was an experimental relationship. "Worship meant life" and everyday choices and interactions must honor God (West, 1962: 8). The challenge for Anabaptist New Testament Christians was to follow an ethic that was not so much a defined code or set of behaviors as a challenge to live the "dynamic, inclusive, impartial nature of God's love, a love that includes the just and the unjust, the good and the evil" (Brown, 2003: 28). Union with God, they believed, is possible only when the life one leads reflects God's nature – and God's nature is love. As with the early church martyrs, Anabaptists and Quakers understood themselves to be called to live out the commandments of Christ despite persecution or hardship. When faced with a choice between obeying God's law and Caesar's, they would heed God.

For Anabaptists and Quakers, the Scriptures held the answers to the central questions about how to live a moral life. The New Testament texts, they believed, provide the basis for personal and social ethics that give form and meaning to the call to live a Christian life. The teachings of Jesus called them to a radical discipleship, in which faithfulness (with all of its uncertainties and risks) meant following the teachings of Jesus rather than the laws of the state. They believed that for Christians, living like Jesus meant loving their enemies, turning the other cheek, and believing in the power of redemptive love, trusting that God's purposes will prevail (Yoder, 2010). As Dale Brown (2003: 23) says,

> The paradox of being strangers who are alien to our culture and taking seriously the biblical call to identify, suffer and love all people, even our enemies, will be integral to our journey to discover how the "Bible tells us so."

When asked to identify the greatest commandment in the law, Jesus replied, "'Love the Lord your God with all your heart and with all your soul and with all your mind.' This is the first and greatest commandment. And the second is like it: 'Love your neighbor as yourself'" (Matthew 22:37–39). The first commandment affirms the power of faith.

The second outlines a personal and social ethic that expands the notion of neighbor to include one's enemies. There is no limit on who counts as a neighbor. To the neighbor one is called to extend the redeeming power of love and forgiveness. This ethic is further expressed in the Gospels in terms of behavior.

> You have heard that it was said, 'Eye for eye, and tooth for tooth.' But I tell you, Do not resist an evil person. If someone strikes you on the right cheek, turn to him the other also. And if someone wants to sue you and take your tunic, let him have your cloak as well. If someone forces you to go one mile, go with him two miles. Give to the one who asks you, and do not turn away from the one who wants to borrow from you. (Matthew 5:38–42)

For Quakers, early Anabaptists, and other communities that inhabited the pacifist tradition as a minority tradition within Christianity from the Middle Ages onward, pacifism was an expression of their spirituality that required a nonviolent way of being in the world (Chatfield, 1996). Their path was to follow Christ's example and to espouse the redemptive power of suffering love, the way of the cross (Brown, 1992).

Nonresistance

Many of the groups that comprised the Historic Peace Churches (although not all) adopted a stance of nonresistance. Early Anabaptists distinguished between the respective realms of the "redeemed" and the "unredeemed" as a way to live out their understanding of radical discipleship in the midst of a fallen world (Brown, 1992). They acknowledged the need for the sword in unredeemed society where the state ruled. But within the community of the redeemed, believers should follow Jesus's standard of nonresistance. They did not challenge the right of the secular state to assert its power with violence, but they themselves resolutely refused to use or sanction the use of violence in any context.

In many instances, faith communities maintained the consistency of their beliefs and practices by removing themselves from the dominant culture, living in separate communities, and refusing to participate in activities that might require them to violate their understanding of Christ's teaching: voting, holding public office, participating in war, paying war taxes.[3] An ethic for Christians and an ethic for "Caesar" remained (Brown, 2003; Yoder, 2009). This self-imposed separation had less to do with defensively isolating themselves from the evils of the dominant culture than with living a life that would bear witness to their faith and express the reality of God's kingdom. For them, living in community provided an opportunity to express a distinctively Christian love, *agape* love, as the way to build God's "kingdom here and now" (Friedmann, 1957: 113).

From Nonresistance to Nonviolent Resistance

In the second half of the nineteenth and continuing into the twentieth century, a number of social forces begin to push the Historic Peace Churches away from their traditional nonresistance stance. A growing sense of responsibility for social reform and the need to resist the social injustices of the times, a desire among pacifists to influence public policy, and a number of new voices in the call to follow Jesus's teachings on violence all precipitated a shift from nonresistance to direct action (Chatfield, 1996).

Issues such as slavery, war, and poverty pressed Christians to consider the relevance and responsibility of their nonresistance stance in the face of human evil. They asked difficult questions: While I may choose to offer my own life rather than kill, what must I do when the innocent are threatened? "Can I refuse to kill others and still be morally responsible when violent, aggressive groups threaten other people" (Johansen, 2008: 1)? This struggle between individual choice and collective responsibility came to the fore in the Abolition movement of the nineteenth century, which felt chastened by the challenge of the seeming ineffectiveness of pacifism against slavery. It continued into the twentieth century in several prominent ways: the draft for the First World War, which called into question the right of individuals to refuse to bear arms on behalf of the state; the challenges created by the rise of Hitler and the atrocities of the Second World War; the realities of segregation, racism, and poverty, not only in the United States but around the world; and the brutal repression of innocents by dictatorships.

The Historic Peace Churches responded to these challenges by shifting away from the Anabaptist separatist stance toward what Brown calls a "nonviolent transformationist stance" (Brown, 1992: 207). The peace witness became a witness for the possibility of the "promised peaceable kingdom" (Brown, 1992: 208). This conceptual shift took a variety of forms, including aid and service projects like the Heifer project; relief and refugee work around the world through the Mennonite Central Committee; the American Friends Service Committee; Brethren Volunteer Service; and Conscientious Objector support networks, culminating in the Civilian Public Service (CPS) agency (Durnbaugh, 1992; Chatfield, 1993).

Members of mainline Christian churches added their voices to the call for direct resistance. They expressed their convictions in many ways, including overt support for movements like Abolition and Suffrage led by Lucretia Mott, William Lloyd Garrison, Sojourner Truth, and Frederick Douglas. Roman Catholics joined in the witness through various organizations, one of the most prominent being the Catholic Worker, founded in 1933 by Dorothy Day and Peter Maurin, an organization that worked on issues of hunger, poverty, and pacifism in a movement that "imported a radical social conscience into the church while enveloping social concerns in religious faith" (Chatfield, 1996: 5). Others, such as Jane Addams, worked to establish international organizations whose goals included finding transnational means for ending war and implementing international law. Numerous organizations whose projects were anchored in Christian principles – including the National Association for the Advancement of Colored People (NAACP, 1909), the Fellowship of Reconciliation (FOR, 1915), the American Friends Service Committee (AFSC, 1917), and the Women's International League for Peace and Freedom (WILPF, 1919) – worked to challenge the dominant culture of the United States (Chatfield, 1996).

Christians felt keenly the need to act on the call to "do for the least of these" (Matthew 25) by responding to various forms of injustice, including the overt violence of war, the implicit violence expressed structurally in racism and poverty, or the moral culpability of a church that was complacent in the face of suffering. They met the challenge to be responsible and effective by returning to the radical Jesus of the Gospels, arguing that Jesus's message about the redemptive power of suffering love was not a call to silence or inaction. During his lifetime, Jesus challenged the status quo in many ways. He criticized the rich, the powerful, and the religious, and he challenged social norms by reaching out to the poor, the rejected, and the untouchables of his time. His model of action inspired the shift from nonresistance to direct, nonviolent resistance.

The shift from nonresistance to nonviolent resistance was shaped by thinkers and activists such as Adin Ballou (1801–1890), Leo Tolstoy (1829–1910), Mohandas Gandhi (1869–1948), Martin Luther King, Jr. (1929–1968), and Walter Wink (b. 1935), who articulated a principled nonviolent resistance for the twentieth and twenty-first centuries. The nonviolence they advocated interpreted Jesus's teachings as a call to a new humanity, a new way of being in the world. Their viewpoint was rooted in a distinctive spirituality – in Yoder's words, "a distinctive way of seeing oneself and one's neighbor under God" (Yoder, 2010: 41) – that embodied a moral commitment that eventually became a strategy for social reform. Their work not only challenged conventional thinking about the means by which change should be brought about, but also provided new ways of thinking about how to measure the effectiveness of the struggle (Wink, 1996; Yoder, 2010).

Ballou challenged the limitations of the nonresistance stance using the teachings of Jesus. He began by arguing that, although Jesus says "not to resist evil with evil," one is permitted to resist evil. In *Christian Non-Resistance* (2003), he argued that nonresistance does not mean either inaction or passivity. Christians are expected to avoid any form of retaliation – responding to injury with injury, "evil with evil." But responses that resist evil using moral resistance (based on love and truth) along with "uninjurious" physical force are not only permitted but required. For Ballou, nonresistance "requires various kinds and degrees of moral and physical strength, according to circumstances" (Ballou, 2003: 6). One's duty is to resist in all ways possible, short of doing injury to the other. To the list of biblical texts that give him guidance, he adds the mandate to "overcome evil with good" (Romans 12:21), the "text that transforms a position of nonresistance into nonviolent resistance" (Brown, 2003: 47). Ballou regarded nonresistance as a force that can change society.

> Non-Resistance explodes this horrible delusion; announces the impossibility of overcoming evil with evil; and, making its appeal directly to all the injured of the human race, enjoins on them, in the name of God, never more to resist injury with injury, assuring them that by adhering to the law of love under all provocations, and scrupulously suffering wrong, rather than inflicting it, they shall gloriously "overcome evil with good," and exterminate all their enemies by turning them into faithful friends. (Ballou, 2003: 6)

Ballou's writings anticipated the work of Walter Wink. Wink (1996) offered an analysis of the Sermon on the Mount that he called "Jesus' Third Way." Grounding his analysis of the biblical texts in the customs of Jesus's time, he challenged traditional interpretations of Matthew 5:39 ("But I say to you, Do not resist an evildoer. But if anyone strikes you on the right cheek, turn the other also"), which treat this passage as a call for passivity. Some Christians understood this passage to prohibit nonviolent direct action, because it is coercive and therefore violates the teachings of Jesus. Both non-Christians and Christian "realists" have used it to argue that the nonresistance position is naive and irresponsible in the face of evil (Yoder, 2009). Wink offered a "third way." By turning the other cheek, Wink argued, servants or slaves invited the master to strike them with his fist (an act of one equal against another) rather than with a backhanded slap (a demeaning act of a superior toward a subordinate). Turning the other cheek, he contended, constituted an act of resistance that challenged the master's right to mistreat the servant. By offering the other cheek, the servant in effect says, "I am a human being . . . I refuse to be humiliated . . . I am your equal. I am a child of God" (Wink, 1996: 104). Wink's interpretation judged turning the other cheek to be an act of defiance that provided the basis for the "makings of a social revolution" (Wink, 1996: 104).

Wink also argued that Jesus provides Christians a way to resist evil that, "judo-like," uses the "momentum of the system" to challenge the system (Wink, 1996: 109). Jesus does not call his followers to passive inaction, but to active, courageous, revolutionary action that refuses to let "evil dictate the terms of opposition." For Wink, this type of action goes beyond "murderous counterviolence" (Wink, 1996: 108) and offers a third way, a response based in love, "that promises to liberate the oppressed from evil even as it frees the oppressor from sin" (Wink, 1996: 108). Wink believed that Jesus's mandate in Matthew 5:39 provides the biblical foundation for nonviolent resistance.

Leo Tolstoy, most familiar as a great literary figure, played a leading role in the development of nonviolence in the twentieth century. Tolstoy's reading of the scriptures led him to proclaim nonresistance as the fundamental teaching of Jesus, most clearly articulated in the calls to love one's enemies (Matthew 5:44), not to resist evil (Matthew 5:39), and to treat others as one would want to be treated (Matthew 7:12). For Tolstoy, faith requires placing one's complete trust in God's judgments, not the fallible judgments of human beings. Tolstoy believed that human judgment is fallible in part because it is clouded by a desire to dominate others, a desire that fuels other kinds of injustice. For Tolstoy, responding to evil with evil means participating in this system of domination and thus contributing to the cycle of violence (Yoder, 2010: 22). Tolstoy believed that the cycle can be broken only by acts of nonresistance. Jesus commanded us not to resist, and there are no exceptions to his commandment. He refused to let the existence of evil define acceptable Christian behavior and instead held fast to his belief in the redemptive power of suffering love (Tolstoy, 1987).

Tolstoy corresponded with Mohandas K. Gandhi, the most influential practitioner of nonviolence of the twentieth century. Gandhi led the nonviolent struggle for Indian independence against the British Empire from 1914–1947. A Hindu himself, Gandhi was captivated by the Christian notion of suffering love and its capacity to defeat evil. "Jesus lived and died in vain if He did not teach us to regulate the whole of life by the eternal law of love" (Gandhi, 1964: 26). Gandhi developed his notion of *satyagraha*, truth force or soul force, as an explicit articulation of the power of truth and suffering to bring pressure on his opponents. In the practice of nonviolence, he explained why suffering works: soul force exerts a spiritual power by winning him over the adversary, not by defeating him or her. Nonviolence as a strategy refuses to give up on the possibility of reconciliation; there is no enemy, only neighbors who must find a way to heal broken relationships. The power of nonviolence lies in the capacity to reveal truth, to deny the oppressor justification for further violence, to reveal the injustice that exists in the world, and to point toward a more just set of social relations. Gandhi understood that violence could not result in the better world that he wanted for India. He challenged the notion that means and ends are disconnected, arguing that it is impossible to use evil means for a good end. He rejected the "pragmatism of necessary but lesser evils" (Yoder, 2010: 45).

The experience of Gandhi in India illuminates how suffering love works and adds tactical strategy and organizational skill to the mix, a combination that set the stage for the civil rights movement in the United States. Gandhi became the "reference point for US advocates of modern nonviolence" (Chatfield, 1999: 287) and directly influenced the civil rights movement in the United States. As Martin Luther King, Jr. said:

> I came to see for the first time the Christian doctrine of love operating through the Gandhian method of nonviolence as one of the most potent weapons available to oppressed people in their struggle for freedom. (King, 1986: 38)

The civil rights movement exemplifies the synthesis of Christianity and social change movements. In this synthesis, the faithful are called to critically evaluate the world in which they live. Economic, political, and social institutions are judged by the moral standards of the faith, and religion provides the basis for the moral imperatives to love one another, to fight for peace and justice, and to expect equality. The Church also provides the symbols, ideologies, and organizational resources necessary for mobilizing the masses (Smith, 1996). The Southern Christian Leadership Council (SCLC), created in 1957, of which King was president, became one of the leading forces in the civil rights movement because black churches were situated at the heart of the struggle. Since the time of slavery, black spirituality had been a source of resistance to white oppression. In the United States of the 1950s and 1960s, black clergy provided leadership through the black churches, which were the foundation of black communities. Black churches provided not only strength, courage, organization, and inspiration, but also the people who would form the heart of the movement (Morris, 1996).

As a leader in the movement, King developed a theology of the cross and a sense of the social power of nonviolent resistance. The movement was aided by a number of other leaders – including James Lawson (who had been to India to study Gandhian techniques), Bayard Rustin, A.J. Muste, Glen Smiley, Ella Baker, Jo Ann Gibson Robinson, James Farmer, A. Philip Randolph, and others – who brought understandings of nonviolence to the movement (Chatfield, 1999). As the movement struggled on and nonviolence encountered violent responses, King articulated Tolstoy's key insight.

> to meet hate with retaliatory hate would do nothing but intensify the distance of evil in the universe. Hate begets hate; violence begets violence; we must meet the forces of hate with the power of love; we must meet physical force with soul force. Our aim must never be to defeat or humiliate the white man, but to win his friendship and understanding. (King, 1986: 74)

Both the Indian independence movement and the civil rights movement in the United States were grounded in religious principles. Violence was not avoided simply for tactical reasons, nor was nonviolent resistance practiced simply as a social strategy. Grounded as it was in a religious vision, nonviolent resistance embodied both faith and strategy. As such, it proved to be a risky endeavor. No small number of participants lost their lives, many were imprisoned, and others lost their jobs, their means of livelihood. People took these risks because they believed there to be a link between what Yoder calls "suffering and the purposes of God" (Yoder, 2010: 42). They acted on the conviction that the commandment to love one's neighbor as oneself (Mark 12:31) binds means and ends. Thus, nonviolent resisters felt compelled to abandon violence as a means toward a nonviolent end. As Yoder puts it, if they had disregarded the "dignity of the neighbor" and disrespected "the social fabric" of the society they hoped to transform, they would have planted the "seeds for the failure of [their] own enterprise. Only fidelity to love as means can be an instrument for love as end" (Yoder, 2010: 46). The successes of the civil rights movement stand forth as compelling examples of a form of nonviolent resistance based on the practice of returning love for evil. It is a movement that answers the question of how to protect the innocent in a way that is both morally right and socially effective.

The Christian nonviolent experiment continued from the middle of the twentieth century into the twenty-first century, expanding in numerous directions. Antinuclear groups developed along side the civil rights movement (the Committee for Nonviolence Action [CNVA] formed on the 1957 anniversary of Hiroshima) and led into opposition to the war in Vietnam. Longstanding groups like FOR, AFSC, and SCLC worked with emergent groups like Women Strike for Peace, Clergy and Laymen Concerned about Vietnam, Another Mother for Peace, and groups that had begun as antinuclear groups, like SANE (Committee for Sane Nuclear Policy) and PAX Christie. These groups used traditional tactics (teach-ins, education, petitions, vigils, boycotts) and pushed the boundaries of nonviolent resistance, engaging in more radicalized tactics and escalating civil disobedience into "what some called 'ultraresistance'" (Chatfield, 1996: 11). These included actions of people like the priests Daniel and Philip Berrigan, who burned draft cards and poured blood on them, guerrilla theater, blockading draft boards, draft evasion, and in some rare cases, self-immolation (Chatfield, 1999).

In the 1980s these actions turned to challenging the production of nuclear weapons in symbolic acts of transformation, turning swords into plowshares (Isaiah 2:4) by pouring blood on warheads, damaging and disarming missiles and launchers, and breaking into factories, bases and warships, risking arrest and imprisonment to do so. In the words of one member of the ANZUS (Australia, New Zealand, and United States) Plowshares movement, "our disarmament would be both actual and symbolic" acts of prophecy (O'Reilly, 1996: 172). The goal of prophecy is to link the future and the present by instilling in the present hopes for a future defined by peace, justice, and freedom, and to resist present dangerous trends. "It is our responsibility to prophecy, to witness, to resist; it is up to the Holy Spirit to convert (O'Reilly, 1996: 172).

In addition to movements focused on the United States, nonviolent resistance movements have become increasingly transnational. Nonviolence becomes a "weapon of the weak" in battles against repression, corruption, militarism, human rights abuses, and poverty, and in pro-democracy and self-determination movements. Transnational nonviolent resistance links local actors and actions with international supporters. It takes expression in cross-border alliances designed to increase leverage, protect against repression, grant access to greater resources, and increase solidarity (Clark, 2009). The success of these alliances is seen in movements like Witness for Peace, Sanctuary, the Anti-Apartheid campaign, Voices in the Wilderness, Women in Black, and Jubilee 2000, which link majority and minority voices in the fight against injustice.

In recent years, groups such as Christian Peacemaker Teams (CPT) have taken nonviolence a step further, developing a nonviolent interventionist strategy grounded in the belief that Christian witness carries a responsibility to stand with those who cannot stand for themselves. Based in the Historic Peace Churches, CPT began in 1986 with the goal of becoming a "peaceful presence, standing between or alongside opposing factions to prevent bloodshed and to attempt dialogue" (Schirch, 2006: 21). Its members work to reduce violence by embedding teams trained in mediation and nonviolence in communities in crisis. Their peace presence is designed to provide protection against acts of violence, and their work includes documenting atrocities, supporting local peacemakers, attempting dialogue with all groups in the conflict, and providing information to Christian congregations "back home" (Schirch, 2006).

Conclusion

Yoder argues that an examination of early Christian heritage reveals "not a simple moral rigor about not shedding blood but a robust alternative holistic social system" (Yoder, 1996: 80). Christian life in the early decades of the church, he argues, is not a story of withdrawal based on a desire for moral purity, but rather withdrawal as an act of resistance, a path of nonconformity, the aim of which was to create a society based on justice and honoring God. Early Christian groups sought to transform society by embodying and living out certain Christian principles. They sought to be communities that nurtured a culture of dialogue and consensus; that believed the Spirit was alive and present where the many were gathered; that offered forgiveness rather than vengeance to the offender; and that welcomed everyone without regard to class, gender, age, or social status. These core values shaped an image of the beloved community where Christians struggle to enact Jesus's teaching in the here and now.

Wink (1996) argues that the church's vocation is nonviolence. Yoder (1996) argues that "fidelity to its own vocation" (Yoder, 1996: 86) is the right way for the church to witness to the world. The "third way" of Jesus is not theoretical, but a clear path that denies the moral purity of withdrawal from society and the realist challenge that to respond effectively to evil in the world one must take up the sword.

Nonviolent resistance as a Christian practice means that social strategy is also prayer, religious processions are a form of protest, a planning meeting includes worship and preaching, song is both solidarity and praise (Yoder, 2010). Christian nonviolent resistance is action and belief that refuses to divide the world into "us" and "them" and asks that the believer recognize the humanity in all: in oneself, so that there is a willingness to demand recognition and rights, as well as in the other, so that there is a refusal to make them the enemy. It denies that evil cannot be opposed without being mimicked. It is a belief in the redemptive power of suffering love. It is the way of Jesus.

Notes

1 It is not possible in this short space to do justice to the hundreds of movements or the hundreds of thousands of people who have participated in these struggles and sacrificed for a vision of a just society grounded in the teachings of their faith traditions.
2 Some scholars contest this idea, arguing the refusal to fight was based on the requirement to swear allegiance to Caesar and to pagan gods. Thus the objection was about idolatry not violence. Yoder and others reject this argument (Yoder, 2009).
3 There are clear exceptions to this position, most notably the Quakers in the New World. William Penn was granted land in the Americas by King Charles II, and Quakers managed the territory from the 1680s until 1756.

References

Ballou, Adin (2003) *Christian Non-Resistance*, L. Gordon Hughes (ed.), Blackstone Editions, Providence, RI.

Brock, Peter (1981) *The Roots of War Resistance: Pacifism from the Early Church to Tolstoy*, Fellowship of Reconciliation, Nyack, NY.

Brown, Dale W. (2003) *Biblical Pacifism*, Brethren Press, Elgin, IL.

Brown, Dale W. (1992) What has happened to our peace witness?, in *Brethren in Transition: 20th Century Directions and Dilemmas*, Emmert F. Bittinger (ed.), Penobscot Press, Camden, ME, pp. 205–213.

Chatfield, Charles (1993) Nonviolence and United States history: Insofar as, in *Nonviolent America: History through the Eyes of Peace*, Louise Hawkley and James C. Juhnke (eds.), Mennonite Press, Newton, KS, pp. 250–265.

Chatfield, Charles (1996) The Catholic Worker in the United States peace tradition, in *American Catholic Pacifism: The Influence of Dorothy Day and the Catholic Worker Movement*, Anne Klejment and Nancy Roberts (eds.), Praeger, Westport, CT, pp. 1–13.

Chatfield, Charles (1999) Nonviolent social movements in the United States: A historical overview, in *Nonviolent Social Movements: A Geographical Perspective*, Stephen Zunes, Lester R. Kurtz, and Sarah Beth Asher (eds.), Blackwell, Malden, MA, pp. 293–301.

Clark, Howard (ed.) (2009) Introduction, in *People Power: Unarmed Resistance and Global Solidarity*, Pluto Press, London, pp. 1–20.

Cooney, Robert, and Michalowski, Helen (1987) *The Power of the People: Active Nonviolence in the United States*, New Society Publishers, Philadelphia.

Cortright, David (2006) *Gandhi and Beyond: Nonviolence for an Age of Terrorism*, Paradigm Publishers, Boulder, CO.

Durnbaugh, Donald F. (1992) *Brethren Beginnings: The Origin of the Church of the Brethren in Early Eighteenth-Century Europe*, Brethren Encyclopedia, Philadelphia.

Friedmann, Robert (1957) The Hutterian brethren and community of goods, in *The Recovery of the Anabaptist Vision*, Guy Hershberger (ed.), Herald Press, Scottsdale, PA, pp. 83–90.

Gandhi, Mohandas K. (1964) *Gandhi on Non-Violence*, Thomas Merton (ed.), New Directions Publishing, New York.

Johansen, Robert C. (2008) The politics of love and war: What is our responsibility? *Journal of Religion, Conflict, and Peace* 2(1), http://

www.religionconflictpeace.org/node/42 (accessed April 19, 2011).

King, Martin Luther (1986) *A Testament of Hope: The Essential Writings and Speeches of Martin Luther King, Jr.*, James M. Washington (ed.), Harper Collins, New York.

Lynd, Staughton and Lynd, Alice (eds.) (1995) *Nonviolence in America: A Documentary History*, Orbis Books, Maryknoll, NY.

Morris, Aldon (1996) The black church in the civil rights movement: The SCLC as the decentralized, radical arm of the black church, in *Disruptive Religion: The Force of Faith in Social Movement Activism*, Christian Smith (ed.), Routledge, New York, pp. 29–46.

O'Reilly, Ciaron (1996) ANZUS plowshares: A nonviolent campaign, in *American Catholic Pacifism: The Influence of Dorothy Day and the Catholic Worker Movement*, Anne Klejment and Nancy Roberts (eds.), Praeger, Westport, CT, pp. 171–186.

Schirch, Lisa (2006) *Civilian Peacekeeping: Preventing Violence and Making Space for Democracy*, Life and Peace Institute, Ostervala, Sweden.

Smith, Christian (1996) Introduction, in *Disruptive Religion: The Force of Faith in Social Movement Activism*, Christian Smith (ed.), Routledge, New York, pp. 1–25.

Tolstoy, Leo (1987) Letter to Ernest Howard Crosby, in *Writings on Civil Disobedience and Nonviolence*, Aylmer Maude (trans.), New Society Publishers, Philadelphia, pp. 241–253.

West, Jessamyn (ed.) (1962) *The Quaker Reader*, Viking Press, New York.

Wink, Walter (1996) Beyond just war and pacifism, in *War and Its Discontents: Pacifism and Quietism in the Abrahamic Traditions*, J. Patout Burns (ed.), Georgetown University Press, Washington, DC, pp. 102–121.

Yoder, John H. (1996) On not being in charge, in *War and Its Discontents: Pacifism and Quietism in the Abrahamic Traditions*, J. Patout Burns (ed.), Georgetown University Press, Washington, DC, pp. 74–90.

Yoder, John H. (2009) *Christian Attitudes to War, Peace, and Revolution*, T. Koontz and A. Alexis-Baker (eds.), Brazos Press, Grand Rapids.

Yoder, John H. (2010) *Nonviolence – A Brief History: The Warsaw Lectures*, P.H. Martens, M. Porter, and M. Werntz (eds.), Baylor University Press, Waco, TX.

Zunes, Stephen, Kurtz, Lester R., and Asher, Sarah Beth (eds.) (1999) *Nonviolent Social Movements in the United States: A Historical Overview*, Blackwell, Malden, MA.

CHAPTER 43
Building Peace in the Pursuit of Social Justice

Mohammed Abu-Nimer

Peacebuilding (PB) is an umbrella term that encompasses at least three main fields of study and practice: conflict resolution, peace studies, and alternative dispute resolution (ADR). There have been some attempts to bridge the gaps between these three areas, for example expanding conflict resolution processes to include transformative methodologies and processes that link areas to wider social change approaches. Nevertheless, certain distinctions between these three areas of PB remain, especially with regards to the ways in which practitioners and scholars in each of these areas define the causes of conflict, processes of intervention, and outcomes (criteria of success).

Developments in the PB field in the last two decades indicate that, as a field, it is no longer in its infancy or birth phase, but rather has moved into its adolescence. Thus there are vibrant debates about its identity and relationship to other disciplines and professions. Today, there are about twenty masters programs, four PhD programs, and hundreds of undergraduate programs in peace and conflict resolution. According to a recent survey, conflict resolution programs are in the majority (58%), ADR programs make up 24%, and peace studies 14% of the field (see Polkinghorn *et al.*, 2008). In addition, new subfields are emerging with their own literatures, practices, and organizations. These include media and PB, religion and PB, foreign policy and PB, and development and PB.[1]

Despite its accelerated growth, the field of PB has not yet reached a point of clarity regarding the use and application of its basic terms. Boutros-Ghali's United Nations (UN) Agenda for Peace document, in 1992, has helped to create a distinction between peacemaking, peacekeeping, and PB. Since then, many scholars and organizations have used PB to refer to activities and actions that are launched to reconstruct, rehabilitate, and reconcile societies in postwar contexts (mainly after reaching a political agreement or the ending of a war). Another group of scholars and practitioners tend to use PB as an umbrella term that relates to actions that attempt to bring closure to a conflict, and

---

The Wiley Blackwell Companion to Religion and Social Justice, First Edition. Edited by Michael D. Palmer and Stanley M. Burgess.
© 2012 John Wiley & Sons Ltd. Published 2020 by John Wiley & Sons Ltd.

that include both peace and conflict resolution activities, regardless of whether they take place after or before a peace agreement is signed. However, the term is also used to describe peace activities (social, economic, or political) carried out in a postpolitical agreement. "Peacemaking" is too a broad term, referring to all efforts (often by third parties) that bring parties together to establish peace through integrated activities performed by both professional diplomats and nondiplomats alike.

By early 2000, PB, both the field and the concept, had evolved to include a wide range of activities performed to achieve durable peace, including security, political economic activities, and legal institution building. In fact, Miall *et al.* (1999) have charted a framework for PB objectives and methods or tools that are categorized by their short-term, medium-term, and long-term measures. In a more extensive review and itemization of PB tools, Lund (2001) identified 92 policy tools that can be applied in PB and classified them according to categories such as official diplomacy, nonofficial conflict management; military; economic and social; political and governance; judicial and legal; and communication and education. Regardless of the different ways in which scholars and practitioners conceptualize PB, it is obvious that the term has developed to indicate a more holistic approach than its early conception by UN Secretary General Boutros-Ghali.

On the practical level, two major accomplishments have taken place in the last two decades. First, in the last ten years, many western governments and some southern government agencies have adopted the language and terminology of peace and conflict resolution. The majority of these major governmental institutions have incorporated the language of PB into their international development statements and funding requirements.[2] Second, a solid network of nongovernmental organizations (NGOs) have developed and been institutionalized in such a way that PB organizations have become an integral part of civil society sectors in many countries around the globe. Thus, organizations such as Catholic Relief Services (CRS), World Vision (WV), CARE International, and UN agencies in general have adopted PB approaches and processes, and have even created special units to oversee the mainstreaming of such strategies and processes into their organizational operations.

Basic Assumptions and Principles of PB

In the context of this essay, as a working definition, the expression "PB approaches" refers to processes and concepts that assume the following:

- Nonviolent methods of solving conflicts are more effective and less costly than the use of violent methods.
- PB processes and outcomes can be more effective and sustainable when they are able to challenge institutional and structural power imbalances in any given conflict context.
- Empowerment of underprivileged groups is an essential tool in achieving peace and justice in the reality of conflict, especially in contexts involving deep-rooted conflict.

- PB processes aim to contribute to the macrocultural transformation processes of societies; specifically, in building a global culture of peace based on the protection and preservation of the basic human needs and rights of all people.
- In most conflicts, at least one of the parties (perhaps all of them) has experienced a certain degree of injustice. Only by addressing this sense of injustice can genuine resolution of the conflict be achieved.

There is a set of principles within PB that can be utilized in responding to injustice and contributing to achieving social justice. Such principles need to be carefully considered when practitioners and policy makers design their intervention strategies in conflict situations, especially in identity-based conflicts that involve religious factors.

However, it is necessary to clarify the expressions "conflict management and settlement," "resolution," and "transformation." These expressions have been used interchangeably in the last two decades, but in fact there are both common and divergent expectations of the three terms.

Conflict management and settlement

This term was developed in the 1960s and 1970s to refer to activities often involving a third-party actor, which are intended to provide a temporary set of arrangements to a conflict, with the main purpose of reducing tensions in the short term and identifying partial agreements on certain conflict issues. For example, when African Americans (a minority group that had long been the object of racial discrimination) were offered affirmative action in the 1970s in the United States, the arrangement was aimed at managing racial tension, but did not address the root causes of the conflict.

Conflict resolution

This term emerged in the mid-1980s to define long-term solutions that address the root causes of conflict (Burton, 1990). Within this process, the structural obstacles of a conflict can be removed and substituted with new arrangements with which the parties are more satisfied and that can fulfill basic human needs. For example, when apartheid in South Africa was abolished and replaced with a new governance system, a resolution was found for the conflict.

Conflict transformation

This term was developed in the late 1990s to describe deep-level changes in the structural and individual aspects of conflict. It also implies a preventative element that focuses on relationship building. Thus, transformation processes and strategies aim at long-term macro changes in societies, structures, and individuals. For example, the European Union's (EU) economic and political system can be viewed as a new arrangement that contributes to the comprehensive transformation of European societies, as opposed to their pre–Second World War relationships.

Due to various factors, including the fast-growing field of PB and competition over scarce resources, disconnects have developed between the different practitioners that engage in PB activities and these different tools and processes. One of these disconnects is in the field of human rights, with nonviolent resistance activists on the one hand, and certain alternative dispute resolution mediators and arbitrators on the other. Human rights activists generally engage in nonviolent resistance, advocacy, and confrontation on issues of justice; mediators and conflict resolution practitioners, who work at both diplomatic and domestic levels, attempt to avoid imposing their own values in the interest of remaining impartial and neutral. Consequently, human rights activists often believe that mediators are passive participants in conflict. However, mediators are trained to interact in quite different environments than are activists. Rather than focus on their different approaches, it is important to reinforce the similarities of the root values that these different actors share (desire for social change, social justice, empowerment, and a culture of peace). Through their varied interventions, their efforts can and should be linked to avoid unproductive fragmentation of the PB field.

There is a wide range of tools and processes in PB that can be utilized to address conflicts and contribute to social justice. Intervention strategies include negotiation, mediation, arbitration, facilitation, problem solving, dialogue, advocacy, nonviolent resistance, and peace education. In addition, there are other forms of intervention such as capacity building through PB training. Training can be a tool of social healing, in which the individual, social, and relational changes necessary for peace can be achieved. Training workshops have been further developed as a form of intervention, not only to provide skills but also to offer a space in which individuals affected by conflict can begin to engage in negotiation and social healing. All training in the above processes (e.g., negotiation and mediation) can provide participants with: new peace-promoting attitudes, knowledge, and skills; reinforcement of culturally relevant peace-promoting attitudes, knowledge, and skills; and the opportunity to redirect or erase negative or divisive attitudes, knowledge, and skills that are deemed to inhibit growth.

Strategies of Peace-Building Intervention

Regardless of whether the focus of PB interventions is on institution building or perceptional and attitudinal changes (collective and individual), both assume that a transformation of the relational aspects of conflict is necessary to sustain peace among the conflicted parties. The PB methods that focus on changing relationships recognize the need for in-depth change in the minds of individuals and in the social structures of the parties in conflict in order to achieve peace. In cases involving deep-rooted conflict (including those involving clashes among people with different religious identities), the transformative process will focus on replacing the old perspectives and values that fueled the conflict with new concepts and values of equality, dignity, and human rights, thereby countering the dehumanization that commonly accompanies violent conflict, and as sometimes occurs when conflicting identities are mobilized.

The Twelve Elements of Social PB, a program developed by the Institute for Multi-Track Diplomacy (IMTD), aims to promote a systematic approach to PB and to facilitate the transformation of deep-rooted social conflict. It recognizes that in order for a conflict-habituated system to move to a peace system, it is necessary to remove from those systems the elements that cause and maintain the conflict and to stimulate or introduce elements that transcend and transform habitual patterns. These "transcenders" address four basic needs – identity, security, community, and vitality – and comprise the 12 elements of social PB. These transcending elements are hope, trust, nourishment, power, community, learning, healing, creativity, will, diversity, complexity, and myth deconstruction.

When practitioners of PB adopt these principles and allow them to guide their intervention designs, they will capture the complexity of the situation, emphasize the possibility of change by replacing old myths, and deconstruct old ways of perceiving other community groups.

Hope

By sharing positive stories of change, examples of success from other conflict areas, and creative ways to build relationships, PB processes can provide people in a conflict situation that seems hopeless with sense of hope and possibility. For example, while working with *madrasah* teachers in Pakistan and sharing with them alternative ways to teach their students Islamic peace and conflict resolution methods, teachers expressed hope and insisted on learning more stories about other Muslim teachers who have faced similar challenges.[3]

Trust

In conflict contexts that are ridden with distrust and antagonism, PB activities aim to restore or build trust. In Sri Lanka, even Buddhist monks have joined the militant nationalistic narrative and have encouraged followers to disconnect their relationship with Hindus, Christians, and Muslims in the war zone. However, through PB programs, some monks joined in with peace activists and created the Interreligious Peace Foundation, a PB network to rebuild trust among the various communities. The leaders of these programs have suffered a great deal in promoting such activities; nevertheless, they have achieved a certain degree of success in their local communities. The leading monk and a Christian priest of this group managed to show these communities, through joint cultural, religious, and political activities, that it is possible to trust people in other communities.

Nourishment

War and conflict leave people physically and psychologically malnourished. Joint PB programs in which people from various faith groups gather to share their hopes and fears and build joint projects to contribute to their wounded communities produce a sense of spiritual and psychological nourishment among the participants. In Bosnia, women from different faith groups continued to meet after the war and established a local network to help other women survivors (Hart, 2008).

Power

It is often the case that during wars, especially in intractable and deep-rooted conflicts, the power of people has been seized or abused by corrupt political leaders, and people are led to believe that they have no power to influence the situation. In some contexts, even religious beliefs are deployed to support such messages. Some Christian and Muslim clergy in the Middle East have preached for withdrawal from active political engagement and encourage their followers to focus exclusively on their religious duties of worship. PB activities that include nonviolent action and resistance and learning new tools for change provide people with a sense of empowerment, by which they can regain their self-confidence and local capacity to change their personal and sometimes their communities' conditions. In Mindanao, Philippines, a mixed grassroots group of Christian and Muslims activists created a network for peace activists (Peace Weavers) to monitor the ceasefire agreement between the Moro Liberation Front and the Philippine Government. The group also gained access to the negotiation panel and the Malaysian third-party representative.[4]

Community

In many conflict areas and deeply divided societies, political and military regimes often control people on each side by disconnecting and fragmenting them during the conflict. PB interventions are intended to connect people with each other and to sustain such connections through activities and programs across borders, as in Cyprus, Northern Ireland, and Israel–Palestine. In the context of the conflicts in these regions, peace activists have managed to create peace networks and physical and virtual spaces in which people were able to connect with each other and form new joint communities to confront the social and human fragmentation and alienation that had resulted from conflicts. In some cases, religious leaders utilized their roles and places of worship to form such communities. For example, the United Religious Initiative (URI) is a global network of more than 67 different religions and spiritual practices who have joined to create over 400 circles around the world (in over than 100 countries). These interfaith circles aim to promote understanding between religious, peace, and development groups according to the guiding principles of the URI.[5]

Learning

In many deep-rooted conflict situations, people often have been socialized to believe that they have nothing to learn about the other side or their enemies. They have been kept in the dark or given misleading information about the "other." Many grow up to believe that they know the other side and have "read about them." In a religious conflict context, some clergy may be the source of such misleading knowledge. Religious rituals and symbols are sometimes utilized to emphasize the superiority of one faith over the other. As a result, in their first few encounters some members of Abrahamic dialogue groups were shocked to learn about the many similarities between Christianity, Islam, and Judaism. These PB activities become a space to humanize and learn from the other. Following the 9/11 events in the United States, many Christian churches began inviting Muslim speakers to educate their followers about Islam.

Healing

Everyone's life is affected by the conflict. Many are wounded either physically or psychologically. Thus, PB interventions often aim at eliciting an acknowledgment of the need for repair and rehabilitation. After the war in Bosnia in 1994, to facilitate healing, Serbian, Croatian, and Muslim women created a joint teacher project in which they explored their past and future relationships. In many trauma healing and PB programs in postwar societies, clergy have offered their spiritual space to host such initiatives. A classic example is the Catholic Church in Rwanda in 1995, which launched spiritual healing programs to assist its constituencies to recover from the horrendous genocide that even some of its members had intentionally or unintentionally aided (Kubai, 1995).

Creativity

The success and sustainability of PB are often shaped by the degree of creativity that each program can bring to the conflict dynamics. In conflicts that encompass decades, even centuries, of dehumanization and violence, many people find it nearly impossible to cultivate the energy necessary to reestablish peace. However, practitioners of PB have generated many creative methods and activities to inject new energy and hope into the heart and minds of their participants. Creativity is an essential tool and skill that aids conflict resolution practitioners in their various intervention programs. Arai (2009) describes the power of creativity in the conflict resolution context:

> Unconventional viability lies at the heart of creativity for transcending seemingly intractable inter-communal conflicts. More specifically, conflict resolution creativity is a social and epistemological process, whereby actors involved in a given social conflict learn to formulate an unconventional resolution option or procedure.

Will

In the reality of conflict, people often lose hope and the will to change, especially in a conflict that has extended over generations. Often, leaders are authoritarian and corrupt, and significant power disparities exist between the parties. Calls for change are frequently met with dismissal and distrust. However, the will for change can be renewed and nurtured by PB activities and different leaders, particularly those religious leaders who can mobilize their constituencies and provide a role model for the possibility of change. For example, Bishop Desmond Tutu in South Africa played an important role not only in the campaign against apartheid, but also in the subsequent work of the Truth and Reconciliation Commission (TRC).

Diversity

"They are all the same" is a statement usually echoed by people who live and experience trans-generational, deep-rooted conflict. Their perception of the other side is one-sided and polarized by such generalizations. However, PB programs can break this impasse of perceiving the other side as homogenous with no diversity of opinion or variation of belief. Arab participants in dialogue groups are often surprised to discover that there are Israeli Jews who opposed the Occupation and who have devoted their lives to achieve peace and justice with their Palestinian neighbors. Similarly, Israeli Jews are shocked when they discover that there are Palestinians who have fully accepted the right of Jews to self-determination and statehood in the Holy Land.

Complexity

The systemic violence and lack of space for joint activities and interactions in deep-rooted conflict generate high degrees of misperceptions of alternative options for solution. When viewing the "other," people have been indoctrinated by agents that cultivate fear, suspicion, and dehumanizing behavior. Thus, children as well as adults commonly perceive their conflict through distorted lenses that prevent them from envisioning alternative possibilities. PB activities remove these tunnel-vision spectacles to reveal a broader, less polarized view of reality. For example, one of the important insights gained by participants in dialogue groups between Tamils, Muslims, and the Sinhalese in Sri Lanka was that there is no simple solution to the conflict. Whether the war is won by the government or the rebels, there is still a need to negotiate arrangements to satisfy the needs of the deprived communities. Similarly, Jewish and Arab participants of dialogue groups realized that the conflict in the Middle East is complex and cannot be solved by expulsion or extermination of the other side (Abu-Nimer, 2004).

Demythologizing

In conflict, demonizing the other is an activity engrained in individuals such that they are not aware of their accepted myths. Certain religious teachings have been manipulated to create and even sustain such processes of demonization and negative myth creation, especially in dealing with or portraying indigenous traditions. So, for example, colonial ideologies and cultures have spread myths about Africans and Native Americans and have supported them by biblical interpretations. In the religious PB context, such negative myths are challenged and even shattered by offering new interpretations that focus on humanization of the "other" and fostering respect for and acceptance of alternative spiritual expressions. The positive contact between Muslim and Christian youth participants in Mindanao assisted in breaking the hold of negative myths by the parties about the allegedly "vicious Moro" and the "Christian settlers." As a result of the long history of violence and dehumanization between Catholic settlers and Muslims in Mindanao, many of these young people grew up in separate enclaves and hardly had an opportunity to interact with members of the other community. Thus, when an interfaith dialogue group for youth engaged them, they confessed to harboring "negative myths and stories" about the other side, which they learned from media, history, religious figures, or other socialization agents in their communities.

Religion, PB, and Social Justice

Despite the long history of religious PB, only in the last two decades has the relationship between religion and PB been academically and professionally explored in more depth (Appleby, 2000; Gopin, 2002; Abu-Nimer, 2008; Little, 2008). Scholars and practitioners are examining the potentially constructive roles that religious actors and institutions can play in conflicts, especially deep-rooted conflicts. In general, these efforts are focused on the assumption that religious PB has a claim to an integral part of the field of PB. However, despite this growth in the literature and professional organizations, the links between religion, PB, and social justice remain relatively unexplored. A significant segment of the efforts to articulate the religious PB field have focused on the roles of religious actors as bridge builders between fighting or divided communities; therefore, they often adopt a "harmonizer role." Thus, in the last two decades, interfaith dialogue has emerged as a central method of religious PB. In the field of interreligious PB, there is little emphasis on nonviolent resistance, liberation theology, or issues of social justice and structural violence.[6]

However, a promising development took place in the Parliament of World's Religions' 2009 Conference in Australia, the largest international gathering of religious PB. At this conference, social justice was adopted as a theme for its annual gathering:

> Peace and justice are within the world's grasp. But they must be pursued together, as one vision. This essential interdependence will be a key focus at the Parliament. Indeed, there is a growing recognition that by addressing pressing issues of social justice, religious and spiritual communities may be more effective than ever before.

Beyond this statement, the program's content was significantly more focused on linkages between justice and development than the previous gathering of this parliament in Spain in 2008.

Despite the preceding exceptional focus, the majority of interreligious PB activities continue to be promoted in the form of interfaith dialogue processes, especially in the context of post–9/11 realities in which a widening perceptual gap between Muslim and western societies has been identified as a root cause of "Islamic global terrorism." There are only a few interreligious PB initiatives that focus on addressing issues of injustice and nonviolent resistance related to this divide between Muslims and western societies and governments. Such an agenda, if adopted by other interfaith and interreligious organizations, would require them to make certain stands against governmental policies. It would also require interreligious organizations to engage with political actors or decision makers while advocating for justice, in addition to preaching harmony, religious understanding, and basic respect of religious practices.

It is obvious that dialogue, understanding, and tolerance of diverse religious practices are important and provide essential norms and messages to be spread in every society. However, interreligious actors can often be trapped in this discourse of harmony without realizing the complexity of the conflict dynamics and the need to tackle the structural causes of the violence, especially when religious institutions are involved. For example, in the early 1990s, the Bishop and Ulama in Mindanao, Philippines called for an interfaith dialogue initiative through the Bishop Ulama Forum (BUF). It took members of this forum several years to realize that their theological conversations and elite interfaith dialogues were disconnected from the concerns of people at the grassroots level, all of whom had suffered for decades from the war between the army and rebel groups. Later, the BUF launched a priest–imam program to spread interfaith dialogue among their constituencies. Nevertheless, the BUF remained to some extent disconnected from the peace activist networks and organizations in Mindanao, which had been fighting against structural violence and war and had initiated development and relief programs to respond to the needs of people in their communities.

For interreligious PB actors to strive toward social justice, their programs or interventions need to be carefully designed so as to avoid their being manipulated by the dominant majority institutions and discourses. Social justice can be advanced in a conflict situation when PB activities are not utilized as tools by the government or donors to achieve their particular agendas. In recent years, Middle Eastern and western governments have initiated interreligious PB programs focusing on dialogue and pluralism.[7] In many cases these governments have political agendas that aim narrowly at preserving order and security or delegitimizing any form of violence.

A similar pattern exists among many of the interfaith PB programs involved with the conflict in Israel–Palestine. Israeli or American-Jewish organizations often carry out interreligious programs disconnected from social and political justice. Thus, they define their agendas as apolitical and distance themselves from confronting the existing economic, political, and military structures that are central to the conflict. As a result, the design and content of the Arab–Jewish interfaith conversation often remain detached from the concerns of minority groups. Similar patterns have developed in interfaith dialogue groups in the United States post–9/11, between Muslims and Jews or between Muslims and Christians. The parties agree to talk about domestic religious and nonreligious issues, but leave out the difficult questions of Israel–Palestine, Iraq, and Iran. The same dynamic exists among Egyptian Muslims and Copts, who meet to explore their relationships but conspicuously omit political issues or questions related to the status of Christians in a Muslim majority state (Abu-Nimer *et al.*, 2007).

Confronting power imbalances in institutional or social structures in a conflict is a necessary condition for interfaith PB to advance the agenda for social justice. Otherwise, such activities of interreligious dialogue and PB run the risk of supporting the status quo or imbalance of power, which in turn usually perpetuates tension and violence despite the interfaith efforts. Such an approach would be equivalent to South African religious groups calling for dialogue between white and black churches without discussing the apartheid structure.

Religion, PB, and Development

Among the many areas for future research in linking PB, religion, and social justice, there is a need to link these concepts and processes with the field of social and economic development. For the majority of the world's population, social justice is deeply connected to the need to reduce poverty and improve basic economic and social conditions. If we accept the notion that "religion is a conceptual framework for humans to understand the world and their place in it" (Bradley, 2007: 14), religious institutions around the world have assumed a major role in framing these needs and ways to address them. When reviewing literature on development and religion, one notices an obvious lack of attention to the potential transformative role that faith-based organizations (FBOs) can play in sustainable development. The extent of the disconnect is clearly reflected in the lack of direct engagement between religion and the major government aid agencies, such as the United States Agency for International Development (USAID), United Kingdom Department for International Development (DFID), Canadian International Development Agency (CIDA), Swedish International Development Agency (SIDA), and the FBOs. In the last decade, there have been few initiatives to promote linkages between development and religion. The British government aid agency supported the largest research program in this area to explore the relationship between development and religion from the perspectives of many scholarly disciplines. In addition, the World Bank launched its faith and development initiative in 1998, led by Katherine Marshal, who continued this exploration through the World Faiths Development Dialogue.[8] Despite these efforts, there is still a disconnect between government development agencies, major international donors, and religious organizations and actors in conflict areas.

The potential to facilitate, understand, and promote a positive role for major FBOs (Muslim, Christian, Buddhist, Hindu, and others), which constitute the largest number of community-based organizations in the world and always operate in conflict and disaster areas, has not been conceptualized or formalized by either the development or PB fields. Exploration and systematic linkages between these three areas of religion, development, and PB in any given context will enhance the capacities of practitioners and social change agents to contribute to social justice outcomes. For example, without the engagement of Muslim FBOs in Iraq, Afghanistan, Somalia, or Egypt, in both development and PB, it is unlikely that any of these countries can achieve stable peace or social justice. Unfortunately, in all of these areas, the majority of the development efforts are either being designed and implemented by secular and foreign actors, which have so far failed to appreciate the need to engage FBOs in PB and development, or by faith-based organizations that are implementing their programs without explicit and conscious linkages to PB principles.

Conclusion

PB is a fast-growing field of scholarship and practice. It has established itself in both academic institutions and professional development organizations. As an emerging field of study, PB is still exploring its relationship with other disciplines and fields of scholarship and practice. Its interdisciplinary linkages to religion have been explored through various scholarly publications in the last two decades; however, many gaps remain unexplored, especially in the context of how PB and religion can establish social justice through economic and material development. Key questions require attention: What are the most strategic intervention models to engage religious actors in peace processes? How can PB strategies be more effective and sustained despite the scarcity of resources? How can locally based PB strategies be developed to affect national and regional conflicts?

Finally, values, principles, and strategies for achieving social justice can be found at the heart of all world religions and indigenous traditions. Religious actors, PB professional practitioners and scholars, and policy makers all bear responsibility for systematically engaging each other to advance community, national, and international PB processes.

Notes

1 For more details about the PB field, see the Association for Conflict Resolution (www.acrnet.org) and CR Info (http://www.crinfo.org/action/browse.jsp?nid=2326; accessed October 3, 2011).
2 For example, USAID, the Department for International Development (DFID), the Canadian International Development Agency (CIDA), and the World Bank, and other major international institutions, have adopted PB frameworks for conflict assessment as part of their operations in conflict zones.
3 See more details at Salam Institute for Peace and Justice, Training Madrassa Teachers in Pakistan: An Assessment Report, www.salaminstitute.org.
4 For further information see http://www.cbcsi.org/a/index.php?option=com_content&view=article&id=159:mindanao-peace-weavers-uphold-the-primacy-of-the-peace-process&catid=37:cso-statements&Itemid=16 (accessed October 3, 2011).
5 Each circle has at least seven members and at least three different religions, indigenous traditions, or spiritual expressions; see http://www.uri.org/Cooperation_Circles.html (accessed October 3, 2011).
6 A quick review of the Parliament of World's Religion Conference in 2009 reveals that it featured 56 speakers on interfaith issues and hosted 13 panels on interfaith dialogue, but only 4 speakers on nonviolence and 2 sessions on nonviolence (one of them a film screening).

7   See initiatives of interfaith as part of "counter-terrorism" campaigns in Saudi Arabia, Morocco, Qatar, Egypt, Britain, France, Spain, and the United States.
8   For full details of this pioneer initiative see Religion and Development Research Programme, http://www.rad.bham.ac.uk/index.php?section=1 (accessed October 3, 2011).

References

Abu-Nimer, Mohammed (2004) Education for coexistence and Arab-Jewish encounters in Israel: Potential and challenges, *Journal of Social Issues*, Special issue: Improving Arab-Jewish Relations in Israel: Theory and Practice in Coexistence Education Programs, 60(2): 405–422.

Abu-Nimer, Mohammed (2008) The role of religious peacebuilders in traumatized societies: From withdrawal to forgiveness, in *Peacebuilding in Traumatized Societies*, Barry Hart (ed.), University Press of America, New York, pp. 239–260.

Abu-Nimer, Mohammed, Khoury, Amal, and Welty, Emily (2007) *Unity in Diversity: Interfaith Dialogue in the Middle East*, USIP, Washington, DC.

Appleby, R. Scott (2000) *The Ambivalence of the Sacred: Religion, Violence, and Reconciliation*, Rowman and Littlefield, Lanham, MD.

Arai, Tatsushi (2009) *Creativity in Conflict Resolution: Alternative Pathways to Peace*, Routledge, New York.

Bradley, Tamsin (2007) The relationship between religion and development: Views from anthropology, Religions and Development Working Paper 5, http://www.research4development.info/PDF/Outputs/ReligionDev_RPC/WP5.pdf (accessed April 19, 2011).

Burton, John (1990) *Conflict Resolution and Prevention*, St. Martin's Press, New York.

Gopin, Marc (2002) *Holy War, Holy Peace: How Religion Can Bring Peace to the Middle East*, Oxford University Press, New York.

Hart, Barry (ed.) (2008) *Peacebuilding in Traumatized Societies*, University Press of America, New York.

Kubai, Anne (1995) *Being Church in Post-genocide Rwanda: The Challenge of Forgiveness and Reconciliation*, Life and Peace Institute, Uppsala, Sweden.

Little, David (ed.) (2008) *Peacemakers in Action: Profiles of Religion in Conflict Resolution*, Cambridge University Press, Cambridge.

Lund, Michael (2001) A toolbox for responding to conflicts and building peace, in *Peacebuilding: A Field Guide*, Luc Reychler and Thania Paffenholz (eds.), Lynne Rienner, Boulder, CO.

Miall, Hugh, Ramsbothan, Oliver, and Woodhouse, Thomas (1999) *Contemporary Conflict Resolution*, Policy Press, Cambridge.

Polkinghorn, B., La Chance, Haleigh, and La Chance, Robert (2008) Understanding of developmental trends in graduate conflict resolution programs in the United States, *Research in Social Movements, Conflicts, and Change* 29: 235–265.

Bibliography

Khan, Ajaz A., Tahmazov, Ismayil, and Abuarqub, Mamoun (2009) *Translating Faith into Development*, Islamic Relief Worldwide, Birmingham, http://www.islamic-relief.com/indepth/downloads/Translating%20faith%20into%20development.pdf (accessed April 19, 2011).

Sibomana, Andre (1999) *Hope for Rwanda: Conversations with Laure Guilbert and Herve Deguine*, Carina Tertsakian (trans.), Pluto Press, London. Originally published in French by Desclee de Brouwer, 1997.

Index

abolitionist movement, 56, 496, 607, 612
Aborigines, 6, 361–72
abortion, 57, 62, 68, 538, 539, 541, 549–51
Africa, 460–1
African diaspora religions, 224
African Independent Churches, 62, 462, 466, 469, 472, 474
African liberation theology, 476
Aggadah, 192
Aggañña Sutta, 21
AIDS, 62, 66, 275, 482–94
Aisyiyah (women's organization in the Muhammadiyah), 246–8
al-Afghani, Jamal al-Din, 154–5, 244
Almed Khan, 155
almsgiving, 6, 140, 158, 319–28
Alternative Dispute Resolution (ADR), 461, 620, 623
Anabaptists, 609
ancestors, 10, 107, 208, 235, 243, 257–66, 274, 310, 354, 358, 382, 412, 423, 442, 463, 464, 467, 470
animals, justice for, 196, 601–2
Anthony, Susan B., 536
"Arab Spring," 402, 409, 410
Arya Samaj, 118, 127
Aryans, 18
Asante (Ghana), 6, 256–67

Aśoka, 27–8, 284
assisted reproductive technologies (ARTs), 551–5
Atiśa, 271
Australia, 361–72

Bahá'í, 2, 11, 210–21
Bahá'u'lláh, 210–12
Barmen Declaration, 68
Bartholomew, Ecumenical Patriarch, 64
Bartolomé de Las Casas, 51
Basil of Cappadocia, 48–9
Basiliad, 49
Bedward, Alexander, 230
behaviorism, 578
Bell, Daniel, 106–7
Benedict XVI, Pope (2005–), 56
Berger, Peter, 98
Bhakti (devotion), 117
birth control, 547–9
Boesak, Allan, 67
Boff, Leonardo, 600
Bonhoeffer, Dietrich, 64–5
Booth, Catherine, 54–5
Booth, William, 54–5
Boutros-Ghali, Boutros, 620
Brahmans, 111, 120
Brahmo Samaj, 118, 127

Brown, John, 522–3
Buddhism, 17–43
  death and dying, 568–9
  engaged, 30, 34
  Five Mindfulness Trainings, 41
  Five Precepts, 28, 32, 283
  Mahāyāna Buddhism, 25–6
  monastic ideal, 32, 272
  "Noble Eightfold Path," 31
  Tibetan monastics, 268–77
  under communism, 273
  Vajrayāna Buddhism, 26
  women, 539

Cakkavatti Sīhanāda Sutta, 22
Calvin, John, 52, 550
Canaanites, 66
capitalism, 52, 55, 58–9, 78, 96, 98, 101, 103, 104, 138, 166, 180, 181, 186, 236, 237, 382, 458, 473, 599, 601
CARE International, 621
cashmaye, 350
caste system, 2, 18, 110–21
Catherine of Sienna, 50
Catholic Relief Services (CRS), 621
Charter for Compassion, 342
Chávez, César, 69
Chicago Declaration of Evangelical Social Concern, 68
Child, Lydia Marie, 56
Chippewa, 347, 416, 427, 428
Christian Coalition, 68
Christian Community Development Association, 73
Christianity, 46–75
  beginning of life, 547
  death and dying, 570–2
  disabilities, 583–6
  hospitality, 308–10
  nonviolence, 605–18
  Paul and social justice, 47, 304
  Philemon, 47
Christians for Biblical Equality (CBE), 72
Chrysostom, John, 48
Chrysostomos, Metropolitan of Zákynthos, 75
civil rights, 53, 73, 134, 174, 198, 313, 454, 496–9, 501–3, 505, 519–22, 525–30, 536, 595, 596
Civil Rights Act, Protection of, 126, 129, 130, 445

civil rights movement, 65, 68, 71, 72, 74, 499–503, 505, 521, 596, 607, 615, 616
climate justice, 342, 591
cloning, 555–7
colonialism, 456–66, 470
conflict management and settlement, 622
conflict resolution, 622
conflict transformation, 622
Confucian perspective on social justice, 90–1
Confucianism, 77–108
Confucius, 16, 77

Dalai Lama, 31, 274
Daly, Mary, 537
Darby, John Nelson, 526
Day, Dorothy, 67, 73
death and dying, 561–73
development and peace building, 630–1
Diola, the, 7–8, 347–8, 350–60
Douglass, Frederick, 56
Dreaming, the, 364–6, 367, 429
DuBois, W.E.B., 500–1, 519, 528

ecology and environment (eco-justice), 591–604
enstoolment (coronation), 261
Environmental Protection Agency, 598
Erga Migrantes Caritas Christi (*The Love of Chrsit towards the Migrants*), 312–14
Essenes, the, 302, 582
euthanasia, 561, 564, 565, 567, 569–73
evangelicalism (American), 519–31

Fair Trade movement, 603
faith-based organizations (FBOs), 517–18, 630–1
Fan, Ruiping, 102–4
Farsi, 403
Feuerstein, Reuven, 583
Finney, Charles, 522
Fleischacker, Samuel, 81
Francis of Assisi, 50–1

Galbraith, John Kenneth, 58
Gamaliel I, 298
Gamaliel II, 300–2
Gandhi, Mohandas K. (Mahatma), 114, 119, 125, 129, 567, 607, 614–15
Garnet, Henry Highland, 56
Garrison, William Lloyd, 56

Gebara, Ivone, 600
Geevarghese Mar Osthathios, 58
gender and sexuality, 535–45
Gertrude of Helfta, 50
Ghotul, 443
Gifford, Paul, 478
Gonds, the, 6, 438–49
Gondwana, 440
Gutierrez, Gustavo, 65

halakhah, 170, 177–8, 192, 582
Hamer, Fannie Lou, 67, 75, 503–4
Hasan al-Banna, 156, 157–8
Hasidism, 190–1
healing, 230
Heschel, Abraham Joshua, 190–202
Hillel the Elder, 295–8
Hinduism, 110–35
   Achhoot (untouchables), 114
   dalits, 2, 118, 125, 126, 128, 135
   death and dying, 566–8
   Dharma, 33, 114–15
   disabilities, 580–1
   Harijans (untouchables, "children of God"), 114, 119
   karma, 19, 23, 115, 567, 580–1
homosexuality, 541
hospice care, 563
hospitality, 6, 306–17
human rights, 2, 8, 9, 62, 64, 69, 98, 120, 125, 138, 142 161, 164, 165, 215, 219, 220, 250, 265, 289, 310, 336, 337, 363, 384, 407–10, 453–5, 465, 483–6, 494, 503, 507–18, 542, 594, 604, 616

indigenous peoples, 4, 66, 347, 350–450
Indo-European, 18
Institute of Multi-Track Diplomacy (IMTD)
Interfaith Power and Light (IPL), 342
Interreligious Peace Foundation, 624
Iraq, 402
Islam, 137–67
   "civil Islam," 253
   death and dying, 572–3
   disabilities, 586–8
   environment, 165–7
   five pillars, 140
   gender, 158–62
   philanthropy, 165
   Sunni and Shi'a Muslims, 404–5

Jainism, 16
Jamaica, 224–38
Jati, 111–12
Jawaharlal Nehru University, 131
Jawaharlal Nehru, 134
Jesus, 63–4, 331, 385, 526, 531, 570, 584, 608–10, 613–14
   and disabilities, 46–7, 584–5
   and social justice, 46–7, 304
Jiang Qing, 99–101
John the Baptist, 303
jubilee years, 63, 200
Judaism, 16, 170–202
   charity, 182–5
   covenant, 176
   disabilities, 581–3
   death and dying, 569–70
   food justice, 602–3
   g'meelut chasadim (deeds of kindness), 6, 292–305
   Hebrew Scriptures, 171–6
   nobility of human creation, 171, 308
   philanthropy, 305
   wealth, 177–8, 181
justice
   compensatory, 4, 6, 9
   distributive, 4, 5–6, 51, 77, 79, 81, 91, 99, 143, 315, 552, 554, 602
   procedural, 4, 8, 597, 598
   prophetic, 193, 357
   restorative, 4, 9, 509, 597
   retributive, 4, 7–8, 148, 149
   social, 3–11, 25, 46, 64, 81, 94, 114, 143, 162, 173, 235, 353, 370, 405, 431, 457, 483, 562, 577, 628
   universal, 196–7

Kabirdas, 127
Kairos Document, 68–9, 70, 477
Kang Xiaoguang, 101–2
Kang Youwei, 94–6
Kempe, Margery, 50
King, Martin Luther, Jr., 67, 501–2
Kinsey Reports, 543
Kook, Abraham Isaac, 190–202
Krishna, Lord, 117
Kshatriyas, 111, 112, 117–18, 122
Kurdish Women: Action Against Honor Killing (KWAHK), 410

Kurds, 402–10
  in Armenia and Azerbaijan, 409
  in Syria, 408
Kurdistan
  in Iran, 408
  in Iraq, 406
  in Turkey, 406–7

Lausanne Movement, 67
lead paint controversies, 595–7
Leo XIII, Pope (1878–1903), 51, 55
Lewis, H.D., 7
Liang Shuming, 97
liberation theology, 65, 600
"Life and Work" movement, 332
Lotus, 38
Luther, Martin, 51–2

Maathai, Wangari, 600
madrasah, 244–6
Mahatma Phule, 128
Maimonides, Moses ben, 172, 174, 176, 178–9, 182–3, 184–5, 186–7, 304, 549
Māori, 6, 412–23
Marshal, Katherine, 630
matrilineal society, 257
"Memphis Miracle," 70
Mencius, 77–8, 83–9
Menno Simons, 52
Methodism, 52–3
Metropolitan Community Churches, 542
Metta Sutta, 20
mishpat, 172, 197
Moody, D.L., 527–8
Moral Majority, 68
Morris, Aldon D., 503
Moses Cordovero, 304
Mother Teresa, 73
Mou Zongsan, 97–8
Mtimkulu, Siphiwo, 513–14
Muhammad 'Abduh, 155
Muhammadiyah, 241–54
  women in, 246–8
Müntzer, Thomas, 52
Muslim Brotherhood, 156
Myanmar, 287–8

Nash, Ronald, 58
National Conference of Christians and Jews, 333
National Council of Churches of Christ in the USA, 337
National Council of Jewish Women, 538
National Religious Partnership for the Environment, 593
Nazi regime, 201
New Zealand Settlement Act (1863), 416
New Zealand, 412–23
NGOs, 475
Nhất Hanh, Thich, 30, 31, 34–44, 275, 594
Niti, 115
non-resistance, 611–17
non-violence, 607–18
Nozick, Robert, 177, 179
Nyaya, 114, 115, 116

Obeah, 225, 228, 230, 235, 237
Oberlin College, 520, 522
Ojibwe, 6, 425–36
Onan, 547

Packer, Herbert, 8
Pali Canon, 21, 23
Parks, Rosa, 75
Parliament of World Religions, 628
peacebuilding (PB), 620–31
Peace Weavers, 625
Pentecostal, Pentecostals, Pentecostalism, 15, 62, 64, 70, 74, 225, 231, 392–8, 477, 478–9, 521
philanthropy, 523–4
Pius XI, Pope (1903–1913), 55
Plato, 10
polygyny, 462–3
Ponce de Leon, 578
potlatch, 4–6, 315–18
poverty, 20, 23, 47, 48, 61, 82, 145, 147, 151, 179, 181, 185, 186, 217, 237, 244, 253, 276, 312, 322, 328, 339, 349, 354, 384–6, 434, 444, 446, 469–72, 476, 479, 486, 492, 493, 513, 578, 593, 596, 603, 612, 617, 620
Promotion of National Unity and Reconciliation Act, 510
Protection of Civil Rights Act (1955), 130
Punarjanma (rebirth), 115, 116
Purusha Sūkta, 18

Qasim Amin, 155–6
Quakers, 610
Qur'an, 139
    social justice in, 143–9

Radical Reformation, 52
Raja Ram Mohan Roy, 118, 127, 133
Rasmussen, Larry, 601
Rawls, John, 6, 79, 175, 177, 439, 483, 484
reconciliation, 8, 9, 30, 38–43, 67, 70, 71, 74, 149, 212, 216, 218, 220, 299, 420, 457, 477, 508, 509–18, 563, 570, 584, 585, 609, 615
religion and peacebuilding, 620–31
Religions for Peace, 339
reparation, 515–18
Republic, Plato's, 10
revival (Creole religion in Haiti), 224–38
Rig Veda, 18
Roberts, Oral, 586
Romero, Oscar, 67
Ruether, Rosemary Radford, 599

sabbatical years, 181, 200
sadaqa, 320, 321–2, 324, 325, 326, 327, 594
Sagan, Carl, 592
Salvation Army, 54–5
Sangha, 32, 33, 208, 275, 280–90, 543, 568
Sarvodaya ("awakening of all"), 43, 114
Sati (burning of widows), 118, 133–4
Sayyid Qutb, 156–7, 158
scheduled castes, 125–6, 439
Secretariat for Non-Christians (Roman Catholic), 335
Shamans, 443
Shintōism, 16
Shudras, 111–12, 113, 114, 116–17, 119, 125
Shuttlesworth, Fred, 503
slave trade, 458, 470
smrities (recollected wisdom), 116
Social Darwinism, 473
Social Justice and the Christian Church (Nash), 58
Sojourners (magazine), 73
Songtsen Gampo (Tibetan king), 269
South Africa, 507–18

Sri Lanka, 285–7
St. Patrick, 48
Stanton, Elizabeth Cady, 57, 536
storytelling, 429
Sub-Saharan Africa, 482–94
Sun Yatsen, 96
sunyata (emptiness), 33
Sushrutha, 580
Swift, Jonathan, 578

Tan, Sor-hoon, 104–6
Taparelli, Luigi, 4, 55
Tappan, Lewis and Arthur, 523–4
Thomas Aquinas, 4, 51
Tibet, 268–77
Truth and Reconciliation Commission (TRC), 8, 508–9
tsadakah (almsgiving), 293–4
tsedek (justice), 197
Tu Wei-ming, 98
Tutu, Bishop Desmond, 508
Twelve Elements of Social Peacebuilding, 624

United Nations Agenda for Peace, 620
United Religious Initiative (URI), 625

Vaishyas, 111
Vandana Shiva, 599
Varna, 110–12, 113, 120
Vasudhaivkutumbakam, 113
Vedas, 18, 118, 132, 581
vegetarianism, 196
Vincent de Paul, 51

Waitangi, Treaty of, 412–13
Walker, David, 56
Walker, Theodore, 601
Wallis, Jim, 59, 67, 74
Weber, Max, 98
Wesley, John, 52–3
Wheaton College, 520, 528
Wilberforce, William, 51
witches, witchcraft, 354, 355–7, 432, 442–3, 598
withdrawing life supports, 562
Women's Bible, 57, 536
women's issues, 2, 535
women's mosque, 246
World Conference of Churches (WCC), 332

World Faiths Development Dialogue, 630
World Health Organization (WHO), 481–5
World Missionary Conference (1910), 331
World Vision, 621

Xunzi, 78, 80–1, 83, 85, 89–9

Yancey, Phillip, 530
Yochanan ben Zakkai, 298–300

zakat (almsgiving), 6, 140, 158, 319–28
Zhang Junmai, 96
Zoroastrianism, 16

www.ingramcontent.com/pod-product-compliance
Lightning Source LLC
LaVergne TN
LVHW081522060526
800LV00044B/1975